Time for Old Magic

compiled by

May Hill Arbuthnot and Mark Taylor

Illustrated by John Averill,
Wade Ray, Seymour Rosofsky,
Debi Sussman, and Rainey Bennett

A representative collection of folk tales, fables, myths,
and epics to be used in the classroom, home, or camp;
especially planned for college classes in children's
literature; with section introductions, headnotes for
the individual stories, and a special section titled
"Old Magic and Children"

Scott, Foresman and Company

FOREWORD

Mark Taylor, well known to the children and teachers of southern California as a spellbinding storyteller and singer of old songs, has shown remarkable versatility in his accomplishments. His university classes in children's literature were extremely popular. Children, parents, and teachers remember appreciatively his CBS-Hollywood television series "Tell It Again," for which he told stories and sang. His reviews of books for children in the Los Angeles *Times* are discriminating and well written. Moreover, he has coauthored three literature texts for grades four, five, and six. Now his picture stories are making his name equally well known from the Pacific to the Atlantic.

Most teachers and librarians who have heard him speak or have attended one of his workshops in children's literature value Mark Taylor for his knowledge and love of folklore and for his unique ability to make fantasy very much alive. It is therefore with special pleasure that I present Mark Taylor as coauthor of *Time for Old Magic* and *Time for New Magic*. May other worlds live again in these pages.

May Hill Arbuthnot

Cleveland, 1969

Library of Congress Catalog Card Number 73–91952

PREFACE

Time for Old Magic is a collection of folk tales, fables, myths, and epics. It is designed for use in the home, around the campfire, with playground groups, and in the classroom, and its content will appeal to children from four to fourteen years of age. Essentially, the book is an expansion of the section titled "Old Magic" in *Time for Fairy Tales*.[1] By devoting a separate volume to traditional tales and another to modern fanciful stories (*Time for New Magic*[2]), it has been possible in each volume to include a greater number of selections, to expand upon the suggestions for using the stories with children, and to enlarge the Bibliography.

Part One, Tales of Old Magic, comprises folklore from all over the world. To the 111 old favorites—folk tales, fables, myths, and epics—retained from *Time for Fairy Tales*, 36 selections have been added, many from countries or cultures not previously represented. New nations have come into prominence in recent years, particularly in Africa and Asia, stimulating an interest in their history and culture, an interest reflected in the inclusion of nine folk tales from Africa and two from Vietnam. There are also new folk tales from Bolivia, Jamaica, Haiti, the South Seas, Australia, Armenia, Latvia, Sweden, and Cornwall and two new Eskimo tales. Excerpts from two epics of recent publication have also been included. The first is from *Gilgamesh,* which is believed to be the oldest legend known to man, dating back 3000 years before Christ; the other excerpt is from *The Hound of Ulster,* which comes from northern Ireland and is built largely around the hero Cuchulain. These are great hero tales, and it is hoped that hearing these excerpts and the ones from *Robin Hood* and the *Odyssey* will so spellbind children that they will promptly demand the books themselves.

[1] May Hill Arbuthnot, *Time for Fairy Tales,* Scott, Foresman and Company, 1961
[2] May Hill Arbuthnot and Mark Taylor, *Time for New Magic,* Scott, Foresman and Company

Introductions precede the folk tales, the fables, the myths, and the epics and each of the main divisions within the folk tales, fables, and myths. Almost every selection is preceded by a brief headnote.

Part Two, Old Magic and Children, is intended to help the adult view the several kinds of folk literature in fuller perspective and to offer guidance on how best to use these materials with children.

In a century marked by profound changes in all areas of society, a century in which man has harnessed the atom and broken free of the bonds of earth, traditional approaches to the arts appear subject to stress and fracture. Newly identified needs of children and new aims of education, together with a rising revolution in technology, not only challenge but also enhance the traditional forms and uses of literature. The old folk tales, thought by some to be the remnants of now irrelevant ways of life and thought, show surprising vitality in their enduring appeal to youngsters, as well as in their application to contemporary situations of the individual and of society. We continue to gain fresh insight into the significance of the "old" literature and of our need for "old magic" in an age of scientific miracle. Thus, we find that, in the midst of exciting developments in instructional technology (including educational television and the multi-media listening post concept), two fundamental ways of presenting literature to children, *reading aloud* and *storytelling,* are more important and more effective than ever before. For this reason, considerable space is devoted to these two techniques which every teacher should master and employ.

The use of films, filmstrips, television, and computers, together with all the forms of art, shows promise of providing an integrated system for improving all aspects of the teaching program—literature included. This is discussed in as much detail as is feasible, remembering that the present era is one of innovation and experimentation.

Adults using this collection of old tales will also find helpful the glossary and pronunciation guide at the back of the book. It includes words and phrases whose meanings may be obscure or whose pronunciations differ from those one would expect of their spellings. For the most part, the entries in the glossary and pronunciation guide are terms and expressions that belong to the place (or time, perhaps) of a story's origin. Such expressions enrich the flavor of an old tale, and the storyteller will want to be familiar with them.

Part Three, the Bibliography, is a thoroughly revised and greatly expanded version of the Bibliography from *Time for Fairy Tales*. New editions vie with older editions—some retellings have questionable changes, some excellent but old editions are out of print. The trend to present individual folk tales in picture-book format lengthens the list. Making new collections of classic but out-of-print collections has become a compiler's game that is both welcome and distressing. Many old and excellent favorites are culled from a multi-volume series and put into a new single-volume edition, but many good tales are left behind. Often an out-of-print collection of tales contains better stories than one that is similar and in print. Our effort has been to select the best of all of these, while favoring in-print materials. Also, in view of the growing awareness that the folk song is an integral part of the folk-tale tradition, a few first-choice collections of folk songs for children and young people have been listed.

Even though we are in the midst of a revolution in communication and technology, the desire to hear the old tales and old songs seems to be stronger than ever. While there is much to distract children and to draw them away from folk tales at an early age, children seem to have a heightened awareness of the world and a greater-than-ever readiness to be interested in the life and thought of other peoples. Since folk tales echo the heartbeat of humanity, it is vital that children hear, read, and savor them. *Time for Old Magic* is offered to all children and adults who want to stop for a while and listen with delight as the races of man tell how it was and how it happened *once upon a time*.

MHA
MT

CONTENTS

Part One

Tales of Old Magic

Folk Tales

Fables

Myths

Epics

In all tongues and in all times since man began, the most familiar words of childhood have probably been *tell me a story*. And the stories have been told, not really for children but for men. As they always do, children have listened in, beyond the edge of the fire's light, to hear what tales were being told. Those they could grasp, they took to themselves, until, over the stretch of centuries, certain stories have become their own. Unfortunately, with the rise of the modern world, grownups have increasingly abandoned the folk tales of simpler times and quieter places as fit only for the young. Now folk tales are mainly the province of children and scholars, but surely anyone who knows the folk tales will agree with Horace: "Change the name and the tale is about you." The *tale* is all tales men have ever told; the *you* is all of us.

THE FOLK TALES

It is curious in an age as realistic and mechanized as ours that the magic of the folk tales still casts its spell on modern children. Witches and dragons, talking beasts and rebellious pancakes, flying carpets and cloaks of darkness, fairies and wise women, spells and enchantments are accepted as casually by children as airplanes and television.

It is true that the modern child becomes interested in fairy tales later than people used to think, and perhaps he wears them out a little sooner. Except for a few of the simplest nursery tales of "The Little Red Hen" and "The Story of the Three Little Pigs" variety, the peak of children's interest in tales of magic seems to be reached around eight or nine years of age and not earlier. After nine there is a continued but steadily diminishing interest in such stories through the ages of ten, eleven, and twelve years.

Only a small fraction of the folk tales were composed for and told to children. A majority of the tales mirror the mature lives, customs, beliefs, and emotions of peoples all over the world, and their adult themes make large numbers of them totally unsuited to children. There still remain, however, enough stories with lively plots, plenty of action, and conclusions which satisfy children's liking for justice and successful achievement, to account for their continued popularity with young people.

The arrangement of the folk tales in *Time for Old Magic* is an arbitrary one calculated to assist the user of this volume and not to reflect scholarly schematics. As indicated in the table of contents, the five broad divisions are continents and geographical regions—Europe, Africa, Asia, Oceania and Australia, North and South America. Within these broad divisions (excepting those of Africa and Oceania and Australia, which are not subdivided), the tales are grouped (1) according to geographical proximity, an example being the Danish, Norwegian, and Swedish tales grouped under Scandinavia; (2) by individual countries, such as Spain or Czechoslovakia; and (3) according to cultural identity, for example, "United States: Tall Tales."

A quick glance will show that most of the folk tales presented here are from Europe and lands colonized by Europeans. Until recently, the most thorough investigation and recording of folk tales took place in Europe and in countries closely bound to her by language and tradition. Even today, when we speak of folk and fairy tales, most people immediately think of such stories as "The Story of the Three Bears," "Cinderella," and "Snow-White and the Seven Dwarfs." Happily, all this is changing. As new nations arise in the world, students of literature, folklore, and the arts are taking an interest in the culture of "new" peoples. Just in the nick of time, they are writing down and tape-recording the old tales before the rush of the twentieth century sweeps away the old patterns of life and with them all the tales and songs which were once a vital part of the daily life of a people. How fortunate that they are doing so, for after the tidal wave of modernism has changed the cultural contours of a group, the scholar can sometimes find only battered remnants in the debris of a folk-tale tradition.

For the most part, the folk tales in this book are the simpler, merrier ones from the great collections. Each of the large groups, such as the English, French, German, and Norwegian, begins with easier stories, most of them with nursery tales for the youngest children. They progress through tales of magic for the sevens, eights, and nines to the more mature stories which will command the respect of the elevens and twelves.

Grownups will discover likenesses in some of the stories from the different national and racial groups, and these likenesses sometimes interest children. See "Tom Tit Tot" and "Rumpelstiltzkin"; "Mr. Vinegar" and "Gudbrand"; "Cinderella," "Tattercoats," and "Little Burnt-Face"; "Beauty and the Beast" and "East o' the Sun and West o' the Moon"; "Sadko" and "Urashima Taro and the Princess of the Sea."

Remember that the folk tales were created and kept alive by the oral tradition of gifted storytellers. Read them aloud if you must, but tell them if you can, for in the spontaneity of good storytelling, these tales come most vividly to life for you and your children.

Of course, tales of magic should never be used exclusively or in too great numbers, but in balanced proportion to realistic fiction and informational reading. Use the folk tales in connection with the study of a people—the Chinese, English, or East Indian, for example. Use them to stimulate the children's creative urge to paint or dramatize or write. The tall tales have often set children to creating their own "whoppers" and illustrating them.

Above all, use these stories for sheer delight. They have humor, nonsense, romance, and poetic beauty. They will help to break up the tight literalness that overtakes some children. They also reiterate moral truths that are important for children to know. "Be of good cheer," these stories seem to say. "Use your head, keep a kindly heart, a civil tongue, and a fearless spirit and you will surely find the water of life and your heart's desire."

Great Britain

*Nowhere, amid the grand diversity of English, Scottish, Welsh, and
Cornish folklore, together with that of Northern Ireland, can one find the
typical British tale. Furthermore, it is pointless to try to determine from
the texts available to children the salient features of English folklore, say, as
against Cornish folklore. We do know that the Piskies are a fairy folk
found frequently in Cornish tales, but they are next of kin to English brownies
and Scottish kelpies. What is important is that from the various corners
of the British Isles there come to us tales like those found in this anthology.
Our greatest selection of stories is from English folklore. Most of the
tales were garnered in the late nineteenth century and were retold most
notably by Joseph Jacobs. His retelling of these tales has given generations
of children access to the essence of the English oral narrative, with its memorably
intrepid giant-killers (not included here) and its classics of the
nursery—the accumulative tale like "The Old Woman and Her Pig," the
humorous anecdote as found in "Master of All Masters," and the simple
talking beast story like "The Story of the Three Little Pigs." Jacobs had a child
audience in mind and intended, he said, "to write as a good old nurse will
speak, when she tells Fairy Tales." How well he succeeded! The humor, the
swinging prose rhythms, and the blending of practicality and wonder
in the tales still provide a rare and indispensable literary treat for successive
generations of four- to ten-year-old youngsters.*

THE OLD WOMAN AND HER PIG

(English)

*This accumulative tale falls naturally into a
kind of chant, which the children soon try to repeat with you. Humorous it already is, but it becomes funnier for the children if you speed up
the returning sequence as it builds item by item.*

An old woman was sweeping her house, and
she found a little crooked sixpence. "What," said
she, "shall I do with this little sixpence? I will go
to market and buy a little pig."

As she was coming home, she came to a stile:
but the piggy wouldn't go over the stile.

She went a little further, and she met a dog. So
she said to him: "Dog! dog! bite pig; piggy won't
go over the stile; and I shan't get home to-
night." But the dog wouldn't.

She went a little further, and she met a stick.
So she said: "Stick! stick! beat dog; dog won't
bite pig; piggy won't get over the stile; and I
shan't get home to-night." But the stick
wouldn't.

She went a little further, and she met a fire. So
she said: "Fire! fire! burn stick; stick won't beat
dog; dog won't bite pig; piggy won't get over the
stile; and I shan't get home to-night." But the
fire wouldn't.

She went a little further, and she met some
water. So she said: "Water! water! quench fire;
fire won't burn stick; stick won't beat dog; dog
won't bite pig; piggy won't get over the stile;
and I shan't get home to-night." But the water
wouldn't.

She went a little further, and she met an ox.
So she said: "Ox! ox! drink water; water won't
quench fire; fire won't burn stick; stick won't
beat dog; dog won't bite pig; piggy won't get over
the stile; and I shan't get home to-night." But
the ox wouldn't.

"The Old Woman and Her Pig." *From English Fairy
Tales,* collected by Joseph Jacobs. Third edition, revised.
David Nutt, London, 1907

She went a little further, and she met a butcher. So she said: "Butcher! butcher! kill ox; ox won't drink water; water won't quench fire; fire won't burn stick; stick won't beat dog; dog won't bite pig; piggy won't get over the stile; and I shan't get home to-night." But the butcher wouldn't.

She went a little further, and she met a rope. So she said: "Rope! rope! hang butcher; butcher won't kill ox; ox won't drink water; water won't quench fire; fire won't burn stick; stick won't beat dog; dog won't bite pig; piggy won't get over the stile; and I shan't get home to-night." But the rope wouldn't.

She went a little further, and she met a rat. So she said: "Rat! rat! gnaw rope; rope won't hang butcher; butcher won't kill ox; ox won't drink water; water won't quench fire; fire won't burn stick; stick won't beat dog; dog won't bite pig; piggy won't get over the stile; and I shan't get home to-night." But the rat wouldn't.

She went a little further, and she met a cat. So she said: "Cat! cat! kill rat; rat won't gnaw rope; rope won't hang butcher; butcher won't kill ox; ox won't drink water; water won't quench fire; fire won't burn stick; stick won't beat dog; dog won't bite pig; piggy won't get over the stile; and I shan't get home to-night."

But the cat said to her, "If you will go to yonder cow and fetch me a saucer of milk, I will kill the rat." So away went the old woman to the cow.

But the cow said to her, "If you will go to yonder hay-stack and fetch me a handful of hay, I'll give you the milk." So away went the old woman to the hay-stack, and she brought the hay to the cow.

As soon as the cow had eaten the hay, she gave the old woman the milk; and away she went with it in a saucer to the cat.

As soon as the cat had lapped up the milk, the cat began to kill the rat; the rat began to gnaw the rope; the rope began to hang the butcher; the butcher began to kill the ox; the ox began to drink the water; the water began to quench the fire; the fire began to burn the stick; the stick began to beat the dog; the dog began to bite the pig; the little pig in a fright jumped over the stile; and so the old woman got home that night.

THE STORY
OF THE THREE BEARS

(English)

This version of "The Three Bears" is from the tale as originally written by Robert Southey (1774–1843). Although the version by Flora Annie Steel remains the better known, the Southey original has a saucy verve which, after more than a century since its first appearance, is refreshing. Here is an example of an authored story which was taken into oral tradition. You may prefer to substitute the more universally known Goldilocks for the old Woman and to eliminate the remark about sending her to the House of Correction.

Once upon a time there were three bears who lived together in a house of their own in a wood. One of them was a Little, Small, Wee Bear; one was a Middle-sized Bear; and the other was a Great, Huge Bear. They had each a pot for their porridge: a little pot for the Little, Small, Wee Bear; a middle-sized pot for the Middle Bear; and a great pot for the Great, Huge Bear. And they had each a chair to sit in: a little chair for the Little, Small, Wee Bear; a middle-sized chair for the Middle Bear; and a great chair for the Great, Huge Bear. And they had each a bed to sleep in: a little bed for the Little, Small, Wee Bear; a middle-sized bed for the Middle Bear; and a great bed for the Great, Huge Bear.

One day, after they had made the porridge for their breakfast and poured it into their porridge-pots, they walked out into the wood while the porridge was cooling, that they might not burn their mouths by beginning too soon to eat it. And while they were walking, a little old Woman came to the house. She could not have been a good, honest old Woman, for first she looked in at the window and then she peeped in at the keyhole, and, seeing nobody in the house, she lifted the latch. The door was not fastened, because the bears were good bears, who did nobody any harm and never suspected that any-

"The Story of the Three Bears." From *English Fairy Tales,* collected by Joseph Jacobs. Third edition, revised. David Nutt, London, 1907

body would harm them. So the little old Woman opened the door and went in, and well pleased she was when she saw the porridge on the table. If she had been a good little old Woman, she would have waited till the bears came home, and then, perhaps, they would have asked her to breakfast, for they were good bears—a little rough or so, as the manner of bears is, but for all that very good-natured and hospitable. But she was an impudent, bad old Woman and set about helping herself.

So first she tasted the porridge of the Great, Huge Bear, and that was too hot for her, and she said a bad word about that. Then she tasted the porridge of the Middle Bear, and that was too cold for her, and she said a bad word about that too. And then she went to the porridge of the Little, Small, Wee Bear and tasted that, and that was neither too hot nor too cold, but just right. She liked it so well that she ate it all up, but the naughty old Woman said a bad word about the little porridge-pot, because it did not hold enough for her.

Then the little old Woman sat down in the chair of the Great, Huge Bear, and that was too hard for her. Then she sat down in the chair of the Middle Bear, and that was too soft for her. And then she sat down in the chair of the Little, Small, Wee Bear, and that was neither too hard nor too soft, but just right. So she seated herself in it, and there she sat till the bottom of the chair came out, and down she came, plump upon the ground. And the naughty old Woman said a wicked word about that too.

Then the little old Woman went upstairs into the bedchamber in which the three bears slept. And first she lay down upon the bed of the Great, Huge Bear, but that was too high at the head for her. Next she lay down upon the bed of the Middle Bear, and that was too high at the foot for her. And then she lay down upon the bed of the Little, Small, Wee Bear, and that was neither too high at the head nor too high at the foot, but just right. So she covered herself up comfortably and lay there till she fell fast asleep.

By this time the three bears thought their porridge would be cool enough, so they came home to breakfast. Now the little old Woman had left the spoon of the Great, Huge Bear, standing in his porridge.

"SOMEBODY HAS BEEN AT MY POR-RIDGE!" said the Great, Huge Bear in his great, rough, gruff voice. And when the Middle Bear looked at his, he saw that the spoon was standing in it too. They were wooden spoons; if they had been silver ones, the naughty old Woman would have put them in her pocket.

"SOMEBODY HAS BEEN AT MY PORRIDGE!" said the Middle Bear in his middle voice.

Then the Little, Small, Wee Bear looked at his, and there was the spoon in the porridge-pot, but the porridge was all gone.

"Somebody has been at my porridge and has eaten it all up!" said the Little, Small, Wee Bear in his little, small, wee voice.

Upon this the three bears, seeing that some one had entered their house and eaten up the Little, Small, Wee Bear's breakfast, began to look about them. Now the little old Woman had not put the hard cushion straight when she rose from the chair of the Great, Huge Bear.

"SOMEBODY HAS BEEN SITTING IN MY CHAIR!" said the Great, Huge Bear in his great, rough, gruff voice.

And the little old Woman had squatted down the soft cushion of the Middle Bear.

"SOMEBODY HAS BEEN SITTING IN MY CHAIR!" said the Middle Bear in his middle voice.

And you know what the little old Woman had done to the third chair.

"Somebody has been sitting in my chair and has sat the bottom out of it!" said the Little, Small, Wee Bear in his little, small, wee voice.

Then the three bears thought it necessary that they should make farther search, so they went upstairs into their bedchamber. Now the little old Woman had pulled the pillow of the Great, Huge Bear out of its place.

"SOMEBODY HAS BEEN LYING IN MY BED!" said the Great, Huge Bear in his great, rough, gruff voice.

And the little old Woman had pulled the bolster of the Middle Bear out of its place.

"SOMEBODY HAS BEEN LYING IN MY BED!" said the Middle Bear in his middle voice.

And when the Little, Small, Wee Bear came to look at his bed, there was the bolster in its place, and the pillow in its place upon the bolster; and upon the pillow was the little old Woman's ugly, dirty head—which was not in its place, for she had no business there.

"Somebody has been lying in my bed—and here she is!" said the Little, Small, Wee Bear in his little, small, wee voice.

The little old Woman had heard in her sleep the great, rough, gruff voice of the Great, Huge Bear, but she was so fast asleep that it was no more to her than the roaring of wind or the rumbling of thunder. And she had heard the middle voice of the Middle Bear, but it was only as if she had heard some one speaking in a dream. But when she heard the little, small, wee voice of the Little, Small, Wee Bear, it was so sharp and so shrill that it awakened her at once. Up she started and when she saw the three bears on one side of the bed, she tumbled herself out at the other and ran to the window. Now the window was open, because the bears, like good, tidy bears, as they were, always opened their bedchamber window when they got up in the morning. Out the little old Woman jumped; and whether she broke her neck in the fall, or ran into the wood and was lost there, or found her way out of the wood and was taken up by the constable and sent to the House of Correction for a vagrant as she was, I cannot tell. But the three bears never saw anything more of her.

THE STORY
OF THE THREE LITTLE PIGS

(English)

It is likely that this story is the top favorite of all five-year-olds who know it.

Once upon a time when pigs spoke rhyme
And monkeys chewed tobacco,
And hens took snuff to make them tough,
And ducks went quack, quack, quack, O!

There was an old sow with three little pigs, and as she had not enough to keep them, she sent them out to seek their fortune. The first that went off met a man with a bundle of straw and said to him:

"The Story of the Three Little Pigs." From *English Fairy Tales,* collected by Joseph Jacobs. Third edition, revised. David Nutt, London, 1907

"Please, man, give me that straw to build me a house."

Which the man did, and the little pig built a house with it. Presently came along a wolf who knocked at the door and said:

"Little pig, little pig, let me come in."

To which the pig answered:

"No, no, by the hair of my chinny chin chin."

The wolf then answered to that:

"Then I'll huff, and I'll puff, and I'll blow your house in."

So he huffed, and he puffed, and he blew the house in and ate up the little pig.

The second little pig met a man with a bundle of furze and said:

"Please, man, give me that furze to build a house."

Which the man did, and the pig built his house. Then along came the wolf and said:

"Little pig, little pig, let me come in."

"No, no, by the hair of my chinny chin chin."

"Then I'll puff, and I'll huff, and I'll blow your house in."

So he huffed, and he puffed, and he puffed, and he huffed, and at last he blew the house down, and he ate up the little pig.

The third little pig met a man with a load of bricks, and said:

"Please, man, give me those bricks to build a house with."

So the man gave him the bricks, and the pig built his house with them. So the wolf came, as he did to the other little pigs, and said:

"Little pig, little pig, let me come in."

"No, no, by the hair of my chinny chin chin."

"Then I'll huff, and I'll puff, and I'll blow your house in."

Well, he huffed, and he puffed, and he huffed, and he puffed, and he puffed and huffed; but he could *not* get the house down. When he found that he could not, with all his huffing and puffing, blow the house down, he said:

"Little pig, I know where there is a nice field of turnips."

"Where?" said the little pig.

"Oh, in Mr. Smith's home-field. If you will be ready tomorrow morning, I will call for you, and we will go together and get some for dinner."

"Very well," said the little pig, "I will be ready. What time do you mean to go?"

"Oh, at six o'clock."

Well, the little pig got up at five and got the turnips before the wolf came (which he did about six) and said:

"Little pig, are you ready?"

The little pig said, "Ready! I have been and come back again, and got a nice potful for dinner."

The wolf felt very angry at this, but thought that he would be up to the little pig somehow or other, so he said:

"Little pig, I know where there is a nice apple tree."

"Where?" said the pig.

"Down at Merry-garden," replied the wolf, "and if you will not deceive me, I will come for you at five o'clock tomorrow, and we will get some apples."

Well, the little pig bustled up the next morning at four o'clock and went off for the apples, hoping to get back before the wolf came; but he had further to go and had to climb the tree, so that just as he was coming down from it, he saw the wolf coming, which, as you may suppose, frightened him very much. When the wolf came up he said:

"Little pig! What! Are you here before me? Are they nice apples?"

"Yes, very," said the little pig. "I will throw one down to you."

And he threw it so far that while the wolf was gone to pick it up, the little pig jumped down and ran home. The next day the wolf came again, and said to the little pig:

"Little pig, there is a fair at Shanklin this afternoon. Will you go?"

"Oh yes," said the pig, "I will go. What time shall you be ready?"

"At three," said the wolf. So the little pig went off before the time as usual and got to the fair

and bought a butter-churn, which he was going home with, when he saw the wolf coming. Then he could not tell what to do. So he got into the churn to hide and by so doing turned it round, and it rolled down the hill with the pig in it, which frightened the wolf so much that he ran home without going to the fair. He went to the little pig's house and told him how frightened he had been by a great round thing which came down the hill past him. Then the little pig said:

"Hah, I frightened you then. I had been to the

fair and bought a butter-churn, and when I saw you, I got into it and rolled down the hill."

Then the wolf was very angry indeed. He declared he *would* eat up the little pig and that he would get down the chimney after him. When the little pig saw what the wolf was about, he hung on the pot full of water and made up a blazing fire and, just as the wolf was coming down, took off the cover, and in fell the wolf. So the little pig put on the cover again in an instant, boiled him up, and ate him for supper and lived happy ever afterwards.

HENNY-PENNY

(English)

Here is the perfect example of a story whose ancestry reaches far back in time—all the way back to the early Buddhistic literature of India. It has something to say to all ages, yet, like its cousins "The Pancake" and "The Gingerbread Boy," it is a favorite of very young children. Versions of it are to be found in many lands, and its gentle lesson is always contemporary.

One day Henny-Penny was picking up corn in the cornyard when—whack!—something hit her upon the head. "Goodness gracious me!" said Henny-Penny. "The sky's a-going to fall. I must go and tell the king."

So she went along, and she went along, and she went along, till she met Cocky-Locky. "Where are you going to, Henny-Penny?" said Cocky-Locky.

"Oh! I'm going to tell the king the sky's a-falling," said Henny-Penny.

"May I come with you?" said Cocky-Locky.

"Certainly," said Henny-Penny. So Henny-Penny and Cocky-Locky went to tell the king the sky was falling.

They went along, and they went along, and they went along, till they met Ducky-Daddles. "Where are you going to, Henny-Penny and Cocky-Locky?" said Ducky-Daddles.

"Oh! We're going to tell the king the sky's a-falling," said Henny-Penny and Cocky-Locky.

"May I come with you?" said Ducky-Daddles.

"Certainly," said Henny-Penny and Cocky-Locky. So Henny-Penny, Cocky-Locky, and Ducky-Daddles went to tell the king the sky was a-falling.

So they went along, and they went along, and they went along, till they met Goosey-Poosey. "Where are you going to, Henny-Penny, Cocky-Locky, and Ducky-Daddles?" said Goosey-Poosey.

"Oh! We're going to tell the king the sky's a-falling," said Henny-Penny and Cocky-Locky and Ducky-Daddles.

"May I come with you?" said Goosey-Poosey.

"Certainly," said Henny-Penny, Cocky-Locky, and Ducky-Daddles. So Henny-Penny, Cocky-Locky, Ducky-Daddles, and Goosey-Poosey went to tell the king the sky was a-falling.

So they went along, and they went along, and they went along, till they met Turkey-Lurkey. "Where are you going, Henny-Penny, Cocky-Locky, Ducky-Daddles, and Goosey-Poosey?" said Turkey-Lurkey.

"Oh! We're going to tell the king the sky's a-falling," said Henny-Penny, Cocky-Locky, Ducky-Daddles, and Goosey-Poosey.

"May I come with you, Henny-Penny, Cocky-

"Henny-Penny." From *English Fairy Tales,* collected by Joseph Jacobs. Third edition, revised. David Nutt, London, 1907

Locky, Ducky-Daddles, and Goosey-Poosey?" said Turkey-Lurkey.

"Oh, certainly, Turkey-Lurkey," said Henny-Penny, Cocky-Locky, Ducky-Daddles, and Goosey-Poosey. So Henny-Penny, Cocky-Locky, Ducky-Daddles, Goosey-Poosey, and Turkey-Lurkey all went to tell the king the sky was a-falling.

So they went along, and they went along, and they went along, till they met Foxy-Woxy, and Foxy-Woxy said to Henny-Penny, Cocky-Locky, Ducky-Daddles, Goosey-Poosey, and Turkey-Lurkey: "Where are you going, Henny-Penny, Cocky-Locky, Ducky-Daddles, Goosey-Poosey, and Turkey-Lurkey?"

And Henny-Penny, Cocky-Locky, Ducky-Daddles, Goosey-Poosey, and Turkey-Lurkey said to Foxy-Woxy: "We're going to tell the king the sky's a-falling."

"Oh! But this is not the way to the king, Henny-Penny, Cocky-Locky, Ducky-Daddles, Goosey-Poosey, and Turkey-Lurkey," said Foxy-Woxy. "I know the proper way. Shall I show it to you?"

"Oh certainly, Foxy-Woxy," said Henny-Penny, Cocky-Locky, Ducky-Daddles, Goosey-Poosey, and Turkey-Lurkey. So Henny-Penny, Cocky-Locky, Ducky-Daddles, Goosey-Poosey, Turkey-Lurkey, and Foxy-Woxy all went to tell the king the sky was a-falling.

So they went along, and they went along, and they went along, till they came to a narrow and dark hole. Now this was the door of Foxy-Woxy's cave. But Foxy-Woxy said to Henny-Penny, Cocky-Locky, Ducky-Daddles, Goosey-Poosey, and Turkey-Lurkey: "This is the short way to the king's palace. You'll soon get there if you follow me. I will go first, and you come after, Henny-Penny, Cocky-Locky, Ducky-Daddles, Goosey-Poosey, and Turkey-Lurkey."

"Why of course, certainly, without doubt, why not?" said Henny-Penny, Cocky-Locky, Ducky-Daddles, Goosey-Poosey, and Turkey-Lurkey.

So Foxy-Woxy went into his cave, and he didn't go very far, but turned round to wait for Henny-Penny, Cocky-Locky, Ducky-Daddles, Goosey-Poosey, and Turkey-Lurkey.

So at last at first Turkey-Lurkey went through the dark hole into the cave. He hadn't got far when "Hrumph," Foxy-Woxy snapped off Turkey-Lurkey's head and threw his body over his left shoulder. Then Goosey-Poosey went in, and "Hrumph," off went her head, and Goosey-Poosey was thrown beside Turkey-Lurkey. Then Ducky-Daddles waddled down, and "Hrumph," snapped Foxy-Woxy, and Ducky-Daddles' head was off, and Ducky-Daddles was thrown alongside Turkey-Lurkey and Goosey-Poosey. Then Cocky-Locky strutted down into the cave and he hadn't gone far when "Snap, Hrumph!" went Foxy-Woxy, and Cocky-Locky was thrown alongside of Turkey-Lurkey, Goosey-Poosey, and Ducky-Daddles.

But Foxy-Woxy had made two bites at Cocky-Locky, and when the first snap only hurt Cocky-Locky, but didn't kill him, he called out to Henny-Penny. But she turned tail and off she ran home, so she never told the king the sky was a-falling.

THE COCK, THE MOUSE, AND THE LITTLE RED HEN

(English)

"It's never too late to mend," said the little Red Hen. Her cheerful philosophy and unbegrudging ways are the very antidote to laziness and evil. Félicité LeFèvre's retelling is a small classic.

Once upon a time there was a hill, and on the hill there was a pretty little house.

It had one little green door, and four little windows with green shutters, and in it there lived a COCK, and A MOUSE, and A LITTLE RED HEN. On another hill close by, there was another little house. It was very ugly. It had a door that wouldn't shut, and two broken windows, and all the paint was off the shutters. And in this house there lived A BOLD BAD FOX and FOUR BAD LITTLE FOXES.

One morning these four bad little foxes came to the big bad Fox and said:

"Oh, Father, we're so hungry!"

"We had nothing to eat yesterday," said one.

"And scarcely anything the day before," said another.

"The Cock, the Mouse, and the Little Red Hen." By Félicité LeFèvre

The big bad Fox shook his head, for he was thinking. At last he said in a big gruff voice:

"On the hill over there I see a house. And in that house there lives a Cock."

"And a Mouse!" screamed two of the little foxes.

"And a little Red Hen," screamed the other two.

"And they are nice and fat," went on the big bad Fox. "This very day I'll take my sack and I will go up that hill and in at that door, and into my sack I will put the Cock, and the Mouse, and the little Red Hen."

So the four little foxes jumped for joy, and the big bad Fox went to get his sack ready to start upon his journey.

But what was happening to the Cock, and the Mouse, and the little Red Hen, all this time?

Well, sad to say, the Cock and the Mouse had both got out of bed on the wrong side that morning. The Cock said the day was too hot, and the Mouse grumbled because it was too cold.

They came grumbling down to the kitchen, where the good little Red Hen, looking as bright as a sunbeam, was bustling about.

"Who'll get some sticks to light the fire with?" she asked.

"I shan't," said the Cock.

"I shan't," said the Mouse.

"Then I'll do it myself," said the little Red Hen.

So off she ran to get the sticks. "And now, who'll fill the kettle from the spring?" she asked.

"I shan't," said the Cock.

"I shan't," said the Mouse.

"Then I'll do it myself," said the little Red Hen.

And off she ran to fill the kettle.

"And who'll get the breakfast ready?" she asked, as she put the kettle on to boil.

"I shan't," said the Cock.

"I shan't," said the Mouse.

"I'll do it myself," said the little Red Hen.

All breakfast time the Cock and the Mouse quarrelled and grumbled. The Cock upset the milk jug, and the Mouse scattered crumbs upon the floor.

"Who'll clear away the breakfast?" asked the poor little Red Hen, hoping they would soon leave off being cross.

"I shan't," said the Cock.

"I shan't," said the Mouse.

"Then I'll do it myself," said the little Red Hen.

So she cleared everything away, swept up the crumbs, and brushed up the fireplace.

"And now, who'll help me to make the beds?"

"I shan't," said the Cock.

"I shan't," said the Mouse.

"Then I'll do it myself," said the little Red Hen.

And she tripped away upstairs.

But the lazy Cock and Mouse each sat down in a comfortable arm-chair by the fire, and soon fell fast asleep.

Now the bad Fox had crept up the hill and into the garden, and if the Cock and Mouse hadn't been asleep, they would have seen his sharp eyes peeping in at the window.

"Rat tat tat! Rat tat tat!" the Fox knocked at the door.

"Who can that be?" said the Mouse, half opening his eyes.

"Go and look for yourself, if you want to know," said the rude Cock.

"It's the postman perhaps," thought the Mouse to himself, "and he may have a letter for me." So without waiting to see who it was, he lifted the latch and opened the door.

As soon as he opened it, in jumped the big Fox.

"Oh! oh! oh!" squeaked the Mouse, as he tried to run up the chimney.

"Doodle doodle do!" screamed the Cock, as he jumped on the back of the biggest arm-chair.

But the Fox only laughed, and without more ado he took the little Mouse by the tail, and popped him into the sack, and seized the Cock by the neck and popped him in too.

Then the poor little Red Hen came running downstairs to see what all the noise was about, and the Fox caught her and put her into the sack with the others.

Then he took a long piece of string out of his pocket, wound it round, and round, and round the mouth of the sack, and tied it very tight indeed. After that he threw the sack over his back, and off he set down the hill, chuckling to himself.

"Oh, I wish I hadn't been so cross," said the

Cock, as they went bumping about.

"Oh! I wish I hadn't been so lazy," said the Mouse, wiping his eyes with the tip of his tail.

"It's never too late to mend," said the little Red Hen. "And don't be too sad. See, here I have my little work-bag, and in it there is a pair of scissors, and a little thimble, and a needle and thread. Very soon you will see what I am going to do."

Now the sun was very hot, and soon Mr. Fox began to feel his sack was heavy, and at last he thought he would lie down under a tree and go to sleep for a little while. So he threw the sack down with a big bump, and very soon fell fast asleep.

Snore, snore, snore, went the Fox.

As soon as the little Red Hen heard this, she took out her scissors, and began to snip a hole in the sack just large enough for the Mouse to creep through.

"Quick," she whispered to the Mouse, "run as fast as you can and bring back a stone just as large as yourself."

Out scampered the Mouse, and soon came back, dragging the stone after him.

"Push it in here," said the little Red Hen, and he pushed it in, in a twinkling.

Then the little Red Hen snipped away at the hole, till it was large enough for the Cock to get through.

"Quick," she said, "run and get a stone as big as yourself."

Out flew the Cock, and soon came back quite out of breath, with a big stone, which he pushed into the sack too.

Then the little Red Hen popped out, got a stone as big as herself, and pushed it in. Next she put on her thimble, took out her needle and thread, and sewed up the hole as quickly as ever she could.

When it was done, the Cock and the Mouse and the little Red Hen ran home very fast, shut the door after them, drew the bolts, shut the shutters, and drew down the blinds and felt quite safe.

The bad Fox lay fast asleep under the tree for some time, but at last he awoke.

"Dear, dear," he said, rubbing his eyes and then looking at the long shadows on the grass, "how late it is getting. I must hurry home."

So the bad Fox went grumbling and groaning down the hill, till he came to the stream. Splash! In went one foot. Splash! In went the other, but the stones in the sack were so heavy that at the very next step, down tumbled Mr. Fox into a deep pool. And then the fishes carried him off to their fairy caves and kept him a prisoner there, so he was never seen again. And the four greedy little foxes had to go to bed without any supper.

But the Cock and the Mouse never grumbled again. They lit the fire, filled the kettle, laid the breakfast, and did all the work, while the good little Red Hen had a holiday, and sat resting in the big arm-chair.

No foxes ever troubled them again, and for all I know they are still living happily in the little house with the green door and green shutters, which stands on the hill.

THE TRAVELS OF A FOX

(English)

There are some amusing phrases in this story which you must make the most of—"while I go to Squintum's," for example. The children like to roll that one under their tongues. When told well, with a touch of slyness, this tale can be hilarious.

One day a fox was digging behind a stump and he found a bumblebee; and the fox put the bumblebee in a bag and took the bag over his shoulder and travelled.

At the first house he came to, he went in and said to the mistress of the house, "Can I leave my bag here while I go to Squintum's?"

"Yes," said the woman.

"Then be careful not to open the bag," said the fox.

But as soon as he was out of sight the woman said to herself, "Well, I wonder what the fellow has in his bag that he is so careful about. I will look and see. It can't do any harm, for I shall tie the bag right up again."

However, the moment she unloosed the string,

"The Travels of a Fox." From *The Oak Tree Fairy Book*, edited by Clifton Johnson, copyright 1933. Reprinted by permission of Roger Johnson

out flew the bumblebee, and the rooster caught him and ate him all up.

After a while the fox came back. He took up his bag and knew at once that his bumblebee was gone, and he said to the woman, "Where is my bumblebee?"

And the woman said, "I untied the string just to take a little peep to find out what was in your bag, and the bumblebee flew out and the rooster ate him."

"Very well," said the fox; "I must have the rooster, then."

So he caught the rooster and put him in his bag and travelled.

At the next house he came to, he went in and said to the mistress of the house, "Can I leave my bag here while I go to Squintum's?"

"Yes," said the woman.

"Then be careful not to open the bag," said the fox.

But as soon as he was out of sight the woman said to herself, "Well, I wonder what the fellow has in his bag that he is so careful about. I will look and see. It can't do any harm, for I shall tie the bag right up again."

However, the moment she unloosed the string the rooster flew out and the pig caught him and ate him all up.

After a while the fox came back. He took up his bag and knew at once that his rooster was gone, and he said to the woman, "Where is my rooster?"

And the woman said, "I untied the string just to take a little peep to find out what was in your bag, and the rooster flew out and the pig ate him."

"Very well," said the fox, "I must have the pig, then."

So he caught the pig and put him in his bag and travelled.

At the next house he came to, he went in and said to the mistress of the house, "Can I leave my bag here while I go to Squintum's?"

"Yes," said the woman.

"Then be careful not to open the bag," said the fox.

But as soon as he was out of sight the woman said to herself, "Well, I wonder what the fellow has in his bag that he is so careful about. I will look and see. It can't do any harm, for I shall tie the bag right up again."

However, the moment she unloosed the string, the pig jumped out and the ox gored him.

After a while the fox came back. He took up his bag and knew at once that his pig was gone, and he said to the woman, "Where is my pig?"

And the woman said, "I untied the string just to take a little peep to find out what was in your bag, and the pig jumped out and the ox gored him."

"Very well," said the fox, "I must have the ox, then."

So he caught the ox and put him in his bag and travelled.

At the next house he came to, he went in and said to the mistress of the house, "Can I leave my bag here while I go to Squintum's?"

"Yes," said the woman.

"Then be careful not to open the bag," said the fox.

But as soon as he was out of sight the woman said to herself, "Well, I wonder what the fellow has in his bag that he is so careful about. I will look and see. It can't do any harm, for I shall tie the bag right up again."

However, the moment she unloosed the string, the ox got out, and the woman's little boy chased the ox out of the house and across a meadow and over a hill, clear out of sight.

After a while the fox came back. He took up his bag and knew at once that his ox was gone, and he said to the woman, "Where is my ox?"

And the woman said, "I untied the string just to take a little peep to find out what was in your bag, and the ox got out and my little boy chased him out of the house and across a meadow and over a hill, clear out of sight."

"Very well," said the fox, "I must have the little boy, then."

So he caught the little boy and put him in his bag and travelled.

At the next house he came to, he went in and said to the mistress of the house, "Can I leave my bag here while I go to Squintum's?"

"Yes," said the woman.

"Then be careful not to open the bag," said the fox.

The woman had been making cake, and when it was baked she took it from the oven, and her children gathered around her teasing for some of it.

"Oh, ma, give me a piece!" said one, and "Oh, ma, give me a piece!" said each of the others.

And the smell of the cake came to the little boy in the bag, and he heard the children beg for the cake, and he said, "Oh, mammy, give me a piece!"

Then the woman opened the bag and took the little boy out; and she put the house-dog in the bag in the little boy's place, and the little boy joined the other children.

After a while the fox came back. He took up his bag and he saw that it was tied fast and he thought that the little boy was safe inside. "I have been all day on the road," said he, "without a thing to eat, and I am getting hungry. I will just step off into the woods now and see how this little boy I have in my bag tastes."

So he put the bag on his back and travelled deep into the woods. Then he sat down and untied the bag, and if the little boy had been in there things would have gone badly with him.

But the little boy was at the house of the woman who made the cake, and when the fox untied the bag the house-dog jumped out and killed him.

MASTER OF ALL MASTERS

(English)

Most youngsters find this story absolutely rib-tickling—especially if you say or read the last paragraph as fast as you can.

A girl once went to the fair to hire herself for servant. At last a funny-looking old gentleman engaged her and took her home to his house. When she got there, he told her that he had something to teach her, for that in his house he had his own names for things.

"Master of All Masters." From *English Fairy Tales*, collected by Joseph Jacobs. Third edition, revised. David Nutt, London, 1907

He said to her, "What will you call me?"

"Master or mister, or whatever you please, sir," says she.

He said, "You must call me 'master of all masters.' And what would you call this?" pointing to his bed.

"Bed or couch, or whatever you please, sir."

"No, that's my 'barnacle.' And what do you call these?" said he, pointing to his pantaloons.

"Breeches or trousers, or whatever you please, sir."

"You must call them 'squibs and crackers.' And what would you call her?" pointing to the cat.

"Cat or kit, or whatever you please, sir."

"You must call her 'white-faced simminy.' And this now," showing the fire, "what would you call this?"

"Fire or flame, or whatever you please, sir."

"You must call it 'hot cockalorum,' and what this?" he went on, pointing to the water.

"Water or wet, or whatever you please, sir."

"No, 'pondalorum' is its name. And what do you call all this?" asked he, as he pointed to the house.

"House or cottage, or whatever you please, sir."

"You must call it 'high topper mountain.'"

That very night the servant woke her master up in a fright and said: "Master of all masters, get out of your barnacle and put on your squibs and crackers. For white-faced simminy has got a spark of hot cockalorum on its tail, and unless you get some pondalorum, high topper mountain will be all on hot cockalorum" . . . . .
. . . . That's all.

MR. VINEGAR

(English)

Gudbrand in the Scandinavian version of this tale was a luckier man than Mr. Vinegar, for in spite of Gudbrand's follies his wife remained loyal and loving and his foolish adventures had a happy conclusion. Perhaps this version is more realistic.

Mr. and Mrs. Vinegar were very poor, and they lived in a shabby little house that they had built with their own hands. It was made of old boards and other rubbish which they had picked up, and it rattled and shook in every high wind. One morning, Mrs. Vinegar, who was a very good housewife, was busily sweeping her kitchen floor when an unlucky thump of the broom against the walls brought down the whole house, clitter-clatter about her ears. Mr. Vinegar had gone to a neighboring thicket to gather some fagots, and she hurried off with much weeping and wailing to tell him of the disaster.

When she found him she exclaimed, "Oh, Mr. Vinegar! Mr. Vinegar! we are ruined, we are ruined! I have knocked the house down and it is all to pieces!"

"My dear," said Mr. Vinegar, "pray do not weep any more. I will go back with you and see what can be done."

So they returned, and Mr. Vinegar said, "Yes, wife, the house is all in bits and we can never live in it again; but here is the door. I will take that on my back and we will go forth to seek our fortune."

With his wife's help he got the door on his back, and off they started. They walked all that day, and by nightfall they were both very tired. They had now come to a thick forest and Mr. Vinegar said, "My love, I will climb up into a tree with this door and you shall follow after."

So he climbed up among the branches of a great tree, and when he had adjusted the door at a level Mrs. Vinegar climbed up also, and they stretched their weary limbs on it and were soon fast asleep.

But in the middle of the night Mr. Vinegar was awakened by the sound of voices directly below him. He looked down and, to his dismay, saw that a party of robbers were met under the tree to divide some money they had stolen.

"Jack," said one, "here's five pounds for you; and Bill, here's ten pounds for you; and Bob, here's three pounds for you."

Mr. Vinegar was so frightened he could listen no longer, and he trembled so violently that he shook the door off the branches on which it lay, and he and Mrs. Vinegar had to cling to the tree to save themselves from a bad tumble. When the door began to drop, the noise it made startled

"Mr. Vinegar." From *The Oak Tree Fairy Book*, edited by Clifton Johnson, copyright 1933. Reprinted by permission of Roger Johnson

the robbers and they looked up to learn the cause, but no sooner did they do this than the door came down on their heads and they all ran away greatly terrified.

Mr. and Mrs. Vinegar, however, dared not quit their tree till broad daylight. Then Mr. Vinegar scrambled down.

"I hope the door was not broken by its fall," said he as he lifted it.

Just then he espied a number of golden guineas that had been beneath the door where they had been dropped on the ground by the robbers in their haste to get away.

"Come down, Mrs. Vinegar!" he cried, "come down, I say! Our fortune is made! Come down, I say!"

Mrs. Vinegar came down as quickly as she could and saw the money with great delight, and when they counted it they found they were the possessors of forty guineas. "Now, my dear," said she, "I'll tell you what you shall do. You must take these forty guineas and go to the nearest town and buy a cow. I can make butter and cheese which you shall sell at market, and we shall then be able to live very comfortably."

"I will do as you say," replied Mr. Vinegar, "and you can stay here till I return."

So he took the money and went off to the nearest town; and there was a fair in the town, and crowds of people. When he arrived he walked about until he saw a beautiful red cow that he thought would just suit him.

"Oh, if I only had that cow," said Mr. Vinegar, "I should be the happiest man alive."

Then he offered the forty guineas for the cow and the owner was quite ready to part with it at that price, and the bargain was made. Mr. Vinegar was proud of his purchase, and he led the cow backwards and forwards to show it. But by and by he saw a man playing some bagpipes— tweedledum, tweedledee. The children followed after the bagpipe man, and he appeared to be pocketing a great deal of money.

"What a pleasant and profitable life that musician must lead," said Mr. Vinegar. "If I had that instrument I should be the happiest man alive, and I could earn far more than with this cow."

So he went up to the man and said, "Friend, what a charming instrument that is, and what a deal of money you must make!"

"Why, yes," said the man; "I make a great deal of money, to be sure, and it is a wonderful instrument."

"Oh!" cried Mr. Vinegar, "how I should like to possess it!"

"Well," said the man, "I will exchange it for your red cow."

"Done!" said the delighted Mr. Vinegar.

So the beautiful red cow was given for the bagpipes. Mr. Vinegar walked up and down with his purchase, but in vain he attempted to play a tune, and the children, instead of giving him pennies, hooted and laughed at him. The day was chilly and poor Mr. Vinegar's fingers grew very cold. At last, heartily ashamed and mortified, he was leaving the town when he met a man wearing a fine, thick pair of gloves.

"Oh, my fingers are so very cold!" said Mr. Vinegar to himself. "If I had those warm gloves I should be the happiest man alive."

Then he went up to the man and said to him, "Friend, you seem to have a capital pair of gloves there."

"Yes, truly," replied the man, "these are excellent gloves."

"Well," said Mr. Vinegar, "I should like to have them. I will give you these bagpipes for them."

"All right," said the man, and he took the bagpipes and Mr. Vinegar put on the gloves and felt entirely contented as he trudged along toward the forest.

But the farther he walked the more tired he became, until presently he saw a man coming toward him with a good stout cane in his hand. "Oh!" said Mr. Vinegar, "if I had that cane I should be the happiest man alive."

Then he said to the man, "Friend, what a rare good cane you have."

"Yes," the man responded, "I have used it for many a mile and it has been a great help."

"How would it suit you to give it to me in exchange for these gloves?" asked Mr. Vinegar.

"I will do so willingly," replied the man.

"My hands had become perfectly warm," said Mr. Vinegar as he went on with his cane, "and my legs were very weary. I could not have done better."

As he drew near the forest where he had left his wife he heard an owl on a tree laughing,

"Hoo, hoo, hoo!" Then it called out his name and he stopped to ask what it wanted.

"Mr. Vinegar," said the owl, "you foolish man, you blockhead, you simpleton! you went to the fair and laid out all your money in buying a cow. Not content with that, you changed the cow for some bagpipes on which you could not play and which were not worth one tenth as much as the cow. Ah, foolish, foolish man! Then you no sooner had the bagpipes than you changed them for the gloves that were worth not one quarter as much as the bagpipes; and when you got the gloves you exchanged them for a cane, and now for your forty guineas you have nothing to show but that poor miserable stick which you might have cut in any hedge. Hoo, hoo, hoo, hoo, hoo!"

The bird laughed loud and long, and Mr. Vinegar became very angry and threw his cane at its head. The cane lodged in the tree, and Mr. Vinegar returned to his wife without money, cow, bagpipes, gloves, or stick, and she said things to him that he liked even less than what the bird had said.

TATTERCOATS

(English)

This is one of the prettiest of the 300 or more variants of the "Cinderella" theme.

In a great palace by the sea there once dwelt a very rich old lord, who had neither wife nor children living, only one little granddaughter, whose face he had never seen in all her life. He hated her bitterly, because at her birth his favourite daughter died; and when the old nurse brought him the baby, he swore that it might live or die as it liked, but he would never look on its face as long as it lived.

So he turned his back and sat by his window, looking out over the sea and weeping great tears for his lost daughter, till his white hair and beard grew down over his shoulders and twined round his chair and crept into the chinks of the floor, and his tears, dropping on to the window-ledge, wore a channel through the stone and

"Tattercoats." From *More English Fairy Tales,* collected and edited by Joseph Jacobs. David Nutt, London, 1894

ran away in a little river to the great sea. And, meanwhile, his granddaughter grew up with no one to care for her or clothe her; only the old nurse, when no one was by, would sometimes give her a dish of scraps from the kitchen or a torn petticoat from the rag-bag; while the other servants of the palace would drive her from the house with blows and mocking words, calling her "Tattercoats" and pointing at her bare feet and shoulders, till she ran away crying, to hide among the bushes.

And so she grew up, with little to eat or to wear, spending her days in the fields and lanes, with only the gooseherd for a companion, who would play to her so merrily on his little pipe, when she was hungry or cold or tired, that she forgot all her troubles and fell to dancing, with his flock of noisy geese for partners.

But one day people told each other that the king was travelling through the land, and in the town nearby was to give a great ball to all the lords and ladies of the country, when the prince, his only son, was to choose a wife.

One of the royal invitations was brought to the palace by the sea, and the servants carried it up to the old lord who still sat by his window, wrapped in his long white hair and weeping into the little river that was fed by his tears.

But when he heard the king's command, he dried his eyes and bade them bring shears to cut him loose, for his hair had bound him a fast prisoner and he could not move. And then he sent them for rich clothes and jewels, which he put on; and he ordered them to saddle the white horse with gold and silk, that he might ride to meet the king.

Meanwhile, Tattercoats had heard of the great doings in the town, and she sat by the kitchen door, weeping because she could not go to see them. And when the old nurse heard her crying, she went to the lord of the palace and begged him to take his granddaughter with him to the king's ball.

But he only frowned and told her to be silent, while the servants laughed and said, "Tattercoats is happy in her rags, playing with the gooseherd. Let her be—it is all she is fit for."

A second, and then a third time, the old nurse begged him to let the girl go with him, but she was answered only by black looks and fierce words, till she was driven from the room by the jeering servants, with blows and mocking words.

Weeping over her ill-success, the old nurse went to look for Tattercoats; but the girl had been turned from the door by the cook and had run away to tell her friend, the gooseherd, how unhappy she was because she could not go to the king's ball.

But when the gooseherd had listened to her story, he bade her cheer up and proposed that they should go together into the town to see the king and all the fine things; and when she looked sorrowfully down at her rags and bare feet, he played a note or two upon his pipe, so gay and merry that she forgot all about her tears and her troubles, and before she well knew, the herdboy had taken her by the hand, and she and he, and the geese before them, were dancing down the road towards the town.

Before they had gone very far, a handsome young man, splendidly dressed, rode up and stopped to ask the way to the castle where the king was staying; and when he found that they too were going thither, he got off his horse and walked beside them along the road.

The herdboy pulled out his pipe and played a low sweet tune, and the stranger looked again and again at Tattercoats' lovely face till he fell deeply in love with her and begged her to marry him.

But she only laughed and shook her golden head.

"You would be finely put to shame if you had a goose-girl for your wife!" said she. "Go and ask one of the great ladies you will see tonight at the king's ball, and do not flout poor Tattercoats."

But the more she refused him, the sweeter the pipe played and the deeper the young man fell in love; till at last he begged her, as a proof of his sincerity, to come that night at twelve to the king's ball, just as she was, with the herdboy and his geese, and in her torn petticoat and bare feet, and he would dance with her before the king and the lords and ladies, and present her to them all, as his dear and honoured bride.

So when night came, and the hall in the castle was full of light and music, and the lords and ladies were dancing before the king, just as the clock struck twelve, Tattercoats and the herdboy, followed by his flock of noisy geese, entered at the great doors and walked straight up the ballroom, while on either side the ladies whispered, the lords laughed, and the king seated at the far end stared in amazement.

But as they came in front of the throne, Tattercoats' lover rose from beside the king and came to meet her. Taking her by the hand, he kissed her thrice before them all and turned to the king.

"Father!" he said, for it was the prince him-

self, "I have made my choice, and here is my bride, the loveliest girl in all the land, and the sweetest as well!"

Before he had finished speaking, the herdboy put his pipe to his lips and played a few low notes that sounded like a bird singing far off in the woods; and as he played, Tattercoats' rags were changed to shining robes sewn with glittering jewels, a golden crown lay upon her golden hair, and the flock of geese behind her became a crowd of dainty pages, bearing her long train.

And as the king rose to greet her as his daughter, the trumpets sounded loudly in honour of the new princess, and the people outside in the street said to each other:

"Ah! Now the prince has chosen for his wife the loveliest girl in all the land!"

But the gooseherd was never seen again, and no one knew what became of him; while the old lord went home once more to his palace by the sea, for he could not stay at court, when he had sworn never to look on his granddaughter's face.

So there he still sits by his window, if you could only see him, as you some day may, weeping more bitterly than ever, as he looks out over the sea.

TOM TIT TOT

(English)

This is a humorous variant of the German "Rumpelstiltzkin." No one knows which came first. Children who hear both generally like this one best, and it is unquestionably one of the finest tales from English oral tradition. Try to keep its touch of Suffolk dialect, which Jacobs skillfully "reduced."

Once upon a time there was a woman, and she baked five pies. And when they came out of the oven, they were that overbaked the crusts were too hard to eat. So she says to her daughter:

"Darter," says she, "put you them there pies on the shelf, and leave 'em there a little, and they'll come again." She meant, you know, the crust would get soft.

"Tom Tit Tot." From *English Fairy Tales,* collected by Joseph Jacobs. Third edition, revised. David Nutt, London, 1907

But the girl, she says to herself, "Well, if they'll come again, I'll eat 'em now." And she set to work and ate 'em all, first and last.

Well, come supper time the woman said, "Go you, and get one o' them there pies. I dare say they've come again now."

The girl went and she looked, and there was nothing but the dishes. So back she came and says she, "Noo, they ain't come again."

"Not one of 'em?" says the mother.

"Not one of 'em," says she.

"Well, come again, or not come again," said the woman, "I'll have one for supper."

"But you can't, if they ain't come," said the girl.

"But I can," says she. "Go you, and bring the best of 'em."

"Best or worst," says the girl, "I've ate 'em all, and you can't have one till that's come again."

Well, the woman she was done, and she took her spinning to the door to spin, and as she span she sang:

"My darter ha' ate five, five pies to-day.
My darter ha' ate five, five pies to-day."

The king was coming down the street, and he heard her sing, but what she sang he couldn't hear, so he stopped and said:

"What was that you were singing, my good woman?"

The woman was ashamed to let him hear what her daughter had been doing, so she sang, instead of that:

"My darter ha' spun five, five skeins to-day.
My darter ha' spun five, five skeins to-day."

"Stars o' mine!" said the king, "I never heard tell of anyone that could do that."

Then he said: "Look you here, I want a wife, and I'll marry your daughter. But look you here," says he, "eleven months out of the year she shall have all she likes to eat, and all the gowns she likes to get, and all the company she likes to keep; but the last month of the year she'll have to spin five skeins every day, and if she don't I shall kill her."

"All right," says the woman, for she thought what a grand marriage that was. And as for the five skeins, when the time came, there'd be plenty of ways of getting out of it, and likeliest, he'd have forgotten all about it.

Well, so they were married. And for eleven months the girl had all she liked to eat, and all the gowns she liked to get, and all the company she liked to keep.

But when the time was getting over, she began to think about the skeins and to wonder if he had 'em in mind. But not one word did he say about 'em, and she thought he'd wholly forgotten 'em.

However, the last day of the last month he takes her to a room she'd never set eyes on before. There was nothing in it but a spinning-wheel and a stool. And says he: "Now, my dear, here you'll be shut in tomorrow with some victuals and some flax, and if you haven't spun five skeins by the night, your head'll go off."

And away he went about his business.

Well, she was that frightened, she'd always been such a gatless girl that she didn't so much as know how to spin, and what was she to do tomorrow with no one to come nigh her to help her? She sat down on a stool in the kitchen, and law! how she did cry!

However, all of a sudden she heard a sort of a knocking low down on the door. She upped and oped it, and what should she see but a small little black thing with a long tail. That looked up at her right curious, and that said:

"What are you a-crying for?"

"What's that to you?" says she.

"Never you mind," that said, "but tell me what you're a-crying for."

"That won't do me no good if I do," says she.

"You don't know that," that said, and twirled that's tail round.

"Well," says she, "that won't do no harm, if that don't do no good," and she upped and told about the pies, and the skeins, and everything.

"This is what I'll do," says the little black thing, "I'll come to your window every morning and take the flax and bring it spun at night."

"What's your pay?" says she.

That looked out of the corner of that's eyes, and that said, "I'll give you three guesses every night to guess my name, and if you haven't guessed it before the month's up, you shall be mine."

Well, she thought she'd be sure to guess that's name before the month was up. "All right," says she, "I agree."

"All right," that says, and law! how that twirled that's tail.

Well, the next day, her husband took her into the room, and there was the flax and the day's food.

"Now there's the flax," says he, "and if that ain't spun up this night, off goes your head." And then he went out and locked the door.

He'd hardly gone, when there was a knocking against the window.

She upped and she oped it, and there sure enough was the little old thing sitting on the ledge.

"Where's the flax?" says he.

"Here it be," says she. And she gave it to him.

Well, come the evening a knocking came again to the window. She upped and she oped it, and there was the little old thing with five skeins of flax on his arm.

"Here it be," says he, and he gave it to her.

"Now, what's my name?" says he.

"What, is that Bill?" says she.

"Noo, that ain't," says he, and he twirled his tail.

"Is that Ned?" says she.

"Noo, that ain't," says he, and he twirled his tail.

"Well, is that Mark?" says she.

"Noo, that ain't," says he, and he twirled his tail harder, and away he flew.

Well, when her husband came in, there were the five skeins ready for him. "I see I shan't have to kill you tonight, my dear," says he. "You'll have your food and your flax in the morning," says he, and away he goes.

Well, every day the flax and the food were brought, and every day that there little black impet used to come mornings and evenings. And all the day the girl sat trying to think of names to say to it when it came at night. But she never hit on the right one. And as it got towards the end of the month, the impet began to look so maliceful, and that twirled that's tail faster and faster each time she gave a guess.

At last it came to the last day but one. The impet came at night along with the five skeins, and that said:

"What, ain't you got my name yet?"

"Is that Nicodemus?" says she.

"Noo, t'ain't," that says.

"Is that Sammle?" says she.

"Noo, t'ain't," that says.

"A-well, is that Methusalem?" says she.

"Noo, t'ain't that neither," that says.

Then that looks at her with that's eyes like a coal o'fire, and that says, "Woman, there's only tomorrow night, and then you'll be mine!" And away it flew.

Well, she felt that horrid. However, she heard the king coming along the passage. In he came, and when he sees the five skeins, he says, says he:

"Well, my dear," says he. "I don't see but what you'll have your skeins ready tomorrow night as well, and as I reckon I shan't have to kill you, I'll have supper in here tonight." So they brought supper, and another stool for him, and down the two sat.

Well, he hadn't eaten but a mouthful or so, when he stops and begins to laugh.

"What is it?" says she.

"A-why," says he, "I was out a-hunting today, and I got away to a place in the wood I'd never seen before. And there was an old chalk-pit. And I heard a kind of a sort of a humming. So I got off my hobby, and I went right quiet to the pit, and I looked down. Well, what should there be but the funniest little black thing you ever set eyes on. And what was that doing, but that had a little spinning wheel, and that was spinning wonderful fast, and twirling that's tail. And as that span that sang:

> "Nimmy nimmy not
> My name's Tom Tit Tot."

Well, when the girl heard this, she felt as if she could have jumped out of her skin for joy, but she didn't say a word.

Next day that there little thing looked so maliceful when he came for the flax. And when night came, she heard that knocking against the window panes. She oped the window, and that come right in on the ledge. That was grinning from ear to ear, and Oo! that's tail was twirling round so fast.

"What's my name?" that says, as that gave her the skeins.

"Is that Solomon?" she says, pretending to be afeard.

"Noo, t'ain't," that says, and that came further into the room.

"Well, is that Zebedee?" says she again.

"Noo, 'tain't," says the impet. And then that laughed and twirled that's tail till you couldn't hardly see it.

"Take time, woman," that says; "next guess, and you're mine." And that stretched out that's black hands at her.

Well, she backed a step or two, and she looked at it, and then she laughed out, and says she, pointing her finger at it:

> "Nimmy nimmy not
> Your name's Tom Tit Tot."

Well, when that heard her, that gave an awful shriek and away that flew into the dark, and she never saw it any more.

THE BLACK BULL OF NORROWAY

(English)

Here is a somber and beautiful story of a black spell which is broken at last by the faithful love of a girl. The rhymes add much to its charm.

Long ago in Norroway there lived a lady who had three daughters. Now they were all pretty, and one night they fell a-talking of whom they meant to marry.

And the eldest said, "I will have no one lower than an Earl."

And the second said, "I will have no one lower than a Lord."

But the third, the prettiest and the merriest, tossed her head and said, with a twinkle in her eye, "Why so proud? As for me I would be content with the Black Bull of Norroway."

At that the other sisters bade her be silent and

"The Black Bull of Norroway." Reprinted with permission of The Macmillan Company from *English Fairy Tales* by Flora Annie Steel. Copyright 1918 by The Macmillan Company, renewed 1946 by Mabel H. Webster. Used by permission of Macmillan & Co. Ltd.

not talk lightly of such a monster. For, see you, is it not written:

> To wilder measures now they turn,
>   The black black Bull of Norroway;
> Sudden the tapers cease to burn,
>   The minstrels cease to play.

So, no doubt, the Black Bull of Norroway was held to be a horrid monster.

But the youngest daughter would have her laugh, so she said three times that she would be content with the Black Bull of Norroway.

Well! It so happened that the very next morning a coach-and-six came swinging along the road, and in it sat an Earl who had come to ask the hand of the eldest daughter in marriage. So there were great rejoicings over the wedding, and the bride and bridegroom drove away in the coach-and-six.

Then the next thing that happened was that a coach-and-four with a Lord in it came swinging along the road; and he wanted to marry the second daughter. So they were wed, and there were great rejoicings, and the bride and bridegroom drove away in the coach-and-four.

Now after this there was only the youngest, the prettiest and the merriest, of the sisters left, and she became the apple of her mother's eye. So you may imagine how the mother felt when one morning a terrible bellowing was heard at the door, and there was a great big Black Bull waiting for his bride.

She wept and she wailed, and at first the girl ran away and hid herself in the cellar for fear, but there the Bull stood waiting, and at last the girl came up and said:

"I promised I would be content with the Black Bull of Norroway, and I must keep my word. Farewell, mother, you will not see me again."

Then she mounted on the Black Bull's back, and it walked away with her quite quietly. And ever it chose the smoothest paths and the easiest roads, so that at last the girl grew less afraid. But she became very hungry and was nigh to faint when the Black Bull said to her, in quite a soft voice that wasn't a bellow at all:

> "Eat out of my left ear,
>   Drink out of my right,

> And set by what you leave
>   To serve the morrow's night."

So she did as she was bid, and, lo and behold! the left ear was full of delicious things to eat, and the right was full of the most delicious drinks, and there was plenty left over for several days.

Thus they journeyed on, and they journeyed on, through many dreadful forests and many lonely wastes, and the Black Bull never paused for bite or sup, but ever the girl he carried ate out of his left ear and drank out of his right, and set by what she left to serve the morrow's night. And she slept soft and warm on his broad back.

Now at last they reached a noble castle where a large company of lords and ladies were assembled, and greatly the company wondered at the sight of these strange companions. And they invited the girl to supper, but the Black Bull they turned into the field, and left to spend the night after his kind.

But when the next morning came, there he was ready for his burden again. Now, though the girl was loth to leave her pleasant companions, she remembered her promise, and mounted on his back, so they journeyed on, and journeyed on, and journeyed on, through many tangled woods and over many high mountains. And ever the Black Bull chose the smoothest paths for her and set aside the briars and brambles, while she ate out of his left ear and drank out of his right.

So at last they came to a magnificent mansion where Dukes and Duchesses and Earls and Countesses were enjoying themselves. Now the company, though much surprised at the strange companions, asked the girl in to supper; and the Black Bull they would have turned into the park for the night, but that the girl, remembering how well he had cared for her, asked them to put him into the stable and give him a good feed.

So this was done, and the next morning he was waiting before the hall-door for his burden; and she, though somewhat loth at leaving the fine company, mounted him cheerfully enough, and they rode away, and they rode away, and they rode away, through thick briar brakes and up fearsome cliffs. But ever the Black Bull trod the brambles underfoot and chose the easiest paths, while she ate out of his left ear and drank out of his right, and wanted for nothing, though he had neither bite nor sup. So it came to pass that he grew tired and was limping with one foot when, just as the sun was setting, they came to a beautiful palace where Princes and Princesses were disporting themselves with ball on the green grass. Now, though the company greatly wondered at the strange companions, they asked the girl to join them, and ordered the grooms to lead away the Black Bull to a field.

But she, remembering all he had done for her, said, "Not so! He will stay with me!" Then seeing a large thorn in the foot with which he had been limping, she stooped down and pulled it out.

And, lo and behold! in an instant, to every one's surprise, there appeared, not a frightful monstrous bull, but one of the most beautiful Princes ever beheld, who fell at his deliverer's feet, thanking her for having broken his cruel enchantment.

A wicked witch-woman who wanted to marry him had, he said, spelled him until a beautiful maiden of her own free will should do him a favour.

"But," he said, "the danger is not all over. You have broken the enchantment by night; that by day has yet to be overcome."

So the next morning the Prince had to resume the form of a bull, and they set out together; and they rode, and they rode, and they rode, till they came to a dark and ugsome glen. And here he bade her dismount and sit on a great rock.

"Here you must stay," he said, "while I go yonder and fight the Old One. And mind! move neither hand nor foot whilst I am away, else I shall never find you again. If everything around you turns blue, I shall have beaten the Old One; but if everything turns red, he will have conquered me."

And with that, and a tremendous roaring bellow, he set off to find his foe.

Well, she sat as still as a mouse, moving neither hand nor foot, nor even her eyes, and waited, and waited, and waited. Then at last everything turned blue. But she was so overcome with joy to think that her lover was victorious that she forgot to keep still, and lifting one of her feet, crossed it over the other!

So she waited, and waited, and waited. Long

she sat, and aye she wearied; and all the time he was seeking for her, but he never found her.

At last she rose and went she knew not whither, determined to seek for her lover through the whole wide world. So she journeyed on, and she journeyed on, and she journeyed on, until one day in a dark wood she came to a little hut where lived an old, old woman who gave her food and shelter, and bid her Godspeed on her errand, giving her three nuts, a walnut, a filbert, and a hazel nut, with these words:

"When your heart is like to break,
    And once again is like to break,
Crack a nut and in its shell
    That will be that suits you well."

After this she felt heartened up, and wandered on till her road was blocked by a great hill of glass; and though she tried all she could to climb it, she could not; for aye she slipped back, and slipped back, and slipped back; for it was like ice.

Then she sought a passage elsewhere, and round and about the foot of the hill she went sobbing and wailing, but ne'er a foothold could she find. At last she came to a smithy; and the smith promised if she would serve him faithfully for seven years and seven days, that he would make her iron shoon wherewith to climb the hill of glass.

So for seven long years and seven short days she toiled, and span, and swept, and washed in the smith's house. And for wage he gave her a pair of iron shoon, and with them she clomb the glassy hill and went on her way.

Now she had not gone far before a company of fine lords and ladies rode past her talking of all the grand doings that were to be done at the young Duke of Norroway's wedding. Then she passed a number of people carrying all sorts of good things which they told her were for the Duke's wedding. And at last she came to a palace castle where the courtyards were full of cooks and bakers, some running this way, some running that, and all so busy that they did not know what to do first.

Then she heard the horns of hunters and cries of "Room! Room for the Duke of Norroway and his bride!"

And who should ride past but the beautiful Prince she had but half unspelled, and by his side was the witch-woman who was determined to marry him that very day.

Well! at the sight she felt that her heart was indeed like to break, and over again was like to break, so that the time had come for her to crack one of the nuts. So she broke the walnut, as it was the biggest, and out of it came a wonderful wee woman carding wool as fast as ever she could card.

Now when the witch-woman saw this wonderful thing she offered the girl her choice of anything in the castle for it.

"If you will put off your wedding with the Duke for a day, and let me watch in his room to-night," said the girl, "you shall have it."

Now, like all witch-women, the bride wanted everything her own way, and she was so sure she had her groom safe, that she consented; but before the Duke went to rest she gave him, with her own hands, a posset so made that any one who drank it would sleep till morning.

Thus, though the girl was allowed alone into the Duke's chamber, and though she spent the livelong night sighing and singing:

> "Far have I sought for thee,
> Long have I wrought for thee,
> Near am I brought to thee,
> Dear Duke o' Norroway;
> Wilt thou say naught to me?"

the Duke never wakened, but slept on. So when day came the girl had to leave him without his ever knowing she had been there.

Then once again her heart was like to break, and over and over again like to break, and she cracked the filbert nut, because it was the next biggest. And out of it came a wonderful wee, wee woman spinning away as fast as ever she could spin. Now when the witch-bride saw this wonderful thing she once again put off her wedding so that she might possess it. And once again the girl spent the livelong night in the Duke's chamber sighing and singing:

> "Far have I sought for thee,
> Long have I wrought for thee,
> Near am I brought to thee,

> Dear Duke o' Norroway;
> Wilt thou say naught to me?"

But the Duke, who had drunk the sleeping-draught from the hands of his witch-bride, never stirred, and when dawn came the girl had to leave him without his ever knowing she had been there.

Then, indeed, the girl's heart was like to break, and over and over and over again like to break, so she cracked the last nut—the hazel nut —and out of it came the most wonderful wee, wee, wee-est woman reeling away at yarn as fast as she could reel.

And this marvel so delighted the witch-bride that once again she consented to put off her wedding for a day, and allow the girl to watch in the Duke's chamber the night through, in order to possess it.

Now it so happened that when the Duke was dressing that morning he heard his pages talking amongst themselves of the strange sighing and singing they had heard in the night; and he said to his faithful old valet, "What do the pages mean?"

And the old valet, who hated the witch-bride, said:

"If the master will take no sleeping-draught to-night, mayhap he may also hear what for two nights has kept me awake."

At this the Duke marvelled greatly, and when the witch-bride brought him his evening posset, he made excuse it was not sweet enough, and while she went away to get honey to sweeten it withal, he poured away the posset and made believe he had swallowed it.

So that night when dark had come, and the girl stole in to his chamber with a heavy heart thinking it would be the very last time she would ever see him, the Duke was really broad awake. And when she sat down by his bedside and began to sing:

> "Far have I sought for thee,"

he knew her voice at once, and clasped her in his arms.

Then he told her how he had been in the power of the witch-woman and had forgotten everything, but that now he remembered all and that the spell was broken for ever and aye.

So the wedding feast served for their marriage, since the witch-bride, seeing her power was gone, quickly fled the country and was never heard of again.

WHITTINGTON AND HIS CAT

(English)

The story of Dick Whittington is a popular legend, a hero tale, and a success story! It is over-long and will be improved by a free telling of the main incidents, cutting the details. Younger children will enjoy Marcia Brown's picture-story of Dick, and older children will appreciate the Italian version, "The Priceless Cats."

In the reign of the famous King Edward III, there was a little boy called Dick Whittington, whose father and mother died when he was very young. As poor Dick was not old enough to work, he was very badly off; he got but little for his dinner, and sometimes nothing at all for his breakfast; for the people who lived in the village were very poor indeed, and could not spare him much more than the parings of potatoes, and now and then a hard crust of bread.

Now Dick had heard many, many very strange things about the great city called London; for the country people at that time thought that folks in London were all fine gentlemen and ladies; and that there was singing and music there all day long; and that the streets were all paved with gold.

One day a large waggon and eight horses, all with bells at their heads, drove through the village while Dick was standing by the sign-post. He thought that this waggon must be going to the fine town of London; so he took courage and asked the waggoner to let him walk with him by the side of the waggon. As soon as the waggoner heard that poor Dick had no father or mother and saw by his ragged clothes that he could not be worse off than he was, he told him he might go if he would, so off they set together.

So Dick got safe to London and was in such a hurry to see the fine streets paved all over with

gold that he did not even stay to thank the kind waggoner, but ran off as fast as his legs would carry him, through many of the streets, thinking every moment to come to those that were paved with gold; for Dick had seen a guinea three times in his own little village and remembered what a deal of money it brought in change; so he thought he had nothing to do but to take up some little bits of the pavement, and should then have as much money as he could wish for.

Poor Dick ran till he was tired and had quite forgot his friend the waggoner; but at last, finding it grow dark, and finding that every way he turned he saw nothing but dirt instead of gold, he sat down in a dark corner and cried himself to sleep.

Little Dick was all night in the streets; and next morning, being very hungry, he got up and walked about and asked everybody he met to give him a halfpenny to keep him from starving; but nobody stayed to answer him, and only two or three gave him a halfpenny; so that the poor boy was soon quite weak and faint for the want of victuals.

In this distress he asked charity of several people, and one of them said crossly: "Go to work for an idle rogue." "That I will," said Dick, "I will to go work for you, if you will let me." But the man only cursed at him and went on.

At last a good-natured looking gentleman saw how hungry he looked. "Why don't you go to work, my lad?" said he to Dick.

"Whittington and His Cat." From *English Fairy Tales*, collected by Joseph Jacobs. Third edition, revised. David Nutt, London, 1907

"That I would, but I do not know how to get any," answered Dick.

"If you are willing, come along with me," said the gentleman, and took him to a hay-field, where Dick worked briskly and lived merrily till the hay was made.

After this he found himself as badly off as before; and being almost starved again, he laid himself down at the door of Mr. Fitzwarren, a rich merchant. Here he was soon seen by the cook-maid, who was an ill-tempered creature, and happened just then to be very busy dressing dinner for her master and mistress; so she called out to poor Dick: "What business have you there, you lazy rogue? There is nothing else but beggars. If you do not take yourself away, we will see how you will like a sousing of some dish-water. I have some here hot enough to make you jump."

Just at that time Mr. Fitzwarren himself came home to dinner; and when he saw a dirty ragged boy lying at the door, he said to him: "Why do you lie there, my boy? You seem old enough to work. I am afraid you are inclined to be lazy."

"No, indeed, sir," said Dick to him, "that is not the case, for I would work with all my heart, but I do not know anybody, and I believe I am very sick for the want of food."

"Poor fellow, get up; let me see what ails you."

Dick now tried to rise, but was obliged to lie down again, being too weak to stand, for he had not eaten any food for three days and was no longer able to run about and beg a halfpenny of people in the street. So the kind merchant ordered that he be taken into the house, given a good dinner, and kept to do what work he was able to do for the cook.

Little Dick would have lived very happy in this good family if it had not been for the ill-natured cook. She used to say: "You are under me, so look sharp; clean the spit and the dripping-pan, make the fires, wind up the jack, and do all the scullery work nimbly, or——" and she would shake the ladle at him. Besides, she was so fond of basting that when she had no meat to baste, she would baste poor Dick's head and shoulders with a broom, or anything else that happened to fall in her way. At last her ill-usage of him was told to Alice, Mr. Fitzwarren's daugh-

ter, who told the cook she should be turned away if she did not treat him kinder.

The behaviour of the cook was now a little better; but besides this Dick had another hardship to get over. His bed stood in a garret, where there were so many holes in the floor and the walls that every night he was tormented with rats and mice. A gentleman having given Dick a penny for cleaning his shoes, he thought he would buy a cat with it. The next day he saw a girl with a cat and asked her, "Will you let me have that cat for a penny?" The girl said: "Yes, that I will, master, though she is an excellent mouser."

Dick hid his cat in the garret and always took care to carry a part of his dinner to her; and in a short time he had no more trouble with the rats and mice, but slept quite sound every night.

Soon after this, his master had a ship ready to sail; and as it was the custom that all his servants should have some chance for good fortune as well as himself, he called them all into the parlour and asked them what they would send out.

They all had something that they were willing to venture except poor Dick, who had neither money nor goods and therefore could send nothing. For this reason he did not come into the parlour with the rest; but Miss Alice guessed what was the matter and ordered him to be called in. She then said, "I will lay down some money for him, from my own purse."

But her father told her: "This will not do, for it must be something of his own."

When poor Dick heard this, he said, "I have nothing but a cat which I bought for a penny some time since of a little girl."

"Fetch your cat then, my lad," said Mr. Fitzwarren, "and let her go."

Dick went upstairs and brought down poor puss, with tears in his eyes, and gave her to the captain. "For," he said, "I shall now be kept awake all night by the rats and mice." All the company laughed at Dick's odd venture; and Miss Alice, who felt pity for him, gave him some money to buy another cat.

This, and many other marks of kindness shown him by Miss Alice, made the ill-tempered cook jealous of poor Dick, and she began to use him more cruelly than ever and always made game of him for sending his cat to sea. She asked him, "Do you think your cat will sell for as much money as would buy a stick to beat you?"

At last poor Dick could not bear this usage any longer, and he thought he would run away from his place; so he packed up his few things and started very early in the morning, on All-hallows Day, the first of November. He walked as far as Holloway and there sat down on a stone, which to this day is called "Whittington's Stone," and began to think to himself which road he should take.

While he was thinking what he should do, the Bells of Bow Church, which at that time were only six, began to ring, and their sound seemed to say to him:

"Turn again, Whittington,
Thrice Lord Mayor of London."

"Lord Mayor of London!" said he to himself. "Why, to be sure, I would put up with almost anything now, to be Lord Mayor of London and ride in a fine coach when I grow to be a man! Well, I will go back and think nothing of the cuffing and scolding of the old cook, if I am to be Lord Mayor of London at last."

Dick went back and was lucky enough to get into the house and set about his work before the old cook came downstairs.

We must now follow Mrs. Puss to the coast of Africa. The ship, with the cat on board, was a long time at sea and was at last driven by the winds on a part of the coast of Barbary, where the only people were the Moors, unknown to the English. The people came in great numbers to see the sailors, because they were of different colour from themselves, and treated them civilly; and, when they became better acquainted, were very eager to buy the fine things that the ship was loaded with.

When the captain saw this, he sent patterns of the best things he had to the king of the country, who was so much pleased with them that he sent for the captain to the palace. Here they were placed, as it is the custom of the country, on rich carpets flowered with gold and silver. The king and queen were seated at the upper end of the room, and a number of dishes were brought in for dinner. They had not sat long, when a vast number of rats and mice rushed in and devoured all the meat in an instant. The captain wondered at this and asked if these vermin were not unpleasant.

"Oh yes," said they, "very offensive; and the king would give half his treasure to be freed of them, for they not only destroy his dinner, as you see, but they assault him in his chamber, and even in bed, so that he is obliged to be watched while he is sleeping, for fear of them."

The captain jumped for joy; he remembered poor Whittington and his cat, and told the king he had a creature on board the ship that would despatch all these vermin immediately. The king jumped so high at the joy which the news gave him, that his turban dropped off his head. "Bring this creature to me," says he; "vermin are dreadful in a court, and if she will perform what you say, I will load your ship with gold and jewels in exchange for her."

The captain, who knew his business, took this opportunity to set forth the merits of Mrs. Puss. He told his majesty: "It is not very convenient to part with her, as, when she is gone, the rats and mice may destroy the goods in the ship—but to oblige your majesty, I will fetch her."

"Run, run!" said the queen. "I am impatient to see the dear creature."

Away went the captain to the ship, while another dinner was got ready. He put Puss under his arm, and arrived at the palace just in time to see the table full of rats. When the cat saw them, she did not wait for bidding, but jumped out of the captain's arms, and in a few minutes laid almost all the rats and mice dead at her feet. The rest of them in their fright scampered away to their holes.

The king was quite charmed to get rid so easily of such plagues, and the queen desired that the creature who had done them so great a kindness might be brought to her, that she might look at her. Upon which the captain called, "Pussy, pussy, pussy!" and she came to him. He then presented her to the queen, who started back, and was afraid to touch a creature who had made such a havoc among the rats and mice. However, when the captain stroked the cat and called, "Pussy, pussy," the queen also touched her and cried, "Putty, putty," for she had not learned English. He then put her down on the queen's lap, where she purred and played with

sending him such a prosperous voyage.

They then told the story of the cat, and showed the rich present that the king and queen had sent for her to poor Dick. As soon as the merchant heard this, he called out to his servants:

"Go send him in, and tell him of his fame;
Pray call him Mr. Whittington by name."

Mr. Fitzwarren now showed himself to be a good man; for when some of his servants said so great a treasure was too much for Dick, he answered: "God forbid I should deprive him of the value of a single penny. It is his own, and he shall have it to a farthing."

He then sent for Dick, who at that time was scouring pots for the cook and was quite dirty. He would have excused himself from coming into the counting-house, saying, "The room is swept, and my shoes are dirty and full of hobnails." But the merchant ordered him to come in.

Mr. Fitzwarren ordered a chair to be set for him, and so he began to think they were making game of him, at the same time said to them: "Do not play tricks with a poor simple boy, but let me go down again, if you please, to my work."

"Indeed, Mr. Whittington," said the merchant, "we are all quite in earnest with you, and I most heartily rejoice in the news that these gentlemen have brought you; for the captain has sold your cat to the King of Barbary and brought you in return for her more riches than I possess in the whole world; and I wish you may long enjoy them!"

Mr. Fitzwarren then told the men to open the great treasure they had brought with them; and said: "Mr. Whittington has nothing to do but to put it in some place of safety."

Poor Dick hardly knew how to behave himself for joy. He begged his master to take what part of it

her majesty's hand, and then purred herself to sleep.

The king, having seen the exploits of Mrs. Puss, and being informed that her kittens would stock the whole country and keep it free from rats, bargained with the captain for the whole ship's cargo, and then gave him ten times as much for the cat as all the rest amounted to.

The captain then took leave of the royal party and set sail with a fair wind for England, and after a happy voyage arrived safe in London.

One morning, early, Mr. Fitzwarren had just come to his counting-house and seated himself at the desk to count over the cash and settle the business for the day, when somebody came tap, tap, at the door. "Who's there?" said Mr. Fitzwarren.

"A friend," answered the other; "I come to bring you good news of your ship *Unicorn*." The merchant, bustling up in such a hurry that he forgot his gout, opened the door, and who should he see waiting but the captain and factor, with a cabinet of jewels and a bill of lading. When he looked at this the merchant lifted up his eyes and thanked Heaven for

he pleased, since he owed it all to his kindness. "No, no," answered Mr. Fitzwarren, "this is all your own; and I have no doubt but you will use it well."

Dick next asked his mistress, and then Miss Alice, to accept a part of his good fortune; but they would not, and at the same time told him they felt great joy at his good success. But this poor fellow was too kind-hearted to keep it all to himself; so he made a present to the captain, the mate, and the rest of Mr. Fitzwarren's servants; and even to the ill-natured old cook.

After this Mr. Fitzwarren advised him to send for a proper tailor and get himself dressed like a gentleman; and told him he was welcome to live in his house till he could provide himself with a better.

When Whittington's face was washed, his hair curled, his hat cocked, and he was dressed in a nice suit of clothes, he was as handsome and genteel as any young man who visited at Mr. Fitzwarren's; so that Miss Alice, who had once been so kind to him and thought of him with pity, now looked upon him as fit to be her sweetheart; and the more so, no doubt, because Whittington was now always thinking what he could do to oblige her and making her the prettiest presents that could be.

Mr. Fitzwarren soon saw their love for each other and proposed to join them in marriage, and to this they both readily agreed. A day for the wedding was soon fixed; and they were attended to church by the Lord Mayor, the court of aldermen, the sheriffs, and a great number of the richest merchants in London, whom they afterwards treated with a very rich feast.

History tells us that Mr. Whittington and his lady lived in great splendour, and were very happy. They had several children. He was Sheriff of London, thrice Lord Mayor, and received the honour of knighthood by Henry V.

He entertained this king and his queen at dinner after his conquest of France so grandly that the king said: "Never had prince such a subject"; when Sir Richard heard this, he said: "Never had subject such a prince."

The figure of Sir Richard Whittington with his cat in his arms, carved in stone, was to be seen till the year 1780 over the archway of the old prison of Newgate, which he built for criminals.

THE GOOD HOUSEWIFE

AND HER NIGHT LABORS

(Scottish)

Slightly reminiscent of "Tom Tit Tot," this Scottish tale shows the irony in sometimes getting what you wish for and tells, in brisk style and with a bit of chant, the way to rid oneself of overhelpful fairies. As with the Irish tales, one gets from the Scottish stories the impression that the "wee folk" are all about and sometimes underfoot.

Once upon a time there was in Scotland a farmer who had a very thrifty wife. She was so thrifty that she would gather the little bits of wool that grazing sheep left here and there on the moorland and bring them to her cottage. After her family had gone to bed, the goodwife, whose name was Inary, sat up late, carding the wool and spinning it into yarn. Then she would weave the yarn into warm cloth, to make garments for her children.

With all this late work, Inary became weary. One night, sitting at her loom, she was so tired that she lay down her shuttle, buried her head in her hands, and burst out weeping.

"The Good Housewife and Her Night Labors." From *Favorite Fairy Tales Told in Scotland* by Virginia Haviland, by permission of Little, Brown and Co. Text Copyright © 1963 by Virginia Haviland

"Oh, if only someone would come, from near or far, from land or sea, to help make my cloth," she sobbed.

No sooner had the words left her lips than she heard a knocking on her door.

"Who is there?" she cried, placing her ear to the keyhole.

"Inary, good housewife, open your door to me. As long as I have, you'll get," spoke a strange voice.

Inary hesitated, but then she opened the door. There on the threshold stood an odd, wee woman, dressed all in green, with a white cap on her head.

In her astonishment, Inary only stood and stared. But the wee visitor, without another word, ran straight to the spinning wheel and began to make it whir.

The goodwife shut the door and turned away. Then she heard another knock, even louder. When she asked who was there, a shrill voice repeated the same strange words she had heard before: "Inary, good housewife, open your door to me. As long as I have, you'll get."

When Inary opened the door this time she saw another queer, wee woman standing on the threshold.

This creature, too, ran into the house without waiting to say by-your-leave. She sat herself at the loom and began to throw the weaving shuttle back and forth.

Before the goodwife could shut her door this time, a funny little man in green trousers came out of the darkness. He seized hold of a handful of wool and began to card it. Another wee woman followed him, and then another, and another, until it seemed to the good housewife that all the fairies and pixies in Scotland were entering her house.

The kitchen was alive with eager, busy fairies. Some of them were hanging the great pot on the fire to boil the fulling water for washing the dirty wool. Some were combing and untangling the clean wool. Others were spinning it into yarn, and plying the shuttle to weave the yarn into great webs of cloth.

The din and rattle of their work was like to deafen the good housewife, and to awaken her husband who was sleeping away as if under a spell. *Splash-splash! Whirr-whirr! Clack-clack!*

. . . The water in the pot bubbled over. The spinning wheel whirred round and round. The shuttle flew backwards and forwards in the loom. . . . It seemed as if Inary would be deafened by the clatter!

The worst of the noise was their shrill crying for something to eat. The goodwife put on her griddle and baked bannocks as fast as she could. But the bannocks were eaten up the moment they came off the fire, and the visitors shouted for more and more.

Good Inary became far more tired than she had been to begin with. At last she went to rouse her husband, to see if he could not get rid of this tumult.

To her horror, Inary found that, although she shook her husband with all her might, she could not wake him. It was plain to see that he was bewitched by the Wee Folk.

Terrified by this, Inary left the fairies eating her last batch of bannocks and stole out of the house. She ran as fast as she could over the moor to the cottage of a certain wise man.

Inary knocked at his door until he put his head out of the window to see who was there.

The man listened in silence as Inary told him the whole story. Then he shook his head at her gravely.

"Let this be a lesson to you, foolish woman, never to pray for things that you do not need. Before your husband can be freed from the fairies' spell, you must get them out of the house and you must pour over him the fulling water in which they have boiled the wool.

"But first you must run to the top of the little hill behind your cottage. Some people call it Burg Hill; others call it the Fairie Knowe, for that is where the Little People live. There you must shout three times with all your might: *'Burg Hill is on fire!'*

"All the fairies will run out to see if it be true that their hill is burning. When they are out of your cottage, you must quickly bar the door and turn the kitchen topsy-turvy. You must upset everything that the fairies have worked with. If not, the things that their fingers have touched will open the door and let them in, in spite of you."

The housewife went away. She climbed to the

top of the hill and three times cried with all her might: *"Burg Hill is on fire!"*

Almost before she had finished saying these words, the door of the cottage was flung wide open. All of the Little Folk came running out, knocking one another over in their eagerness to be home first at the hill. Each was calling for the things which he valued most and had left behind him in the Fairie Knowe.

Their cries sounded like this:

"Fetlock and cow
Distaff and thread,
Butter-kegs and cheese,
My big meal chest;
My sons and daughters,
My wool cards and comb,
My anvil and hammer,
My harrows and hoard;
My horses and traces,
My pigstys and pigs!
Burg Hill is on fire,
And if Burg Hill be burned
Our happy home
And merry life
Is gone."

While the Wee Folk were rushing and crying, the housewife slipped away down the back of the Knowe, and ran as fast as she could to her cottage. When she was once inside, it did not take her long to bar the door and turn everything upside down.

She took the band off the spinning wheel, and twisted the head of the distaff the opposite way. She lifted the pot of fulling water off the fire, turned the weaving loom topsy-turvy, and threw down the carding combs.

When she had done everything she could think of, she put the griddle once more on the fire, and set to work to bake a griddleful of bannocks for her husband's breakfast, for the fairies had eaten up every bite of bread in the house.

She was busy at this when the Little Folk trooped back. They had soon found out that Burg Hill was not on fire at all.

"Good housewife, let us in," they cried as they knocked on the door.

"I cannot open the door," she answered, "for my hands are fast in the dough."

Then the fairies began to call to the things which their fingers had touched.

"Good Spinning Wheel, get up and open the door," they whispered.

"How can I?" answered the spinning wheel. "My band is undone."

"Kind Distaff! Open the door for us."

"That would I gladly do," said the distaff, "but I cannot walk, for my head is turned the wrong way."

"Weaving Loom! Have pity, and open the door."

"I am all topsy-turvy, and cannot help myself, far less help anyone else," sighed the loom.

"Pot of Fulling Water! Open the door," they implored.

"I am off the fire," growled the water, "and all my strength is gone."

The fairies became tired and impatient.

"Is there nothing that will come to our aid, and open the door?" they cried.

"I will," said a little barley bannock that was lying toasting on the hearth, and it rose and trundled quickly across the floor.

But, luckily, the housewife saw it. She nipped it between her finger and thumb, just as it was halfway across the kitchen. Because it was only half-baked, it fell with a *splatch* on the cold floor.

The fairies now gave up trying to enter the kitchen. Instead, they climbed through the windows into the room where the good housewife's husband was sleeping. They swarmed up on his bed, and tickled him until he became quite giddy. He talked nonsense and flung himself about, as if he had a fever.

What in the world shall I do now? said the housewife to herself. She wrung her hands in despair.

All of a sudden, she remembered what the wise man had said about the fulling water. She ran to the kitchen and lifted a cupful out of the pot. Back she rushed and threw it over her husband.

In an instant the husband woke up. Jumping out of bed, he ran across the room and opened the door. The fairies vanished, and they have never been seen there from that day to this.

SKERRY-WERRY

(Cornish)

A good Cornish tale is hard to find—at least in print and in a collection for children. "Skerry-Werry" is a haunted and haunting tale, brimful of Cornish words and the Cornish fairies that are known by such names as piskies *and* dinkies. *Retold from traditional sources by a Cornish writer who loved these tales, "Skerry-Werry" has the mystery and dark beauty appropriate to the Celtic spirit and isolated mood of "the land outside England."*

On a great wind-swept moor in King Arthur's country stood a gray stone cottage with a shaggy roof of straw. The cottage was occupied by a widow woman named Nance Pencarrow. Nance was up in years, but in spite of her age her heart was young and she loved children dearly. She was also fond of animals, especially of her golden cat whom she called Tommie Cat.

The moor was a lonely spot, but Nance had gone there when she was first married, and now that she was old she did not want to live anywhere else. Besides, she was too busy to feel the loneliness for she had to get her own living which she did by spinning wool and flax.

When her day's work was done and she had had her supper, she went outside her cottage to enjoy the view. The moor was beautiful to her in all seasons and in all weathers, but particularly so at sundown when the setting sun made the brown moorland streams like rivers of gold.

One evening late in the summer, when the moor was like amethyst fire with heather, there was an unusually fine sunset. The sky behind the sinking sun was a background of pale yellow on which stood out, in sharp relief, great clouds of all wonderful shapes and sizes and every color. Nance watched, enchanted, until the sun was a mere speck on the distant, glittering sea. She was so charmed that she never thought of going into her cottage till the last glimmer of the afterglow had pulsed out of the sky and the stars began to show themselves.

The night seemed unnaturally dark after such splendor, and, as the old woman turned to go in, she was startled to hear a little voice piping, "I've got no mammie to mammie me. Oh dear, what shall I do?"

"My dear senses!" Nance ejaculated. "Whatever is that crying?"

The voice, small as it was, seemed to fill all the silence, and the despair in it went straight to the old woman's kind heart. She listened intently but could not tell whence the cry came. One minute it seemed to be on her right, the next on her left, then it seemed to be away in the distance.

"The little mammieless thing is like a quail, you never can tell where it is," said Nance to herself as the tiny voice once more piped its mournful pipe.

"I'll go in and light my lantern and try to find the poor little cheeld," said the old woman as she hastened into the cottage. Entering it she noticed that her fire had burned down, so she poked it into a blaze, threw on furze and turf, lit her lantern, and went out again on to the moor. The fire leaped and flamed as she went and sent a warm glow after her through the open door.

"Where be 'ee, my little dear?" called the old woman, holding her lantern close to the ground.

As she held it the tiny voice wailed out again, "I've got no mammie to mammie me. Oh dear, what shall I do?"

Nance looked down and close to her feet, on a small bank of wild thyme, was a white face set in a frame of wind-blown hair. Tiny as the eyes were, Nance could see that they were blue as bluest milkworts.

"Why, you be a little bit of a cheeld!" cried Nance astonished. "You be that small 'twas no wonder I couldn't see 'ee. How did 'ee get out here on this lone moor all by your little self?"

The tiny creature with shining hair and blue eyes made no answer but again wailed out, "I've got no mammie to mammie me. Oh dear——"

"Where is your mammie?" interrupted Nance in great concern. "Shame upon her to leave 'ee in this lone place, if she did leave 'ee," Nance added as the child did not speak. "You be a little woman-cheeld by the looks of 'ee."

"I've got no——" began the tiny voice once

more while the pathos in it filled Nance's kind heart with pity.

"I shall mammie you if you will let me," she said, going down on her knees beside the little creature. "I shall dearly love to mammie you for I have nothing of my own to love except Tommie, my cat, an' the little moor birds."

"Will you really mammie me?" asked the child softly.

"Iss fy, I will, the same as if you was my own cheeld. You shall lack for nothing if I can help it."

"Then you shall mammie me till you can't hold me on your lap," said the child.

"That's a bargain," cried Nance, smiling all over her comely old face. "Come along with me into my cottage an' warm your dinky self by the fire."

The tiny creature tripped lightly after the old woman into the cottage. At the door they were met by the big golden cat, who held his tail aloft and purred loudly.

"Tommie Cat is pleased to see 'ee," said Nance in great delight. "He is a very particular gentleman an' don't like anybody except his ould mistress. So you must be in his good graces."

The child, who was not much taller than the golden cat when he stood on his hind legs, went straight to the fire and sat down on a small cricket. Tommie Cat sat by her side and purred yet more loudly while Nance gave the child a slice of buttered brown bread and a cup of goat's milk.

The little maid took it gratefully. When she had eaten and drank, she looked up at Nance and said, "Please, what must I call you?"

"Call me Mammie Pencarrow, if you please, my dear," returned the old woman.

"I will," replied the child. "Now, will you take me upon your lap and mammie me, Mammie Pencarrow?"

"Gladly," cried Nance, and seating herself in her elbow-chair she lifted the tiny creature onto her ample lap.

"My dear life, how heavy you be!" she exclaimed. "Whoever would have believed you was such a lump of a cheeld!"

The old woman, holding the child, petted her and called her by every endearing name she could think of till the fire died down and the cat began to mew.

"Tommie Cat thinks 'tis time we was in bed," said Nance at last. "'Tis just upon midnight, I reckon."

"I never sleep in a bed," said the child. "I sleep on the heather."

"I picked some heather only yesterday to dry for my fire," replied Nance. "I shall make a bed with it in the corner of my little chamber, an' I'll cover 'ee over with a quilt which the Small People made for my ould grandmother's firstborn."

"Then I shall be snug and warm," said the child, "and safer than little moorbirds under their mothers' wings."

Nance made haste to make a bed of heather, then she took the quilt from a chest, and soon the tiny stranger was lying fast asleep under the coverlet which was many-hued like the bow in the cloud and almost as soft. The child did not sleep long, and almost before the larks left their nests in the dewy turf she was awake, merry as a grig with her talk and laughter.

All that day Nance could hardly spin for watching the child dancing, until at last she exclaimed to her, "You can dance like the Dinkies!"

"Did you ever see the Dinkies dance?" the child asked quickly.

"No, but my ould grannie did," Nance replied. "I sometimes wish I had the gift of second sight as she had."

"Do you?" cried the little maid. "Perhaps you will grow new eyes, Mammie Pencarrow, and see even more wonderful things than your grannie saw."

When evening came Nance put aside her spinning wheel and got the supper ready for herself, the child, and Tommie Cat. After they had eaten, all three went to the door of the cottage and looked out over the great moor. The child soon got tired of standing still and began to dance like a gnat in the sunshine. As twilight spread over the earth the child ceased from her dancing and gazed toward the east where great boulder-crowned hills stood up against the evening sky.

"Be 'ee looking for your mammie?" asked Nance, noticing her eager gaze.

"No, I am looking for something I think you

will like to see. It is traveling fast over the moors from the tor country. Look, Mammie Pencarrow, look."

Mammie Pencarrow looked but saw nothing save the will-o'-the-wisp. "I can see nothing but Piskey lights whipping along," she said laughing. "I have seen Piskey lights times without number."

"Look, all the same," begged the child, "and keep your eyes fixed on the first light."

The old woman did as she was bidden and saw a teeny tiny white hand holding a lantern the size of a sloan.

"My goodness gracious," Nance exclaimed, "if my ould eyes didn't deceive me, I saw a dinky hand holding a teeny tiny light flip by my door. 'Twas a lovely little hand, sure 'nough, an' white as a moon daisy."

"You have begun to grow new eyes," laughed the child, clapping her hands.

"The dinky hand must be the hand of a Little Body like my ould grannie used to see," said Nance. "How I wish I could see the rest of her!"

"You will see lots of wonderful things if you get new eyesight," the child murmured.

The following evening again found the old woman, the little maid, and Tommie Cat outside the cottage. The child danced till the sun had set and the stars were reflected in all their silvery whiteness in the moorland pools. Then the dancing ceased, and the child sent her glance toward the tor country.

"There is something coming along," she said softly. "It will be here in a minute. Look hard at it when it comes near."

The old woman looked hard. When it came close to the cottage she exclaimed, "My dear life, I see two dinky feet dancing along! The feet do match the hand I saw yesterday eve. What darling little feet they be!"

"They are dancing like the Dinkies you told me about yesterday," said the child. "Oh, I am so glad you have seen the little feet for now I know that you are growing new eyes."

The next day it was wet. The rain fell quietly on the moor, bringing out the fragrance of the wild thyme, the mints, and many another moorland plant till the great open space with its multitude of flowers was full of sweetness.

"I'm afraid the Piskey lights won't come whipping over the moor in the dummuts this evening for 'tis raining an' will rain till tomorrow if I can tell the weather," said Nance as she sat at her spinning wheel and watched the child playing with the yellow cat. "An' I do so want to see the Little Body. I want to see her all to once unless she goes about in bits!"

The rain did not leave off, and the sun went down behind gray clouds. At eventide, when they went to the door and looked out, there was nothing to be seen save a heavy veil of mist.

"The mist is as thick as a hedge," said Nance. "We may as well go in an' sit by the fire."

"We will," cried the child, "and you shall hold me on your lap."

When the old woman had taken her seat in the elbow-chair she took the child on her lap, but to her astonishment she found her grown heavier. "Why, if you get much heavier I shan't be able to hold 'ee," Nance exclaimed. "I can't understand how you're such a great weight. You en't growing no bigger nuther. If my ould eyes tell me true, you have gone smaller!"

The child laughed mischievously.

"Somebody must have stepped over 'ee when you was a croom of a baby," Nance went on, "or you have stepped over a ling broom. If that was the case, you will always be a little go-by-the-ground like the Small People." Then she added tenderly, "but you will always be a little skerry-werry."

"What is a skerry-werry?" asked the child.

"A little body, quick an' light on her feet," said the old woman, "an' you be ever so quick on your dinky feet. I think I shall call 'ee Skerry-Werry."

"Do," said the child, "it is a nice name. Now, sing to me, Mammie Pencarrow, sing to Skerry-Werry."

Nance began to sing, but her voice was so loud and harsh that the cat left the hearthstone and jumped up on the window seat, and the child put her hands over her ears.

"My voice is harsher than corncraiks," said the old woman, "but I was willing to oblige 'ee, my dear. Sing to Mammie Pencarrow instead, won't 'ee now?"

Nothing loath, the little maid opened wide her red mouth and began to sing. Her voice was so bewitching that the old woman could not keep still. Her head went niddle noddle, her hands tried to keep time to the tune, the crock on the brandis went twirling, and the cloam on the gaily painted dresser started to dance, the cricket tapped on the floor, and Tommie Cat stood on his legs in the window seat.

"Stop singing, I beg of 'ee," Nance implored, "or I don't know what will happen. My little house will go dancing away over the moor unless 'ee stop."

The child stopped but she seemed surprised. "Was my voice harsh as a corncraik's?" she asked.

"No fy, it wasn't, I never heard such singing in all my life, but what it was about I have no more idea than Tommie Cat. You sang in a strange language, my dear, there wasn't a word of Cornish in it!"

The day that followed was a beautiful one. Skerry-Werry danced till Nance's head went spinning like her wheel and the big golden cat sat on his tail and looked amazed. At the setting of the sun all three went out on the moor. The child did not dance and the cat was as still as if he were sitting by a mousehole. The twilight came quickly after the sun had dropped into the sea.

"The Piskey lights have left the tor country," the child said. "Look, Mammie Pencarrow, look."

The Piskey lights came nearer and nearer. When they were quite close, Nance saw a teeny tiny woman about the height of her thumb at the head of the lights. Her face was white and shiny like a wren's egg fresh from the nest, her hair was as yellow as a sunbeam and as silky as cotton grass. Her dress was green and all of a glimmer like glowworm light. In her hand she held a lantern the size of a sloan, and the light that came from it was as silvery as the dew's crystal beads. She smiled as the old woman gazed down at her when she whipped past.

"My dear soul an' body, what a lovely little lady!" Nance exclaimed. "She must have been one of the Small People my ould grannie used to see."

"I'm ever so glad you have seen a Dinky," cried Skerry-Werry. "You really are getting your grandmother's gift, Mammie Pencarrow, the gift of second sight."

"There's more Piskey lights traveling over the moor," said the old woman, and keeping her gaze fixed on them she saw a teeny tiny horse's head with a golden mane which the head tossed as it flew by the cottage.

"My dear senses, whatever shall I see next?" laughed Nance with the glee of a child. "Now I wish I could see the rest of the little horse, his little tail and all! He must be a handsome critter judging by his head."

"I'm so glad you have seen the head of a dinky horse," piped the child, "for now I am certain that you have grown your new eyes."

For a long time they kept their faces turned toward the east, but they saw no more that night, and when the dummuts changed to darkness they went into the cottage.

The next evening, when the sun had gone under the water, the old woman faced the tor country to watch for Piskey lights. For a long time she watched in vain, then out of the twilight appeared four tiny lights which came galloping over the ground. When they came near she saw four horse's feet.

"I expect 'tis the feet of the dinky horse whose head I saw last night," cried Nance, holding up her hands.

"I wonder what you will see next," said Skerry-Werry.

"I wonder," echoed the old woman.

The next day it was misty, but for heat and not for rain. The mist lay white as hoar frost on the turf and heather, and the great hills were wrapped in gray.

"This sort of weather won't prevent the Piskey lights from whipping about if they're so minded," said Nance as she sat at her wheel.

"They will be minded, Mammie Pencarrow."

"How do you know, Skerry-Werry?" Nance asked.

"Because you mammied me," was the answer.

The moment supper was over and the things put away, Mammie Pencarrow, Skerry-Werry, and Tommie Cat went outside the cottage. The setting sun shone behind a thin veiling of mist. Through an eyelet in the fog could be seen the curve of the new moon. The evening was hot and sultry even on the open moor.

"I fear there won't be anything out of the

common for my ould eyes to see tonight," said Nance.

"Perhaps not for your *old* eyes to see, but there may be something lovely for your *new* eyes."

As Skerry-Werry was speaking, out of the mist came a teeny tiny prancing horse as bright as the crescent moon, with a golden tail that swept the ground. He was not half so big as Tommie Cat, but he was perfect, bare as a colt and as full of life and grace. His golden mane flew out as he came, and he galloped so fast that he was out of sight almost as soon as they saw him.

"My dear heart alive, I have seen the whole of the dinky horse!" Nance exclaimed. "Whoever would have believed there were such things as horses not so big as Tommie Cat!"

"It isn't everybody who can see a dinky horse," said Skerry-Werry. "Not one in a million. But the fog is lifting, and in the clearness I can see something coming. Look, Mammie Pencarrow, look."

Nance, sending her glance to where the child pointed, saw a long train of golden light coming over the turf. The cat shot out his ears, and his eyes became balls of green fire. The light was many yards in length and out of it appeared a hundred tiny horses. On every horse rode a tiny horseman dressed in a bright green coat and breeches and a red hat.

The old woman was too astonished to utter a word and sat, staring, with her eyes and mouth wide open. Behind the horses, which all had long manes and sweeping tails, came a teeny tiny carriage drawn by twelve horses as white as ewe's cream. In the carriage sat a teeny tiny woman with a very sad face. She looked so sorrowful that Nance's kind eyes filled with tears. As she gazed at her, the golden carriage and the prancing horses were almost lost sight of in her pity for the sad-faced woman.

"Nobody is too dinky to have sorrow," said the old woman softly to herself, "an' even the Small People must have their little sorrows, I s'pose."

"You have got the second sight," cried Skerry-Werry, "and you have seen more than your grandmother ever saw!"

"How do you know what my ould grannie saw or did not see?" asked Nance, gazing at the child.

"You're only a croom of a cheeld, or look like one, but you do talk like an ancient woman. You be'nt one of the Little Ancients, be 'ee, Skerry-Werry?"

"Why, Mammie Pencarrow, what will you say next?" laughed the child. "Shall we go into the cottage?"

"If you please," murmured the old woman.

Into the little dwelling they went, taking their places by the fire which was blazing on the hearthstone and sending a warm glow over the room.

"Won't you mammie me and call me pretty names like you did the first night I came?" asked the child.

Nance smiled. "I love to mammie you and say pretty things to you." Stooping down, she lifted the child on her lap, but the tiny maid was so heavy it nearly broke Nance's back.

"What a terrible weight you be," she groaned. "I don't believe I shall be able to hold 'ee on my lap more than a minute. The weight of 'ee is breaking my poor ould knees. 'Tis fine an' queer that a little bit of a cheeld like you should be so heavy. You be getting smaller as you be getting heavier. I can't understand it. There! my ould knees have given out already, iss fy, they have!"

As Nance spoke, Skerry-Werry slipped from her knees and fell face down on the cat, who looked as flat as a baking iron when the dinky maid picked herself up.

"I hope I did not hurt you, Tommie Cat," she whispered, patting him, "but I can't have hurt you so much as it hurts me to know that Mammie Pencarrow can no longer hold me on her lap and mammie me."

"I can mammie you in everything else," said Nance stoutly. "Sit on your cricket now an' warm your toes by the fire before we go to bed."

The child seated herself on the stool and sat gazing into the fire, her tiny white face resting on her hands. Her hair, which looked wind-blown even indoors, was a cloud of gold above her brow. The old woman sat and watched her. The cat, who had quickly recovered being fallen upon, got up and sat at his mistress' feet, but he did not purr.

Nance and Skerry-Werry were silent a long

time, and everything was very still in the cottage and out. The fire blazed brighter and brighter, its shine and the shadows playing on the whitewashed walls. Suddenly the silence was broken by a sad voice crying outside.

"I have lost my little cheeld-whidden. Ah me, what shall I do?"

The old woman started but said never a word. The cat looked toward the door. The child did not move.

In a little while the silence was again broken by the small, sad voice. "I have lost my little cheeld-whidden. Ah me, what shall I do?"

The old woman clutched the elbows of her chair. The cat turned his face to the door. The child sat still, gazing into the fire.

Suddenly Skerry-Werry looked up and said, "Whoever was that crying outside the door?"

"I don't know, my dear, unless it was a nighthawk," returned the old woman.

"I thought a nighthawk's note was a *churrrr,* and now and again a *wh-ip, wh-ip,*" said the child. "The voice I heard outside the door was not like a nighthawk's."

"Perhaps it was a moorhen calling her children to her," said the old woman.

"Perhaps it was," said the child, "but I thought a moorhen's call was *krek-rerk-rerk.* The voice outside the door did not cry *krek-rerk-rerk.*"

"Maybe it was a quail," said the old woman. "His voice is almost as sweet as a flute."

"I know it is," said the child, "for I have heard him often. But, all the same, it is not half so sweet as the voice I heard crying outside the door."

"Perhaps it was a horny-wink," said the old woman.

"I think it could not have been a horny-wink," said the child, "for a horny-wink cries *pet-wit, pet-wit.*"

"It might have been a moor owl we heard."

"The moor owl's flight is soft and silent, but his cry is a scream."

"Perhaps it was a great black raven we heard," said the old woman, "as he was flying across the moors to his home on the cliffs."

"Perhaps it was," said the child, "but I thought a raven's voice was hoarse and loud, and that he called *cawk, cawk.* The voice I heard outside the door was crying as if it had *lost* something."

"Then it must have been a poor mother cow crying out for her baby calf," said the old woman.

"The cow mother says *moo-moo-moo,* and the voice we heard was not crying like that. But perhaps we shall hear the voice again, Mammie Pencarrow."

"I hope not," said the old woman, "for it do hurt like pain."

"Did I hurt you like pain when I cried and said I had no mammie to mammie me?" asked the child.

"No fy, you didn't. I wanted only to find the little mammieless thing."

"Did you?" said the child, gazing up into Nance's face, which was looking troubled.

As she was gazing at the old woman, the sad voice was heard again outside the door. "I have lost my little cheeld-whidden. Ah me, what shall I do?"

"It is surely a shorn lamb shivering on the moor, bleating an' crying for its warm soft fleece," said the old woman loud and quickly as if she wanted to drown the voice outside her door.

"I thought a shorn lamb said *baa, baa, b-a-a,*" said the child. "The voice we heard did not say *baa, b-a-a.*"

"It must have been a mare whinnying for its foal," said the old woman louder and quicker than before.

"The voice I heard did not whinny," said the child.

"Then what did it say?" cried the old woman. "I want you to tell me."

"P'raps it was the cry of a hare caught in the cruel teeth of a gin," said the old woman.

"If you thought that, you would go out in the dark and set the poor hare free," said the child.

"P'raps it's your own mammie come back to mammie you," said the old woman, and her voice was almost as full of sadness as the little voice she had heard outside.

"Look and see," said the child.

Nance turned her face toward the door. There, standing on the drexel, was a beautiful little lady, the same little lady she had seen sitting in the golden carriage drawn by the twelve white horses. As she looked at her, the teeny tiny person lifted up her voice and wrung her hands, "Ah me, I have lost my little cheeld-whidden, what shall I do?" Her voice, pathetic in its woe yet sweeter than music, went straight to Nance's heart.

"If you be her little cheeld-whidden—an' I believe you be," she said, turning to the child, "why don't you run to her? She have got the greater right to you, my little Skerry-Werry," Nance added with a sob in her voice.

"I am her little cheeld-whidden," said the child, "and now that I am too heavy for you to hold on your lap I will go to her to mammie me."

Skerry-Werry got up from the cricket and went toward the door, and as she went she grew visibly smaller. By the time she had reached the little lady standing on the drexel she was only daisy high.

"My little cheeld, my own dear teeny tiny skilly-widden," cried the yearning voice of the mother. "I have found you at last."

The gladness in her voice filled Nance's heart with gladness, and Tommie Cat purred as he had never purred before.

"I must have mammied a Little Body's cheeld," said the old woman softly. "I'm fine an' glad she has got her own dinky mammie instead of me but, oh dear, oh dear, whatever shall I do without my little Skerry-Werry?"

Nance Pencarrow and Tommie Cat went to the door and looked out into the night. At first they saw nothing save the dark and the soft shining of stars. Then, out of the darkness, came the sound of silvery voices and happy laughter. As the old woman looked toward the sound, she saw that the darkness was lit up with a pale green light. Sitting on the turf were hundreds and hundreds of Small People and there in the center, dancing like a butterfly, was her Skerry-Werry!

Ireland

How is it possible to characterize the hero tales, the sorrowful romances, the drolls, the strange half-world of faëry with its enchantments and spells that mark the Celtic fairy tales? Great variety of plot and beauty of style have come from the lips of Irish storytellers, and far less humor than most people seem to expect. Indeed, so few and far between are the drolls and so numerous the somber tales of heroism and romance which come to tragic ends that the Irish tales are almost more popular with adults than with children. Ireland stands alone in the zeal and thoroughness with which its folk tales are sought out from among the people and recorded. The three examples given here differ widely in plot and style. "King O'Toole" is amusing and reflects a widespread European Catholic convention, while "The Peddler of Ballaghadereen" is, according to Ruth Sawyer who brought it to this country, traceable to Hebrew legend and was a tale told by the Irish seanachies. "Connla and the Fairy Maiden" is much more representative of the purely Gaelic tradition—pagan, romantic, and bardic.

KING O'TOOLE AND HIS GOOSE

Stories of the saints walking the earth and taking part in men's affairs were fairly common in the Middle Ages. Usually they were serious stories, but here is an amusing exception. In spite of the unfamiliar and rather difficult nineteenth- *century Irish style of speech, older children will get the sense and the humor of the tale.*

Och, I thought all the world, far and near, had heerd of King O'Toole—well, well, but the darkness of mankind is untellible! Well, sir, you must know, as you didn't hear it afore, that there was a king, called King O'Toole, who was a fine old king in the old ancient times, long ago; and it was he that owned the churches in the early days. The king, you see, was the right sort; he was the real boy and loved sport as he loved his life, and hunting in particular; and from the rising o' the sun, up he got, and away he went over the mountains after the deer; and fine times they were.

Well, it was all mighty good, as long as the king had his health; but, you see, in the course of time the king grew old, by raison he was stiff in his limbs, and when he got stricken in years, his heart failed him, and he was lost entirely for want o' diversion, because he couldn't go a-hunting no longer; and, by dad, the poor king was obliged at last to get a goose to divert him. Oh, you may laugh, if you like, but it's truth I'm telling you; and the way the goose diverted him was this-a-way: You see, the goose used to swim across the lake, and go diving for trout, and catch fish on a Friday for the king, and flew every other day round about the lake, diverting the poor king. All went on mighty well until, by dad, the goose got stricken in years like her master, and couldn't divert him no longer, and then it was that the poor king was lost entirely. The king was walkin' one mornin' by the edge of the lake, lamentin' his cruel fate, and thinking of drowning himself, that could get no diversion in life, when all of a sudden, turning round the corner, who should he meet but a mighty decent young man coming up to him.

"God save you," says the king to the young man.

"God save you kindly, King O'Toole," says the young man.

"True for you," says the king. "I am King O'Toole," says he, "prince and plennypenny-tinchery of these parts," says he; "but how came ye to know that?" says he.

"Oh, never mind," says St. Kavin.

You see it was Saint Kavin, sure enough—the saint himself in disguise, and nobody else. "Oh, never mind," says he, "I know more than that. May I make bold to ask how is your goose, King O'Toole?" says he.

"King O'Toole and His Goose." From *Celtic Fairy Tales*, selected and edited by Joseph Jacobs. David Nutt, London, 1892

"Blur-an-agers, how came ye to know about my goose?" says the king.

"Oh, no matter; I was given to understand it," says Saint Kavin.

After some more talk the king says, "What are you?"

"I'm an honest man," says Saint Kavin.

"Well, honest man," says the king, "and how is it you make your money so aisy?"

"By makin' old things as good as new," says Saint Kavin.

"Is it a tinker you are?" says the king.

"No," says the saint; "I'm no tinker by trade, King O'Toole; I've a better trade than a tinker," says he. "What would you say," says he, "if I made your old goose as good as new?"

My dear, at the word of making his goose as good as new, you'd think the poor old king's eyes were ready to jump out of his head. With that the king whistled, and down came the poor goose, just like a hound, waddling up to the poor cripple, her master, and as like him as two peas. The minute the saint clapt his eyes on the goose, "I'll do the job for you," says he, "King O'Toole."

"By *Jaminee!*" says King O'Toole, "if you do, I'll say you're the cleverest fellow in the seven parishes."

"Oh, by dad," says St. Kavin, "you must say more nor that—my horn's not so soft all out," says he, "as to repair your old goose for nothing; what'll you gi' me if I do the job for you?— that's the chat," says St. Kavin.

"I'll give you whatever you ask," says the king; "isn't that fair?"

"Divil a fairer," says the saint; "that's the way to do business. Now," says he, "this is the bargain I'll make with you, King O'Toole: will you gi' me all the ground the goose flies over, the first offer, after I make her as good as new?"

"I will," says the king.

"You won't go back o' your word?" says St. Kavin.

"Honour bright!" says King O'Toole, holding out his fist.

"Honour bright!" says St. Kavin, back agin, "it's a bargain. Come here!" says he to the poor old goose, "come here, you unfortunate ould cripple, and it's I that'll make you the sporting bird." With that, my dear, he took up the goose by the two wings. "Criss o' my cross an you," says he, markin' her to grace with the blessed sign at the same minute—and throwing her up in the air, "whew," says he, jist givin' her a blast to help her; and with that, my jewel, she took to her heels, flyin' like one o' the eagles themselves, and cutting as many capers as a swallow before a shower of rain.

Well, my dear, it was a beautiful sight to see the king standing with his mouth open, looking at his poor old goose flying as light as a lark, and better than ever she was; and when she lit at his feet, patted her on the head, and *"Ma vourneen,"* says he, "but you are the *darlint* o' the world."

"And what do you say to me," says Saint Kavin, "for making her the like?"

"By Jabers," says the king, "I say nothing beats the art o' man, barring the bees."

"And do you say no more nor that?" says Saint Kavin.

"And that I'm beholden to you," says the king.

"But will you gi'e me all the ground the goose flew over?" says Saint Kavin.

"I will," says King O'Toole, "and you're welcome to it," says he, "though it's the last acre I have to give."

"But you'll keep your word true," says the saint.

"As true as the sun," says the king.

"It's well for you, King O'Toole, that you said that word," says he; "for if you didn't say that word, the divil the bit o' your goose would ever fly agin."

When the king was as good as his word, Saint Kavin was pleased with him, and then it was that he made himself known to the king. "And," says he, "King O'Toole, you're a decent man, for I only came here to try you. You don't know me," says he, "because I'm disguised."

"Musha! then," says the king, "who are you?"

"I'm Saint Kavin," said the saint, blessing himself.

"Oh, queen of heaven!" says the king, making the sign of the cross between his eyes, and falling down on his knees before the saint; "is it the great Saint Kavin," says he, "that I've been discoursing all this time without knowing it," says

he, "all as one as if he was a lump of a *gossoon* —and so you're a saint?" says the king.

"I am," says Saint Kavin.

"By Jabers, I thought I was only talking to a dacent boy," says the king.

"Well, you know the difference now," says the saint. "I'm Saint Kavin," says he, "the greatest of all the saints."

And so the king had his goose as good as new, to divert him as long as he lived; and the saint supported him after he came into his property, as I told you, until the day of his death—and that was soon after; for the poor goose thought he was catching a trout one Friday; but, my jewel, it was a mistake he made—and instead of a trout, it was a thieving horse-eel; and instead of the goose killing a trout for the king's supper

—by dad, the eel killed the king's goose—and small blame to him; but he didn't ate her, because he darn't ate what Saint Kavin had laid his blessed hands on.

CONNLA AND

THE FAIRY MAIDEN

This is an ancient story that goes back to the pre-Christian times of the Druids. Its roots not only reach even further back in time, but run through much of the world's folklore. The gift of the apple, according to Robert Graves, "records an ancient ritual situation, outgrown by the time of Homer and Hesiod," [1] *thus dating back to the neolithic and Bronze ages. The theme of the hero traveling to the Land of the Ever Young is found in a later Irish legend about the hero Oisin, and in the Japanese tale of Urashima Taro (See p. 213).*

Connla of the Fiery Hair was son of Conn of the Hundred Fights. One day as he stood by the side of his father on the height of Usna, he saw a maiden clad in strange attire towards him coming.

"Whence comest thou, maiden?" said Connla.

"I come from the Plains of the Ever Living," she said, "there where is neither death nor sin. There we keep holiday alway, nor need we help from any in our joy. And in all our pleasure we have no strife. And because we have our homes in the round green hills, men call us the Hill Folk."

The king and all with him wondered much to hear a voice when they saw no one. For save Connla alone, none saw the Fairy Maiden.

"To whom art thou talking, my son?" said Conn the king.

Then the maiden answered, "Connla speaks to a young, fair maid, whom neither death nor old age awaits. I love Connla, and now I call him away to the Plain of Pleasure, Moy Mell, where Boadag is king for aye, nor has there been sorrow

"Connla and the Fairy Maiden." From *Celtic Fairy Tales*, selected and edited by Joseph Jacobs. David Nutt, London, 1892
[1] Robert Graves, *The Greek Myths*, Volume One, George Braziller, Inc., 1955, page 21

or complaint in that land since he held the kingship. Oh, come with me, Connla of the Fiery Hair, ruddy as the dawn, with thy tawny skin. A fairy crown awaits thee to grace thy comely face and royal form. Come, and never shall thy comeliness fade, nor thy youth, till the last awful day of judgment."

The king in fear at what the maiden said, which he heard though he could not see her, called aloud to his Druid, Coran by name.

"Oh, Coran of the many spells," he said, "and of the cunning magic, I call upon thy aid. A task is upon me too great for all my skill and wit, greater than any laid upon me since I seized the kingship. A maiden unseen has met us, and by her power would take from me my dear, my comely son. If thou help not, he will be taken from thy king by woman's wiles and witchery."

Then Coran the Druid stood forth and chanted his spells towards the spot where the maiden's voice had been heard. And none heard her voice again, nor could Connla see her longer. Only as she vanished before the Druid's mighty spell, she threw an apple to Connla.

For a whole month from that day Connla would take nothing, either to eat or to drink, save only from that apple. But as he ate, it grew again and always kept whole. And all the while there grew within him a mighty yearning and longing after the maiden he had seen.

But when the last day of the month of waiting came, Connla stood by the side of the king his father on the Plain of Arcomin, and again he saw the maiden come towards him, and again she spoke to him.

" 'Tis a glorious place, forsooth, that Connla holds among shortlived mortals awaiting the day of death. But now the folk of life, the ever-living ones, beg and bid thee come to Moy Mell, the Plain of Pleasure, for they have learnt to know thee, seeing thee in thy home among thy dear ones."

When Conn the king heard the maiden's voice he called to his men aloud and said:

"Summon swift my Druid Coran, for I see she has again this day the power of speech."

Then the maiden said: "Oh, mighty Conn, Fighter of a Hundred Fights, the Druid's power is little loved; it has little honour in the mighty land, peopled with so many of the upright. When the Law comes, it will do away with the Druid's magic spells that issue from the lips of the false black demon."

Then Conn the king observed that since the coming of the maiden, Connla his son spoke to none that spake to him. So Conn of the Hundred Fights said to him, "Is it to thy mind what the woman says, my son?"

" 'Tis hard upon me," said Connla; "I love my own folk above all things; but yet a longing seizes me for the maiden."

When the maiden heard this, she answered and said: "The ocean is not so strong as the waves of thy longing. Come with me in my curragh, the gleaming, straight-gliding crystal canoe. Soon can we reach Boadag's realm. I see the bright sun sink, yet far as it is, we can reach it before dark. There is, too, another land worthy of thy journey, a land joyous to all that seek it. Only wives and maidens dwell there. If thou wilt, we can seek it and live there alone together in joy."

When the maiden ceased to speak, Connla of the Fiery Hair rushed away from his kinsmen and sprang into the curragh, the gleaming, straight-gliding crystal canoe. And then they all, king and court, saw it glide away over the bright sea towards the setting sun, away and away, till eye could see it no longer. So Connla and the Fairy Maiden went forth on the sea and were no more seen, nor did any know whither they came.

THE PEDDLER

OF BALLAGHADEREEN

This story was learned by Ruth Sawyer from an Irish seanachie (storyteller), and it is another example of a widespread European folklore theme. Ruth Sawyer has recorded this tale, telling it as she heard it told.

More years ago than you can tell me and twice as many as I can tell you, there lived a peddler in Ballaghadereen. He lived at the crossroads, by

"The Peddler of Ballaghadereen." From *The Way of the Storyteller* by Ruth Sawyer. Copyright 1942 by Ruth Sawyer. Reprinted by permission of The Viking Press, Inc., and the Bodley Head

himself in a bit of a cabin with one room to it, and that so small that a man could stand in the middle of the floor and, without taking a step, he could lift the latch on the front door, he could lift the latch on the back door, and he could hang the kettle over the turf. That is how small and snug it was.

Outside the cabin the peddler had a bit of a garden. In it he planted carrots and cabbages, onions and potatoes. In the center grew a cherry tree—as brave and fine a tree as you would find anywhere in Ireland. Every spring it flowered, the white blossoms covering it like a fresh falling of snow. Every summer it bore cherries as red as heart's blood.

But every year, after the garden was planted the wee brown hares would come from the copse near by and nibble-nibble here, and nibble-nibble there, until there was not a thing left, barely, to grow into a full-sized vegetable that a man could harvest for his table. And every summer as the cherries began to ripen the blackbirds came in whirling flocks and ate the cherries as fast as they ripened.

The neighbors that lived thereabouts minded this and nodded their heads and said: "Master Peddler, you're a poor, simple man, entirely. You let the wild creatures thieve from you without lifting your hand to stop them."

And the peddler would always nod his head back at them and laugh and answer: "Nay, then, 'tis not thieving they are at all. They pay well for what they take. Look you—on yonder cherry tree the blackbirds sing sweeter nor they sing on any cherry tree in Ballaghadereen. And the brown hares make good company at dusk-hour for a lonely man."

In the country roundabout, every day when there was market, a wedding, or a fair, the peddler would be off at ring-o'-day, his pack strapped on his back, one foot ahead of the other, fetching him along the road. And when he reached the town diamond he would open his pack, spread it on the green turf, and, making a hollow of his two hands, he would call:

"Come buy a trinket—come buy a brooch—
Come buy a kerchief of scarlet or yellow!"

In no time at all there would be a great crowding of lads and lasses and children about him, searching his pack for what they might be wanting. And like as not, some barefooted lad would hold up a jack-knife and ask: "How much for this, Master Peddler?"

And the peddler would answer: "Half a crown."

And the lad would put it back, shaking his head dolefully. "Faith, I haven't the half of that, nor likely ever to have it."

And the peddler would pull the lad over to him and whisper in his ear: "Take the knife—'twill rest a deal more easy in your pocket than in my pack."

Then, like as not, some lass would hold up a blue kerchief to her yellow curls and ask: "Master Peddler, what is the price of this?"

And the peddler would answer: "One shilling sixpence."

And the lass would put it back, the smile gone from her face, and she turning away.

And the peddler would catch up the kerchief again and tie it himself about her curls and laugh and say: "Faith, there it looks far prettier than ever it looks in my pack. Take it, with God's blessing."

So it would go—a brooch to this one and a top to that. There were days when the peddler took in little more than a few farthings. But after those days he would sing his way homeward; and the shrewd ones would watch him passing by and wag their fingers at him and say: "You're a poor, simple man, Master Peddler. You'll never be putting a penny by for your old age. You'll end your days like the blackbirds, whistling for crumbs at our back doors. Why, even the vagabond dogs know they can wheedle the half of the bread you are carrying in your pouch, you're that simple."

Which likewise was true. Every stray, hungry dog knew him the length and breadth of the county. Rarely did he follow a road without one tagging his heels, sure of a noonday sharing of bread and cheese.

There were days when he went abroad without his pack, when there was no market-day, no wedding or fair. These he spent with the children, who would have followed him about like the dogs, had their mothers let them. On these days he would sit himself down on some doorstep and when a crowd of children had gathered he would tell them tales—old tales of Ireland—tales of the good folk, of the heroes, of the saints. He knew them all, and he knew how to tell them, the way the children would never be forgetting one of them, but carry them in their hearts until they were old.

And whenever he finished a tale he would say, like as not, laughing and pinching the cheek of some wee lass: "Mind well your manners, whether you are at home or abroad, for you can never be telling what good folk, or saint, or hero you may be fetching up with on the road—or who may come knocking at your doors. Aye, when Duirmuid, or Fionn or Oisin or Saint Patrick walked the earth they were poor and simple and plain men; it took death to put a grand memory on them. And the poor and the simple and the old today may be heroes tomorrow—you never can be telling. So keep a kind word for all, and a gentling hand."

Often an older would stop to listen to the scraps of words he was saying; and often as not he would go his way, wagging his finger and mumbling: "The poor, simple man. He's as foolish as the blackbirds."

Spring followed winter in Ireland, and sum-

mer followed close upon the heels of both. And winter came again and the peddler grew old. His pack grew lighter and lighter, until the neighbors could hear the trinkets jangling inside as he passed, so few things were left. They would nod their heads and say to one another: "Like as not his pockets are as empty as his pack. Time will come, with winter at hand, when he will be at our back doors begging crumbs, along with the blackbirds."

The time did come, as the neighbors had prophesied it would, smug and proper, when the peddler's pack was empty, when he had naught in his pockets and naught in his cupboard. That night he went hungry to bed.

Now it is more than likely that hungry men will dream; and the peddler of Ballaghadereen had a strange dream that night. He dreamed that there came a sound of knocking in the middle of the night. Then the latch on the front door lifted, the door opened without a creak or a cringe, and inside the cabin stepped Saint Patrick. Standing in the doorway the good man pointed a finger; and he spoke in a voice tuned as low as the wind over the bogs. "Peddler, peddler of Ballaghadereen, take the road to Dublin town. When you get to the bridge that spans the Liffey you will hear what you were meant to hear."

On the morrow the peddler awoke and remembered the dream. He rubbed his stomach and found it mortal empty; he stood on his legs and found them trembling in under him; and he said to himself: "Faith, an empty stomach and weak legs are the worst traveling companions a man can have, and Dublin is a long way. I'll bide where I am."

That night the peddler went hungrier to bed, and again came the dream. There came the knocking on the door, the lifting of the latch. The door opened and Saint Patrick stood there, pointing the road: "Peddler, peddler of Ballaghadereen, take the road that leads to Dublin Town. When you get to the bridge that spans the Liffey you will hear what you were meant to hear!"

The second day it was the same as the first. The peddler felt the hunger and the weakness stronger in him, and stayed where he was. But when he woke after the third night and the third

coming of the dream, he rose and strapped his pack from long habit upon his back and took the road to Dublin. For three long weary days he traveled, barely staying his fast, and on the fourth day he came into the city.

Early in the day he found the bridge spanning the river and all the lee-long day he stood there, changing his weight from one foot to the other, shifting his pack to ease the drag of it, scanning the faces of all who passed by. But although a great tide of people swept this way, and a great tide swept that, no one stopped and spoke to him.

At the end of the day he said to himself: "I'll find me a blind alley, and like an old dog I'll lay me down in it and die." Slowly he moved off the bridge. As he passed by the Head Inn of Dublin, the door opened and out came the landlord.

To the peddler's astonishment he crossed the thoroughfare and hurried after him. He clapped a strong hand on his shoulder and cried: "Arra, man, hold a minute! All day I've been watching you. All day I have seen you standing on the bridge like an old rook with rent wings. And of all the people passing from the west to the east, and of all the people passing from the east to the west, not one crossing the bridge spoke aught with you. Now I am filled with a great curiosity entirely to know what fetched you here."

Seeing hunger and weariness on the peddler, he drew him toward the inn. "Come; in return for having my curiosity satisfied you shall have rest in the kitchen yonder, with bread and cheese and ale. Come."

So the peddler rested his bones by the kitchen hearth and he ate as he hadn't eaten in many days. He was satisfied at long last and the landlord repeated his question. "Peddler, what fetched you here?"

"For three nights running I had a dream——" began the peddler, but he got no further.

The landlord of the Head Inn threw back his head and laughed. How he laughed, rocking on his feet, shaking the whole length of him!

"A dream you had, by my soul, a dream!" He spoke when he could get his breath. "I could be telling you were the cut of a man to have dreams, and to listen to them, what's more. Rags on your back and hunger in your cheeks and age upon you, and I'll wager not a farthing in your pouch. Well, God's blessing on you and your dreams."

The peddler got to his feet, saddled his pack, and made for the door. He had one foot over the sill when the landlord hurried after him and again clapped a hand on his shoulder.

"Hold, Master Peddler," he said, "I too had a dream, three nights running." He burst into laughter again, remembering it. "I dreamed there came a knocking on this very door, and the latch lifted, and, standing in the doorway, as you are standing, I saw Saint Patrick. He pointed with one finger to the road running westward and he said: 'Landlord, Landlord of the Head Inn, take *that* road to Ballaghadereen. When you come to the crossroads you will find a wee cabin, and beside the cabin a wee garden, and in the center of the garden a cherry tree. Dig deep under the tree and you will find gold—much gold.' "

The landlord paused and drew his sleeve across his mouth to hush his laughter.

"Ballaghadereen! I never heard of the place. Gold under a cherry tree—whoever heard of gold under a cherry tree! There is only one dream that I hear, waking or sleeping, and it's the dream of gold, much gold, in my own pocket. Aye, listen, 'tis a good dream." And the landlord thrust a hand into his pouch and jangled the coins loudly in the peddler's ear.

Back to Ballaghadereen went the peddler, one foot ahead of the other. How he got there I cannot be telling you. He unslung his pack, took up a mattock lying near by, and dug under the cherry tree. He dug deep and felt at last the scraping of the mattock against something hard and smooth. It took him time to uncover it and he found it to be an old sea chest, of foreign pattern and workmanship, bound around with bands of brass. These he broke, and lifting the lid he found the chest full of gold, tarnished and clotted with mold; pieces-of-six and pieces-of-eight and Spanish doubloons.

I cannot begin to tell the half of the goodness that the peddler put into the spending of that gold. But this I know. He built a chapel at the crossroads—a resting-place for all weary travelers, journeying thither.

And after he had gone the neighbors had a statue made of him and placed it facing the crossroads. And there he stands to this day, a pack on his back and a dog at his heels.

Germany

The German folk tales were known to English-speaking children in translation long before the tales of the British Isles and of other parts of the Western world were available. Since their first translation into English, the fairy tales of Jacob and Wilhelm Grimm have been published in most of the languages of the civilized world and are the beloved heritage of children everywhere. Because the Grimms were students of the German language, they collected their tales either directly from the lips of untutored story-tellers or, as they were able to get them, from reliable printed sources. It can be said that with their work the science of folklore was born, and that they did much to shape its early methods. Although at the outset they insisted on setting down the tales exactly as they were told, they eventually began to rewrite the tales from a number of oral and printed sources, so that some of their best-loved stories, like "Snow White and the Seven Dwarfs," represent their own literary retelling and not the folk teller's. The stories range from simple little tales for the nursery to mature themes for adults. They are dramatic, exciting, and full of suspense and smashing climaxes. Indeed, over the years many adults have questioned some of the more violent and cruel episodes. But children have made the Grimms' original and scholarly work their own possession, and these now classic tales are some of the most popular and best fairy tales ever told.

THE WOLF AND
THE SEVEN LITTLE KIDS

"The Story of the Three Little Pigs" can be used with five-year-olds, but this similar tale is a bit more alarming and is better for the sevens. The joyful conclusion makes everything all right. Felix Hoffmann's picture-book treatment was chosen as an American Library Association notable book in 1959.

There was once on a time an old goat who had seven little kids and loved them with all the love of a mother for her children. One day she wanted to go into the forest and fetch some food. So she called all seven to her and said, "Dear children, I have to go into the forest; be on your guard against the wolf; if he comes in, he will devour you all—skin, hair, and all. The wretch often disguises himself, but you will know him at once by his rough voice and his black feet." The kids said, "Dear mother, we will take good care of ourselves; you may go away without any anxiety." Then the old one bleated, and went on her way with an easy mind.

It was not long before some one knocked at the house-door and cried, "Open the door, dear children; your mother is here, and has brought something back with her for each of you." But the little kids knew that it was the wolf, by the rough voice. "We will not open the door," cried they, "You are not our mother. She has a soft, pleasant voice, but your voice is rough; you are the wolf!" Then the wolf went away to a shop-keeper and bought himself a great lump of chalk, ate this and made his voice soft with it. Then he came back, knocked at the door of the house, and cried, "Open the door, dear children, your mother is here and has brought something back with her for each of you." But the wolf had laid his black paws against the window, and the children saw them and cried, "We will not open the door; our mother has not black feet like you: you are the wolf!" Then the wolf ran to a baker and said, "I have hurt my feet, rub some dough over them for me." And when the baker had rubbed his feet over, he ran to the miller and

said, "Strew some white meal over my feet for me." The miller thought to himself, "The wolf wants to deceive some one," and refused; but the wolf said, "If you will not do it, I will devour you." Then the miller was afraid and made his paws white for him. Truly men are like that.

So now the wretch went for the third time to the house-door, knocked at it, and said, "Open the door for me, children, your dear little mother has come home and has brought every one of you something back from the forest with her." The little kids cried, "First show us your paws that we may know if you are our dear little mother." Then he put his paws in through the window, and when the kids saw that they were white, they believed that all he said was true, and opened the door. But who should come in but the wolf! They were terrified and wanted to hide themselves. One sprang under the table, the second into the bed, the third into the stove, the fourth into the kitchen, the fifth into the cupboard, the sixth under the washing-bowl, and the seventh into the clock-case. But the wolf found all but one and used no great ceremony; one after the other he swallowed them down his throat. The youngest in the clock-case was the only one he did not find. When the wolf had satisfied his appetite, he took himself off, laid himself down under a tree in the green meadow outside, and began to sleep. Soon afterwards the old goat came home again from the forest. Ah! what a sight she saw there! The house-door stood wide open. The table, chairs, and benches were thrown down, the washing-bowl lay broken to pieces, and the quilts and pillows were pulled off the bed. She sought her children, but they were nowhere to be found. She called them one after another by name, but no one answered. At last, when she came to the youngest, a soft voice cried, "Dear mother, I am in the clock-case." She took the kid out, and it told her that the wolf had come and had eaten all the others. Then you may imagine how she wept over her poor children.

At length in her grief she went out, and the youngest kid ran with her. When they came to the meadow, there lay the wolf by the tree and snored so loud that the branches shook. She looked at him on every side and saw that something was moving and struggling in his gorged

"The Wolf and the Seven Little Kids." From *Grimm's Household Tales,* translated by Margaret Hunt body. "Ah, heavens," said she, "is it possible that my poor children whom he has swallowed down for his supper can be still alive?" Then the kid had to run home and fetch scissors, and a needle and thread, and the goat cut open the monster's stomach, and hardly had she made one cut, than one little kid thrust its head out, and when she had cut farther, all six sprang out one after another, and were all still alive, and had suffered no injury whatever, for in his greediness the monster had swallowed them down whole. What rejoicing there was! Then they embraced their dear mother, and jumped like a tailor at his wedding. The mother, however, said, "Now go and look for some big stones, and we will fill the wicked beast's stomach with them while he is still asleep." Then the seven kids dragged the stones thither with all speed, and put as many of them into his stomach as they could get in; and the mother sewed him up again in the greatest haste, so that he was not aware of anything and never once stirred.

When the wolf at length had had his sleep out, he got on his legs, and as the stones in his stomach made him very thirsty, he wanted to go to a well to drink. But when he began to walk and to move about, the stones in his stomach knocked against each other and rattled. Then cried he,

> "What rumbles and tumbles
> Against my poor bones?
> I thought 'twas six kids,
> But it's naught but big stones."

And when he got to the well and stooped over the water and was just about to drink, the heavy stones made him fall in and there was no help, but he had to drown miserably. When the seven kids saw that, they came running to the spot and cried aloud, "The wolf is dead! The wolf is dead!" and danced for joy round about the well with their mother.

THE ELVES
AND THE SHOEMAKER

This story has an excellent plot and appears in similar form in many lands, but the style here is rather dull, unless one turns the narrative into direct conversation. It lends itself well to simple dramatization or to a puppet play. Adrienne Adams' The Shoemaker and the Elves gives it added charm and substance as a picture story.

There was once a shoemaker who worked very hard and was very honest; but still he could not earn enough to live upon, and at last all he had in the world was gone, except just leather enough to make one pair of shoes.

Then he cut them all ready to make up the next day, meaning to get up early in the morning to work. His conscience was clear and his heart light amidst all his troubles; so he went peaceably to bed, left all his cares to heaven, and fell asleep.

In the morning, after he had said his prayers, he set himself down to his work, when to his great wonder, there stood the shoes, all ready made, upon the table. The good man knew not what to say or think of this strange event. He looked at the workmanship; there was not one false stitch in the whole job, and all was so neat and true that it was a complete masterpiece.

That same day a customer came in, and the shoes pleased him so well that he willingly paid a price higher than usual for them; and the poor shoemaker with the money bought leather enough to make two pairs more. In the evening he cut out the work, and went to bed early that he might get up and begin betimes next day. But he was saved all the trouble, for when he got up in the morning the work was finished ready to his hand.

Presently in came buyers, who paid him handsomely for his goods, so that he bought leather enough for four pairs more. He cut out the work again over night, and found it finished in the morning as before; and so it went on for some time; what was got ready in the evening was always done by daybreak, and the good man soon became thriving and prosperous again.

One evening about Christmas time, as he and his wife were sitting over the fire chatting together, he said to her, "I should like to sit up and watch to-night, that we may see who it is that comes and does my work for me." The wife liked the thought; so they left a light burning,

"The Elves and the Shoemaker." From *Grimm's Popular Stories*, translated by Edgar Taylor

and hid themselves in the corner of the room behind a curtain and watched to see what would happen.

As soon as it was midnight, there came two little naked dwarfs; and they sat themselves upon the shoemaker's bench, took up all the work that was cut out, and began to ply with their little fingers, stitching and rapping and tapping away at such a rate that the shoemaker was all amazement, and could not take his eyes off for a moment. And on they went till the job was quite finished, and the shoes stood ready for use upon the table. This was long before daybreak; and then they bustled away as quick as lightning.

The next day the wife said to the shoemaker, "These little wights have made us rich, and we ought to be thankful to them, and do them a good office in return. I am quite vexed to see them run about as they do; they have nothing upon their backs to keep off the cold. I'll tell you what, I will make each of them a shirt, and a coat and waistcoat, and a pair of pantaloons into the bargain; do you make each of them a little pair of shoes."

The thought pleased the good shoemaker very much; and one evening, when all the things were ready, they laid them on the table instead of the work that they used to cut out, and then went and hid themselves to watch what the little elves would do.

About midnight the elves came in and were going to sit down to their work as usual; but when they saw the clothes lying for them, they

laughed and were greatly delighted. Then they dressed themselves in the twinkling of an eye, and danced and capered and sprang about as merry as could be, till at last they danced out at the door and over the green; and the shoemaker saw them no more; but everything went well with him from that time forward, as long as he lived.

THE FOUR MUSICIANS

This story is wonderful to tell, to illustrate, and to dramatize! It has many variants and is universally popular and funny. In another amusing version, the cock crows, "Cuck, cuck, cuck, cucdoo-oo!" and the robber thinks a fellow is calling, "Cut the man in two-oo!" The story lends itself to simple dramatization by six- or seven-year-olds in a classroom, playroom, or yard. A few bandannas will make the robbers, and the animals may be costumed or not, depending upon the formality or spontaneity of the occasion.

There was once a donkey who had worked for his master faithfully many years, but his strength at last began to fail, and every day he became more and more unfit for work. Finally his master concluded it was no longer worth while to keep him and was thinking of putting an end to him. But the donkey saw that mischief was brewing and he ran away.

"I will go to the city," said he, "and like enough I can get an engagement there as a musician; for though my body has grown weak, my voice is as strong as ever."

So the donkey hobbled along toward the city, but he had not gone far when he spied a dog lying by the roadside and panting as if he had run a long way. "What makes you pant so, my friend?" asked the donkey.

"Alas!" replied the dog, "my master was going to knock me on the head because I am old and weak and can no longer make myself useful to him in hunting. So I ran away; but how am I to gain a living now, I wonder?"

"Hark ye!" said the donkey. "I am going to

"The Four Musicians." From *The Oak Tree Fairy Book,* edited by Clifton Johnson, copyright 1933. Reprinted by permission of Roger Johnson

the city to be a musician. You may as well keep company with me and try what you can do in the same line."

The dog said he was willing, and they went on together. Pretty soon they came to a cat sitting in the middle of the road and looking as dismal as three wet days. "Pray, my good lady," said the donkey, "what is the matter with you, for you seem quite out of spirits?"

"Ah me!" responded the cat, "how can I be cheerful when my life is in danger? I am getting old, my teeth are blunt, and I like sitting by the fire and purring better than chasing the mice about. So this morning my mistress laid hold of me and was going to drown me. I was lucky enough to get away from her; but I do not know what is to become of me, and I'm likely to starve."

"Come with us to the city," said the donkey, "and be a musician. You understand serenading, and with your talent for that you ought to be able to make a very good living."

The cat was pleased with the idea and went along with the donkey and the dog. Soon afterward, as they were passing a farmyard, a rooster flew up on the gate and screamed out with all his might, "Cock-a-doodle-doo!"

"Bravo!" said the donkey, "upon my word you make a famous noise; what is it all about?"

"Oh," replied the rooster, "I was only foretelling fine weather for our washing-day; and that I do every week. But would you believe it! My mistress doesn't thank me for my pains, and she has told the cook that I must be made into broth for the guests that are coming next Sunday."

"Heaven forbid!" exclaimed the donkey; "come with us, Master Chanticleer. It will be better, at any rate, than staying here to have your head cut off. We are going to the city to be musicians; and—who knows?—perhaps the four of us can get up some kind of a concert. You have a good voice, and if we all make music together, it will be something striking. So come along."

"With all my heart," said the cock; and the four went on together.

The city was, however, too far away for them to reach it on the first day of their travelling, and when, toward night, they came to a thick woods, they decided to turn aside from the highway and pass the night among the trees. So they found a dry, sheltered spot at the foot of a great oak and the donkey and dog lay down on the ground beneath it; but the cat climbed up among the branches, and the rooster, thinking the higher he sat the safer he would be, flew up to the very top. Before he went to sleep the rooster looked around him to the four points of the compass to make sure that everything was all right. In so doing he saw in the distance a little light shining, and he called out to his companions, "There must be a house no great way off, for I can see a light."

"If that be the case," said the donkey, "let us get up and go there. Our lodging here is not what I am used to, and the sooner we change it for better the more pleased I shall be."

"Yes," said the dog, "and perhaps I might be able to get a few bones with a little meat on them at that house."

"And very likely I might get some milk," said the cat.

"And there ought to be some scraps of food for me," said the rooster.

So the cat and the rooster came down out of the tree and they all walked off with Chanticleer in the lead toward the spot where he had seen the light.

At length they drew near the house, and the donkey, being the tallest of the company, went up to the lighted window and looked in.

"Well, what do you see?" asked the dog.

"What do I see?" answered the donkey. "I see that this is a robber's house. There are swords and pistols and blunderbusses on the walls, and there are chests of money on the floor, and all sorts of other plunder lying about. The robbers are sitting at a table that is loaded with the best of eatables and drinkables, and they are making themselves very comfortable and merry."

"Those eatables and drinkables would just suit us," declared the rooster.

"Yes, indeed they would," said the donkey, "if we could only get at them; but that will never be, unless we can contrive to drive away the robbers first."

Then they consulted together and at last hit on a plan. The donkey stood on his hind legs with his forefeet on the window-sill, the dog got on the donkey's shoulders, the cat mounted the back of the dog, and the rooster flew up and perched on the back of the cat. When all was ready they began their music.

"Hehaw! hehaw! hehaw!" brayed the donkey.

"Bow-wow! bow-wow!" barked the dog.

"Meow! meow!" said the cat.

"Cock-a-doodle-doo!" crowed the rooster.

Then they all burst through the window into the room, breaking the glass with a frightful clatter. The robbers, not doubting that some hideous hobgoblin was about to devour them, fled to the woods in great terror.

The donkey and his comrades now sat down at the table and made free with the food the robbers had left, and feasted as if they had been hungry for a month. When they had finished they put out the lights and each sought a sleeping-place to his own liking. The donkey laid himself down on some straw in the yard, the dog stretched himself on a mat just inside the door, the cat curled up on the hearth near the warm ashes, and the rooster flew up on the roof and settled himself on the ridge beside the chimney. They were all tired and soon fell fast asleep.

About midnight the robbers came creeping back to the house. They saw that no lights were burning and everything seemed quiet. "Well, well," said the robber captain, "we need not have been so hasty. I think we ran away without reason. But we will be cautious. The rest of you stay here while I go and find out if we are likely to have any more trouble."

So he stepped softly along to the house and entered the kitchen. There he groped about until he found a candle and some matches on the mantel over the fireplace. The cat had now waked up and stood on the hearth watching the robber with shining eyes. He mistook those eyes for two live coals and reached down to get a light by touching a match to them. The cat did not fancy that sort of thing and flew into his face, spitting and scratching. Then he cried out in fright and ran toward the door, and the dog, who was lying there, bit the robber's leg. He managed, however, to get out in the yard, and there the donkey struck out with a hind foot and gave him a kick that knocked him down, and Chanticleer who had been roused by the noise, cried out "Cock-a-doodle-doo! Cock-a-doodle-doo!"

The robber captain had barely strength to crawl away to the other robbers. "We cannot live at that house any more," said he. "In the kitchen is a grewsome witch, and I felt her hot breath and her long nails on my face, and by the door there stood a man who stabbed me in the leg, and in the yard is a black giant who beat me with a club, and on the roof is a little fellow who kept shouting, 'Chuck him up to me! Chuck him up to me!'"

So the robbers went away and never came back, and the four musicians found themselves so well pleased with their new quarters that they did not go to the city, but stayed where they were; and I dare say you would find them there at this very day.

MOTHER HOLLE

One little girl approved the justice of the conclusion of this tale by remarking sternly, "It served that girl right to get pitch on her. She was a real mean girl." This tale may easily be traced from one of its earliest appearances in print (in Perrault's collection of French fairy tales in 1697) to English folklore and on to the Appalachian and Ozark mountains of the United States where, in one version from Arkansas, it is called "The Good Girl and the Ornery Girl."

There was once a widow who had two daughters—one of whom was pretty and industrious, whilst the other was ugly and idle. But she was much fonder of the ugly and idle one, because she was her own daughter; and the other, who was a step-daughter, was obliged to do all the work, and be the Cinderella of the house. Every day the poor girl had to sit by a well, in the highway, and spin and spin till her fingers bled.

Now it happened that one day the shuttle was marked with her blood, so she dipped it in the well, to wash the mark off; but it dropped out of her hand and fell to the bottom. She began to weep, and ran to her step-mother and told her of the mishap. But she scolded her sharply, and was so merciless as to say, "Since you have let the shuttle fall in, you must fetch it out again."

"Mother Holle." From *Grimm's Household Tales,* translated by Margaret Hunt

So the girl went back to the well, and did not know what to do; and in the sorrow of her heart she jumped into the well to get the shuttle. She lost her senses; and when she awoke and came to herself again, she was in a lovely meadow where the sun was shining and many thousands of flowers were growing. Across this meadow she went, and at last came to a baker's oven full of bread, and the bread cried out, "Oh, take me out! take me out! or I shall burn; I have been baked a long time!" So she went up to it, and took out all the loaves one after another with the bread-shovel. After that she went on till she came to a tree covered with apples, which called out to her, "Oh, shake me! shake me! we apples are all ripe!" So she shook the tree till the apples fell like rain, and went on shaking till they were all down, and when she had gathered them into a heap, she went on her way.

At last she came to a little house, out of which an old woman peeped; but she had such large teeth that the girl was frightened, and was about to run away. But the old woman called out to her, "What are you afraid of, dear child? Stay with me; if you will do all the work in the house properly, you shall be the better for it. Only you must take care to make my bed well, and to shake it thoroughly till the feathers fly—for then there is snow on the earth. I am Mother Holle."

As the old woman spoke so kindly to her, the girl took courage and agreed to enter her service. She attended to everything to the satisfaction of her mistress, and always shook her bed so vigorously that the feathers flew about like snowflakes. So she had a pleasant life with her; never an angry word; and to eat she had boiled or roast meat every day.

She stayed some time with Mother Holle, before she became sad. At first she did not know what was the matter with her, but found at length that it was home-sickness: although she was many thousand times better off here than at home, still she had a longing to be there. At last she said to the old woman: "I have a longing for home; and however well off I am down here, I cannot stay any longer; I must go up again to my own people." Mother Holle said, "I am pleased that you long for your home again, and as you have served me so truly, I myself will take you up again." Thereupon she took her by the hand, and led her to a large door. The door was opened, and just as the maiden was standing beneath the doorway, a heavy shower of golden rain fell, and all the gold remained sticking to her, so that she was completely covered over with it.

"You shall have that because you have been so industrious," said Mother Holle; and at the same time she gave her back the shuttle which she had let fall into the well. Thereupon the door closed, and the maiden found herself up above upon the earth, not far from her mother's house.

And as she went into the yard the cock was sitting on the well, and cried——

"Cock-a-doodle-doo!
Your golden girl's come back to you!"

So she went in to her mother, and as she arrived thus covered with gold, she was well received, both by her and her sister.

The girl told all that had happened to her; and as soon as the mother heard how she had come by so much wealth, she was very anxious to obtain the same good luck for the ugly and lazy daughter. She had to seat herself by the well and spin; and in order that her shuttle might be stained with blood, she stuck her hand into a thorn bush and pricked her finger. Then she threw her shuttle into the well, and jumped in after it.

She came, like the other, to the beautiful meadow and walked along the very same path. When she got to the oven the bread again cried, "Oh, take me out! take me out! or I shall burn; I have been baked a long time!" But the lazy thing answered, "As if I had any wish to make myself dirty!" and on she went. Soon she came to the apple-tree, which cried, "Oh, shake me! shake me! we apples are all ripe!" But she answered, "I like that! one of you might fall on my head," and so went on.

When she came to Mother Holle's house she was not afraid, for she had already heard of her big teeth, and she hired herself to her immediately.

The first day she forced herself to work diligently, and obeyed Mother Holle when she told her to do anything, for she was thinking of all the gold that she would give her. But on the second day she began to be lazy, and on the third day still more so, and then she would not get up in the morning at all. Neither did she make Mother Holle's bed as she ought, and did not shake it so as to make the feathers fly up. Mother Holle was soon tired of this, and gave her notice to leave. The lazy girl was willing enough to go, and thought that now the golden rain would come. Mother Holle led her also to the great door; but while she was standing beneath it, instead of the gold a big kettleful of pitch was emptied over her. "That is the reward for your service," said Mother Holle, and shut the door.

So the lazy girl went home; but she was quite covered with pitch, and the cock by the well-side, as soon as he saw her, cried out——

"Cock-a-doodle-doo!
Your pitchy girl's come back to you!"

But the pitch stuck fast to her, and could not be got off as long as she lived.

THE HUT IN THE FOREST

This tale has all the familiar devices of many folk tales—three sisters (brothers would do as well), the youngest of whom is kind and true; a test of character repeated three times; an enchanted prince; and a strong sermon, which it largely serves to illustrate.

A poor wood-cutter lived with his wife and three daughters in a little hut on the edge of a lonely forest. One morning as he was about to go to his work, he said to his wife, "Let my dinner be brought into the forest to me by my eldest daughter, or I shall never get my work done, and in order that she may not miss her way," he added, "I will take a bag of millet with me and strew the seeds on the path." When, therefore, the sun was just above the centre of the forest, the girl set out on her way with a bowl of soup, but the field-sparrows, and wood-sparrows, larks and finches, blackbirds and siskins had picked up the millet long before, and the girl could not find the track. Then trusting to chance, she went on and on, until the sun sank and night began to fall. The trees rustled in the darkness, the owls hooted, and she began to be afraid. Then in the distance she perceived a light which glimmered between the trees. "There ought to be some people living there, who can take me in for the night," thought she, and went up to the light. It was not long before she came to a house the windows of which were all lighted up. She knocked, and a rough voice from the inside cried, "Come in." The girl stepped into the dark entrance and knocked at the door of the room. "Just come in," cried the voice, and when she opened the door, an old grey-haired man was sitting at the table, supporting his face with both hands, and his white beard fell down over the table almost as far as the ground. By the stove lay three animals, a hen, a cock, and a brindled cow. The girl told her story to the old man, and begged for shelter for the night. The man said,

"Pretty little hen,
Pretty little cock,
And pretty brindled cow,
What say ye to that?"

"Duks," answered the animals, and that must have meant, "We are willing," for the old man

"The Hut in the Forest." From *Grimm's Household Tales,* translated by Margaret Hunt

said, "Here you shall have shelter and food; go to the fire, and cook us our supper." The girl found in the kitchen abundance of everything, and cooked a good supper, but had no thought of the animals. She carried the full dishes to the table, seated herself by the grey-haired man, ate and satisfied her hunger. When she had had enough, she said, "But now I am tired, where is there a bed in which I can lie down, and sleep?" The animals replied,

"Thou hast eaten with him,
 Thou hast drunk with him,
 Thou hast had no thought for us,
 So find out for thyself where thou canst pass the
    night."

Then said the old man, "Just go upstairs, and thou wilt find a room with two beds; shake them up, and put white linen on them, and then I, too, will come and lie down to sleep." The girl went up, and when she had shaken the beds and put clean sheets on, she lay down in one of them without waiting any longer for the old man. After some time, however, the grey-haired man came, took his candle, looked at the girl and shook his head. When he saw that she had fallen into a sound sleep, he opened a trap-door, and let her down into the cellar.

Late at night the wood-cutter came home and reproached his wife for leaving him to hunger all day. "It is not my fault," she replied, "the girl went out with your dinner, and must have lost herself, but she is sure to come back tomorrow." The wood-cutter, however, arose before dawn to go into the forest, and requested that the second daughter should take him his dinner that day. "I will take a bag with lentils," said he; "the seeds are larger than millet; the girl will see them better, and can't lose her way." At dinner-time, therefore, the girl took out the food, but the lentils had disappeared. The birds of the forest had picked them up as they had done the day before, and had left none. The girl wandered about in the forest until night, and then she too reached the house of the old man, was told to go in, and begged for food and a bed. The man with the white beard again asked the animals,

"Pretty little hen,
 Pretty little cock,

And pretty brindled cow,
 What say ye to that?"

The animals again replied "Duks," and everything happened just as it had happened the day before. The girl cooked a good meal, ate and drank with the old man, and did not concern herself about the animals, and when she inquired about her bed they answered,

"Thou hast eaten with him,
 Thou hast drunk with him,
 Thou hast had no thought for us,
 So find out for thyself where thou canst pass the
    night."

When she was asleep the old man came, looked at her, shook his head, and let her down into the cellar.

On the third morning the wood-cutter said to his wife, "Send our youngest child out with my dinner today, she has always been good and obedient, and will stay in the right path, and not run about after every wild humble-bee, as her sisters did." The mother did not want to do it, and said, "Am I to lose my dearest child, as well?"

"Have no fear," he replied, "the girl will not go astray; she is too prudent and sensible; besides I will take some peas with me, and strew them about. They are still larger than lentils, and will show her the way." But when the girl went out with her basket on her arm, the wood-pigeons had already got all the peas in their crops, and she did not know which way she was to turn. She was full of sorrow and never ceased to think how hungry her father would be, and how her good mother would grieve, if she did not go home.

At length when it grew dark, she saw the light and came to the house in the forest. She begged quite prettily to be allowed to spend the night there, and the man with the white beard once more asked his animals,

"Pretty little hen,
 Pretty little cock,
 And beautiful brindled cow,
 What say ye to that?"

"Duks," said they. Then the girl went to the stove where the animals were lying, and petted the cock and hen, and stroked their smooth feathers with her hand, and caressed the brindled cow between her horns; and when, in obedience to the old man's orders, she had made ready some good soup, and the bowl was placed upon the table, she said, "Am I to eat as much as I want, and the good animals to have nothing? Outside is food in plenty, I will look after them first."

So she went and brought some barley and strewed it for the cock and hen, and a whole armful of sweet-smelling hay for the cow. "I hope you will like it, dear animals," said she, "and you shall have a refreshing draught in case you are thirsty." Then she fetched in a bucketful of water, and the cock and hen jumped on to the edge of it and dipped their beaks in, and then held up their heads as the birds do when they drink, and the brindled cow also took a hearty draught. When the animals were fed, the girl seated herself at the table by the old man and ate what he had left. It was not long before the cock and the hen began to thrust their heads beneath their wings, and the eyes of the cow likewise began to blink. Then said the girl, "Ought we not to go to bed?"

> "Pretty little hen,
> Pretty little cock,
> And pretty brindled cow,
> What say ye to that?"

The animals answered "Duks,"

> "Thou hast eaten with us,
> Thou hast drunk with us,
> Thou hast had kind thought for all of us,
> We wish thee good-night."

Then the maiden went upstairs, shook the feather-beds, and laid clean sheets on them, and when she had done it the old man came and lay down on one of the beds, and his white beard reached down to his feet. The girl lay down on the other, said her prayers, and fell asleep.

She slept quietly till midnight, and then there was such a noise in the house that she awoke.

There was a sound of cracking and splitting in every corner, and the doors sprang open, and beat against the walls. The beams groaned as if they were being torn out of their joints, it seemed as if the staircase were falling down, and at length there was a crash as if the entire roof had fallen in. As, however, all grew quiet once more, and the girl was not hurt, she stayed quietly lying where she was, and fell asleep again.

But when she woke up in the morning with the brilliancy of the sunshine, what did her eyes behold? She was lying in a vast hall, and everything around her shone with royal splendour; on the walls, golden flowers grew up on a ground of green silk, the bed was of ivory, and the canopy of red velvet, and on a chair close by, was a pair of shoes embroidered with pearls. The girl believed that she was in a dream, but three richly clad attendants came in, and asked what orders she would like to give? "If you will go," she replied, "I will get up at once and make ready some soup for the old man, and then I will feed the pretty little hen, and the cock, and the beautiful brindled cow." She thought the old man was up already, and looked round at his bed; he, however, was not lying in it, but a stranger.

And while she was looking at him, and becoming aware that he was young and handsome, he awoke, sat up in bed, and said, "I am a king's son, and was bewitched by a wicked witch, and made to live in this forest, as an old grey-haired man; no one was allowed to be with me but my three attendants in the form of a cock, a hen, and a brindled cow. The spell was not to be broken until a girl came to us whose heart was so good that she showed herself full of love, not only towards mankind, but towards animals— and that you have done, and by you at midnight we were set free, and the old hut in the forest was changed back again into my royal palace."

And when they had arisen, the king's son ordered the three attendants to set out and fetch the father and mother of the girl to the marriage feast. "But where are my two sisters?" inquired the maiden. "I have locked them in the cellar, and to-morrow they shall be led into the forest, and shall live as servants to a charcoal-burner, until they have grown kinder, and do not leave poor animals to suffer hunger."

THE FROG-KING

Here is an enchantment not broken by the love of the princess but by the king's stern insistence that what she has promised she must perform. The author of The Hobbit, *J. R. R. Tolkien, writes of it: ". . . the point of the story lies not in thinking frogs possible mates, but in the necessity of keeping promises (even those with intolerable consequences) that, together with observing prohibitions, runs through all Fairyland."* [1] *The final episode with Faithful Henry remains a curious addition.*

In olden times when wishing still helped one, there lived a king whose daughters were all beautiful, but the youngest was so beautiful that the sun itself, which has seen so much, was astonished whenever it shone in her face. Close by the King's castle lay a great dark forest, and under an old lime-tree in the forest was a well, and when the day was very warm, the King's child went out into the forest and sat down by the side of the cool fountain; and when she was bored she took a golden ball, and threw it up on high and caught it; and this ball was her favourite plaything.

Now it so happened that on one occasion the princess's golden ball did not fall into the little hand which she was holding up for it, but on to the ground beyond, and rolled straight into the water. The King's daughter followed it with her eyes, but it vanished, and the well was deep, so deep that the bottom could not be seen. At this she began to cry, and cried louder and louder, and could not be comforted. And as she thus lamented, some one said to her, "What ails you, King's daughter? You weep so that even a stone would show pity." She looked round to the side from whence the voice came, and saw a frog stretching forth its thick, ugly head from the water. "Ah! old water-splasher, is it you?" said she; "I am weeping for my golden ball, which has fallen into the well."

"Be quiet, and do not weep," answered the frog, "I can help you, but what will you give me

if I bring your plaything up again?" "Whatever you will have, dear frog," said she—"my clothes, my pearls and jewels, and even the golden crown which I am wearing."

The frog answered: "I do not care for your clothes, your pearls and jewels, nor for your golden crown; but if you will love me and let me be your companion and play-fellow, and sit by you at your little table, and eat off your little golden plate, and drink out of your little cup, and sleep in your little bed—if you will promise me this I will go down below, and bring your golden ball up again."

"Oh, yes," said she, "I promise you all you wish, if you will but bring me my ball back again." But she thought: "How the silly frog does talk! He lives in the water with the other frogs, and croaks, and can be no companion to any human being!"

But the frog when he had received this promise, put his head into the water and sank down, and in a short while came swimming up again with the ball in his mouth, and threw it on the grass. The King's daughter was delighted to see her pretty plaything once more, and picked it up, and ran away with it. "Wait, wait," said the frog. "Take me with you. I can't run as you can." But what did it avail him to scream his croak, croak, after her, as loudly as he could? She did not listen to it, but ran home and soon forgot the poor frog, who was forced to go back into his well again.

The next day when she had seated herself at table with the King and all the courtiers, and was eating from her little golden plate, something came creeping splish splash, splish splash, up the marble staircase, and when it had got to the top, it knocked at the door and cried, "Princess, youngest princess, open the door for me." She ran to see who was outside, but when she opened the door, there sat the frog in front of it. Then she slammed the door to, in great haste, sat down to dinner again, and was quite frightened. The King saw plainly that her heart was beating violently, and said, "My child, what are you so afraid of? Is there perchance a giant outside who wants to carry you away?" "Ah, no," replied she, "it is no giant, but a disgusting frog."

"What does the frog want with you?" "Ah, dear father, yesterday when I was in the forest

"The Frog-King." From *Grimm's Household Tales,* translated by Margaret Hunt
[1] J. R. R. Tolkien, "On Fairy-Stories," in *Essays Presented to Charles Williams,* Oxford, 1947

sitting by the well, playing, my golden ball fell into the water. And because I cried so, the frog brought it out again for me; and because he insisted so on it, I promised him he should be my companion, but I never thought he would be able to come out of his water! And now he is outside there, and wants to come in to me."

In the meantime it knocked a second time, and cried:

"Princess! youngest princess!
Open the door for me!
Do you not know what you said to me
Yesterday by the cool waters of the fountain?
Princess, youngest princess!
Open the door for me!"

Then said the King, "That which you have promised must you perform. Go and let him in." She went and opened the door, and the frog hopped in and followed her, step by step, to her chair. There he sat still and cried: "Lift me up beside you." She delayed, until at last the King commanded her to do it. Once the frog was on the chair he wanted to be on the table, and when he was on the table he said: "Now, push your little golden plate nearer to me that we may eat together." She did this, but it was easy to see that she did not do it willingly. The frog enjoyed what he ate, but almost every mouthful she took choked her. At length he said, "I have eaten and am satisfied; now I am tired, carry me into your little room and make your little silken bed ready, and we will both lie down and go to sleep."

The King's daughter began to cry, for she was afraid of the cold frog which she did not like to touch, and which was now to sleep in her pretty, clean little bed. But the King grew angry and said, "He who helped you when you were in trouble ought not afterwards to be despised by you." So she took hold of the frog with two fingers, carried him upstairs, and put him in a corner.

But when she was in bed he crept to her and said: "I am tired, I want to sleep as well as you, lift me up or I will tell your father." Then she was terribly angry, and took him up and threw him with all her might against the wall. "Now, you will be quiet, odious frog," said she. But when he fell down he was no frog but a king's son with kind and beautiful eyes. He by her father's will was now her dear companion and husband. Then he told her how he had been bewitched by a wicked witch, and how no one could have delivered him from the well but herself, and that to-morrow they would go together into his kingdom.

Then they went to sleep, and next morning when the sun awoke them, a carriage came driving up with eight white horses, which had white ostrich feathers on their heads, and were harnessed with golden chains, and behind stood the young King's servant, faithful Henry. Faithful Henry had been so unhappy when his master was changed into a frog, that he had caused three iron bands to be laid round his heart, lest it should burst with grief and sadness. The carriage was to conduct the young King into his kingdom. Faithful Henry helped them both in, and placed himself behind again, and was full of joy because of this deliverance. And when they had driven a part of the way, the King's son heard a cracking behind him as if something had broken. So he turned round and cried: "Henry, the carriage is breaking."

"No, master, it is not the carriage. It is a band from my heart, which was put there in my great pain when you were a frog and imprisoned in the well." Again and once again while they were on their way something cracked, and each time the King's son thought the carriage was breaking; but it was only the bands which were springing from the heart of faithful Henry because his master was set free and was happy.

HANSEL AND GRETTEL

A prime fear of many children is one of being abandoned. Here it is dealt with bluntly, but the aesthetic distance it acquires in story form, together with its happy ending, reassures young-sters. This is a favorite story to illustrate and dramatize.

Once upon a time there dwelt on the outskirts of a large forest a poor woodcutter with his wife and two children; the boy was called Hansel and the girl Grettel. He had always little enough to live on, and once, when there was a great famine in the land, he couldn't even provide them with daily bread. One night, as he was tossing about in bed, full of cares and worry, he sighed and said to his wife: "What's to become of us? How are we to support our poor children, now that we have nothing more for ourselves?"

"I'll tell you what, husband," answered the woman, who was the children's step-mother. "Early tomorrow morning we'll take the chil-dren out into the thickest part of the wood; there we shall light a fire for them and give them each a piece of bread; then we'll go on to our work and leave them alone. They won't be able to find their way home, and we shall thus be rid of them."

"No, wife," said her husband, "that I won't do; how could I find it in my heart to leave my children alone in the wood? The wild beasts would soon come and tear them to pieces."

"Oh! you fool," said she, "then we must all four die of hunger, and you may just as well go and plane the boards for our coffins"; and she left him no peace till he consented.

"But I can't help feeling sorry for the poor children," added the husband.

The children, too, had not been able to sleep for hunger, and had heard what their step-mother had said to their father. Grettel wept bit-terly and spoke to Hansel: "Now it's all up with us."

"No, no, Grettel," said Hansel, "don't fret yourself; I'll be able to find a way of escape, no fear." And when the old people had fallen asleep

"Hansel and Grettel." From *The Blue Fairy Book,* edited by Andrew Lang. Longmans, Green, and Co., Lon-don, 1889

he got up, slipped on his little coat, opened the back door and stole out.

The moon was shining clearly, and the white pebbles which lay in front of the house glittered like bits of silver. Hansel bent down and filled his pocket with as many of them as he could cram in. Then he went back and said to Grettel, "Be comforted, my dear little sister, and go to sleep. God will not desert us"; and he lay down in bed again.

At daybreak, even before the sun was up, the woman came and woke the two children: "Get up, you lie-abeds, we're all going to the forest to fetch wood." She gave them each a bit of bread and spoke: "There's something for your lun-cheon, but don't eat it up before, for it's all you'll get."

Grettel took the bread under her apron, as Hansel had the stones in his pocket. Then they all set out together on the way to the forest. After they had walked for a little, Hansel stood still and looked back at the house, and this manœuvre he repeated again and again.

His father observed him, and spoke: "Hansel, what are you gazing at there, and why do you al-ways remain behind? Take care, and don't lose your footing."

"Oh! Father," said Hansel, "I am looking back at my white kitten, which is sitting on the roof, waving me a farewell."

The woman exclaimed: "What a donkey you are! That isn't your kitten, that's the morning sun shining on the chimney." But Hansel had not looked back at his kitten, but had always dropped one of the white pebbles out of his pocket onto the path.

When they had reached the middle of the for-est the father said: "Now, children, go and fetch a lot of wood, and I'll light a fire that you mayn't feel cold."

Hansel and Grettel heaped up brushwood till they had made a pile nearly the size of a small hill. The brushwood was set fire to, and when the flames leaped high the woman said: "Now lie down at the fire, children, and rest yourselves; we are going into the forest to cut down wood; when we've finished we'll come back and fetch you."

Hansel and Grettel sat down beside the fire, and at midday ate their little bits of bread. They heard the strokes of the axe, so they thought their father was quite near. But it was no axe they heard, but a bough he had tied onto a dead tree, and that was blown about by the wind. And when they had sat for a long time their eyes closed with fatigue, and they fell fast asleep. When they awoke at last, it was pitch dark.

Grettel began to cry, and said: "How are we ever to get out of the wood?"

But Hansel comforted her. "Wait a bit," he said, "till the moon is up, and then we'll find our way sure enough." And when the full moon had risen he took his sister by the hand and followed the pebbles, which shone like new threepenny bits, and showed them the path. They walked all through the night, and at daybreak reached their father's house again.

They knocked at the door, and when the woman opened it she exclaimed: "You naughty children, what a time you've slept in the wood! We thought you were never going to come back." But the father rejoiced, for his conscience had reproached him for leaving his children behind by themselves.

Not long afterwards there was again great dearth in the land, and the children heard their step-mother address their father thus in bed one night: "Everything is eaten up once more; we have only half a loaf in the house, and when that's done it's all up with us. The children must be got rid of; we'll lead them deeper into the wood this time, so that they won't be able to find their way out again. There is no other way of saving ourselves."

The man's heart smote him heavily, and he thought: "Surely it would be better to share the last bite with one's children!" But his wife wouldn't listen to his arguments, and did nothing but scold and reproach him. If a man yields once, he's done for, and so, because he had given in the first time, he was forced to do so the second.

But the children were awake, and had heard the conversation. When the old people were asleep Hansel got up, and wanted to go out and pick up pebbles again, as he had done the first time; but the woman had barred the door, and Hansel couldn't get out. But he consoled his little sister, and said: "Don't cry, Grettel, and sleep peacefully, for God is sure to help us."

At early dawn the woman came and made the children get up. They received their bit of bread, but it was even smaller than the time before. On the way to the wood Hansel crumbled it in his pocket, and every few minutes he stood still and dropped a crumb on the ground.

"Hansel, what are you stopping and looking about you for?" said the father.

"I'm looking back at my little pigeon, which is sitting on the roof waving me a farewell," answered Hansel.

"Fool!" said the wife. "That isn't your pigeon, it's the morning sun glittering on the chimney." But Hansel gradually threw all his crumbs onto the path. The woman led the children still deeper into the forest, farther than they had ever been in their lives before.

Then a big fire was lit again, and the step-mother said: "Just sit down there, children, and if you're tired you can sleep a bit; we're going into the forest to cut down wood, and in the evening when we're finished we'll come back to fetch you."

At midday Grettel divided her bread with Hansel, for he had strewed his all along their path. Then they fell asleep, and evening passed away, but nobody came to the poor children.

They didn't awake till it was pitch dark, and Hansel comforted his sister, saying: "Only wait, Grettel, till the moon rises, then we shall see the bread crumbs I scattered along the path; they will show us the way back to the house." When the moon appeared they got up, but they found no crumbs, for the thousands of birds that fly about the woods and fields had picked them all up.

"Never mind," said Hansel to Grettel. "You'll see, we'll still find a way out." But all the same they did not.

They wandered about the whole night, and the next day, from morning till evening, but they could not find a path out of the wood. They were very hungry, too, for they had nothing to eat but a few berries they found growing on the ground. And at last they were so tired that their legs refused to carry them any longer, so they lay down under a tree and fell fast asleep.

On the third morning after they had left their father's house they set about their wandering again, but only got deeper and deeper into the wood, and now they felt that if help did not come to them soon they must perish. At midday they saw a beautiful little snow-white bird sitting on a branch, which sang so sweetly that they stopped still and listened to it. And when its song was finished it flapped its wings and flew on in front of them. They followed it and came to a little house, on the roof of which it perched; and when they came quite near they saw that the cottage was made of bread and roofed with cakes, while the window was made of transparent sugar.

"Now we'll set to," said Hansel, "and have a regular blow-out. I'll eat a bit of the roof, and you, Grettel, can eat some of the window, which you'll find a sweet morsel."

Hansel stretched up his hand and broke off a little bit of the roof to see what it was like, and Grettel went to the casement and began to nibble at it. Thereupon a shrill voice called out from the room inside:

"Nibble, nibble, little mouse,
Who's nibbling my house?"

The children answered:

" 'Tis Heaven's own child,
The tempest wild,"

and went on eating, without putting themselves about. Hansel, who thoroughly appreciated the roof, tore down a big bit of it, while Grettel pushed out a whole round window-pane, and sat down the better to enjoy it. Suddenly the door opened, and an ancient dame leaning on a staff hobbled out. Hansel and Grettel were so terrified that they let what they had in their hands fall.

But the old woman shook her head and said: "Oh, ho! you dear children, who led you here? Just come in and stay with me, no ill shall befall you." She took them both by the hand and led them into the house, and laid a most sumptuous dinner before them—milk and sugared pancakes, with apples and nuts. After they had finished, two beautiful little white beds were prepared for them, and when Hansel and Grettel lay down in them they felt as if they had got into heaven.

The old woman had appeared to be most friendly, but she was really an old witch who had waylaid the children, and had only built the little bread house in order to lure them in. When anyone came into her power she killed, cooked, and ate him, and held a regular feast-day for the occasion. Now witches have red eyes, and cannot see far, but, like beasts, they have a keen sense of smell, and know when human beings pass by. When Hansel and Grettel fell into her hands she laughed maliciously, and said jeeringly: "I've got them now; they shan't escape me."

Early in the morning, before the children were awake, the old woman rose up, and when she saw them both sleeping so peacefully, with their round rosy cheeks, she muttered to herself, "That'll be a dainty bite."

Then she seized Hansel with her bony hand and carried him into a little stable, and barred the door on him. He might scream as much as he liked, it did him no good.

Then she went to Grettel, shook her till she awoke, and cried: "Get up, you lazy-bones, fetch water and cook something for your brother. When he's fat I'll eat him up." Grettel began to cry bitterly, but it was of no use: she had to do what the wicked witch bade her.

So the best food was cooked for poor Hansel, but Grettel got nothing but crab-shells. Every morning the old woman hobbled out to the stable and cried: "Hansel, put out your finger, that I may feel if you are getting fat." But Hansel always stretched out a bone, and the old dame, whose eyes were dim, couldn't see it, and thinking always it was Hansel's finger, wondered why he fattened so slowly. When four weeks passed and Hansel still remained thin, she lost patience and determined to wait no longer.

"Hi! Grettel," she called to the girl, "be quick and get some water. Hansel may be fat or thin, I'm going to kill him tomorrow and cook him." Oh! how the poor little sister sobbed as she carried the water, and how the tears rolled down her cheeks!

"Kind heaven help us now!" she cried. "If only the wild beasts in the wood had eaten us, then at least we should have died together."

"Just hold your peace," said the old hag. "Crying won't help you."

Early in the morning Grettel had to go out

and hang up the kettle full of water, and light the fire. "First we'll bake," said the old dame. "I've heated the oven already and kneaded the dough." She pushed Grettel out to the oven, from which fiery flames were already issuing. "Creep in," said the witch, "and see if it's properly heated, so that we can shove in the bread." For when she had got Grettel in she meant to close the oven and let the girl bake, that she might eat her up too.

But Grettel perceived her intention, and spoke: "I don't know how I'm to do it; how do I get in?"

"You silly goose!" said the hag. "The opening is big enough. See, I could get in myself." And she crawled toward it, and poked her head into the oven. Then Grettel gave her a shove that sent her right in, shut the iron door, and drew the bolt. Gracious! how she yelled! it was quite horrible; but Grettel fled, and the wretched old woman was left to perish miserably.

Grettel flew straight to Hansel, opened the little stable-door, and cried: "Hansel, we are free; the old witch is dead."

Then Hansel sprang like a bird out of a cage when the door is opened. How they rejoiced, and fell on each other's necks, and jumped for joy, and kissed one another! And as they had no longer any cause for fear, they went into the old hag's house, and there they found, in every corner of the room, boxes with pearls and precious stones.

"These are even better than pebbles," said Hansel, and crammed his pockets full of them.

Grettel said: "I too will bring something home"; and she filled her apron full.

"But now," said Hansel, "let's go and get well away from the witches' wood."

When they had wandered about for some hours they came to a big lake. "We can't get over," said Hansel; "I see no bridge of any sort or kind."

"Yes, and there's no ferry-boat either," answered Grettel; "but look, there swims a white duck; if I ask her she'll help us over"; and she called out:

"Here are two children, mournful very,
Seeing neither bridge nor ferry;

Take us upon your white back,
And row us over, quack, quack!"

The duck swam toward them, and Hansel got on her back and bade his little sister sit beside him.

"No," answered Grettel, "we should be too heavy a load for the duck; she shall carry us across separately."

The good bird did this, and when they were landed safely on the other side and had gone on for a while, the wood became more and more familiar to them, and at length they saw their father's house in the distance. Then they set off to run and, bounding into the room, fell on their father's neck. The man had not passed a happy hour since he left them in the wood, but the woman had died. Grettel shook out her apron so that the pearls and precious stones rolled about the room, and Hansel threw down one handful after the other out of his pocket. Thus all their troubles were ended, and they all lived happily ever afterwards.

My story is done. See! there runs a little mouse. Anyone who catches it may make himself a large fur cap out of it.

SNOW-WHITE AND ROSE-RED

A great lovable bear, domestic tranquillity, and two kind sisters (who prove an exception to the sibling rivalry found in many folk tales) make this a warm story to savor and tuck away in one's memories of childhood.

There was once a poor widow who lived in a lonely cottage. In front of the cottage was a garden wherein stood two rose-trees, one of which bore white and the other red roses. She had two children who were like the two rose-trees, and one was called Snow-White, and the other Rose-Red. They were as good and happy, as busy and cheerful as ever two children in the world were, only Snow-White was more quiet and gentle than Rose-Red. Rose-Red liked better to run

"Snow-White and Rose-Red." From *Grimm's Household Tales,* translated by Margaret Hunt

about in the meadows and fields seeking flowers and catching butterflies; but Snow-White sat at home with her mother, and helped her with her house-work, or read to her when there was nothing to do.

The two children were so fond of each other that they always held each other by the hand when they went out together, and when Snow-White said, "We will not leave each other," Rose-Red answered, "Never so long as we live," and their mother would add, "What one has she must share with the other."

They often ran about the forest alone and gathered red berries, and no beasts did them any harm, but came close to them trustfully. The little hare would eat a cabbage-leaf out of their hands, the roe grazed by their side, the stag leapt merrily by them, and the birds sat still upon the boughs, and sang whatever they knew.

No mishap overtook them; if they had stayed too late in the forest, and night came on, they laid themselves down near one another upon the moss, and slept until morning came, and their mother knew this and had no distress on their account.

Once when they had spent the night in the wood and the dawn had roused them, they saw a beautiful child in a shining white dress sitting near their bed. He got up and looked quite kindly at them, but said nothing and went away into the forest. And when they looked round they found that they had been sleeping quite close to a precipice, and would certainly have fallen into it in the darkness if they had gone only a few paces further. And their mother told them that it must have been the angel who watches over good children.

Snow-White and Rose-Red kept their mother's little cottage so neat that it was a pleasure to look inside it. In the summer Rose-Red took care of the house, and every morning laid a wreath of flowers by her mother's bed before she awoke, in which was a rose from each tree. In the winter Snow-White lit the fire and hung the kettle on the wrekin. The kettle was of copper and shone like gold, so brightly was it polished. In the evening, when the snowflakes fell, the mother said, "Go, Snow-White, and bolt the door," and then they sat round the hearth, and the mother took her spectacles and read aloud out of a large

book, and the two girls listened as they sat and span. And close by them lay a lamb upon the floor, and behind them upon a perch sat a white dove with its head hidden beneath its wings.

One evening, as they were thus sitting comfortably together, some one knocked at the door as if he wished to be let in. The mother said, "Quick, Rose-Red, open the door, it must be a traveller who is seeking shelter." Rose-Red went and pushed back the bolt, thinking that it was a poor man, but it was not; it was a bear that stretched his broad, black head within the door.

Rose-Red screamed and sprang back, the lamb bleated, the dove fluttered, and Snow-White hid herself behind her mother's bed. But the bear began to speak and said, "Do not be afraid, I will do you no harm! I am half-frozen, and only want to warm myself a little beside you."

"Poor bear," said the mother, "lie down by the fire, only take care that you do not burn your coat." Then she cried, "Snow-White, Rose-Red, come out, the bear will do you no harm, he means well." So they both came out, and by-and-by the lamb and dove came nearer, and were not afraid of him. The bear said, "Here, children, knock the snow out of my coat a little"; so they brought the broom and swept the bear's hide clean; and he stretched himself by the fire and growled contentedly and comfortably. It was not long before they grew quite at home, and played tricks with their clumsy guest. They tugged his hair with their hands, put their feet upon his back and rolled him about, or they took a hazel-switch and beat him, and when he growled they laughed. But the bear took it all in good part, only when they were too rough he called out, "Leave me alive, children,

"Snowy-White, Rosy-Red,
Will you beat your lover dead?"

When it was bed-time, and the others went to bed, the mother said to the bear, "You can lie there by the hearth, and then you will be safe from the cold and the bad weather." As soon as day dawned the two children let him out, and he trotted across the snow into the forest.

Henceforth the bear came every evening at the same time, laid himself down by the hearth, and let the children amuse themselves with him as much as they liked; and they got so used to him that the doors were never fastened until their black friend had arrived.

When spring had come and all outside was green, the bear said one morning to Snow-White, "Now I must go away, and cannot come back for the whole summer." "Where are you going, then, dear bear?" asked Snow-White. "I must go into the forest and guard my treasures from the wicked dwarfs. In the winter, when the earth is frozen hard, they are obliged to stay below and cannot work their way through; but now, when the sun has thawed and warmed the earth, they break through it, and come out to pry and steal; and what once gets into their hands, and in their caves, does not easily see daylight again."

Snow-White was quite sorry for his going away, and as she unbolted the door for him, and the bear was hurrying out, he caught against the bolt and a piece of his hairy coat was torn off, and it seemed to Snow-White as if she had seen gold shining through it, but she was not sure about it. The bear ran away quickly, and was soon out of sight behind the trees.

A short time afterwards the mother sent her children into the forest to get fire-wood. There they found a big tree which lay felled on the ground, and close by the trunk something was jumping backwards and forwards in the grass, but they could not make out what it was. When they came nearer they saw a dwarf with an old withered face and a snow-white beard a yard long. The end of the beard was caught in a crevice of the tree, and the little fellow was jumping backwards and forwards like a dog tied to a rope, and did not know what to do.

He glared at the girls with his fiery red eyes and cried, "Why do you stand there? Can you not come here and help me?" "What are you about there, little man?" asked Rose-Red. "You stupid, prying goose!" answered the dwarf; "I was going to split the tree to get a little wood for cooking. The little bit of food that one of us wants gets burnt up directly with thick logs; we do not swallow so much as you coarse, greedy folk. I had just driven the wedge safely in, and everything was going as I wished; but the wretched wood was too smooth and suddenly sprang asunder, and the tree closed so quickly that I could not pull out my beautiful white

beard; so now it is tight in and I cannot get away, and the silly, sleek, milk-faced things laugh! Ugh! how odious you are!"

The children tried very hard, but they could not pull the beard out, it was caught too fast. "I will run and fetch some one," said Rose-Red. "You senseless goose!" snarled the dwarf; "why should you fetch some one? You are already two too many for me; can you not think of something better?" "Don't be impatient," said Snow-White, "I will help you," and she pulled her scissors out of her pocket, and cut off the end of the beard.

As soon as the dwarf felt himself free he laid hold of a bag which lay amongst the roots of the tree, and which was full of gold, and lifted it up, grumbling to himself, "Uncouth people, to cut off a piece of my fine beard. Bad luck to you!" and then he swung the bag upon his back, and went off without even once looking at the children.

Some time after that Snow-White and Rose-Red went to catch a dish of fish. As they came near the brook they saw something like a large grasshopper jumping towards the water, as if it were going to leap in. They ran to it and found it was the dwarf. "Where are you going?" said Rose-Red; "you surely don't want to go into the water?" "I am not such a fool!" cried the dwarf; "don't you see that the accursed fish wants to pull me in?" The little man had been sitting there fishing, and unluckily the wind had twisted his beard with the fishing-line; just then a big fish bit, and the feeble creature had not strength to pull it out; the fish kept the upper hand and pulled the dwarf towards him. He held on to all the reeds and rushes, but it was of little good, he was forced to follow the movements of the fish, and was in urgent danger of being dragged into the water.

The girls came just in time; they held him fast and tried to free his beard from the line, but all in vain, beard and line were entangled fast together. Nothing was left but to bring out the scissors and cut the beard, whereby a small part of it was lost. When the dwarf saw that he screamed out, "Is that civil, you toad-stool, to disfigure one's face? Was it not enough to clip off the end of my beard? Now you have cut off the best part of it. I cannot let myself be seen by my people. I wish you had been made to run the soles off your shoes!" Then he took out a sack of pearls which lay in the rushes, and without saying a word more he dragged it away and disappeared behind a stone.

It happened that soon afterwards the mother sent the two children to the town to buy needles and thread, and laces and ribbons. The road led them across a heath upon which huge pieces of rock lay strewn here and there. Now they noticed a large bird hovering in the air, flying slowly round and round above them; it sank lower and lower, and at last settled near a rock not far off. Directly afterwards they heard a loud, piteous cry. They ran up and saw with horror that the eagle had seized their old acquaintance the dwarf, and was going to carry him off.

The children, full of pity, at once took tight hold of the little man, and pulled against the eagle so long that at last he let his booty go. As soon as the dwarf had recovered from his first fright he cried with his shrill voice, "Could you not have done it more carefully! You dragged at my brown coat so that it is all torn and full of holes, you helpless clumsy creatures!" Then he took up a sack full of precious stones, and slipped away again under the rock into his hole. The girls, who by this time were used to his thanklessness, went on their way and did their business in the town.

As they crossed the heath again on their way home they surprised the dwarf, who had emptied out his bag of precious stones in a clean spot, and had not thought that any one would come there so late. The evening sun shone upon the brilliant stones; they glittered and sparkled with all colours so beautifully that the children stood still and looked at them. "Why do you stand gaping there?" cried the dwarf, and his ashen-grey face became copper-red with rage. He was going on with his bad words when a loud growling was heard, and a black bear came trotting towards them out of the forest. The dwarf sprang up in a fright, but he could not get to his cave, for the bear was already close. Then in the dread of his heart he cried, "Dear Mr. Bear, spare me, I will give you all my treasures; look, the beautiful jewels lying there! Grant me my life; what do you want with such a slender little fellow as I? You would not feel me between your teeth.

Come, take these two wicked girls, they are tender morsels for you, fat as young quails; for mercy's sake eat them!" The bear took no heed of his words, but gave the wicked creature a single blow with his paw, and he did not move again.

The girls had run away, but the bear called to them, "Snow-White and Rose-Red, do not be afraid; wait, I will come with you." Then they knew his voice and waited, and when he came up to them suddenly his bearskin fell off, and he stood there a handsome man, clothed all in gold. "I am a King's son," he said, "and I was bewitched by that wicked dwarf, who had stolen my treasures; I have had to run about the forest as a savage bear until I was freed by his death. Now he has got his well-deserved punishment."

Snow-White was married to him, and Rose-Red to his brother, and they divided between them the great treasure which the dwarf had gathered together in his cave. The old mother lived peacefully and happily with her children for many years. She took the two rose-trees with her, and they stood before her window, and every year bore the most beautiful roses, white and red.

CLEVER ELSIE

This story is pure slapstick. Elsie is such a dolt she provokes amused protest, but she has a host of equally weak-minded cousins in folk tales around the world.

There was once a man who had a daughter who was called Clever Elsie. And when she had grown up, her father said, "We will get her married." "Yes," said the mother, "if only any one would come who would have her." At length a man came from a distance and wooed her, who was called Hans; but he stipulated that Clever Elsie should be really wise. "Oh," said the father, "she's sharp enough"; and the mother said, "Oh, she can see the wind coming up the street, and hear the flies coughing." "Well," said Hans, "if she is not really wise, I won't have her." When they were sitting at dinner and had eaten, the

"Clever Elsie." From *Grimm's Household Tales,* translated by Margaret Hunt

mother said, "Elsie, go into the cellar and fetch some beer."

Then Clever Elsie took the pitcher from the wall, went into the cellar, and tapped the lid briskly as she went, so that the time might not appear long. When she was below she fetched herself a chair, and set it before the barrel so that she had no need to stoop, and did not hurt her back or do herself any unexpected injury. Then she placed the can before her, and turned the tap, and while the beer was running she would not let her eyes be idle, but looked up at the wall, and after much peering here and there, saw a pick-axe exactly above her, which the masons had accidently left there.

Then Clever Elsie began to weep and said, "If I get Hans, and we have a child, and he grows big, and we send him into the cellar here to draw beer, then the pick-axe will fall on his head and kill him." Then she sat and wept and screamed with all the strength of her body, over the misfortune which lay before her. Those upstairs waited for the drink, but Clever Elsie still did not come. Then the woman said to the servant, "Just go down into the cellar and see where Elsie is." The maid went and found her sitting in front of the barrel, screaming loudly. "Elsie, why do you weep?" asked the maid. "Ah," she answered, "have I not reason to weep? If I get Hans, and we have a child, and he grows big, and has to draw beer here, the pick-axe will perhaps fall on his head, and kill him." Then said the maid, "What a clever Elsie we have!" and sat down beside her and began loudly to weep over the misfortune.

After a while, as the maid did not come back, and those upstairs were thirsty for the beer, the man said to the boy, "Just go down into the cellar and see where Elsie and the girl are." The boy went down, and there sat Clever Elsie and the girl both weeping together. Then he asked, "Why are you weeping?" "Ah," said Elsie, "have I not reason to weep? If I get Hans, and we have a child, and he grows big, and has to draw beer here, the pick-axe will fall on his head and kill him." Then said the boy, "What a clever Elsie we have!" and sat down by her, and likewise began to howl loudly.

Upstairs they waited for the boy, but as he still did not return, the man said to the woman, "Just go down into the cellar and see where Elsie is!" The woman went down, and found all three in the midst of their lamentations, and inquired what was the cause; then Elsie told her also that her future child was to be killed by the pick-axe, when it grew big and had to draw beer, and the pick-axe fell down. Then said the mother likewise, "What a clever Elsie we have!" and sat down and wept with them.

The man upstairs waited a short time, but as his wife did not come back and his thirst grew ever greater, he said, "I must go into the cellar myself and see where Elsie is." But when he got into the cellar, and they were all sitting together crying, and he heard the reason, and that Elsie's child was the cause, and that Elsie might perhaps bring one into the world some day, and that he might be killed by the pick-axe, if he should happen to be sitting beneath it, drawing beer just at the very time when it fell down, he cried, "Oh, what a clever Elsie!" and sat down, and likewise wept with them.

The bridegroom stayed upstairs alone for a long time; then as no one would come back he thought, "They must be waiting for me below: I too must go there and see what they are about." When he got down, the five of them were sitting screaming and lamenting quite piteously, each out-doing the other. "What misfortune has happened then?" asked he. "Ah, dear Hans," said Elsie, "if we marry each other and have a child, and he is big, and we perhaps send him here to draw something to drink, then the pick-axe which has been left up there might dash his brains out if it were to fall down, so have we not reason to weep?" "Come," said Hans, "more understanding than that is not needed for my household; as you are such a clever Elsie, I will have you," and he seized her hand, took her upstairs with him, and married her.

After Hans had had her some time, he said, "Wife, I am going out to work and earn some money for us; go into the field and cut the corn that we may have some bread." "Yes, dear Hans, I will do that." After Hans had gone away, she cooked herself some good broth and took it into the field with her. When she came to the field she said to herself, "What shall I do; shall I cut first, or shall I eat first? Oh, I will eat first." Then she drank her cup of broth, and when she was fully satisfied, she once more said, "What shall I do? Shall I cut first, or shall I sleep first? I will sleep first." Then she lay down among the corn and fell asleep. Hans had been at home for a long time, but Elsie did not come; then said he, "What a clever Elsie I have; she is so industrious that she does not even come home to eat."

But when evening came and she still stayed away, Hans went out to see what she had cut, but nothing was cut, and she was lying among the corn asleep. Then Hans hastened home and brought a fowler's net with little bells and hung it round about her, and she still went on sleeping. Then he ran home, shut the house-door, and sat down in his chair and worked.

At length, when it was quite dark, Clever Elsie awoke and when she got up there was a jingling all round about her, and the bells rang at each step which she took. Then she was alarmed, and became uncertain whether she really was Clever Elsie or not, and said, "Is it I, or is it not I?" But she knew not what answer to make to this, and stood for a time in doubt; at length she thought: "I will go home and ask if it be I, or if it be not I, they will be sure to know." She ran to the door of her own house, but it was shut; then she knocked at the window and cried, "Hans, is Elsie within?" "Yes," answered Hans, "she is within."

Hereupon she was terrified, and said, "Ah, heavens! Then it is not I," and went to another door; but when the people heard the jingling of the bells they would not open it, and she could get in nowhere. Then she ran out of the village, and no one has seen her since.

SNOW-WHITE AND THE SEVEN DWARFS

This may well be one of the most famous of folk tales, and Snow-White truly belongs in the distinguished company of Cinderella and Sleeping Beauty.

It was in the middle of winter, when the broad flakes of snow were falling around, that a certain queen sat working at a window, the frame of which was made of fine black ebony; and as she was looking out upon the snow, she pricked her finger, and three drops of blood fell upon it. Then she gazed thoughtfully upon the red drops which sprinkled the white snow, and said, "Would that my little daughter may be as white as that snow, as red as the blood, and as black as the ebony window-frame!"

And so the little girl grew up. Her skin was as white as snow, her cheeks as rosy as blood, and her hair as black as ebony; and she was called Snow-White.

But this queen died; and the king soon married another wife, who was very beautiful, but so proud that she could not bear to think that any one could surpass her. She had a magical mirror, to which she used to go and gaze upon herself in it, and say,

"Mirror, Mirror on the wall
Who is fairest of us all?"

And the glass answered,

"Thou, queen, art fairest of them all."

But Snow-White grew more and more beautiful; and when she was seven years old, she was as

"Snow-White and the Seven Dwarfs." From *Grimm's Popular Stories,* translated by Edgar Taylor (slightly adapted)

bright as the day, and fairer than the queen herself. Then the glass one day answered the queen, when she went to consult it as usual,

"Queen, you are full fair, 'tis true,
But Snow-White fairer is than you."

When the queen heard this she turned pale with rage and envy; and called to one of her servants and said, "Take Snow-White away into the wide wood, that I may never see her more." Then the servant led Snow-White away; but his heart melted when she begged him to spare her life, and he said, "I will not hurt thee, thou pretty child." So he left her by herself, and though he thought it most likely that the wild beasts would tear her in pieces, he felt as if a great weight were taken off his heart when he had made up his mind not to kill her, but leave her to her fate.

Then poor Snow-White wandered along through the wood in great fear; and the wild beasts roared about her, but none did her any harm. In the evening she came to a little cottage, and went in there to rest herself, for her little feet would carry her no further. Everything was spruce and neat in the cottage. On the table was spread a white cloth, and there were seven little plates with seven little loaves, and seven little glasses, and knives and forks laid in order; and by the wall stood seven little beds. Then, as she was very hungry, she picked a little piece off each loaf, and drank a very little from each glass; and after that she thought she would lie down and rest. So she tried all the little beds; and one was

too long, and another was too short, till at last the seventh suited her; and there she laid herself down, and went to sleep.

Presently in came the masters of the cottage, who were seven little dwarfs that lived among the mountains, and dug and searched about for gold. They lighted up their seven lamps, and saw directly that all was not right. The first said, "Who has been sitting on my stool?" The second, "Who has been eating off my plate?" The third, "Who has been picking my bread?" The fourth, "Who has been meddling with my spoon?" The fifth, "Who has been handling my fork?" The sixth, "Who has been cutting with my knife?" The seventh, "Who has been drinking from my glass?" Then the first looked round and said, "Who has been lying on my bed?" And the rest came running to him, and every one cried out that somebody had been upon his bed. But the seventh saw Snow-White, and called all his brethren to come and see her; and they cried out with wonder and astonishment, and brought their lamps to look at her, and said, "Oh, what a lovely child she is!" And they were delighted to see her, and took care not to wake her; and the seventh dwarf slept an hour with each of the other dwarfs in turn, till the night was gone.

In the morning Snow-White told them all her story; and they pitied her, and said if she would keep all things in order, and cook and wash, and knit and spin for them, she might stay where she was, and they would take good care of her. Then they went out all day long to their work, seeking for gold and silver in the mountains; and Snow-White remained at home; and they warned her,

and said, "The queen will soon find out where you are, so take care and let no one in."

But the queen, now that she thought Snow-White was dead, believed that she was certainly the handsomest lady in the land; and she went to her mirror and said,

> "Mirror, Mirror on the wall
> Who is fairest of us all?"

And the mirror answered,

> "Queen, thou art of beauty rare,
> But Snow-White living in the glen
> With the seven little men,
> Is a thousand times more fair."

Then the queen was very much alarmed; for she knew that the glass always spoke the truth, and was sure that the servant had betrayed her. And she could not bear to think that any one lived who was more beautiful than she was; so she disguised herself as an old pedlar and went her way over the hills to the place where the dwarfs dwelt. Then she knocked at the door, and cried, "Fine wares to sell!" Snow-White looked out at the window, and said, "Good-day, good-woman; what have you to sell?" "Good wares, fine wares," said she; "laces and bobbins of all colors." "I will let the old lady in; she seems to be a very good sort of body," thought Snow-White; so she ran down, and unbolted the door. "Bless me!" said the old woman, "how badly your stays are laced! Let me lace them up with one of my nice new laces." Snow-White did not dream of any mischief; so she stood up before the old woman, who set to work so nimbly, and pulled the lace so tight, that Snow-White lost her breath, and fell down as if she were dead. "There's an end of all thy beauty," said the spiteful queen, and went away home.

In the evening the seven dwarfs returned; and I need not say how grieved they were to see their faithful Snow-White stretched upon the ground motionless, as if she were quite dead. However, they lifted her up, and when they found what was the matter, they cut the lace; and in a little time she began to breathe, and soon came to life again. Then they said, "The old woman was the queen herself; take care another time, and let no one in when we are away."

When the queen got home, she went straight to her glass, and spoke to it as usual; but to her great surprise it still said,

> "Queen, thou art of beauty rare,
> But Snow-White living in the glen
> With the seven little men,
> Is a thousand times more fair."

Then the blood ran cold in her heart with spite and malice to see that Snow-White still lived; and she dressed herself up again in a disguise, but very different from the one she wore before, and took with her a poisoned comb. When she reached the dwarfs' cottage, she knocked at the door, and cried, "Fine wares to sell!" But Snow-White said, "I dare not let any one in." Then the queen said, "Only look at my beautiful combs"; and gave her the poisoned one. And it looked so pretty that Snow-White took it up and put it into her hair to try it. But the moment it touched her head the poison was so powerful that she fell down senseless. "There you may lie," said the queen, and went her way. But by good luck the dwarfs returned very early that evening, and when they saw Snow-White lying on the ground, they guessed what had happened, and soon found the poisoned comb. When they took it away, she recovered, and told them all that had passed; and they warned her once more not to open the door to any one.

Meantime the queen went home to her glass, and trembled with rage when she received exactly the same answer as before; and she said, "Snow-White shall die, if it costs me my life." So she went secretly into a chamber, and prepared a poisoned apple. The outside looked very rosy and tempting, but whoever tasted it was sure to die. Then she dressed herself up as a peasant's wife, and travelled over the hills to the dwarfs' cottage, and knocked at the door; but Snow-White put her head out of the window and said, "I dare not let any one in, for the dwarfs have told me not." "Do as you please," said the old woman, "but at any rate take this pretty apple; I will make you a present of it." "No," said Snow-White, "I dare not take it." "You silly girl!" answered the other, "what are you afraid of? Do you think it is poisoned? Come! Do you eat one part, and I will eat the other." Now the apple was so prepared that one side was good, though the other side was poisoned. Then Snow-White was very much tempted to taste, for the apple looked exceedingly nice; and when she saw the old woman eat, she could refrain no longer. But she had scarcely put the piece into her mouth, when she fell down dead upon the ground. "This time nothing will save you," said the queen; and she went home to her glass and at last it said,

"Thou, queen, art the fairest of them all."

And then her envious heart was glad, and as happy as such a heart could be.

When evening came, and the dwarfs returned home, they found Snow-White lying on the ground. No breath passed her lips, and they were afraid that she was quite dead. They lifted her up, and combed her hair, and washed her face with water; but all was in vain, for the little girl seemed quite dead. So they laid her down upon a bier, and all seven watched and bewailed her three whole days; and then they proposed to bury her; but her cheeks were still rosy, and her face looked just as it did while she was alive; so they said, "We will never bury her in the cold ground." And they made a coffin of glass, so that they might still look at her, and wrote her name upon it, in golden letters, and that she was a king's daughter. And the coffin was placed upon the hill, and one of the dwarfs always sat by it and watched. And the birds of the air came too, and bemoaned Snow-White; first of all came an owl, and then a raven, but at last came a dove.

And thus Snow-White lay for a long, long time, and still looked as though she were only asleep; for she was even now as white as snow, and as red as blood, and as black as ebony. At last a prince came and called at the dwarfs' house; and he saw Snow-White, and read what was written in golden letters. Then he offered the dwarfs money, and earnestly prayed them to let him take her away; but they said, "We will not part with her for all the gold in the world." At last, however, they had pity on him, and gave him the coffin; but the moment he lifted it up to carry it home with him, the piece of apple fell from between her lips, and Snow-White awoke, and said, "Where am I?" And the prince an-swered, "Thou art safe with me." Then he told her all that had happened, and said, "I love you better than all the world. Come with me to my father's palace, and you shall be my wife." And Snow-White consented, and went home with the prince; and everything was prepared with great pomp and splendour for their wedding.

To the feast was invited, among the rest, Snow-White's old enemy, the queen; and as she was dressing herself in fine rich clothes, she looked in the glass, and said,

"Mirror, Mirror on the wall,
Who is fairest of us all?"

And the glass answered,

"O Queen, although you are of beauty rare
The young queen is a thousand times more fair."

When she heard this, she started with rage; but her envy and curiosity were so great, that she could not help setting out to see the bride. And when she arrived, and saw that it was no other than Snow-White, who, as she thought, had been dead a long while, she choked with passion, and fell ill and died. But Snow-White and the prince lived and reigned happily over that land many, many years.

THE FISHERMAN AND HIS WIFE

There is another version of the rhyme, by Wanda Gág, that goes: "Manye, Manye, Timpie Tee,/Fishye, Fishye in the sea,/Ilsebill my wilful wife/Does not want my way of life." Try that to create a somber spell in the telling. You may want to cut an episode or two from the story to keep it from seeming unduly long. Its moral has a lifelong application.

There was once upon a time a Fisherman who lived with his wife in a miserable hovel close by the sea, and every day he went out fishing. And once as he was sitting with his rod, looking at the clear water, his line suddenly went down, far

"The Fisherman and His Wife." From *Grimm's Household Tales,* translated by Margaret Hunt

down below, and when he drew it up again, he brought out a large Flounder. Then the Flounder said to him, "Hark you, Fisherman, I pray you, let me live. I am no Flounder really, but an enchanted prince. What good will it do you to kill me? I should not be good to eat. Put me in the water again, and let me go." "Come," said the Fisherman, "there is no need for so many words about it—a fish that can talk I should certainly let go, anyhow." With that he put him back again into the clear water, and the Flounder went to the bottom, leaving a long streak of blood behind him. Then the Fisherman got up and went home to his wife in the hovel.

"Husband," said the woman, "have you caught nothing to-day?" "No," said the man, "I did catch a Flounder, who said he was an enchanted prince, so I let him go again," "Did you not wish for anything first?" said the woman. "No," said the man; "what should I wish for?" "Ah," said the woman, "it is surely hard to have to live always in this dirty hovel; you might have wished for a small cottage for us. Go back and call him. Tell him we want to have a small cottage; he will certainly give us that." "Ah," said the man, "why should I go there again?" "Why," said the woman, "you did catch him, and you let him go again; he is sure to do it. Go at once." The man still did not quite like to go, but did not like to oppose his wife either, and went to the sea.

When he got there the sea was all green and yellow, and no longer so smooth; so he stood and said,

> "Flounder, flounder in the sea,
> Come, I pray thee, here to me;
> For my wife, good Ilsabil,
> Wills not as I'd have her will."

Then the Flounder came swimming to him and said: "Well, what does she want then?" "Ah," said the man, "I did catch you, and my wife says I really ought to have wished for something. She does not like to live in a wretched hovel any longer; she would like to have a cottage." "Go, then," said the Flounder, "she has it already."

When the man went home, his wife was no longer in the hovel, but instead of it there stood a small cottage, and she was sitting on a bench be-

fore the door. Then she took him by the hand and said to him, "Just come inside. Look, now isn't this a great deal better?" So they went in, and there was a small porch, and a pretty little parlour and bedroom, and a kitchen and pantry, with the best of furniture, and fitted up with the most beautiful things made of tin and brass, whatsoever was wanted. And behind the cottage there was a small yard, with hens and ducks, and a little garden with flowers and fruit. "Look," said the wife, "is not that nice!" "Yes," said the husband, "and so we must always think it—now we will live quite contented." "We will think about that," said the wife. With that they ate something and went to bed.

Everything went well for a week or a fortnight, and then the woman said, "Hark you, husband, this cottage is far too small for us, and the garden and yard are little; the Flounder might just as well have given us a larger house. I should like to live in a great stone castle; go to the Flounder, and tell him to give us a castle." "Ah, wife," said the man, "the cottage is quite good enough; why should we live in a castle?" "What!" said the woman; "just go there, the Flounder can always do that." "No, wife," said the man, "the Flounder has just given us the cottage. I do not like to go back so soon; it might make him angry." "Go," said the woman, "he can do it quite easily, and will be glad to do it; just you go to him."

The man's heart grew heavy, and he would not go. He said to himself, "It is not right," and yet he went. And when he came to the sea the water was quite purple and dark-blue, and grey and thick, and no longer so green and yellow, but it was still quiet. And he stood there and said,

> "Flounder, flounder in the sea,
> Come, I pray thee, here to me;
> For my wife, good Ilsabil,
> Wills not as I'd have her will."

"Well, what does she want, then?" said the Flounder. "Alas," said the man, half scared, "she wants to live in a great stone castle." "Go to it, then, she is standing before the door," said the Flounder.

Then the man went away, intending to go home, but when he got there, he found a great stone palace, and his wife was just standing on the steps going in, and she took him by the hand and said: "Come in." So he went in with her, and in the castle was a great hall paved with marble, and many servants, who flung wide the doors; and the walls were all bright with beautiful hangings, and in the rooms were chairs and tables of pure gold, and crystal chandeliers hung from the ceiling, and all the rooms and bedrooms had carpets, and food and wine of the very best were standing on all the tables, so that they nearly broke down beneath it. Behind the house, too, there was a great court-yard, with stables for horses and cows, and the very best of carriages; there was a magnificent large garden, too, with the most beautiful flowers and fruit-trees, and a park quite half a mile long, in which were stags, deer, and hares, and everything that could be desired. "Come," said the woman, "isn't that beautiful?" "Yes, indeed," said the man, "now let it be; and we will live in this beautiful castle and be content." "We will consider about that," said the woman, "and sleep upon it"; thereupon they went to bed.

Next morning the wife awoke first, and it was just daybreak, and from her bed she saw the beautiful country lying before her. Her husband was still stretching himself, so she poked him in the side with her elbow, and said, "Get up, husband, and just peep out of the window. Look you, couldn't we be the King over all that land? Go to the Flounder; we will be the King." "Ah, wife," said the man, "why should we be King? I do not want to be King." "Well," said the wife, "if you won't be King, I will; go to the Flounder, for I will be King." "Ah, wife," said the man, "why do you want to be King? I do not like to say that to him." "Why not?" said the woman; "go to him this instant; I must be King!" So the man went, and was quite unhappy because his wife wished to be King. "It is not right; it is not right," thought he. He did not wish to go, but yet he went.

And when he came to the sea, it was quite dark-grey, and the water heaved up from below, and smelt putrid. Then he went and stood by it, and said,

"Flounder, flounder in the sea,
Come, I pray thee, here to me;

For my wife, good Ilsabil,
Wills not as I'd have her will."

"Well, what does she want, then?" said the Flounder. "Alas," said the man, "she wants to be King." "Go to her; she is King already."

So the man went, and when he came to the palace, the castle had become much larger, and had a great tower and magnificent ornaments, and the sentinel was standing before the door, and there were numbers of soldiers with kettle-drums and trumpets. And when he went inside the house, everything was of real marble and gold, with velvet covers and great golden tassels. Then the doors of the hall were opened, and there was the court in all its splendour, and his wife was sitting on a high throne of gold and diamonds, with a great crown of gold on her head, and a sceptre of pure gold and jewels in her hand, and on both sides of her stood her maids-in-waiting in a row, each of them always one head shorter than the last.

Then he went and stood before her, and said: "Ah, wife, and now you are King." "Yes," said the woman, "now I am King." So he stood and looked at her, and when he had looked at her thus for some time, he said, "And now that you are King, let all else be. Now we will wish for nothing more." "No, husband," said the woman, quite anxiously, "I find time passes very heavily. I can bear it no longer. Go to the Flounder—I am King, but I must be Emperor, too." "Oh, wife, why do you wish to be Emperor?" "Husband," said she, "go to the Flounder. I will be Emperor." "Alas, wife," said the man, "he cannot make you Emperor; I may not say that to the fish. There is only one Emperor in the land. An Emperor the Flounder cannot make you! I assure you he cannot."

"What!" said the woman, "I am the King, and you are nothing but my husband; will you go this moment? Go at once! If he can make a king he can make an emperor. I will be Emperor; go instantly." So he was forced to go. As the man went, however, he was troubled in mind, and thought to himself: "It will not end well; it will not end well! Emperor is too shameless! The Flounder will at last be tired out."

With that he reached the sea, and the sea was quite black and thick, and began to boil up from below, so that it threw up bubbles, and such a sharp wind blew over it that it curdled, and the man was afraid. Then he went and stood by it, and said,

"Flounder, flounder in the sea,
Come, I pray thee, here to me;
For my wife, good Ilsabil,
Wills not as I'd have her will."

"Well, what does she want, then?" said the Flounder. "Alas, Flounder," said he, "my wife wants to be Emperor." "Go to her," said the Flounder; "she is Emperor already."

So the man went, and when he got there the whole palace was made of polished marble with alabaster figures and golden ornaments, and soldiers were marching before the door blowing trumpets, and beating cymbals and drums; and in the house, barons, and counts, and dukes were going about as servants. Then they opened the doors to him, which were of pure gold. And when he entered, there sat his wife on a throne, which was made of one piece of gold, and was quite two miles high; and she wore a great golden crown that was three yards high, and set with diamonds and carbuncles, and in one hand she had the sceptre, and in the other the imperial orb; and on both sides of her stood the yeomen of the guard in two rows, each being smaller than the one before him, from the biggest giant, who was two miles high, to the very smallest dwarf, just as big as my little finger. And before it stood a number of princes and dukes.

Then the man went and stood among them, and said, "Wife, are you Emperor now?" "Yes," said she, "now I am Emperor." Then he stood and looked at her well, and when he had looked at her thus for some time, he said, "Ah, wife, be content, now that you are Emperor." "Husband," said she, "why are you standing there? Now, I am Emperor, but I will be Pope too; go to the Flounder." "Oh, wife," said the man, "what will you not wish for? You cannot be Pope; there is but one in Christendom; he cannot make you Pope." "Husband," said she, "I will be Pope. Go immediately; I must be Pope this very day." "No, wife," said the man, "I do not like to say that to him; that would not do. It

is too much; the Flounder can't make you Pope." "Husband," said she, "what nonsense! If he can make an emperor, he can make a pope. Go to him directly. I am Emperor, and you are nothing but my husband; will you go at once?"

Then he was afraid and went; but he was quite faint, and shivered and shook, and his knees and legs trembled. And a high wind blew over the land, and the clouds flew, and towards evening all grew dark, and the leaves fell from the trees, and the water rose and roared as if it were boiling, and splashed upon the shore; and in the distance he saw ships which were firing guns in their sore need, pitching and tossing on the waves. And yet in the midst of the sky there was still a small bit of blue, though on every side it was as red as in a heavy storm. So, full of despair, he went and stood in much fear and said,

"Flounder, flounder in the sea,
Come, I pray thee, here to me;
For my wife, good Ilsabil,
Wills not as I'd have her will."

"Well, what does she want, now?" said the Flounder. "Alas," said the man, "she wants to be Pope." "Go to her then," said the Flounder; "she is Pope already."

So he went, and when he got there, he saw what seemed to be a large church surrounded by palaces. He pushed his way through the crowd. Inside, however, everything was lighted up with thousands and thousands of candles, and his wife was clad in gold, and she was sitting on a much higher throne, and had three great golden crowns on, and round about her there was much ecclesiastical splendour; and on both sides of her was a row of candles the largest of which was as tall as the very tallest tower, down to the very smallest kitchen candle, and all the emperors and kings were on their knees before her, kissing her shoe. "Wife," said the man, and looked attentively at her, "are you now Pope?" "Yes," said she, "I am Pope." So he stood and looked at her, and it was just as if he was looking at the bright sun. When he had stood looking at her thus for a short time, he said: "Ah, wife, if you are Pope, do let well alone!" But she looked as stiff as a post, and did not move or show any signs of life. Then said he, "Wife, now that you are Pope, be satisfied; you cannot become anything greater now." "I will consider about that," said the woman. Thereupon they both went to bed, but she was not satisfied, and greediness let her have no sleep, for she was continually thinking what there was left for her to be.

The man slept well and soundly, for he had run about a great deal during the day; but the woman could not fall asleep at all, and flung herself from one side to the other the whole night through, thinking always what more was left for her to be, but unable to call to mind anything else. At length the sun began to rise, and when the woman saw the red of dawn, she sat up in bed and looked at it. And when, through the window, she saw the sun thus rising, she said, "Cannot I, too, order the sun and moon to rise?" "Husband," she said, poking him in the ribs with her elbows, "wake up! Go to the Flounder, for I wish to be even as God is." The man was still half asleep, but he was so horrified that he fell out of bed. He thought he must have heard amiss, and rubbed his eyes, and said, "Alas, wife, what are you saying?" "Husband," said she, "if I can't order the sun and moon to rise, and have to look on and see the sun and moon rising, I can't bear it. I shall not know what it is to have another happy hour, unless I can make them rise myself." Then she looked at him so terribly that a shudder ran over him, and said, "Go at once; I wish to be like unto God." "Alas, wife," said the man, falling on his knees before her, "the Flounder cannot do that; he can make an emperor and a pope; I beseech you, go on as you are, and be Pope." Then she fell into a rage, and her hair flew wildly about her head, and she cried, "I will not endure this, I'll not bear it any longer; will you go this instant?" Then he put on his trousers and ran away like a madman. But outside a great storm was raging, and blowing so hard that he could scarcely keep his feet; houses and trees toppled over, the mountains trembled, rocks rolled into the sea, the sky was pitch black, and it thundered and lightened, and the sea came in with black waves as high as church-towers and mountains, and all with crests of white foam at the top. Then he cried, but could not hear his own words,

"Flounder, flounder in the sea,
Come, I pray thee, here to me;

For my wife, good Ilsabil,
Wills not as I'd have her will."

"Well, what does she want, then?" said the Flounder. "Alas," said he, "she wants to be like unto God." "Go to her, and you will find her back again in the dirty hovel." And there they are still living to this day.

RUMPELSTILTZKIN

This makes a splendid story for dramatization with puppets, either string puppets or hand. The children can cast the story into acts, line up their characters, and as they make the puppets, try out the dialogue with them. With children under ten years old, hand puppets are easier to make and the dialogue is usually kept fluid. Children over ten may want to write parts of their dialogue or all of it.

There was once upon a time a poor miller who had a very beautiful daughter. Now it happened one day that he had an audience with the King, and in order to appear a person of some importance he told him that he had a daughter who could spin straw into gold.

"Now that's a talent worth having," said the King to the miller. "If your daughter is as clever as you say, bring her to my palace to-morrow, and I'll put her to the test."

When the girl was brought to him he led her into a room full of straw, gave her a spinning-wheel and spindle, and said: "Now set to work and spin all night till early dawn, and if by that time you haven't spun the straw into gold you shall die." Then he closed the door behind him and left her alone inside.

So the poor miller's daughter sat down, and didn't know what in the world she was to do. She hadn't the least idea of how to spin straw into gold, and became at last so miserable that she began to cry.

Suddenly the door opened, and in stepped a

"Rumpelstiltzkin." From *The Blue Fairy Book*, edited by Andrew Lang. Longmans, Green, and Co., London, 1889

tiny little man and said: "Good-evening, Miss Miller-maid; why are you crying so bitterly?"

"Oh!" answered the girl, "I have to spin straw into gold, and haven't a notion how it's done."

"What will you give me if I spin it for you?" asked the manikin.

"My necklace," replied the girl.

The little man took the necklace, sat himself down at the wheel, and whir, whir, whir, the wheel went round three times, and the bobbin was full. Then he put on another, and whir, whir, whir, the wheel went round three times, and the second too was full; and so it went on till the morning, when all the straw was spun away, and all the bobbins were full of gold.

As soon as the sun rose the King came, and when he perceived the gold he was astonished and delighted, but his heart only lusted more than ever after the precious metal. He had the miller's daughter put into another room full of straw, much bigger than the first, and bade her, if she valued her life, spin it all into gold before the following morning.

The girl didn't know what to do, and began to cry; then the door opened as before, and the tiny little man appeared and said: "What'll you give me if I spin the straw into gold for you?"

"The ring from my finger," answered the girl. The manikin took the ring, and whir! round went the spinning-wheel again, and when morning broke he had spun all the straw into glittering gold.

The King was pleased beyond measure at the sight, but his greed for gold was still not satisfied, and he had the miller's daughter brought into a yet bigger room full of straw, and said: "You must spin all this away in the night; but if you succeed this time you shall become my wife."

"She's only a miller's daughter, it's true," he thought; "but I couldn't find a richer wife if I were to search the whole world over."

When the girl was alone the little man appeared for the third time, and said: "What'll you give me if I spin the straw for you once again?"

"I've nothing more to give," answered the girl.

"Then promise me when you are Queen to give me your first child."

"Who knows what mayn't happen before that?" thought the miller's daughter; and besides, she saw no other way out of it, so she promised the manikin what he demanded, and he set to work once more and spun the straw into gold. When the King came in the morning, and found everything as he had desired, he straightway made her his wife, and the miller's daughter became a queen.

When a year had passed a beautiful son was born to her, and she thought no more of the little man, till all of a sudden one day he stepped into her room and said, "Now give me what you promised." The Queen was in a great state, and offered the little man all the riches in her kingdom if he would only leave her the child.

But the manikin said: "No, a living creature is dearer to me than all the treasures in the world."

Then the Queen began to cry and sob so bitterly that the little man was sorry for her, and said: "I'll give you three days to guess my name, and if you find it out in that time you may keep your child."

Then the Queen pondered the whole night over all the names she had ever heard, and sent a messenger to scour the land and to pick up far and near any names he should come across. When the little man arrived on the following day she began with Kasper, Melchior, Belshazzar, and all the other names she knew, in a string, but at each one the manikin called out, "That's not my name."

The next day she sent to inquire the names of all the people in the neighbourhood, and had a long list of the most uncommon and extraordinary for the little man when he made his appearance. "Is your name, perhaps, Sheepshanks, Cruickshanks, Spindleshanks?"

But he always replied, "That's not my name."

On the third day the messenger returned and announced: "I have not been able to find any new names, but as I came upon a high hill round the corner of the wood, where the foxes and hares bid each other good night, I saw a little house, and in front of the house burned a fire, and round the fire sprang the most grotesque little man, hopping on one leg and crying:

> 'To-morrow I brew, to-day I bake,
> And then the child away I'll take;
> For little deems my royal dame
> That Rumpelstiltzkin is my name!' "

You may imagine the Queen's delight at hearing the name, and when the little man stepped in shortly afterwards and asked, "Now, my lady Queen, what's my name?" she asked first: "Is your name Conrad?"

"No."

"Is your name Harry?"

"No."

"Is your name, perhaps, Rumpelstiltzkin?"

"Some demon has told you that, some demon has told you that," screamed the little man, and in his rage drove his right foot so far into the ground that it sank in up to his waist. Then in a passion he seized the left foot with both hands and tore himself in two.

ONE-EYE, TWO-EYES, AND THREE-EYES

Listen carefully and you will find here "Cinderella" in a rather interesting disguise.

There was once a woman who had three daughters, the eldest of whom was called One-Eye, because she had only one eye in the middle of her forehead, and the second, Two-Eyes, because she had two eyes like other folks, and the youngest, Three-Eyes, because she had three eyes; and her third eye was also in the centre of her forehead. However, as Two-Eyes saw just as other human beings did, her sisters and her mother could not endure her. They said to her, "You, with your two eyes, are no better than the common people; you do not belong to us!" They pushed her about, and threw old clothes to her, and gave her nothing to eat but what they left, and did everything that they could to make her unhappy. It came to pass that Two-Eyes had to go out into the fields and tend the goat, but she was still quite hungry, because her sisters had given her so little to eat. So she sat down on a ridge and began to weep, and so bitterly that two streams ran down from her eyes. And once when she looked up in her grief, a woman was standing beside her, who said, "Why are you weeping, little Two-Eyes?" Two-Eyes answered, "Have I not reason to weep, when I have two eyes like other people, and my sisters and mother hate me for it, and push me from one corner to another, throw old clothes at me, and give me nothing to eat but the scraps they leave? To-day they have given me so little that I am still quite hungry." Then the wise woman said, "Wipe away your tears, Two-Eyes, and I will tell you something to stop you ever suffering from hunger again; just say to your goat,

> 'Bleat, my little goat, bleat,
> Cover the table with something to eat,'

and then a clean well-spread little table will stand before you, with the most delicious food upon it of which you may eat as much as you are

"One-Eye, Two-Eyes, and Three-Eyes." From *Grimm's Household Tales*, translated by Margaret Hunt

inclined for; and when you have had enough, and have no more need of the little table, just say,

'Bleat, bleat, my little goat, I pray,
And take the table quite away,'

and then it will vanish again from your sight." Hereupon the wise woman departed. But Two-Eyes thought, "I must instantly make a trial, and see if what she said is true, for I am far too hungry," and she said,

"Bleat, my little goat, bleat,
Cover the table with something to eat,"

and scarcely had she spoken the words than a little table, covered with a white cloth, was standing there, and on it was a plate with a knife and fork, and a silver spoon; and the most delicious food was there also, warm and smoking as if it had just come out of the kitchen. Then Two-Eyes said the shortest prayer she knew, "Lord God, be with us always, Amen," and helped herself to some food, and enjoyed it. And when she was satisfied, she said, as the wise woman had taught her,

"Bleat, bleat, my little goat, I pray,
And take the table quite away,"

and immediately the little table and everything on it was gone again. "That is a delightful way of keeping house!" thought Two-Eyes, and was quite glad and happy.

In the evening, when she went home with her goat, she found a small earthenware dish with some food, which her sisters had set ready for her, but she did not touch it. Next day she again went out with her goat, and left the few bits of broken bread which had been handed to her, lying untouched. The first and second time that she did this, her sisters did not remark it at all, but as it happened every time, they did observe it, and said, "There is something wrong about Two-Eyes; she always leaves her food untasted, and she used to eat up everything that was given her; she must have discovered other ways of getting food." In order that they might learn the truth, they resolved to send One-Eye with Two-

Eyes when she went to drive her goat to the pasture, to observe what Two-Eyes did when she was there, and whether any one brought her anything to eat and drink. So when Two-Eyes set out the next time, One-Eye went to her and said, "I will go with you to the pasture, and see that the goat is well taken care of, and driven where there is food." But Two-Eyes knew what was in One-Eye's mind, and drove the goat into high grass and said, "Come, One-Eye, we will sit down, and I will sing something to you." One-Eye sat down and was tired with the unaccustomed walk and the heat of the sun, and Two-Eyes sang constantly,

"One eye, wakest thou?
One eye, sleepest thou?"

until One-Eye shut her one eye, and fell asleep, and as soon as Two-Eyes saw that One-Eye was fast asleep, and could discover nothing, she said,

"Bleat, my little goat, bleat,
Cover the table with something to eat,"

and seated herself at her table and ate and drank until she was satisfied, and then she again cried,

"Bleat, bleat, my little goat, I pray,
And take the table quite away,"

and in an instant all was gone. Two-Eyes now awakened One-Eye, and said, "One-Eye, you want to take care of the goat, and go to sleep while you are doing it, and in the meantime the goat might run all over the world. Come, let us go home again." So they went home, and again Two-Eyes let her little dish stand untouched, and One-Eye could not tell her mother why she would not eat it, and to excuse herself said, "I fell asleep when I was out."

Next day the mother said to Three-Eyes, "This time you shall go and observe if Two-Eyes eats anything when she is out, and if any one fetches her food and drink, for she must eat and drink in secret." So Three-Eyes went to Two-Eyes, and said, "I will go with you and see if the goat is taken proper care of, and driven where there is food." But Two-Eyes knew what was in Three-Eyes' mind, and drove the goat into high grass and said, "We will sit down, and I will sing something to you, Three-Eyes." Three-Eyes sat down and was tired with the walk and with the heat of the sun, and Two-Eyes began the same song as before, and sang,

"Three eyes, are you waking?"

but then, instead of singing,

"Three eyes, are you sleeping?"

as she ought to have done, she thoughtlessly sang,

"Two eyes, are you sleeping?"

and sang all the time,

"Three eyes, are you waking?
Two eyes, are you sleeping?"

Then two of the eyes which Three-Eyes had, shut and fell asleep, but the third, as it had not been named in the song, did not sleep. It is true that Three-Eyes shut it, but only in her cunning, to pretend it was asleep too, but it blinked, and could see everything very well. And when Two-Eyes thought that Three-Eyes was fast asleep, she used her little charm,

"Bleat, my little goat, bleat,
Cover the table with something to eat,"

and ate and drank as much as her heart desired, and then ordered the table to go away again,

"Bleat, bleat, my little goat, I pray,
And take the table quite away,"

and Three-Eyes had seen everything. Then Two-Eyes came to her, waked her and said, "Have you been asleep, Three-Eyes? You are a good caretaker! Come, we will go home." And when they got home, Two-Eyes again did not eat, and Three-Eyes said to the mother, "Now, I know why that high-minded thing there does not eat. When she is out, she says to the goat,

'Bleat, my little goat, bleat,
Cover the table with something to eat,'

and then a little table appears before her covered with the best of food, much better than any we have here, and when she has eaten all she wants, she says,

'Bleat, bleat, my little goat, I pray,
And take the table quite away,'

and all disappears. I watched everything closely. She put two of my eyes to sleep by using a certain form of words, but luckily the one in my forehead kept awake." Then the envious mother cried, "Dost thou want to fare better than we do? The desire shall pass away," and she fetched a butcher's knife, and thrust it into the heart of the goat, which fell down dead.

When Two-Eyes saw that, she went out full of trouble, seated herself on the ridge of grass at the edge of the field, and wept bitter tears. Suddenly the wise woman once more stood by her side, and said, "Two-Eyes, why are you weeping?" "Have I not reason to weep?" she answered. "The goat which covered the table for me every day when I spoke your charm has been killed by my mother, and now I shall again have to bear hunger and want." The wise woman said, "Two-Eyes, I will give you a piece of good advice; ask your sisters to give you the entrails of the slaughtered goat, and bury them in the ground in front of the house, and your fortune will be made." Then she vanished, and Two-Eyes went home and said to her sisters, "Dear sisters, do give me some part of my goat; I don't wish for what is good, but give me the entrails." Then they laughed and said, "If that's all you want, you can have it." So Two-Eyes took the entrails and buried them quietly in the evening, in front of the house-door, as the wise woman had counseled her to do.

Next morning, when they all awoke, and went to the house-door, there stood a strangely magnificent tree with leaves of silver, and fruit of gold hanging among them, so that in all the wide world there was nothing more beautiful or precious. They did not know how the tree could have come there during the night, but Two-Eyes saw that it had grown up out of the entrails of the goat, for it was standing on the exact spot where she had buried them. Then the mother said to One-Eye, "Climb up, my child, and gather some of the fruit of the tree for us." One-Eye climbed up, but when she was about to get hold of one of the golden apples, the branch escaped from her hands, and that happened each time, so that she could not pluck a single apple, let her do what she might. Then said the mother, "Three-Eyes, do you climb up; you with your three eyes can look about you better than One-Eye." One-Eye slipped down, and Three-Eyes climbed up. Three-Eyes was not more skilful, and might search as she liked, but the golden apples always escaped her. At length the mother grew impatient, and climbed up herself, but could get hold of the fruit no better than One-Eye and Three-Eyes, for she always clutched empty air.

Then said Two-Eyes, "I will just go up, perhaps I may succeed better." The sisters cried, "You indeed, with your two eyes, what can you do?" But Two-Eyes climbed up, and the golden apples did not get out of her way, but came into her hand of their own accord, so that she could pluck them one after the other, and brought a whole apronful down with her. The mother took them away from her, and instead of treating poor Two-Eyes any better for this, she and One-Eye and Three-Eyes were only envious, because Two-Eyes alone had been able to get the fruit, and they treated her still more cruelly.

It so befell that once when they were all standing together by the tree, a young knight came up. "Quick, Two-Eyes," cried the two sisters, "creep under this, and don't disgrace us!" and with all speed they turned an empty barrel which was standing close by the tree over poor Two-Eyes, and they pushed the golden apples, which she had been gathering, under it too. When the knight came nearer he was a handsome lord, who stopped and admired the magnificent gold and silver tree, and said to the two sisters, "To whom does this fine tree belong? Any one who would bestow one branch of it on me might in return for it ask whatsoever he desired." Then One-Eye and Three-Eyes replied that the tree belonged to them, and that they would give him a branch. They both took great trouble, but they were not able to do it, for the branches and fruit both moved away from them every time. Then said the knight, "It is very strange that the tree should belong to you, and

that you should still not be able to break a piece off." They again asserted that the tree was their property.

Whilst they were saying so, Two-Eyes rolled out a couple of golden apples from under the barrel to the feet of the knight, for she was vexed with One-Eye and Three-Eyes for not speaking the truth. When the knight saw the apples, he was astonished, and asked where they came from. One-Eye and Three-Eyes answered that they had another sister, who was not allowed to show herself, for she had only two eyes like any common person. The knight, however, desired to see her, and cried, "Two-Eyes, come forth." Then Two-Eyes, quite comforted, came from beneath the barrel, and the knight was surprised at her great beauty, and said, "Thou, Two-Eyes, canst certainly break off a branch from the tree for me." "Yes," replied Two-Eyes, "that I certainly shall be able to do, for the tree belongs to me." And she climbed up, and with the greatest ease, broke off a branch with beautiful silver leaves and golden fruit, and gave it to the knight. Then said the knight, "Two-Eyes, what shall I give thee for it?" "Alas!" answered Two-Eyes, "I suffer from hunger and thirst, grief and want, from early morning till late night; if you would take me with you, and deliver me from these things, I should be happy."

So the knight lifted Two-Eyes on to his horse and took her home with him to his father's castle, and there he gave her beautiful clothes, and meat and drink to her heart's content; and as he loved her so much he married her, and the wedding was solemnized with great rejoicing. When Two-Eyes was thus carried away by the handsome knight, her two sisters grudged her good fortune in downright earnest. "The wonderful tree, however, still remains with us," thought they, "and even if we can gather no fruit from it, still every one will stand still and look at it, and come to us and admire it. Who knows what good things may be in store for us?" But next morning, the tree had vanished, and all their hopes were at an end. When Two-Eyes looked out of the window of her own little room, to her great delight it was standing in front of it, and so it had followed her.

Two-Eyes lived a long time in happiness. Once two poor women came to her in her castle, and begged for alms. She looked in their faces, and recognized her sisters, One-Eye and Three-Eyes, who had fallen into such poverty that they had to wander about and beg their bread from door to door. Two-Eyes, however, made them welcome, and was kind to them, and took care of them, so that they both with all their hearts repented the evil that they had done their sister in their youth.

THE GOOSE-GIRL

This is a somber romance in spite of the happy ending. The little rhyme the goose-girl says over Conrad's hat is certainly a powerful charm!

There was once upon a time an old Queen whose husband had been dead for many years, and she had a beautiful daughter. When the princess grew up she was betrothed to a prince who lived at a great distance. When the time came for her to be married, and she had to journey forth into the distant kingdom, the aged Queen packed up for her many costly vessels of silver and gold, and trinkets also of gold and silver; and cups and jewels, in short, everything which appertained to a royal dowry, for she loved her child with all her heart. She likewise sent her maid in waiting, who was to ride with her, and hand her over to the bridegroom, and each had a horse for the journey, but the horse of the King's daughter was called Falada, and could speak. So when the hour of parting had come, the aged mother went into her bedroom, took a small knife and cut her finger with it until it bled. Then she held a white handkerchief to it into which she let three drops of blood fall, gave it to her daughter and said, "Dear child, preserve this carefully, it will be of service to you on your way."

So they took a sorrowful leave of each other; the princess put the piece of cloth in her bosom, mounted her horse, and then went away to her bridegroom. After she had ridden for a while she felt a burning thirst, and said to her waiting-maid, "Dismount, and take my cup which you

"The Goose-Girl." From *Grimm's Household Tales*, translated by Margaret Hunt

have brought with you for me, and get me some water from the stream, for I should like to drink." "If you are thirsty," said the waiting-maid, "get off your horse yourself, and lie down and drink out of the water, I don't choose to be your servant." So in her great thirst the princess alighted, bent down over the water in the stream and drank, and was not allowed to drink out of the golden cup. Then she said: "Ah, Heaven!" and the three drops of blood answered: "If this your mother knew, her heart would break in two." But the King's daughter was humble, said nothing, and mounted her horse again. She rode some miles further, but the day was warm, the sun scorched her, and she was thirsty once more, and when they came to a stream of water, she again cried to her waiting-maid, "Dismount, and give me some water in my golden cup," for she had long ago forgotten the girl's ill words. But the waiting-maid said still more haughtily: "If you wish to drink, drink as you can. I don't choose to be your maid." Then in her great thirst the King's daughter alighted, bent over the flowing stream, wept and said, "Ah, Heaven!" and the drops of blood again replied, "If this your mother knew, her heart would break in two."

And as she was thus drinking and leaning right over the stream, the handkerchief with the three drops of blood fell out of her bosom, and floated away with the water without her observing it, so great was her trouble. The waiting-maid, however, had seen it, and she rejoiced to think that she had now power over the bride, for since the princess had lost the drops of blood, she had become weak and powerless. So now when she wanted to mount her horse again, the one that was called Falada, the waiting-maid said, "Falada is more suitable for me, and my nag will do for you," and the princess had to be content with that. Then the waiting-maid, with many hard words, bade the princess exchange her royal apparel for her own shabby clothes; and at length she was compelled to swear by the clear sky above her, that she would not say one word of this to anyone at the royal court, and if she had not taken this oath she would have been killed on the spot. But Falada saw all this, and observed it well.

The waiting-maid now mounted Falada, and

the true bride the bad horse, and thus they traveled onwards, until at length they entered the royal palace. There were great rejoicings over her arrival, and the prince sprang forward to meet her, lifted the waiting-maid from her horse, and thought she was his consort. She was conducted upstairs, but the real princess was left standing below.

Then the old King looked out of the window and saw her standing in the courtyard, and noticed how dainty and delicate and beautiful she was, and instantly went to the royal apartment, and asked the bride about the girl she had with her who was standing down below in the courtyard, and who she was. "I picked her up on my way for a companion; give the girl something to work at, that she may not stand idle." But the old King had no work for her, and knew of none, so he said, "I have a little boy who tends the geese, she may help him." The boy was called Conrad, and the true bride had to help him to tend the geese.

Soon afterwards the false bride said to the young King, "Dearest husband, I beg you to do me a favour." He answered, "I will do so most willingly." "Then send for the knacker, and have the head of the horse on which I rode here cut off, for it vexed me on the way." In reality, she was afraid that the horse might tell how she had behaved to the King's daughter. Then she succeeded in making the King promise that it should be done, and the faithful Falada was to die; this came to the ears of the real princess, and she secretly promised to pay the knacker a piece of gold if he would perform a small service for her. There was a great dark-looking gateway in the town, through which morning and evening she had to pass with the geese: would he be so good as to nail up Falada's head on it, so that she might see him again, more than once. The knacker's man promised to do that, and cut off the head, and nailed it fast beneath the dark gateway.

Early in the morning, when she and Conrad drove out their flock beneath this gateway, she said in passing,

"Alas, Falada, hanging there!"

Then the head answered,

"Alas, young Queen, how ill you fare!
If this your tender mother knew,
Her heart would surely break in two."

Then they went still further out of the town, and drove their geese into the country. And when they had come to the meadow, she sat down and unbound her hair which was like pure gold, and Conrad saw it and delighted in its brightness, and wanted to pluck out a few hairs. Then she said,

"Blow, blow, thou gentle wind, I say,
Blow Conrad's little hat away,
And make him chase it here and there,
Until I have braided all my hair,
And bound it up again."

And there came such a violent wind that it blew Conrad's hat far away across country, and he was forced to run after it. When he came back she had finished combing her hair and was putting it up again, and he could not get any of it. Then Conrad was angry, and would not speak to her, and thus they watched the geese until the evening, and then they went home.

Next day when they were driving the geese out through the dark gateway, the maiden said,

"Alas, Falada, hanging there!"

Falada answered,

"Alas, young Queen, how ill you fare!
If this your tender mother knew,
Her heart would surely break in two."

And she sat down again in the field and began to comb out her hair, and Conrad ran and tried to clutch it, so she said in haste,

"Blow, blow, thou gentle wind, I say,
Blow Conrad's little hat away,
And make him chase it here and there,
Until I have braided all my hair,
And bound it up again."

Then the wind blew, and blew his little hat off his head and far away, and Conrad was forced to run after it, and when he came back, her hair had been put up a long time, and he could get none of it, and so they looked after the geese till evening came.

But in the evening after they had got home, Conrad went to the old King, and said, "I won't tend the geese with that girl any longer!" "Why not?" inquired the aged King. "Oh, because she vexes me the whole day long." Then the aged King commanded him to relate what it was that she did to him. And Conrad said, "In the morning when we pass beneath the dark gateway with the flock, there is a sorry horse's head on the wall, and she says to it,

'Alas, Falada, hanging there!'

And the head replies,

'Alas, young Queen, how ill you fare!
If this your tender mother knew,
Her heart would surely break in two.'"

And Conrad went on to relate what happened on the goose pasture and how when there he had to chase his hat.

The aged King commanded him to drive his flock out again next day, and as soon as morning came, he placed himself behind the dark gateway, and heard how the maiden spoke to the head of Falada, and then he too went into the country, and hid himself in the thicket in the meadow. There he soon saw with his own eyes the goose-girl and the goose-boy bringing their flock, and how after a while she sat down and unplaited her hair, which shone with radiance. And soon she said,

"Blow, blow, thou gentle wind, I say,
Blow Conrad's little hat away,
And make him chase it here and there,
Until I have braided all my hair,
And bound it up again."

Then came a blast of wind and carried off Conrad's hat, so that he had to run far away, while the maiden quietly went on combing and plaiting her hair, all of which the King observed. Then, quite unseen, he went away, and when the goose-girl came home in the evening, he called her aside, and asked why she did all these things.

"I may not tell that, and I dare not lament my sorrows to any human being, for I have sworn not to do so by the heaven which is above me; if I had not done that, I should have lost my life." He urged her and left her no peace, but he could draw nothing from her. Then said he, "If you will not tell me anything, tell your sorrows to the iron-stove there," and he went away. Then she crept into the iron-stove, and began to weep and lament, and emptied her whole heart, and said, "Here am I deserted by the whole world, and yet I am a King's daughter, and a false waiting-maid has by force brought me to such a pass that I have been compelled to put off my royal apparel, and she has taken my place with my bridegroom, and I have to perform menial service as a goose-girl. If my mother did but know that, her heart would break."

The aged King, however, was standing outside by the pipe of the stove, and was listening to what she said, and heard it. Then he came back again, and bade her come out of the stove. And royal garments were placed on her, and it was marvellous how beautiful she was! The aged King summoned his son, and revealed to him that he had got the false bride who was only a waiting-maid, but that the true one was standing there, as the sometime goose-girl. The young King rejoiced with all his heart when he saw her beauty and youth, and a great feast was made ready to which all the people and all good friends were invited. At the head of the table sat the bridegroom with the King's daughter at one side of him, and the waiting-maid on the other, but the waiting-maid was blinded, and did not recognize the princess in her dazzling array. When they had eaten and drunk, and were merry, the aged King asked the waiting-maid as a riddle, what punishment a person deserved who had behaved in such and such a way to her master, and at the same time related the whole story, and asked what sentence such a person merited. Then the false bride said, "She deserves no better fate than to be stripped entirely naked, and put in a barrel which is studded inside with pointed nails, and two white horses should be harnessed to it, which will drag her along through one street after another, till she is dead." "It is you," said the aged King, "and you have pronounced your own sentence, and thus shall it be done unto you." And when the sentence had been carried out, the young King married his true bride, and both of them reigned over their kingdom in peace and happiness.

RAPUNZEL

Rapunzel is so ill-starred that her eventual happiness seems almost anticlimactic. When telling the story to children, try using this rhyme each time the witch and the prince ask Rapunzel to let them up: "Rapunzel, Rapunzel, let down your long hair/ That I may climb up by a golden stair." An air of tragic romanticism hangs over this tale, making it perhaps more suitable for older girls; but when it is told well, it creates for most children a somber spell that lingers long after the final lines have been spoken.

In a little German village lived a man and his wife. They had long wished for a child, and now at last they had reason to hope that their wish would be granted.

In their back yard was a shed which looked out upon their neighbor's garden. Often the woman would stand and look at this garden, for it was well kept and flourishing, and had lovely flowers and luscious vegetables laid out in the most tempting manner. The garden was surrounded by a high stone wall but, wall or no wall, there was not much danger of any one entering it. This was because it belonged to Mother Gothel, who was a powerful witch and was feared in all the land.

One summer's day, as the witch's garden was at its very best, the woman was again gazing from the window of her little shed. She feasted her eyes on the gay array of flowers, and she looked longingly at the many kinds of vegetables which were growing there. Her mouth watered as her eyes traveled from the long, crisp beans to the fat, green peas; from the cucumbers to the crinkly lettuce; from the carrots to the waving turnip tops. But when her glance fell upon a fine big bed of rampion (which in that country is

called *rapunzel*) a strange feeling came over her. She had always been fond of rampion salad, and these plants in the witch's garden looked so fresh, so green, so tempting, that she felt she must have some, no matter what the cost.

But then she thought to herself, "It's no use. No one can ever get any of the witch's vegetables. I might as well forget about it."

Still, try as she would, she could not, could not forget. Every day she looked at the fresh green rampion, and every day her longing for it increased. She grew thinner and thinner, and began to look pale and miserable.

Her husband soon noticed this, and said, "Dear wife, what is the matter with you?"

"Oh," said she, "I have a strange desire for some of that rampion in Mother Gothel's garden, and unless I get some, I fear I shall die."

At this the husband became alarmed and as he loved her dearly, he said to himself, "Before you let your wife die, you'll get her some of those plants, no matter what the risk or cost."

Therefore, that evening at twilight, he climbed over the high wall and into the witch's garden. Quickly he dug up a handful of rampion plants and brought them to his ailing wife. She was overjoyed, and immediately made a big juicy salad which she ate with great relish, one might almost say with greed.

In fact she enjoyed it so much that, far from being satisfied, her desire for the forbidden vegetable had now increased threefold. And although she looked rosier and stronger after she had eaten the rampion salad, in a few days she became pale and frail once more.

There was nothing for the man to do but go over to the witch's garden again; and so he went, at twilight as before. He had reached the rampion patch and was about to reach out for the plants, when he stopped short, horrified. Before him stood the witch, old Mother Gothel herself!

"Oh, Mother Gothel," said the man, "please be merciful with me. I am not really a thief and have only done this to save a life. My wife saw your rampion from that window yonder, and now her longing for it is so strange and strong that I fear she will die if she cannot get some of it to eat."

At this the witch softened a little and said, "If

it is as you say, I will let you take as many of the plants as are needed to make her healthy again. But only on one condition: when your first child is born, you must give it to me. I won't hurt it and will care for it like a mother."

The man had been so frightened that he hardly knew what he was doing, and so in his terror, he made this dreadful promise.

Soon after this, the wife became the mother of a beautiful baby girl, and in a short time Mother Gothel came and claimed the child according to the man's promise. Neither the woman's tears nor the man's entreaties could make the witch change her mind. She lifted the baby out of its cradle and took it away with her. She called the girl Rapunzel after those very plants in her garden which had been the cause of so much trouble.

Rapunzel was a winsome child, with long luxuriant tresses, fine as spun gold. When she was twelve years old, the witch took her off to the woods and shut her up in a high tower. It had neither door nor staircase but at its very top was one tiny window. Whenever Mother Gothel came to visit the girl, she stood under this window and called:

Rapunzel, Rapunzel,
Let down your hair.

As soon as Rapunzel heard this, she took her long braids, wound them once or twice around a hook outside the window, and let them fall twenty ells downward toward the ground. This made a ladder for the witch to climb, and in that way she reached the window at the top of the tower.

Thus it went for several years, and Rapunzel was lonely indeed, hidden away in the high tower.

One day a young Prince was riding through the forest when he heard faint music in the distance. That was Rapunzel, who was trying to lighten her solitude with the sound of her own sweet voice.

The Prince followed the sound, but all he found was a tall, forbidding tower. He was eager to get a glimpse of the mysterious singer but he looked in vain for door or stairway. He saw the little window at the top but could think of no

way to get there. At last he rode away, but Rapunzel's sweet singing had touched his heart so deeply that he came back evening after evening and listened to it.

Once, as he was standing there as usual, well hidden by a tree—he saw a hideous hag come hobbling along. It was old Mother Gothel. She stopped at the foot of the tower and called:

Rapunzel, Rapunzel,
Let down your hair.

Now a pair of golden-yellow braids tumbled down from the window. The old hag clung to them and climbed up, up, up, and into the tower window.

"Well!" thought the Prince. "If that is the ladder to the songbird's nest then I, too, must try my luck some day."

The next day at dusk, he went back to the tower, stood beneath it and called:

Rapunzel, Rapunzel,
Let down your hair.

The marvelous tresses were lowered at once. The Prince climbed the silky golden ladder, and stepped through the tiny window up above.

Rapunzel had never seen a man, and at first she was alarmed at seeing this handsome youth enter her window. But the Prince looked at her with friendly eyes and said softly, "Don't be afraid. When I heard your sweet voice, my heart was touched so deeply that I could not rest until I had seen you."

At that Rapunzel lost her fear and they talked happily together for a while. Then the Prince said, "Will you take me for your husband, and come away with me?"

At first Rapunzel hesitated. But the youth was so pleasant to behold and seemed so good and gentle besides, that she thought to herself: "I am sure he will be much kinder to me than Mother Gothel."

So she laid her little hand in his and said, "Yes, I will gladly go with you, but I don't know how I can get away from here. If you come every day, and bring each time a skein of silk, I will weave it into a long, strong ladder. When it is finished I will climb down on it, and then you can take me away on your horse. But come only in the evening," she added, "for the old witch always comes in the daytime."

Every day the Prince came and brought some silk. The ladder was getting longer and stronger, and was almost finished. The old witch guessed nothing, but one day Rapunzel forgot herself and said, "How is it, Mother Gothel, that it takes you so long to climb up here, while the Prince can do it in just a minute—oh!"

"What?" cried the witch.

"Oh nothing, nothing," said the poor girl in great confusion.

"You wicked, wicked child!" cried the witch angrily. "What do I hear you say? I thought I had kept you safely hidden from all the world, and now you have deceived me!"

In her fury, she grabbed Rapunzel's golden hair, twirled it once or twice around her left hand, snatched a pair of scissors with her right, and ritsch, rotsch, the beautiful braids lay on the floor. And she was so heartless after this, that she dragged Rapunzel to a waste and desolate place, where the poor girl had to get along as best she could, living in sorrow and want.

On the evening of the very day in which Rapunzel had been banished, the old witch fastened Rapunzel's severed braids to the window hook, and then she sat in the tower and waited. When the Prince appeared with some silk, as was his wont, he called:

Rapunzel, Rapunzel,
Let down your hair.

Swiftly Mother Gothel lowered the braids. The Prince climbed up as usual, but to his dismay he found, not his dear little Rapunzel, but the cruel witch who glared at him with angry, venomous looks.

"Aha!" she cried mockingly. "You have come to get your dear little wife. Well, the pretty bird is no longer in her nest, and she'll sing no more. The cat has taken her away, and in the end that same cat will scratch out your eyes. Rapunzel is lost to you; you will never see her again!"

The Prince was beside himself with grief, and in his despair he leaped out of the tower window. He escaped with his life, but the thorny thicket into which he fell, blinded him.

Now he wandered, sad and sightless, from place to place, ate only roots and berries, and could do nothing but weep and grieve for the loss of his dear wife.

So he wandered for a whole year in deepest misery until at last he chanced upon the desolate place whither Rapunzel had been banished. There she lived in wretchedness and woe with her baby twins—a boy and a girl—who had been born to her in the meantime.

As he drew near, he heard a sweet and sorrowful song. The voice was familiar to him and he hurried toward it.

When Rapunzel saw him, she flew into his arms and wept with joy. Two of her tears fell on the Prince's eyes—in a moment they were healed and he could see as well as before.

Now they were happy indeed! The Prince took his songbird and the little twins too, and together they rode away to his kingdom. There they all lived happily for many a long year.

France

France has given us not only several of the best-known and most popular of folk tales, but also what is probably the first great collection of folk tales published for young people. This was the famous book of eight fairy tales published by Charles Perrault in 1697 (popularly known as Contes de ma Mère l'Oye—Tales of Mother Goose)*, which anticipated by more than a hundred years the work of the Brothers Grimm and the serious interest in folklore which swept Europe afterwards. Of those first bright tales from Perrault we have here "The Sleeping Beauty in the Wood," "Cinderella," and "The Master Cat." Of the three other stories, two—"Beauty and the Beast" and "The White Cat"—are by well-known French women of the eighteenth century and stand somewhere between the folk tale and the modern fanciful tale. Mme. de Beaumont wisely kept her "Beauty and the Beast" close to the simplicity of the traditional tale. "The White Cat," by Mme. d'Aulnoy, is more elaborate and sophisticated but still retains a basic folk-tale construction. Little has been done in this century toward compiling French folk tales that are suitable for children and of recent vintage. Barbara Leonie Picard's collection is almost the only one to offer "new" French stories in English. It is to be hoped that someday soon the immortal tales of Perrault will be joined by equally splendid folk tales of France that reflect more recent expressions of the humorous wisdom of her people.*

THE SLEEPING BEAUTY IN THE WOOD

The idea of an enchanted sleep reaches back to Greek mythology and beyond. Here is its most perfect and romantic expression. This version omits the second episode in which the ogress proposes to eat up Beauty's children and threatens Beauty. Although such barbarism has a humorous undertone in Perrault's telling, it is neither suitable nor necessary for children. The adult is well advised to read this and the other seven Perrault tales in their original form.

There were formerly a king and a queen who were so sorry that they had no children; so sorry that it cannot be expressed. They went to all the waters in the world; vows, pilgrimages, all ways were tried, and all to no purpose.

At last, however, the Queen had a daughter. There was a very fine christening; and the Princess had for her god-mothers all the fairies they could find in the whole kingdom (they found

"The Sleeping Beauty in the Wood." From *The Blue Fairy Book*, edited by Andrew Lang. Longmans, Green, and Co., London, 1889

seven), that every one of them might give her a gift, as was the custom of fairies in those days. By this means the Princess had all the perfections imaginable.

After the ceremonies of the christening were over, all the company returned to the King's palace, where was prepared a great feast for the fairies. There was placed before every one of them a magnificent cover with a case of massive gold, wherein were a spoon, knife, and fork, all of pure gold set with diamonds and rubies. But as they were all sitting down at the table they saw come into the hall a very old fairy, whom they had not invited because it was over fifty years since she had been out of a certain tower, and she was believed to be either dead or enchanted.

The King ordered her a cover, but could not furnish her with a case of gold as the others, because they had seven only made for the seven fairies. The old Fairy fancied she was slighted, and muttered some threats between her teeth. One of the young fairies who sat by her overheard how she grumbled and, judging that she might give the little Princess some unlucky gift, went, as soon as they rose from table, and hid herself behind the hangings, that she might speak last and repair, as much as she could, the evil which the old Fairy might intend.

In the meanwhile all the fairies began to give their gifts to the Princess. The youngest gave her for gift that she should be the most beautiful person in the world; the next, that she should have the wit of an angel; the third, that she should have a wonderful grace in everything she did; the fourth, that she should dance perfectly well; the fifth, that she should sing like a nightingale; and the sixth, that she should play all kinds of music to the utmost perfection.

The old Fairy's turn came next. With her head shaking more with spite than age, she said that the Princess should have her hand pierced with a spindle and die of the wound. This terrible gift made the whole company tremble, and everybody fell a-crying.

At this very instant the young Fairy came out from behind the hangings, and spake these words aloud:

"Assure yourselves, O King and Queen, that your daughter shall not die of this disaster. It is true, I have no power to undo entirely what my elder has done. The Princess shall indeed pierce her hand with a spindle; but, instead of dying, she shall only fall into a profound sleep, which shall last a hundred years, at the expiration of which a king's son shall come and awake her."

The King, to avoid the misfortune foretold by the old Fairy, caused immediately proclamation to be made, whereby everybody was forbidden, on pain of death, to spin with a distaff and spindle, or to have so much as any spindle in their houses. About fifteen or sixteen years after, the King and Queen being gone to one of their houses of pleasure, the young Princess happened one day to divert herself by running up and down the palace; when going up from one apartment to another, she came into a little room on the top of the tower, where a good old woman, alone, was spinning with her spindle. This good woman had never heard of the King's proclamation against spindles.

"What are you doing there, goody?" said the Princess.

"I am spinning, my pretty child," said the old woman, who did not know who she was.

"Ha!" said the Princess, "this is very pretty; how do you do it? Give it to me, that I may see if I can do so."

She had no sooner taken it than it ran into her hand, and she fell down in a swoon.

The good old woman, not knowing very well what to do in this affair, cried out for help. People came in from every quarter in great numbers; they threw water upon the Princess' face, unlaced her, struck her on the palms of her hands, and rubbed her temples with Hungary-water, but nothing would bring her to herself.

And now the King, who came up at the noise, bethought himself of the prediction of the fairies, and, judging very well that this must necessarily come to pass, since the fairies had said it, caused the Princess to be carried into the finest apartment in his palace, and to be laid upon a bed all embroidered with gold and silver.

One would have taken her for a little angel, she was so very beautiful, for her swooning away had not diminished one bit of her complexion: her cheeks were carnation, and her lips were coral; indeed her eyes were shut, but she was heard to breathe softly, which satisfied those about her that she was not dead. The King commanded that they should not disturb her, but let her sleep quietly till her hour of awakening was come.

The good Fairy who had saved her life by condemning her to sleep a hundred years was in the kingdom of Matakin, twelve thousand leagues off, when this accident befell the Princess; but she was instantly informed of it by a little dwarf, who had boots of seven leagues, that is, boots with which he could tread over seven leagues of ground in one stride. The Fairy came away immediately, and she arrived, about an hour after, in a fiery chariot drawn by dragons.

The King handed her out of the chariot, and she approved everything he had done; but as she had very great foresight, she thought when the Princess should awake she might not know what to do with herself, being all alone in this old palace; and this was what she did: she touched with her wand everything in the palace—except the King and the Queen—governesses, maids of honour, ladies of the bedchamber, gentlemen, officers, stewards, cooks, undercooks, scullions, guards, with their beefeaters, pages, footmen; she likewise touched all the horses which were in the stables, the great dogs in the outward court, and pretty little Mopsey too, the Princess' little spaniel, which lay by her on the bed.

Immediately upon her touching them they all fell asleep that they might not awake before their mistress and that they might be ready to wait upon her when she wanted them. The very spits at the fire, as full as they could hold of partridges and pheasants, did fall asleep also. All this was done in a moment. Fairies are not long in doing their business.

And now the King and the Queen, having kissed their dear child without waking her, went out of the palace and put forth a proclamation that nobody should dare to come near it.

This, however, was not necessary, for in a quarter of an hour's time there grew up all round about the park such a vast number of trees, great and small, bushes and brambles, twining one within another, that neither man nor beast could pass through; so that nothing could be seen but the very top of the towers of the palace; and that either, unless it was a good way off. Nobody doubted but the Fairy gave herein a very extraordinary sample of her art, insuring that the Princess, while she continued sleeping, might have nothing to fear from any curious people.

When a hundred years were gone and passed, the son of the King then reigning, who was of another family from that of the sleeping Princess, being gone a-hunting on that side of the country, asked:

"What were those towers I saw in the middle of a great thick wood?"

Everyone answered according as they had heard. Some said that it was a ruinous old castle, haunted by spirits; others, that all the sorcerers and witches of the country kept there their sabbath or night's meeting. The common opinion was that an ogre lived there and that he carried thither all the little children he could catch, without anybody being able to follow him because only he had the power to pass through the wood.

The Prince was at a stand, not knowing what to believe, when a very aged countryman spake to him thus:

"May it please your royal highness, it is now about fifty years since I heard from my father, who heard my grandfather say, that there was then in this castle a princess, the most beautiful was ever seen; that she must sleep there a hundred years, and should be waked by a king's son, for whom she was reserved."

The young Prince was all on fire at these words, believing, without weighing the matter, that he could put an end to this rare adventure; and, pushed on by love and honour, resolved that moment to look into it.

Scarce had he advanced towards the wood when all the great trees, the bushes, and brambles gave way of themselves to let him pass through; he walked up to the castle, which he saw at the end of a large avenue, and he went in. What a little surprised him was that none of his people could follow him, because the trees closed again as soon as he had passed through them. However, he did not cease from continuing his way; a young and amorous prince is always valiant.

He came into a spacious outward court, where everything he saw might have frozen up the most fearless person with horror. There reigned over all a most frightful silence; the image of death everywhere showed itself, and there was nothing to be seen but stretched-out bodies of men and animals, all seeming to be dead. He, however, very well knew, by the ruby faces and pimpled noses of the beefeaters, that they were only asleep; and their goblets, wherein still remained some drops of wine, showed plainly that they fell asleep in their cups.

He then crossed a court paved with marble, went up the stairs, and came into the guard chamber, where guards were standing in their ranks, with their muskets upon their shoulders, and snoring as loud as they could. After that he went through several rooms full of gentlemen and ladies, all asleep, some standing, others sitting. At last he came into a chamber all gilded with gold, where he saw upon a bed, the curtains of which were all open, the finest sight was ever beheld—a princess, who appeared to be about fifteen or sixteen years of age, and whose bright and, in a manner, resplendent beauty, had somewhat in it divine. He approached with trembling and admiration, and fell down before her upon his knees.

And now, as the enchantment was at an end,

the Princess awaked, and looking on him with eyes more tender than the first view might seem to admit of:

"Is it you, my Prince?" said she to him. "You have waited a long while."

The Prince, charmed with these words, and much more with the manner in which they were spoken, knew not how to show his joy and gratitude. He assured her that he loved her better than he did himself. Their discourse was not well connected, they did weep more than talk—little eloquence, a great deal of love. He was more at a loss than she, and we need not wonder at it: she had time to think on what to say to him, for it is very probable (though history mentions nothing of it) that the good Fairy, during so long a sleep, had given her very agreeable dreams. In short, they talked four hours together, and yet they said not half what they had to say.

In the meanwhile all the palace awaked; everyone thought upon their particular business, and as all of them were not in love they were ready to die for hunger. The chief lady of honour, being as sharp set as other folks, grew very impatient, and told the Princess aloud that supper was served up. The Prince helped the Princess to rise. She was entirely dressed, and very magnificently, but his royal highness took care not to tell her that she was dressed like his great-grandmother and had a point band peeping over a high collar. She looked not a bit the less charming and beautiful for all that.

They went into the great hall of looking-glasses, where they supped, and were served by the Princess' officers. The violins and hautboys played old tunes, but very excellent, though it was now above a hundred years since they had played. And after supper, without losing any time, the lord almoner performed the wedding ceremony for Beauty and the Prince in the chapel of the castle. A short time thereafter, the Prince took Beauty to his own kingdom where they lived happily ever after.

CINDERELLA or

THE LITTLE GLASS SLIPPER

Here is the favorite theme of fiction writers of every age—the misunderstood, lowly maiden who finally comes into her own. It is no wonder that in 1893 Marian Cox was able to list 345 variants of this story. The count has undoubtedly grown since then. Although Perrault's version is the best known, the story had already appeared in somewhat similar form in Italy and has since been retold by many others, most notably Walter de la Mare.

Once there was a gentleman who married, for his second wife, the proudest and most haughty woman that was ever seen. She had, by a former husband, two daughters of her own humour, who were, indeed, exactly like her in all things. He had likewise, by another wife, a young daughter, but of unparalleled goodness and sweetness of temper, which she took from her mother, who was the best creature in the world.

No sooner were the ceremonies of the wedding over but the step-mother began to show herself in her true colours. She could not bear the good qualities of this pretty girl, and the less because they made her own daughters appear the more odious. She employed her in the meanest work of the house. The girl scoured the dishes, tables, etc., and scrubbed madam's chamber, and those of misses, her daughters; she lay up in a sorry garret, upon a wretched straw bed, while her sisters lay in fine rooms, with floors all inlaid, upon beds of the very newest fashion, and where they had looking-glasses so large that they might see themselves at their full length from head to foot.

The poor girl bore all patiently and dared not tell her father, who would have rattled her off; for his wife governed him entirely. When she had done her work, she used to go into the chimney-corner and sit down among cinders and ashes, which made her commonly be called *Cinderwench*; but the youngest, who was not so rude and uncivil as the eldest, called her Cinderella. However, Cinderella, notwithstanding her mean apparel, was a hundred times handsomer than her sisters, though they were always dressed very richly.

It happened that the King's son gave a ball,

"Cinderella or The Little Glass Slipper." From *The Blue Fairy Book,* edited by Andrew Lang. Longmans, Green, and Co., London, 1889

and invited all persons of fashion· to it. Our young misses were also invited, for they cut a very grand figure among the quality. They were mightily delighted at this invitation, and wonderfully busy in choosing out such gowns, petticoats, and head-clothes as might become them. This was a new trouble to Cinderella; for it was she who ironed her sisters' linen, and plaited their ruffles; they talked all day long of nothing but how they should be dressed.

"For my part," said the eldest, "I will wear my red velvet suit with French trimming."

"And I," said the youngest, "shall have my usual petticoat; but then, to make amends for that, I will put on my gold-flowered manteau and my diamond stomacher, which is far from being the most ordinary one in the world."

They sent for the best tire-woman they could get to make up their head-dresses and adjust their double pinners, and they had their red brushes and patches from Mademoiselle de la Poche.

Cinderella was likewise called up to them to be consulted in all these matters, for she had excellent notions, and advised them always for the best, nay, and offered her services to dress their heads, which they were very willing she should do. As she was doing this, they said to her:

"Cinderella, would you not be glad to go to the ball?"

"Alas!" said she, "you only jeer me; it is not for such as I am to go thither."

"Thou art in the right of it," replied they; "it would make the people laugh to see a Cinder-wench at a ball."

Anyone but Cinderella would have dressed their heads awry, but she was very good, and dressed them perfectly well. They were almost two days without eating, so much they were transported with joy. They broke above a dozen laces in trying to be laced up close, that they might have a fine slender shape, and they were continually at their looking-glass. At last the happy day came; they went to court, and Cinderella followed them with her eyes as long as she could, and when she had lost sight of them, she fell a-crying.

Her godmother, who saw her all in tears, asked her what was the matter.

"I wish I could—I wish I could——" she was not able to speak the rest, being interrupted by her tears and sobbing.

This godmother of hers, who was a fairy, said to her, "You wish you could go to the ball; is it not so?"

"Y—es," cried Cinderella, with a great sigh.

"Well," said her godmother, "be but a good girl, and I will contrive that you shall go." Then she took her into her chamber, and said to her, "Run into the garden, and bring me a pumpkin."

Cinderella went immediately to gather the finest she could get, and brought it to her godmother, not being able to imagine how this pumpkin could make her go to the ball. Her godmother scooped out all the inside of it, having left nothing but the rind; which done, she struck it with her wand, and the pumpkin was instantly turned into a fine coach, gilded all over with gold.

She then went to look into her mouse-trap, where she found six mice, all alive, and ordered Cinderella to lift up a little the trapdoor, when, giving each mouse, as it went out, a little tap with her wand, the mouse was that moment turned into a fine horse, which altogether made a very fine set of six horses of a beautiful mouse-coloured dapple-grey. Being at a loss for a coachman, Cinderella said, "I will go and see if there is never a rat in the rat-trap—we may make a coachman of him."

"You are right," replied her godmother; "go and look."

Cinderella brought the trap to her, and in it there were three huge rats. The fairy made choice of one of the three which had the largest beard, and, having touched him with her wand, he was turned into a fat, jolly coachman, who had the smartest whiskers eyes ever beheld.

After that, she said to her: "Go again into the garden, and you will find six lizards behind the watering-pot. Bring them to me."

She had no sooner done so but her godmother turned them into six footmen, who skipped up immediately behind the coach, with their liveries all bedaubed with gold and silver, and clung as close behind each other as if they had done nothing else their whole lives. The fairy then said to Cinderella:

"Well, you see here an equipage fit to go to

the ball with; are you not pleased with it?"

"Oh! yes," cried she; "but must I go thither as I am, in these nasty rags?"

Her godmother only just touched her with her wand, and, at the same instant, her clothes were turned into cloth of gold and silver, all beset with jewels. This done, she gave her a pair of glass slippers, the prettiest in the whole world. Being thus decked out, she got up into her coach; but her godmother, above all things, commanded her not to stay till after midnight, telling her, at the same time, that if she stayed one moment longer, the coach would be a pumpkin again, her horses mice, her coachman a rat, her footmen lizards, and her clothes become just as they were before.

She promised her godmother she would not fail of leaving the ball before midnight; and then away she drove, scarce able to contain herself for joy. The King's son, who was told that a great princess, whom nobody knew, was come, ran out to receive her; he gave her his hand as she alighted from the coach, and led her into the hall, among all the company. There was immediately a profound silence. The dancing stopped, and the violins ceased to play, so eager was everyone to contemplate the singular beauties of the unknown new-comer. Nothing was then heard but a confused noise of: "Ha! how handsome she is! Ha! how handsome she is!"

The King himself, old as he was, could not help watching her and telling the Queen softly that it was a long time since he had seen so beautiful and lovely a creature.

All the ladies were busied in considering her clothes and head-dress, that they might have some made next day after the same pattern, provided they could meet with such fine materials and as able hands to make them.

The King's son conducted her to the most honourable seat, and afterwards took her out to dance with him; she danced so very gracefully that they all more and more admired her. A fine collation was served up, whereof the young prince ate not a morsel, so intently was he busied in gazing on her.

She went and sat down by her sisters, showing them a thousand civilities, giving them part of the oranges and citrons which the Prince had presented her with, which very much surprised

them, for they did not know her. While Cinderella was thus amusing her sisters, she heard the clock strike eleven and three-quarters, whereupon she immediately made a curtsy to the company and hastened away as fast as she could.

Upon arriving home, she ran to seek out her godmother, and, after having thanked her, she said she could not but heartily wish she might go next day to the ball, because the King's son had invited her.

As she was eagerly telling her godmother whatever had passed at the ball, her two sisters knocked at the door, which Cinderella ran and opened.

"How long you have stayed!" cried she, gaping, rubbing her eyes and stretching herself as if she had been just waked out of her sleep; she had not, of course, had any inclination to sleep since they went from home.

"If you had been at the ball," said one of her sisters, "you would not have been tired with it. There came thither the finest princess, the most beautiful ever was seen with mortal eyes; she showed us a thousand civilities, and gave us oranges and citrons."

Cinderella seemed very indifferent in the matter; indeed, she asked them the name of that princess; but they told her they did not know it, and that the King's son was very uneasy on her account and would give all the world to know who she was. At this Cinderella, smiling, replied:

"She must, then, be very beautiful indeed; how happy you have been! Could not I see her? Ah! dear Miss Charlotte, do lend me your yellow suit of clothes which you wear every day."

"Ay, to be sure!" cried Miss Charlotte; "lend my clothes to such a dirty Cinderwench as you! I should be a fool."

Cinderella, indeed, expected well such answer, and was very glad of the refusal; for she would have been sadly put to it if her sister had lent her what she asked for jestingly.

The next day the two sisters were at the ball, and so was Cinderella, but dressed more magnificently than before. The King's son was always by her, and never ceased his compliments and kind speeches to her; to whom all this was so far from being tiresome that she quite forgot what her godmother had recommended to her; so that she, at last, counted the clock striking twelve when she took it to be no more than eleven; she then rose up and fled, as nimble as a deer. The Prince followed, but could not overtake her. She left behind one of her glass slippers, which the Prince took up most carefully. She got home, but quite out of breath, and in her nasty old clothes, having nothing left her of all her finery but one of the little slippers, fellow to that she dropped.

The guards at the palace gate were asked if they had not seen a princess go out. They said they had seen nobody go out but a young girl, very meanly dressed, who had more the air of a poor country wench than a gentlewoman.

When the two sisters returned from the ball Cinderella asked them if they had been well diverted, and if the fine lady had been there. They told her that she had, but that she hurried away immediately when it struck twelve, and with so much haste that she dropped one of her little glass slippers, the prettiest in the world, which the King's son had taken up; that he had done nothing but look at her all the time at the ball, and that most certainly he was very much in love with the beautiful person who owned the glass slipper.

What they said was very true; for a few days after, the King's son caused it to be proclaimed, by sound of trumpet, that he would marry her whose foot this slipper would just fit. They whom he employed began to try it upon the princesses, then the duchesses and all the court, but in vain; it was brought to the two sisters, who did all they possibly could to thrust their foot into the slipper, but they could not effect it.

Cinderella, who saw all this, and knew her slipper, said to them, laughing: "Let me see if it will not fit me."

Her sisters burst out a-laughing, and began to banter her. The gentleman who was sent to try the slipper looked earnestly at Cinderella, and, finding her very handsome, said it was but just that she should try, and that he had orders to let everyone make trial.

He obliged Cinderella to sit down, and, putting the slipper to her foot, he found it went on very easily, and fitted her as if it had been made of wax. The astonishment of her two sisters was excessively great, but still abundantly greater when Cinderella pulled out of her pocket the

other slipper and put it on her foot. Thereupon, in came her godmother, who, having touched with her wand Cinderella's clothes, made them richer and more magnificent than any of those she had before.

And now her two sisters found her to be that fine, beautiful lady whom they had seen at the ball. They threw themselves at her feet to beg pardon for all the ill-treatment they had made her undergo. Cinderella took them up, and, as she embraced them, cried that she forgave them with all her heart, and desired them always to love her.

She was conducted to the young Prince, dressed as she was; he thought her more charming than ever and, a few days after, married her. Cinderella, who was no less good than beautiful, gave her two sisters lodgings in the palace, and that very same day matched them with two great lords of the court.

THE MASTER CAT or PUSS IN BOOTS

Of all the wise and resourceful fairy animals of the folk tales, Puss in Boots is the cleverest. It will be interesting to compare Gustave Doré's romantic illustration of Puss with the one shown here and with the interpretations of two distinguished modern illustrators, Marcia Brown and Hans Fischer, each of whom has published the story in picture-book form. There is good reason to believe that Perrault invented the boots for Puss, a brilliant stroke if so!

There was a miller who left no more estate to the three sons he had than his mill, his ass, and his cat. The partition was soon made. Neither the scrivener nor attorney was sent for. They would soon have eaten up all the poor patrimony. The eldest had the mill, the second the ass, and the youngest nothing but the cat.

The poor young fellow was quite comfortless at having so poor a lot. "My brothers," said he, "may get their living handsomely enough by joining their stocks together; but, for my part,

"The Master Cat or Puss in Boots." From *The Blue Fairy Book,* edited by Andrew Lang. Longmans, Green, and Co., London, 1889

when I have eaten up my cat, and made me a muff of his skin, I must die of hunger."

The cat, who heard all this, but made as if he did not, said to him with a grave and serious air: "Do not thus afflict yourself, my good master; you have nothing else to do but to give me a bag, and get a pair of boots made for me, that I may scamper through the dirt and the brambles, and you shall see that you have not so bad a portion of me as you imagine."

The cat's master did not build very much upon what he said; he had, however, often seen him play a great many cunning tricks to catch rats and mice; as when he used to hang by the heels, or hide himself in the meal, and make as if he were dead; so that he did not altogether despair of his affording him some help in his miserable condition. When the cat had what he asked for, he booted himself very gallantly, and, putting his bag about his neck, he held the strings of it in his two forepaws, and went into a warren where was great abundance of rabbits. He put bran and sow-thistle into his bag, and, stretching out at length, as if he had been dead, he waited for some young rabbits, not yet acquainted with the deceits of the world, to come and rummage his bag for what he had put into it.

Scarce had he lain down but he had what he wanted: a rash and foolish young rabbit jumped into his bag, and Monsieur Puss, immediately drawing close the strings, took and killed him without pity. Proud of his prey, he went with it to the palace, and asked to speak with his majesty. He was shown upstairs into the king's apartment, and, making a low reverence, said to him:

"I have brought you, sir, a rabbit of the warren, which my noble Lord, the Master of Carabas"—for that was the title which Puss was pleased to give his master—"has commanded me to present to Your Majesty from him."

"Tell thy master," said the king, "that I thank him, and that he does me a great deal of pleasure."

Another time he went and hid himself among some standing corn, holding his bag open; and, when a brace of partridges ran into it, he drew the strings, and so caught them both. He went and made a present of these to the king, as he had done before with the rabbit which he took

in the warren. The king, in like manner, received the partridges with great pleasure, and ordered some money to be given to Puss.

The cat continued for two or three months thus to carry his majesty, from time to time, game of his master's taking. One day in particular, when he knew for certain that he was to take the air along the river-side with his daughter, the most beautiful princess in the world, he said to his master:

"If you will follow my advice your fortune is made. You have nothing else to do but go and wash yourself in the river, in that part I shall show you, and leave the rest to me."

The Marquis of Carabas did what the cat advised him to, without knowing why or wherefore. While he was washing, the king passed by, and the cat began to cry out: "Help! help! My Lord Marquis of Carabas is going to be drowned."

At this noise the king put his head out of the coach-window, and, finding it was the cat who had so often brought him such good game, he commanded his guards to run immediately to the assistance of his lordship the Marquis of Carabas. While they were drawing the poor marquis out of the river, the cat came up to the coach and told the king that, while his master was washing, there came by some rogues who went off with his clothes, though he had cried out: "Thieves! thieves!" several times, as loud as he could.

This cunning cat had hidden them under a great stone. The king immediately commanded the officers of his wardrobe to run and fetch one of his best suits for the Lord Marquis of Carabas.

The fine clothes the king had given him extremely set off his good mien (for he was well made and very handsome in his person), and the king's daughter took a secret inclination to him, and the Marquis of Carabas had no sooner cast two or three respectful and somewhat tender glances but she fell in love with him to distraction. The king would needs have him come into the coach and take part of the airing.

The cat, quite over-joyed to see his project begin to succeed, marched on before and, meeting with some countrymen who were mowing a meadow, he said to them: "Good people, you who are mowing, if you do not tell the king that the meadow you mow belongs to my Lord Marquis of Carabas, you shall be chopped as small as herbs for the pot."

The king did not fail asking of the mowers to whom the meadow they were mowing belonged.

"To my Lord Marquis of Carabas," answered they altogether, for the cat's threats had made them terribly afraid.

"You see, sir," said the marquis, "this is a meadow which never fails to yield a plentiful harvest every year."

The Master Cat, who went still on before, met with some reapers and said to them:

"Good people, you who are reaping, if you do not tell the king that all this corn belongs to the Marquis of Carabas, you shall be chopped as small as herbs for the pot."

The king, who passed by a moment after, would needs know to whom all that corn, which he then saw, did belong.

"To my Lord Marquis of Carabas," replied the reapers, and the king was very well pleased with it, as well as the marquis, whom he congratulated thereupon. The Master Cat, who went always before, said the same words to all he met, and the king was astonished at the vast estates of my Lord Marquis of Carabas.

Monsieur Puss came at last to a stately castle, the master of which was an ogre, the richest had ever been known; for all the lands which the king had then gone over belonged to this castle.

The cat, who had taken care to inform himself who this ogre was and what he could do, asked to speak with him, saying he could not pass so near his castle without having the honour of paying his respects to him.

The ogre received him as civilly as an ogre could do, and made him sit down.

"I have been assured," said the cat, "that you have the gift of being able to change yourself into all sorts of creatures you have a mind to; you can, for example, transform yourself into a lion, or elephant, and the like."

"That is true," answered the ogre very briskly "and to convince you, you shall see me now become a lion."

Puss was so sadly terrified at the sight of a lion so near him that he immediately got into the gutter, not without abundance of trouble and danger, because of his boots, which were of no use at all to him in walking upon the roof tiles. Shortly after, when Puss saw that the ogre had resumed his natural form, he came down, and owned he had been very much frightened.

"I have been moreover informed," said the cat, "but I know not how to believe it, that you have also the power to take on you the shape of the smallest animals; for example, to change yourself into a rat or a mouse; but I must own to you I take this to be impossible."

"Impossible!" cried the ogre; "you shall see that presently."

And at the same time he changed himself into a mouse, and began to run about the floor. Puss no sooner perceived this but he fell upon him and ate him up.

Meanwhile the king, who saw, as he passed, this fine castle of the ogre's, had a mind to go into it. Puss, who heard the noise of his majesty's coach running over the draw-bridge, ran out, and said to the king: "Your Majesty is welcome to this castle of my Lord Marquis of Carabas."

"What! my Lord Marquis," cried the king, "and does this castle also belong to you? There can be nothing finer than this court and all the stately buildings which surround it; let us go into it, if you please."

The marquis gave his hand to the princess, and followed the king, who went first. They passed into a spacious hall, where they found a magnificent collation, which the ogre had prepared for his friends, who were that very day to visit him, but dared not to enter, knowing the king was there. His majesty was perfectly charmed with the good qualities of my Lord Marquis of Carabas, as was his daughter, who had fallen in love with him, and, seeing the vast estate he possessed, said to him: "It will be owing to yourself only, my Lord Marquis, if you are not my son-in-law."

The marquis, making several low bows, accepted the honour which his majesty conferred upon him, and forthwith, that very same day, married the princess.

Puss became a great lord, and never ran after mice any more but only for his diversion.

BEAUTY AND THE BEAST

This story, very similar in theme to the Norse "East o' the Sun and West o' the Moon" and the Greek "Cupid and Psyche," has a unique charm of its own. Perhaps part of its appeal lies in Beauty's compassion for her poor Beast and her ability to see beyond his ugly exterior to his goodness. Andrew Lang derived his telling from that of Mme. Villeneuve (printed sometime between 1785 and 1789), a widely read adaptation of Mme. de Beaumont's earlier telling.

Once upon a time, in a very far-off country, there lived a merchant who had been so fortunate in all his undertakings that he was enormously rich. As he had, however, six sons and six daughters, he found that his money was not too much to let them all have everything they fancied, as they were accustomed to do.

But one day a most unexpected misfortune befell them. Their house caught fire and was speedily burnt to the ground, with all the splendid furniture, the books, pictures, gold, silver, and precious goods it contained; and this was only the beginning of their troubles. Their father, who had until this moment prospered in all ways, suddenly lost every ship he had upon the sea, either by dint of pirates, shipwreck, or fire. Then he heard that his clerks in distant countries, whom he trusted entirely, had proved unfaithful; and at last from great wealth he fell into the direst poverty.

"Beauty and the Beast." From *The Blue Fairy Book*, edited by Andrew Lang. Longmans, Green, and Co., London, 1889.

All that he had left was a little house in a desolate place at least a hundred leagues from the town in which he had lived, and to this he was forced to retreat with his children, who were in despair at the idea of leading such a different life. Indeed, the daughters at first hoped that their friends, who had been so numerous while they were rich, would insist on their staying in their houses now they no longer possessed one. But they soon found that they were left alone. Their former friends even attributed their misfortunes to their own extravagance and showed no intention of offering any help. So nothing was left for them but to take their departure to the cottage, which stood in the midst of a dark forest and seemed to be the most dismal place upon the face of the earth. As they were too poor to have any servants, the girls had to work hard and the sons, for their part, cultivated the fields to earn their living. Roughly clothed and living in the simplest way, the girls regretted unceasingly the luxuries and amusements of their former life; only the youngest tried to be brave and cheerful. She had been as sad as anyone when misfortune first overtook her father, but, soon recovering her natural gaiety, she set to work to make the best of things, to amuse her father and brothers as well as she could, and to try to persuade her sisters to join her in dancing and singing. But they would do nothing of the sort, and because she was not as doleful as themselves, they declared that this miserable life was all she was fit for. But she was really far prettier and cleverer than they were; indeed, she was so lovely that she was always called Beauty. After two years, when they were all beginning to get used to their new life, something happened to disturb their tranquillity. Their father received the news that one of his ships, which he had believed to be lost, had come safely into port with a rich cargo. All the sons and daughters at once thought that their poverty was at an end and wanted to set out directly for the town; but their father, who was more prudent, begged them to wait a little, and, though it was harvest-time and he could ill be spared, determined to go himself first, to make inquiries. Only the youngest daughter had any doubt but that they would soon again be as rich as they were before, or at least rich enough to live comfortably in some town where they would find amusement and gay companions once more. So they all loaded their father with commissions for jewels and dresses which it would have taken a fortune to buy; only Beauty, feeling sure that it was of no use, did not ask for anything. Her father, noticing her silence, said: "And what shall I bring for you, Beauty?"

"The only thing I wish for is to see you come home safely," she answered.

But this reply vexed her sisters, who fancied she was blaming them for having asked for such costly things. Her father, however, was pleased, but as he thought that at her age she certainly ought to like pretty presents, he told her to choose something.

"Well, dear Father," she said, "as you insist upon it, I beg that you will bring me a rose. I have not seen one since we came here, and I love them so much."

So the merchant set out and reached the town as quickly as possible, but only to find that his former companions, believing him to be dead, had divided between them the goods which the ship had brought; and after six months of trouble and expense he found himself as poor as when he started, having been able to recover only just enough to pay the cost of his journey. To make matters worse, he was obliged to leave the town in the most terrible weather, so that by the time he was within a few leagues of his home he was almost exhausted with cold and fatigue. Though he knew it would take some hours to get through the forest, he was so anxious to be at his journey's end that he resolved to go on; but night overtook him, and the deep snow and bitter frost made it impossible for his horse to carry him any further. Not a house was to be seen; the only shelter he could get was the hollow trunk of a great tree, and there he crouched all the night, which seemed to him the longest he had ever known. In spite of his weariness the howling of the wolves kept him awake, and even when at last the day broke he was not much better off, for the falling snow had covered up every path, and he did not know which way to turn.

At length he made out some sort of track, and though at the beginning it was so rough and slippery that he fell down more than once, it presently became easier, and led him into an avenue of trees which ended in a splendid castle. It seemed to the merchant very strange that no snow had fallen in the avenue, which was entirely composed of orange trees, covered with flowers and fruit. When he reached the first court of the castle he saw before him a flight of agate steps. He went up them and passed through several splendidly furnished rooms. The pleasant warmth of the air revived him, and he felt very hungry; but there seemed to be nobody in all this vast and splendid palace whom he could ask to give him something to eat. Deep silence reigned everywhere, and at last, tired of roaming through empty rooms and galleries, he stopped in a room smaller than the rest, where a clear fire was burning and a couch was drawn up cosily close to it. Thinking that this must be prepared for someone who was expected, he sat down to wait till he should come, and very soon fell into a sweet sleep.

When his extreme hunger wakened him after several hours, he was still alone; but a little table, upon which was a good dinner, had been drawn up close to him, and, as he had eaten nothing for twenty-four hours, he lost no time in beginning his meal, hoping that he might soon have an opportunity of thanking his considerate entertainer, whoever it might be. But no one appeared, and even after another long sleep, from which he awoke completely refreshed, there was no sign of anybody, though a fresh meal of dainty cakes and fruit was prepared upon the little table at his elbow. Since he was naturally timid, the silence began to terrify him, and he resolved to search once more through all the rooms; but it was of no use. Not even a servant was to been seen; there was no sign of life in the palace! He began to wonder what he should do and to amuse himself by pretending that all the treasures he saw were his own and considering how he would divide them among his children. Then he went down into the garden, and though it was winter everywhere else, here the sun shone, the birds sang, the flowers bloomed, and the air was soft and sweet. The merchant, in ecstasies with all he saw and heard, said to himself:

"All this must be meant for me. I will go this minute and bring my children to share all these delights."

In spite of being so cold and weary when he reached the castle, he had taken his horse to the stable and fed it. Now he thought he would saddle it for his homeward journey, and he turned down the path which led to the stable. This path had a hedge of roses on each side of it, and the merchant thought he had never seen or smelt such exquisite flowers. They reminded him of his promise to Beauty, and he stopped and had just gathered one to take to her when he was startled by a strange noise behind him. Turning round, he saw a frightful Beast, which seemed to be very angry and said, in a terrible voice:

"Who told you that you might gather my roses? Was it not enough that I allowed you to be in my palace and was kind to you? This is the way you show your gratitude, by stealing my flowers! But your insolence shall not go unpunished." The merchant, terrified by these furious words, dropped the fatal rose, and, throwing himself on his knees, cried: "Pardon me, noble sir. I am truly grateful to you for your hospitality, which was so magnificent that I could not imagine that you would be offended by my taking such a little thing as a rose." But the Beast's anger was not lessened by this speech.

"You are very ready with excuses and flattery," he cried; "but that will not save you from the death you deserve."

"Alas!" thought the merchant, "if my daughter Beauty could only know what danger her rose has brought me into!"

And in despair he began to tell the Beast all his misfortunes, and the reason of his journey, not forgetting to mention Beauty's request.

"A king's ransom would hardly have procured all that my other daughters asked," he said; "but I thought that I might at least take Beauty her rose. I beg you to forgive me, for you see I meant no harm."

The Beast considered for a moment, and then he said, in a less furious tone:

"I will forgive you on one condition—that is, that you will give me one of your daughters."

"Ah!" cried the merchant, "if I were cruel enough to buy my own life at the expense of one of my children's, what excuse could I invent to bring her here?"

"No excuse would be necessary," answered the Beast. "If she comes at all she must come willingly. On no other condition will I have her. See if any one of them is courageous enough and

loves you well enough to come and save your life. You seem to be an honest man, so I will trust you to go home. I give you a month to see if any of your daughters will come back with you and stay here, to let you go free. If none of them is willing, you must come alone, after bidding them good-bye for ever, for then you will belong to me. And do not imagine that you can hide from me, for if you fail to keep your word I will come and fetch you!" added the Beast grimly.

The merchant accepted this proposal, though he did not really think any of his daughters would be persuaded to come. He promised to return at the time appointed, and then, anxious to escape from the presence of the Beast, he asked permission to set off at once. But the Beast answered that he could not go until the next day.

"Then you will find a horse ready for you," he said. "Now go and eat your supper, and await my orders."

The poor merchant, more dead than alive, went back to his room, where the most delicious supper was already served on the little table which was drawn up before a blazing fire. But he was too terrified to eat, and only tasted a few of the dishes, for fear the Beast should be angry if he did not obey his orders. When he had finished he heard a great noise in the next room, which he knew meant that the Beast was coming. As he could do nothing to escape his visit, the only thing that remained was to seem as little afraid as possible; so when the Beast appeared and asked roughly if he had supped well, the merchant answered humbly that he had, thanks to his host's kindness. Then the Beast warned him to remember their agreement and to prepare his daughter exactly for what she had to expect.

"Do not get up to-morrow," he added, "until you see the sun and hear a golden bell ring. Then you will find your breakfast waiting for you here, and the horse you are to ride will be ready in the courtyard. He will also bring you back again when you come with your daughter a month hence. Farewell. Take a rose to Beauty, and remember your promise!"

The merchant was only too glad when the Beast went away, and though he could not sleep for sadness, he lay down until the sun rose. Then, after a hasty breakfast, he went to gather Beauty's rose, and mounted his horse, which carried him off so swiftly that in an instant he had lost sight of the palace, and he was still wrapped in gloomy thoughts when it stopped before the door of the cottage.

His sons and daughters, who had been very uneasy at his long absence, rushed to meet him, eager to know the result of his journey, which, seeing him mounted upon a splendid horse and wrapped in a rich mantle, they supposed to be favourable. But he hid the truth from them at first, only saying sadly to Beauty as he gave her the rose:

"Here is what you asked me to bring you; you little know what it has cost."

But this excited their curiosity so greatly that presently he told them his adventures from beginning to end, and then they were all very unhappy. The girls lamented loudly over their lost hopes, and the sons declared that their father should not return to this terrible castle, and began to make plans for killing the Beast if it should come to fetch him. But he reminded them that he had promised to go back. Then the girls were very angry with Beauty, and said it was all her fault, and that if she had asked for something sensible this would never have happened, and complained bitterly that they should have to suffer for her folly.

Poor Beauty, much distressed, said to them:

"I have indeed caused this misfortune, but I assure you I did it innocently. Who could have guessed that to ask for a rose in the middle of summer would cause so much misery? But as I did the mischief it is only just that I should suffer for it. I will therefore go back with my father to keep his promise."

At first nobody would hear of this arrangement, and her father and brothers, who loved her dearly, declared that nothing should make them let her go; but Beauty was firm. As the time drew near she divided all her little possessions among her sisters, and said good-bye to everything she loved, and when the fatal day came she encouraged and cheered her father as they mounted together the horse which had brought him back. It seemed to fly rather than gallop, but so smoothly that Beauty was not frightened; indeed, she would have enjoyed the journey if she had not feared what might happen to her at the end of it. Her father still tried to persuade her to go back, but in vain. While they were talking the night fell, and then, to their great surprise, wonderful coloured lights began to shine in all directions, and splendid fireworks blazed out before them; all the forest was illuminated by them, and even felt pleasantly warm,

though it had been bitterly cold before. This lasted until they reached the avenue of orange trees, where were statues holding flaming torches, and when they got nearer to the palace they saw that it was illuminated from the roof to the ground, and music sounded softly from the courtyard. "The Beast must be very hungry," said Beauty, trying to laugh, "if he makes all this rejoicing over the arrival of his prey."

But, in spite of her anxiety, she could not help admiring all the wonderful things she saw.

The horse stopped at the foot of the flight of steps leading to the terrace, and when they had dismounted her father led her to the little room he had been in before, where they found a splendid fire burning, and the table daintily spread with a delicious supper.

The merchant knew that this was meant for them, and Beauty, who was rather less frightened now that she had passed through so many rooms and seen nothing of the Beast, was quite willing to begin, for her long ride had made her very hungry. But they had hardly finished their meal when the noise of the Beast's footsteps was heard approaching, and Beauty clung to her father in terror, which became all the greater when she saw how frightened he was. But when the Beast really appeared, though she trembled at the sight of him, she made a great effort to hide her horror, and saluted him respectfully.

This evidently pleased the Beast. After looking at her he said, in a tone that might have struck terror into the boldest heart, though he did not seem to be angry: "Good-evening, old man. Good-evening, Beauty."

The merchant was too terrified to reply, but Beauty answered sweetly: "Good-evening, Beast."

"Have you come willingly?" asked the Beast. "Will you be content to stay here when your father goes away?"

Beauty answered bravely that she was quite prepared to stay.

"I am pleased with you," said the Beast. "As you have come of your own accord, you may stay. As for you, old man," he added, turning to the merchant, "at sunrise to-morrow you will take your departure. When the bell rings get up quickly and eat your breakfast, and you will find the same horse waiting to take you home; but remember that you must never expect to see my palace again."

Then turning to Beauty, he said:

"Take your father into the next room, and help him to choose everything you think your brothers and sisters would like to have. You will find two travelling-trunks there; fill them as full as you can. It is only just that you should send them something very precious as a remembrance of yourself."

Then he went away, after saying, "Good-bye, Beauty; good-bye, old man;" and though Beauty was beginning to think with great dismay of her father's departure, she was afraid to disobey the Beast's orders; and they went into the next room, which had shelves and cupboards all round it. They were greatly surprised at the riches it contained. There were splendid dresses fit for a queen, with all the ornaments that were to be worn with them; and when Beauty opened the cupboards she was quite dazzled by the gorgeous jewels that lay in heaps upon every shelf. After choosing a vast quantity, which she divided between her sisters—for she had made a heap of the wonderful dresses for each of them—she opened the last chest, which was full of gold.

"I think, Father," she said, "that as the gold will be more useful to you, we had better take out the other things again and fill the trunks with it." So they did this; but the more they put in, the more room there seemed to be, and at last they put back all the jewels and dresses they had taken out, and Beauty even added as many more of the jewels as she could carry at once; and then the trunks were not too full, but they were so heavy that an elephant could have not have carried them!

"The Beast was mocking us," cried the merchant; "he must have pretended to give us all these things, knowing that I could not carry them away."

"Let us wait and see," answered Beauty. "I cannot believe that he meant to deceive us. All we can do is to fasten them up and leave them ready."

So they did this and returned to the little room, where, to their astonishment, they found breakfast ready. The merchant ate his with a good appetite, as the Beast's generosity made him believe that he might perhaps venture to come back soon and see Beauty. But she felt sure that her father was leaving her forever, so she was very sad when the bell rang sharply for the second time, and warned them that the time was come for them to part. They went down into the courtyard, where two horses were waiting, one loaded with the two trunks, the other for him to ride. They were pawing the ground in their impatience to start, and the merchant was forced to bid Beauty a hasty farewell; and as soon as he was mounted he went off at such a pace that she lost sight of him in an instant. Then Beauty began to cry, and wandered sadly back to her own room. But she soon found that she was very sleepy, and as she had nothing better to do she lay down and instantly fell asleep. And then she dreamed that she was walking by a brook bordered with trees and lamenting her sad fate, when a young prince, handsomer than anyone she had ever seen and with a voice that went straight to her heart, came and said to her, "Ah, Beauty! you are not so unfortunate as you suppose. Here you will be rewarded for all you have suffered elsewhere. Your every wish shall be gratified. Only try to find me out, no matter how I may be disguised, as I love you dearly, and in making me happy you will find your own happiness. Be as true-hearted as you are beautiful, and we shall have nothing left to wish for."

"What can I do, Prince, to make you happy?" said Beauty.

"Only be grateful," he answered, "and do not trust too much to your eyes. And, above all, do not desert me until you have saved me from my cruel misery."

After this she thought she found herself in a room with a stately and beautiful lady, who said to her:

"Dear Beauty, try not to regret all you have left behind you, for you are destined to a better fate. Only do not let yourself be deceived by appearances."

Beauty found her dreams so interesting that she was in no hurry to awake, but presently the clock roused her by calling her name softly twelve times, and then she got up and found her dressing-table set out with everything she could possibly want; and when her toilet was finished she found dinner was waiting in the room next to hers. But dinner does not take very long when you are all by yourself, and very soon she sat down cosily in the corner of a sofa, and began to think about the charming Prince she had seen in her dream.

"He said I could make him happy," said Beauty to herself.

"It seems, then, that this horrible Beast keeps him a prisoner. How can I set him free? I wonder why they both told me not to trust to appearances? I don't understand it. But, after all, it was only a dream, so why should I trouble myself about it? I had better go and find something to do to amuse myself."

So she got up and began to explore some of the many rooms of the palace.

The first she entered was lined with mirrors, and Beauty saw herself reflected on every side, and thought she had never seen such a charming room. Then a bracelet which was hanging from a chandelier caught her eye, and on taking it down she was greatly surprised to find that it held a portrait of her unknown admirer, just as she had seen him in her dream. With great delight she slipped the bracelet on her arm and went on into a gallery of pictures, where she soon found a portrait of the same handsome Prince, as large as life, and so well painted that as she studied it he seemed to smile kindly at her. Tearing herself away from the portrait at last, she passed through into a room which contained every musical instrument under the sun, and here she amused herself for a long while in trying some of them, and singing until she was tired. The next room was a library, and she saw everything she had ever wanted to read, as well as everything she had read, and it seemed to her that a whole lifetime would not be enough even to read the names of the books, there were so many. By this time it was growing dusk, and wax candles in diamond and ruby candlesticks were beginning to light themselves in every room.

Beauty found her supper served just at the time she preferred to have it, but she did not see anyone or hear a sound, and, though her father had warned her that she would be alone, she began to find it rather dull.

But presently she heard the Beast coming and wondered tremblingly if he meant to eat her up now.

However, as he did not seem at all ferocious,

and only said gruffly, "Good-evening, Beauty," she answered cheerfully and managed to conceal her terror. Then the Beast asked her how she had been amusing herself, and she told him all the rooms she had seen.

Then he asked if she thought she could be happy in his palace; and Beauty answered that everything was so beautiful that she would be very hard to please if she could not be happy. And after about an hour's talk Beauty began to think that the Beast was not nearly so terrible as she had supposed at first. Then he got up to leave her, and said in his gruff voice:

"Do you love me, Beauty? Will you marry me?"

"Oh! what shall I say?" cried Beauty, for she was afraid to make the Beast angry by refusing.

"Say yes or no without fear," he replied.

"Oh! no, Beast," said Beauty hastily.

"Since you will not, good-night, Beauty," he said.

And she answered, "Good-night, Beast," very glad to find that her refusal had not provoked him. And after he was gone she was very soon in bed and asleep, and dreaming of her unknown Prince. She thought he came and said to her:

"Ah, Beauty! why are you so unkind to me? I fear I am fated to be unhappy for many a long day still."

And then her dreams changed, but the charming Prince figured in them all; and when morning came her first thought was to look at the portrait and see if it was really like him, and she found that it certainly was.

This morning she decided to amuse herself in the garden, for the sun shone, and all the fountains were playing; but she was astonished to find that every place was familiar to her, and presently she came to the brook where the myrtle trees were growing where she had first met the Prince in her dream, and that made her think more than ever that he must be kept a prisoner by the Beast. When she was tired she went back to the palace, and found a new room full of materials for every kind of work—ribbons to make into bows, and silks to work into flowers. Then there was an aviary full of rare birds, which were so tame that they flew to Beauty as soon as they saw her, and perched upon her shoulders and her head.

"Pretty little creatures," she said, "how I wish that your cage was nearer to my room, that I might often hear you sing!"

So saying she opened a door, and found to her delight that it led into her own room, though she had thought it was quite the other side of the palace.

There were more birds in a room farther on, parrots and cockatoos that could talk, and they greeted Beauty by name; indeed, she found them so entertaining that she took one or two back to her room, and they talked to her while she was at supper; after which the Beast paid her his usual visit, and asked the same questions as before, and then with a gruff "good-night" he took his departure, and Beauty went to bed to dream of her mysterious Prince. The days passed swiftly in different amusements, and after a while Beauty found out another strange thing in the palace, which often pleased her when she was tired of being alone. There was one room which she had not noticed particularly; it was empty, except that under each of the windows stood a very comfortable chair; and the first time she had looked out of the window it had seemed to her that a black curtain prevented her from seeing anything outside. But the second time she went into the room, happening to be tired, she sat down in one of the chairs, when instantly the curtain was rolled aside, and a most amusing pantomine was acted before her; there were dances, and coloured lights, and music, and pretty dresses, and it was all so gay that Beauty was in ecstasies. After that she tried the other seven windows in turn, and there was some new and surprising entertainment to be seen from each of them, so that Beauty never could feel lonely any more. Every evening after supper the Beast came to see her, and always before saying good-night asked her in his terrible voice:

"Beauty, will you marry me?"

And it seemed to Beauty, now she understood him better, that when she said, "No, Beast," he went away quite sad. But her happy dreams of the handsome young Prince soon made her forget the poor Beast, and the only thing that at all disturbed her was to be constantly told to distrust appearances, to let her heart guide her, and not her eyes, and many other equally perplexing things, which, consider as she would, she could not understand.

So everything went on for a long time, until at last, happy as she was, Beauty began to long for the sight of her father and her brothers and sisters; and one night, seeing her look very sad, the Beast asked her what was the matter. Beauty had quite ceased to be afraid of him. Now she knew that he was really gentle in spite of his ferocious looks and his dreadful voice. So she answered that she was longing to see her home once more. Upon hearing this the Beast seemed sadly distressed, and cried miserably:

"Ah! Beauty, have you the heart to desert an unhappy Beast like this? What more do you want to make you happy? Is it because you hate me that you want to escape?"

"No, dear Beast," answered Beauty softly, "I do not hate you, and I should be very sorry never to see you any more, but I long to see my father again. Only let me go for two months, and I promise to come back to you and stay for the rest of my life."

The Beast, who had been sighing dolefully while she spoke, now replied:

"I cannot refuse you anything you ask, even though it should cost me my life. Take the four boxes you will find in the room next to your own, and fill them with everything you wish to take with you. But remember your promise and come back when the two months are over, or you may have cause to repent it, for if you do not come in good time you will find your faithful Beast dead. You will not need any chariot to bring you back. Only say good-bye to all your brothers and sisters the night before you come away, and when you have gone to bed turn this ring round upon your finger and say firmly: 'I wish to go back to my palace and see my Beast again.' Good-night, Beauty. Fear nothing, sleep peacefully, and before long you shall see your father once more."

As soon as Beauty was alone she hastened to fill the boxes with all the rare and precious things she saw about her, and only when she was tired of heaping things into them did they seem to be full.

Then she went to bed, but could hardly sleep for joy. And when at last she did begin to dream of her beloved Prince she was grieved to see him stretched upon a grassy bank sad and weary, and hardly like himself.

"What is the matter?" she cried.

But he looked at her reproachfully, and said: "How can you ask me, cruel one? Are you not leaving me to my death perhaps?"

"Ah! don't be so sorrowful," cried Beauty; "I am only going to assure my father that I am safe and happy. I have promised the Beast faithfully that I will come back, and he would die of grief if I did not keep my word!"

"What would that matter to you?" said the Prince. "Surely you would not care?"

"Indeed I should be ungrateful if I did not care for such a kind Beast," cried Beauty indignantly. "I would die to save him from pain. I assure you it is not his fault that he is so ugly."

Just then a strange sound woke her—someone was speaking not very far away; and opening her eyes she found herself in a room she had never seen before, which was certainly not nearly so splendid as those she was used to in the Beast's palace. Where could she be? She got up and dressed hastily, and then saw that the boxes she had packed the night before were all in the room. While she was wondering by what magic the Beast had transported them and herself to this strange place she suddenly heard her father's voice, and rushed out and greeted him joyfully. Her brothers and sisters were all astonished at her appearance, as they had never expected to see her again, and there was no end to the questions they asked her. She had also much to hear about what had happened to them while she was away, and of her father's journey home. But when they heard that she had only come to be with them for a short time, and then must go back to the Beast's palace forever, they lamented loudly. Then Beauty asked her father what he thought could be the meaning of her strange dreams, and why the Prince constantly begged her not to trust to appearances. After much consideration he answered: "You tell me yourself that the Beast, frightful as he is, loves you dearly, and deserves your love and gratitude for his gentleness and kindness; I think the Prince must mean you to understand that you ought to reward him by doing as he wishes you to, in spite of his ugliness."

Beauty could not help seeing that this seemed

very probable; still, when she thought of her dear Prince who was so handsome, she did not feel at all inclined to marry the Beast. At any rate, for two months she need not decide, but could enjoy herself with her sisters. But though they were rich now, and lived in a town again, and had plenty of acquaintances, Beauty found that nothing amused her very much; and she often thought of the palace, where she was so happy, especially as at home she never once dreamed of her dear Prince, and she felt quite sad without him.

Then her sisters seemed to have got quite used to being without her, and even found her rather in the way, so she would not have been sorry when the two months were over but for her father and brothers, who begged her to stay and seemed so grieved at the thought of her departure that she had not the courage to say good-bye to them. Every day when she got up she meant to say it at night, and when night came she put it off again, until at last she had a dismal dream which helped her to make up her mind. She thought she was wandering in a lonely path in the palace gardens, when she heard groans which seemed to come from some bushes hiding the entrance of a cave, and running quickly to see what could be the matter, she found the Beast stretched out upon his side, apparently dying. He reproached her faintly with being the cause of his distress, and at the same moment a stately lady appeared, and said very gravely:

"Ah! Beauty, you are only just in time to save his life. See what happens when people do not keep their promises! If you had delayed one day more, you would have found him dead."

Beauty was so terrified by this dream that the next morning she announced her intention of going back at once, and that very night she said good-bye to her father and all her brothers and sisters, and as soon as she was in bed she turned her ring round upon her finger, and said firmly:

"I wish to go back to my palace and see my Beast again," as she had been told to do.

Then she fell asleep instantly, and only woke up to hear the clock saying, "Beauty, Beauty," twelve times in its musical voice, which told her at once that she was really in the palace once more. Everything was just as before, and her birds were so glad to see her! But Beauty thought she had never known such a long day, for she was so anxious to see the Beast again that she felt as if supper-time would never come.

But when it did come and no Beast appeared she was really frightened; so, after listening and waiting for a long time, she ran down into the garden to search for him. Up and down the paths and avenues ran poor Beauty, calling him in vain, for no one answered, and not a trace of him could she find; until at last, quite tired, she stopped for a minute's rest, and saw that she was standing opposite the shady path she had seen in her dream. She rushed down it, and, sure enough, there was the cave, and in it lay the Beast—asleep, as Beauty thought. Quite glad to have found him, she ran up and stroked his head, but to her horror he did not move or open his eyes.

"Oh! he is dead; and it is all my fault," said Beauty, crying bitterly.

But then, looking at him again, she fancied he still breathed, and, hastily fetching some water from the nearest fountain, she sprinkled it over his face, and to her great delight he began to revive.

"Oh! Beast, how you frightened me!" she cried. "I never knew how much I loved you until just now, when I feared I was too late to save your life."

"Can you really love such an ugly creature as I am?" said the Beast faintly. "Ah! Beauty, you only came just in time. I was dying because I thought you had forgotten your promise. But go back now and rest, I shall see you again by-and-by."

Beauty, who had half expected that he would be angry with her, was reassured by his gentle voice, and went back to the palace, where supper was awaiting her; and afterwards the Beast came in as usual, and talked about the time she had spent with her father, asking if she had enjoyed herself and if they had all been very glad to see her.

Beauty answered politely, and quite enjoyed telling him all that had happened to her. And when at last the time came for him to go, and he asked, as he had so often asked before:

"Beauty, will you marry me?" she answered softly:

"Yes, dear Beast."

As she spoke a blaze of light sprang up before the windows of the palace; fireworks crackled and guns banged, and across the avenue of orange trees, in letters all made of fire-flies, was written: "Long live the Prince and his Bride."

Turning to ask the Beast what it could all mean, Beauty found that he had disappeared, and in his place stood her long-loved Prince! At the same moment the wheels of a chariot were heard upon the terrace, and two ladies entered the room. One of them Beauty recognized as the stately lady she had seen in her dreams; the other was also so grand and queenly that Beauty hardly knew which to greet first.

But the one she already knew said to her companion:

"Well, Queen, this is Beauty, who has had the courage to rescue your son from the terrible enchantment. They love one another, and only your consent to their marriage is wanting to make them perfectly happy."

"I consent with all my heart," cried the Queen. "How can I ever thank you enough, charming girl, for having restored my dear son to his natural form?"

And then she tenderly embraced Beauty and the Prince, who had meanwhile been greeting the Fairy and receiving her congratulations.

"Now," said the Fairy to Beauty, "I suppose you would like me to send for all your brothers and sisters to dance at your wedding?"

And so she did, and the marriage was celebrated the very next day with the utmost splendour, and Beauty and the Prince lived happily ever after.

THE WHITE CAT

The White Cat and Other Old French Fairy Tales is a handsome book illustrated by Elizabeth MacKinstry and serves as the source of this version. It was reissued in a facsimile edition in 1967.

Once upon a time there was a King who had three sons. The day came when they were grown so big and strong that he began to fear they would be planning to rule in his place. This would cause trouble among themselves and his subjects. Now the King was not so young as he

once had been but nevertheless he had no notion of giving up his kingdom then and there. So after much thought he hit upon a scheme which should keep them too busily occupied to interfere in the affairs of state. Accordingly he called the three into his private apartments where he spoke to them with great kindliness and concern of his plans for the future.

"I am planning to retire from the affairs of state. But I do not wish my subjects to suffer from this change. Therefore, while I am still alive, I shall transfer my crown to one of you. I shall not follow the usual custom of leaving the crown to my eldest son, but whichever one of you shall bring me the handsomest and most intelligent little dog shall become my heir."

The Princes were greatly surprised by this strange request, but they could not very well refuse to humor their father's whim; and since there was luck in it for the two younger sons and the elder of the three was a timid, rather spiritless fellow, they agreed readily enough. The King then bade them farewell after first distributing jewels and money among them and adding that a year from that day at the same place and hour they should return to him with their little dogs.

Within sight of the city gates stood a castle where the three often spent many days in company with their young companions. Here they agreed to part and to meet again in a year before proceeding with their trophies to the King; and so having pledged their good faith, and changing their names that they might not be known, each set off upon a different road.

It would take far too long to recount the adventures of all three Princes so I shall tell only of those that befell the youngest, for a more gay and well-mannered Prince never lived, nor one so handsome and accomplished.

Scarcely a day passed that he did not buy a dog or two, greyhounds, mastiffs, bloodhounds, pointers, spaniels, water dogs, lapdogs; but the instant he found a handsomer one he let the first go and kept the new purchase, since it would have been impossible for him to carry them all

"The White Cat." Reprinted with permission of The Macmillan Company from *The White Cat and Other Old French Fairy Tales* by Mme. La Comtesse D'Aulnoy, arranged by Rachel Field. Copyright 1928 by The Macmillan Company. Used by permission of Arthur Pederson

on his journeyings. He went without fixed plan or purpose and so he continued for many days until at last darkness and a terrible storm overtook him at nightfall in a lonely forest. Thunder and lightning rumbled and flashed; rain fell in torrents; the trees seemed to close more densely about him until at last he could no longer find his way. When he had wandered thus for some time he suddenly saw a glint of light between the tree trunks. Feeling certain that this must mean a shelter of some sort he pressed on till he found himself approaching the most magnificent castle he had ever seen. The gate was of gold and covered with jewels of such brilliance that it was their light which had guided him to the spot. In spite of the rain and storm he caught glimpses of walls of finest porcelain decorated with pictures of the most famous fairies from the beginning of the world up to that very day: Cinderella, Graciosa, Sleeping Beauty, and a hundred others. As he admired all this magnificence he noticed a rabbit's foot fastened to the golden gates by a chain of diamonds. Marveling greatly at such a lavish display of precious gems, the young Prince pulled at the rabbit's foot and straightway an unseen bell of wonderful sweetness rang; the gate was opened by hundreds of tiny hands and others pushed him forward while he hesitated amazed upon the threshold. He moved on wonderingly, his hand on the hilt of his sword until he was reassured by two voices singing a welcome. Again he felt himself being pushed, this time toward a gate of coral opening upon an apartment of mother-of-pearl from which he passed into others still more richly decorated and alight with wax candles and great chandeliers sparkling with a thousand rainbows.

He had passed through perhaps sixty such rooms when the hands that guided him made a sign for him to stop. He saw a large armchair moving by itself toward a fireplace at the same moment that the fire began to blaze and the hands, which he now observed to be very small and white, carefully drew off his wet clothes and handed him others so fine and richly embroidered they seemed fit for a wedding day. The hands continued to dress him, until at last, powdered and attired more handsomely than he had ever been in his life before, the Prince was led into a banquet hall. Here the four walls were decorated solely with paintings representing famous cats, Puss-in-Boots and others whom he was quick to recognize. Even more astonishing than this was the table set for two with its gold service and crystal cups.

There was an orchestra composed entirely of cats. One held a music book with the strangest notes imaginable; another beat time with a little baton; and all the rest strummed tiny guitars.

While the Prince stared in amazement, each cat suddenly began to mew in a different key and to claw at the guitar strings. It was the strangest music ever heard! The Prince would have thought himself in bedlam had not the palace itself been so marvelously beautiful. So he stopped his ears and laughed heartily at the various poses and grimaces of these strange musicians. He was meditating upon the extraordinary sights he had already seen in the castle, when he beheld a little figure entering the hall. It was scarcely more than two feet in height and wrapped in a long gold crêpe veil. Before it walked two cats dressed in deep mourning and wearing cloaks and swords, while still others followed, some carrying rat-traps full of rats and mice in cages.

By this time the Prince was too astonished to think. But presently the tiny pink figure approached him and lifted its veil. He now beheld the most beautiful little white cat that ever was or ever will be. She had such a very youthful and melancholy air and a mewing so soft and sweet that it went straight to the young Prince's heart.

"Son of a King," she said to him, "thou art welcome; my mewing Majesty beholds thee with pleasure."

"Madam," responded the Prince, bowing as low as possible before her, "it is very gracious of you to receive me with so much attention, but you do not appear to me to be an ordinary little cat. The gift of speech which you have and this superb castle you inhabit are certainly evidence to the contrary."

"Son of a King," rejoined the White Cat, "I pray that you will cease to pay me compliments. I am plain in my speech and manners, but I have a kind heart. Come," she added, to her attendants, "let them serve supper and bid the concert cease, for the Prince does not understand what they are singing."

"And are they singing words, madam?" he asked incredulously.

"Certainly," she answered, "we have very gifted poets here, as you will see if you remain long enough."

Supper was then served to them by the same hands that had guided him there, and a very strange meal it was. There were two dishes of each course—one soup, for instance, being of savory pigeons while the other had been made of nicely fattened mice. The sight of this rather took away the Prince's appetite until his hostess, who seemed to guess what was passing in his mind, assured him that his own dishes had been specially prepared and contained no rats and mice of any kind. Her charming manners convinced the Prince that the little Cat had no wish to deceive him, so he began to eat and drink with great enjoyment. During their meal he happened to observe that on one paw she wore a tiny miniature set in a bracelet. This surprised him so that he begged her to let him examine it more closely. He had supposed it would be the picture of Master Puss, but what was his astonishment to find it the portrait of a handsome young man who bore a strange resemblance to himself! As he stared at it, the White Cat was heard to sigh so deeply and with such profound sadness that the Prince became even more curious; but he dared not question one so affected. Instead he entertained her with tales of court life, with which, to his surprise, he found her well acquainted.

After supper the White Cat led her guest into another Hall, where upon a little stage twelve cats and twelve monkeys danced in the most fantastic costumes. So the evening ended in great merriment; and after the Cat had bade the Prince a gracious good night the same strange hands conducted him to his own apartment, where in spite of the softness of his bed he spent half the night trying to solve the mystery of the castle and his extraordinary little hostess.

But when morning came he was no nearer to an answer to his questionings, so he allowed the pair of hands to help him dress and lead him into the palace courtyard. Here a vast company of cats in hunting costume were gathering to the sound of the horn. A fête day indeed! The White Cat was going to hunt and wished the Prince to accompany her. Now the mysterious hands presented him with a wooden horse. He made some objection to mounting it, but it proved to be an excellent charger, and a tireless galloper. The White Cat rode beside him on a monkey, the handsomest and proudest that ever was seen. She had thrown off her long veil and wore a military cap which made her look so bold that she frightened all the mice in the neighborhood. Never was there a more successful hunt. The cats outran all the rabbits and hares and a thousand skillful feats were performed to the gratification of the entire company. Tiring of the hunt at last the White Cat took up a horn no bigger than the Prince's little finger and blew upon it with so loud and clear a tone it could be heard ten leagues away. Scarcely had she sounded two or three flourishes when all the cats in the countryside seemed to appear. By land and sea and through the air they all came flocking to her call, dressed in every conceivable costume. So, followed by this extraordinary train, the Prince rode back with his hostess to the castle.

That night the White Cat put on her gold veil again and they dined together as before. Being very hungry the Prince ate and drank heartily, and this time the food had a strange effect upon him. All recollection of his father and the little dog he was to find for him slipped from his mind. He no longer thought of anything but of gossiping with the White Cat and enjoying her kind and gracious companionship. So the days passed in pleasant sport and amusement and the night in feasting and conversation. There was scarcely one in which he did not discover some new charm of the little White Cat. Now he had forgotten even the land of his birth. The hands continued to wait upon him and supply every want till he began to regret that he could not become a cat himself to live forever in such pleasant company.

"Alas," he confessed to the White Cat at last, "how wretched it makes me even to think of leaving you! I have come to love you so dearly. Could you not become a woman or else make me a cat?"

But though she smiled at his wish, the look she turned upon him was very strange.

A year passes away quickly when one has neither pain nor care, when one is merry and in good health. The Prince took no thought of time, but the White Cat was not so forgetful.

"There are only three days left to look for the little dog you were to bring to the King, your father," she reminded him. "Your two brothers have already found several very beautiful ones."

At her words the Prince's memory returned to him and he marveled at his strange forgetfulness.

"What spell would have made me forget what was most important to me in the whole world?" he cried in despair. "My honor and my fortune are lost unless I can find a dog that will win a kingdom for me and a horse swift enough to carry me home again in this short time!"

So, believing this to be impossible, he grew very sorrowful. Then the White Cat spoke to him with great reassurance.

"Son of a King," she said, "do not distress yourself so. I am your friend. Remain here another day, and though it is five hundred leagues from here to your country the good wooden horse will carry you there in less than twelve hours' time."

"But it is not enough for me to return to my father, dear Cat," said the Prince. "I must take him a little dog as well."

"And so you shall," replied she. "Here is a walnut which contains one more beautiful than the Dog Star."

"Your Majesty jests with me," he protested.

"Put the walnut to your ear then," insisted the Cat, "and you will hear it bark."

He obeyed her, and as he held the walnut to his ear a faint "Bow-wow" came from within, more tiny and shrill than a cricket on a winter night. The Prince could scarcely believe his ears or contain his curiosity to see so diminutive a creature. But he was wise enough to follow the White Cat's advice not to open the walnut till he should reach his father's presence.

It was a sad leave-taking between the Prince and the White Cat. A thousand times he thanked her, but though he urged her to return to court with him, she only shook her head and sighed deeply as upon the night of his arrival. So he galloped away at last on the wooden horse, which bore him more swiftly than the wind to the appointed place.

He reached the castle even before his two brothers and enjoyed the sight of their surprise at seeing a wooden horse champing at the bit in the courtyard. The two brothers were so busy telling of their various adventures that they took little note of their younger brother's silence concerning his, but when the time came to show one another their dogs the two were vastly amused at sight of an ugly cur which the young Prince had brought along, pretending to consider it a marvel of beauty. Needless to say the elder Princes smiled with secret satisfaction to think how far superior were their own dogs, for though they wished their brother no ill luck, they had no wish to see him ruling over the kingdom.

Next morning the three set out together in the same coach. The two eldest brothers carried baskets filled with little dogs too delicate and beautiful to be touched, while the youngest carried the poor cur as if it also was precious. By no outward sign did he betray the presence of the walnut with its precious occupant which was safely hidden in his pocket. No sooner did the three set foot in the palace than all the court crowded around to welcome the returned travelers and see the results of their journeyings. The King received them with great joy, professing delight over the little dogs his two elder sons brought out for his inspection. But the more he studied their merits, the more puzzled he became, so nearly were they alike in beauty and grace. The two brothers were already beginning to dispute with one another as to which deserved the crown when the younger brother stepped forward, holding upon the palm of his hand the walnut so lately presented to him by the White Cat. Opening it without more ado, he revealed a tiny dog lying upon cotton. So perfectly formed was it and so small that it could pass through a little finger ring without touching any part of it. It was more delicate than thistledown and its coat shone with colors of the rainbow. Nor was this all; immediately it was released from its kennel, the little creature arose on its hind legs and began to go through the steps of a tarantella, with tiny castanets and all the airs and graces of a Spanish dancer!

The King was dumbfounded and even the two brothers were forced to acknowledge that such a beautiful and gifted dog had never been seen before. But their father was in no mood to give up his kingdom, so he announced that he had decided upon another test of their skill. This time he would give them a year to travel over land and sea in search of a piece of cloth so fine it would pass through the eye of the finest Venetian-point lace needle.

So the Prince remounted his wooden horse and set off at full speed, for now he knew exactly where he wanted to go. So great was his eagerness to see the beautiful White Cat once more that he could scarcely contain himself until her castle came into view. This time every window was alight to welcome him and the faithful pair of hands which had waited on him so well before were ready to take the bridle of the wooden horse and lead it back to the stable while the Prince hurried to the White Cat's private apartments.

He found her lying on a little couch of blue satin with many pillows. Her expression was sad until she caught sight of him. Then she sprang up and began to caper about him delightedly.

"Oh, dear Prince," cried she, "I had scarcely dared to hope for your return. I am generally so unfortunate in matters that concern me."

A thousand times must the grateful Prince caress her and recount his adventures, which perhaps she knew more about than he guessed. And now he told her of his father's latest whim—how he had set his heart upon having a piece of cloth that could pass through the eye of the finest needle. For his own part he did not believe it was possible to find such a thing, but he believed that if any one could help him in this quest it would be his dear White Cat. She listened attentively to all he told her and finally explained with a thoughtful air that this was a matter demanding careful consideration. There were, it seemed, some cats in her castle who could spin with extraordinary skill, and she added that she would also put a paw to the work herself so that he need not trouble himself to search farther.

The Prince was only too delighted to accept this offer and he and his charming hostess sat down to supper together, after which a magnificent display of fireworks was set off in his honor. And once more the days passed in enchanted succession. The ingenious White Cat knew a thousand different ways of entertaining her guest, so that he never once thought of missing human so-ciety. Indeed, he was probably the first person in the world to spend a whole year of complete contentment with only cats for company.

The second year slipped away as pleasantly as the first. The Prince could scarcely think of anything that the tireless hands did not instantly supply, whether books, jewels, pictures, old things or new. In short, he had but to say, "I want a certain gem that is in the cabinet of the Great Mogul, or the King of Persia, or such and such a statue in Corinth or any part of Greece," and he saw it instantly before him, without knowing how it came or who brought it. It is not unpleasant at all to find oneself able to possess any treasure in the world. No wonder our Prince was happy!

But the White Cat who was ever watchful of his welfare, warned him that the hour of departure was approaching and that he might make himself easy in his mind about the piece of cloth, for she had a most wonderful one for him. She added that it was her intention this time to furnish him with an equipage worthy of his high birth, and without waiting for his reply, beckoned him to the window overlooking the castle courtyard. Here he saw an open coach of gold and flame-color with a thousand gallant devices to please the mind and eye. It was drawn by twelve horses as white as snow, four-and-four abreast, with harnesses of flaming velvet embroidered with diamonds and gold. A hundred other coaches, each with eight horses and filled with superbly attired noblemen followed, escorted by a thousand bodyguards whose uniforms were so richly embroidered you could not see the material beneath. But the most remarkable part of this cavalcade was that a portrait of the White Cat was to be seen everywhere, in coach device, uniform, or worn as a decoration on the doublets of those who rode in the train, as if it were some newly created order that had been conferred upon them.

"Go now," said the White Cat to the Prince. "Appear at the court of the King, your father, in such magnificence that he cannot fail to be impressed and to bestow upon you the crown which you deserve. Here is another walnut. Crack it in his presence and you will find the piece of cloth you asked of me."

"Oh, dear White Cat," he answered tenderly,

"I am so overcome by your goodness that I would gladly give up my hopes of power and future grandeur to stay here with you the rest of life."

"Son of a King," she answered, "I am convinced of your kindness of heart. A kind heart is a rare thing among princes who would be loved by all, yet not love any one themselves. But you are the proof that there is an exception to this rule. I give you credit for the affection you have shown to a little white cat that after all is good for nothing but to catch mice."

So the Prince kissed her paw and departed.

This time the two brothers arrived at their father's palace before him, congratulating themselves that their young brother must be dead or gone for good. They lost no time in displaying the cloths they had brought, which were indeed so fine that they could pass through the eye of a large needle but not through the small eye of the needle the King had already selected. At this there arose a great murmuring at court. The friends of the two Princes took sides among themselves as to which had fulfilled the bargain better. But this was interrupted by a flourish of trumpets announcing the arrival of their younger brother.

The magnificence of his train fairly took away the breath of the King and his court, but their astonishment grew even greater when, after saluting his father, the young Prince brought out the walnut. This he cracked with great ceremony only to find, instead of the promised piece of cloth, a cherry stone. At sight of this the King and the court exchanged sly smiles. Nothing daunted, the Prince cracked the cherry stone, only to find a kernel inside. Jeers and murmurs ran through the great apartment. The Prince must be a fool indeed! He made no answer to them, but even he began to doubt the White Cat's words as he found next a grain of wheat and within that the smallest millet seed. "Oh, White Cat, White Cat! Have you betrayed me?" he muttered between his teeth. Even as he spoke he felt a little scratch upon his hand, so sharp that it drew blood. Taking this to be some sort of sign, the Prince proceeded to open the millet seed. Before the incredulous eyes of the whole court he drew out of it a piece of cloth four hundred yards long and marvelously embroidered with colored birds and beasts, with trees and fruits and flowers, with shells and jewels and even with suns and moons and countless stars. There were also portraits of Kings and Queens of the past upon it and of their children and children's children, not forgetting the smallest child, and each dressed perfectly in the habit of his century.

The sight of this was almost too much for the King. He could scarcely find the needle. Through its eye the wonderful piece of cloth was able to pass not only once, but six times, before the jealous gaze of the two older Princes. But the King was still far from ready to give up his kingdom. Once more he turned to his children.

"I am going to put your obedience to a new and final test," he told them. "Go and travel for another year and whichever one of you brings back with him the most beautiful Princess shall marry her and be crowned King on his wedding day. I pledge my honor that after this I shall ask no further favors of you."

So off the three went again, the youngest Prince still in a good humor although he had the least cause to be since he had twice been the acknowledged winner of the wager. But he was not one to dispute his father's will, so soon he and all his train were taking the road back to his dear White Cat. She knew the very day and hour of his arrival, and all along the way flowers had been strewn and perfume made the air sweet. Once more the castle gate was opened to him and the strange hands took him in charge while all the cats climbed into the trees to welcome their returning visitor.

"So, my Prince," said the White Cat when he reached her side at last, "once more you have returned without the crown. But no matter," she added as he opened his lips to explain. "I know that you are bound to take back the most beautiful Princess to court and I will find one for you, never fear. Meantime, let us amuse ourselves and be merry."

The third year passed for the young Prince as had the two others, and since nothing runs away faster than time passed without trouble or care, it is certain that he would have completely forgotten the day of his return to court had not the White Cat reminded him of it. This time, however, she told him that upon him alone depended his fate. He must promise to do whatever she asked of him. The Prince agreed readily enough until he heard her command him to cut off her head and tail and fling them into the fire.

"I!" cried the Prince, aghast, "I be so barbarous as to kill my dear White Cat? This is some trick to try my heart, but you should be sure of its gratitude."

"No, no, Son of a King," she answered, "I know your heart too well for that. But fate is stronger than either of us, and you must do as I bid you. It is the only way; and you must believe me, for I swear it on the honor of a Cat."

Tears came into the eyes of the Prince at the mere thought of cutting off the head of so amiable and pretty a creature. He tried to say all the most tender things he could think of, hoping to distract her. But she persisted that she wished to die by his hand because it was the only means of preventing his brothers from winning the crown. So piteously did she beg him that at last, all of a tremble, he drew his sword. With faltering hand he cut off the head and tail of his dear White Cat.

Next moment the most remarkable transformation took place before his very eyes. The body of the little White Cat suddenly changed into that of a young girl, the most graceful ever seen. But this was as nothing compared to the beauty and sweetness of her face, where only the shining brightness of the eyes gave any hint of the cat she had so recently been. The Prince was struck dumb with surprise and delight. He opened his eyes wider still to look at her, and what was his amazement to behold a troop of lords and ladies entering the apartment, each with a cat's skin flung over an arm. They advanced, and throwing themselves at the feet of their Queen, expressed their joy at seeing her once more restored to her natural form. She received them with great affection, but presently she desired them to leave her alone with the Prince.

"Behold, my dear Prince," she said as soon as they had done so, "I am released of a terrible enchantment, too long a tale to tell you now. Suffice it to say that this portrait which you saw upon my paw when I was a cat, was given to me by my guardian fairies during the time of my trial. I supposed it was of my first, unhappy love who was so cruelly taken from me and whose re-

semblance to you is so striking. Conceive my joy then, to find that it is of the Prince who has my entire heart and who was destined to rescue me from my enchantment."

And she bowed low before our Prince, who was so filled with joy and wonder that he would have remained there forever telling her of his love, had she not reminded him that the hour for his return to his father's court was almost upon them. Taking him by the hands, she led him into the courtyard to a chariot even more magnificent than the one she had provided before. The rest were equally gorgeous, the horses shod with emeralds held in place by diamond nails, with such gold and jeweled trappings as were never seen before or since. But the young Prince had eyes for nothing beyond the beauty of his companion.

Just before they reached the outskirts of the city, they sighted the Prince's two brothers with their trains driving toward them from opposite directions. At this the Princess hid herself in a small throne of rock crystal and precious gems while the Prince remained alone in the coach. His two brothers, each accompanied by a charming lady, greeted him warmly but expressed surprise and curiosity that he should be alone. To these questions he replied that he had been so unfortunate as not to have met with any lady of sufficient beauty to bring with him to court. He added, however, that he had instead a very rare and gifted White Cat. At this the brothers laughed loudly and exchanged pleased glances, for now they were convinced that he was indeed a simpleton and they need have no fears of his outwitting them a third time.

Through the streets of the city the two elder Princes rode with their ladies in open carriages, while the youngest Prince came last. Behind him was borne the great rock crystal, at which every one gazed in wonder.

The two Princes eagerly charged up the palace stairs with their Princesses, so anxious were they for their father's approval. The King received them graciously, but once more had difficulty in deciding which should have the prize. So he turned to his youngest son, who stood alone before him. "Have you returned empty-handed this time?" he asked.

"In this rock your Majesty will find a little

White Cat," he answered, "one which mews so sweetly and has such velvet paws that you cannot but be delighted with it."

But before the surprised King could reach the crystal, the Princess touched an inner spring. It flew open revealing her in all her beauty, more dazzling than the sun itself. Her hair fell in golden ringlets; she was crowned with flowers and she moved with incomparable grace in her gown of white and rose-colored gauze. Even the King himself could not resist such loveliness, but hastened to acknowledge her undisputed right to wear the crown.

"But I have not come to deprive your Majesty of a throne which you fill so admirably," she said, bowing before him graciously. "I was born the heiress to six kingdoms of my own, so permit me to offer one to you and to each of your elder sons. I ask no other favors of you than your friendship and that your youngest son shall be my husband. Three kingdoms will be quite enough for us."

And so in truth they found them.

THE GREY PALFREY

Kind beasts often come to the aid of the struggling heroes or heroines of folk tales, but never more romantically than in this tale.

In the county of Champagne there once lived a knight. He was young and handsome and brave, and indeed he was all things that a good knight should be; but he was poor, owning little land and only one small manor set in a forest, among the trees and away from the road.

This young knight went much to the tourneying, often going many miles from his home to where tournaments were being held, not only for the sake of the honour he would gain by his courage and skill, but for the prizes and for the ransoms he might ask from those he overthrew, for it was by these ransoms that he lived and bought all that was needed for himself and for his servants and his few followers. Though his garments were always neat and his helmet and

"The Grey Palfrey." From *French Legends, Tales and Fairy Stories* by Barbara Leonie Picard. Reprinted by permission of Henry Z. Walck, Inc., and Oxford University Press

his hauberk polished bright, his clothes were plain and his armour none of the best, and the food he ate, though there was enough of it, was no rich fare.

But one thing this knight owned that would not have shamed the wealthiest lord, and that was a grey palfrey, the favourite among his few horses, with sleek and glossy hide and a mane and a tail like flowing silver, so that no one, seeing it, did not stop to admire. Very fleet was this palfrey, and it had not its match in all Champagne. It was the envy of the countryside, and many were the rich lords who sought to buy it from the knight. Yet poor as he was, not for all the wealth in the world would he have parted with his palfrey, for he counted it his friend; and so indeed it proved to be.

Some two miles from this knight's manor, beside the road which ran through the forest, stood the castle of a duke. Old he was, and rich, and very miserly, forever seeking to add wealth to wealth. He had one daughter, the only young and gracious thing in all his castle, and it was this maiden whom the poor knight loved, and she loved him in return. But because he was poor, though of good repute, her father would never have considered him as a suitor; and since the maiden was never permitted to leave the castle, they might only speak together secretly, through a crack in the castle wall.

Every day at the same hour, when he was not at the tourneying, the knight would ride on the grey palfrey from his manor to the castle of the Duke, by a secret path through the forest which he alone used. And every day when she might, the maiden would await his coming at the castle wall, and they would talk of their love for a few happy moments. But not every day could she leave her father's side, or steal away unobserved, so on many days the knight would wait in vain to see her before riding sadly home along the secret path. Yet this made the times when they met all the sweeter.

One day the knight could bear it no longer, and since he knew the maiden cared nothing for riches, and would have been content as his wife had he been a peasant and lived in a hovel, he went to the castle and asked to speak with her father. The old Duke welcomed him courteously, since fair words cost nothing, and the young knight said, "Lord, there is a favour I would ask of you."

"And what might it be?" said the Duke.

"I am poor," said the knight, "but I am nobly born, and my honour is unquestioned, and no man has ever been able to speak ill of me. I love your daughter and I know that she loves me. I am here to ask for her hand in marriage."

The old Duke went as pale as his white beard in his anger. "There is not a lord in all France, nor a prince in all Christendom, whom I could not buy for my daughter, if I wished her to marry. She is not for a poor knight such as you. Now begone from my castle and never speak to me of such matters again."

Heavy at heart, the knight rode home, but since the maiden loved him he did not lose all hope, and a day or two later he rode to a distant town where a great tournament was to be held, thinking that there he might win a small measure of those riches, which, if carefully saved, might cause the old Duke to relent.

At that time a lord, wealthy and old as the Duke himself, came to visit him, and after they had talked long together of the things they had done when young and the memories they had in common, the lord said, "We are both rich, but were our riches combined, they would be even greater. Were you to give me your daughter as a wife, I would ask no dowry with her, but you and I, thus linked by a marriage, might share our wealth for the rest of our days. What say you to this, my old friend?"

The Duke was glad and rubbed his hands together and nodded many times. "You have spoken well, it shall be as you say. In all France there will be none richer than we two."

The Duke set about preparations for the marriage and cared nothing for his daughter's tears, inviting some score or more guests for the wedding, old friends of his and the bridegroom's, greybeards all. And because of his avarice, he sent to his neighbours in the countryside, asking the loan of a horse or two from each, that there might be mounts enough to carry the guests and their squires along the road through the forest to the church. And so little shame he had, that he sent to the young knight to borrow his grey palfrey, that his daughter might ride to her wedding on the finest horse in all Champagne.

The young knight had returned from the tourneying, well pleased enough with life, for he had easily been the best of all the knights gathered there, and every prize he had carried home to his little manor in the forest; so that it seemed to him he was perhaps a step nearer that which he had set his heart upon. When he heard the Duke's message, he asked, "Why does your master wish to borrow my horse?"

And the Duke's servant answered, "So that my master's daughter may ride upon it tomorrow to her wedding at the church."

When the young knight learnt how the maiden he loved was to marry the old lord, he thought that his heart would break, and at first he would have refused with indignation the Duke's request. But then he thought, "Not for the sake of her father, but to do honour to the lady I love, will I lend my palfrey. It is I whom she loves, she will have no joy of this marriage, and perhaps it will comfort her a little if I send her the palfrey which is my friend." So he saddled and bridled the palfrey and gave it to the serving-man, and then he went to his own room and would neither eat nor drink, but flung himself down upon his bed and wept.

In the Duke's castle, on the eve of the wedding, his guests made merry, feasting and drinking deep, and since they were, like himself, all old, when the time came for them to go to rest, they were in truth most weary. But very early in the morning, before dawn indeed, while the moon still shown brightly, the watchman roused them that they might be at the church betimes. Grumbling and half asleep, the guests clothed themselves and gathered in the courtyard where their horses waited. Yawning, they climbed into the saddles and set out upon their way, with the Duke and the old lord at their head. And after all the others came the maiden on the grey palfrey, with her father's old seneschal to watch over her. She was clad in a fair gown, and over it a scarlet mantle trimmed with costly fur, but her face was pale and she wept, and she had not slept all night for sorrow.

In the moonlight they left the castle and took the forest road which led to the church; yet since the way was narrow and branches overhung the track, they might not ride two abreast, but followed each other one by one through the forest, with the old seneschal at the very end, after the weeping bride.

A little way along the road, from habit, the palfrey turned aside, taking the secret path that its master had so often used; and because the old seneschal was nodding and dozing as he rode, he never missed the maiden. Deep into the forest, along the secret way went the palfrey, and in terror the maiden looked about her. But though she was fearful, she did not cry out, for she thought, "I had rather be lost in the forest and devoured by the wild beasts, than live without the knight I love." And she let the palfrey carry her where it would.

After two miles, in the dim light of early dawn, the palfrey stopped before a small manor set among the trees and waited for the gate to be opened. The watchman peeped out through a grille and called, "Who is there?" And, trembling, the maiden answered, "I am alone and lost in the forest. Have pity on me and give me shelter till sunrise."

But the watchman, looking closely knew his master's palfrey, and made all haste to where he was. "Lord," he said, "at the gate stands your palfrey, and on its back is a lady so lovely that I think she can be no mortal maid. Is it your will that I should let her in?"

The young knight leapt off his bed and ran to the gate and flung it wide and caught the maiden in his arms. When they had done with kissing and weeping for joy, he asked her, "How did you come here?" And she answered, "It was your grey palfrey that brought me, for I should not have known the way."

"Since you are here," said the knight, "here shall you stay, if you will it."

"It is all I ask, to be with you for ever," she said.

So the knight called for his chaplain, and with no delay he and the maiden were married, and in all the manor there was great rejoicing.

When the Duke and the old lord and their friends reached the church they found that the maiden was not with them, and they set themselves to search for her, all about the forest. But by the time the Duke came upon the little manor set among the trees, his daughter was a wife, and there was nothing he could do about it, save give the marriage his blessing, which he did with an ill grace. But little the young knight and his lady cared for that.

The Scandinavian Countries

The Scandinavian folk tales can be traced as a continuous tradition
for more than a thousand years, but the first serious study and collection of them
was begun in Sweden in 1630. When we speak of Scandinavia we
mean the present-day countries of Norway, Sweden, and Denmark (Iceland and
Finland not included), although the Norse traditions reach into
Finland, Iceland, Russia, the British Isles, and Northern Europe. The tales and
myths from the Scandinavian peoples are among the most prominent
in European literature. Although the temper of Scandinavian folk tales is, in the
main, serious, the stories have a drollery that equals that of the English tales.
Peter Christian Asbjörnsen and Jörgen Moe, like the Grimm brothers, collected
their stories from the lips of old storytellers, thus capturing the dramatic and
forthright quality that invariably characterizes such spontaneous narration. These
tales were also fortunate in their translator, Sir George Webbe Dasent, who
put them into such clear, vigorous English that their folk flavor and even the
feeling of spontaneity are preserved. These qualities make them easy to
tell and the stories should not be read if it is possible to learn them for telling.
Since Dasent's day, Gudrun Thorne-Thomsen and Ingri d'Aulaire, both
Norwegians, have retold these stories in even simpler style. Unhappily, the
Thorne-Thomsen book is out of print, although it may still be found
in many libraries and gives consistently the best versions for telling.

THE MOST OBEDIENT WIFE

(Danish)

This tale is among those collected by Svend Grundtvig, a well-known Danish folklorist of the nineteenth century. The Danes, to all who know them, exhibit a remarkable sense of humor, which seems to be almost a national trait. Although this variant on "The Taming of the Shrew" theme is but one of many, the Danish wit heightens its comedy. For the sake of the girls, be sure to follow it with the Czech "Clever Manka."

Long ago there was a rich farmer who had three daughters, all grown up and marriageable, and all three very pretty. The eldest of them was the prettiest, and she was also the cleverest, but she was so quarrelsome and obstinate, that there was never any peace in the house. She constantly contradicted her father, who was a kind, peace-loving man, and she quarrelled with her sisters, although they were very good-natured girls.

Many wooers came to the farm, and one of them wished to marry the eldest daughter. The farmer said that he had no objection to him as a son-in-law, but at the same time he thought it his duty to tell the suitor the truth. Accordingly he warned him that his eldest daughter was so violent and strong-minded that no one could live in peace with her. As some compensation for these faults, she would receive three hundred pounds more in her dowry than would her two sisters. That was, of course, very attractive, but the young man thought over the matter and, after he had been visiting the house for some time, he altered his mind and asked for the hand of the second daughter. The daughter accepted him, and, as her father was willing, the two became man and wife and lived very happily together.

Then came another wooer, from another part of the country, and he also wanted to marry the eldest daughter. The father warned him, as he had cautioned the first wooer; telling him that she would receive three hundred pounds more than her youngest sister, but that he must be careful, for she was so stubborn and quarrelsome that nobody could live in peace with her. So the second wooer changed his mind and asked for the hand of the youngest daughter. They married shortly after and lived happily and peacefully together.

The eldest sister was now alone with her father, but she did not treat him any better than before, and grew even more ill-humoured because her two sisters had found favour in the eyes of the first two wooers. She was obstinate and quarrelsome, violent and bad-tempered, and she grew more so from day to day.

At last another wooer came, and he was neither from their own district nor even from their country, but from a distant land. He went to the farmer and asked for the hand of his eldest daughter. "I do not want her to marry at all," said the father. "It would be a shame to allow her to do so; she is so ill-tempered and violent that no human being could live in peace with her and I do not want to be the cause of such unhappiness." But the wooer remained firm; he wanted her, he said, whatever her faults might be. At length the father yielded, provided that his daughter were willing to marry the young man, for, after all, he would be glad to get rid of her, and as he had told the suitor the whole truth about her, his conscience was clear. Accordingly, the young man wooed the girl, and she did not hesitate long, but accepted the offer, for she was tired of sitting at home a despised and spurned spinster.

The wooer said that he had no time to remain with them just then, as he must return home at once, and, as soon as the wedding day was fixed, he rode away. He also told them not to wait for him at the farm on the day of the wedding, he would appear in good time at the church. When the day came the farmer drove with his daughter to the church, where a great company of wedding guests had assembled; the bride's sisters and brothers-in-law were there, and all the village people arrived in their Sunday clothes. The bridegroom was there also, but in ordinary travelling garments; and so the couple walked up to the altar and were married.

As soon as the ceremony was over, the bridegroom took his young wife by the hand and led her out of the church. He sent a message to his

"The Most Obedient Wife." From *Danish Fairy Tales*, by Svend Grundtvig. Reprinted by permission of the publishers, Thomas Y. Crowell Company, New York

father-in-law asking him to excuse their absence from the marriage feast, as they had no time to waste. He had not driven in a coach, as is the custom at weddings, but travelled on horseback, on a fine big grey horse, with an ordinary saddle, and a couple of pistols in the saddlebags. He had brought no friends or relations with him, only a big dog, that lay beside the horse during the ceremony. The bridegroom lifted his bride on to the pommel, as if she had been a feather, jumped into the saddle, put the spurs to his horse and rode off with the dog trotting behind. The marriage party standing at the church door looked after them, and shook their heads in amazement. Then they got into their carriages, drove back-to the house, and partook of the marriage feast without bride or bridegroom.

The bride did not like this at all, but as she did not want to quarrel with her bridegroom so soon, she held her tongue for a time; but as he did not speak either, she at last broke the ice and said that it was a very fine horse they were riding. "Yes," he replied; "I have seven other horses at home in my stables, but this is my favourite; it is the most valuable of all, and I like it best." Then she remarked that she liked the beautiful dog also. "It is indeed a jewel of a dog," he said, "and has cost me a lot of money."

After a while they came to a forest, where the bridegroom sprang from his horse and cut a thin switch from a willow-tree. This he wound three times round his finger, then tied it with a thread and gave it to his bride, saying: "This is my wedding gift to you. Take good care of it, and carry it about with you always! You will not repent it." She thought it a strange wedding gift, but put it in her pocket, and they rode on again. Presently the bride dropped her glove, and the bridegroom said to the dog: "Pick it up, Fido!" But the dog took no notice, and left the glove on the ground. Then his master drew his pistol from the holster, shot the dog, and rode on, leaving it lying dead. "How could you be so cruel?" said his bride. "I never say a thing twice," was the reply, and they journeyed on in silence.

After some time they came to a running stream that they had to cross. There being only a ford, and no bridge, the man said to his horse: "Take good care! Not a drop must soil my bride's dress!" When they had crossed, however, the dress was badly soiled, and the husband lifted his bride from the horse, drew out the other pistol and shot the horse, so that it fell dead to the ground. "Oh, the poor horse!" cried the bride. "Yes, but I never say a thing twice," answered her husband. Then he took saddle, bridle, and cover from the horse; bridle and cover he carried himself, but the saddle he gave to his young wife, and said: "You can carry that; we shall soon be home." He walked on in silence, and the bride quickly put the saddle on her back and followed him; she had no desire to make him say it twice.

Soon they arrived at his dwelling place, a very fine farm. The menservants and maidservants rushed to the door and received them, and the husband said to them: "See, this is my wife and your mistress. Whatever she tells you, you are to do, just as if I had ordered it." Then he led her indoors and showed her everything—living-rooms and bedrooms, kitchen and cellar, brew-house and dairy—and said to her: "You will look after everything indoors, I attend to everything out-of-doors," and then they sat down to supper, and soon after went to bed.

Days, weeks and months passed; the young wife attended to all household matters while her husband looked after the farm, and not a single angry word passed between them. The servants had been accustomed to obey their master implicitly, and now they obeyed their mistress likewise, and so six months passed without there having arisen any necessity for the husband to say the same thing twice to his wife. He was always kind and polite to her, and she was always gentle and obedient.

One day he said to her: "Would you not like to visit your relations?" "Yes, dear husband, I should like to do so very much, if it is convenient," she replied. "It is quite convenient," he said, "but you have never mentioned it. It shall be done at once; get ready, while I have the horses put to the carriage." He went to the stable and saw to everything, while his wife ran upstairs to dress as quickly as possible for the journey. The husband drove up, cracked his whip and asked: "Are you ready?" "Yes, dear," came the reply, and she came running out and entered the carriage. She had not quite finished dressing and carried some of her things in her hand, and these she put on in the carriage.

Then they started. When they had driven nearly half the distance, they saw a great flock of ravens flying across the road. "What beautiful white birds!" said the husband. "No, they are black, dear!" said his wife. "I think it is going to rain," he said, turned the horses, and drove home again. She understood perfectly why he had done so; it was the first time that she had contradicted him, but she showed no resentment, and the two conversed in quite a friendly fashion all the way home. The horses were put into the stable—and it did not rain.

When a month had passed, the husband said one morning: "I believe it is going to be fine to-day. Would you not like to visit your relations?" She wished to do so very much indeed, and she hastened a little more than the last time, so that when her husband drove up and cracked his whip, she was quite ready and mounted the carriage beside him. They had driven considerably more than half the distance, when they met a large flock of sheep and lambs. "What a fine pack of wolves!" said the husband. "You mean sheep, dear!" said the wife. "I think it will rain before evening," said the husband, looking up at the sky. "It will be better for us to drive home again." With these words he turned the horses and drove back home. They conversed in a friendly manner until they reached home; but it did not rain.

When another month had passed, the husband said one morning to his wife: "We really must see whether we cannot manage to visit your relations. What do you say to our driving across to-day? It looks as though the day would be fine." His wife thought so too; she was ready very soon and they set out. They had not travelled far when they saw a great flock of swans flying along over their heads. "That was a fine flock of storks," said the husband. "Yes, so it was, dear," said his wife, and they drove on; there was no change in the weather that day, so that they reached her father's farm in due course. He received them joyfully and sent at once for his two other daughters and their husbands, and a very merry family meeting it was.

The three married sisters went into the kitchen together, because they could talk more freely there, and they had a great deal to tell each other; the two younger ones in particular had many questions to ask their elder sister, because they had not seen her for a very long time. Then they helped to prepare the dinner; it goes without saying that nothing was too good for this festive occasion.

The three brothers-in-law sat meanwhile with their father-in-law in the sitting-room and they, too, had much to tell and ask each other. Then said the old farmer: "This is the first time that you have all three been gathered together under my roof, and I should like to ask you frankly how you are pleased with your wives." The husbands who had married the two younger, good-tempered sisters said at once that they were perfectly satisfied and lived very happily. "But how do you get on with yours?" the father-in-law asked the husband of the eldest sister. "Nobody ever married a better wife than I did," was the reply. "Well, I should like to see which of you has the most obedient wife," said the father-in-law, and then he fetched a heavy silver jug and filled it to the top with gold and silver coins. This he placed in the middle of the table before the three men, and said that he would give it to him who had the most obedient wife.

They put the matter to the test at once. The husband who had married the youngest sister went to the kitchen door and called: "Will you come here a moment, Gerda, please; as quickly as possible!" "All right, I am coming," she answered, but it was some time before she came, because as she explained, she had first to talk about something with one of her sisters. "What do you want with me?" she asked. The husband made some excuse, and she went out again.

Now it was the turn of the man who had married the middle sister. "Please come here a moment, Margaret!" he called. She also answered: "Yes, I am coming at once," but it was a good while before she came; she had had something in her hands and was compelled to put it down first. The husband invented some excuse, and she went out again.

Then the third husband went to the kitchen door, opened it slightly and just said: "Christine!"—"Yes!" she answered, as she stood there with a large dish of food in her hands. "Take this from me!" she said quickly to her sisters, but they looked at her in amazement and did not take the dish. Bang! she dropped it right on the middle of the kitchen floor, rushed into the room and asked: "What do you wish, dear?"—"Oh, I only wanted to see you," he said, "but since you are here, you may as well take that jug standing on the table; it is yours, with all that is in it.—You might also show us what you got from me as a marriage gift on your wedding day."—"Yes, dear, here it is," she said, and drew the willow ring from her bosom, where she had kept it ever since. The husband handed it to his father-in-law and asked: "Can you put that ring straight?"—No, that was impossible without breaking it. "Well, you see now," said the husband, "if I had not bent the twig when it was green, I could not have made it into this shape."

After that they sat down to a merry meal, then the husband of the oldest sister returned home with her, and they lived for many years very happily together.

THE THREE
BILLY-GOATS GRUFF
(Norwegian)

This is a matchless little tale to tell, admirable in plot and economy of words. You will probably want to substitute for the big billy-goat Gruff's gruesome verse, the simpler, "Well, come along. I've two big spears to fight you with," and explain to the children, "By spears, of course, he meant his horns." This is fun for the five-year-olds to dramatize informally without any special costuming.

Once on a time there were three billy-goats, who were to go up to the hill-side to make themselves fat, and the name of all three was "Gruff."

On the way up was a bridge over a burn they had to cross; and under the bridge lived a great ugly troll, with eyes as big as saucers, and a nose as long as a poker.

"The Three Billy-Goats Gruff." From *Popular Tales from the Norse*, by Peter Christian Asbjörnsen and Jörgen Moe, translated by Sir George Webbe Dasent. David Douglas, Edinburgh, 1888

So first of all came the youngest billy-goat Gruff to cross the bridge.

"Trip, trap! trip, trap!" went the bridge.

"WHO'S THAT tripping over my bridge?" roared the troll.

"Oh, it is only I, the tiniest billy-goat Gruff; and I'm going up to the hill-side to make myself fat," said the billy-goat, with such a small voice.

"Now, I'm coming to gobble you up," said the troll.

"Oh, no! pray don't take me. I'm too little, that I am," said the billy-goat. "Wait a bit till the second billy-goat Gruff comes. He's much bigger."

"Well, be off with you;" said the troll.

A little while after came the second billy-goat Gruff to cross the bridge.

"TRIP, TRAP! TRIP, TRAP! TRIP, TRAP!" went the bridge.

"WHO'S THAT tripping over my bridge?" roared the troll.

"Oh, it's the second billy-goat Gruff, and I'm going up to the hill-side to make myself fat," said the billy-goat, who hadn't such a small voice.

"Now I'm coming to gobble you up," said the troll.

"Oh, no! don't take me. Wait a little till the big billy-goat Gruff comes. He's much bigger."

"Very well! be off with you," said the troll.

But just then up came the big billy-goat Gruff.

"TRIP, TRAP! TRIP, TRAP! TRIP, TRAP!" went the bridge, for the billy-goat was so heavy that the bridge creaked and groaned under him.

"WHO'S THAT tramping over my bridge?" roared the troll.

"IT'S I! THE BIG BILLY-GOAT GRUFF," said the billy-goat, who had an ugly hoarse voice of his own.

"Now I'm coming to gobble you up," roared the troll.

"Well, come along! I've got two spears,
And I'll poke your eyeballs out at your ears;
I've got besides two curling-stones,
And I'll crush you to bits, body and bones."

That was what the big billy-goat said; and so he flew at the troll, and poked his eyes out with his horns, and crushed him to bits, body and bones, and tossed him out into the burn, and after that he went up to the hill-side. There the billy-goats got so fat they were scarce able to walk home again; and if the fat hasn't fallen off them, why, they're still fat; and so—

"Snip, snap, snout.
This tale's told out."

THE PANCAKE

(Norwegian)

How many versions of this tale there are!— such as the Russian "Mr. Bun" and Ruth Sawyer's Journey-Cake, Ho! *Although the beginning here is rather long and exacting, one can simplify it for very young children to "Once there was a mother who had seven hungry children." The ending is much more effective if the story-teller, as he utters the pig's "Ouf, ouf," will mime the pig's gulping down the hapless, haughty pancake.*

Once on a time there was a goody who had seven hungry bairns, and she was frying a pancake for them. It was a sweet-milk pancake, and there it lay in the pan bubbling and frizzling so thick and good, it was a sight for sore eyes to look at. And the bairns stood round about, and the goodman sat by and looked on.

"Oh, give me a bit of pancake, mother, dear; I am so hungry," said one bairn.

"Oh, darling mother," said the second.

"Oh, darling good mother," said the third.

"Oh, darling, good, nice mother," said the fourth.

"Oh, darling, pretty, good, nice mother," said the fifth.

"Oh, darling, pretty, good, nice, clever mother," said the sixth.

"Oh, darling, pretty, good, nice, clever, sweet mother," said the seventh.

So they begged for the pancake all round, the one more prettily than the other; for they were so hungry and so good.

"Yes, yes, bairns, only bide a bit till it turns it-self,"—she ought to have said "till I can get it turned,"—"and then you shall all have some—a lovely sweet-milk pancake; only look how fat and happy it lies there."

When the pancake heard that, it got afraid, and in a trice it turned itself all of itself, and tried to jump out of the pan; but it fell back into it again t'other side up, and so when it had been fried a little on the other side too, till it got firmer in its flesh, it sprang out on the floor and rolled off like a wheel through the door and down the hill.

"Holloa! Stop, pancake!" and away went the goody after it, with the frying-pan in one hand and the ladle in the other, as fast as she could, and her bairns behind her, while the goodman limped after them last of all.

"Hi! won't you stop? Seize it. Stop, pancake," they all screamed out, one after the other, and tried to catch it on the run and hold it; but the pancake rolled on and on, and in the twinkling of an eye it was so far ahead that they couldn't see it, for the pancake was faster on its feet than any of them.

So when it had rolled awhile it met a man.

"Good-day, pancake," said the man.

"God bless you, Manny Panny!" said the pancake.

"Dear pancake," said the man, "don't roll so fast; stop a little and let me eat you."

"The Pancake." From *Tales from the Fjeld,* from the Norse of Peter Christian Asbjörnsen and Jörgen Moe, translated by Sir George Webbe Dasent. Chapman and Hall, London, 1874

"When I have given the slip to Goody Poody, and the goodman, and seven squalling children, I may well slip through your fingers, Manny Panny," said the pancake, and rolled on and on till it met a hen.

"Good-day, pancake," said the hen.

"The same to you, Henny Penny," said the pancake.

"Pancake, dear, don't roll so fast; bide a bit and let me eat you up," said the hen.

"When I have given the slip to Goody Poody, and the goodman, and seven squalling children, and Manny Panny, I may well slip through your claws, Henny Penny," said the pancake, and so it rolled on like a wheel down the road.

Just then it met a cock.

"Good-day, pancake," said the cock.

"The same to you, Cocky Locky," said the pancake.

"Pancake, dear, don't roll so fast, but bide a bit and let me eat you up."

"When I have given the slip to Goody Poody, and the goodman, and seven squalling children, and to Manny Panny, and Henny Penny, I may well slip through your claws, Cocky Locky," said the pancake, and off it set rolling away as fast as it could; and when it had rolled a long way it met a duck.

"Good-day, pancake," said the duck.

"The same to you, Ducky Lucky."

"Pancake, dear, don't roll away so fast; bide a bit and let me eat you up."

"When I have given the slip to Goody Poody, and the goodman, and seven squalling children, and Manny Panny, and Henny Penny, and Cocky Locky, I may well slip through your fingers, Ducky Lucky," said the pancake, and with that it took to rolling and rolling faster than ever; and when it had rolled a long, long while, it met a goose.

"Good-day, pancake," said the goose.

"The same to you, Goosey Poosey."

"Pancake, dear, don't roll so fast; bide a bit and let me eat you up."

"When I have given the slip to Goody Poody, and the goodman, and seven squalling children, and Manny Panny, and Henny Penny, and Cocky Locky, and Ducky Lucky, I can well slip through your feet, Goosey Poosey," said the pancake, and off it rolled.

So when it had rolled a long, long way farther, it met a gander.

"Good-day, pancake," said the gander.

"The same to you, Gander Pander," said the pancake.

"Pancake, dear, don't roll so fast; bide a bit and let me eat you up."

"When I have given the slip to Goody Poody, and the goodman, and seven squalling children, and Manny Panny, and Henny Penny, and Cocky Locky, and Ducky Lucky, and Goosey Poosey, I may well slip through your feet, Gander Pander," said the pancake, which rolled off as fast as ever.

So when it had rolled a long, long time, it met a pig.

"Good-day, pancake," said the pig.

"The same to you, Piggy Wiggy," said the pancake, which, without a word more, began to roll and roll like mad.

"Nay, nay," said the pig, "you needn't be in such a hurry; we two can then go side by side and see one another over the wood; they say it is not too safe in there."

The pancake thought there might be something in that, and so they kept company. But when they had gone awhile, they came to a brook. As for piggy, he was so fat he swam safe across, it was nothing to him; but the poor pancake couldn't get over.

"Seat yourself on my snout," said the pig, "and I'll carry you over."

So the pancake did that.

"Ouf, ouf," said the pig, and swallowed the pancake at one gulp; and then, as the poor pancake could go no farther, why—this story can go no farther either.

WHY THE BEAR IS STUMPY-TAILED

(Norwegian)

It has been said that all over the world, wherever there are bears, this story occurs. The folk tales are always warning the unwary against the folly of credulity.

"Why the Bear Is Stumpy-Tailed." From *Popular Tales from the Norse*, by Peter Christian Asbjörnsen and Jörgen Moe, translated by Sir George Webbe Dasent. David Douglas, Edinburgh, 1888

One day the bear met the fox, who came slinking along with a string of fish he had stolen.

"Whence did you get those from?" asked the bear.

"Oh! my Lord Bruin, I've been out fishing and caught them," said the fox.

So the bear had a mind to learn to fish too, and bade the fox tell him how he was to set about it.

"Oh! it's an easy craft for you," answered the fox, "and soon learnt. You've only got to go upon the ice and cut a hole and stick your tail down into it; and so you must go on holding it there as long as you can. You're not to mind if your tail smarts a little; that's when the fish bite. The longer you hold it there the more fish you'll get; and then all at once out with it, with a cross pull sideways, and with a strong pull too."

Yes; the bear did as the fox had said, and held his tail a long, long time down in the hole, till it was fast frozen in. Then he pulled it out with a cross pull, and it snapped short off. That's why Bruin goes about with a stumpy tail this very day.

THE LAD WHO WENT TO THE NORTH WIND

(Norwegian)

Although the lad is determined to get his rights, he is vulnerable to losing them. This story is easy to tell and seems to be a great favorite with children. Perhaps they feel sympathy and admiration for the humble lad who stands up to power and wins out against trickery.

Once on a time there was an old widow who had one son; and as she was poorly and weak, her son had to go up into the safe to fetch meal for cooking; but when he got outside the safe, and was just going down the steps, there came the North Wind, puffing and blowing, caught up the meal, and so away with it through the air. Then the lad went back into the safe for more; but when he came out again on the steps, if the North Wind didn't come again and carry off the meal with a puff; and more than that, he did so the third time. At this the lad got very angry, and as he thought it hard that the North Wind should behave so, he thought he'd just look him up and ask him to give up his meal.

So off he went, but the way was long and he walked and walked, but at last he came to the North Wind's house.

"Good day!" said the lad, "thank you for coming to see us yesterday."

"Good day!" answered the North Wind, for his voice was loud and gruff, "and thanks for coming to see me. What do you want?"

"Oh!" answered the lad, "I only wished to ask you to be so good as to let me have back that meal you took from me on the safe steps, for we haven't much to live on; and if you're to go on snapping up the morsel we have there'll be nothing for it but to starve."

"I haven't got your meal," said the North Wind; "but if you are in such need, I'll give you a cloth which will get you everything you want, if you only say, 'Cloth, spread yourself, and serve up all kinds of good dishes!' "

With this the lad was well content. But, as the way was so long he couldn't get home in one day, he turned into an inn on the way; and when they were going to sit down to supper, he laid the cloth on a table which stood in the corner and said, "Cloth, spread yourself, and serve up all kinds of good dishes."

He had scarce said so before the cloth did as it was bid; and all who stood by thought it a fine thing, but most of all the landlady. So, when all were fast asleep, at dead of night, she took the lad's cloth, and put another in its stead, just like the one he had got from the North Wind, but which couldn't so much as serve up a bit of dry bread.

So, when the lad woke, he took his cloth and went off with it, and that day he got home to his mother.

"Now," said he, "I've been to the North Wind's house, and a good fellow he is, for he gave me this cloth, and when I only say to it, 'Cloth, spread yourself, and serve up all kinds of good dishes,' I get any sort of food I please."

"All very true, I daresay," said his mother; "but seeing is believing, and I shan't believe it till I see it."

So the lad made haste, drew out a table, laid the cloth on it, and said, "Cloth, spread yourself, and serve up all kinds of good dishes."

But never a bit of dry bread did the cloth serve up.

"Well," said the lad, "there's no help for it but to go to the North Wind again." And away he went.

So he came to where the North Wind lived late in the afternoon.

"Good evening!" said the lad.

"Good evening!" said the North Wind.

"I want my rights for that meal of ours which you took," said the lad; "for as for that cloth I got, it isn't worth a penny."

"I've got no meal," said the North Wind; "but yonder you have a ram which coins nothing but golden ducats as soon as you say to it, 'Ram, ram! make money!' "

So the lad thought this a fine thing; but as it was too far to get home that day, he turned in for the night to the same inn where he had slept before.

"The Lad Who Went to the North Wind." From *Popular Tales from the Norse*, by Peter Christian Asbjörnsen and Jörgen Moe, translated by Sir George Webbe Dasent. David Douglas, Edinburgh, 1888

Before he called for anything, he tried the truth of what the North Wind had said of the ram, and found it all right; but when the landlord saw that, he thought it was a famous ram and, when the lad had fallen asleep, he took another which couldn't coin gold ducats, and changed the two.

Next morning off went the lad; and when he got home to his mother, he said, "After all, the North Wind is a jolly fellow; for now he has given me a ram which can coin golden ducats if I only say, 'Ram, ram! make money!'"

"All very true, I daresay," said his mother; "but I shan't believe any such stuff until I see the ducats made."

"Ram, ram! make money!" said the lad; but if the ram made anything, it wasn't money.

So the lad went back again to the North Wind, and blew him up, and said the ram was worth nothing, and he must have his rights for the meal.

"Well," said the North Wind; "I've nothing else to give you but that old stick in the corner yonder; but it's a stick of that kind that if you say, 'Stick, stick! lay on!' it lays on till you say, 'Stick, stick! now stop!'"

So, as the way was long, the lad turned in this night too to the landlord; but as he could pretty well guess how things stood as to the cloth and the ram, he lay down at once on the bench and began to snore, as if he were asleep.

Now the landlord, who easily saw that the stick must be worth something, hunted up one which was like it, and when he heard the lad snore, was going to change the two, but just as the landlord was about to take it the lad bawled out, "Stick, stick! lay on!"

So the stick began to beat the landlord, till he jumped over chairs, and tables, and benches, and yelled and roared, "Oh my! oh my! bid the stick be still, else it will beat me to death, and you shall have back both your cloth and your ram."

When the lad thought the landlord had got enough, he said, "Stick, stick! now stop!"

Then he took the cloth, put it into his pocket, and went home with his stick in his hand, leading the ram by a cord round its horns; and so he got his rights for the meal he had lost.

BOOTS AND HIS BROTHERS

(*Norwegian*)

The name "Boots" came into the English versions of the Norwegian tales by way of the distinguished British translator, Sir George Webbe Dasent. "Boots" is the English equivalent for a boy who blacks boots and does odds and ends of work. Perhaps it is enough to say to the children the first time you tell the story, "There was a poor man who had three sons, Peter, Paul, and John. And because John was the youngest son and had to black the boots of others, he was often called Boots, but usually he was just called Jack." Mrs. Thorne-Thomsen and the d'Aulaires translate the name as Espen Cinderlad, others as Ashlad, so take your choice. At any rate, Boots, Cinderella, Espen Cinderlad, Jack, Juan Bobo, and Jean are all members of the world family of underdogs who succeed. As for the clipping of ears, children readily accept it as a just punishment for dullard aspirants to half a kingdom, especially if the storyteller does not emphasize it.

Once on a time there was a man who had three sons, Peter, Paul, and John. John was Boots, of course, because he was the youngest. I can't say the man had anything more than these three sons, for he hadn't one penny to rub against another; and so he told his sons over and over again they must go out into the world and try to earn their bread, for there at home there was nothing to be looked for but starving to death.

Now, a bit off the man's cottage was the King's palace, and you must know, just against the King's windows a great oak had sprung up, which was so stout and big that it took away all the light from the King's palace. The King had said he would give many, many dollars to the man who could fell the oak, but no one was man enough for that, for as soon as ever one chip of the oak's trunk flew off, two grew in its stead. A

"Boots and His Brothers." From *Popular Tales from the Norse*, by Peter Christian Asbjörnsen and Jörgen Moe, translated by Sir George Webbe Dasent. David Douglas, Edinburgh, 1888

well, too, the King wanted, which was to hold water for the whole year; for all his neighbours had wells, but he hadn't any, and that he thought a shame. So the King said he would give any one who could dig him such a well as would hold water for a whole year round, both money and goods; but no one could do it, for the King's palace lay high, high up on a hill, and they hadn't dug a few inches before they came upon the living rock.

But as the King had set his heart on having these two things done, he had it given out far and wide, in all the churches of his kingdom, that he who could fell the big oak in the King's courtyard, and get him a well that would hold water the whole year round, should have the Princess and half the kingdom. Well, you may easily know there was many a man who came to try his luck; but for all their hacking and hewing, and all their digging and delving, it was no good. The oak got bigger and stouter at every stroke, and the rock didn't get softer either. So one day those three brothers thought they'd set off and try too, and their father hadn't a word against it; for even if they didn't get the Princess and half the kingdom, it might happen they might get a place somewhere with a good master; and that was all he wanted. So when the brothers said they thought of going to the palace, their father said "yes" at once. So Peter, Paul, and Jack went off from their home.

Well, they hadn't gone far before they came to a fir-wood, and up along one side of it rose a steep hill-side, and as they went, they heard something hewing and hacking away up on the hill among the trees.

"I wonder now what it is that is hewing away up yonder," said Jack.

"You're always so clever with your wonderings," said Peter and Paul both at once. "What wonder is it, pray, that a woodcutter should stand and hack up on a hill-side?"

"Still, I'd like to see what it is, after all," said Jack; and up he went.

"Oh, if you're such a child, 'twill do you good to go and take a lesson," bawled out his brothers after him.

But Jack didn't care for what they said; he climbed the steep hill-side towards where the noise came, and when he reached the place, what

do you think he saw? Why, an axe stood there hacking and hewing, all of itself, at the trunk of a fir.

"Good day!" said Jack. "So you stand here all alone and hew, do you?"

"Yes, here I've stood and hewed and hacked a long, long time, waiting for you," said the axe.

"Well, here I am at last," said Jack, as he took the axe, pulled it off its haft, and stuffed both head and haft into his wallet.

So when he got down again to his brothers, they began to jeer and laugh at him.

"And now, what funny thing was it you saw up yonder on the hill-side?" they said.

"Oh, it was only an axe we heard," said Jack.

So when they had gone a bit farther, they came under a steep spur of rock, and up there they heard something digging and shovelling.

"I wonder now," said Jack, "what it is digging and shovelling up yonder at the top of the rock."

"Ah, you're always so clever with your wonderings," said Peter and Paul again, "as if you'd never heard a woodpecker hacking and pecking at a hollow tree."

"Well, well," said Jack, "I think it would be a piece of fun just to see what it really is."

And so off he set to climb the rock, while the others laughed and made game of him. But he didn't care a bit for that; up he climbed, and when he got near the top, what do you think he saw? Why, a spade that stood there digging and delving.

"Good day!" said Jack. "So you stand here all alone, and dig and delve!"

"Yes, that's what I do," said the spade, "and that's what I've done this many a long day, waiting for you."

"Well, here I am," said Jack again, as he took the spade and knocked it off its handle, and put it into his wallet, and then went down again to his brothers.

"Well, what was it, so rare and strange," said Peter and Paul, "that you saw up there at the top of the rock?"

"Oh," said Jack, "nothing more than a spade; that was what we heard."

So they went on again a good bit, till they came to a brook. They were thirsty, all three, after their long walk, and so they lay down beside the brook to have a drink.

"I wonder now," said Jack, "where all this water comes from."

"I wonder if you're right in your head," said Peter and Paul in one breath. "If you're not mad already, you'll go mad very soon, with your wonderings. Where the brook comes from, indeed! Have you never heard how water rises from a spring in the earth?"

"Yes, but still I've a great fancy to see where this brook comes from," said Jack.

So up alongside the brook he went, in spite of all that his brothers bawled after him. Nothing could stop him. On he went. So, as he went up and up, the brook got smaller and smaller, and at last, a little way farther on, what do you think he saw? Why, a great walnut, and out of that the water trickled.

"Good-day!" said Jack again. "So you lie here, and trickle and run down all alone?"

"Yes, I do," said the walnut; "and here have I trickled and run this many a long day, waiting for you."

"Well, here I am," said Jack, as he took up a lump of moss, and plugged up the hole, that the water mightn't run out. Then he put the walnut into his wallet, and ran down to his brothers.

"Well, now," said Peter and Paul, "have you found out where the water comes from? A rare sight it must have been!"

"Oh, after all, it was only a hole it ran out of," said Jack; and so the others laughed and made game of him again, but Jack didn't mind that a bit.

"After all, I had the fun of seeing it," said he.

So when they had gone a bit farther, they came to the King's palace; but as every one in the kingdom had heard how they might win the Princess and half the realm, if they could only fell the big oak and dig the King's well, so many had come to try their luck that the oak was now twice as stout and big as it had been at first, for two chips grew for every one they hewed out with their axes, as I daresay you all bear in mind. So the King had now laid it down as a punishment, that if any one tried and couldn't fell the oak, he should be put on a barren island, and both his ears were to be clipped off. But the two brothers didn't let themselves be scared by that; they were quite sure they could fell the oak, and Peter, as he was eldest, was to try his hand first; but it went with him as with all the rest who had hewn at the oak; for every chip he cut out, two grew in its place. So the King's men seized him, and clipped off both his ears, and put him out on the island.

Now Paul was to try his luck, but he fared just the same; when he had hewn two or three strokes, they began to see the oak grow, and so the King's men seized him too, and clipped his ears, and put him out on the island; and his ears they clipped closer, because they said he ought to have taken a lesson from his brother.

So now Jack was to try.

"If you *will* look like a marked sheep, we're quite ready to clip your ears at once, and then you'll save yourself some bother," said the King, for he was angry with him for his brothers' sake.

"Well, I'd like just to try first," said Jack, and so he got leave. Then he took his axe out of his wallet and fitted it to its haft.

"Hew away!" said he to his axe; and away it hewed, making the chips fly again, so that it wasn't long before down came the oak.

When that was done, Jack pulled out his spade, and fitted it to its handle.

"Dig away!" said he to the spade; and so the spade began to dig and delve till the earth and rock flew out in splinters, and so he had the well soon dug out, you may think.

And when he had got it as big and deep as he chose, Jack took out his walnut and laid it in one corner of the well, and pulled the plug of moss out.

"Trickle and run," said Jack; and so the nut trickled and ran, till the water gushed out of the hole in a stream, and in a short time the well was brimfull.

Then Jack had felled the oak which shaded the King's palace, and dug a well in the palace-yard, and so he got the Princess and half the kingdom, as the King had said; but it was lucky for Peter and Paul that they had lost their ears, else they had heard each hour and day how every one said, "Well, after all, Jack wasn't so much out of his mind when he took to wondering."

PRINCESS ON
THE GLASS HILL

(Norwegian)

If this story seems overly long, let Boots find only the horse with the golden trappings and ride up the hill only once.

Once on a time there was a man who had a meadow, which lay high up on the hill-side, and in the meadow was a barn, which he had built to keep his hay in. Now, I must tell you there hadn't been much in the barn for the last year or two, for every St. John's night, when the grass stood greenest and deepest, the meadow was eaten down to the very ground the next morning, just as if a whole drove of sheep had been there feeding on it over night. This happened once, and it happened twice; so at last the man grew weary of losing his crop of hay, and said to his sons—for he had three of them, and the youngest was nicknamed Boots, of course—that now one of them must just go and sleep in the barn in the outlying field when St. John's night came, for it was too good a joke that his grass should be eaten, root and blade, this year, as it had been the last two years. So whichever of them went must keep a sharp lookout; that was what their father said.

Well, the eldest son was ready to go and watch the meadow; trust him for looking after the grass! It shouldn't be his fault if man or beast, or the fiend himself, got a blade of grass. So, when evening came, he set off to the barn, and lay down to sleep; but a little later on in the night came such a clatter, and such an earthquake, that walls and roof shook, and groaned, and creaked; then up jumped the lad, and took to his heels as fast as ever he could; nor dared he once look round till he reached home; and as for the hay, why it was eaten up this year just as it had been twice before.

The next St. John's night, the man said again it would never do to lose all the grass in the outlying field year after year in this way, so one

"Princess on the Glass Hill." From *Popular Tales from the Norse*, by Peter Christian Asbjörnsen and Jörgen Moe, translated by Sir George Webbe Dasent. David Douglas, Edinburgh, 1888

of his sons must just trudge off to watch it, and watch it well too. Well, the next oldest son was ready to try his luck, so he set off, and lay down to sleep in the barn as his brother had done before him; but as night wore on there came on a rumbling and quaking of the earth, worse even than on the last St. John's night, and when the lad heard it he got frightened, and took to his heels as though he were running a race.

Next year the turn came to Boots; but when he made ready to go, the other two began to laugh, and to make game of him, saying,

"You're just the man to watch the hay, that you are; you who have done nothing all your life but sit in the ashes and toast yourself by the fire."

But Boots did not care a pin for their chattering, and stumped away, as evening drew on, up the hill-side to the outlying field. There he went inside the barn and lay down; but in about an hour's time the barn began to groan and creak, so that it was dreadful to hear.

"Well," said Boots to himself, "if it isn't worse than this, I can stand it well enough."

A little while after came another creak and an earthquake, so that the litter in the barn flew about the lad's ears.

"Oh!" said Boots to himself, "if it isn't worse than this, I daresay I can stand it out."

But just then came a third rumbling, and a third earthquake, so that the lad thought walls and roof were coming down on his head; but it passed off, and all was still as death about him.

"It'll come again, I'll be bound," thought Boots; but no, it did not come again; still it was and still it stayed; but after he had lain a little while he heard a noise as if a horse were standing just outside the barn-door, and cropping the grass. He stole to the door, and peeped through a chink, and there stood a horse feeding away. So big, and fat, and grand a horse, Boots had never set eyes on; by his side on the grass lay a saddle and bridle, and a full set of armour for a knight, all of brass, so bright that the light gleamed from it.

"Ho, ho!" thought the lad; "it's you, is it, that eats up our hay? I'll soon put a spoke in your wheel; just see if I don't."

So he lost no time, but took the steel out of his tinder-box, and threw it over the horse; then it had no power to stir from the spot, and became so tame that the lad could do what he liked with it. So he got on its back and rode off with it to a place which no one knew of, and there he put up the horse. When he got home his brothers laughed and asked how he had fared.

"You didn't lie long in the barn, even if you had the heart to go so far as the field."

"Well," said Boots, "all I can say is, I lay in the barn till the sun rose, and neither saw nor heard anything; I can't think what there was in the barn to make you both so afraid."

"A pretty story!" said his brothers; "but we'll soon see how you have watched the meadow"; so they set off; but when they reached it, there stood the grass as deep and thick as it had been over night.

Well, the next St. John's eve it was the same story over again; neither of the elder brothers dared to go out to the outlying field to watch the crop; but Boots, he had the heart to go, and everything happened just as it had happened the year before. First a clatter and an earthquake, then a greater clatter and another earthquake, and so on a third time; only this year the earthquakes were far worse than the year before. Then all at once everything was as still as death, and the lad heard how something was cropping the grass outside the barn-door, so he stole to the door, and peeped through a chink; and what do you think he saw? Why, another horse standing right up against the wall, and chewing and champing with might and main. It was far finer and fatter than that which came the year before, and it had a saddle on its back, and a bridle on its neck, and a full suit of mail for a knight lay by its side, all of silver, and as grand as you would wish to see.

"Ho, ho!" said Boots to himself; "it's you that gobbles up our hay, is it? I'll soon put a spoke in your wheel"; and with that he took the steel out of his tinder-box, and threw it over the crest of the horse, which stood as still as a lamb. Well, the lad rode this horse, too, to the hiding-place where he kept the other one, and after that he went home.

"I suppose you'll tell us," said one of his brothers, "there's a fine crop this year too, up in the hayfield."

"Well, so there is," said Boots; and off ran the others to see, and there stood the grass thick and deep, as it was the year before; but they didn't give Boots softer words for all that.

Now, when the third St. John's eve came, the two elder still hadn't the heart to lie out in the barn and watch the grass, for they had got so scared at heart the night they lay there before, that they couldn't get over the fright; but Boots, he dared to go; and, to make a long story short, the very same thing happened this time as had happened twice before. Three earthquakes came, one after the other, each worse than the one which went before, and when the last came, the lad danced about with the shock from one barn wall to the other; and after that, all at once, it was still as death. Now when he had lain a little while he heard something tugging away at the grass outside the barn, so he stole again to the door-chink, and peeped out, and there stood a horse close outside—far, far bigger and fatter than the two he had taken before.

"Ho, ho!" said the lad to himself, "it's you, is it, that comes here eating up our hay? I'll soon stop that—I'll soon put a spoke in your wheel." So he caught up his steel and threw it over the horse's neck, and in a trice it stood as if it were nailed to the ground, and Boots could do as he pleased with it. Then he rode off with it to the hiding-place where he kept the other two, and then went home. When he got home his two brothers made game of him as they had done before, saying they could see he had watched the grass well, for he looked for all the world as if he were walking in his sleep, and many other spiteful things they said, but Boots gave no heed to them, only asking them to go and see for themselves; and when they went, there stood the grass as fine and deep this time as it had been twice before.

Now, you must know that the king of the country where Boots lived had a daughter, whom he would only give to the man who could ride up over the hill of glass, for there was a high, high hill, all of glass, as smooth and slippery as ice, close by the king's palace. Upon the tip-top of the hill the king's daughter was to sit, with three golden apples in her lap, and the man who could ride up and carry off the three golden apples was to have half the kingdom, and the Princess to wife. This the king had stuck up on all the church-doors in his realm, and had given it out in many other kingdoms besides. Now, this Princess was so lovely that all who set eyes on her fell over head and ears in love with her whether they would or no. So I needn't tell you how all the princes and knights who heard of her were eager to win her to wife, and half the kingdom beside; and how they came riding from all parts of the world on high prancing horses, and clad in the grandest clothes, for there wasn't one of them who hadn't made up his mind that he, and he alone, was to win the Princess.

So when the day of trial came, which the king had fixed, there was such a crowd of princes and knights under the glass hill, that it made one's head whirl to look at them; and everyone in the country who could even crawl along was off to the hill, for they all were eager to see the man who was to win the Princess. So the two elder brothers set off with the rest; but as for Boots, they said outright he shouldn't go with them, for if they were seen with such a dirty changeling, all begrimed with smut from cleaning their shoes and sifting cinders in the dusthole, they said folk would make game of them.

"Very well," said Boots, "it's all one to me. I can go alone, and stand or fall by myself."

Now when the two brothers came to the hill of glass the knights and princes were all hard at it, riding their horses till they were all in a foam; but it was no good, by my troth; for as soon as ever the horses set foot on the hill, down they slipped, and there wasn't one who could get a yard or two up; and no wonder, for the hill was as smooth as a sheet of glass, and as steep as a house-wall. But all were eager to have the Princess and half the kingdom. So they rode and slipped, and slipped and rode, and still it was the same story over again. At last all their horses were so weary that they could scarce lift a leg, and in such a sweat that the lather dripped from them, and so the knights had to give up trying any more. So the king was just thinking that he would proclaim a new trial for the next day, to see if they would have better luck, when all at once a knight came riding up on so brave a steed that no one had ever seen the like of it in his born days, and the knight had mail of brass, and the horse a brass bit in his mouth, so bright that the sunbeams shone from it. Then all the others

called out to him he might just as well spare himself the trouble of riding at the hill, for it would lead to no good; but he gave no heed to them, and put his horse at the hill, and went up it like nothing for a good way, about a third of the height; and when he had got so far, he turned his horse round and rode down again. So lovely a knight the Princess thought she had never yet seen; and while he was riding, she sat and thought to herself,

"Would to heaven he might only come up, and down the other side."

And when she saw him turning back, she threw down one of the golden apples after him, and it rolled down into his shoe. But when he got to the bottom of the hill he rode off so fast that no one could tell what had become of him. That evening all the knights and princes were to go before the king, that he who had ridden so far up the hill might show the apple which the Princess had thrown, but there was no one who had anything to show. One after the other they all came, but not a man of them could show the apple.

At even the brothers of Boots came home too, and had such a long story to tell about the riding up the hill.

"First of all," they said, "there was not one of the whole lot who could get so much as a stride up; but at last came one who had a suit of brass mail, and a brass bridle and saddle, all so bright that the sun shone from them a mile off. He was a chap to ride, just! He rode a third of the way up the hill of glass, and he could easily have ridden the whole way up, if he chose; but he turned round and rode down, thinking, maybe, that was enough for once."

"Oh! I should so like to have seen him, that I should," said Boots, who sat by the fireside, and stuck his feet into the cinders as was his wont.

"Oh!" said his brothers, "you would, would you? You look fit to keep company with such high lords, nasty beast that you are, sitting there amongst the ashes."

Next day the brothers were all for setting off again, and Boots begged them this time, too, to let him go with them and see the riding; but no, they wouldn't have him at any price, he was too ugly and nasty, they said.

"Well, well!" said Boots; "if I go at all, I must go by myself. I'm not afraid."

So when the brothers got to the hill of glass, all the princes and knights began to ride again, and you may fancy they had taken care to shoe their horses sharp; but it was no good—they rode and slipped, and slipped and rode, just as they had done the day before, and there was not one who could get so far as a yard up the hill. And when they had worn out their horses, so that they could not stir a leg, they were all forced to give it up as a bad job. So the king thought he might as well proclaim that the riding should take place the day after for the last time, just to give them one chance more; but all at once it came across his mind that he might as well wait a little longer, to see if the knight in brass mail would come this day too. Well, they saw nothing of him; but all at once came one riding on a steed, far, far, braver and finer than that on which the knight in brass had ridden, and he had silver mail, and a silver saddle and bridle, all so bright that the sunbeams gleamed and glanced from them far away. Then the others shouted out to him again, saying he might as well hold hard, and not try to ride up the hill, for all his trouble would be thrown away; but the knight paid no heed to them, and rode straight at the hill, and right up it, till he had gone two-thirds of the way, and then he wheeled his horse round and rode down again. To tell the truth, the Princess liked him still better than the knight in brass, and she sat and wished he might only be able to come right up to the top, and down the other side; but when she saw him turning back, she threw the second apple after him, and it rolled down and fell into his shoe. But as soon as ever he had come down from the hill of glass, he rode off so fast that no one could see what became of him.

At even, when all were to go in before the king and the Princess, that he who had the golden apple might show it, in they went, one after the other, but there was no one who had any apple to show, and the two brothers, as they had done on the former day, went home and told how things had gone, and how all had ridden at the hill and none got up.

"But, last of all," they said, "came one in a silver suit, and his horse had a silver saddle and a silver bridle. He was just a chap to ride; and he got two-thirds up the hill, and then turned back. He was a fine fellow and no mistake; and the Princess threw the second gold apple to him."

"Oh!" said Boots, "I should so like to have seen him too, that I should."

"A pretty story!" they said. "Perhaps you think his coat of mail was as bright as the ashes you are always poking about and sifting, you nasty dirty beast."

The third day everything happened as it had happened the two days before. Boots begged to go and see the sight, but the two wouldn't hear of his going with them. When they got to the hill there was no one who could get so much as a yard up it; and now all waited for the knight in silver mail, but they neither saw nor heard of him. At last came one riding on a steed, so brave that no one had ever seen his match; and the knight had a suit of golden mail, and a golden saddle and bridle, so wondrous bright that the sunbeams gleamed from them a mile off. The other knights and princes could not find time to call out to him not to try his luck, for they were amazed to see how grand he was. So he rode right at the hill, and tore up it like nothing, so that the Princess hadn't even time to wish that he might get up the whole way. As soon as ever he reached the top, he took the third golden apple from the Princess' lap, and then turned his horse and rode down again. As soon as he got down, he rode off at full speed, and was out of sight in no time.

Now, when the brothers got home at even, you may fancy what long stories they told, how the riding had gone off that day; and amongst other things, they had a deal to say about the knight in golden mail.

"He just was a chap to ride!" they said; "so grand a knight isn't to be found in the wide world."

"Oh!" said Boots, "I should so like to have seen him; that I should."

"Ah!" said his brothers, "his mail shone a deal brighter than the glowing coals which you are always poking and digging at; nasty dirty beast that you are."

Next day all the knights and princes were to pass before the king and the Princess—it was too late to do so the night before, I suppose—that he who had the gold apple might bring it forth; but one came after another, first the princes and then the knights, and still no one could show the gold apple.

"Well," said the king, "some one must have it, for it was something that we all saw with our own eyes, how a man came and rode up and bore it off."

So he commanded that every one who was in the kingdom should come up to the palace and see if they could show the apple. Well, they all came, one after another, but no one had the golden apple, and after a long time the two brothers of Boots came. They were the last of all, so the king asked them if there was no one else in the kingdom who hadn't come.

"Oh, yes," said they; "we have a brother, but he never carried off the golden apple. He hasn't stirred out of the dust-hole on any of the three days."

"Never mind that," said the king; "he may as well come up to the palace like the rest."

So Boots had to go up to the palace.

"How, now," said the king; "have you got the golden apple? Speak out!"

"Yes, I have," said Boots; "here is the first, and here is the second, and here is the third too"; and with that he pulled all three golden apples out of his pocket, and at the same time threw off his sooty rags, and stood before them in his gleaming golden mail.

"Yes!" said the king; "you shall have my daughter, and half my kingdom, for you well deserve both her and it."

So they got ready for the wedding, and Boots got the Princess to wife, and there was great merry-making at the bridal-feast, you may fancy, for they could all be merry though they couldn't ride up the hill of glass; and all I can say is, if they haven't left off their merry-making yet, why, they're still at it.

GUDBRAND ON THE HILL-SIDE

(Norwegian)

This story was retold in inimitable fashion by Hans Christian Andersen in his "What the Good-Man Does Is Sure to Be Right!" and is also found in the folklore of many European countries. The sly humor and tenderness of "Gud-brand on the Hill-Side" are beautifully interpreted by Mrs. Gudrun Thorne-Thomsen in her recording of it for the American Library Association.

Once on a time there was a man whose name was Gudbrand; he had a farm which lay far, far away, upon a hill-side, and so they called him Gudbrand on the Hill-side.

Now, you must know this man and his goodwife lived so happily together, and understood one another so well, that all the husband did the wife thought so well done, there was nothing like it in the world, and she was always glad whatever he turned his hand to. The farm was their own land, and they had a hundred dollars lying at the bottom of their chest, and two cows tethered up in a stall in their farmyard.

So one day his wife said to Gudbrand, "Do you know, dear, I think we ought to take one of our cows into town and sell it; that's what I think; for then we shall have some money in hand, and such well-to-do people as we ought to have ready money like the rest of the world. As for the hundred dollars at the bottom of the chest yonder, we can't make a hole in them, and I'm sure I don't know what we want with more than one cow. Besides, we shall gain a little in another way, for then I shall get off with only looking after one cow, instead of having, as now, to feed and litter and water two."

Well, Gudbrand thought his wife talked right good sense, so he set off at once with the cow on his way to town to sell her; but when he got to the town, there was no one who would buy his cow.

"Well, well! never mind," said Gudbrand, "at the worst, I can only go back home again with my cow. I've both stable and tether for her, I should think, and the road is no farther out than in"; and with that he began to toddle home with his cow.

But when he had gone a bit of the way, a man met him who had a horse to sell, so Gudbrand thought 'twas better to have a horse than a cow, so he swopped with the man. A little farther on he met a man walking along and driving a fat

"Gudbrand on the Hill-Side." From *Popular Tales from the Norse*, by Peter Christian Asbjörnsen and Jörgen Moe, translated by Sir George Webbe Dasent. David Douglas, Edinburgh, 1888

pig before him, and he thought it better to have a fat pig than a horse, so he swopped with the man. After that he went a little farther, and a man met him with a goat; so he thought it better to have a goat than a pig, and he swopped with the man that owned the goat. Then he went on a good bit till he met a man who had a sheep, and he swopped with him too, for he thought it always better to have a sheep than a goat. After a while he met a man with a goose, and he swopped away the sheep for the goose; and when he had walked a long, long time, he met a man with a cock, and he swopped with him, for he thought in this wise, " 'Tis surely better to have a cock than a goose." Then he went on till the day was far spent, and he began to get very hungry, so he sold the cock for a shilling, and bought food with the money, for, thought Gudbrand on the Hill-side, " 'Tis always better to save one's life than to have a cock."

After that he went on home till he reached his nearest neighbour's house, where he turned in.

"Well," said the owner of the house, "how did things go with you in town?"

"Rather so so," said Gudbrand. "I can't praise my luck, nor do I blame it either," and with that he told the whole story from first to last.

"Ah!" said his friend, "you'll get nicely called over the coals, that one can see, when you get home to your wife. Heaven help you, I wouldn't stand in your shoes for something."

"Well," said Gudbrand on the Hill-side, "I think things might have gone much worse with me; but now, whether I have done wrong or not, I have so kind a goodwife, she never has a word to say against anything that I do."

"Oh!" answered his neighbour, "I hear what you say, but I don't believe it for all that."

"Shall we lay a bet upon it?" asked Gudbrand on the Hill-side. "I have a hundred dollars at the bottom of my chest at home; will you lay as many against them?"

Yes, the friend was ready to bet; so Gudbrand stayed there till evening, when it began to get dark, and then they went together to his house, and the neighbour was to stand outside the door and listen, while the man went in to see his wife.

"Good evening!" said Gudbrand on the Hill-side.

"Good evening!" said the goodwife. "Oh, is that you? Now God be praised."

Yes, it was he. So the wife asked how things had gone with him in town.

"Oh, only so so," answered Gudbrand; "not much to brag of. When I got to the town there was no one who would buy the cow, so you must know I swopped it away for a horse."

"For a horse," said his wife; "well, that is good of you; thanks with all my heart. We are so well-to-do that we may drive to church, just as well as other people; and if we choose to keep a horse we have a right to get one, I should think. So run out, child, and put up the horse."

"Ah!" said Gudbrand, "but you see I've not got the horse after all; for when I got a bit farther on the road I swopped it away for a pig."

"Think of that, now!" said the wife; "you did just as I should have done myself; a thousand thanks! Now I can have a bit of bacon in the house to set before people when they come to see me, that I can. What do we want with a horse? People would only say we had got so proud that we couldn't walk to church. Go out, child, and put up the pig in the stye."

"But I've not got the pig either," said Gudbrand; "for when I got a little farther on I swopped it away for a milch goat."

"Bless us!" cried his wife, "how well you manage everything! Now I think it over, what should I do with a pig? People would only point at us and say, 'Yonder they eat up all they have got.' No! now I have got a goat, and I shall have milk and cheese, and keep the goat too. Run out, child, and put up the goat."

"Nay, but I haven't got the goat either," said Gudbrand, "for a little farther on I swopped it away, and got a fine sheep instead."

"You don't say so!" cried his wife; "why, you do everything to please me, just as if I had been with you; what do we want with a goat! If I had it I should lose half my time in climbing up the hills to get it down. No, if I have a sheep, I shall have both wool and clothing, and fresh meat in the house. Run out, child, and put up the sheep."

"But I haven't got the sheep any more than the rest," said Gudbrand; "for when I had gone a bit farther I swopped it away for a goose."

"Thank you! thank you! with all my heart," cried his wife; "what should I do with a sheep? I have no spinning-wheel, nor carding-comb, nor should I care to worry myself with cutting and shaping and sewing clothes. We can buy clothes now, as we have always done; and now I shall have roast goose, which I have longed for so often; and, besides, down to stuff my little pillow with. Run out, child, and put up the goose."

"Ah!" said Gudbrand, "but I haven't the goose either; for when I had gone a bit farther I swopped it away for a cock."

"Dear me!" cried his wife, "how you think of everything! just as I should have done myself. A cock! think of that! why it's as good as an eight-day clock, for every morning the cock crows at four o'clock, and we shall be able to stir our stumps in good time. What should we do with a goose? I don't know how to cook it; and as for my pillow, I can stuff it with cotton-grass. Run out, child, and put up the cock."

"But after all I haven't got the cock," said Gudbrand; "for when I had gone a bit farther, I got as hungry as a hunter, so I was forced to sell the cock for a shilling, for fear I should starve."

"Now, God be praised that you did so!" cried his wife; "whatever you do, you do it always just after my own heart. What should we do with the cock? We are our own masters, I should think, and can lie a-bed in the morning as long as we like. Heaven be thanked that I have got you safe back again; you who do everything so well that I want neither cock nor goose; neither pigs nor kine."

Then Gudbrand opened the door and said, "Well, what do you say now? Have I won the hundred dollars?" and his neighbour was forced to allow that he had.

THE HUSBAND WHO WAS TO MIND THE HOUSE

(*Norwegian*)

Wanda Gág made a delightful little book of this story and called it Gone Is Gone. *There is also an American folk-song version called "The Old Man in the Wood."*

Once on a time there was a man, so surly and cross, he never thought his wife did anything right in the house. So one evening, in hay-making time, he came home, scolding and swearing, and showing his teeth and making a dust.

"Dear love, don't be so angry; there's a good man," said his goody; "to-morrow let's change our work. I'll go out with the mowers and mow, and you shall mind the house at home."

Yes, the husband thought that would do very well. He was quite willing, he said.

So, early next morning, his goody took a scythe over her neck, and went out into the hay-field with the mowers and began to mow; but the man was to mind the house, and do the work at home.

First of all he wanted to churn the butter; but when he had churned a while, he got thirsty, and went down to the cellar to tap a barrel of ale. So, just when he had knocked in the bung, and was putting the tap into the cask, he heard overhead the pig come into the kitchen. Then off he ran up the cellar steps, with the tap in his hand, as fast as he could, to look after the pig, lest it

"The Husband Who Was to Mind the House." From *Popular Tales from the Norse,* by Peter Christian Asbjörnsen and Jörgen Moe, translated by Sir George Webbe Dasent. David Douglas, Edinburgh, 1888

should upset the churn; but when he got up he saw that the pig had already knocked the churn over and was routing and grunting amongst the cream, which was running all over the floor. He got so wild with rage that he quite forgot the ale-barrel, and ran at the pig as hard as he could. He caught it, too, just as it ran out of doors, and gave it such a kick that piggy lay for dead on the spot. Then all at once he remembered he had the tap in his hand; but when he got down to the cellar, every drop of ale had run out of the cask.

Then he went into the dairy and found enough cream left to fill the churn again, and so he began to churn, for butter they must have at dinner. When he had churned a bit, he remembered that their milking cow was still shut up in the byre, and hadn't had a bit to eat or a drop to drink all the morning, though the sun was high. Then all at once he thought 'twas too far to take her down to the meadow, so he'd just get her up on the house-top—for the house, you must know, was thatched with sods, and a fine crop of grass was growing there. Now their house lay close up against a steep down, and he thought if he laid a plank across to the thatch at the back he'd easily get the cow up.

But still he couldn't leave the churn, for there was his little babe crawling about on the floor, and "if I leave it," he thought, "the child is safe to upset it." So he took the churn on his back, and went out with it; but then he thought he'd better first water the cow before he turned her out on the thatch; so he took up a bucket to draw water out of the well; but, as he stooped down at the well's brink, all the cream ran out of the churn over his shoulders, and so down into the well.

Now it was near dinner-time, and he hadn't even got the butter yet; so he thought he'd best boil the porridge. He filled the pot with water and hung it over the fire. When he had done that, he thought the cow might perhaps fall off the thatch and break her legs or her neck. So he got up on the house to tie her up. One end of the rope he made fast to the cow's neck, and the other he slipped down the chimney and tied round his own thigh; and he had to make haste, for the water now began to boil in the pot, and he had still to grind the oatmeal.

So he began to grind away; but while he was hard at it, down fell the cow off the house top after all, and as she fell, she dragged the man up the chimney by the rope. There he stuck fast; and as for the cow, she hung halfway down the wall, swinging between heaven and earth, for she could neither get down nor up.

And now the goody had waited seven lengths and seven breadths for her husband to come and call them home to dinner; but never a call they had. At last she thought she'd waited long enough, and went home. But when she got there and saw the cow hanging in such an ugly place, she ran up and cut the rope in two with her scythe. But as she did this, down came her husband out of the chimney; and so when his old dame came inside the kitchen, there she found him standing on his head in the porridge-pot.

THE PRINCESS WHO COULD NOT BE SILENCED

(Norwegian)

For once a woman does not have the last word!—but no one much minds, since the ending is obviously happy for everybody. As in "Boots and His Brothers," the punishment of ear clipping or ear branding is one which children easily accept, if it is told matter-of-factly. Besides, the focus here is on the marvelous wit of the genial and intrepid Espen. Tell this with all the offhand dash of Espen himself.

There was once a king, and he had a daughter who was so cross and crooked in her words that no one could silence her, and so he gave it out that he who could do it should marry the princess and have half the kingdom, too. There were plenty of those who wanted to try it, I can tell you, for it is not every day that you can get a princess and half a kingdom. The gate to the king's palace did not stand still a minute. They came in great crowds from the East and the

"The Princess Who Could Not Be Silenced." From *East o' the Sun and West o' the Moon* by Gudrun Thorne-Thomsen. Reprinted with permission of Harper & Row, Publishers, Evanston

West, both riding and walking. But there was not one of them who could silence the princess.

At last the king had it given out that those who tried, and failed, should have both ears marked with the big red-hot iron with which he marked his sheep. He was not going to have all that flurry and worry for nothing.

Well, there were three brothers, who had heard about the princess, and, as they did not fare very well at home, they thought they had better set out to try their luck and see if they could not win the princess and half the kingdom. They were friends and good fellows, all three of them, and they set off together.

When they had walked a bit of the way, Espen picked up something.

"I've found—I've found something!" he cried.

"What did you find?" asked the brothers.

"I found a dead crow," said he.

"Ugh! Throw it away! What would you do with that?" said the brothers, who always thought they knew a great deal.

"Oh, I haven't much to carry, I might as well carry this," said Espen.

So when they had walked on a bit, Espen again picked up something.

"I've found—I've found something!" he cried.

"What have you found now?" said the brothers.

"I found a willow twig," said he.

"Dear, what do you want with that? Throw it away!" said they.

"Oh, I haven't much to carry, I might as well carry that," said Espen.

So when they had walked a bit, Espen picked up something again. "Oh, lads, I've found—I've found something!" he cried.

"Well, well, what did you find this time?" asked the brothers.

"A piece of a broken saucer," said he.

"Oh, what is the use of that? Throw it away!" said they.

"Oh, I haven't much to carry, I might as well carry that," said Espen.

And when they had walked a bit farther, Espen stooped down again and picked up something else.

"I've found—I've found something, lads!" he cried.

"And what is it now?" said they.

"Two goat horns," said Espen.

"Oh! Throw them away. What could you do with them?" said they.

"Oh, I haven't much to carry, I might as well carry them," said Espen.

In a little while he found something again.

"Oh, lads, see, I've found—I've found something," he cried.

"Dear, dear, what wonderful things you do find! What is it now?" said the brothers.

"I've found a wedge," said he.

"Oh, throw it away. What do you want with that?" said they.

"Oh, I haven't much to carry, I might as well carry that," said Espen.

And now, as they walked over the fields close up to the King's palace, Espen bent down again and held something in his fingers.

"Oh, lads, lads, see what I've found!" he cried.

"If you only found a little common sense, it would be good for you," said they. "Well, let's see what it is now."

"A worn-out shoe sole," said he.

"Pshaw! Well, that was something to pick up! Throw it away! What do you want with that?" said the brothers.

"Oh, I haven't much to carry, I might as well carry that, if I am to win the princess and half the kingdom," said Espen.

"Yes, you are likely to do that—you," said they.

And now they came to the king's palace. The eldest one went in first.

"Good-day," said he.

"Good-day to you," said the princess, and she twisted and turned.

"It's awfully hot here," said he.

"It is hotter over there in the hearth," said the princess. There lay the red-hot iron ready awaiting. When he saw that he forgot every word he was going to say, and so it was all over with him.

And now came the next eldest one. "Good-day," said he.

"Good-day to you," said she, and she turned and twisted herself.

"It's awfully hot here," said he.

"It's hotter over there in the hearth," said she. And when he looked at the red-hot iron he, too, couldn't get a word out, and so they marked his ears and sent him home again.

Then it was Espen's turn. "Good-day," said he.

"Good-day to you," said she, and she twisted and turned again.

"It's nice and warm in here," said Espen.

"It's hotter in the hearth," said she, and she was no sweeter, now the third one had come.

"That's good, I may bake my crow there, then?" asked he.

"I'm afraid she'll burst," said the princess.

"There's no danger; I'll wind this willow twig around," said the lad.

"It's too loose," said she.

"I'll stick this wedge in," said the lad, and took out the wedge.

"The fat will drop off," said the princess.

"I'll hold this under," said the lad, and pulled out the broken bit of the saucer.

"You are crooked in your words, that you are," said the princess.

"No, I'm not crooked, but this is crooked," said the lad, and he showed her the goat's horn.

"Well, I never saw the like!" cried the princess.

"Oh, here is the like of it," said he, and pulled out the other.

"Now, you think you'll wear out my soul, don't you?" said she.

"No, I won't wear out your soul, for I have a sole that's worn out already," said the lad, and pulled out the shoe sole.

Then the princess hadn't a word to say.

"Now, you're mine," said Espen. And so she was.

LITTLE FREDDY
WITH HIS FIDDLE

(Norwegian)

The Scandinavian tales are full of magic objects which assist those resourceful persons who learn how to use them. Freddy's fiddle is one of the gayest of these.

Once on a time there was a cottager who had an only son, and this lad was weakly and hadn't much health to speak of; so he couldn't go out to work in the field.

His name was Freddy, and undersized he was, too; and so they called him Little Freddy. At home there was little either to bite or sup, and so his father went about the country trying to bind him over as a cowherd or an errand-boy; but there was no one who would take his son till he came to the sheriff, and he was ready to take him, for he had just packed off his errand-boy, and there was no one who would fill his place, for the story went that he was a skinflint.

But the cottager thought it was better there than nowhere: Freddy would get his food, for all he was to get was his board—there was nothing said about wages or clothes. So when the lad had served three years he wanted to leave, and then the sheriff gave him all his wages at one time. He was to have a penny a year. "It couldn't well be less," said the sheriff. And so he got threepence in all.

As for little Freddy, he thought it was a great sum, for he had never owned so much; but for all that he asked if he wasn't to have something more.

"You have already had more than you ought to have," said the sheriff.

"Sha'n't I have anything, then, for clothes?" asked little Freddy; "for those I had on when I came here are worn to rags, and I have had no new ones."

And, to tell the truth, he was so ragged that the tatters hung and flapped about him.

"When you have got what we agreed on," said the sheriff, "and three whole pennies beside, I have nothing more to do with you. Be off!"

But for all that he got leave just to go into the kitchen and get a little food to put in his scrip; and after that he set off on the road to buy himself more clothes. He was both merry and glad, for he had never seen a penny before; and every now and then he felt in his pockets as he went along to see if he had them all three. So when he

"Little Freddy with His Fiddle." From *Tales from the Fjeld,* from the Norse of Peter Christian Asbjörnsen and Jörgen Moe, translated by Sir George Webbe Dasent. Chapman and Hall, London, 1874

had gone far, and farther than far, he got into a narrow dale, with high fells on all sides, so that he couldn't tell if there were any way to pass out; and he began to wonder what there could be on the other side of those fells, and how he ever should get over them.

But up and up he had to go, and on he strode; he was not strong on his legs, and had to rest every now and then—and then he counted and counted how many pennies he had got. So when he had got quite up to the very top, there was nothing but a great plain overgrown with moss. There he sat him down, and began to see if his money were all right; and before he was aware of him a beggarman came up to him—and he was so tall and big that the lad began to scream and screech when he got a good look of him and saw his height and length.

"Don't you be afraid," said the beggarman; "I'll do you no harm; I only beg for a penny, in God's name."

"Heaven help me!" said the lad. "I have only three pennies, and with them I was going to the town to buy clothes."

"It is worse for me than for you," said the beggarman. "I have got no penny, and I am still more ragged than you."

"Well! then you shall have it," said the lad.

So when he had walked on awhile he got weary, and sat down to rest again. But when he looked up there he saw another beggarman, and he was still taller and uglier than the first; and so when the lad saw how very tall and ugly and long he was he fell a-screeching.

"Now, don't you be afraid of me," said the beggar; "I'll not do you any harm. I only beg for a penny, in God's name."

"Now, may heaven help me!" said the lad. "I've only got two pence, and with them I was going to the town to buy clothes. If I had only met you sooner, then——"

"It's worse for me than for you," said the beggarman. "I have no penny, and a bigger body and less clothing."

"Well, you may have it," said the lad.

So he went awhile farther, till he got weary, and then he sat down to rest; but he had scarce sat down than a third beggarman came to him. He was so tall and ugly and long, that the lad had to look up and up, right up to the sky. And

when he took him all in with his eyes, and saw how very, very tall and ugly and ragged he was he fell a-screeching and screaming again.

"Now, don't you be afraid of me, my lad," said the beggarman. "I'll do you no harm; for I am only a beggarman, who begs for a penny in God's name."

"May heaven help me!" said the lad. "I have only one penny left, and with it I was going to the town to buy clothes. If I had only met you sooner, then—"

"As for that," said the beggarman, "I have no penny at all—that I haven't, and a bigger body and less clothes, so it is worse for me than for you."

"Yes!" said little Freddy, he must have the penny then—there was no help for it; for so each would have what belonged to him, and he would have nothing.

"Well!" said the beggarman, "since you have such a good heart that you gave away all that you had in the world, I will give you a wish for each penny." For you must know it was the same beggarman who had got them all three; he had only changed his shape each time, that the lad might not know him again.

"I have always had such a longing to hear a fiddle go, and see folk so glad and merry that they couldn't help dancing," said the lad; "and so, if I may wish what I choose, I will wish myself such a fiddle, that everything that has life must dance to its tune."

"That you may have," said the beggarman; "but it was a sorry wish. You must wish something better for the other two pennies."

"I have always had such a love for hunting and shooting," said little Freddy; "so if I may wish what I choose, I will wish myself such a gun that I shall hit everything I aim at, were it ever so far off."

"That you may have," said the beggarman; "but it was a sorry wish. You must wish better for the last penny."

"I have always had a longing to be in company with folk who were kind and good," said little Freddy; "and so, if I could get what I wish, I would wish it to be so that no one can say nay to the first thing I ask."

"That wish was not so sorry," said the beggarman; and off he strode between the hills, and he saw him no more. And so the lad laid down to sleep, and the next day he came down from the fell with his fiddle and his gun.

First he went to the storekeeper and asked for clothes, and at one farm he asked for a horse, and at another for a sledge; and at this place he asked for a fur-coat, and no one said him nay—even the stingiest folk were all forced to give him what he asked for. At last he went through the country as a fine gentleman, and had his horse and his sledge; and so when he had gone a bit he met the sheriff with whom he had served.

"Good-day, master," said little Freddy, as he pulled up and took off his hat.

"Good-day," said the sheriff. And then he went on, "When was I ever your master?"

"Oh, yes!" said little Freddy. "Don't you remember how I served you three years for three pence?"

"Heaven help us!" said the sheriff. "How you have got on all of a hurry! And pray how was it that you got to be such a fine gentleman?"

"Oh, that's telling!" said little Freddy.

"And are you full of fun, that you carry a fiddle about with you?" asked the sheriff.

"Yes! yes!" said Freddy. "I have always had such a longing to get folk to dance; but the funniest thing of all is this gun, for it brings down almost anything that I aim at, however far it may be off. Do you see that magpie yonder, sitting in the spruce fir? What'll you bet I don't bag it, as we stand here?"

On that the sheriff was ready to stake horse and groom, and a hundred dollars besides, that he couldn't do it; but, as it was, he would bet all the money he had about him; and he would go to fetch it when it fell—for he never thought it

possible for any gun to carry so far.

But as the gun went off down fell the magpie, and into a great bramble thicket; and away went the sheriff up into the brambles after it, and he picked it up and showed it to the lad. But in a trice little Freddy began to scrape his fiddle, and the sheriff began to dance, and the thorns to tear him; but still the lad played on, and the sheriff danced and cried and begged till his clothes flew to tatters, and he scarce had a thread to his back.

"Yes!" said little Freddy; "now I think you're about as ragged as I was when I left your service. So now you may get off with what you have got."

But, first of all, the sheriff had to pay him what he had wagered that he could not hit the magpie.

So when the lad came to the town he turned aside into an inn, and he began to play, and all who came danced, and he lived merrily and well. He had no care, for no one could say him nay to anything he asked.

But just as they were all in the midst of their fun, up came the watchmen to drag the lad off to the town-hall; for the sheriff had laid a charge against him, and said he had waylaid him and robbed him, and nearly taken his life. And now he was to be hanged—they would not hear of anything else. But little Freddy had a cure for all trouble, and that was his fiddle. He began to play on it, and the watchmen fell a-dancing, till they lay down and gasped for breath.

So they sent soldiers and the guard on their way; but it was no better with them than with the watchmen. As soon as ever little Freddy scraped his fiddle, they were all bound to dance,

so long as he could lift a finger to play a tune; but they were half dead long before he was tired. At last they stole a march on him, and took him while he lay asleep by night; and when they had caught him he was doomed to be hanged on the spot, and away they hurried him to the gallows-tree.

There a great crowd of people flocked together to see this wonder, and the sheriff, too, was there; and he was so glad at last at getting amends for the money and the skin he had lost, and that he might see him hanged with his own eyes. But they did not get little Freddie to the gallows very fast, for he was always weak on his legs, and now he made himself weaker still. His fiddle and his gun he had with him also—it was hard to part him from them; and so, when he came to the gallows and had to mount the steps, he halted on each step; and when he got to the top he sat down, and asked if they could deny him a wish, and if he might have leave to do one thing? He had such a longing, he said, to scrape a tune and play a bar on his fiddle before they hanged him.

"No! no!" they said. "It were sin and shame to deny him that." For, you know, no one could gainsay what he asked.

But the sheriff he begged them, for God's sake, not to let him have leave to touch a string, else it was all over with them altogether; and if the lad got leave, the sheriff begged them to bind him to the birch that stood there.

So little Freddy was not slow in getting his fiddle to speak, and all that were there fell a-dancing at once—those who went on two legs, and those who went on four; both the dean and the parson, and the lawyer, and the bailiff, and the sheriff; masters and men, dogs and swine, they all danced and laughed and screeched at one another. Some danced till they lay for dead; some danced till they fell into a swoon. It went badly with all of them, but worst of all with the sheriff, for there he stood bound to the birch, and he danced and scraped great bits off his back against the trunk. There was not one of them who thought of doing anything to little Freddy, and away he went with his fiddle and his gun, just as he chose; and he lived merrily and happily all his days, for there was no one who could say him nay to the first thing he asked for.

EAST O' THE SUN AND WEST O' THE MOON

(Norwegian)

This story, which is "Cupid and Psyche" in Norse dress, might well be a fragment of an ancient myth, with the polar bear an obvious symbol of winter in a northern country. The tale is also pure romance and fulfills the usual desires for food, warmth, luxury, security, and love.

Once on a time there was a poor husbandman who had so many children that he hadn't much of either food or clothing to give them. Pretty children they all were, but the prettiest was the youngest daughter, who was so lovely there was no end to her loveliness.

So one day, 'twas on a Thursday evening late at the fall of the year, the weather was so wild and rough outside, and it was so cruelly dark, and rain fell and wind blew, till the walls of the cottage shook again. There they all sat round the fire busy with this thing and that. But just then, all at once something gave three taps on the window-pane. Then the father went out to see what was the matter; and, when he got out of doors, what should he see but a great big White Bear.

"Good evening to you," said the White Bear.

"The same to you," said the man.

"Will you give me your youngest daughter? If you will, I'll make you as rich as you are now poor," said the Bear.

Well, the man would not be at all sorry to be so rich; but still he thought he must have a bit of a talk with his daughter first; so he went in and told them how there was a great White Bear waiting outside, who had given his word to make them so rich if he could only have the youngest daughter.

The lassie said "No!" outright. Nothing could get her to say anything else; so the man went out and settled it with the White Bear, that he should come again the next Thursday evening and get an answer. Meantime he talked his daughter over, and kept on telling her of all the riches they would get, and how well off she would be herself; and so at last she thought bet-

"East o' the Sun and West o' the Moon." From *Popular Tales from the Norse*, by Peter Christian Asbjörnsen and Jörgen Moe, translated by Sir George Webbe Dasent. David Douglas, Edinburgh, 1888

ter of it, and washed and mended her rags, made herself as smart as she could, and was ready to start. I can't say her packing gave her much trouble.

Next Thursday evening came the White Bear to fetch her, and she got upon his back with her bundle, and off they went. So, when they had gone a bit of the way, the White Bear said, "Are you afraid?"

No! she wasn't.

"Well! mind and hold tight by my shaggy coat, and then there's nothing to fear," said the Bear.

So she rode a long, long way, till they came to a great steep hill. There, on the face of it, the White Bear gave a knock, and a door opened, and they came into a castle, where there were many rooms all lit up; rooms gleaming with silver and gold; and there too was a table ready laid, and it was all as grand as grand could be. Then the White Bear gave her a silver bell; and when she wanted anything, she was only to ring it, and she would get it at once.

Well, after she had eaten and drunk, and evening wore on, she got sleepy after her journey, and thought she would like to go to bed, so she rang the bell; and she had scarce taken hold of it before she came into a chamber, where there was a bed made, as fair and white as any one would wish to sleep in, with silken pillows and curtains, and gold fringe. All that was in the room was gold or silver; but when she had gone to bed, and put out the light, she heard someone come into the next room. That was the White Bear, who threw off his beast shape at night; but she never saw him, for he always came after she had put out the light, and before the day dawned he was up and off again. So things went on happily for a while, but at last she began to get silent and sorrowful; for there she went about all day alone, and she longed to go home to see her father and mother and brothers and sisters. So one day, when the White Bear asked what it was that she lacked, she said it was so dull and lonely there that she longed to go home to see her father and mother and brothers and sisters, and that was why she was so sad and sorrowful, because she couldn't get to them.

"Well, well!" said the Bear, "perhaps there's a cure for all this; but you must promise me one thing, not to talk alone with your mother, but only when the rest are by to hear; for she'll take you by the hand and try to lead you into a room alone to talk; but you must mind and not do that, else you'll bring bad luck on both of us."

So one Sunday the White Bear came and said now they could set off to see her father and mother. Well, off they started, she sitting on his back; and they went far and long. At last they came to a grand house, and there her brothers and sisters were running about out of doors at play, and everything was so pretty, 'twas a joy to see.

"This is where your father and mother live now," said the White Bear; "but don't forget what I told you, else you'll make us both unlucky."

"No! bless me, I'll not forget." And when she had reached the house, the White Bear turned right about and left her.

Then when she went in to see her father and mother, there was such joy, there was no end to it. None of them thought they could thank her enough for all she had done for them. Now, they had everything they wished, as good as good could be, and they all wanted to know how she got on where she lived.

Well, she said, it was very good to live where she did; she had all she wished. What she said besides I don't know; but I don't think any of them had the right end of the stick, or that they got much out of her. But so in the afternoon, after they had done dinner, all happened as the White Bear had said. Her mother wanted to talk with her alone in her bed-room; but she minded what the White Bear had said, and wouldn't go up stairs.

"Oh, what we have to talk about will keep," she said, and put her mother off. But somehow or other, her mother got round her at last, and she had to tell her the whole story. So she said that every night, when she had gone to bed, someone came into the next room as soon as she had put out the light, and that she never saw him, because he was always up and away before the morning dawned; and how she went about woeful and sorrowing, for she thought she should so like to see him, and that all day long she walked about there alone, and that it was dull and dreary and lonesome.

"My!" said her mother; "it may well be a troll you heard! But now I'll teach you a lesson how to set eyes on him. I'll give you a bit of candle, which you can carry home in your bosom; just light that while he is asleep, but take care not to drop the tallow on him."

Yes! she took the candle, and hid it in her bosom, and as night drew on, the White Bear came and fetched her away.

But when they had gone a bit of the way, the White Bear asked if all hadn't happened as he had said.

Well, she couldn't say it hadn't.

"Now, mind," said he, "if you have listened to your mother's advice, you have brought bad luck on us both, and then, all that has passed between us will be as nothing."

"No," she said, "I didn't listen to my mother's advice."

So when she reached home, and had gone to bed, it was the old story over again. There came someone into the next room; but at dead of night, when she heard he slept, she got up and struck a light, lit the candle, went into the room, and let the light shine on him, and so she saw that he was the loveliest prince one ever set eyes on, and she fell so deep in love with him on the spot, that she thought she couldn't live if she didn't give him a kiss there and then. And so she did, but as she kissed him, she dropped three hot drops of tallow on his shirt, and he woke up.

"What have you done?" he cried; "now you have made us both unlucky, for had you held out only this one year, I had been freed. For I have a stepmother who has bewitched me, so that I am a white bear by day, and a man by night. But now all ties are snapt between us; now I must set off from you to her. She lives in a castle which stands EAST O' THE SUN AND WEST O' THE MOON, and there, too, is a princess, with a nose three ells long, and she's the wife I must have now."

She wept and took it ill, but there was no help for it; go he must.

Then she asked if she mightn't go with him.

No, she mightn't.

"Tell me the way, then," she said, "and I'll search you out; *that* surely I may get leave to do."

"Yes, you might do that," he said; "but there is no way to that place. It lies EAST O' THE SUN AND WEST O' THE MOON, and thither you'd never find your way."

So next morning, when she woke up, both prince and castle were gone, and then she lay on a little green patch, in the midst of the gloomy thick wood, and by her side lay the same bundle of rags she had brought with her from her old home.

So when she had rubbed the sleep out of her eyes, and wept till she was tired, she set out on her way, and walked many, many days, till she came to a lofty crag. Under it sat an old hag, who played with a gold apple which she tossed about. Her the lassie asked if she knew the way to the prince, who lived with his stepmother in the castle that lay EAST O' THE SUN AND WEST O' THE MOON, and who was to marry the princess with a nose three ells long.

"How did you come to know about him?" asked the old hag; "But maybe you are the lassie who ought to have had him?"

Yes, she was.

"So, so; it's you, is it?" said the old hag. "Well, all I know about him is that he lives in the castle that lies EAST O' THE SUN AND WEST O' THE MOON, and thither you'll come, late or never; but still you may have the loan of my horse, and on him you can ride to my next neighbour. Maybe she'll be able to tell you; and when you get there, just give the horse a switch under the left ear, and beg him to be off home; and, stay, this gold apple you may take with you."

So she got upon the horse, and rode a long, long time, till she came to another crag, under which sat another old hag, with a gold carding-comb. Her the lassie asked if she knew the way to the castle that lay EAST O' THE SUN AND WEST O' THE MOON, and she answered, like the first old hag, that she knew nothing about it, except it was east o' the sun and west o' the moon.

"And thither you'll come, late or never; but you shall have the loan of my horse to my next neighbour; maybe she'll tell you all about it; and when you get there, just switch the horse under the left ear, and beg him to be off home."

And this old hag gave her the golden carding-comb; it might be she'd find some use for it, she said. So the lassie got up on the horse, and rode a far, far way, and a weary time; and so at last she came to another great crag, under which sat another old hag, spinning with a golden spinning-wheel. Her, too, she asked if she knew the way to the prince, and where the castle was that lay EAST O' THE SUN AND WEST O' THE MOON. So it was the same thing over again.

"Maybe it's you who ought to have had the prince?" said the old hag.

Yes, it was.

But she, too, didn't know the way a bit better than the other two. "East o' the sun and west o' the moon it was," she knew—that was all.

"And thither you'll come, late or never; but I'll lend you my horse, and then I think you'd best ride to the East Wind and ask him; maybe he knows those parts, and can blow you thither. But when you get to him, you need only give the horse a switch under the left ear, and he'll trot home of himself."

And so, too, she gave her the gold spinning-wheel. "Maybe you'll find a use for it," said the old hag.

Then on she rode many, many days, a weary time, before she got to the East Wind's house, but at last she did reach it, and then she asked the East Wind if he could tell her the way to the prince who dwelt east o' the sun and west o' the moon. Yes, the East Wind had often heard tell of it, the prince, and the castle, but he couldn't tell the way, for he had never blown so far.

"But, if you will, I'll go with you to my brother the West Wind. Maybe he knows, for he's much stronger. So, if you will just get on my back, I'll carry you thither."

Yes, she got on his back, and I should just think they went briskly along.

So when they got there, they went into the West Wind's house, and the East Wind said the lassie he had brought was the one who ought to have had the prince who lived in the castle EAST O' THE SUN AND WEST O' THE MOON; and so she had set out to seek him, and how he had come with her, and would be glad to know if the West Wind knew how to get to the castle.

"Nay," said the West Wind, "so far I've never blown; but if you will, I'll go with you to our brother the South Wind, for he's much stronger than either of us, and he has flapped his wings far and wide. Maybe he'll tell you. You can get

on my back, and I'll carry you to him."

Yes! she got on his back, and so they travelled to the South Wind, and weren't so very long on the way, I should think.

When they got there, the West Wind asked him if he could tell her the way to the castle that lay EAST O' THE SUN AND WEST O' THE MOON, for it was she who ought to have had the prince who lived there.

"You don't say so! That's she, is it?" said the South Wind.

"Well, I have blustered about in most places in my time, but so far have I never blown; but if you will, I'll take you to my brother the North Wind; he is the oldest and strongest of the whole lot of us, and if he doesn't know where it is, you'll never find any one in the world to tell you. You can get on my back, and I'll carry you thither."

Yes! she got on his back, and away he went from his house at a fine rate. And this time, too, she wasn't long on her way.

So when they got to the North Wind's house, he was so wild and cross, cold puffs came from him a long way off.

"BLAST YOU BOTH, WHAT DO YOU WANT?" he roared out to them ever so far off, so that it struck them with an icy shiver.

"Well," said the South Wind, "you needn't be so foul-mouthed, for here I am, your brother, the South Wind, and here is the lassie who ought to have had the prince who dwells in the castle that lies EAST O' THE SUN AND WEST O' THE MOON, and now she wants to ask you if you ever were there, and can tell her the way, for she would be so glad to find him again."

"YES, I KNOW WELL ENOUGH WHERE IT IS," said the North Wind. "Once in my life I blew an aspen-leaf thither, but I was so tired I couldn't blow a puff for ever so many days after. But if you really wish to go thither, and aren't afraid to come along with me, I'll take you on my back and see if I can blow you thither."

Yes! with all her heart; she must and would get thither if it were possible in any way; and as for fear, however madly he went, she wouldn't be at all afraid.

"Very well, then," said the North Wind, "but you must sleep here to-night, for we must have the whole day before us, if we're to get thither at all."

Early next morning the North Wind woke her, and puffed himself up, and blew himself out, and made himself so stout and big, 'twas gruesome to look at him; and so off they went high up through the air, as if they would never stop till they got to the world's end.

Down here below there was such a storm; it threw down long tracts of wood and many houses, and when it swept over the great sea, ships foundered by hundreds.

So they tore on and on—no one can believe how far they went—and all the while they still went over the sea, and the North Wind got more and more weary, and so out of breath he could scarce bring out a puff, and his wings drooped and drooped, till at last he sunk so low that the crests of the waves dashed over his heels.

"Are you afraid?" said the North Wind.

No, she wasn't.

But they weren't very far from land; and the North Wind had still so much strength left in him that he managed to throw her up on the shore under the windows of the castle which lay EAST O' THE SUN AND WEST O' THE MOON; but then he was so weak and worn out, he had to

stay there and rest many days before he could get home again.

Next morning the lassie sat down under the castle window, and began to play with the gold apple; and the first person she saw was the long-nose who was to have the prince.

"What do you want for your gold apple, you lassie?" said the long-nose, and threw up the window.

"It's not for sale, for gold or money," said the lassie.

"If it's not for sale for gold or money, what is it that you will sell it for? You may name your own price," said the princess.

"Well! if I may get to the prince, who lives here, and be with him to-night, you shall have it," said the lassie whom the North Wind had brought.

Yes! she might; that could be done. So the princess got the gold apple; but when the lassie came up to the prince's bed-room at night he was fast asleep; she called him and shook him, and between whiles she wept sore; but all she could do she couldn't wake him up. Next morning as soon as day broke, came the princess with the long nose, and drove her out again.

So in the day-time she sat down under the castle windows and began to card with her golden carding-comb, and the same thing happened. The princess asked what she wanted for it; and she said it wasn't for sale for gold or money, but if she might get leave to go up to the prince and be with him that night, the princess should have it. But when she went up she found him fast asleep again, and all she called, and all she shook, and wept, and prayed, she couldn't get life into him; and as soon as the first gray peep of day came, then came the princess with the long nose and chased her out again.

So in the day-time the lassie sat down outside under the castle window, and began to spin with her golden spinning-wheel, and that, too, the princess with the long nose wanted to have. So she threw up the window and asked what she wanted for it. The lassie said, as she had said twice before, it wasn't for sale for gold or money; but if she might go up to the prince who was there, and be with him alone that night, she might have it.

Yes! she might do that and welcome. But now

you must know there were some folk who had been carried off thither, and as they sat in their room, which was next the prince, they had heard how a woman had been in there, and wept and prayed, and called to him two nights running, and they told that to the prince.

That evening, when the princess came with her sleepy drink, the prince made as if he drank, but threw it over his shoulder, for he could guess it was a sleepy drink. So, when the lassie came in, she found the prince wide awake; and then she told him the whole story how she had come thither.

"Ah," said the Prince, "you've just come in the very nick of time, for to-morrow is to be our wedding-day; but now I won't have the long-nose, and you are the only woman in the world who can set me free. I'll say I want to see what my wife is fit for, and beg her to wash the shirt which has the three spots of tallow on it; she'll say yes, for she doesn't know 'tis you who put them there; but that's a work only for Christian folk, and not for such a pack of trolls, and so I'll say that I won't have any other for my bride than the woman who can wash them out, and ask you to do it."

Next day, when the wedding was to be, the prince said, "First of all, I'd like to see what my bride is fit for."

"Yes!" said the step-mother, with all her heart.

"Well," said the prince, "I've got a fine shirt which I'd like for my wedding shirt, but somehow or other it has got three spots of tallow on it, which I must have washed out; and I have sworn never to take any other bride than the woman who's able to do that. If she can't, she's not worth having."

Well, that was no great thing they said, so they agreed, and she with the long nose began to wash away as hard as she could, but the more she rubbed and scrubbed, the bigger the spots grew.

"Ah!" said the old hag, her mother, "you can't wash; let me try."

But she hadn't long taken the shirt in hand, before it got far worse than ever, and with all her rubbing and wringing and scrubbing, the spots grew bigger and blacker, and the darker and uglier was the shirt.

Then all the other trolls began to wash, but the longer it lasted, the blacker and uglier the shirt grew, till at last it was as black all over as if it had been up the chimney.

"Ah!" said the prince, "you're none of you worth a straw; you can't wash. Why there, outside, sits a beggar lassie. I'll be bound she knows how to wash better than the whole lot of you. COME IN, LASSIE!" he shouted.

Well, in she came.

"Can you wash this shirt clean, lassie, you?" said he.

"I don't know," she said, "but I think I can."

And almost before she had taken it and dipped it in the water, it was as white as driven snow, and whiter still.

"Yes; you are the lassie for me," said the prince.

At that the old hag flew into such a rage, she burst on the spot, and the princess with the long nose after her, and the whole pack of trolls after her—at least I've never heard a word about them since.

As for the prince and princess, they set free all the folk who had been carried off and shut up there; and they took with them all the silver and gold, and flitted away as far as they could from the castle that lay EAST O' THE SUN AND WEST O' THE MOON.

THE OLD WOMAN AND THE TRAMP

(Swedish)

As this tale well demonstrates, greedy people may be crafty, but they are essentially stupid. This idea is handled with a light touch. Marcia Brown's Stone Soup *presents it in terms of three French soldiers, who, in pursuit of a good meal, outwit an entire village.*

A tramp was once plodding along on his way through a forest. The distance between the

"The Old Woman and the Tramp." From *Favorite Fairy Tales Told in Sweden* by Virginia Haviland, by permission of Little, Brown and Co. Text Copyright © 1966 by Virginia Haviland

houses there was so great that he knew he had little hope of finding shelter before night set in. But all of a sudden he saw bright lights shining between the trees. He discovered a cottage with a brisk fire burning on the hearth. How good it would be, he thought, to toast himself before that blaze, and to find a bite of food! With this in mind, he dragged himself over to the cottage.

An old woman appeared at the door.

"Good evening, and well met!" said the tramp.

"Good evening," said the woman. "And where do you come from?"

"South of the sun, and east of the moon," said the tramp. "And now I am on the way home again, for I have been all over the world except in this parish."

"You must be a great traveler indeed," said the woman. "What may be your business here?"

"Oh, I want only a shelter for the night."

"I thought as much," said the woman. "But you may as well go away at once, for my husband is not at home and my cottage is not an inn."

"My good woman," said the tramp, "you must not be so hard-hearted. We are both human beings. It is written that we should help one another."

"Help one another?" said the woman. "Help? Did you ever hear of such a thing? Who will help me, do you think? I haven't a morsel in the house! No, you must look for shelter elsewhere."

But the tramp was like the rest of his kind. He would not consider himself beaten at the first rebuff. Although the old woman grumbled, he kept at it. He begged like a starved dog, until at last she gave in and granted him permission to lie on the floor for the night.

That was very kind, he thought, and he thanked her for it.

"It is better to lie on the floor without sleep than to suffer cold in the forest deep," he said. He was a merry fellow, this tramp, and always ready with a rhyming word.

When he entered the cottage he could see that the woman was not so badly off as she had pretended to be. She was just stingy and complaining.

The tramp tried to make himself agreeable as he asked her for something to eat.

"Where shall I get it?" asked the woman. "I haven't tasted a morsel the whole day."

But the tramp was a cunning fellow, he was.

"Poor old granny, you must be starving. Well, well, I suppose I shall have to ask you to have something with me, then."

"Have something with you!" said the woman. "You don't look as if you could ask anyone to have anything! What have you to offer, I should like to know?"

"He who far and wide does roam sees many things not known at home; and he who many things has seen has wits about him and senses keen," said the tramp, with more of his rhymes. "Better dead than to lose one's head! Lend me a pot, granny!"

The old woman had now grown curious, as you may guess. She let him have a big pot.

The tramp filled the pot with water and hung it over the fire. Then he blew and blew till the fire flared up brightly all around it. He took a four-inch nail from his pocket, carefully turned it around three times in his hand, and dropped it into the pot.

The woman stared. "What is this going to be?" she asked.

"Nail broth," said the tramp, and began to stir the water with the porridge whisk.

"Nail broth?" asked the woman.

"Yes, nail broth," said the tramp.

The old woman had seen and heard a good deal in her time, but that anybody could make broth with a nail, well, she had never heard the like of this before.

"That's something for poor people to know," she said, "and I should like to learn how to make it."

"That which is not worth having will always go a-begging," said the tramp.

But if she wanted to learn to make it she had only to watch him, he said, and went on stirring the broth.

The old woman squatted near the hearth, her hands clasping her knees and her eyes following the tramp's hand as he stirred the broth.

"This generally makes good broth," he said; "but this time it will very likely be rather thin, for this whole week I have been making broth with the same nail. If only I had a handful of sifted meal to add, that would make it all right. But what one has to go without, it's no use thinking more about," and once again he stirred the broth.

"Well, I think I have a scrap of flour somewhere," said the old woman. She went to fetch it, and it was both good and fine.

The tramp began stirring the flour into the broth and went on stirring and stirring, while the woman sat, staring now at him and then at the pot, until her eyes seemed nearly to burst from their sockets.

"This broth would be good enough for company," the tramp now announced, putting in one handful of flour after another, "if only I had a bit of salted beef and a few potatoes to add. Indeed, it would be fit for gentlefolk, however particular they might be. But what one has to go without, it's no use thinking more about."

The old woman began to consider this, and she remembered she had a few potatoes, and perhaps there was a bit of beef as well. These she found and gave to the tramp, who went on stirring and stirring, while she sat and stared as hard as ever.

"This will be grand enough for the best in the land," he said at last.

"Well, I never!" said the woman. "And just fancy—all that with a nail!"

"If we had only a little barley and a drop of milk, we could ask the King himself to sup some of this. This is what he has every evening. That I know, for I have been in service under the King's cook," he said.

"Dear me! Ask the King to have some! Well, I never!" exclaimed the woman, slapping her knees. She was quite overcome by the tramp and his grand connections.

"But what one has to go without, it's no use thinking more about," said the tramp.

And then the woman remembered she had a little barley. And as for milk, well, she wasn't quite out of that, she said, for her best cow had just calved. She went to fetch both the one and the other.

The tramp went on with his stirring, and the woman with her staring, one moment at him and the next at the pot.

Suddenly the tramp took out the nail.

"Now it's ready, and we'll have a real feast. But with this kind of soup the King and the Queen always have something to drink, and one sandwich at least. And then they always have a cloth on the table when they eat," he added. "But what one has to go without, it's no use thinking more about."

By this time the old woman herself had begun to feel quite grand, I can tell you. If that was all that was wanted to make the soup just as the King had it, she thought it would be nice to have it just the same way for once, and play at being King and Queen with the tramp. So she went to a cupboard and brought out a bottle and glasses, butter and cheese, smoked beef and veal, until at last the table looked as if it were decked out for company.

Never in her life had the old woman eaten such a grand feast, and never had she tasted such broth. Just fancy, made only with a nail! She was in such a merry humor at having learned such an economical way of making broth that she could not do enough for the tramp who had taught her such a useful thing.

The old woman and the tramp then ate and drank, and drank and ate, until their hunger was satisfied.

The tramp was ready to lie down on the floor to sleep. But that would never do, thought the old woman. No, that was impossible. Such a grand person must have a bed to lie in.

The tramp did not need much urging. "It's just like the sweet Christmas time. Happy are they who meet such good people." And he lay on the bed she offered him and went to sleep.

Next morning when the tramp awoke, the old woman was ready with coffee for him. And as he was leaving, she gave him a bright dollar piece.

"And thanks, many thanks, for what you have taught me," she said. "Now I shall live in comfort, since I have learned how to make broth with a nail."

"Well, it isn't very difficult, if one only has something good to add to it," said the tramp as he went on his way.

The woman stood at the door staring after him.

"Such people don't grow on every bush," she said.

Finland

*Of all the national groups, the Finns are said to have the largest collection
of folk tales in manuscript form. Unfortunately for us, most of these materials
are in Finnish or German or Swedish. The history of folklore and
folk-tale study in Finland is impressive and, as one scholar has said, predates the
actual establishment of Finland as an independent nation. The outstandingly
great name in the Finnish folklore study movement is that of Elias Lönnrot, who
published the illustrious* Kalevala, *a collection in two volumes of ancient
poetry and incantations. They make up a great folk epic that influenced the meter
of Longfellow's* Hiawatha. *Almost every Finn knows the* Kalevala *and
owns a copy of it. The Finnish "historic-geographic" method for folk-tale research
and study, developed in the late nineteenth century, has shaped much of the
folklore research that goes on in Europe, the United States, and other parts of the
world. For the highly literate Finns, as for no other people, folklore and folk
tales and folk songs are part and parcel of the national spirit, education, and pride.*

HIDDEN LAIVA or
THE GOLDEN SHIP

Men's dreams of flying are so graphically expressed in this story from Tales of a Finnish Tupa *that parts of it sound like a report of an airplane flight. The romance has some amusing ups and downs, but the princess seems to improve with age. A* tupa, *by the way, is a Finnish cottage, whose kitchen boasts an open fire, warmth, good food, and cheer, and is the center of most household life.*

In olden days there lived a woodsman whose name was Toivo. Every day, with his bow and arrows slung across his shoulder, he used to wander through the wild forests of Finland. One day in his wanderings he came to a high jagged mountain where no man had ever set foot before. For this was the mountain where the Gnomes lived, and there in a dark hidden cavern lay Hiitola, the Gnomes' home.

When the Gnomes saw Toivo, they all crowded round him and began shouting: "You come at just the right moment! If you will settle our quarrel and help us to divide our gold fairly between us, we will give you money and a golden ship."

"Hidden Laiva or the Golden Ship" from *Tales of a Finnish Tupa* by James Cloyd Bowman and Margery Bianco, through permission of Albert Whitman and Company

It happened that the parents of these Gnomes had died just a few days before, and the Gnomes had fallen heir to all their wealth. They were very busy trying to divide it up. The whole mountain side was strewn with golden spoons and golden dishes and golden carriages. There was a lot of money, too, great shining gold pieces lying all about. The Gnomes were very greedy; each wanted to have more than his own share and so they couldn't come to any agreement about it all.

Toivo stared about him at all this wealth strewn around. More beautiful than the dishes or carriages was a ship of gold that stood on a high rock shining in the sun. The ship caught Toivo's eye at once.

"How do you make this ship go?" he asked the Gnomes.

The largest of the Gnomes stepped forward. He had a turned-up nose, a shaggy pointed red beard and short bandy legs. He hopped into the golden ship and said:

"Why, you just lift this upper what-you-may-call-it with your hand, and push the lower one with your foot, and the ship will race with the wind like a wild tern."

As soon as Toivo had learned the trick, he made a bargain with the Gnomes.

"If you will give me the golden ship and fill it with golden spoons and dishes, and fill my pockets with money, I'll show you how to settle your quarrel."

"Agreed!" shouted the Gnomes, and they began scrambling about in a great hurry to do as he asked.

Toivo set an arrow to his bow and said:

"I am going to shoot an arrow, and the first one to find it will be your King. He will settle your affairs."

"That's wonderful! Now we'll be happy again," shouted the Gnomes.

Toivo stretched his bow and sent the arrow whistling through the air. All the Gnomes went rushing after it. Then Toivo jumped into the golden ship, he pulled with his hand and he pushed with his foot, there was a loud whir-rr, and the ship leaped down the steep mountain and far out across the sea.

Soon after, Toivo brought it to a perfect landing before the King's castle.

It happened that the King's daughter was on the castle steps at that very moment. She was sitting with her chin in her hands, dreaming of the day that some brave prince would come riding up to marry her, when all at once she saw the golden ship.

"This must surely be a prince from some wonderful country," she said to herself, "to come riding over land and sea in a ship like that!"

And she came dancing down the castle steps.

"Take me in your golden ship, dear Prince," she said, "and I will be your bride!"

But Toivo could only stammer, "Sweet Princess, you're making a big mistake. I'm merely Toivo, a common woodsman. I'm not good enough to touch the shoes on your feet. There are plenty of Kings' sons who would be glad and proud to be your husband!"

But the Princess was so excited about the golden ship and the golden spoons and the golden dishes that she didn't care whether Toivo was only a woodsman or what he was.

"It doesn't matter a bit," she said. "Take me in your ship, that's all, and I'll be your bride."

"You're making fun of me," Toivo answered her. "No one but a King's son would be good enough for the likes of you."

The Princess ran into the castle and back again, her arms heaped with costly clothes.

"Dress up in these," she laughed, "and you'll be a Prince too!" And back she ran to fetch food and drink.

Toivo was so humble he dared not even lay a finger on those fine clothes. He felt that he was not even good enough to be the Princess' servant. And he gazed at her in fear and trembling as she paced back and forth before the golden ship, begging him to marry her.

But at the end of seven days he saw that she was really unhappy because he refused her, so he said:

"Gentle Princess, if you really want to make a bargain with a humble woodsman, step into the ship."

As soon as she was seated, he fell on his knees and asked:

"Where would you like to sail, gentle Princess, in this golden ship?"

"To the very middle of the sea. I've heard tell there is an island there ten miles long where the berry bushes are loaded to the ground with red and purple fruit, and where the birds sing day and night."

Toivo pushed with his hand and pulled with his foot, and off flew the golden ship over land and sea. Soon it dived from the sky, right down to the center of an island, and stopped there. Toivo jumped out and ran to look for the purple and red berries.

The first berries that he found were yellow. Toivo tasted them, and before he knew what was happening he fell to the ground in a deep sleep. The Princess waited impatiently for him to come back. At first she thought he was lost. But after

three days she decided that he had deserted her, and she grew very angry.

"Die here, you low-bred knave!" she cried. "I shall turn the golden ship round and sail right home again."

So she pulled with her hand and pushed with her foot, and flew back to the castle, while poor Toivo still lay sprawled out on the ground fast asleep.

At the end of another day, Toivo woke up. He searched everywhere, but he could not find the golden ship nor the Princess. His beautiful golden spoons and dishes were gone, too. All he had left was a pocketful of money.

As he hunted high and low, he grew faint with hunger. Before him was a bush laden with purple berries. Toivo filled his left pocket with the fruit, thrust a berry into his mouth and began crunching it between his teeth. All at once he felt horns growing out from his head, monstrous pronged horns like the antlers of a wild moose. They were heavy and they hurt terribly.

"It would be better if I'd stayed hungry," he thought. "These horns are driving me crazy! If a ship should come, the sailors will take me for a wild beast and shoot me."

As he looked for some safe place in which to hide, he saw a bush with red berries on it. He filled his right pocket this time, and crunched one of the red berries between his teeth. No sooner had he done so than the heavy horns fell by magic from his head and he became the most handsome man in the world.

Next day a ship appeared over the edge of the sea. Toivo ran up and down the beach shouting to the sailors. "Take me with you, good friends, take me away before I die on this island. Bring me to the King's castle and I will pay you well."

The sailors gladly took Toivo and set him down before the King's castle. There he walked through the garden and came to a clear sparkling pool. He sat down on the edge of the pool and dipped his tired feet in the water.

It so happened that the King's Butler was coming to draw water. He said to Toivo:

"My good man, tired you may be, but if the King hears that you've been dipping your dusty feet into his drinking water, he'll have your head cut off!"

"My good sir," said Toivo, "the water will soon be clear again, but I'm sorry for my mistake. Let me show you a secret."

And he took a shining red berry from his right pocket and gave it to the Butler. The Butler crunched the berry between his teeth, and at once became the handsomest man in the kingdom, next of course to Toivo himself. He was so delighted that he hid Toivo in a corner of the pantry where the King would not find him.

At dinner time the Princess saw how wonderfully changed the Butler was in his looks, and it made her very curious.

"What has made you so handsome all of a sudden?" she asked him.

"I met a man in the garden who gave me a shining red berry," he whispered. "I ate it, and the charm worked. I became as you now see me."

"Find that man," the Princess said. "Tell him if he'll only make me beautiful too, I'll marry him."

"I'm afraid he's gone," the Butler said. "He wanted to hide, because he was afraid someone would cut his head off if they found him here."

"Tell him not to be frightened," the Princess said. "I will protect him. Bring him into the secret chamber and I'll give him food and drink."

The Butler went to fetch Toivo, and when they returned they found the Princess waiting with food and drink all set out. When the Princess saw Toivo, he was so handsome that she did not know him at all. While he was eating she said:

"If you can make me as beautiful as you are handsome, I'll be your bride."

Toivo became hot with anger, for he thought the Princess had grown tired of him on the island and had run away, stealing his golden ship and leaving him there to die. He did not know of the long time she had waited there.

"No, gentle Princess," he said. "I'm only a poor servant. There is many a King's son who would gladly marry you."

"Only believe me," she said. "I will dress you in a uniform of a General in the King's Army. I will fill your pockets with gold. I will give you a magic golden ship! Only please, please make me as beautiful as you are handsome, and let us be married."

"Very well," said Toivo at last. "Have it your way. Eat this berry."

He took a purple berry from his left pocket, and as the Princess crunched the berry between her teeth a pair of monstrous pronged horns grew out from her head, as heavy and huge as the horns of a wild elk!

As for Toivo, he got very frightened at what he had done, and ran off to hide.

The Princess set up a great hullabaloo, and everyone came running. When the King saw the horns he tried to cut them away, but they were hard as iron and firmly fixed to her head. So then he ordered his two strongest soldiers to follow behind the Princess everywhere she went and carry the weight of the horns while she walked.

No wonder the whole court was upset! The King and the Queen and all the ladies and gentlemen in waiting could talk of nothing but the poor Princess and her terrible plight. In despair the King at last sent soldiers into every part of his kingdom with this message:

"Whoever will cure the King's daughter by removing her monstrous horns shall receive the hand of the King's daughter in marriage and be

raised to the highest command in the King's Army."

From every part of the kingdom came doctors and healers and magicians. They tried all their medicines and potions, all their spells and wonders. But it was wasted work, for the horns still remained.

At last, after many days, Toivo came forward from the crowd and knelt before the King, saying:

"O King, please let me try my cure."

"I doubt if you can do anything, my lad," the King said. "You can see for yourself how all these wise men have failed, one after another. They have eaten and drunk to their own luck, but my poor daughter remains the same."

"But, King, I am the only one who knows the right charm," Toivo begged. "If you'll let me try, I'm sure I can take away the horns."

"Try, then, and if the horns do fall from my daughter's head, I'll make you the highest general in my army."

"Send all these doctors and healers away," said Toivo, "and command your soldiers to make merry, for I will surely make your daughter the most beautiful woman in the kingdom!"

So the King commanded all the doctors and healers and magicians to go home, and the soldiers to make merry, while Toivo was left alone to work his cure.

Toivo said to the maidservant:

"Go, girl, and put dry sticks in the *sauna* (bath house) hearth. Make a hot fire to heat the stones in the Princess's bath house."

And to the page boy he said:

"Run quick to the deep wild forest, boy, and fetch me three long straight willow twigs. With these I will make the horns disappear."

The *sauna* was made ready with warm water and heated stones. The long straight willow twigs were brought and laid in the bath house, too. Then Toivo called for the Princess. He sent the maidservant outside and shut the door. He set the Princess on a bench. He tore the clothing from her shoulders and began to beat her soundly with the willow twigs.

"I'll teach you to run away with my golden ship and leave me to die in the middle of the sea!" he shouted between the strokes. "I'll teach you, you cruel woman, to steal my golden spoons and my golden dishes! I am Toivo, the man you promised to marry if I would take you to a far-off island! I'll teach you!"

The Princess's shoulders were soon red and welted from the blows of the willow twigs. She cried:

"Stop beating me, stop beating me, poor man, and I'll explain everything. Only stop, and I promise never to harm you again!"

"Very well then, explain," said Toivo gruffly.

"It was like this," the Princess began. "For three long days and nights I waited for you. I can't tell you how lonely it seemed, there on that island in the middle of the sea. Every moment I expected some horrible monster to come and swallow me alive. I felt sure you had deserted me, and you can't blame me for being so frightened that I flew back home in your golden ship. How can you doubt that I loved you from the very beginning, and still do!"

When Toivo heard this he threw away the willow twigs and fell on his knees before her. "Forgive me, forgive me for being angry with you, gentle Princess! I will never lift my hand against you again."

As he spoke, Toivo drew a shining red berry from his right pocket. The Princess crunched it between her teeth; at once the ugly horns fell from her head and her face became as fair as a new-blown rose.

Toivo called the maidservant. She dressed the Princess in fine linen; upon her head she set the tall bridal crown, covered with jewels, and upon her feet soft shoes woven of the finest white birch bark in all the King's land.

When the people saw the Princess in her white robe, her thick golden braids falling to her knees, her blue eyes shining and her skin like the fairest rose-petal, they knew she had become the most beautiful woman in the kingdom.

The King was so happy he declared a holiday throughout the whole land. Everywhere people ate, drank and danced all night long.

Toivo became the King's highest general. He married his Princess and they all lived happily ever after.

Spain

The folklore of Spain, as well as of Portugal, is richly varied, laced as it is with strong strains from the Moorish and Moslem civilizations and from a fervent, deep-reaching Christian heritage. Spain has also exerted a tremendous influence on the language, literature, and lore of Spanish-speaking America and has in turn been influenced by New World folklore as well as by the general European traditions. Interestingly enough, folklore research in Spain is well organized and quite thorough, and has been underway for a very long time. However, the collections of Spanish folk tales for children are rather few in number. One notable feature of Spanish folklore is the frequent occurrence of stories about the saints, marked by a deep faith and a strong sense of morality. A typically Spanish beginning for the tales is often used by Ruth Sawyer: "Once there was and was not. . . ." It makes an effective beginning and offers a change from "Once upon a time. . . ."

THE HALF-CHICK

This selfish creature has his counterparts in many folk tales. The tale is really a variant of the English "The Old Woman and Her Pig," or perhaps it is the other way around. Before telling it, explain what a weather vane is and show children the picture of the weathercock (p. 149).

Once upon a time there was a handsome black Spanish hen, who had a large brood of chickens. They were all fine, plump little birds, except the youngest, who was quite unlike his brothers and sisters. Indeed, he was such a strange, queer-look-

"The Half-Chick." From *The Green Fairy Book*, edited by Andrew Lang. Longmans, Green, and Co., London, 1892

ing creature, that when he first chipped his shell his mother could scarcely believe her eyes, he was so different from the twelve other fluffy, downy, soft little chicks who nestled under her wings. This one looked just as if he had been cut in two. He had only one leg, and one wing, and one eye, and he had half a head and half a beak. His mother shook her head sadly as she looked at him and said:

"My youngest born is only a half-chick. He can never grow up a tall handsome cock like his brothers. They will go out into the world and rule over poultry yards of their own; but this poor little fellow will always have to stay at home with his mother." And she called him Medio Pollito, which is Spanish for half-chick.

Now though Medio Pollito was such an odd, helpless-looking little thing, his mother soon found that he was not at all willing to remain under her wing and protection. Indeed, in character he was as unlike his brothers and sisters as he was in appearance. They were good, obedient chickens, and when the old hen chicked after them, they chirped and ran back to her side. But Medio Pollito had a roving spirit in spite of his one leg, and when his mother called to him to return to the coop, he pretended that he could not hear, because he had only one ear.

When she took the whole family out for a walk in the fields, Medio Pollito would hop away by himself, and hide among the Indian corn. Many an anxious minute his brothers and sisters had looking for him, while his mother ran to and fro cackling in fear and dismay.

As he grew older he became more self-willed and disobedient, and his manner to his mother was often very rude, and his temper to the other chickens very disagreeable.

One day he had been out for a longer expedition than usual in the fields. On his return he strutted up to his mother with the peculiar little hop and kick which was his way of walking, and cocking his one eye at her in a very bold way he said:

"Mother, I am tired of this life in a dull farmyard, with nothing but a dreary maize field to look at. I'm off to Madrid to see the King."

"To Madrid, Medio Pollito!" exclaimed his mother; "why, you silly chick, it would be a long journey for a grown-up cock, and a poor little

thing like you would be tired out before you had gone half the distance. No, no, stay at home with your mother, and some day, when you are bigger, we will go a little journey together."

But Medio Pollito had made up his mind, and he would not listen to his mother's advice, nor to the prayers and entreaties of his brothers and sisters.

"What is the use of our all crowding each other up in this poky little place?" he said. "When I have a fine courtyard of my own at the King's palace, I shall perhaps ask some of you to come and pay me a short visit," and scarcely waiting to say good-bye to his family, away he stumped down the high road that led to Madrid.

"Be sure that you are kind and civil to everyone you meet," called his mother, running after him; but he was in such a hurry to be off, that he did not wait to answer her, or even to look back.

A little later in the day, as he was taking a short cut through a field, he passed a stream. Now the stream was all choked up and overgrown with weeds and water-plants, so that its waters could not flow freely.

"Oh! Medio Pollito," it cried, as the half-chick hopped along its banks, "do come and help me by clearing away these weeds."

"Help you, indeed!" exclaimed Medio Pollito, tossing his head, and shaking the few feathers in his tail. "Do you think I have nothing to do but to waste my time on such trifles? Help yourself, and don't trouble busy travellers. I am off to Madrid to see the King," and hoppity-kick, hoppity-kick, away stumped Medio Pollito.

A little later he came to a fire that had been left by some gypsies in a wood. It was burning very low, and would soon be out.

"Oh! Medio Pollito," cried the fire, in a weak, wavering voice as the half-chick approached, "in a few minutes I shall go quite out, unless you put some sticks and dry leaves upon me. Do help me, or I shall die!"

"Help you, indeed!" answered Medio Pollito. "I have other things to do. Gather sticks for yourself, and don't trouble me. I am off to Madrid to see the King," and hoppity-kick, hoppity-kick, away stumped Medio Pollito.

The next morning, as he was getting near Madrid, he passed a large chestnut tree, in whose branches the wind was caught and entangled.

"Oh! Medio Pollito," called the wind, "do hop up here, and help me to get free of these branches. I cannot come away, and it is so uncomfortable."

"It is your own fault for going there," answered Medio Pollito. "I can't waste all my morning stopping here to help you. Just shake yourself off, and don't hinder me, for I am off to Madrid to see the King," and hoppity-kick, hoppity-kick, away stumped Medio Pollito in great glee, for the towers and roofs of Madrid were now in sight.

When he entered the town he saw before him a great splendid house, with soldiers standing before the gates. This he knew must be the King's palace, and he determined to hop up to the front gate and wait there until the King came out. But as he was hopping past one of the back windows the King's cook saw him:

"Here is the very thing I want," he exclaimed, "for the King has just sent a message to say that he must have chicken broth for his dinner," and opening the window he stretched out his arm, caught Medio Pollito, and popped him into the broth-pot that was standing near the fire. Oh! how wet and clammy the water felt as it went over Medio Pollito's head, making his feathers cling to his side.

"Water, water!" he cried in his despair, "do have pity upon me and do not wet me like this."

"Ah! Medio Pollito," replied the water, "you would not help me when I was a little stream away on the fields; now you must be punished."

Then the fire began to burn and scald Medio Pollito, and he danced and hopped from one side of the pot to the other, trying to get away from the heat, and crying out in pain:

"Fire, fire! do not scorch me like this; you can't think how it hurts."

"Ah! Medio Pollito," answered the fire, "you would not help me when I was dying away in the wood. You are being punished."

At last, just when the pain was so great that Medio Pollito thought he must die, the cook lifted up the lid of the pot to see if the broth was ready for the King's dinner.

"Look here!" he cried in horror, "this chicken is quite useless. It is burnt to a cinder. I can't send it up to the royal table." And opening the window he threw Medio Pollito out into the

street. But the wind caught him up, and whirled him through the air so quickly that Medio Pollito could scarcely breathe, and his heart beat against his side till he thought it would break.

"Oh, wind!" at last he gasped out, "if you hurry me along like this you will kill me. Do let me rest a moment, or——" but he was so breathless that he could not finish his sentence.

"Ah! Medio Pollito," replied the wind, "when I was caught in the branches of the chestnut tree you would not help me; now you are punished." And he swirled Medio Pollito over the roofs of the houses till they reached the highest church in the town, and there he left him fastened to the top of the steeple.

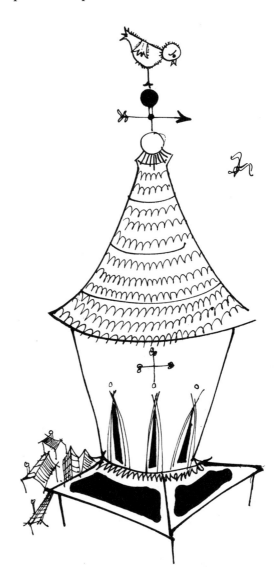

And there stands Medio Pollito to this day. And if you go to Madrid, and walk through the streets till you come to the highest church, you will see Medio Pollito perched on his one leg on the steeple, with his one wing drooping at his side, and gazing sadly out of his one eye over the town.

THE JOKES OF SINGLE-TOE

Padre Porko is a unique character in Spanish folklore. He is the gentlemanly pig, wise, witty, and urbane. He solves his own and his neighbors' problems with nonchalance. Look up the other stories in the book that bears his name. They are all good to tell.

"Chestnuts are ripening and falling on the other side of the canal," said the black-headed sparrow, teetering on the edge of the table.

"Oh, but it's too early for chestnuts," observed the Padre. "It takes two or three frosty nights to open the prickles."

"Well, if you can't believe me," said the sparrow, ruffling his collar, "ask the squirrel. He keeps track of the nuts."

So the Padre asked Single-Toe (so named because he had only one on his left front foot). The squirrel put his paw beside his nose as though he were trying to think up an answer to a riddle. "I'll try to let you know in three days," he mumbled, "but don't do anything about chestnuts until you see me again." And he went off in such a rush that even the good Padre grew suspicious.

An hour later he laid down his pipe and beckoned to Mrs. Wren. "Do you mind having a little fly around the wood to see what the squirrel family is up to this morning?"

She came back twittering all over. "The squirrels, for miles around, are all in the grove across the canal, throwing down the chestnuts for dear life. Single-Toe is making them work all the harder, and giggling at something he seems to think very funny."

"Oh, the rascal," chuckled the Padre. "The sly

little one-toed sinner! He will give me an answer in three days, will he? Yes, indeed, after he has gathered all the best nuts." He called to his housekeeper. "Mrs. Hedge-Hog, bring me three of the oatmeal sacks from the cupboard and some strong string." And folding the bags inside his belt, he trotted off, pushing his wheelbarrow.

Up among the leaves, busy pulling the polished nuts out of the burrs, Single-Toe and his relatives did not hear the Padre arrive. Patter, plop, plop, plop, patter—the brown nuts were falling on the grass.

"What a lark," beamed the Padre, stuffing four or five into his mouth at once. "And this year they are sweeter and juicier than they have been for a long time." He made little piles of the biggest ones, and began filling his sacks. Finally he had all the wheelbarrow would carry. Bouncing the last bag up and down so he could tie the string around the top, he called out in his silkiest voice, "Many thanks, Single-Toe. You will see that I have taken only the big ones. I do hope that the prickers haven't made your paws sore."

There was a sudden calm in the chestnut grove. The squirrels came leaping down to a low bough, from where they could send sour looks after the Padre, trundling his barrow along toward the bridge. He was singing,

> With chestnuts roasting in a row,
>   I love to hear them sizzle.
> I care not how the winds may blow,
>   Nor how the rain-drops drizzle.
> I welcome every Jack and Jill
>   Who knocks upon my door.
> We toast our toes and eat our fill,
>   For there are plenty more.

One day three or four weeks later the Padre was doing a little carpentering under the umbrella pine, when something behind him sniffed. He jumped, and dropped two nails out of his mouth. There, under the table, tears running down their noses, were Mrs. Single-Toe and the four children.

"Bless my blue-eyed buttons," exclaimed the Padre, spitting out the rest of the nails. "What can be as wrong as all that?"

"It's Papa," said the oldest boy. "He's been in a hole by the old oak for four days, and is almost starved."

"The Jokes of Single-Toe" from *Padre Porko* by Robert Davis. Copyright 1939, 1948, by Robert Davis. Reprinted by permission of Holiday House, Inc.

"But why doesn't he come home?" said the Padre. "The oak isn't far away."

"The fox won't let him," sobbed Madame Single-Toe.

"And why not?"

"He's mad because of Papa's jokes," the youngest child explained.

The Padre's mouth opened in a wide grin. "More of the jokes that other people don't find funny, eh? Well, I'll take a stroll by the twisted oak and have a talk with the fox." As he started off, he called over his shoulder, "Mrs. Hedge-Hog, you might give these youngsters a couple of the pickled chestnuts we keep for company." He winked solemnly at Mrs. Single-Toe, who blushed.

The fox was lying with his muzzle just an inch from the hole. He did not budge, nor lift his eye when the Padre wished him good morning. "I've got him this time," he snarled. "Four days I've been watching this hole. My mother brings my meals and keeps guard while I eat. He'll not get away *this* time!"

"He is a nuisance with his jokes, I admit," said the Padre peaceably, "but he doesn't do any real harm. Don't you think a good scare would be enough for him?"

"No, I don't," snapped the fox. "And don't you mix in this business, Padre, with your talk about kindness. What I've suffered from that little pest you'd never believe. First he dropped a tomato on my nose—a tomato that was too ripe. And then he dribbled pitch all over my head and neck while I was asleep. So don't waste your time." The fox advanced his red tongue hungrily to the very edge of the hole.

The Padre walked away, deep in thought. His generous heart was very unhappy. What should he say to the near-orphans in his kitchen? There must be some way to save him. Suddenly he saw some crows gossiping in a dead pine. "Will one of you black boys do me a favor, in a great hurry?" he called.

"Certainly, Don Porko," they all cawed.

"Fly low through the woods, and tell every rabbit you see that I want their road commissioner to come to my house for dinner. Say that I'm going to have celery root and cabbage, chopped in parsley."

The Padre's guest was promptness itself. He used a turnip leaf as a napkin, and when he had wiped his whiskers, ate the napkin. "It makes less for Ma'am Hedge-Hog to clear up," he explained.

"Now for serious business," said the Padre, leading the way to the garden, when they had finished their second glass of dandelion wine. "I have invited you here as an expert. We will draw a map." He made a cross in the soft earth with a stick. "Here is the oak that the lightning split. And here in front of it, so, is a rabbit hole that was begun, but never finished. Do you follow me?"

The road commissioner nodded. "I know it perfectly. The workman was caught by an owl when he came up with some dirt."

"Now," continued the Padre, "how far is the bottom of this unfinished hole from one of your regular tunnels, and how long would it take to dig up to it?"

"About half a jump," replied the road commissioner. "The 'Alley to the Ivy Rock' runs very close to that unfinished hole. A good digger can do a medium-sized jump of tunnel in half a day. I should say it would take two hours to dig upwards from 'Ivy Rock Alley' and join the hole."

The Padre beckoned the road commissioner to follow him to the cellar. Scraping away the sand, he laid bare ten carrots, each as smooth and straight as an orange-colored candle. "These are yours, Mr. Commissioner, if you will do this little job of digging for me."

The bargain was soon struck. "One thing more," said the Padre, as the commissioner was lolloping away. "You will find a friend of mine in the unfinished hole. Don't let him make a noise, but bring him here the moment you can get him free. I'll be waiting."

Daylight was fading when the rabbit returned, covered with damp earth to his armpits. He was supporting a hoarse, hungry, and grimy red squirrel. The Padre welcomed them, pointing to the cupboard. "Sh-h-h-sh, go and see what's inside, Single-Toe."

One might have thought a hundred squirrels were behind the cupboard door, such was the hugging and chattering, the rubbing of noses, and the scratching of ears. Single-Toe was invited to stay for a light lunch, even after the road commissioner had left for his burrow, the biggest carrot in his mouth.

Safe, fed, and warmed, the red squirrel became his own gay self again. He began to chuckle, then to shake with merriment. "Ha, ha, ha! That silly old fox is still there, watching an empty hole! Won't it be a priceless joke, if I climb the oak and drop a rotten egg on his nose?"

At the word "joke," Mrs. Single-Toe, the four little squirrels, and the good Padre, all stiffened.

"Don't you ever say that word again," said his wife. "Do you hear, no more jokes, never, never."

Single-Toe wilted. "Yes," he confessed, not daring to meet the Padre's eye, "jokes aren't always so terribly funny, are they? Not even for the joker."

Italy

Italy figures as the place in Europe where predecessors of many famous folk tales first appeared in print. In the work of Giambattista Basile (Il Pentamerone) and of Giovanni Francesco Straparola (Le Piacevoli Notti) we can find the prefigurings of "Cinderella," "Puss in Boots," and many others. But until recent years, Italian folk tales compiled for English-speaking children were few and seemed to be more generally European than typically Italian. This was mainly because few of the primary source materials were, or are, available in English. Also, it would be hard to find a "typical" Italian folk tale when one considers the various Italian provinces which were once independent kingdoms, and the islands of Corsica, Sardinia, and Sicily. "March and the Shepherd" and "The Most Precious Possession" are from Domenico Vittorini's Old Italian Tales, a treasury for the storyteller. Some of the stories are adapted from oral sources, but one is taken from Boccaccio (whose stories were from oral tradition and from his own imagination and cannot always be identified as having come from one or the other). The entire Vittorini collection of twenty tales has unusual variety, an earthy sort of humor, and a vigorous sense of justice. Told with simplicity and with respect for sources, these lively tales prove again how little human nature differs from country to country. "King Clothes" is from Jagendorf's The Priceless Cats, which, with other compilations like Haviland's Favorite Fairy Tales Told in Italy, adds to the number of good Italian folk tales retold for young people's enjoyment.

MARCH AND THE SHEPHERD

This duel of wits between two tricksters, with the shepherd always the winner, makes the wry humor of the conclusion quite acceptable.

One morning, in the very beginning of spring, a shepherd led his sheep to graze, and on the way he met March.

"March and the Shepherd." Reprinted by permission of David McKay Company, Inc., from *Old Italian Tales*, retold by Domenico Vittorini; copyright © 1958 by Domenico Vittorini

"Good morning," said March. "Where are you going to take your sheep to graze today?"

"Well, March, today I am going to the mountains."

"Fine, Shepherd. That's a good idea. Good luck." But to himself March said, "Here's where I have some fun, for today I'm going to fix you."

And that day in the mountains the rain came down in buckets; it was a veritable deluge. The shepherd, however, had watched March's face very carefully and noticed a mischievous look on it. So, instead of going to the mountains, he had remained in the plains. In the evening, upon returning home, he met March again.

"Well, Shepherd, how did it go today?"

"It couldn't have been better. I changed my mind and went to the plains. A very beautiful day. Such a lovely warm sun."

"Really? I'm glad to hear it," said March, but he bit his lip in vexation. "Where are you going tomorrow?"

"Tomorrow I'm going to the plains, too. With this fine weather, I would be crazy if I went to the mountains."

"Oh, really? Fine! Farewell."

And they parted.

But the shepherd didn't go to the plains again; he went to the mountains. And on the plains March brought rain and wind and hail—a punishment indeed from heaven. In the evening he met the shepherd homeward bound.

"Good evening, Shepherd. How did it go today?"

"Very well indeed. Do you know? I changed my mind again and went to the mountains after all. It was heavenly there. What a day! What a sky! What a sun!"

"I'm really happy to hear it, Shepherd. And where are you going tomorrow?"

"Well, tomorrow I'm going to the plains. I see dark clouds over the mountains. I wouldn't

want to find myself too far from home."

To make a long story short, whenever the shepherd met March, he always told him the opposite of what he planned to do the next day, so March was never able to catch him. The end of the month came and on the last day, the thirtieth, March said to the shepherd, "Well, Shepherd, how is everything?"

"Things couldn't be any better. This is the end of the month and I'm out of danger. There's nothing to fear now; I can begin to sleep peacefully."

"That's true," said March. "And where are you going tomorrow?"

The shepherd, certain that he had nothing to fear, told March the truth. "Tomorrow," he said, "I shall go to the plains. The distance is shorter and the work less hard."

"Fine. Farewell."

March hastened to the home of his cousin April and told her the whole story. "I want you to lend me at least one day," he said. "I am determined to catch this shepherd." Gentle April was unwilling, but March coaxed so hard that finally she consented.

The following morning the shepherd set off for the plains. No sooner had his flock scattered when there arose a storm that chilled his very heart. The sharp wind howled and growled; snow fell in thick icy flakes; hail pelted down. It was all the shepherd could do to get his sheep back into the fold.

That evening as the shepherd huddled in a corner of his hearth, silent and melancholy, March paid him a visit.

"Good evening, Shepherd," he said.

"Good evening, March."

"How did it go today?"

"I'd rather not talk about it," said the shepherd. "I can't understand what happened. Not even in the middle of January have I ever seen a storm like the one on the plains today. It seemed as if all the devils had broken loose from hell. Today I had enough rough weather to last me the whole year. And, oh, my poor sheep!"

Then at last was March satisfied.

And from that time on March has had thirty-one days because, as it is said in Tuscany, the rascal never returned to April the day he borrowed from her.

THE MOST PRECIOUS

POSSESSION

This tale starts off as if it were to be a variant of "Dick Whittington" without the rags-to-riches theme, but the conclusion is different. The story is also similar to "The Priceless Cats" in Jagendorf's collection of the same name.

There was a time when Italian traders and explorers, finding the way to the East blocked by the Turks, turned west in their search for new lands to trade with—a search that led to the discovery of the New World.

In those days there lived in Florence a merchant by the name of Ansaldo. He belonged to the Ormanini family, known not only for its wealth but for the daring and cunning of its young men. It happened that on one of his trips in search of adventure and trade, Ansaldo ventured beyond the Strait of Gibraltar and, after battling a furious storm, landed on one of the Canary Islands.

The king of the island welcomed him cordially, for the Florentines were well known to him. He ordered a magnificent banquet prepared and arranged to have it served in the sumptuous hall, resplendent with mirrors and gold, in which he had received Ansaldo.

When it was time to serve the meal, Ansaldo noticed with surprise that a small army of

"The Most Precious Possession." Reprinted by permission of David McKay Company, Inc., from *Old Italian Tales,* retold by Domenico Vittorini; copyright © 1958 by Domenico Vittorini

youths, carrying long stout sticks, entered and lined up against the walls of the banquet hall. As each guest sat down, one of the youths took up a place directly behind him, the stick held in readiness to strike.

Ansaldo wondered what all this meant and wracked his brain for some clue to these odd goings-on. He didn't have long to wait. Suddenly, a horde of huge ferocious rats poured into the hall and threw themselves upon the food that was being served. Pandemonium broke loose as the boys darted here and there, wielding the sticks.

For many years the Florentines had enjoyed the reputation of being the cleverest people on earth, able to cope with any situation. Ansaldo saw a chance to uphold the tradition. He asked the king's permission to go back to his ship, and returned shortly with two big Persian cats. These animals were much admired and loved by the Florentines and Venetians who had first seen them in the East and who had brought many of them back to Italy. Ever since, one or two cats always completed the crew of a ship when it set out on a long journey.

Ansaldo let the cats go and before long the entire hall was cleared of the revolting and destructive rats.

The astonished and delighted king thought he was witnessing a miracle. He could not find words enough to thank Ansaldo whom he hailed as the saviour of the island, and when Ansaldo made him a present of the cats, his gratitude knew no bounds.

After a pleasant visit, Ansaldo made ready to

sail for home. The king accompanied him to his ship and there he showered him with rich and rare gifts, much gold and silver, and many precious stones of all kinds and colors—rubies, topazes, and diamonds.

Ansaldo was overwhelmed not only by these costly gifts but by the king's gratitude and the praises he heaped upon him and on the cats. As for the latter, they were regarded with awe by all the islanders and as their greatest treasure by the king and the entire royal household.

When Ansaldo returned home he regaled his friends with the account of his strange adventure. There was among them a certain Giocondo de' Fifanti who was as rich in envy as he was poor in intelligence. He thought: "If the island king gave Ansaldo all these magnificent gifts for two mangy cats, what will he not give me if I present him with the most beautiful and precious things that our city of Florence has to offer?" No sooner said than done. He purchased lovely belts, necklaces, bracelets studded with diamonds, exquisite pictures, luxurious garments and many other expensive gifts and took ship for the now famous Canary Islands.

After an uneventful crossing he arrived in port and hastened to the royal palace. He was received with more pomp than was Ansaldo. The king was greatly touched by the splendor of Giocondo's gifts and wanted to be equally generous. He held a long consultation with his people and then informed Giocondo happily that they had decided to let him share with his visitor their most precious possession. Giocondo could hardly contain his curiosity. However, the day of departure finally arrived and found Giocondo on his ship, impatiently awaiting the visit of the king. Before long, the king, accompanied by the entire royal household and half the islanders, approached the ship. The king himself carried the precious gift on a silken cushion. With great pride he put the cushion into Giocondo's outstretched greedy hands. Giocondo was speechless. On the cushion, curled up in sleepy, furry balls, were two of the kittens that had been born to the Persian cats Ansaldo had left on the island.

The old story does not go on to say whether Giocondo, on his return to Florence, ever regaled his friends with the tale of *his* adventure!

KING CLOTHES

No happy ending here! The tale is a rather sharp commentary on certain human foibles. There are many stories in Italy about the peasant boy who is both foolish and wise, and his name varies from one area to the next. In Sicily he is called Giufa.

It is told that years ago there lived in Sicily, the largest island in all the Mediterranean, a young fellow named Giufa, who was so silly that, as the saying goes, he wasn't sure of the weather when it was raining in buckets. That is what folks said, but I'm not sure they were right. For people lived in Sicily before they lived anywhere in Italy, and there must have been silly fellows before him.

Giufa wore rags for clothes and never had shoes, so the dust on the road jumped between his toes. And who looks at a fellow who is dressed in rags? Nobody. Doors were closed in his face, and sometimes people wouldn't ever talk to him. He was never asked to a wedding or a feast. Life was not too pleasant for Giufa.

One sunny day his mother sent him to take something to the farm that was next to theirs.

Giufa went off whistling, kicking the dust on the road. Sometimes he stopped to speak to a bird or a butterfly. Soon he came to the farmhouse. At the gate stood the wife of the farmer.

"Good day, mistress," Giufa said politely. "My mother sent me to give you this," and he held out a basket to her.

The woman took one look at his ragged clothes and dusty face and feet.

"Drop it right there," she cried, "and go quickly. You look like a scarecrow, and the dogs will be after you."

Giufa did not say anything. What could he say? Besides, it was dinnertime just then, and his stomach was empty and growling. So he turned sadly toward home.

Though kith and kin said he was a noodlehead, he had sense enough to think that the farmwoman could have been a little nicer and could have asked him in to have a piece of bread and cheese.

When he reached home he told his mother how he had been treated, adding: "I could smell the bean soup out at the gate. They could have been good Christians and asked me to have a plate. They talk to me like that because I don't wear fine breeches and a velvet coat."

Giufa's mother worried about this, and a few weeks later she once again had to send her son with something to that same farm. Not wanting to put the boy to shame, she dressed him in a fine white shirt, good breeches, a nice blue coat, and good shoes.

You should have seen Giufa! He looked like a different fellow. He almost could not recognize himself.

Off he went, whistling gaily and joking with bird and beast until he came to the farmer's house. There stood both the farmer and his wife, and neither one recognized Giufa in his fine clean clothes.

"I have something for you," he cried.

It was noon then, and so they greeted him pleasantly and invited him into the farmhouse.

They asked him to sit down to hot steaming minestrone soup that was filled with fresh vegetables and good sharp cheese. With it came crisp fresh bread and rich red wine.

Giufa ate and joked and had the best time of his life. At the end of the meal, the farmer sat back and asked the boy to tell him about this and that. But instead of doing so, Giufa stood up and put some of the cheese and bread in the pockets of his coat and breeches and into his hat. The farmer and his wife laughed because they thought this was so funny. Then Giufa bowed low and, looking down at his bulging pockets and over at his hat, said:

"Here is food for you, my good clothes and fine hat, and I want to thank you from the bottom of my heart, for it is you who were treated like a king, and it is because of you, my good clothes and fine hat, that I had a fine meal. When I came here the last time without you, fine clothes, I was treated like a crazy dog."

Then he turned around and walked out. You can guess what the farmer and his wife thought and said! Maybe they remembered the saying: "Dress up a stick and folks'll think it's a nobleman."

Poland

If the Polish people seem to have their roots in things both Slavic and German, so does Polish folklore. The tales of Poland are distinctly Polish, but that Polish-ness is enriched by Jewish folklore, by the folk-tale traditions of various Slavic countries, and by the traditions of Germany and Western Europe. The tales, which seem to be mostly about the common folk who use their cleverness to get ahead, are enlivened with laughter and a warm, graceful piety. Tailors, peasant boys, kings, princesses, saints, and sinners make up the human parade in the stories, accompanied by a generous mixture of animals, witches, ghosts, and devils. Perhaps the going and coming of invaders has done painful things to Polish territory, but it has also enriched the tales of a gentle land whose people persist though their country's borders tremble and shift with the crosscurrents of history. There are few collections of Polish tales in English. The best known are those retold by Lucia Borski, as she presented them from her own background to boys and girls in the United States. Josephine Bernhard also compiled Polish tales in the 1930's. Some of the Borski and Bernhard tales are to be found in Virginia Haviland's more recent Favorite Fairy Tales Told in Poland.

KING BARTEK

Young girls will like this romantic story of a royal disguise that serves to reveal both the haughty hypocrite and the true-hearted maiden.

On the outskirts of a village, in a hut fallen almost to ruins, there lived a very poor widow with her two daughters, Bialka and Spiewna. Both of them were so beautiful that their fame spread over seven mountains, over seven seas. Even at the King's palace the rumors were heard. Many of the knights wished to go at once and woo the girls.

The King disliked to lose his knights, as he had planned a great war, and besides he did not have much faith in the rumors. Instead of granting permission to the knights to go, he sent some of his faithful messengers to see the maidens and bring back pictures of Bialka and Spiewna.

The rumors were true. The pictures brought back by the messengers exceeded everybody's expectations. Spiewna was a true sister to the lily; Bialka, to the red rose. The first had azure eyes, the other, eyes dark as the Black Sea; one was proud of her long, golden braids, the other of her raven black braids. The first one had the beauty of a sunny day in her face, the other, the charm of a May night. The knights became enamored of the maidens; no one could keep them from departing. Even the King himself, as he was young and thought of marriage, scratched himself behind the ear and looked at the pictures with great pleasure. The war was put off, the court was desolated, and only the King and his Jester, Pieś, who was old and ugly like the seven mortal sins, were left there.

For a long, long time the knights did not come back. They were enjoying themselves; or it might be the other way around, Bialka and Spiewna, sure of their beauty, might be taking their time picking and choosing, like sparrows in poppy seeds. The knights in love unwound entangled thread, killed partridges in the air, and sang serenades. Be it as it may, their long ab-

"King Bartek." Reprinted by permission of David McKay Company, Inc., from *The Jolly Tailor and Other Fairy Tales Translated from the Polish* by Lucia Merecka Borski and Kate B. Miller. Copyright 1928, 1956 by Lucia Merecka Borski and John F. Miller

sence annoyed the King and he grew impatient and ill-tempered.

"Pieś," he once addressed the Jester, "do you know what I am thinking about?"

"I know, Your Lordship!"

"How?"

"Because our thoughts walk the same paths."

"I wonder!" laughed the King.

"Your Lordship wishes to go to the widow's daughters."

"You guessed!" cried the young King, rejoicing.

"Then we shall go together," said Pieś. "But we must change our places; I, a King; Your Lordship, a Jester."

"What an idea!" said the young ruler, shocked a bit.

"There won't be much of a difference," smiled the Jester.

"No, I shall not do it! You may, if you wish, become a King, but I shall put on a peasant's garb and call myself Bartek."

"As you please!" answered Pieś. "Something unpleasant may come of it though."

"Why?" asked the King, now Bartek.

"A King, be he as ugly and humpbacked as I am, will always have preference over Bartek. And then who knows? Your Highness may fall in love with either Spiewna or Bialka."

The youthful lord became alarmed.

"So much the better!" he said after a while, and added in a whisper, "The heart that loves will not fool itself."

They went on their journey.

In the meantime the widow's hut was as noisy as a beehive. One brought musicians, another singers. The hut changed into a music box adorned with garlands and flowers, as if in celebration of a holiday. The knights reveled, the girls danced, song followed song, and jokes, one after another. The mother's white bonnet swung on her white hair from one ear to the other from happiness.

Bialka liked Przegoń (Pshegon) more than all the others. Spiewna chose none as yet. Neither her mother's persuasion nor her sister's scoffs did any good. The girl's heart had not awakened yet, and without love she did not wish to marry even the richest of knights.

The betrothal of Przegoń to Bialka was announced. She had her wedding dress made, goods for which were brought by Przegoń. The jewelry, one could not describe, it could be gathered in measures.

Bialka was overwhelmed with joy, was triumphant with her success. She looked down on her sister with haughtiness and consoled her mother with scornful words.

"Do not worry, Mother! Spiewna awaits a prince. She will become wiser when she has to grow rue, and then I, Przegoń's wife, will try to get her an organist. Also I shall find a suitable nook for you, Mother."

Her mother's heart grieved, but what could she answer?

Then one day a golden carriage drove up before the door. All three of them ran quickly to the window, and Bialka shouted:

"The King has come!"

Sudden confusion possessed the hut. The old widow trotted to the kitchen to prepare some fowl for His Majesty, the King, while Bialka snatched a hand-mirror and a comb and turning to her sister called in a commanding voice:

"Don't you dare to call the King's attention to yourself!"

Spiewna stopped in astonishment.

"Do you hear me?" shouted Bialka.

"I hear, but I don't understand."

"You don't understand—you don't understand!"

"For—how—" began Spiewna.

"Don't dare to call the King's attention to yourself!"

"What do you care about the King when you have Przegoń?"

"Have I or not, that is nothing to you!" grumbled Bialka. "And better take my advice, otherwise—you shall see!"

His Majesty, the King, was far from good looking. He was ugly, old, his right arm was higher than the left, and he was also limping. But all this was covered with the golden crown, was concealed by the purple cloak and was straightened by the long robe richly embroidered with pearls. Upon seeing the sisters, he at once laid his royal gifts at their feet, and loaded them with compliments. Spiewna refused all the gifts; she accepted only a white rose, which she pinned into her hair.

"How beautiful he is!" whispered Bialka.

"How ridiculous he is!" replied Spiewna.

Bialka looked at her with anger.

Among the King's numerous attendants, there was a young and handsome page, called Bartek. Spiewna's eyes met the youth's gaze. Bartek, dazzled with the girl's beauty, did not take his eyes off her, and when the King offered jewels to Bialka, he came near Spiewna and said:

"All my riches is this fife. It plays beautifully and the time will come when I shall present you with its song."

Spiewna, standing on the threshold, blushed like a rose, and Bialka seeing this, maliciously whispered in her ear:

"Just the kind of a husband for you. Keep away from the King!"

"And Przegoń?" questioned Spiewna.

"You may have him," threw out Bialka.

Przegoń did not see the King, but he learned of his arrival and of his gifts to Bialka. He wished to speak to Bialka, but she, busy with her guest, who exaggerated his compliments and promised golden mountains, did not care to see him. He stayed away from his unfaithful sweetheart and waited to see what time would bring forth.

One night, and 'twas a night with the full moon, a scented intoxicating night, under the window of the room where both sisters slept, there came sounds of a guitar accompanied by a song.

"The King!" murmured Bialka and she jumped to the window.

The King sang:

Out of the mist thou shalt have palaces,
For thy comfort and pleasures I will care
And pay with gold for thy every smile.
Attired, bejewelled like a peacock
Thou shalt be Queen in the royal gardens.

"Do you hear, do you hear?" said Bialka to Spiewna. "Thus sings the King!"

Then later under the window fluted the country fife. Bialka looked out of the window and noticed Bartek. Seeing her sister moved by the sad and sweet tones of the fife, she roared with laughter.

The fife stopped playing and they heard this song:

Do not come to me with pretense
But with love in thy pure eyes
That knows another's love.
Be not touched with a royal gown
That is worn by a fool's soul,
A soul that knows not what is love.

"Thus sings Bartek!" called Spiewna.

"Ha-ha-ha!" rang out Bialka's venomous laughter. She leaned over the window and called aloud into the silent night:

"Drive away the fool, Your Majesty, who has the boldness to interrupt your song and insult your royal soul! Order him away, for he steals from us this beautiful night!"

"I will punish him more severely than you think," was the answer, "because to-morrow he will marry your sister."

"And when we?" asked Bialka.

"Even now. Come to me!"

Bialka jumped out of the window, and there she met face to face with Przegoń.

"What are you doing here?" she asked him haughtily.

"I came to wish you happiness with this—king's Jester," replied Przegoń pointing to Pies̀.

"What? What?" cried Bialka, looking with frightened eyes at the splendid dress, like a king's.

And in the room, where Spiewna remained, Bartek's fife rang out followed by a song:

'Tis hard to find true love
Under an alluring purple gown,
Infirmity shall remain in heart
With all the roses torn aside.
Ugly looks and lameness and a hump
May all be covered with a royal cloak.
The King wished for a true heart;
The fool desired fun and laughter;
And both are satisfied.
Therefore the fool dressed like a King;
The King put on the peasant's garb.
Now, maiden, cry for thy alluring loss
And understand these prophesying words:
That people are not judged by looks
But by their hearts and deeds.

The golden carriage came to the door, a thousand torches were lighted, a thousand knights with Przegoń at the head surrounded the royal carriage, into which Spiewna was led with her bridesmaids, and they all went to the King's palace to celebrate the wedding. The mother rejoiced at Spiewna's happiness, but she grieved over the neglected Bialka, who had to grow sixteen beds of rue before she married an old organist.

Czechoslovakia

Present-day Czechoslovakia is the home of several groups of people—
the largest groups being the Czechs and Moravians in the west and the Slovaks in
the east. They are Slavic peoples, but for a long part of their history
they were dominated by the Magyars of Hungary. At different times Germany
also greatly influenced Czech life and customs. All this is reflected in
Czechoslovakian folklore, although it is not easily discernible in the folk tales.
Only one collection of Czechoslovakian tales is relatively recent,
Virginia Haviland's Favorite Fairy Tales Told in Czechoslovakia *(1966), and*
its five tales are from collections made before 1930. Fortunately, Parker
Fillmore's The Shoemaker's Apron *(1920), in which the two selections here first*
appeared, gave us fine stories told in clear, vigorous English that
preserves the Czechoslovakian folk feeling with its strong current of humor.

BUDULINEK

It is interesting to note the numbers of stories which warn children not to let anyone in the house when they are alone. This is an exceptionally exciting story for the seven- and eight-year-olds and readily lends itself to amusing illustration. It is easy to set the organ-grinder's chant to one's own simple melody.

There was once a little boy named Budulinek. He lived with his old Granny in a cottage near a forest.

Granny went out to work every day. In the morning when she went away she always said:

"There, Budulinek, there's your dinner on the table and mind, you mustn't open the door no matter who knocks!"

One morning Granny said:

"Now, Budulinek, today I'm leaving you some soup for your dinner. Eat it when dinner time comes. And remember what I always say: don't open the door no matter who knocks."

She went away and pretty soon Lishka, the sly old mother fox, came and knocked on the door.

"Budulinck!" she called. "You know me! Open the door! Please!"

Budulinek called back:

"No, I mustn't open the door."

But Lishka, the sly old mother fox, kept on knocking.

"Listen, Budulinek," she said: "if you open the door, do you know what I'll do? I'll give you a ride on my tail!"

Now Budulinek thought to himself:

"Oh, that would be fun to ride on the tail of Lishka, the fox!"

So Budulinek forgot all about what Granny said to him every day and opened the door.

Lishka, the sly old thing, came into the room and what do you think she did? Do you think she gave Budulinek a ride on her tail? Well, she didn't. She just went over to the table and gobbled up the bowl of soup that Granny had put

there for Budulinek's dinner and then she ran away.

When dinner time came Budulinek hadn't anything to eat.

In the evening when Granny came home, she said:

"Budulinek, did you open the door and let anyone in?"

Budulinek was crying because he was so hungry, and he said:

"Yes, I let in Lishka, the old mother fox, and she ate up all my dinner, too!"

Granny said:

"Now, Budulinek, you see what happens when you open the door and let some one in. Another time remember what Granny says and don't open the door."

The next morning Granny cooked some porridge for Budulinek's dinner and said:

"Now, Budulinek, here's some porridge for your dinner. Remember, while I'm gone you must not open the door no matter who knocks."

Granny was no sooner out of sight than Lishka came again and knocked on the door.

"Oh, Budulinek!" she called. "Open the door and let me in!"

But Budulinek said:

"No, I won't open the door!"

"Oh, now, Budulinek, please open the door!" Lishka begged. "You know me! Do you know what I'll do if you open the door? I'll give you a ride on my tail! Truly I will!"

Budulinek thought to himself:

"This time maybe she will give me a ride on her tail."

So he opened the door.

Lishka came into the room, gobbled up Budulinek's porridge, and ran away without giving him any ride at all.

When dinner time came Budulinek hadn't anything to eat.

In the evening when Granny came home she said:

"Budulinek, did you open the door and let anyone in?"

Budulinek was crying again because he was so hungry, and he said:

"Yes, I let in Lishka, the old mother fox, and she ate up all my porridge, too!"

"Budulinek, you're a bad boy!" Granny said. "If you open the door again, I'll have to spank you! Do you hear?"

The next morning before she went to work, Granny cooked some peas for Budulinek's dinner.

As soon as Granny was gone he began eating the peas, they were so good.

Presently Lishka, the fox, came and knocked on the door.

"Budulinek!" she called. "Open the door! I want to come in!"

But Budulinek wouldn't open the door. He took his bowl of peas and went to the window and ate them there where Lishka could see him.

"Oh, Budulinek!" Lishka begged. "You know me! Please open the door! This time I promise you I'll give you a ride on my tail! Truly I will!"

She just begged and begged until at last Budulinek opened the door. Then Lishka jumped into the room and do you know what she did? She put her nose right into the bowl of peas and gobbled them all up!

Then she said to Budulinek:

"Now get on my tail and I'll give you a ride!"

So Budulinek climbed on Lishka's tail and Lishka went running around the room faster and faster until Budulinek was dizzy and just had to hold on with all his might.

Then, before Budulinek knew what was happening, Lishka slipped out of the house and ran off swiftly into the forest, home to her hole, with Budulinek still on her tail! She hid Budulinek down in her hole with her own three children and she wouldn't let him out. He had to stay there with the three little foxes and they all teased him and bit him. And then wasn't he sorry he had disobeyed his Granny! And, oh, how he cried!

When Granny came home she found the door open and no little Budulinek anywhere. She looked high and low, but no, there was no little Budulinek. She asked everyone she met had they seen her little Budulinek, but nobody had. So poor Granny just cried and cried, she was so lonely and sad.

One day an organ-grinder with a wooden leg began playing in front of Granny's cottage. The music made her think of Budulinek.

"Organ-grinder," Granny said, "here's a penny for you. But, please, don't play any more. Your music makes me cry."

"Why does it make you cry?" the organ-grinder asked.

"Because it reminds me of Budulinek," Granny said, and she told the organ-grinder all about Budulinek and how somebody had stolen him away.

The organ-grinder said:

"Poor Granny! I tell you what I'll do: as I go around and play my organ I'll keep my eyes open for Budulinek. If I find him I'll bring him back to you."

"Will you?" Granny cried. "If you bring me back my little Budulinek I'll give you a measure of rye and a measure of millet and a measure of poppy seed and a measure of everything in the house!"

So the organ-grinder went off and everywhere he played his organ he looked for Budulinek. But he couldn't find him.

At last one day while he was walking through the forest he thought he heard a little boy crying. He looked around everywhere until he found a fox's hole.

"Oho!" he said to himself. "I believe that wicked old Lishka must have stolen Budulinek! She's probably keeping him here with her own three children! I'll soon find out."

So he put down his organ and began to play. And as he played he sang softly:

> "One old fox
> And two, three, four,

And Budulinek
He makes one more!"

Old Lishka heard the music playing and she said to her oldest child:

"Here, son, give the old man a penny and tell him to go away because my head aches."

So the oldest little fox climbed out of the hole and gave the organ-grinder a penny and said:

"My mother says, please will you go away because her head aches."

As the organ-grinder reached over to take the penny, he caught the oldest little fox and stuffed him into a sack. Then he went on playing and singing:

> "One old fox
> And two and three
> And Budulinek
> Makes four for me!"

Presently Lishka sent out her second child with a penny and the organ-grinder caught the second little fox in the same way and stuffed it also into the sack. Then he went on grinding his organ and softly singing:

> "One old fox
> And another for me,
> And Budulinek
> He makes the three."

"I wonder why that old man still plays his organ," Lishka said and sent out her third child with a penny.

So the organ-grinder caught the third little fox and stuffed it also into the sack. Then he kept on playing and singing softly:

> "One old fox—
> I'll soon get you!—
> And Budulinek
> He makes just two."

At last Lishka herself came out. So he caught her, too, and stuffed her in with her children. Then he sang:

"Four naughty foxes
Caught alive!
And Budulinek
He makes the five!"

The organ-grinder went to the hole and called down:

"Budulinek! Budulinek! Come out!"

As there were no foxes left to hold him back, Budulinek was able to crawl out.

When he saw the organ-grinder he cried and said:

"Oh, please, Mr. Organ-Grinder, I want to go home to my Granny!"

"I'll take you home to your Granny," the organ-grinder said, "but first I must punish these naughty foxes."

The organ-grinder cut a strong switch and gave the four foxes in the sack a terrible beating until they begged him to stop and promised that they would never again do anything to Budulinek.

Then the organ-grinder let them go and he took Budulinek home to Granny.

Granny was delighted to see her little Budulinek and she gave the organ-grinder a measure of rye and a measure of millet and a measure of poppy seed and a measure of everything else in the house.

And Budulinek never again opened the door!

CLEVER MANKA

This is a good example of the humor in Czech stories. It especially delights girls after hearing "The Most Obedient Wife." Riddles abounded in songs, tales, and morality plays during the Middle Ages, and this tale is but one example of how they have persisted and shaped later folk tales. Generally the riddles had to do with Christ and the Devil playing for a poor sinner's soul. Echoes of this may also be found in the Ethiopian tale "The Fire on the Mountain" and in the American tale "Young Melvin," though it is unlikely that they have any connection whatsoever with medieval moralities.

There was once a rich farmer who was as grasping and unscrupulous as he was rich. He was always driving a hard bargain and always getting the better of his poor neighbors. One of these neighbors was a humble shepherd who in return for service was to receive from the farmer a heifer. When the time of payment came the farmer refused to give the shepherd the heifer and the shepherd was forced to lay the matter before the burgomaster.

The burgomaster, who was a young man and as yet not very experienced, listened to both sides and when he had deliberated he said:

"Instead of deciding this case, I will put a riddle to you both and the man who makes the best answer shall have the heifer. Are you agreed?"

The farmer and the shepherd accepted this proposal and the burgomaster said:

"Well then, here is my riddle: What is the swiftest thing in the world? What is the sweetest thing? What is the richest? Think out your answers and bring them to me at this same hour tomorrow."

The farmer went home in a temper.

"What kind of a burgomaster is this young fellow!" he growled. "If he had let me keep the heifer I'd have sent him a bushel of pears. But now I'm in a fair way of losing the heifer for I can't think of any answer to his foolish riddle."

"What is the matter, husband?" his wife asked.

"It's that new burgomaster. The old one would have given me the heifer without any argument, but this young man thinks to decide the case by asking us riddles."

When he told his wife what the riddle was, she cheered him greatly by telling him that she knew the answers at once.

"Why, husband," said she, "our gray mare must be the swiftest thing in the world. You know yourself nothing ever passes us on the road. As for the sweetest, did you ever taste honey any sweeter than ours? And I'm sure there's nothing richer than our chest of golden ducats that we've been laying by these forty years."

The farmer was delighted.

"You're right, wife, you're right! That heifer remains ours!"

The shepherd when he got home was downcast and sad. He had a daughter, a clever girl named Manka, who met him at the door of his cottage and asked:

"What is it, father? What did the burgomaster say?"

The shepherd sighed.

"I'm afraid I've lost the heifer. The burgomaster set us a riddle and I know I shall never guess it."

"Perhaps I can help you," Manka said. "What is it?"

So the shepherd gave her the riddle and the next day as he was setting out for the burgomaster's, Manka told him what answers to make.

When he reached the burgomaster's house, the farmer was already there rubbing his hands and beaming with self-importance.

The burgomaster again propounded the riddle and then asked the farmer his answers.

The farmer cleared his throat and with a pompous air began:

"The swiftest thing in the world? Why, my dear sir, that's my gray mare, of course, for no other horse ever passes us on the road. The sweetest? Honey from my beehives, to be sure. The richest? What can be richer than my chest of golden ducats!"

And the farmer squared his shoulders and smiled triumphantly.

"H'm," said the young burgomaster, dryly. Then he asked:

"What answers does the shepherd make?"

The shepherd bowed politely and said:

"The swiftest thing in the world is thought for thought can run any distance in the twinkling of an eye. The sweetest thing of all is sleep for when a man is tired and sad what can be sweeter? The richest thing is the earth for out of the earth come all the riches of the world."

"Good!" the burgomaster cried. "Good! The heifer goes to the shepherd!"

Later the burgomaster said to the shepherd:

"Tell me, now, who gave you those answers? I'm sure they never came out of your own head."

At first the shepherd tried not to tell, but when the burgomaster pressed him he confessed that they came from his daughter, Manka. The burgomaster, who thought that he would like to make another test of Manka's cleverness, sent for ten eggs. He gave them to the shepherd and said:

"Take these eggs to Manka and tell her to have them hatched out by tomorrow and to bring me the chicks."

When the shepherd reached home and gave Manka the burgomaster's message, Manka laughed and said: "Take a handful of millet and go right back to the burgomaster. Say to him: 'My daughter sends you this millet. She says that if you plant, grow it, and have it harvested by tomorrow, she'll bring you the ten chicks and you can feed them the ripe grain.' "

When the burgomaster heard this, he laughed heartily.

"That's a clever girl of yours," he told the shepherd. "If she's as comely as she is clever, I think I'd like to marry her. Tell her to come to see me, but she must come neither by day nor by night, neither riding nor walking, neither dressed nor undressed."

When Manka received this message she waited until the next dawn when night was gone and day not yet arrived. Then she wrapped herself in a fishnet and, throwing one leg over a goat's back and keeping one foot on the ground, she went to the burgomaster's house.

Now I ask you: did she go dressed? No, she wasn't dressed. A fishnet isn't clothing. Did she go undressed? Of course not, for wasn't she covered with a fishnet? Did she walk to the burgomaster's? No, she didn't walk for she went with one leg thrown over a goat. Then did she ride? Of course she didn't ride for wasn't she walking on one foot?

When she reached the burgomaster's house she called out:

"Here I am, Mr. Burgomaster, and I've come neither by day nor by night, neither riding nor walking, neither dressed nor undressed."

The young burgomaster was so delighted with Manka's cleverness and so pleased with her comely looks that he proposed to her at once and in a short time married her.

"But understand, my dear Manka," he said, "you are not to use that cleverness of yours at my expense. I won't have you interfering in any of my cases. In fact if ever you give advice to any one who comes to me for judgment, I'll turn you out of my house at once and send you home to your father."

All went well for a time. Manka busied herself

in her house-keeping and was careful not to interfere in any of the burgomaster's cases.

Then one day two farmers came to the burgomaster to have a dispute settled. One of the farmers owned a mare which had foaled in the marketplace. The colt had run under the wagon of the other farmer and thereupon the owner of the wagon claimed the colt as his property.

The burgomaster, who was thinking of something else while the case was being presented, said carelessly:

"The man who found the colt under his wagon is, of course, the owner of the colt."

As the owner of the mare was leaving the burgomaster's house, he met Manka and stopped to tell her about the case. Manka was ashamed of her husband for making so foolish a decision and she said to the farmer:

"Come back this afternoon with a fishing net and stretch it across the dusty road. When the burgomaster sees you he will come out and ask you what you are doing. Say to him that you're catching fish. When he asks you how you can expect to catch fish in a dusty road, tell him it's just as easy for you to catch fish in a dusty road as it is for a wagon to foal. Then he'll see the injustice of his decision and have the colt returned to you. But remember one thing: you mustn't let him find out that it was I who told you to do this."

That afternoon when the burgomaster chanced to look out the window he saw a man stretching a fishnet across the dusty road. He went out to him and asked: "What are you doing?"

"Fishing."

"Fishing in a dusty road? Are you daft?"

"Well," the man said, "it's just as easy for me to catch fish in a dusty road as it is for a wagon to foal."

Then the burgomaster recognized the man as the owner of the mare and he had to confess that what he said was true.

"Of course the colt belongs to your mare and must be returned to you. But tell me," he said, "who put you up to this? You didn't think of it yourself."

The farmer tried not to tell but the burgomaster questioned him until he found out that Manka was at the bottom of it. This made him very angry. He went into the house and called his wife.

"Manka," he said, "do you forget what I told you would happen if you went interfering in any of my cases? Home you go this very day. I don't care to hear any excuses. The matter is settled. You may take with you the one thing you like best in my house for I won't have people saying that I treated you shabbily."

Manka made no outcry.

"Very well, my dear husband, I shall do as you say: I shall go to my father's cottage and take with me the one thing I like best in your house. But don't make me go until after supper. We have been very happy together and I should like to eat one last meal with you. Let us have no more words but be kind to each other as we've always been and then part as friends."

The burgomaster agreed to this and Manka prepared a fine supper of all the dishes of which her husband was particularly fond. The burgomaster opened his choicest wine and pledged Manka's health. Then he set to, and the supper was so good that he ate and ate and ate. And the more he ate, the more he drank until at last he grew drowsy and fell sound asleep in his chair. Then without awakening him Manka had him carried out to the wagon that was waiting to take her home to her father.

The next morning when the burgomaster opened his eyes, he found himself lying in the shepherd's cottage.

"What does this mean?" he roared out.

"Nothing, dear husband, nothing!" Manka said. "You know you told me I might take with me the one thing I liked best in your house, so of course I took you! That's all."

For a moment the burgomaster rubbed his eyes in amazement. Then he laughed loud and heartily to think how Manka had outwitted him.

"Manka," he said, "you're too clever for me. Come on, my dear, let's go home."

So they climbed back into the wagon and drove home.

The burgomaster never again scolded his wife but thereafter whenever a very difficult case came up he always said:

"I think we had better consult my wife. You know she's a very clever woman."

Union of Soviet Socialist Republics

The folk tales of the Soviet Union present a formidable subject for study. The great collection by A. N. Afanasiev, Russian Fairy Tales *(1855–1864), is held to be as much a landmark in Russian folk-tale study as was the work of the Grimms in Germany, although Afanasiev took his tales largely from those already collected by others. Since the 1950's a movement has been underway in the Soviet Union to publish its collected folklore in a series that will run to perhaps a hundred volumes or more. Just the strictly Russian folk tales, folk epics, and folk songs would fill many volumes, but the folklore of the other hundred or so nationalities in the Soviet Union is also being systematically recorded. Russian folklore is as dazzling as the history of Russia and is so imaginatively rich that opera and ballet have drawn frequently on its themes and episodes. Violence, beauty, and strangeness are some of the elements that color the tales. Although numerous Russian folk tales are available to children in English, they scarcely do justice to the variety of tales that one may find within Soviet borders. The Bibliography reveals that many individual stories are found in picture-book form, while several other titles are collections that represent separately Armenia, Latvia, Russia, and the Ukraine. A more wide-ranging selection of tales may be found in* Tales of Faraway Folk *and* More Tales of Faraway Folk, *by Babette Deutsch and Avrahm Yarmolinsky. These two books gather up twenty-five tales from Central Asia, Eastern Russia, Estonia, and the Baltic and Caucasus regions.*

THE FOOLISH MAN

(Armenian)

Only part of the Armenian people live in the Soviet Union (Armenian Soviet Socialist Republic) because their ancient homeland is now divided among Turkey, Iran, and the Soviet Union. Most of the Armenian tales have been unknown to children in this country, but the book from which our selection was taken, Once There Was and Was Not, *does something to change that. It is a rare bonanza for storytellers and a beautiful reflection of the Armenian mind and life. This tale is one with a bite, figuratively and literally!*

Once there was and was not in ancient Armenia a poor man who worked and toiled hard from morn till night, but nevertheless remained poor.

Finally one day he became so discouraged that he decided to go in search of God in order to ask

Him how long he must endure such poverty—and to beg of Him a favor.

On his way, the man met a wolf.

"Good day, brother man," asked the wolf. "Where are you bound in such a hurry?"

"I go in search of God," replied the man. "I have a complaint to lodge with Him."

"Well," said the wolf, "would you do me a kindness? When you find God, will you complain to Him for me, too? Tell Him you met a half-starved wolf who searches the woods and fields for food from morning till night—and though he works hard and long, still finds nothing to eat. Ask God why He does not provide for wolves since He created them?"

"I will tell Him of your complaint," agreed the poor man, and continued on his way.

As he hurried over the hills and through the valleys, he chanced to meet a beautiful maid.

"Where do you go in such a hurry, my brother?" asked the maid.

"I go in search of God," replied the man.

"Oh, kind friend, when you find God, would you ask Him something for me? Tell Him you met a maid on your way. Tell Him she is young and fair and very rich—but very unhappy. Ask God why she cannot know happiness. What will become of her? Ask God why He will not help her to be happy."

"I will tell Him of your trouble," promised the poor man, and continued on his way.

Soon he met a tree which seemed all dried up and dying even though it grew by the side of a river.

"Where do you go in such a hurry, O traveler?" called the dry tree.

"I go in search of God," answered the man. "I have a complaint to lodge with Him."

"Wait a moment, O traveler," begged the tree, "I, too, have a question for God.

"Please ask Him why I am dry both in summer and winter. Though I live by this wet river, my leaves do not turn green. Ask God how long I must suffer. Ask Him that for me, good friend," said the tree.

The man listened to the tree's complaint, promised to tell God, and continued once again upon his way.

Finally, the poor man reached the end of his journey. He found God seated beneath the ledge of a cliff.

"Good day," said the man as he approached God.

"Welcome, traveler," God returned his greeting. "Why have you journeyed so far? What is your trouble?"

"Well, I want to know why there is injustice in the world. Is it fair that I toil and labor from morn till night—and yet never seem to earn enough for a full stomach, while many who do not work half as hard as I live and eat as rich men do?"

"Go then," replied God. "I present you the Gift of Luck. Go find it and enjoy it to the end of your days."

"I have yet another complaint, my Lord," continued the man—and he proceeded to list the complaints and requests of the starved wolf, the beautiful maid, and the parched tree.

God gave appropriate answers to each of the three complaints, whereupon the poor man thanked Him and started on his way homeward.

Soon he came upon the dry, parched tree.

"What message did God have for me?" asked the tree.

"He said that beneath your trunk there lies a pot of gold which prevents the water from seeping up your trunk to your leaves. God said your branches will never turn green until the pot of gold is removed."

"Well, what are you waiting for, foolish man!" exclaimed the tree. "Dig up that pot of gold. It will make you rich—and permit me to turn green and live again!"

"Oh, no," protested the man. "I have no time to dig up a pot of gold. God has given me the Gift of Luck. I must hurry and search for it." And he hurried on his way.

Presently, he met the beautiful maid who was waiting for him. "Oh, kind friend, what message did God have for me?"

"God said that you will soon meet a kind man who will prove to be a good life's companion to you. No longer will you be lonely. Happiness and contentment will come to you," reported the poor man.

"In that case, what are you waiting for, foolish man?" exclaimed the maid. "Why don't you stay here and be my life's companion."

"Oh, no! I have no time to stay with you. God has given me the Gift of Luck. I must hurry and search for it." And the man hurried on his way.

Some distance away, the starving wolf impatiently awaited the man's coming, and hailed him with a shout.

"Well, what did God say? What message did He send to me?"

"Brother wolf, so many things have happened since I saw you last," said the man. "I hardly know where to begin. On my way to seek God, I met a beautiful maid who begged me to ask God the reason for her unhappiness. And I met a parched tree who wanted God to explain the dryness of its branches even though it stood by a wet river.

"I told God about these matters. He bade me tell the maid to seek a life's companion in order to find happiness. He bade me warn the tree about a pot of gold buried near its trunk which must be removed before the branches can receive nourishment from the earth.

"On my return, I brought God's answers to the maid and to the tree. The maid asked me to stay and be her life's companion, while the tree asked me to dig up the pot of gold.

"Of course, I had to refuse both since God gave me the Gift of Luck—and I must hurry along to search for it!"

"Ah-h-h, brother man, and what was God's reply to me?" asked the starving wolf.

"As for you," replied the man, "God said that you would remain hungry until you met a silly and foolish man whom you could eat up. Only then, said God, would your hunger be satisfied."

"Hmmmmmm," mused the wolf, "where in the world will I find a man more silly and stupid than you?"

And he ate up the foolish man.

THE DEVIL'S BRIDE

(Latvian)

Like the Armenians, the Latvians are a people whose culture is very old. The Latvian folk tales have much in common with the great body of European folklore, but they reveal, of course, something of Latvian history and attitudes. "The Devil's Bride" is one of hundreds of amusing tales in which the devil is bested.

A long time ago there lived on a farm a farm hand and a milkmaid. They never saw eye to eye, and they fought together like cat and dog. The people around them would watch and smile and say, "Just wait and see! You will marry in the end. Once old John and Lisel, who live on the next farmstead, were just the same. Then they could scarce wait until fall when working people have time to marry. Just at oak-cutting time, the pastor announced their marriage banns, and after three weeks the wedding was celebrated. Now they have grown children who themselves are ready for marriage. Just wait! You will marry in the end!"

Now, the farm hand was no ordinary farm hand. During the winter he served as overseer to the baron's kiln house. He had a horse of his own and money besides. When he heard his

"The Devil's Bride." From *Tit for Tat,* copyright © 1967 by Mae J. Durham. Reprinted by permission of Harcourt, Brace & World, Inc.

neighbors' talk, he would say, "If I take the milkmaid as my wife, may a thief steal my horse!"

And the milkmaid would say, "If I marry the farm hand, may the devil take my soul!"

But indeed! In just a short time, there they were, the farm hand and the milkmaid, married and celebrating their wedding feast.

After the wedding the bride was driven from the church to her new home. It was then that the devil appeared to claim her soul; and it was then that a thief appeared to steal the farm hand's horse. The two met behind the garden fence.

"Where are you going?" asked the devil of the thief.

"I am going to steal that horse," answered the thief. "And where are you going?" asked the thief of the devil.

"I am here to claim the soul of the milkmaid," answered the devil. "But I cannot do it alone. You must help me. When we get inside, I will crawl under the bench, and you will hide behind the stove. The bride will sit on the bench at the head of the table. I will step on her foot. Immediately, she will sneeze, and you are to say, 'The devil take the bride's soul!' After you say this three times, the bride will die, and I can claim her soul. There will be great confusion. Everyone will run about with endless lamenting. In the meantime, you can steal the horse with no trouble at all."

The devil and the thief entered the house where the devil noticed a red-berry tree switch. "Of that, I am afraid. If someone were to flail me with that switch, my bones would shatter into dust."

Once inside the house, the devil crawled under the bench, and the thief hid behind the stove. Just then the bride came into the room and sat down on the bench at the head of the table. The devil stepped on her foot; the bride sneezed so loudly that the entire room resounded. Everyone stood about as though bewitched or dumbstruck. No one had wit enough to say, "God help you!" Only the thief, from behind the stove, called out in a loud voice, "God help you!"

The devil was angry but thought, "Let him say it thus this time; it does not matter so long as the third time he says, 'The devil take the bride's soul!' That will do."

The devil stepped on the bride's foot a second time. The bride sneezed again as loudly as the first time. No one said, "God help you!"—no one but the thief who was still hiding behind the stove. "God help you!"

The devil grew so angry that he was ready to devour the thief. Still, he thought, "There is the third time." He stepped on the bride's foot for the third time. She sneezed so loudly that the entire room trembled, but the wonder of it was no one, not even a chicken, had the sense to say, "God help you!" The bride turned pale. At this, the thief put his head around the corner of the stove and exclaimed at the top of his voice, "God help you!" Immediately, the bride recovered, got up, and started to dance.

The devil turned blue with anger and shouted, "People! People! Look there is a thief behind the stove!"

And the thief called out, "People! People! The devil is under the bride's bench!"

No one looked for the thief. All eyes turned to the bench. No one save the thief could see the devil. Suddenly, the thief remembered what the devil had said about the red-berry tree switch. The thief seized the switch and started to whip the devil. Dust flew in all directions; the devil

was driven out of the door never to be seen again. Everyone surrounded the thief, asking him how he had become mixed up with the devil.

"Why, it was the doing of the farm hand and the milkmaid. Did he not say, 'If I take the milk-maid as my wife, may a thief steal my horse'? And did she not say, 'If I marry the farm hand, may the devil take my soul'?"

The young couple were happy that their quarreling had taken such a happy turn, and they gave the horse to the thief as a wedding-guest gift. They forgot that they did not see eye to eye, and they forgot to fight like cat and dog. So it was that they lived a long and contented life together.

SADKO

(Russian)

This story, which has the strangeness of a dream, inspired an opera and may be dramatized by older children, either with puppet or human actors. At the conclusion of the story, the reintroduction of Maroosia and old Peter seems to shatter the spell of the tale. Why not omit them and end with the speculative, "And what happened after that? Well, some say Sadko took his dulcimer and swam out again. . . ."

In Novgorod in the old days there was a young man—just a boy he was—the son of a rich merchant who had lost all his money and died. So Sadko was very poor. He had not a kopeck in the world, except what the people gave him when he played his dulcimer for their dancing. He had blue eyes and curling hair, and he was strong, and would have been merry; but it is dull work playing for other folk to dance, and Sadko dared not dance with any young girl, for he had no money to marry on, and he did not want to be chased away as a beggar. And the young women of Novgorod, they never looked at the handsome Sadko. No; they smiled with their bright eyes at the young men who danced with them, and if they ever spoke to Sadko, it was just to tell him sharply to keep the music going or to play faster.

So Sadko lived alone with his dulcimer, and

"Sadko." From *Old Peter's Russian Tales* edited by Arthur Ransome. Copyright 1917 by Thomas Nelson & Sons Ltd. Reprinted by permission of the publisher

made do with half a loaf when he could not get a whole, and with crust when he had no crumb. He did not mind so very much what came to him, so long as he could play his dulcimer and walk along the banks of the little river Volkhov [1] that flows by Novgorod, or on the shores of the lake, making music for himself, and seeing the pale mists rise over the water, and dawn or sunset across the shining river.

"There is no girl in all Novgorod as pretty as my little river," he used to say, and night after night he would sit by the banks of the river or on the shores of the lake, playing the dulcimer and singing to himself.

Sometimes he helped the fishermen on the lake, and they would give him a little fish for his supper in payment for his strong young arms.

And it happened that one evening the fishermen asked him to watch their nets for them on the shore, while they went off to take their fish to sell them in the square at Novgorod.

Sadko sat on the shore, on a rock, and played his dulcimer and sang. Very sweetly he sang of the fair lake and the lovely river—the little river that he thought prettier than all the girls of Novgorod. And while he was singing he saw a whirlpool in the lake, little waves flying from it across the water, and in the middle a hollow down into the water. And in the hollow he saw the head of a great man with blue hair and a gold crown. He knew that the huge man was the Tzar of the Sea. And the man came nearer, walking up out of the depths of the lake—a huge, great man, a very giant, with blue hair falling to his waist over his broad shoulders. The little waves ran from him in all directions as he came striding up out of the water.

Sadko did not know whether to run or stay; but the Tzar of the Sea called out to him in a great voice like wind and water in a storm,—

"Sadko of Novgorod, you have played and sung many days by the side of this lake and on the banks of the little river Volkhov. My daughters love your music, and it has pleased me too. Throw out a net into the water, and draw it in, and the waters will pay you for your singing.

[1] The Volkhov would be a big river if it were in England, and Sadko and old Peter called it little only because they loved it.

And if you are satisfied with the payment, you must come and play to us down in the green palace of the sea."

With that the Tzar of the Sea went down again into the waters of the lake. The waves closed over him with a roar, and presently the lake was as smooth and calm as it had ever been.

Sadko thought, and said to himself: "Well, there is no harm done in casting out a net." So he threw a net out into the lake.

He sat down again and played on his dulcimer and sang, and when he had finished his singing the dusk had fallen and the moon shone over the lake. He put down his dulcimer and took hold of the ropes of the net, and began to draw it up out of the silver water. Easily the ropes came, and the net, dripping and glittering in the moonlight.

"I was dreaming," said Sadko; "I was asleep when I saw the Tzar of the Sea, and there is nothing in the net at all."

And then, just as the last of the net was coming ashore, he saw something in it, square and dark. He dragged it out, and found it was a coffer. He opened the coffer, and it was full of precious stones—green, red, gold—gleaming in the light of the moon. Diamonds shone there like little bundles of sharp knives.

"There can be no harm in taking these stones," says Sadko, "whether I dreamed or not."

He took the coffer on his shoulder, and bent under the weight of it, strong though he was. He put it in a safe place. All night he sat and watched by the nets, and played and sang, and planned what he would do.

In the morning the fishermen came, laughing and merry after their night in Novgorod, and they gave him a little fish for watching their nets; and he made a fire on the shore, and cooked it and ate it as he used to do.

"And that is my last meal as a poor man," says Sadko. "Ah me! who knows if I shall be happier?"

Then he set the coffer on his shoulder and tramped away for Novgorod.

"Who is that?" they asked at the gates.

"Only Sadko, the dulcimer player," he replied.

"Turned porter?" said they.

"One trade is as good as another," said Sadko, and he walked into the city. He sold a few of the stones, two at a time, and with what he got for them he set up a booth in the market. Small things led to great, and he was soon one of the richest traders in Novgorod.

And now there was not a girl in the town who could look too sweetly at Sadko. "He has golden hair," says one. "Blue eyes like the sea," says another. "He could lift the world on his shoulders," says a third. A little money, you see, opens everybody's eyes.

But Sadko was not changed by his good fortune. Still he walked and played by the little river Volkhov. When work was done and the traders gone, Sadko would take his dulcimer and play and sing on the banks of the river. And still he said, "There is no girl in all Novgorod as pretty as my little river." Every time he came back from his long voyages—for he was trading far and near, like the greatest of merchants—he went at once to the banks of the river to see how his sweetheart fared. And always he brought some little present for her and threw it into the waves.

For twelve years he lived unmarried in Novgorod, and every year made voyages, buying and selling, and always growing richer and richer. Many were the mothers of Novgorod who would have liked to see him married to their daughters. Many were the pillows that were wet with the tears of the young girls, as they thought of the blue eyes of Sadko and his golden hair.

And then, in the twelfth year since he walked into Novgorod with the coffer on his shoulder, he was sailing a ship on the Caspian Sea, far, far away. For many days the ship sailed on, and Sadko sat on deck and played his dulcimer and sang of Novgorod and of the little river Volkhov that flows under the walls of the town. Blue was the Caspian Sea, and the waves were like furrows in a field, long lines of white under the steady wind, while the sails swelled and the ship shot over the water.

And suddenly the ship stopped.

In the middle of the sea, far from land, the ship stopped and trembled in the waves, as if she were held by a big hand.

"We are aground!" cry the sailors; and the captain, the great one, tells them to take soundings. Seventy fathoms by the bow it was, and seventy fathoms by the stern.

"We are not aground," says the captain, "unless there is a rock sticking up like a needle in the middle of the Caspian Sea!"

"There is magic in this," say the sailors.

"Hoist more sail," says the captain; and up go the white sails, swelling out in the wind, while the masts bend and creak. But still the ship lay shivering, and did not move, out there in the middle of the sea.

"Hoist more sail yet," says the captain; and up go the white sails, swelling and tugging, while the masts creak and groan. But still the ship lay there shivering and did not move.

"There is an unlucky one aboard," says an old sailor. "We must draw lots and find him, and throw him overboard into the sea."

The other sailors agreed to this. And still Sadko sat, and played his dulcimer and sang.

The sailors cut pieces of string, all of a length, as many as there were souls in the ship, and one of those strings they cut in half. Then they made them into a bundle, and each man plucked one string. And Sadko stopped his playing for a moment to pluck a string, and his was the string that had been cut in half.

"Magician, sorcerer, unclean one!" shouted the sailors.

"Not so," said Sadko. "I remember now an old promise I made, and I keep it willingly."

He took his dulcimer in his hand, and leapt from the ship into the blue Caspian Sea. The waves had scarcely closed over his head before the ship shot forward again, and flew over the waves like a swan's feather, and came in the end safely to her harbour.

"And what happened to Sadko?" asked Maroosia.

"You shall hear, little pigeon," said old Peter, and he took a pinch of snuff. Then he went on.

Sadko dropped into the waves, and the waves closed over him. Down he sank, like a pebble thrown into a pool, down and down. First the water was blue, then green, and strange fish with goggle eyes and golden fins swam round him as he sank. He came at last to the bottom of the sea.

And there, on the bottom of the sea, was a palace built of green wood. Yes, all the timbers of all the ships that have been wrecked in all the seas of the world are in that palace, and they are all green, and cunningly fitted together, so that the palace is worth a ten days' journey only to see it. And in front of the palace Sadko saw two big kobbly sturgeons, each a hundred and fifty feet long, lashing their tails and guarding the gates. Now, sturgeons are the oldest of all fish, and these were the oldest of all sturgeons.

Sadko walked between the sturgeons and through the gates of the palace. Inside there was a great hall, and the Tzar of the Sea lay resting in the hall, with his gold crown on his head and his blue hair floating round him in the water, and his great body covered with scales lying along the hall. The Tzar of the Sea filled the hall—and there is room in that hall for a village. And there were fish swimming this way and that in and out of the windows.

"Ah, Sadko," says the Tzar of the Sea, "you took what the sea gave you, but you have been a long time in coming to sing in the palaces of the sea. Twelve years I have lain here waiting for you."

"Great Tzar, forgive," says Sadko.

"Sing now," says the Tzar of the Sea, and his voice was like the beating of waves.

And Sadko played on his dulcimer and sang.

He sang of Novgorod and of the little river Volkhov which he loved. It was in his song that none of the girls of Novgorod were as pretty as the little river. And there was the sound of wind over the lake in his song, the sound of ripples under the prow of a boat, the sound of ripples on the shore, the sound of the river flowing past the tall reeds, the whispering sound of the river at night. And all the time he played cunningly on the dulcimer. The girls of Novgorod had never danced to so sweet a tune when in the old days Sadko played his dulcimer to earn kopecks and crusts of bread.

Never had the Tzar of the Sea heard such music.

"I would dance," said the Tzar of the Sea, and he stood up like a tall tree in the hall.

"Play on," said the Tzar of the Sea, and he strode through the gates. The sturgeons guarding the gates stirred the water with their tails.

And if the Tzar of the Sea was huge in the hall, he was huger still when he stood outside on the bottom of the sea. He grew taller and taller, towering like a mountain. His feet were like small hills. His blue hair hung down to his waist, and he was covered with green scales. And he began to dance on the bottom of the sea.

Great was that dancing. The sea boiled, and ships went down. The waves rolled as big as houses. The sea overflowed its shores, and whole towns were under water as the Tzar danced mightily on the bottom of the sea. Hither and thither rushed the waves, and the very earth shook at the dancing of that tremendous Tzar.

He danced till he was tired, and then he came back to the palace of green wood, and passed the sturgeons, and shrank into himself and came through the gates into the hall, where Sadko still played on his dulcimer and sang.

"You have played well and given me pleasure," says the Tzar of the Sea. "I have thirty daughters, and you shall choose one and marry her, and be a Prince of the Sea."

"Better than all maidens I love my little river," says Sadko; and the Tzar of the Sea laughed and threw his head back, with his blue hair floating all over the hall.

And then there came in the thirty daughters of the Tzar of the Sea. Beautiful they were, lovely, and graceful; but twenty-nine of them passed by, and Sadko fingered his dulcimer and thought of his little river.

There came in the thirtieth, and Sadko cried out aloud. "Here is the only maiden in the world as pretty as my little river!" says he. And she looked at him with eyes that shone like stars reflected in the river. Her hair was dark, like the river at night. She laughed, and her voice was like the flowing of the river.

"And what is the name of your little river?" says the Tzar.

"It is the little river Volkhov that flows by Novgorod," says Sadko; "but your daughter is as fair as the little river, and I would gladly marry her if she will have me."

"It is a strange thing," says the Tzar, "but Volkhov is the name of my youngest daughter."

He put Sadko's hand in the hand of his youngest daughter, and they kissed each other. And as they kissed, Sadko saw a necklace round her neck, and knew it for one he had thrown into the river as a present for his sweetheart.

She smiled, and "Come!" says she, and took him away to a palace of her own, and showed him a coffer; and in that coffer were bracelets and rings and earrings—all the gifts that he had thrown into the river.

And Sadko laughed for joy, and kissed the youngest daughter of the Tzar of the Sea, and she kissed him back.

"O my little river!" says he; "there is no girl in all the world but thou as pretty as my little river."

Well, they were married, and the Tzar of the Sea laughed at the wedding feast till the palace shook and the fish swam off in all directions.

And after the feast Sadko and his bride went off together to her palace. And before they slept she kissed him very tenderly, and she said,—

"O Sadko, you will not forget me? You will play to me sometimes, and sing?"

"I shall never lose sight of you, my pretty one," says he; "and as for music, I will sing and play all the day long."

"That's as may be," says she, and they fell asleep.

And in the middle of the night Sadko happened to turn in bed, and he touched the Princess with his left foot, and she was cold, cold, cold as ice in January. And with that touch of cold he woke, and he was lying under the walls of Novgorod, with his dulcimer in his hand, and one of his feet was in the little river Volkhov, and the moon was shining.

"O grandfather! And what happened to him after that?" asked Maroosia.

"There are many tales," said old Peter. "Some say he went into the town, and lived on alone until he died. But I think with those who say that he took his dulcimer and swam out into the middle of the river, and sank under water again, looking for his little Princess. They say he found her, and lives still in the green palaces of the bottom of the sea; and when there is a big storm, you may know that Sadko is playing on his dulcimer and singing, and that the Tzar of the Sea is dancing his tremendous dance, down there, on the bottom, under the waves."

"Yes, I expect that's what happened," said Ivan. "He'd have found it very dull in Novgorod, even though it is a big town."

THE FIRE-BIRD,
THE HORSE OF POWER,
AND THE PRINCESS VASILISSA

(Russian)

One wonders at the young archer's readiness for despair when he has the horse of power to solve all his problems. But no matter, for this story has the color and the extravagant magic of an Oriental tale that spins on and on. It makes a good introduction to Stravinsky's "Firebird" and indicates how folk tales have inspired musicians and artists. Children may enjoy making a puppet play out of this tale.

Once upon a time a strong and powerful Tzar ruled in a country far away. And among the servants was a young archer, and this archer had a horse—a horse of power—such a horse as belonged to the wonderful men of long ago—a great horse with a broad chest, eyes like fire, and hoofs of iron. There are no such horses nowadays. They sleep with the strong men who rode them, the bogatirs, until the time comes when Russia has need of them. Then the great horses will thunder up from under the ground, and the valiant men leap from the graves in the armour they have worn so long. The strong men will sit those horses of power, and there will be swinging of clubs and thunder of hoofs, and the earth will be swept clean from the enemies of God and the Tzar. So my grandfather used to say, and he was as much older than I as I am older than you, little ones, and so he should know.

Well, one day long ago, in the green time of the year, the young archer rode through the forest on his horse of power. The trees were green; there were little blue flowers on the ground under the trees; the squirrels ran in the branches, and the hares in the undergrowth; but no birds sang. The young archer rode along the forest path and listened for the singing of the birds, but there was no singing. The forest was

"The Fire-Bird, the Horse of Power, and the Princess Vasilissa." From *Old Peter's Russian Tales* edited by Arthur Ransome. Copyright 1917 by Thomas Nelson & Sons Ltd. Reprinted by permission of the publisher

silent, and the only noises in it were the scratching of four-footed beasts, the dropping of fir cones, and the heavy stamping of the horse of power in the soft path.

"What has come to the birds?" said the young archer.

He had scarcely said this before he saw a big curving feather lying in the path before him. The feather was larger than a swan's, larger than an eagle's. It lay in the path, glittering like a flame; for the sun was on it, and it was a feather of pure gold. Then he knew why there was no singing in the forest. For he knew that the fire-bird had flown that way, and that the feather in the path before him was a feather from its burning breast.

The horse of power spoke and said,

"Leave the golden feather where it lies. If you take it you will be sorry for it, and know the meaning of fear."

But the brave young archer sat on the horse of power and looked at the golden feather, and wondered whether to take it or not. He had no wish to learn what it was to be afraid, but he thought, "If I take it and bring it to the Tzar my master, he will be pleased; and he will not send me away with empty hands, for no tzar in the world has a feather from the burning breast of the fire-bird." And the more he thought, the more he wanted to carry the feather to the Tzar. And in the end he did not listen to the words of the horse of power. He leapt from the saddle, picked up the golden feather of the fire-bird, mounted his horse again, and galloped back through the green forest till he came to the palace of the Tzar.

He went into the palace, and bowed before the Tzar and said,—

"O Tzar, I have brought you a feather of the fire-bird."

The Tzar looked gladly at the feather, and then at the young archer.

"Thank you," says he; "but if you have brought me a feather of the fire-bird, you will be able to bring me the bird itself. I should like to see it. A feather is not a fit gift to bring to the Tzar. Bring the bird itself, or, I swear by my sword, your head shall no longer sit between your shoulders!"

The young archer bowed his head and went out. Bitterly he wept, for he knew now what it was to be afraid. He went out into the courtyard, where the horse of power was waiting for him, tossing its head and stamping on the ground.

"Master," says the horse of power, "why do you weep?"

"The Tzar has told me to bring him the fire-bird, and no man on earth can do that," says the young archer, and he bowed his head on his breast.

"I told you," says the horse of power, "that if you took the feather you would learn the meaning of fear. Well, do not be frightened yet, and do not weep. The trouble is not now; the trouble lies before you. Go back to the Tzar and ask him to have a hundred sacks of maize scattered over the open field, and let this be done at midnight."

The young archer went back into the palace and begged the Tzar for this, and the Tzar ordered that at midnight a hundred sacks of maize should be scattered in the open field.

Next morning, at the first redness in the sky, the young archer rode out on the horse of power, and came to the open field. The ground was scattered all over with maize. In the middle of the field stood a great oak with spreading boughs. The young archer leapt to the ground, took off the saddle, and let the horse of power loose to wander as he pleased about the field. Then he climbed up into the oak and hid himself among the green boughs.

The sky grew red and gold, and the sun rose. Suddenly there was a noise in the forest round the field. The trees shook and swayed, and almost fell. There was a mighty wind. The sea piled itself into waves with crests of foam, and the fire-bird came flying from the other side of the world. Huge and golden and flaming in the sun, it flew, dropped down with open wings into the field, and began to eat the maize.

The horse of power wandered in the field. This way he went, and that, but always he came a little nearer to the fire-bird. Nearer and nearer came the horse. He came close up to the fire-bird, and then suddenly stepped on one of its spreading fiery wings and pressed it heavily to the ground. The bird struggled, flapping mightily with its fiery wings, but it could not get away. The young archer slipped down from the tree, bound the fire-bird with three strong ropes, swung it on its back, saddled the horse, and rode to the palace of the Tzar.

The young archer stood before the Tzar, and his back was bent under the great weight of the fire-bird, and the broad wings of the bird hung on either side of him like fiery shields, and there was a trail of golden feathers on the floor. The young archer swung the magic bird to the foot of the throne before the Tzar; and the Tzar was glad, because since the beginning of the world no tzar had seen the fire-bird flung before him like a wild duck caught in a snare.

The Tzar looked at the fire-bird and laughed with pride. Then he lifted his eyes and looked at the young archer, and says he,

"As you have known how to take the fire-bird, you will know how to bring me my bride, for whom I have long been waiting. In the land of Never, on the very edge of the world, where the red sun rises in flame from behind the sea, lives the Princess Vasilissa. I will marry none but her. Bring her to me, and I will reward you with silver and gold. But if you do not bring her, then, by my sword, your head will no longer sit between your shoulders!"

The young archer wept bitter tears, and went

out into the courtyard where the horse of power was stamping the ground with its hoofs of iron and tossing its thick mane.

"Master, why do you weep?" asked the horse of power.

"The Tzar has ordered me to go to the land of Never, and to bring back the Princess Vasilissa."

"Do not weep—do not grieve. The trouble is not yet; the trouble is to come. Go to the Tzar and ask him for a silver tent with a golden roof, and for all kinds of food and drink to take with us on the journey."

The young archer went in and asked the Tzar for this, and the Tzar gave him a silver tent with silver hangings and a gold-embroidered roof, and every kind of rich wine and the tastiest of foods.

Then the young archer mounted the horse of power and rode off to the land of Never. On and on he rode, many days and nights, and came at last to the edge of the world, where the red sun rises in flame from behind the deep blue sea.

On the shore of the sea the young archer reined in the horse of power, and the heavy hoofs of the horse sank in the sand. He shaded his eyes and looked out over the blue water, and there was the Princess Vasilissa in a little silver boat, rowing with golden oars.

The young archer rode back a little way to where the sand ended and the green world began. There he loosed the horse to wander where he pleased, and to feed on the green grass. Then on the edge of the shore, where the green grass ended and grew thin and the sand began, he set up the shining tent, with its silver hangings and its gold-embroidered roof. In the tent he set out the tasty dishes and the rich flagons of wine which the Tzar had given him, and he sat himself down in the tent and began to regale himself, while he waited for the Princess Vasilissa.

The Princess Vasilissa dipped her golden oars in the blue water, and the little silver boat moved lightly through the dancing waves. She sat in the little boat and looked over the blue sea to the edge of the world, and there, between the golden sand and the green earth, she saw the tent standing, silver and gold in the sun. She dipped her oars, and came nearer to see it the better. The nearer she came the fairer seemed the tent, and at last she rowed to the shore and grounded her little boat on the golden sand, and stepped out daintily and came up to the tent. She was a little frightened, and now and again she stopped and looked back to where the silver boat lay on the sand with the blue sea beyond it. The young archer said not a word, but went on regaling himself on the pleasant dishes he had set out there in the tent.

At last the Princess Vasilissa came up to the tent and looked in.

The young archer rose and bowed before her. Says he—

"Good-day to you, Princess! Be so kind as to come in and take bread and salt with me, and taste my foreign wines."

And the Princess Vasilissa came into the tent and sat down with the young archer, and ate sweetmeats with him, and drank his health in a golden goblet of the wine the Tzar had given him. Now this wine was heavy, and the last drop from the goblet had no sooner trickled down her little slender throat than her eyes closed against her will, once, twice, and again.

"Ah me!" says the Princess, "it is as if the night itself had perched on my eyelids, and yet it is but noon."

And the golden goblet dropped to the ground from her little fingers, and she leant back on a cushion and fell instantly asleep. If she had been beautiful before, she was lovelier still when she lay in that deep sleep in the shadow of the tent.

Quickly the young archer called to the horse of power. Lightly he lifted the Princess in his strong young arms. Swiftly he leapt with her into the saddle. Like a feather she lay in the hollow of his left arm, and slept while the iron hoofs of the great horse thundered over the ground.

They came to the Tzar's palace, and the young archer leapt from the horse of power and carried the Princess into the palace. Great was the joy of the Tzar; but it did not last for long.

"Go, sound the trumpets for our wedding," he said to his servants; "let all the bells be rung."

The bells rang out and the trumpets sounded, and at the noise of the horns and the ringing of the bells the Princess Vasilissa woke up and looked about her.

"What is this ringing of bells," says she, "and this noise of trumpets? And where, oh, where is the blue sea, and my little silver boat with its golden oars?" And the princess put her hand to her eyes.

"The blue sea is far away," says the Tzar, "and for your little silver boat I give you a golden throne. The trumpets sound for our wedding, and the bells are ringing for our joy."

But the Princess turned her face away from the Tzar; and there was no wonder in that, for he was old, and his eyes were not kind.

And she looked with love at the young archer; and there was no wonder in that either, for he was a young man fit to ride the horse of power.

The Tzar was angry with the Princess Vasilissa, but his anger was as useless as his joy.

"Why, Princess," says he, "will you not marry me, and forget your blue sea and your silver boat?"

"In the middle of the deep blue sea lies a great stone," says the Princess, "and under that stone is hidden my wedding dress. If I cannot wear that dress I will marry nobody at all."

Instantly the Tzar turned to the young archer, who was waiting before the throne.

"Ride swiftly back," says he, "to the land of Never, where the red sun rises in flame. There—do you hear what the Princess says?—a great stone lies in the middle of the sea. Under that stone is hidden her wedding dress. Ride swiftly. Bring back that dress, or, by my sword, your head shall no longer sit between your shoulders!"

The young archer wept bitter tears, and went out into the courtyard, where the horse of power was waiting for him, champing its golden bit.

"There is no way of escaping death this time," he said.

"Master, why do you weep?" asked the horse of power.

"The Tzar has ordered me to ride to the land of Never, to fetch the wedding dress of the Princess Vasilissa from the bottom of the deep blue sea. Besides, the dress is wanted for the Tzar's wedding, and I love the Princess myself."

"What did I tell you?" says the horse of power. "I told you that there would be trouble if you picked up the golden feather from the fire-bird's burning breast. Well, do not be afraid. The trouble is not yet; the trouble is to come. Up! into the saddle with you, and away for the wedding dress of the Princess Vasilissa!"

The young archer leapt into the saddle, and the horse of power, with his thundering hoofs, carried him swiftly through the green forests and over the bare plains, till they came to the edge of the world, to the land of Never, where the red sun rises in flame from behind the deep blue sea. There they rested, at the very edge of the sea.

The young archer looked sadly over the wide waters, but the horse of power tossed its mane and did not look at the sea, but on the shore. This way and that it looked, and saw at last a huge lobster moving slowly, sideways, along the golden sand.

Nearer and nearer came the lobster, and it was a giant among lobsters, the tzar of all the lobsters; and it moved slowly along the shore, while the horse of power moved carefully and as if by accident, until it stood between the lobster and the sea. Then, when the lobster came close by, the horse of power lifted an iron hoof and set it firmly on the lobster's tail.

"You will be the death of me!" screamed the lobster—as well he might, with the heavy foot of the horse of power pressing his tail into the sand. "Let me live, and I will do whatever you ask of me."

"Very well," says the horse of power; "we will let you live," and he slowly lifted his foot. "But this is what you shall do for us. In the middle of the blue sea lies a great stone, and under that stone is hidden the wedding dress of the Princess Vasilissa. Bring it here."

The lobster groaned with the pain in his tail. Then he cried out in a voice that could be heard all over the deep blue sea. And the sea was disturbed, and from all sides lobsters in thousands made their way towards the bank. And the huge lobster that was the oldest of them all and the tzar of all the lobsters that live between the rising and the setting of the sun, gave them the order and sent them back into the sea. And the young archer sat on the horse of power and waited.

After a little time the sea was disturbed again, and the lobsters in their thousands came to the shore, and with them they brought a golden casket in which was the wedding dress of the Princess Vasilissa. They had taken it from under the great stone that lay in the middle of the sea.

The tzar of all the lobsters raised himself pain-fully on his bruised tail and gave the casket into the hands of the young archer, and instantly the horse of power turned himself about and galloped back to the palace of the Tzar, far, far away, at the other side of the green forests and beyond the treeless plains.

The young archer went into the palace and gave the casket into the hands of the Princess, and looked at her with sadness in his eyes, and she looked at him with love. Then she went away into an inner chamber, and came back in her wedding dress, fairer than the spring itself. Great was the joy of the Tzar. The wedding feast was made ready, and the bells rang, and flags waved about the palace.

The Tzar held out his hand to the Princess, and looked at her with his old eyes. But she would not take his hand.

"No," says she; "I will marry nobody until the man who brought me here has done penance in boiling water."

Instantly the Tzar turned to his servants and ordered them to make a great fire, and to fill a great cauldron with water and set it on the fire, and, when the water should be at its hottest, to take the young archer and throw him into it, to do penance for having taken the Princess Vasilissa away from the land of Never.

There was no gratitude in the mind of that Tzar.

Swiftly the servants brought wood and made a mighty fire, and on it they laid a huge cauldron of water, and built the fire around the walls of the cauldron. The fire burned hot and the water steamed. The fire burned hotter, and the water bubbled and seethed. They made ready to take the young archer, to throw him into the caul-dron.

"Oh, misery!" thought the young archer. "Why did I ever take the golden feather that had fallen from the fire-bird's burning breast? Why did I not listen to the wise words of the horse of power?" And he remembered the horse of power, and he begged the Tzar,

"O lord Tzar, I do not complain. I shall pres-ently die in the heat of the water on the fire. Suffer me, before I die, once more to see my horse."

"Let him see his horse," says the Princess.

"Very well," says the Tzar. "Say good-bye to

your horse, for you will not ride him again. But let your farewells be short, for we are waiting."

The young archer crossed the courtyard· and came to the horse of power, who was scraping the ground with his iron hoofs.

"Farewell, my horse of power," says the young archer. "I should have listened to your words of wisdom, for now the end is come, and we shall never more see the green trees pass above us and the ground disappear beneath us, as we race the wind between the earth and the sky."

"Why so?" says the horse of power.

"The Tzar has ordered that I am to be boiled to death—thrown into that cauldron that is seething on the great fire."

"Fear not," says the horse of power, "for the Princess Vasilissa has made him do this, and the end of these things is better than I thought. Go back, and when they are ready to throw you in the cauldron, do you run boldly and leap yourself into the boiling water."

The young archer went back across the courtyard, and the servants made ready to throw him into the cauldron.

"Are you sure that the water is boiling?" says the Princess Vasilissa.

"It bubbles and seethes," said the servants.

"Let me see for myself," says the Princess, and she went to the fire and waved her hand above the cauldron. And some say there was something in her hand, and some say there was not.

"It is boiling," says she, and the servants laid hands on the young archer; but he threw them from him, and ran and leapt boldly before them all into the very middle of the cauldron.

Twice he sank below the surface, borne around with the bubbles and foam of the boiling water. Then he leapt from the cauldron and stood before the Tzar and the Princess. He had become so beautiful a youth that all who saw cried aloud in wonder.

"This is a miracle," says the Tzar. And the Tzar looked at the beautiful young archer and thought of himself—of his age, of his bent back, and his gray beard, and his toothless gums. "I too will become beautiful," thinks he, and he rose from his throne and clambered into the cauldron, and was boiled to death in a moment.

And the end of the story? They buried the Tzar, and made the young archer Tzar in his place. He married the Princess Vasilissa, and lived many years with her in love and good fellowship. And he built a golden stable for the horse of power, and never forgot what he owed him.

A CLEVER JUDGE

(Russian)

Babette Deutsch, one of the authors of Tales of Faraway Folk, *from which this story is taken, identifies "A Clever Judge" as a Kirghiz folk tale. In the introduction she says: "The people who tell this tale live on the vast steppes or prairies of southwestern Asia. They are herders of cattle, sheep, and goats. And they are clever fellows, too, as you shall see."*

There lived a man in the steppes who was famous for his justice and wisdom. At that time if a man was known for his fairness, people came to him from far and wide to ask him to settle their disputes. And so it was that one day two villagers appeared before this wise man and asked him to settle their quarrel.

"Tell me your story," the judge said to the plaintiff.

"I had to leave my village," said the plaintiff, "for I had business elsewhere. And all my wealth was a hundred gold coins. I did not come by them easily. I had to work hard for them, and I did not want them to be stolen while I was away. Nor did I care to carry so much money with me on my journey. So I entrusted these gold coins for safekeeping to this man here. When I got back from my journey, he denied that he had ever received the money from me."

"And who saw you give him these hundred gold coins?" asked the judge.

"No one saw it. We went together to the heart of the forest and there I handed him the coins."

"What have you to say to this?" the judge asked, turning to the defendant.

The defendant shrugged his shoulders.

"I don't know what he is talking about," said

the man. "I never went to the forest with him. I never saw his gold coins."

"Do you remember the place where you handed over the money?" the judge asked the plaintiff.

"Of course I do. It was under a tall oak. I remember it very well. I can point it out with no trouble at all."

"So you do have a witness, after all," said the judge. "Here, take my signet ring, go to the tall tree under which you stood when you handed over the money, set the seal of my signet ring against the trunk, and bid the tree appear before me to bear out the truth of your story."

The plaintiff took the signet ring and went off to carry out the demand of the judge. The defendant remained behind and waited for his return.

After some time had passed, the judge turned to the defendant and asked, "Do you think he has reached the oak by this time?"

"No, not yet," was the answer.

After further time had passed, the judge again turned to the defendant and asked, "Do you think he has reached the tree by this time?"

"Yes," was the answer, "by now he must have reached it."

Not long after that the plaintiff returned.

"Well?" asked the judge.

"I did just as you said," replied the plaintiff. "I walked as far as the forest and then I went on until I came to the tall oak under which we stood when I handed over my gold coins. I set the seal of your signet ring against the trunk of the tree and I bade it appear before you as a witness. But the tree refused to budge."

"Never mind," said the judge. "The oak has appeared before me and it has borne witness in your favor."

At that the defendant exclaimed, "How can you say such a thing! I have been here all this while and no tree has stalked into the place."

"But," replied the judge, "you said that you had not been in the forest at all. And yet when I asked you whether the plaintiff had reached the oak, first you answered that he could not have reached it, and the second time you said that he must surely have reached it. Therefore, you *were* in the forest and you remembered where the oak was under which you stood when the plaintiff handed his gold coins to you for safekeeping. Now you must not only return him his hundred gold pieces, but you must also pay a fine for having tried to cheat him."

So the tree was a witness without budging, and justice was done.

Turkey

Turkish folklore has an impressive scope and vitality. Until the 1920's, sung-spoken narratives about folk heroes, tales of wonder and magic, ballads, songs, and traditional folk-theater plays were a living legacy of Turkish folkways. However, much of the recorded folklore exists only in Arabic, and with the establishment of the Turkish republic many of the old customs, such as the folk theater, have passed away within the last two generations. The books listed in the Bibliography provide many fine stories from Turkish folk- lore, the most popular being, as they are in Turkey, the tales of the Hodja.

HOW MANY DONKEYS?

Fortunately, many tales about the irresistibly popular Nasr-ed-Din Hodja (spellings will vary) are available in several books for English-speaking boys and girls. The Turks love humorous stories, and the Hodja anecdotes have provided them with a rare character whose adventures *have been told and laughed over for at least five centuries. He is their Paul Bunyan and their Three Sillies all in one. His mixture of wisdom and folly strike such sympathetic chords in us all that he is easily one of the most lovable figures in world folklore.*

There was the tinkle of tiny bells, the sharp clip of small hoofs, the throaty drone of a solitary singer. Nasr-ed-Din Hodja was bringing the donkeys back from the mill, their saddlebags filled with freshly ground wheat. The hot Turkish sun beat down on his turbaned head. The brown dust from the donkeys' hoofs puffed about him. The staccato trot of his donkey jiggled him back and forth. But Nasr-ed-Din Hodja was too pleased to be uncomfortable.

"I'll show them," he chuckled. "They gave me plenty of advice about taking care of their donkeys and their wheat. As though I did not know more about donkeys than any man in Ak Shehir."

His eyes rested lazily on the road ahead. At first it followed the brook running away from Mill Valley, the brook that turned the heavy stones to grind the wheat. Then the road disappeared over a hilltop.

"Just over that hill," he mused contentedly, "is Ak Shehir, where they are waiting for their donkeys. There is not a scratch or a bruise on one of the little creatures. No donkeys in all Turkey have had better treatment today than these nine."

Idly he began counting them.

"What?" he gasped. "Eight donkeys?"

He jumped from his donkey and ran hither and yon, looking behind rocks and over hilltops, but no stray donkey could he see. At last he stood beside the donkeys and counted again. This time there were nine. With a sigh of relief he climbed onto his own donkey and went swinging along the road. His long legs in their baggy pantaloons swung easily back and forth in time to the donkey's trot. Passing through a cluster of trees he thought it time to count the donkeys again.

"One—two—three—" and up to eight he counted, but no ninth donkey was to be seen. Down from his donkey's back he came. Behind all the trees he peered. Not a hair of a donkey could he find.

Again he counted, standing beside his donkeys. There they all were—nine mild little donkeys waiting for orders to move on. Nasr-ed-Din Hodja scratched his poor head in bewilderment. Was he losing his mind or were the donkeys all bewitched? Again he counted. Yes, surely there were nine.

"Ughr-r-r-r," Nasr-ed-Din Hodja gave the low guttural which is Turkish for "Giddap." As he rode on, he looked about him for the evil spirits which must be playing tricks on him. Each donkey wore the blue beads which should drive away the evil spirits. Were there evil spirits abroad stronger even than the blue beads?

He was glad to see a friend coming toward him down the road.

"Oh, Mustapha Effendi," he cried. "Have you seen one of these donkeys? I have lost a donkey and yet I have not lost it."

"What can you mean, Hodja Effendi?" asked Mustapha.

"I left the mill with nine donkeys," explained the Hodja. "Part of the way home there have been nine and part of the way there have been eight. Oh, I am bewitched! Help me! Help me!"

Mustapha was used to the queer ways of the Hodja, but he was surprised. He counted the donkeys silently.

"Let me see you count the donkeys," he ordered the Hodja.

"One—two—three," began the Hodja, pointing at each one as he counted up to eight.

As he said the last number, he stopped and looked at his friend with a face full of helplessness and terror. His terror turned to amazement as Mustapha slapped his knee and laughed until he almost fell from his donkey.

"What is so funny?" asked the Hodja.

"Oh, Hodja Effendi!" Mustapha laughed. "When you are counting your brothers, why, oh why, do you not count the brother on whom you are riding?"

Nasr-ed-Din Hodja was silent for a moment to think through this discovery. Then he kissed the hand of his deliverer, pressed it to his forehead and thanked him a thousand times for his help. He rode, singing, on to Ak Shehir to deliver the donkeys to their owners.

A Tale from "Arabian Nights"

The source of the Arabian Nights *is lost in antiquity. Some of the tales seem to stem from ancient India, others from North Africa, and others from Persia. In the Moslem world, where they were preserved, they were not considered polite literature but circulated in the market places or the coffee houses. The first translation of the stories into French, in 1704, was made by Antoine Galland from a manuscript that came from Syria but was written in Egypt. However confused their source, the "thousand and one tales" have been spellbinding young readers ever since. Today, perhaps because of rival media of entertainment, they are not so much read. Their interminable length is undoubtedly the chief obstacle to their popularity, for they contain stories within stories, episodes upon episodes, magic and more magic. Modern adapters of these tales have practiced an economy of incident that was lacking in the original, but even greatly cut versions have a color, dramatic plot construction, and a use of magic that remain weird and enthralling. Perhaps this sample will send some of the children to a collection of the tales for further reading.*

ALADDIN AND THE WONDERFUL LAMP

This version of "Aladdin and the Wonderful Lamp," by Andrew Lang, is based on his translation from the French of Galland. Until fairly recently, scholars had cause to believe that the story of Aladdin was not part of the original Arabian Nights *but rather had been added by Galland himself from other sources. For the full flavor and spread of the* Arabian Nights, *the adult will do well to turn to the masterful translation from the Arabic by Sir Richard Francis Burton (1821–1890), which is now a literary classic in its own right. It has been published in a three-volume edition (1965) that includes Burton's fascinating scholarly notes.*

There once lived a poor tailor who had a son called Aladdin, a careless, idle boy who would do nothing but play all day long in the streets with little idle boys like himself. This so grieved the father that he died; yet, in spite of his mother's tears and prayers, Aladdin did not mend his ways. One day, when he was playing in the streets as usual, a stranger asked him his age, and if he was not the son of Mustapha the tailor.

"Aladdin and the Wonderful Lamp." From *The Blue Fairy Book,* edited by Andrew Lang. Longmans, Green, and Co., London, 1889

"I am, sir," replied Aladdin; "but he died a long while ago."

On this the stranger, who was a famous African magician, fell on his neck and kissed him, saying: "I am your uncle, and knew you from your likeness to my brother. Go to your mother and tell her I am coming." Aladdin ran home and told his mother of his newly found uncle.

"Indeed, child," she said, "your father had a brother, but I always thought he was dead."

However, she prepared supper, and bade Aladdin seek his uncle, who came laden with wine and fruit. He presently fell down and kissed the place where Mustapha used to sit, bidding Aladdin's mother not to be surprised at not having seen him before, as he had been forty years out of the country. He then turned to Aladdin and asked him his trade, at which the boy hung his head, while his mother burst into tears. On learning that Aladdin was idle and would learn no trade, he offered to take a shop for him and stock it with merchandise. Next day he bought Aladdin a fine suit of clothes and took him all over the city, showing him the sights, and brought him home at nightfall to his mother, who was overjoyed to see her son so fine.

Next day the magician led Aladdin into some beautiful gardens a long way outside the city gates. They sat down by a fountain and the magician pulled a cake from his girdle, which he divided between them. They then journeyed onwards till they almost reached the mountains. Aladdin was so tired that he begged to go back, but the magician beguiled him with pleasant stories and led him on in spite of himself. At last they came to two mountains divided by a narrow valley.

"We will go no farther," said the false uncle. "I will show you something wonderful; only do you gather up sticks while I kindle a fire."

When it was lit the magician threw on it a powder he had about him, at the same time saying some magical words. The earth trembled a little and opened in front of them, disclosing a square flat stone with a brass ring in the middle to raise it by. Aladdin tried to run away, but the magician caught him and gave him a blow that knocked him down.

"What have I done, uncle?" he said piteously; whereupon the magician said more kindly:

"Fear nothing, but obey me. Beneath this stone lies a treasure which is to be yours, and no one else may touch it, so you must do exactly as I tell you."

At the word *treasure* Aladdin forgot his fears, and grasped the ring as he was told, saying the names of his father and grandfather. The stone came up quite easily, and some steps appeared.

"Go down," said the magician; "at the foot of those steps you will find an open door leading into three large halls. Tuck up your gown and go through them without touching anything, or you will die instantly. These halls lead into a garden of fine fruit trees. Walk on till you come to a niche in a terrace where stands a lighted lamp. Pour out the oil it contains, and bring it to me." He drew a ring from his finger and gave it to Aladdin, bidding him prosper.

Aladdin found everything as the magician had said, gathered some fruit off the trees and, having got the lamp, arrived at the mouth of the cave. The magician cried out in a great hurry: "Make haste and give me the lamp." This Aladdin refused to do until he was out of the cave. The magician flew into a terrible passion, and throwing some more powder on to the fire, he said something, and the stone rolled back into its place.

The magician left Persia for ever, which plainly showed that he was no uncle of Aladdin's, but a cunning magician, who had read in

his magic books of a wonderful lamp, which would make him the most powerful man in the world. Though he alone knew where to find it, he could only receive it from the hand of another. He had picked out the foolish Aladdin for this purpose, intending to get the lamp and kill him afterwards.

For two days Aladdin remained in the dark, crying and lamenting. At last he clasped his hands in prayer, and in so doing rubbed the ring, which the magician had forgotten to take from him. Immediately an enormous and frightful genie rose out of the earth, saying: "What wouldst thou with me? I am the Slave of the Ring, and will obey thee in all things."

Aladdin fearlessly replied: "Deliver me from this place!" whereupon the earth opened, and he found himself outside.

As soon as his eyes could bear the light he went home, but fainted on the threshold. When he came to himself he told his mother what had passed, and showed her the lamp and the fruits he had gathered in the garden, which were in reality precious stones. He then asked for some food.

"Alas! child," she said, "I have nothing in the house, but I have spun a little cotton and will go and sell it."

Aladdin bade her keep her cotton, for he would sell the lamp instead. As it was very dirty she began to rub it, that it might fetch a higher price. Instantly a hideous genie appeared, and asked what she would have. She fainted away, but Aladdin, snatching the lamp, said boldly: "Fetch me something to eat!" The genie returned with a silver bowl, twelve silver plates containing rich meats, two silver cups, and two bottles of wine.

Aladdin's mother, when she came to herself, said: "Whence comes this splendid feast?"

"Ask not, but eat," replied Aladdin. So they sat at breakfast till it was dinner-time, and Aladdin told his mother about the lamp. She begged him to sell it, and have nothing to do with devils.

"No," said Aladdin, "since chance hath made us aware of its virtues, we will use it, and the ring likewise, which I shall always wear on my finger."

When they had eaten all the genie had

brought, Aladdin sold one of the silver plates, and so on until none were left. He then had recourse to the genie, who gave him another set of plates, and thus they lived for many years.

One day Aladdin heard that an order from the Sultan proclaimed that everyone was to stay at home and close his shutters while the Princess, his daughter, went to and from the bath. Aladdin was seized by a desire to see her face, which was very difficult, as she always went veiled. He hid himself behind the door of the bath, and peeped through a chink. The Princess lifted her veil as she went in, and looked so beautiful that Aladdin fell in love with her at first sight. He went home so changed that his mother was frightened. He told her he loved the Princess so deeply that he could not live without her and meant to ask her in marriage of her father.

His mother, on hearing this, burst out laughing, but Aladdin at last prevailed upon her to go before the Sultan and carry his request. She fetched a napkin and laid in it the magic fruits from the enchanted garden, which sparkled and shone like the most beautiful jewels. She took these with her to please the Sultan, and set out, trusting in the lamp. The Grand Vizier and the lords of council had just gone in as she entered the hall and placed herself in front of the Sultan. He, however, took no notice of her. She went every day for a week, and stood in the same place.

When the council broke up on the sixth day the Sultan said to his Vizier: "I see a certain woman in the audience-chamber every day carrying something in a napkin. Call her next time, that I may find out what she wants."

Next day, at a sign from the Vizier, she went up to the foot of the throne and remained kneeling till the Sultan said to her: "Rise, good woman, and tell me what you want." She hesitated, so the Sultan sent away all but the Vizier, and bade her speak freely, promising to forgive her beforehand for anything she might say. She then told him of her son's violent love for the Princess.

"I prayed him to forget her," she said, "but in vain; he threatened to do some desperate deed if I refused to go and ask your Majesty for the hand of the Princess. Now I pray you to forgive not me alone, but my son Aladdin."

The Sultan asked her kindly what she had in the napkin, whereupon she unfolded the jewels and presented them. He was thunderstruck, and turning to the Vizier said: "What sayest thou? Ought I not to bestow the Princess on one who values her at such a price?"

The Vizier, who wanted her for his own son, begged the Sultan to withhold her for three months, in the course of which he hoped his son would contrive to make him a richer present. The Sultan granted this, and told Aladdin's mother that, though he consented to the marriage, she must not appear before him again for three months.

Aladdin waited patiently for nearly three months, but after two had elapsed his mother, going into the city to buy oil, found every one rejoicing, and asked what was going on.

"Do you not know," was the answer, "that the son of the Grand Vizier is to marry the Sultan's daughter to-night?"

Breathless, she ran and told Aladdin, who was overwhelmed at first, but presently bethought him of the lamp. He rubbed it, and the genie appeared, saying: "What is thy will?"

Aladdin replied: "The Sultan, as thou knowest, has broken his promise to me, and the Vizier's son is to have the Princess. My command is that to-night you bring hither the bride and bridegroom."

"Master, I obey," said the genie.

Aladdin then went to his chamber, where, sure enough, at midnight the genie transported the bed containing the Vizier's son and the Princess. "Take this new-married man," he said, "and put him outside in the cold, and return at daybreak." Whereupon the genie took the Vizier's son out of bed, leaving Aladdin with the Princess.

"Fear nothing," Aladdin said to her; "you are my wife, promised to me by your unjust father, and no harm shall come to you."

The Princess was too frightened to speak, and passed the most miserable night of her life, while Aladdin lay down beside her and slept soundly. At the appointed hour the genie fetched in the shivering bridegroom, laid him in his place, and transported the bed back to the palace.

Presently the Sultan came to wish his daughter good-morning. The unhappy Vizier's son jumped up and hid himself, while the Princess would not say a word, and was very sorrowful.

The Sultan sent her mother to her, who said: "How comes it, child, that you will not speak to your father? What has happened?"

The Princess sighed deeply, and at last told her mother how, during the night, the bed had been carried into some strange house, and what had passed there. Her mother did not believe her in the least, but bade her rise and consider it an idle dream.

The following night exactly the same thing happened, and next morning, on the Princess's refusing to speak, the Sultan threatened to cut off her head. She then confessed all, bidding him ask the Vizier's son if it were not so. The Sultan told the Vizier to ask his son, who owned the truth, adding that, dearly as he loved the Princess, he had rather die than go through another such fearful night, and wished to be separated from her. His wish was granted, and there was an end of feasting and rejoicing.

When the three months were over, Aladdin sent his mother to remind the Sultan of his promise. She stood in the same place as before, and the Sultan, who had forgotten Aladdin, at once remembered him and sent for her. On seeing her poverty the Sultan felt less inclined than ever to keep his word, and asked his Vizier's advice, who counselled him to set so high a value on the Princess that no man living could come up to it.

The Sultan then turned to Aladdin's mother, saying: "Good woman, a sultan must remember his promises, and I will remember mine, but your son must first send me forty basins of gold brimful of jewels, carried by forty black slaves, led by as many white ones, splendidly dressed. Tell him that I await his answer."

The mother of Aladdin bowed low and went home, thinking all was lost. She gave Aladdin the message, adding: "He may wait long enough for your answer!"

"Not so long, mother, as you think," her son replied. "I would do a great deal more than that for the Princess."

He summoned the genie, and in a few moments the eighty slaves arrived, and filled up the small house and garden. Aladdin made them set out to the palace, two and two, followed by his

mother. They were so richly dressed, with such splendid jewels in their girdles, that everyone crowded to see them and the basins of gold they carried on their heads. They entered the palace, and, after kneeling before the Sultan, stood in a half-circle round the throne with their arms crossed, while Aladdin's mother presented them to the Sultan.

He hesitated no longer, but said: "Good woman, return and tell your son that I wait for him with open arms." She lost no time in telling Aladdin, bidding him make haste. But Aladdin first called the genie.

"I want a scented bath," he said, "a richly embroidered habit, a horse surpassing the Sultan's, and twenty slaves to attend me. Besides this, six slaves, beautifully dressed, to wait on my mother; and lastly, ten thousand pieces of gold in ten purses."

No sooner said than done. Aladdin mounted his horse and passed through the streets, the slaves strewing gold as they went. Those who had played with him in his childhood knew him not, he had grown so handsome. When the Sultan saw him, he came down from his throne, embraced him, and led him into a hall where a feast was spread, intending to marry him to the Princess that very day.

But Aladdin refused, saying, "I must build a palace fit for her," and took his leave.

Once home, he said to the genie: "Build me a palace of the finest marble, set with jasper, agate, and other precious stones. In the middle you shall build me a large hall with a dome, its four walls of massy gold and silver, each side having six windows, whose lattices, all except one which is to be left unfinished, must be set with diamonds and rubies. There must be stables and horses and grooms and slaves; go and see about it!"

The palace was finished by next day, and the genie carried him there and showed him all his orders faithfully carried out, even to the laying of a velvet carpet from Aladdin's palace to the Sultan's. Aladdin's mother then dressed herself carefully, and walked to the palace with her slaves, while he followed her on horseback. The Sultan sent musicians with trumpets and cymbals to meet them, so that the air resounded with music and cheers. She was taken to the Princess, who saluted her and treated her with great honour.

At night the Princess said good-bye to her father, and set out on the carpet for Aladdin's palace, with his mother at her side, and followed by the hundred slaves. She was charmed at the sight

of Aladdin, who ran to receive her.

"Princess," he said, "blame your beauty for my boldness if I have displeased you."

She told him that, having seen him, she willingly obeyed her father in this matter. After the wedding had taken place Aladdin led her into the hall, where a feast was spread, and she supped with him, after which they danced till midnight.

Next day Aladdin invited the Sultan to see the palace. On entering the hall with the four-and-twenty windows, with their rubies, diamonds, and emeralds, he cried: "It is a world's wonder! There is only one thing that surprises me. Was it by accident that one window was left unfinished?"

"No, sir, by design," returned Aladdin. "I wished your Majesty to have the glory of finishing this palace."

The Sultan was pleased, and sent for the best jewellers in the city. He showed them the unfinished window, and bade them fit it up like the others.

"Sir," replied their spokesman, "we cannot find jewels enough."

The Sultan had his own fetched, which they soon used, but to no purpose, for in a month's time the work was not half done. Aladdin, knowing that their task was vain, bade them undo their work and carry the jewels back, and the genie finished the window at his command. The Sultan was surprised to receive his jewels again, and visited Aladdin, who showed him the window finished. The Sultan embraced him, the envious Vizier meanwhile hinting that it was the work of enchantment.

Aladdin had won the hearts of the people by his gentle bearing. He was made captain of the Sultan's armies, and won several battles for him, but remained modest and courteous as before, and lived thus in peace and content for several years.

But far away in Africa the magician remembered Aladdin, and by his magic arts discovered that Aladdin, instead of perishing miserably in the cave, had escaped, and had married a princess, with whom he was living in great honour and wealth. He knew that the poor tailor's son could only have accomplished this by means of the lamp, and travelled night and day till he reached the capital of China, bent on Aladdin's ruin. As he passed through the town he heard people talking everywhere about a marvellous palace.

"Forgive my ignorance," he asked, "what is this palace you speak of?"

"Have you not heard of Prince Aladdin's palace," was the reply, "the greatest wonder of the world? I will direct you if you have a mind to see it."

The magician thanked him who spoke, and having seen the palace knew that it had been raised by the Genie of the Lamp, and became half mad with rage. He determined to get hold of the lamp, and again plunge Aladdin into the deepest poverty.

Unluckily, Aladdin had gone a-hunting for eight days, which gave the magician plenty of time. He bought a dozen copper lamps, put them into a basket, and went to the palace, crying: "New lamps for old!" followed by a jeering crowd. The Princess, sitting in the hall of four-and-twenty windows, sent a slave to find out what the noise was about, who came back laughing, so that the Princess scolded her.

"Madam," replied the slave, "who can help laughing to see an old fool offering to exchange fine new lamps for old ones?"

Another slave, hearing this, said: "There is an old one on the cornice there which he can have."

Now this was the magic lamp, which Aladdin had left there, as he could not take it out hunting with him. The Princess, not knowing its value, laughingly bade the slave take it and make the exchange.

She went and said to the magician: "Give me a new lamp for this."

He snatched it and, amid the jeers of the crowd, bade the slave take her choice. Little he cared, but left off crying his lamps, and went out of the city gates to a lonely place, where he remained till nightfall, when he pulled out the lamp and rubbed it. The genie appeared, and at the magician's command carried him, together with the palace and the Princess in it, to a lonely place in Africa.

Next morning the Sultan looked out of the window towards Aladdin's palace and rubbed his eyes, for it was gone. He sent for the Vizier and asked what had become of the palace. The Vizier looked out too, and was lost in astonishment. He again put it down to enchantment, and this time the Sultan believed him, and sent thirty men on horseback to fetch Aladdin in chains. They met him riding home, bound him, and forced him to go with them on foot. The people, however, who loved him, followed, armed, to see that he came to no harm. He was carried before the Sultan, who ordered the executioner to cut off his head. The executioner made Aladdin kneel down, bandaged his eyes, and raised his scimitar to strike.

At that instant the Vizier, who saw that the crowd had forced their way into the courtyard and were scaling the walls to rescue Aladdin, called to the executioner to stay his hand. The people, indeed, looked so threatening that the Sultan gave way and ordered Aladdin to be unbound, and pardoned him in the sight of the crowd. Aladdin now begged to know what he had done.

"False wretch!" said the Sultan, "come hither," and showed him from the window the place where his palace had stood. Aladdin was so amazed that he could not say a word. "Where is my palace and my daughter?" demanded the Sultan. "For the first I am not so deeply concerned, but my daughter I must have, and you must find her or lose your head."

Aladdin begged for forty days in which to find her, promising if he failed, to return and suffer death at the Sultan's pleasure. His prayer was granted, and he went forth sadly from the Sultan's presence. For three days he wandered about like a madman, asking everyone what had become of his palace, but they only laughed and pitied him. He came to the banks of a river, and knelt down to say his prayers before throwing himself in. In so doing he rubbed the magic ring he still wore. The genie he had seen in the cave appeared, and asked his will.

"Save my life, genie," said Aladdin, "and bring my palace back."

"That is not in my power," said the genie; "I am only the Slave of the Ring; you must ask him of the lamp."

"Even so," said Aladdin, "but thou canst take me to the palace, and set me down under my dear wife's window." He at once found himself in Africa, under the window of the Princess, and fell asleep out of sheer weariness.

He was awakened by the singing of the birds, and his heart was lighter. He saw plainly that all his misfortunes were owing to the loss of the lamp, and vainly wondered who had robbed him of it.

That morning the Princess rose earlier than she had done since she had been carried into Africa by the magician, whose company she was forced to endure once a day. She, however, treated him so harshly that he dared not live there altogether. As she was dressing, one of her women looked out and saw Aladdin. The Princess ran and opened the window, and at the noise she made, Aladdin looked up. She called to him to come to her, and great was the joy of these lovers at seeing each other again.

After he had kissed her, Aladdin said: "I beg of you, Princess, in God's name, before we speak of anything else, for your own sake and mine, tell me what has become of an old lamp I left on the cornice in the hall of four-and-twenty windows, when I went a-hunting."

"Alas!" she said, "I am the innocent cause of our sorrows," and told him of the exchange of the lamp.

"Now I know," cried Aladdin, "that we have to thank the African magician for this! Where is the lamp?"

"He carries it about with him," said the Princess. "I know, for he pulled it out of his breast to show me. He wishes me to break my faith with you and marry him, saying that you were beheaded by my father's command. He is for ever speaking ill of you, but I only reply by my tears. If I persist, I doubt not but he will use violence."

Aladdin comforted her, and left her for a while. He changed clothes with the first person he met in the town, and having bought a certain powder returned to the Princess, who let him in by a little side door.

"Put on your most beautiful dress," he said to her, "and receive the magician with smiles, leading him to believe that you have forgotten me. Invite him to sup with you, and say you wish to taste the wine of his country. He will go for some and while he is gone I will tell you what to do."

She listened carefully to Aladdin and when he left her, arrayed herself gaily for the first time

since she left China. She put on a girdle and head-dress of diamonds and, seeing in a glass that she was more beautiful than ever, received the magician, saying, to his great amazement: "I have made up my mind that Aladdin is dead, and that all my tears will not bring him back to me, so I am resolved to mourn no more, and have therefore invited you to sup with me; but I am tired of the wines of China, and would fain taste those of Africa."

The magician flew to his cellar, and the Princess put the powder Aladdin had given her in her cup. When he returned she asked him to drink her health in the wine of Africa, handing him her cup in exchange for his, as a sign she was reconciled to him. Before drinking the magician made her a speech in praise of her beauty, but the Princess cut him short, saying: "Let us drink first, and you shall say what you will afterwards." She set her cup to her lips and kept it there, while the magician drained his to the dregs and fell back lifeless. The Princess then opened the door to Aladdin, and flung her arms round his neck; but Aladdin put her away, bidding her leave him, as he had more to do. He then went to the dead magician, took the lamp out of his vest, and bade the genie carry the palace and all in it back to China. This was done, and the Princess in her chamber only felt two little shocks, and little thought she was at home again.

The Sultan, who was sitting in his closet, mourning for his lost daughter, happened to look up, and rubbed his eyes, for there stood the palace as before! He hastened thither, and Aladdin received him in the hall of the four-and-twenty windows, with the Princess at his side. Aladdin told him what had happened, and showed him the dead body of the magician, that he might believe. A ten days' feast was proclaimed, and it seemed as if Aladdin might now live the rest of his life in peace; but it was not to be.

The African magician had a younger brother, who was, if possible, more wicked and more cunning than himself. He travelled to China to avenge his brother's death, and went to visit a pious woman called Fatima, thinking she might be of use to him. He entered her cell and clapped a dagger to her breast, telling her to rise and do his bidding on pain of death. He changed clothes with her, coloured his face like hers, put on her veil, and murdered her, that she might tell no tales. Then he went towards the palace of Aladdin, and all the people, thinking he was the holy woman, gathered round him, kissing his hands and begging his blessing. When he got to the palace there was such a noise going on round him that the Princess bade her slave look out of the window and ask what was the matter. The slave said it was the holy woman, curing people by her touch of their ailments, whereupon the Princess, who had long desired to see Fatima, sent for her. On coming to the Princess, the magician offered up a prayer for her health and prosperity. When he had done, the Princess made him sit by her, and begged him to stay with her always. The false Fatima, who wished for nothing better, consented, but kept his veil down for fear of discovery. The Princess showed him the hall, and asked him what he thought of it.

"It is truly beautiful," said the false Fatima. "In my mind it wants but one thing."

"And what is that?" said the Princess.

"If only a roc's egg," replied he, "were hung up from the middle of this dome, it would be the wonder of the world."

After this the Princess could think of nothing but the roc's egg, and when Aladdin returned from hunting he found her in a very ill humour. He begged to know what was amiss, and she told him that all her pleasure in the hall was spoilt for the want of a roc's egg hanging from the dome.

"If that is all," replied Aladdin, "you shall soon be happy." He left her and rubbed the lamp, and when the genie appeared commanded him to bring a roc's egg. The genie gave such a loud and terrible shriek that the hall shook.

"Wretch!" he cried, "is it not enough that I have done everything for you, but you must command me to bring my master and hang him up in the midst of this dome? You and your wife and your palace deserve to be burnt to ashes, but that this request does not come from you, but from the brother of the African magician, whom you destroyed. He is now in your palace disguised as the holy woman—whom he murdered. He it was who put that wish into your wife's head. Take care of yourself, for he means to kill you." So saying, the genie disappeared.

Aladdin went back to the Princess, saying his head ached, and requesting that the holy Fatima should be fetched to lay her hands on it. But when the magician came near, Aladdin, seizing his dagger, pierced him to the heart.

"What have you done?" cried the Princess. "You have killed the holy woman!"

"Not so," replied Aladdin, "but a wicked magician," and told her of how she had been deceived.

After this Aladdin and his wife lived in peace. He succeeded the Sultan when he died, and reigned for many years, leaving behind him a long line of kings.

Africa

*Until as late as 1900 much of the African continent was still a mystery; since
1950 more than two dozen new independent African states have been established!
This unique chapter in history has been reflected in the growing number of
books of African tales. What has until recently been but a trickle promises to
become a great stream of narrative, much of it printed in this country for a
special audience of children. It must be emphasized, however, that in Africa, the
content of the oral narrative represents not only a survival of earlier
customs and thought but also the contemporary and vital expression of long-
established communities and tribes. African storytellers are fond of using
songs within the prose narration and of having a kind of chanted interchange of
phrase and song with their listeners. Moralistic endings are a well-
integrated feature of many of the tales. "Why" stories are frequent. We may also
note a strong sense of ethics and a very sophisticated predilection for
realism, sometimes bordering on the humorously cynical. Whether the tales are
from the Pygmies of the Congo basin, the Bushmen of the Kalahari
Desert, or the Guragé tribes of Ethiopia, they share these qualities. The stories
here will help to some extent to make children aware of the variety,
depth, and uniqueness of the Africans' life and thought, bringing into sharper
focus the common humanity they share with us, as well as their distinctive views.*

ALLAH WILL PROVIDE

(North African)

*It is possible even today to hear stories, maybe
this very one, told by wandering storytellers in
the Moslem countries of North Africa. "Allah
Will Provide" poses a metaphysical question
which it slyly* does *and* does not *answer! Bou
Azza's conclusions and actions certainly seem
foolish, but would he have received his good fortune had he behaved differently? This is good
fun to dramatize with puppets or live actors.*

Bou Azza was an honest woodcutter who
worked hard each day cutting down trees which
he sold in the market place of a small North African village. His efforts were not highly rewarded, however, for he earned barely enough
money to keep his young wife and himself in
food and clothing.

Because he was getting old in body, Bou Azza
wondered with each passing day how much

"Allah Will Provide." From *The Sultan's Fool and
Other North African Tales* by Robert Gilstrap and Irene
Estabrook. Copyright © 1958 by Robert Gilstrap and Irene
Estabrook. Reprinted by permission of Holt, Rinehart and
Winston, Inc.

longer he would be able to work and who would
take care of him and his wife when he was too
old to do so.

One afternoon as the hot sun beat down on
him, Bou Azza gathered together the logs he had
cut that morning, fastened them with a piece of
rope, and slung them over his shoulder. Then he
set out down the hill toward his tiny house on
the outskirts of the village.

Before reaching his home, Bou was forced to
stop and rest beneath an olive tree near the road.
As he wiped the perspiration from his forehead
he suddenly noticed a horned viper curled up on
the ground a few feet away from him. At first the
old woodcutter was very frightened for he knew
that a bite from this reptile would surely kill
him. Carefully he climbed up to a high branch
of the olive tree. But after watching the snake
for a few seconds, Bou Azza realized that he had
nothing to fear. The snake had other interests.

On one of the lower branches of the tree, not
far from where Bou Azza was sitting, there was a
small bird. The snake was staring at the bird
with his beady black eyes, swaying its long, slender body back and forth, and occasionally spitting out its evil-looking, forked tongue.

At first the bird did not notice the snake, but

when she did, her small feathery body was seized with helpless terror. Gripping the fragile little twig on which she rested, she tried to move her wings, but they were frozen with fear. She also tried to sound an alarm, but her beak opened and shut without a sound coming out.

As the snake swayed back and forth, Bou Azza realized that the bird had been hypnotized by the viper's movements, and he watched the two animals with weird fascination.

As Bou Azza looked down, the viper held the bird in its merciless stare, swaying from side to side like the pendulum of a clock, while the helpless victim became more and more paralyzed. Then suddenly the little bird fell from the branch and landed just a few inches from the snake. As Bou Azza watched, the snake ate its prey whole—feathers and all. Then, satisfied, it crawled away looking for new victims.

Bou Azza, rested from his journey, but sickened by what he had just witnessed, headed for home with his wood on his back, and an idea in his head.

As Bou Azza walked home in the twilight, he thought more and more about his idea. After a time he said to himself, "I am a fool! The serpent finds much food without really working for it, thanks to Allah. Whereas I, a man, must work very hard in the hottest part of the day to earn just a mouthful of food. Allah alone is good, and with His help I will be like the serpent. No longer will I work so hard to get food when the serpent gets it for nothing. So shall it be."

And continuing on his way home, Bou Azza wore an expression of contentment over the new way of life that the serpent had revealed to him.

On the following morn, instead of rising before the sun made its way into the sky, Bou Azza stayed in bed until noon. Then he took his grass mat to the rear of the house where he sat under a fig tree.

His wife became worried at his strange behavior, and when she saw that he obviously had no plans to work for the day she went to him and said, "Bou Azza! What is wrong with you today? Are you not going to cut wood to sell in the market?"

"No, wife," said Bou Azza as he stretched in the sun. "I will not leave my mat even if I die of hunger. Yesterday I saw a serpent finding his food without working, and I have decided that if Allah feeds the serpents he will provide me with my bread."

His anxious wife had no idea what her husband was talking about and thought he had gone mad.

"Please get up," she cried, and she tugged at his clothing. But nothing she said or did made any difference, and when twilight came to Bou Azza's home, he was still resting on his mat.

The poor woman was sick with worry for she had always counted on her husband for food and money. But when she realized that he would not change his mind, she hurried to the woods while there was still light to see and looked for mushrooms to sell at the market in the village.

She looked for hours, scraping away leaves, digging under fallen logs, searching everywhere. Suddenly, as she dug into some soft earth her knife hit something hard buried beneath the surface of the ground. Rapidly she dug the dirt away and uncovered a metal cooking pot with a

lid. After working for some time she pried the lid off and discovered that the pot was filled with shimmering gold pieces.

The animals of the forest drew close to watch her struggle helplessly with the giant pot as she shouted with excitement. But it was too heavy for her to lift. She ran as fast as she could to the house crying with happiness. "Oh, Bou Azza," she shouted. "I have found a whole pot of gold. Come with me. Help me bring it to the house."

Actually Bou Azza was impressed with the thought of the gold. But he had made a promise to himself not to move, and now he could not lift his finger.

"Oh, wife," he said, without opening his eyes. "If Allah saw fit to let you find such a treasure surely he will give you the strength to carry it home. Personally I have decided not to move an inch!"

This reply made his wife furious. And she ran to the house of her brothers to see if they would help her carry the pot home. Naturally her brothers were delighted with the prospect of sharing so much gold, and they ran with Bou Azza's wife to the forest and helped her carry it home.

When she and her brothers reached her house, with the giant pot spilling over with gold, she felt sure that her husband would get off his mat and help her count their fortune.

"Get up, you lazy lout!" she shouted, as she stood over her husband who slept peacefully on his straw bed. "I hope you have enough energy to come and count your riches."

"Did I not tell you?" he said sleepily. "I am not going to lift a finger until Allah drops fortunes on my head just as he showered gifts on the serpent."

"Just as you like," the angry wife said, as she filled her skirt with hundreds of heavy gold pieces and poured them over her husband's head.

"Praise be to Allah!" her husband shouted as the gold pieces fell around him. "Praise be to the one and only Allah! Do you not now see, my wife, that serpents and men are all his creatures and he does provide for all of us?"

His wife did not understand, but she did know that for the rest of their lives she and her hus-band would live in luxury and that Bou Azza would never have to work again.

And every time someone came to visit them, Bou Azza told them this story, ending each time with the words, "Why work? Allah will provide."

And although his listeners felt that he was wrong, no one could contradict him.

THE FIRE ON THE MOUNTAIN

(Ethiopian)

The history and character of the Ethiopians are unique, and this fact is reflected in their tales. Like the ancient Egyptians, the Ethiopians were originally Hamites, people who invaded Africa from Asia. Known from Biblical times as Abyssinia, Ethiopia is one of the oldest Christian countries in Africa, but her people include Caucasians, Negroes, and Asians of varying languages and religions. "The Fire on the Mountain" is a magnificent ethical tale which avoids all preaching in favor of vividly dramatizing its point. Read Harold Courlander's introduction and notes in the excellent collection from which this story is taken.

People say that in the old days in the city of Addis Ababa there was a young man by the name of Arha. He had come as a boy from the country of Guragé, and in the city he became the servant of a rich merchant, Haptom Hasei.

Haptom Hasei was so rich that he owned everything that money could buy, and often he was very bored because he had tired of everything he knew, and there was nothing new for him to do.

One cold night, when the damp wind was blowing across the plateau, Haptom called to Arha to bring wood for the fire. When Arha was finished, Haptom began to talk.

"How much cold can a man stand?" he said, speaking at first to himself. "I wonder if it would be possible for a man to stand on the highest peak, Mount Sululta, where the coldest winds blow, through an entire night without blankets or clothing and yet not die?"

"I don't know," Arha said. "But wouldn't it be a foolish thing?"

"Perhaps, if he had nothing to gain by it, it would be a foolish thing to spend the night that way," Haptom said. "But I would be willing to bet that a man couldn't do it."

"I am sure a courageous man could stand naked on Mount Sululta throughout an entire night and not die of it," Arha said. "But as for me, it isn't my affair since I've nothing to bet."

"Well, I'll tell you what," Haptom said. "Since you are so sure it can be done, I'll make a bet with you anyway. If you can stand among the rocks on Mount Sululta for an entire night without food or water, or clothing or blankets or fire, and not die of it, then I will give you ten acres of good farmland for your own, with a house and cattle."

Arha could hardly believe what he had heard.

"Do you really mean this?" he asked.

"I am a man of my word," Haptom replied.

"Then tomorrow night I will do it," Arha said, "and afterwards, for all the years to come, I shall till my own soil."

But he was very worried, because the wind swept bitterly across that peak. So in the morning Arha went to a wise old man from the Guragé tribe and told him of the bet he had made. The old man listened quietly and thoughtfully, and when Arha had finished he said:

"I will help you. Across the valley from Sululta is a high rock which can be seen in the daytime. Tomorrow night, as the sun goes down, I shall build a fire there, so that it can be seen from where you stand on the peak. All night long you must watch the light of my fire. Do not close your eyes or let the darkness creep upon you. As you watch my fire, think of its warmth, and think of me, your friend, sitting there tending it for you. If you do this you will survive, no matter how bitter the night wind."

Arha thanked the old man warmly and went back to Haptom's house with a light heart. He told Haptom he was ready, and in the afternoon Haptom sent him, under the watchful eyes of other servants, to the top of Mount Sululta. There, as night fell, Arha removed his clothes and stood in the damp cold wind that swept across the plateau with the setting sun. Across the valley, several miles away, Arha saw the light of his friend's fire, which shone like a star in the blackness.

The wind turned colder and seemed to pass through his flesh and chill the marrow in his bones. The rock on which he stood felt like ice. Each hour the cold numbed him more, until he thought he would never be warm again, but he kept his eyes upon the twinkling light across the valley, and remembered that his old friend sat there tending a fire for him. Sometimes wisps of fog blotted out the light, and then he strained to see until the fog passed. He sneezed and coughed and shivered, and began to feel ill. Yet all night through he stood there, and only when the dawn came did he put on his clothes and go down the mountain back to Addis Ababa.

Haptom was very surprised to see Arha, and he questioned his servants thoroughly.

"Did he stay all night without food or drink or blankets or clothing?"

"Yes," his servants said. "He did all of these things."

"Well, you are a strong fellow," Haptom said to Arha. "How did you manage to do it?"

"I simply watched the light of a fire on a distant hill," Arha said.

"What! You watched a fire? Then you lose the bet, and you are still my servant, and you own no land!"

"But this fire was not close enough to warm me, it was far across the valley!"

"I won't give you the land," Haptom said. "You didn't fulfill the conditions. It was only the fire that saved you."

Arha was very sad. He went again to his old friend of the Guragé tribe and told him what had happened.

"Take the matter to the judge," the old man advised him.

Arha went to the judge and complained, and the judge sent for Haptom. When Haptom told his story, and the servants said once more that Arha had watched a distant fire across the valley, the judge said:

"No, you have lost, for Haptom Hasei's condition was that you must be without fire."

Once more Arha went to his old friend with the sad news that he was doomed to the life of a servant, as though he had not gone through the ordeal on the mountaintop.

"Don't give up hope," the old man said. "More wisdom grows wild in the hills than in any city judge."

He got up from where he sat and went to find a man named Hailu, in whose house he had been a servant when he was young. He explained to the good man about the bet between Haptom and Arha, and asked if something couldn't be done.

"Don't worry about it," Hailu said after thinking for a while. "I will take care of it for you."

Some days later Hailu sent invitations to many people in the city to come to a feast at his house. Haptom was among them, and so was the judge who had ruled Arha had lost the bet.

When the day of the feast arrived, the guests came riding on mules with fine trappings, their servants strung out behind them on foot. Haptom came with twenty servants, one of whom held a silk umbrella over his head to shade him from the sun, and four drummers played music that signified the great Haptom was here.

The guests sat on soft rugs laid out for them and talked. From the kitchen came the odors of wonderful things to eat: roast goat, roast corn and durra, pancakes called injera, and many tantalizing sauces. The smell of the food only accentuated the hunger of the guests. Time passed. The food should have been served, but they didn't see it, only smelled vapors that drifted from the kitchen. The evening came, and still no food was served. The guests began to whisper among themselves. It was very curious that the honorable Hailu had not had the food brought out. Still the smells came from the kitchen. At last one of the guests spoke out for all the others:

"Hailu, why do you do this to us? Why do you invite us to a feast and then serve us nothing?"

"Why, can't you smell the food?" Hailu asked with surprise.

"Indeed we can, but smelling is not eating, there is no nourishment in it!"

"And is there warmth in a fire so distant that it can hardly be seen?" Hailu asked. "If Arha was warmed by the fire he watched while standing on Mount Sululta, then you have been fed by the smells coming from my kitchen."

The people agreed with him; the judge now saw his mistake, and Haptom was shamed. He thanked Hailu for his advice, and announced that Arha was then and there the owner of the land, the house, and the cattle.

Then Hailu ordered the food brought in, and the feast began.

SON OF THE LONG ONE

(East African)

Here is one of the typical tales from the many told about the hare (in some places called "Sungura"). It deftly builds suspense and has a surprise ending that is funny and satisfying. The storyteller can have a good time with this, and children may learn a point about being afraid of the unknown or about jumping to conclusions.

Sungura, the hare, was out in his garden all morning. When he returned to his house under the roots of a big thorn tree, he saw some very strange-looking tracks in the dust of his doorway, long tracks, as if some huge animal had gone in. Sungura was frightened. He had never seen such tracks and was quite convinced that some monster was inside his house. He called out in a shaky voice, "Hodi, who is inside my house?"

A big voice replied, "I am the warrior son of the long one whose anklets became unfastened in a great battle and are dragging behind. I can crush the mighty rhinoceros to earth and the elephant trembles at my voice. Beware of me!"

Sungura was indeed frightened. What sort of monster is in my house? he thought. He shuddered at the thought of any creature whose anklets dragging could make these tracks. He must be huge and much too strong to be chased away by a hare. Sungura decided to get help from some of his friends and started off into the bush. He had gone only a few feet when he met the jackal, Mbweha. "Oh, clever Mbweha," he cried, "Please help me. Some strange, strong animal is in my house and refuses to come out. Perhaps you who are so cunning can get him to go away."

"Well, I'll talk to this mysterious intruder, but I'm not sure he'll listen."

"Son of the Long One." Reprinted from *Jambo, Sungura, Tales from East Africa* by Eleanor B. Heady. By permission of W. W. Norton & Company, Inc. Text Copyright © 1965 by Eleanor B. Heady.

Sungura and Mbweha approached the door of the house. "See the tracks," said the hare. "Aren't they strange?"

"They are indeed," agreed the jackal. Then he called out, "Hodi, who is in the house of my friend, Sungura?"

Again the big voice answered, "I am the warrior son of the long one whose anklets became unfastened in a great battle and are dragging behind. I can crush the mighty rhinoceros to earth and the elephant trembles at my voice. Beware of me!"

Now Mbweha was as frightened as his friend. "He sounds very ferocious, Sungura. I think we better go away and leave him." So the hare and the jackal trotted into the bush, but Sungura was still determined to get the intruder out of his house.

Next they met a leopard. "Oh, Chui, my friend, I need your help," said Sungura. "Someone very strong is inside my house and refuses to come out."

"Refuses? It's your house, isn't it?"

"Of course, Chui, but he seems to think no one is strong enough to make him leave and now I have no place to sleep tonight. What shall I do?"

"I'll go have a talk with this fellow," said Chui. "Perhaps my reputation for cunning has come to his ears. He will probably go away when I arrive."

The three friends trotted back to the house of the hare and this time, Chui, the leopard, called out, "Who is in the house of my friend, Sungura?"

For a moment there was no answer, then just as before came this reply, "I am the warrior son of the long one whose anklets became unfastened in a great battle and are dragging behind. I can crush the mighty rhinoceros to earth. The elephant trembles at the sound of my voice. Beware of me!"

"What could one as strong as I do against him? He can crush the rhinoceros. I think we better go away and leave him," said Chui. "I have never met such a creature and I have no desire to do so."

"But he has my house," wailed Sungura.

"You'll just have to find another," said Mbweha.

"Of course, you'd be foolish to try to fight with the son of the long one," agreed Chui.

With that the jackal and the leopard ran into the bush, leaving the disappointed hare looking sadly at his house.

Sungura started out again, not quite sure where he was going. Find another house, indeed! That wasn't as easily done as some people seemed to suppose. Then he heard a booming voice above him, "Is that you way down there, Sungura? Thought you usually took a nap in the afternoon. Something wrong?"

Sungura looked up at the huge swaying trunk of Tembo, the elephant. "Something is very wrong, Tembo," he said. "Come with me and I'll show you."

As they walked toward the hare's home, Sungura told the elephant of the intruder and how he refused to leave. "I think I can make him go," said Tembo. "I am the largest animal in the bush. Surely he will be afraid of me."

When they reached the hare's tree Tembo called out, "Hodi, may I come in, you who have taken the house of my friend, Sungura. I am Tembo, king of the bush."

"Ha, ha, ha," laughed the big voice, "Come in indeed! Don't you know that you are much too large to come in? Besides, I am stronger than you. I am the warrior son of the long one whose anklets became unfastened in a great battle and are dragging behind. I can crush the mighty rhinoceros to earth and you, Tembo, should tremble at my voice for I am very mighty."

"I have never heard of such a creature," said Tembo shakily. "Perhaps you will have to let him stay in your house, Sungura. I wouldn't dare try to get him out. He is much too strong for me."

"Well thank you, Tembo," said the hare. "I guess there is no one to help." Sungura hopped sadly off into the bush and sat down on a round stone to think. A huge tear rolled down each cheek. "My lovely home," he sobbed. "How shall I ever find another?"

Just then there was a stirring in the grass and a small rasping voice asked, "What is the trouble? Perhaps I can help."

Sungura looked down into the funny ugly face of Chura, the frog. "Oh, my small friend, you cannot help. Some very strong creature is in my house and will not go away. Mbweha, Chui, and Tembo have all tried to get him to leave, but he refuses. He sounds so terrible. What shall I do?" Sungura began to cry harder.

"There, there, Sungura," croaked the frog. "Don't be so upset. There must be a way to get rid of this house-stealer. He can't be so very large, or he couldn't get into your house."

"True, I didn't think of that," said Sungura.

"Now let's go to your house and I'll see what I can do."

Sungura arose doubtfully and the two friends hopped back to the hole under the tree. The frog looked carefully at the strange tracks and then winked at his friend, calling out in a loud voice, "Who is in the house of my friend, Sungura?"

Once again the intruder replied, "I am the warrior son of the long one whose anklets became unfastened in a great battle. I can crush the mighty rhinoceros to earth and the elephant trembles at the sound of my voice. Beware of me!"

And Chura replied, "I am strong and a leaper. If you don't leave the house of my friend I shall leap upon you and off again before you can harm me. You will not like my leaping."

The voice that came from the hare's house was a much smaller one this time, a voice that sounded frightened. "Please, oh leaper, I am only Nyodu, the caterpillar. I shall come out if you promise not to harm me."

Sungura could hardly believe his eyes when the tiny furry creature crawled slowly out of his house. "And to think all of us were afraid of you —all but Chura, who is very brave."

"Not brave at all," laughed the frog. "I have learned never to believe a thief. If you'll remember that you will save yourself a lot of trouble."

THE GREAT TUG-OF-WAR

(Nigerian)

This tale of a wheeling-dealing rabbit is one to tax the wits. Zomo is the name given to the ubiquitous and wily hare by the Hausa people of Nigeria. Hugh Sturton, compiler of Zomo, the Rabbit, *says that Zomo is the direct ancestor of Brer Rabbit. Mr. Sturton has taken many liberties with the tales of Zomo in order to put them into acceptable and entertaining form. Even though folklorists may object, children will enjoy the results.*

It happens one year that the rains come late and go early so the harvest is poor and food is scarce. Animals who usually reap a hundred baskets of corn find they have only fifty, and animals who usually reap fifty find they have only twenty-five. As for Zomo, who never reaps more than ten, even in the best of seasons, he is left with only five.

"When are you going to fetch the rest of it?" asks his wife when he brings home his five baskets.

"There isn't any more," says Zomo.

"D'you mean to tell me," says his wife, "that this is all we have to eat for the next twelve months?"

"We shall have to manage as best we can," says Zomo.

The corn lasts through most of the dry season but by the time the hot weather comes round, it is nearly finished. First Zomo tries to borrow some more, but the other animals say they have none to lend. Then he tries to borrow money so that he can buy corn in the market, but they remember the last time they lent him money, and so they are sorry but they can't oblige.

When his wife tells him that they have food for only two more days, Zomo reckons that the time has come for him to have a good think. So he goes and sits under the *chediya* tree with his thinking cap on, and in the evening, when his wife calls him in to supper, he tells her that he is going to go and see Giwa the Elephant, who has more corn than he knows what to do with.

Next morning, Zomo puts on his best gown and goes and calls on Giwa. When he reaches the house, he says that he has a message for the master and he is taken into the audience chamber where Giwa is receiving those who come to pay their respects.

"God give you long life," cries Zomo in a loud voice, doing obeisance and looking very respectful.

"Amen, Zomo," says Giwa, who likes to be buttered up.

"I have a message for you," says Zomo. "It is from Dorina the Hippopotamus."

"We don't see much of him since he's taken to living in the river," says Giwa. "Tell me," he goes on, "does he still have that black stallion?"

"That is what the message is about," says Zomo.

"Well, you can tell him from me," says Giwa, "that if he still wants to swap the black for my chestnut, there is nothing doing; but I will buy the black from him any time he likes."

"He is short of corn this year," says Zomo, "and he says that if you can let him have some, he will give you the black in exchange."

"Oho," says Giwa, "so that's how the land lies, is it? Well, how much does he want?"

"He says that he'll let him go for a hundred baskets," says Zomo, "so long as he can keep him until after the festival."

"Whatever does he want to do that for?" asks Giwa.

"He's his favorite mount," says Zomo, "and he likes to ride him in the procession."

"All right," says Giwa, "tell Dorina it's a bargain."

Without more ado, the elephant orders his wife and daughters to measure out a hundred baskets of corn.

"There you are, Zomo," he says when this is done. "If you lead the way, my boys will carry it for you. And tell Dorina," he goes on, "that he can keep the black until the festival, but no longer."

"I'll tell him that," says Zomo. So saying, he takes his leave and sets off with ten young elephants behind him who are each carrying ten baskets of corn.

"All right, put it down here, boys," says Zomo when they reach a place near his house. "You've done your share—I'll get those lazy young hippos to take it the rest of the way."

As soon as the young elephants have gone, Zomo calls to his wife and children and they carry the baskets into his house. When they have finished, his corn-stores are all full and running over.

"Where did you get all this?" asks Zomo's wife when they finish carting the corn.

"Giwa is my friend," says Zomo, "and when he hears that my corn is nearly finished, he insists on giving me some of his. 'Zomo,' he says. 'I won't have you going short.' Naturally I do not wish to offend him and so I accept."

When she hears this, Zomo's wife looks at him as if she doesn't believe a word he says, but she holds her tongue and says nothing.

Next morning, Zomo puts on his best gown again, and this time he makes for the river where Dorina the Hippopotamus has his house. Since Dorina lives in the water, the bad season does not hurt him and he has plenty of food.

When Zomo reaches Dorina's gate, he says that he has a message for him and is taken to the audience chamber.

"God give you victory," Zomo cries in a loud voice, doing obeisance and looking very respectful, just as he does with the elephant.

"Welcome, Zomo," says Dorina. "What brings you to these parts?"

"I have a message," says Zomo, "from Giwa the Elephant."

"Oh?" says Dorina. "What does Giwa want with me?"

"He wants to know," says Zomo, "whether you still want to buy his chestnut."

"Of course I do," says Dorina. "I even offer to swap my black for him, but Giwa will not have it."

"Well, he's changed his mind now," says Zomo, and tells Dorina the same tale that he already told Giwa, right down to the bit about Giwa wishing to keep the chestnut until the festival because it is the horse he likes to ride in the procession. Dorina is so pleased with the proposition that then and there he tells his wife and daughters to prepare a hundred baskets of dried fish.

When the fish is ready, Zomo takes his leave and sets off for dry land with twenty young hippos behind him, each carrying five baskets. By and by they reach a place near his house, and he tells them to put the stuff down and he will get the young elephants, who are fat and lazy he says, to carry it the rest of the way.

As soon as the young hippos have gone back to the river, Zomo fetches his wife and children and they carry the baskets home. Since the larder is already full of corn, the eight youngest rabbits

have to give up their hut to make room for the fish, which fills it right up to the thatch and makes it bulge like a pumpkin.

Soon after this, the rains come and all through the rainy season Zomo keeps his wife and children busy plaiting a rope. It is the biggest rope you ever saw and so strong that you can tie Giwa the Elephant up with it and he won't get loose. His old woman is always asking Zomo what they want with such a rope, but Zomo won't say.

By and by, when the rains are nearly over, the festival comes round. All the animals ride in the procession, and the elephant sees that the hippo is mounted on the black, and the hippo sees that the elephant is mounted on the chestnut.

Next day, bright and early, Zomo takes one end of his rope and sets out for the river. When he comes to the bank, he finds a fig tree and passes the rope round the trunk. Then he goes on to the hippo's house.

"Ah, Zomo," says Dorina when he is ushered into his presence, "you are just the man I wish to see. Do you bring news about my horse?"

"God give you long life," says Zomo, "here is the end of his tethering rope, which Giwa the Elephant tells me to bring to you. When the sun rises tomorrow, he will take him down to the river by the fig tree, and he says when you see the leaves of the fig tree begin to shake, it will be the signal to pull him in on the rope."

"Very well," says Dorina. "We'll be ready."

"God give you victory," Zomo goes on, "Giwa also says to tell you that this chestnut of his is a mighty strong horse and that he can't answer for it if you let him get away."

"Never fear," says Dorina, "my boys will take care of him."

When Zomo leaves the hippo, he goes and gets the other end of the rope and takes it to the elephant's house. "God give you long life," he says to Giwa, and then he spins him the same yarn, right down to the bit about the black being a mighty strong horse and Dorina not answering for it if he lets him get away.

"Not to worry," says Giwa. "My boys will look after him all right."

When Zomo gets home that evening, he tells his wife that people may come asking for him next day, and that if they do, she is to say that he is gone to Gwanja.

"But," says she, "you aren't going to Gwanja, are you?"

"Not I," says Zomo, "but this is what you must say. And furthermore," he goes on, "if they ask how long I shall be away, you are to say six months if not eight."

Early next morning, before the sun rises, Giwa the Elephant lines up his ten sons outside his house. He tells them that the hippo's black is mighty strong and that when he gives the signal they must heave on the rope with all their might. On the river bank Dorina the Hippo is doing the same thing with his twenty sons.

By and by the sun rises, the breeze springs up, and the leaves of all the trees along the river bank begin to shake. But Giwa and Dorina do not notice the other trees because they are only watching the fig tree. As soon as they see its leaves shaking, they both shout, "Heave," and then all the young elephants and all the young hippos begin to pull on the rope as if their lives depend on it.

At first the hippos gain some ground. When the old elephant sees this, he thinks that his horse is getting away and so he becomes very agitated and dances up and down and shouts to his sons to pull harder. Then the elephants begin to gain ground and it is the turn of the old hippo at the other end to become agitated and dance up and down and shout.

While this goes on, Zomo slips out of his house and hides himself in the branches of the fig tree. He has to hold on tight because the elephants and the hippos are pulling it this way and that and at one time he thinks that the tree will come up by the roots. But he waits until the tree is steady because both sides strain so hard, and then he takes out his knife and reaches down and cuts the rope.

When Zomo cuts the rope, the young hippos, who are up on the bank of the river, go toppling back into the water and make such a mighty splash that it stuns all the fish for miles around and even gives old Kada the Crocodile a headache.

As for the young elephants at the other end, they are right in front of their father's house, and so when the rope parts, they all go tumbling backward and knock down the ornamental gateway, which Giwa made for himself the year before, and then go rolling on into the compound where they flatten two huts and a corn-store.

When the old elephant and the old hippo see the rope part, they both think they will lose their horse, and so they both dash out to the fig tree to catch it and there they run into one another. Now Giwa, besides being surprised, is by no means pleased to see Dorina just now. He scowls at him and says that the black broke his tethering rope and that unless Dorina catches him and brings him back he will have to ask for the return of all his corn.

Dorina doesn't care to be scowled at at the best of times, let alone just now when he thinks that his horse has got away, and so he scowls right back and says that he doesn't know about any corn, all he knows is that the chestnut has broken his rope and got away and that unless Giwa catches him and brings him back he will have to ask for the return of all his fish.

Giwa is not used to being spoken to like this, even by Zaki the Lion, and doesn't care for it any more than Dorina cares to be scowled at. "Dorina," he says, "you get above yourself. You

may be a great man among the frogs and fishes, but here on land we don't consider you any great shakes."

This makes Dorina madder than ever because he doesn't like to be reminded that he now lives with frogs and fishes. "Giwa," he says, "the only reason I leave dry land and live in the water is that your belly rumbles so loud at night that it disturbs my children and they don't get their proper sleep."

At this, Giwa calls the hippo a baseborn, bandy-legged bog-trotter, and Dorina says that the elephant is a beady-eyed, swivel-nosed, loppy-lugged lounge-about. If the other animals don't come running up at this moment, they will certainly come to blows but as it is, they are just parted in time.

Later both of them send for Zomo, but they are told that Zomo is gone to Gwanja and won't be back for six months, if not eight. In fact it is much longer than this before Giwa and Dorina are on speaking terms again.

As for Zomo, he lies low and keeps out of everybody's sight. But his wife and children get so fat on Giwa's corn and Dorina's fish that the other animals think that Zomo must be working in Gwanja and sending money back to his family.

"That Zomo," they say to one another, "I do declare that he has turned over a new leaf at last."

ANANSI'S HAT-SHAKING DANCE

(*West African*)

West Africa is the home of many nations and many tribes, among them the countries of Ghana, Guinea, Senegal, and Dahomey and such peoples as the Ashanti and the Wolofs. Kwaku Anansi, the West African spider-man, is becoming more and more popular in the United States, and "Anansi's Hat-Shaking Dance" is one of the best stories for revealing his vanity and his aversion to telling the truth. His character is not at all changed in the Jamaican stories about him.

"Anansi's Hat-Shaking Dance." From *The Hat-Shaking Dance and Other Tales of the Gold Coast* by Harold Courlander and Albert Kofi Prempeh, © 1957 by Harold Courlander and reprinted with permission of Harcourt, Brace & World, Inc. Originally based on one of the tales in Rattray's *Akan-Ashanti Folk Tales* (Clarendon Press)

As a trickster-hero, a liar, and a thief, he is at the same time lovable and forgivable—for in Anansi we find not malice but mischief, not evil but devilment.

If you look closely, you will see that Kwaku Anansi, the spider, has a bald head. It is said that in the old days he had hair, but that he lost it through vanity.

It happened that Anansi's mother-in-law died. When word came to Anansi's house, Aso, his wife, prepared to go at once to her own village for the funeral. But Anansi said to Aso: "You go ahead; I will follow."

When Aso had gone, Anansi said to himself: "When I go to my dead mother-in-law's house, I will have to show great grief over her death. I will have to refuse to eat. Therefore, I shall eat now." And so he sat in his own house and ate a huge meal. Then he put on his mourning clothes and went to Aso's village.

First there was the funeral. Afterwards there was a large feast. But Anansi refused to eat, out of respect for his wife's dead mother. He said: "What kind of man would I be to eat when I am mourning for my mother-in-law? I will eat only after the eighth day has passed."

Now this was not expected of him, because a man isn't required to starve himself simply because someone has died. But Anansi was the kind of person that when he ate, he ate twice as much as others, and when he danced, he danced more vigorously than others, and when he mourned, he had to mourn more loudly than anybody else. Whatever he did, he didn't want to be outdone by anyone else. And although he was very hungry, he couldn't bear to have people think he wasn't the greatest mourner at his own mother-in-law's funeral.

So he said: "Feed my friends, but as for me, I shall do without." So everyone ate—the porcupine, the rabbit, the snake, the guinea fowl, and the others. All except Anansi.

On the second day after the funeral they said to him again: "Eat, there is no need to starve."

But Anansi replied: "Oh no, not until the eighth day, when the mourning is over. What kind of man do you think I am?"

So the others ate. Anansi's stomach was empty, and he was unhappy.

On the third day they said again: "Eat, Kwaku Anansi, there is no need to go hungry."

But Anansi was stubborn. He said: "How can I eat when my wife's mother has been buried only three days?" And so the others ate, while Anansi smelled the food hungrily and suffered.

On the fourth day, Anansi was alone where a pot of beans was cooking over the fire. He smelled the beans and looked in the pot. At last he couldn't stand it any longer. He took a large spoon and dipped up a large portion of the beans, thinking to take it to a quiet place and eat it without anyone's knowing. But just then the dog, the guinea fowl, the rabbit, and the others returned to the place where the food was cooking.

To hide the beans, Anansi quickly poured them in his hat and put it on his head. The other people came to the pot and ate, saying again: "Anansi, you must eat."

He said: "No, what kind of man would I be?"

But the hot beans were burning his head. He jiggled his hat around with his hands. When he saw the others looking at him, he said: "Just at this very moment in my village the hat-shaking festival is taking place. I shake my hat in honor of the occasion."

The beans felt hotter than ever, and he jiggled his hat some more. He began to jump with pain, and he said: "Like this in my village they are doing the hat-shaking dance."

He danced about, jiggling his hat because of the heat. He yearned to take off his hat, but he could not because his friends would see the beans. So he shouted: "They are shaking and jiggling the hats in my village, like this! It is a great festival! I must go!"

They said to him: "Kwaku Anansi, eat something before you go."

But now Anansi was jumping and writhing with the heat of the beans on his head. He shouted: "Oh no, they are shaking hats, they are wriggling hats and jumping like this! I must go to my village! They need me!"

He rushed out of the house, jumping and pushing his hat back and forth. His friends followed after him saying: "Eat before you go on your journey!"

But Anansi shouted: "What kind of man do

you think I am, with my mother-in-law just buried?"

Even though they all followed right after him, he couldn't wait any longer, because the pain was too much, and he tore the hat from his head. When the dog saw, and the guinea fowl saw, and the rabbit saw, and all the others saw what was in the hat, and saw the hot beans sticking to Anansi's head, they stopped chasing him. They began to laugh and jeer.

Anansi was overcome with shame. He leaped into the tall grass, saying: "Hide me." And the grass hid him.

That is why Anansi is often found in the tall grass, where he was driven by shame. And you will see that his head is bald, for the hot beans he put in his hat burned off his hair.

All this happened because he tried to impress people at his mother-in-law's funeral.

THE SLOOGEH DOG
AND THE STOLEN AROMA

(Congolese)

Perhaps this tale originated in North Africa. It is certainly very close in its spirit and lesson to the Ethiopian "The Fire on the Mountain," and variants of it occur in Turkey and Switzerland.

There was once a greedy African who through shrewd and sometimes dishonest dealings had become very rich. He was so rich in ivory that he had a fence of tusks all around his compound. He was so rich in sheep that he dared not count them, lest the evil spirits become jealous and destroy them.

He had so many wives that it took him from sunup to sundown just to walk past the doors of their huts. And he had so many daughters of marriageable age that he kept them in a herd guarded day and night by old women.

The favorite pastime of this rich man was eating. But no guest ever dipped the finger in the

pot with him at mealtime. No pet sat near him waiting to pick up fallen crumbs.

He ate alone in the shade of a big tree near the ivory gate of his compound. He ate much food and he became very fat.

One day as he sat on his eating stool, a procession of wives filed over to him from the cookhouse. Each carried on her head a basket or platter or bowl of food.

Each put her offering before him and backed away to sit on her heels and watch him eat. This day among the delicacies were baked elephant's foot, fried locusts, and rice balls with peanut gravy.

A wonderful aroma came from the steaming food. It flooded the compound and seeped through and over the ivory fence.

Now it happened that, at the very moment the smell of the food was spreading through the jungle, the Sloogeh Dog was coming down a path near the rich man's gate. In his wanderings he had foolishly crossed the hot, barren "hungry country" and he was truly on the verge of starvation.

When the smell of the rich man's food met him, his head jerked up and saliva gathered at the corners of his mouth. New strength came into his long lean body. He trotted, following the scent, straight to the rich man's gate.

The Sloogeh Dog pushed on the gate. It was tied fast, so he peered between the ivory posts. Seeing the man eating meat off a big bone, he made polite little begging sounds deep in his throat.

Saliva made two long threads from the corners of his mouth to the ground.

The sight of the hungry creature at his very gate spoiled the rich man's enjoyment of his food. He threw a vex and bellowed, "Go away from my face, beggar!"

The Sloogeh Dog was outside the fence where anyone was free to be. He knew he didn't have to go away. But he had another idea. He trotted all the way around the compound searching for the pile of rich scraps which he was sure would be somewhere near the fence. He found not so much as a peanut shuck.

However, he didn't forget the wonderful smell of that food. Each day, at mealtime, he would come to sniff and drool at the rich man's gate.

Each day the man would drive him away. And every day his anger grew until one day he left his food and went straight to the Council of Old Men.

He told his story. Then he said, "I want you to arrest that beggar of a dog!"

"On what grounds?" asked one of the old men.

"For stealing the aroma of my food!" said the rich man.

So the dog was arrested, a judge was appointed, and a day was set for the trial.

On the day of the trial, the whole village gathered about the Tree of Justice. From the start, the sympathy of the people was all with the Sloogeh Dog, for there was scarcely one of them who had not been swindled by the rich man.

But the judge was a just man. "I agree that the aroma was part of the food and so belonged to the accuser," he said. "And since the dog came every day to enjoy the smell of the food, one must conclude that it was intentional."

Murmurs of pity came from the crowd.

The Sloogeh Dog yawned nervously.

The judge continued. "If he had stolen only once, the usual punishment would be to cut off his paws!"

The Sloogeh Dog's legs gave way under him and he slithered on his belly to a hiding place back of the Tree of Justice.

"However," cried the judge, "since the crime was a daily habit, I must think about it overnight before I decide on a suitable punishment."

At sunup the next morning the people gathered to hear the sentence. They became very curious when the judge came leading a horse. He dropped the reins to the ground and left the animal standing where the trail enters the village.

Was the horse part of the punishment? Was the judge taking a trip later? He only shrugged when the people questioned him.

The judge called the rich man and the Sloogeh Dog to come before him. Handing a kiboko to the rich man, he said, "The accused will be beaten to death by the accuser!"

The rich man took off his gold-embroidered robe. He made a practice swing through the air with the whip.

The judge held up his hand. "Wait!" he commanded.

Then he turned to the people. "Do the people

agree that it was the invisible part of the food, and therefore its spirit, that was stolen?"

"Ee, ee!" cried the people.

The judge held up his hand again. "Do the people agree that the spirit of the dog is his shadow?"

"Ee, ee!" they said.

"Then," boomed the judge, "since the crime was against the spirit of the food, *only* the spirit of the dog shall be punished!"

The people howled with laughter. Their feet drummed on the hard-packed earth. They slapped each other's backs and shouted, "Esu! Esu!"

The Sloogeh Dog leaped up and licked the judge's nose.

The judge turned to the rich man and, when he could be heard, he said, "The shadow is big now, but you must beat it until the sun is straight up in the sky. When there is nothing left of the shadow, we shall agree that it is dead."

The rich man threw down the whip, picked up his garment, and said, "I withdraw the charges."

The judge shook his head. "You caused the

arrest," he said. "You wanted the trial. Now administer justice. And if the kiboko touches so much as a hair of the Sloogeh Dog, it will be turned upon you!"

There was nothing for the rich man to do but swing the whip hour after hour. The people watched and laughed as the dog leaped and howled, pretending to suffer with his shadow.

As the sun climbed higher and higher, the shadow became smaller and smaller—and much harder to hit. The whip became heavier in the man's flabby hands. He was dripping with sweat and covered with dust stirred up by the whip.

When the man could hardly bear the ordeal any longer, the dog lay down. That made it necessary for the man to get on his knees and put his arm between him and the dog to keep from touching a hair. When he brought down the whip, he hit his arm.

The people screamed with laughter.

The rich man bellowed and threw the kiboko. Then he leaped to the back of the judge's horse and rode headlong out of the village.

"He won't come back," said the oldest Old Man. "He would get *his* paws chopped off if he did. He stole the judge's horse!"

The Sloogeh Dog slunk off toward the rich man's house, his long nose sniffing for a whiff of something cooking beyond the ivory gate.

THE HONEY GATHERER'S
THREE SONS

(Congolese)

It would be more precise to refer to this story and the next as fables. They are only two out of hundreds that are employed to instruct children as well as to amuse all listeners. The ways in which various kinds of folklore are used to teach Congolese children are most interestingly explained in the preface to The Magic Drum, *the collection from which this story is taken.*

A honey gatherer had three sons, all born at the same time. Their names were Hear-it-how-

ever-faint-the-sound, Follow-it-however-great-the-distance and Put-it-together-however-small-the-pieces. These names are sufficient to indicate the skill of these young men, but their friends called them simply Hear, Follow and Piece.

One day the honey gatherer went on a long, long journey into the forest until he came to a tree that was as high as a hill, and the bees that buzzed in and out showed clearly that it must be full of honey. He climbed up, but, treading on a rotten branch, fell to the ground and was broken into ten pieces.

Hear was sitting beside the hut in the village, but he promptly jumped to his feet, saying, "Father has fallen from a tree. Come! Let us go to his help."

His brother Follow set out and led them along the father's tracks until they came upon the body lying in ten pieces. Piece then put all the parts together, fastened them up, and the father walked home while the sons carried his honey.

Next day the honey gatherer again set out to look for honey, while his sons sat at home, each boasting that he was more important than the others.

"You could not have heard him without me," said Hear.

"Though you had heard him you could not have found him without me," said Follow.

"Even though you had found him, you could not have put him together without me," said Piece.

Meanwhile, the old honey gatherer had gone far into the forest till he came to a tree as high as the clouds, and the bees buzzing in and out showed clearly that it must be full of honey. He climbed up, but, treading on a rotten branch, fell to the ground and was broken into a hundred pieces. His sons were sitting at home boasting about their prowess, when Hear jumped up, saying, "Father has fallen!"

Follow reluctantly set out to follow the footprints, and found the hundred pieces on the ground. Pointing to them he said, "See how indispensable I am. I have found him for you."

Piece then put the hundred pieces together very grudgingly, saying, "I, and I alone, have restored Father."

Their father walked home, while the sons carried the honey.

Next day the old honey gatherer went farther than ever into the forest and he found a tree that reached to the stars. The bees buzzing in and out showed that it must be full of honey. He climbed up, but, treading on a rotten branch, fell to the ground and was broken into a thousand pieces.

Hear heard the fall, but would not tell his brothers. Follow knew that there must have been an accident since his father did not return, while Piece realized that his father needed his assistance, but would not condescend to ask his brothers to find him so that he might piece him together.

So the old honey gatherer died, because the selfish sons each thought more of his own reputation than of his father's. In truth, each needed the others, and none was wiser or better than the rest.

LOOK BEHIND
AS WELL AS BEFORE
(Congolese)

Here, for older children, is the African cousin to "The Old Woman and Her Pig." It has an interesting counterpart in the picture book The Camel Who Took a Walk, *by Jack Tworkov, which has been made into a filmstrip by Weston Woods Studios.*

The big white ant, the luswa, wanted to get married and was taking the bride-price to the parents of the girl to whom he was addressing his attentions. He was so occupied with his errand that he did not look behind, or he would have seen a frog following him. The frog was licking his lips as he went after the luswa, and was so intent on the prospect of a feast that he did not see a snake following him. Had the snake looked behind, he would have known that a wooden club was after him. The club was so eager to overtake the snake that he did not see the small white ants doggedly pursuing him. The small white ants, the tuswalandala, did not realize it, but a fowl was on their tracks. The fowl was anxious to feast off the small white ants, but did not know

that a wild cat was slinking after her. The wild cat had his eye on the fowl, otherwise he would have detected a trap that was in his path. The trap was thinking of nothing but the wild cat or he would have seen the bush fire rolling toward him. The bush fire was heaving up sparks and smoke and thus failed to realize that water was barring his way. The water only thought of attacking the fire, and so was not prepared for the drought that was on his heels.

The parents of the prospective bride had cooked a feast, but before they could sit down to it the frog began to eat the big white ant. The snake attacked the frog. The club struck down the snake. The small white ants gnawed into the club, the fowl snapped up the small white ants, the wild cat seized the fowl, the trap fell on the wild cat, the fire consumed the trap, the water put out the fire, the drought dried up the water, and all that was left was a dusty waste. How much better if the white ant had looked behind. And moreover, if you have cruel designs upon another, don't forget that others may have similar designs on you.

WINDBIRD AND THE SUN
(South African)

This typical why *story has been very nicely retold and expanded by Josef Marais. Children might enjoy looking for other tales from around the world that tell why there are rainbows. "Windbird and the Sun" comes from the Hottentots, a rapidly disappearing people who are confined largely to the desert regions of South Africa.*

Once the Queen of the Fountains had a beautiful daughter. Her name was Thashira and the Queen was very proud of her and gave her all that she wished. But nothing made Thashira really happy except bright colors. Gaily-colored flowers, or blankets of yellow, green or blue, or necklaces made of gaudy stones—all these gave Thashira pleasure. Nothing else interested her

"Look Behind as Well as Before." Reprinted from *The Magic Drum* by W. F. P. Burton. By permission of Abelard-Schuman, Ltd. All Rights Reserved

"Windbird and the Sun." From *Koos the Hottentot* by Josef Marais (New York: Alfred A. Knopf, Inc., 1945), pp. 53–62. Reprinted by permission of the author

—in fact the Queen's daughter for most of the time was sad and unpleasant to her friends. She would not help grind corn, or fashion clay pots, as the other girls of the kraal did. She would not take part in the dance ceremonies when harvest time came. All day Thashira sat and stared at the blue of the sky. Flowers seldom bloomed in the dry country and the thorntrees and bushes were mostly bare without any color to delight her eyes. The Queen herself was busy travelling up the mountains to see the fountains, and she was very worried knowing that her daughter was so sad.

The young men of the kraal left Thashira alone. "Who wants such a dull, unpleasant girl for a wife?" they said.

Sometimes Thashira went to the nearby vlei (when there was some water there) and plucked water lilies for a wreath to put on her head. Sometimes she gathered wild berries and decorated her body with the red juice. During these times she was happy and everyone said, "Thashira has found another color," and everyone would smile at her and nod and say, "How pretty you look!" Then she tried mixing the juice of plants with the brown or red clay near the vlei and with that she painted pictures on the rocks. But Thashira tired of all this and spent most of the days lying in the shade of a baobab tree and staring at the bright blue of the sky.

The Sun saw her there one day and said to her, "Beautiful Thashira, I know you love the blue color of the sky. That makes me happy because it is I who give the sky its color." She came out from under the branch of the baobab tree and looked up for a moment at the brilliant Sun and said, "Thank you, you are kind." Then she went back under the shade. She did not even smile.

The Sun sympathized with her, for he too liked colors. Every day he tried placing new and finer colors in the sky when the day was ending and he was ready to sink beyond the koppies to the west. This pleased Thashira and she made a habit of climbing the highest koppie to admire the Sun while he showed her his new glowing colors. So they became very fond of each other, the maiden and the Sun.

But Windbird fell in love with Thashira. As she lay half asleep under the baobab tree he ca-

ressed her hair and cooled her brow. It was not often that Windbird was so gentle. In the dry country he is always in a violent hurry. Most of the time Windbird is very busy journeying back and forth from the seacoast to the great lands in the interior of Africa. Above the ocean he chooses a large cloud and flies with it inland. If the mountains are very high he has to trail the cloud so high that he sometimes loses most of it on the way. Then the people are angry at him for bringing no clouds or rain. Windbird has a quick temper, and if he finds the people are angry and blaming him he gets angry too. Then he blows the dust over the Veld. And people hate him still more.

But when Windbird fell in love with the daughter of the Queen of the Fountains, he blew very gently for weeks. He brought clouds from as far as Cape Agulhas where the Indian and the Atlantic oceans meet. He tore off pieces of clouds while he flew them over the big mountains near the coast, for fear they were too big and might cause hailstones. Thus, just enough rain fell, and the flowers bloomed and the plants sprouted and there were lots of colors for the maiden to enjoy.

"That's all very well," growled Windbird to himself, "but Thashira doesn't know it is I who bring her this pleasure."

So one day while the girl was romping among the chinkerinchees, plucking bunches of the tiny white flowers with their green dotted petals, he approached her and said, "Thashira, I love you. That is why I have brought the clouds to water the ground and give you these fine flowers. I am great and strong. I am Windbird." He thought the maiden would be grateful and impressed by his prowess. But she glanced at him coolly and said, "Thank you, you are kind." Then she continued picking chinkerinchees. Windbird flew into a temper. He blew great blasts of air across the Veld so that the newly-grown grasses and plants swayed until their roots broke. The flowers were torn off their stems. The bushes were uprooted.

"Now you can see my strength," Windbird boasted, and the air currents whistled wildly across Veld and vlei. Thashira was heartbroken. All the brightly-colored plants and blossoms had disappeared. Once more the land was dusty and bare. Again she took to lying in the shade of her baobab tree and gazing at the only color that was left—the blue of the sky. When Windbird came to call on her she scornfully told him to go away.

The Queen of the Fountains returned and found her daughter sadder than ever. Thashira's only companion now was a little dove whose neck was decorated with gaily-colored feathers. When the Sun shone on the little dove her feathers reflected all the colors of the Sun's rays. The Queen saw that Thashira spent her days beneath the baobab tree. She watched Thashira whisper messages to the dove who then flew far away into the blue sky.

"Thashira, my daughter, you are so sad. True, life in this dry land is dreary. What can I do to make you happy?"

"Mother, I love the Sun for he makes the sky blue, and his warmth helps the colorful flowers to bloom."

"Is it to the Sun that you are sending your little dove with messages?" asked the Queen, and Thashira shyly nodded.

"Good—then I will order that a great ladder be built so that you may go up into the blue sky you love so much and stay forever with the Sun," cried the Queen.

The elephants and the hippos and the rhinos and the monkeys rushed to obey the Queen of the Fountains for they knew how much their lives depended on pleasing her. In the distant forests they pulled down the trees. Against all the rules of nature the Queen ordered the rivers to flood over the dry land even for a brief period so that they might bring the great logs to Thashira's home. The people built hundreds and hundreds of ladders and placed them one on top of the other. When they reached so high into the sky that the top ladder could not be seen Thashira sent her little dove with a final message to the Sun, and then while the crowds of people anxiously watched, she placed her foot on the first rung.

Suddenly from the distance came the horrible wail of the wind. Windbird was furious that the Sun had won Thashira. Now his moment for revenge had come.

"So!" Windbird roared in his anger. "You scorned the power of Windbird! Now you shall see who is stronger—the Sun or the Wind." And the dust and bushes flew across the Veld, the loose stones whipped the bodies of the multitude of people. With a tremendous crack the great ladders came tumbling down to earth. The cries of the people mingled with the cruel whistling of Windbird.

The Queen of the Fountains wept for her daughter, Thashira. She wept and wept with sorrow and her tears floated upwards in a great, grey mist. Then the little dove returned from above with one of her wings almost broken from the strong winds; but the colors of her neck feathers were brighter than ever. She alighted on the shoulder of beautiful Thashira. The next moment Thashira with the little dove were floating upward, and the misty vapor from the Queen's tears enveloped them. The Sun burst out in all his brilliance. The whistling of Windbird died down to a whisper . . . then there was dead stillness. The people looked upward and across the sky shone a glorious rainbow of all the colors that anyone could wish.

Thashira is the rainbow and when the Sun

shines on her, she glows with happiness. Though Windbird tries and tries he cannot blow her away. From time to time Windbird breaks into one of his violent fits of temper, but Thashira re- mains steadfast in the sky proudly showing the Sun and the world her gorgeous colors. May Windbird never succeed in blowing Thashira, the rainbow, away!

China

Although China's history and literature reach back at least four thousand years, we actually know very little of her folk tales. Chinese tales have long appeared in collections for young people, but their validity is questionable, since they may have been invented in large part, drawn from some of the few texts of Chinese literature that have been translated into Western tongues, or taken from accounts given by persons in this country—accounts that are not verifiable. It was not until 1917 that efforts were begun to unlock the great treasure of China's folk literature, but these efforts were sporadic until the present Communist era. Now China's tales are assiduously collected from every possible source and published widely for the people, but they are rewritten and distorted to promote the Communist way of life. The two stories here cannot be called true folk tales. They are both taken from Alice Ritchie's The Treasure of Li-Po, *a charming group of six stories that have retained their popularity with American children for almost twenty years and that capture the spirit and inflection of pre-Communist China as we have generally assumed it to be. The titles in the Bibliography are mainly of compilations which purport to be actual folk tales taken from reliable printed sources or from the lips of Chinese storytellers. In all of them we see the China of long ago.*

THE FOX'S DAUGHTER

What a charming way to present a homily on the virtue and reward of serious attention to one's duties!

Nothing is luckier than to be the child of a fox, for, without taking the trouble to learn anything, foxes know as much magic as the man who spends his whole life studying it, and when a fox's child takes human form, as sometimes happens, and becomes a boy or a girl, he knows as much magic as his father.

Liu was a young student who should have been working hard for his examinations, but he was rather idle and much preferred wandering

about his father's estate, or sailing in a boat on the river which ran through it, to sitting indoors over his books.

One day, when he was occupied—if it can be called occupied—in this way, he saw the form of a young girl among the reeds which grew upon a little island in the river. Quickly he jumped into his boat and hurried across the water, and, tying the boat up to a willow tree, he began to search the island for her.

For some time he saw nothing, but he heard mocking laughter to the right and to the left, and, running wildly first in one direction and then in the other, he tore his silk robe and broke the strap of one of his sandals. At last he succeeded in running her down, but she looked so beautiful, leaning against a tree and smiling at him, that even after he had got his breath back he could not speak.

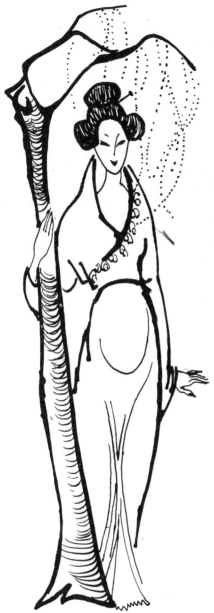

"Alas," said the girl in a clear low voice, looking at his torn robe and flapping sandal, "if Master Liu pursued his studies with the same zeal as he has pursued me, he would take a high place when the candidates go up to the Examination Hall, and some day he would be a man of great importance—but of course he will do nothing of the sort."

Liu eagerly asked her name and how she happened to know all about him, and also how she came to be upon the island, for he could see no boat except his own.

"My name is Feng-Lien," said the maiden, "but as to how I came here, I shall not tell you, and I can go away again as swiftly."

(This was not surprising, because of course she was a fox's daughter, and could appear and disappear at will.) And now she made a movement as if she meant to go, but Liu sprang forward with his hands spread out.

"I beg you to stay," he cried, "or at least tell me where we shall meet again, for you are the most beautiful person I have ever seen."

"Look for me in your books," said the maiden; then, seeing his face become clouded with disappointment, she took a little silver mirror from her girdle and gave it to him. "There," she said, "you shall have something which has belonged to me, but I warn you, you will never see me in it except through your books." And in a moment she had vanished.

Liu went back to his boat feeling very sad, and many times before he reached the house he looked longingly into the silver mirror, but all he saw was the back-view of the beautiful Feng-Lien standing as if she was watching someone going away from her.

As soon as he reached his room, remembering what she had said, he took out the heavy and difficult books which he had never had a mind to study, and laying them on the top of the mirror, he tried to see it through them, but of course he saw nothing, not even its silver handle, buried under those great volumes.

"Feng-Lien meant more than she said," he remarked to himself, and he removed the books from the mirror with a sigh and applied himself earnestly to reading them, refusing to see his friends when they came to the house and not accepting any invitations. After he had spent several days in this way, he looked into the mirror again, and there was Feng-Lien with her face turned towards him, smiling and nodding as if she was pleased.

For a month or more he did nothing but study, looking often into the mirror to be encouraged by the lovely face of Feng-Lien, but presently the fine summer weather came, and he could not force himself to stay in the house. He began once more to wander about the garden and the wild land beside the river, idly enjoying the scent of the newly opened flowers and the sight of the bright birds.

"Perhaps I shall see Feng-Lien again," he said. But he did not find her, and in his heart he knew she would not come while he behaved in this way. Then, one evening after he had been on a fishing expedition all day with some friends, when he pulled out the silver mirror he saw Feng-Lien crying bitterly, and the next morning she had her back turned to him.

"It is clear that there is only one thing to be done," he said to himself. "I must make a habit of working all the time."

He took the silver mirror and nailed it on the wall so that whenever he raised his eyes from his difficult reading he would see Feng-Lien's face. She always looked happy now. This went on for two years, and at the end of that time he went up to the Examination Hall and did so well that he took a high place in the final list.

"Now," he said, "at last, I shall surely be allowed to see Feng-Lien herself."

He took up the mirror and looked for a long time at her reflection, at the arched eyebrows and the beautiful eyes and the smiling mouth, until it seemed to him that her lips parted and she spoke, yes, she seemed to be speaking words of welcome and congratulation, and suddenly the mirror dissolved into a drop of dew and instead of her likeness, Feng-Lien herself stood before him.

"Really," she said, bowing very low, "I am quite frightened of this learned young man."

"The success I have had is entirely owing to you," said Liu.

So they were married, and Liu attained to one of the highest positions in China, but Feng-Lien never again had to use the magic she possessed by reason of being a fox's daughter. She found quite simple ways of keeping her husband, who continued to be by nature somewhat lazy, up to the mark.

TWO OF EVERYTHING

Whether you read aloud or tell this story, it will produce howls of laughter. It is easy to dramatize and guarantees a pleased audience.

"Two of Everything." From *The Treasure of Li-Po* by Alice Ritchie, copyright, 1949 by Harcourt, Brace & World, Inc., and reprinted with their permission and the permission of The Hogarth Press Ltd.

Mr. and Mrs. Hak-Tak were rather old and rather poor. They had a small house in a village among the mountains and a tiny patch of green land on the mountain side. Here they grew the vegetables which were all they had to live on, and when it was a good season and they did not need to eat up everything as soon as it was grown, Mr. Hak-Tak took what they could spare in a basket to the next village which was a little larger than theirs and sold it for as much as he could get and bought some oil for their lamp, and fresh seeds, and every now and then, but not often, a piece of cotton stuff to make new coats and trousers for himself and his wife. You can imagine they did not often get the chance to eat meat.

Now, one day it happened that when Mr. Hak-Tak was digging in his precious patch, he unearthed a big brass pot. He thought it strange that it should have been there for so long without his having come across it before, and he was disappointed to find that it was empty; still, he thought they would find some use for it, so when he was ready to go back to the house in the evening he decided to take it with him. It was very big and heavy, and in his struggles to get his arms round it and raise it to a good position for carrying, his purse, which he always took with him in his belt, fell to the ground, and, to be quite sure he had it safe, he put it inside the pot and so staggered home with his load.

As soon as he got into the house Mrs. Hak-Tak hurried from the inner room to meet him.

"My dear husband," she said, "whatever have you got there?"

"For a cooking-pot it is too big; for a bath a little too small," said Mr. Hak-Tak. "I found it buried in our vegetable patch and so far it has been useful in carrying my purse home for me."

"Alas," said Mrs. Hak-Tak, "something smaller would have done as well to hold any money we have or are likely to have," and she stooped over the pot and looked into its dark inside.

As she stooped, her hairpin—for poor Mrs. Hak-Tak had only one hairpin for all her hair and it was made of carved bone—fell into the pot. She put in her hand to get it out again, and then she gave a loud cry which brought her husband running to her side.

"What is it?" he asked. "Is there a viper in the pot?"

"Oh, my dear husband," she cried. "What can be the meaning of this? I put my hand into the pot to fetch out my hairpin and your purse, and look, I have brought out two hairpins and two purses, both exactly alike."

"Open the purse. Open both purses," said Mr. Hak-Tak. "One of them will certainly be empty."

But not a bit of it. The new purse contained exactly the same number of coins as the old one—for that matter, no one could have said which was the new and which the old—and it meant, of course, that the Hak-Taks had exactly twice as much money in the evening as they had had in the morning.

"And two hairpins instead of one!" cried Mrs. Hak-Tak, forgetting in her excitement to do up her hair which was streaming over her shoulders. "There is something quite unusual about this pot."

"Let us put in the sack of lentils and see what happens," said Mr. Hak-Tak, also becoming excited.

They heaved in the bag of lentils and when they pulled it out again—it was so big it almost filled the pot—they saw another bag of exactly the same size waiting to be pulled out in its turn. So now they had two bags of lentils instead of one.

"Put in the blanket," said Mr. Hak-Tak. "We need another blanket for the cold weather." And, sure enough, when the blanket came out, there lay another behind it.

"Put my wadded coat in," said Mr. Hak-Tak, "and then when the cold weather comes there will be one for you as well as for me. Let us put in everything we have in turn. What a pity we have no meat or tobacco, for it seems that the pot cannot make anything without a pattern."

Then Mrs. Hak-Tak, who was a woman of great intelligence, said, "My dear husband, let us put the purse in again and again and again. If we take two purses out each time we put one in, we shall have enough money by tomorrow evening to buy everything we lack."

"I am afraid we may lose it this time," said Mr. Hak-Tak, but in the end he agreed, and they dropped in the purse and pulled out two, then they added the new money to the old and dropped it in again and pulled out the larger amount twice over. After a while the floor was covered with old leather purses and they decided just to throw the money in by itself. It worked quite as well and saved trouble; every time, twice as much money came out as went in, and every time they added the new coins to the old and threw them all in together. It took them some hours to tire of this game, but at last Mrs. Hak-Tak said, "My dear husband, there is no need for us to work so hard. We shall see to it that the pot does not run away, and we can always make more money as we want it. Let us tie up what we have."

It made a huge bundle in the extra blanket and the Hak-Taks lay and looked at it for a long time before they slept, and talked of all the things they would buy and the improvements they would make in the cottage.

The next morning they rose early and Mr. Hak-Tak filled a wallet with money from the bundle and set off for the big village to buy more things in one morning than he had bought in a whole fifty years.

Mrs. Hak-Tak saw him off and then she tidied up the cottage and put the rice on to boil and had another look at the bundle of money, and made herself a whole set of new hairpins from the pot, and about twenty candles instead of the one which was all they had possessed up to now. After that she slept for a while, having been up so late the night before, but just before the time when her husband should be back, she awoke and went over to the pot. She dropped in a cabbage leaf to make sure it was still working properly, and when she took two leaves out she sat down on the floor and put her arms round it.

"I do not know how you came to us, my dear pot," she said, "but you are the best friend we ever had."

Then she knelt up to look inside it, and at that moment her husband came to the door, and, turning quickly to see all the wonderful things he had bought, she overbalanced and fell into the pot.

Mr. Hak-Tak put down his bundles and ran across and caught her by the ankles and pulled her out, but, oh, mercy, no sooner had he set her carefully on the floor than he saw the kicking legs of another Mrs. Hak-Tak in the pot! What was he to do? Well, he could not leave her there, so he caught her ankles and pulled, and another Mrs. Hak-Tak so exactly like the first that no one would have told one from the other, stood beside them.

"Here's an extraordinary thing," said Mr. Hak-Tak, looking helplessly from one to the other.

"I will not have a second Mrs. Hak-Tak in the house!" screamed the old Mrs. Hak-Tak.

All was confusion. The old Mrs. Hak-Tak shouted and wrung her hands and wept, Mr. Hak-Tak was scarcely calmer, and the new Mrs. Hak-Tak sat down on the floor as if she knew no more than they did what was to happen next.

"One wife is all *I* want," said Mr. Hak-Tak, "but how could I have left her in the pot?"

"Put her back in it again!" cried Mrs. Hak-Tak.

"What? And draw out two more?" said her husband. "If two wives are too many for me, what should I do with three? No! No!" He stepped back quickly as if he was stepping away from the three wives and, missing his footing, lo and behold, he fell into the pot!

Both Mrs. Hak-Taks ran and each caught an ankle and pulled him out and set him on the floor, and there, oh, mercy, was another pair of kicking legs in the pot! Again each caught hold of an ankle and pulled, and soon another Mr. Hak-Tak, so exactly like the first that no one could have told one from the other, stood beside them.

Now the old Mr. Hak-Tak liked the idea of his double no more than Mrs. Hak-Tak had liked the idea of hers. He stormed and raged and scolded his wife for pulling him out of the pot, while the new Mr. Hak-Tak sat down on the floor beside the new Mrs. Hak-Tak and looked as if, like her, he did not know what was going to happen next.

Then the old Mrs. Hak-Tak had a very good idea. "Listen, my dear husband," she said, "now, do stop scolding and listen, for it is really a good thing that there is a new one of you as well as a new one of me. It means that you and I can go on in our usual way, and these new people, who are ourselves and yet not ourselves, can set up house together next door to us."

And that is what they did. The old Hak-Taks built themselves a fine new house with money from the pot, and they built one just like it next door for the new couple, and they lived together in the greatest friendliness, because, as Mrs. Hak-Tak said, "The new Mrs. Hak-Tak is really more than a sister to me, and the new Mr. Hak-Tak is really more than a brother to you."

The neighbors were very much surprised, both at the sudden wealth of the Hak-Taks and at the new couple who resembled them so strongly that they must, they thought, be very close relations of whom they had never heard before. They said: "It looks as though the Hak-Taks, when they so unexpectedly became rich, decided to have two of everything, even of themselves, in order to enjoy their money more."

Japan

The ideals embodied in the Japanese tales are the ones by which the Japanese have lived for centuries, and the beliefs and customs pictured in the stories are very like the present-day ones. Storytellers do not abound in Japan as they do in Turkey or in Africa, but folklorists have found many farmers, villagers, and fishermen who were living repositories of the traditional tales and legends. The average Japanese knows many of his folk tales because they have long been printed in single-story and collected editions for children and because they inform so much of the artistic and cultural life of Japan. As in China, so in Japan much of the traditional folk literature provides the content for the sermons of Buddhist priests, for the plays in such traditional theaters as the Bunraku Doll Theater, and for the work of artists and poets. In reading the tales of Japan, one quickly comes very close to the spirit of her past and her present.

MOMOTARO:

BOY-OF-THE-PEACH

This is one of the most popular stories in Japan, where the word for ogres is "oni." It is uniquely Japanese and has been charmingly retold by Uchida. After hearing this story, children will be pleased to discover the amusing little poem about Momotaro in Time for Poetry.

Once long, long ago, there lived a kind old man and a kind old woman in a small village in Japan.

One fine day, they set out from their little cottage together. The old man went toward the mountains to cut some firewood for their kitchen, and the old woman went toward the river to do her washing.

When the old woman reached the shore of the river, she knelt down beside her wooden tub and began to scrub her clothes on a round, flat stone. Suddenly she looked up and saw something very strange floating down the shallow river. It was a big, big peach; bigger than the round wooden tub that stood beside the old woman.

Rumbley-bump and a-bumpety-bump . . . Rumbley-bump and a-bumpety-bump. The big peach rolled closer and closer over the stones in the stream.

"My gracious me!" the old woman said to herself. "In all my long life I have never seen a peach of such great size and beauty. What a fine present it would make for the old man. I do think I will take it home with me."

Then the old woman stretched out her hand just as far as she could, but no matter how hard she stretched, she couldn't reach the big peach.

"If I could just find a long stick, I would be able to reach it," thought the old woman, looking around, but all she could see were pebbles and sand.

"Oh, dear, what shall I do?" she said to herself. Then suddenly she thought of a way to bring the beautiful big peach to her side. She began to sing out in a sweet, clear voice,

"The deep waters are salty!
The shallow waters are sweet!
Stay away from the salty water,
And come where the water is sweet."

She sang this over and over, clapping her hands in time to her song. Then, strangely enough, the big peach slowly began to bob along toward the shore where the water was shallow.

Rumbley-bump and a-bumpety-bump . . . Rumbley-bump and a-bumpety-bump. The big peach came closer and closer to the old woman and finally came to a stop at her feet.

The old woman was so happy, she picked the big peach up very carefully and quickly carried it home in her arms. Then she waited for the old man to return so she could show him her lovely present. Toward evening the old man came home with a big pack of wood on his back.

"Come quickly, come quickly," the old woman called to him from the house.

"What is it? What is the matter?" the old man asked as he hurried to the side of the old woman.

"Just look at the fine present I have for you," said the old woman happily as she showed him the big round peach.

"My goodness! What a great peach! Where in the world did you buy such a peach as this?" the old man asked.

The old woman smiled happily and told him how she had found the peach floating down the river.

"Well, well, this is a fine present indeed," said the old man, "for I have worked hard today and I am very hungry."

Then he got the biggest knife they had, so he could cut the big peach in half. Just as he was ready to thrust the sharp blade into the peach, he heard a tiny voice from inside.

"Wait, old man! Don't cut me!" it cried, and before the surprised old man and woman could say a word, the beautiful big peach broke in two, and a sweet little boy jumped out from inside. The old man and woman were so surprised, they could only raise their hands and cry out, "Oh, oh! My goodness!"

Now the old man and woman had always wanted a child of their own, so they were very, very happy to find such a fine little boy, and decided to call him "Momotaro," which means boy-of-the-peach. They took very good care of the little boy and grew to love him dearly, for he was a fine young lad. They spent many happy years together, and before long Momotaro was fifteen years old.

One day Momotaro came before the old man and said, "You have both been good and kind to me. I am very grateful for all you have done, and now I think I am old enough to do some good for others too. I have come to ask if I may leave you."

"You wish to leave us, my son? But why?" asked the old man in surprise.

"Oh, I shall be back in a very short time," said Momotaro. "I wish only to go to the Island of the Ogres, to rid the land of those harmful creatures. They have killed many good people, and have stolen and robbed throughout the country. I wish to kill the ogres so they can never harm our people again."

"That is a fine idea, my son, and I will not stop you from going," said the old man.

So that very day, Momotaro got ready to start out on his journey. The old woman prepared some millet cakes for him to take along on his trip, and soon Momotaro was ready to leave. The old man and woman were sad to see him go and called, "Be careful, Momotaro! Come back safely to us."

"Yes, yes, I shall be back soon," he answered. "Take care of yourselves while I am away," he added, and waved as he started down the path toward the forest.

He hurried along, for he was anxious to get to the Island of the Ogres. While he was walking through the cool forest where the grass grew long and high, he began to feel hungry. He sat down at the foot of a tall pine tree and carefully unwrapped the *furoshiki*[1] which held his little millet cakes. "My, they smell good," he thought. Suddenly he heard the tall grass rustle and saw something stalking through the grass toward him. Momotaro blinked hard when he saw what it was. It was a dog as big as a calf! But Momotaro was not frightened, for the dog just said, "Momotaro-san, Momotaro-san, what is it you are eating that smells so good?"

[1] Pronounced foo-ro-shee-kee, a square cloth used to wrap and carry articles.

"I'm eating a delicious millet cake which my good mother made for me this morning," he answered.

The dog licked his chops and looked at the cake with hungry eyes. "Please, Momotaro-san," he said, "just give me one of your millet cakes, and I will come along with you to the Island of the Ogres. I know why you are going there, and I can be of help to you."

"Very well, my friend," said Momotaro. "I will take you along with me," and he gave the dog one of his millet cakes to eat.

As they walked on, something suddenly leaped from the branches above and jumped in front of Momotaro. He stopped in surprise and found that it was a monkey who had jumped down from the trees.

"Greetings, Momotaro-san!" called the monkey happily. "I have heard that you are going to the Island of the Ogres to rid the land of these plundering creatures. Take me with you, for I wish to help you in your fight."

When the dog heard this he growled angrily. "Grruff," he said to the monkey. "*I* am going to help Momotaro-san. We do not need the help of a monkey such as you! Out of our way! Grruff, grruff," he barked angrily.

"How dare you speak to me like that?" shrieked the monkey, and he leaped at the dog, scratching with his sharp claws. The dog and the monkey began to fight each other, biting, clawing, and growling. When Momotaro saw this he pushed them apart and cried, "Here, here, stop it, you two! There is no reason why you both cannot go with me to the Island of the Ogres. I shall have two helpers instead of one!" Then he took another millet cake from his *furoshiki* and gave it to the monkey.

Now there were three of them going down the path to the edge of the woods. The dog in front, Momotaro in the middle, and the monkey walking in the rear. Soon they came to a big field and just as they were about to cross it, a large pheasant hopped out in front of them. The dog jumped at it with a growl, but the pheasant fought back with such spirit that Momotaro ran over to stop the dog. "We could use a brave bird such as you to help us fight the ogres. We are on our way to their island this very day. How would you like to come along with us?"

"Oh, I would like that indeed, for I would like to help you rid the land of these evil and dangerous ogres," said the pheasant happily.

"Then here is a millet cake for you, too," said Momotaro, giving the pheasant a cake, just as he had to the monkey and the dog.

Now there were four of them going to the Island of the Ogres, and as they walked down the path together, they became very good friends.

Before long they came to the water's edge and Momotaro found a boat big enough for all of them. They climbed in and headed for the Island of the Ogres. Soon they saw the island in the distance wrapped in gray, foggy clouds. Dark stone walls rose up above towering cliffs and large iron gates stood ready to keep out any who tried to enter.

Momotaro thought for a moment, then turned to the pheasant and said, "You alone can wing your way over their high walls and gates. Fly into their stronghold now, and do what you can to frighten them. We will follow as soon as we can."

So the pheasant flew far above the iron gates and stone walls and down onto the roof of the ogres' castle. Then he called to the ogres, "Momotaro-san has come to rid the land of you and your many evil deeds. Give up your stolen treasures now, and perhaps he will spare your lives!"

When the ogres heard this, they laughed and shouted. "HO, HO, HO! We are not afraid of a little bird like you! We are not afraid of little Momotaro!"

The pheasant became very angry at this, and flew down, pecking at the heads of the ogres with his sharp, pointed beak. While the pheasant was fighting so bravely, the dog and monkey helped Momotaro to tear down the gates, and they soon came to the aid of the pheasant.

"Get away! Get away!" shouted the ogres, but the monkey clawed and scratched, the big dog growled and bit the ogres, and the pheasant flew about, pecking at their heads and faces. So fierce were they that soon the ogres began to run away. Half of them tumbled over the cliffs as they ran and the others fell pell-mell into the sea. Soon only the Chief of the Ogres remained. He threw up his hands, and then bowed low to Momotaro. "Please spare me my life, and all our stolen trea-

sures are yours. I promise never to rob or kill anyone again," he said.

Momotaro tied up the evil ogre, while the monkey, the dog and the pheasant carried many boxes filled with jewels and treasures down to their little boat. Soon it was laden with all the treasures it could hold, and they were ready to sail toward home.

When Momotaro returned, he went from one family to another, returning the many treasures which the ogres had stolen from the people of the land.

"You will never again be troubled by the Ogres of Ogre Island!" he said to them happily.

And they all answered, "You are a kind and brave lad, and we thank you for making our land safe once again."

Then Momotaro went back to the home of the old man and woman with his arms full of jewels and treasures from Ogre Island. My, but the old man and woman were glad to see him once again, and the three of them lived happily together for many, many years.

URASHIMA TARO AND THE PRINCESS OF THE SEA

This tale, which can be traced back to the eighth century in Japan, bears striking resemblance to such European tales as the Gaelic story of Oisin's sojourn in the Land of the Ever-Young and the Russian "Sadko." It has aptly been called the Japanese "Rip Van Winkle." The simplicity and poetry of the tale have been captured by Taro Yashima in his picture-book version, The Seashore Story, *a runner-up for the Caldecott Award in 1968.*

Long, long ago, in a small village of Japan, there lived a fine young man named Urashima Taro. He lived with his mother and father in a thatched-roof house which overlooked the sea. Each morning he was up before the sun, and went out to sea in his little fishing boat. On days when his luck was good, he would bring back large baskets full of fish which he sold in the village market.

"Urashima Taro and the Princess of the Sea." From *The Dancing Kettle and Other Japanese Folk Tales*, copyright, 1949, by Yoshiko Uchida. Reprinted by permission of Harcourt, Brace & World, Inc.

One day, as he was carrying home his load of fish, he saw a group of shouting children. They were gathered around something on the beach and were crying, "Hit him! Poke him!" Taro ran over to see what was the matter, and there on the sand he saw a big brown tortoise. The children were poking it with a long stick and throwing stones at its hard shell.

"Here, here," called Taro. "That's no way to treat him! Why don't you leave him alone, and let him go back to the sea?"

"But we found him," said one of the children. "He belongs to us!"

"Yes, yes, he is ours," cried all the children.

Now, because Urashima Taro was a fair and kindly young man, he said to them, "Suppose I give each of you something in return for the tortoise?" Then he took ten shiny coins out of a small bag of money and gave one to each child. "Now, isn't that a fair bargain?" he asked. "A coin for each of you, and the tortoise for me."

"Yes, yes. Thank you!" called the children, and away they ran to the village candy shop.

Taro watched the old tortoise crawl away slowly toward the sea and called, "You'd better stay at home in the sea from now on, old fellow!" Then, smiling happily because he had been able to save the tortoise, he turned to go home. There his mother and father were waiting for him with bowls of steaming rice and soup.

Several days passed, and Taro soon forgot all about the tortoise whom he had saved. One day he was sitting in his boat feeling very sad because he could catch no fish. Suddenly he heard a voice from the sea calling, "Urashima-san! Urashima-san!"

"Now who could be calling me here in the middle of the sea?" thought Urashima Taro. He looked high and low, but could see no one. Suddenly, from the crest of a big wave, out popped the head of the old tortoise.

"I came to thank you for saving me the other day," said the tortoise.

"Well, I'm glad you got away safely," said Taro.

"This time I would like to do something for you, Urashima-san," said the tortoise. "How would you like to visit the princess who lives in the Palace of the Sea?"

"The princess of the sea!" shouted Taro. "I have heard often of her beauty, and everyone says her palace is more lovely than any place on earth! But how can I go to the bottom of the sea, and how can I enter her palace?"

"Just leave everything to me," said the old tortoise. "Hop on my back and I will see that you get there safely. I will also take you into the palace, for I am one of the palace guards."

So Urashima Taro jumped onto the smooth round back of the tortoise, and away they went.

Swish, swish . . . the waves seemed to part and make a path for them as the tortoise swam on. Soon Taro felt himself going down . . . down . . . down . . . into the sea, but he wasn't getting wet at all. He heard the waves lapping gently about his ears. "That's strange," thought Taro. "This is just like a dream—a nice happy dream."

Before long, they were at the bottom of the big blue sea. Taro could see bright-colored fish playing hide and seek among the long strands of swaying seaweed. He could see clams and other shellfish shyly peeking out at him from their shells. Soon Taro saw something big and shiny looming in the hazy blue water.

"Is that the palace?" he asked anxiously. "It looks very beautiful."

"Oh, no," answered the tortoise. "That is just the outer gate."

They came to a stop and Taro could see that the gateway was guarded by a fish in armor of silver. "Welcome home," the guard called to the tortoise, as he opened the gate for them to enter.

"See whom I have brought back with me," the tortoise answered happily. The guard in the armor of silver turned to Urashima Taro and bowed most politely. Taro just had time to return the bow when he looked up and saw another gate. This one was even larger than the first, and was made of silver stones and pillars of coral. A row of fish in armor of gold was guarding the second gate.

"Now, Urashima-san, if you will get off and wait here, I will tell the princess that you have come," said the tortoise, and he disappeared into the palace beyond the gate. Taro had never seen such a beautiful sight in all his life. The silver stones in the gate sparkled and glittered as though they were smiling at him. Taro had to blink hard.

Soon the tortoise was back at his side telling him that the princess was waiting to see him. He led Taro through the gate of coral and silver, and up a path of golden stones to the palace. There in front of the palace stood the beautiful princess of the sea with her ladies-in-waiting.

"Welcome to the Palace of the Sea, Urashima Taro," she said, and her voice sounded like the tinkling of little silver bells. "Won't you come with me?" she asked.

Taro opened his mouth to answer, but not a

sound would come forth. He could only look at the beautiful princess and the sparkling emeralds and diamonds and rubies which glittered on the walls of the palace. The princess understood how Taro felt, so she just smiled kindly and led him down a hallway paved with smooth, white pearls. Soon they came to a large room, and in the center of the room was an enormous table and an enormous chair. Taro thought they might have been made for a great king.

"Sit down, Urashima-san," said the princess, and as he sat in the enormous chair, the ladies-in-waiting appeared from all sides. They placed on the table plate after plate of all the delicious things that Taro could think of. "Eat well, my friend," said the princess, "and while you dine, my maids will sing and dance for you." Soon there was music and singing and dancing. The room was filled with laughing voices. Taro felt

like a king now! He thought surely this was all a dream, and that it would end soon. But no, after he had dined, the princess took him all through the beautiful palace. At the very last, she brought him to a room that looked as though it were made of ice and snow. There were creamy pearls and sparkling diamonds everywhere.

"Now, how would you like to see all the seasons of the year?" whispered the princess.

"Oh, I would like that very much," answered Taro, and as he spoke, the east door of the room opened slowly and quietly. Taro could scarcely believe the sight before his eyes. He saw big clouds of pale pink cherry blossoms and tall green willow trees swaying in the breeze. He could hear bluebirds singing, and saw them fly happily into the sky.

"Ah, that is spring," murmured Taro. "What a lovely sunny day!" But before he could say more, the princess led him further on. As she opened the door to the south, Taro could see white lotus blossoms floating on a still green pond. It was a warm summer day, and he could hear crickets chirping lazily, somewhere in the distance. She opened the door to the west and he saw a hillside of maple trees. Their leaves of crimson and yellow were whirling and dancing down among golden chrysanthemums. He had seen such trees each fall in his own little village. When the princess opened the door to the north, Taro felt a blast of cold air. He shivered, and looked up to see snowflakes tumbling down from gray skies. They were putting white caps on all the fence posts and treetops.

"Now you have seen all the seasons of the year," said the princess.

"They were beautiful!" sighed Taro happily. "I have never seen such wonderful sights in all my life! I wish I could stay here always!"

Taro was having such a very good time that he forgot all about his home in the village. He feasted and danced and sang with his friends in the Palace of the Sea, and before he knew it, three long years had gone by. But to Taro they seemed to be just three short days.

At last Taro said to the princess, "Alas, I have been here much too long. I must go home to see my mother and father so they will not worry about me."

"But you will come back?" asked the princess.

"Oh, yes, yes. I will come back," answered Taro.

"Before you go I have something for you," said the princess, and she gave Taro a small jewel box studded with many precious stones.

"Oh, it is beautiful, Princess," said Taro. "How can I thank you for all you have done for me?"

But the princess went on, "There is just one thing about that box," she said. "You must never, never open it if you ever wish to return to the Palace of the Sea. Can you remember that, Urashima Taro?"

"I will never open it, no matter what happens," promised Taro. Then he said good-bye to all his friends in the palace. Once again he climbed on the back of the old tortoise and they sailed toward his village on the seacoast. The princess and her ladies-in-waiting stood at the coral gate and waved to Taro till he could no longer see them. The tortoise swam on and on, and one by one all the little bright-colored fish that had been following them began to turn back. Before long, Taro could see the seacoast where he used to go fishing, and soon they were back on the very beach where Taro had once saved the tortoise. Taro hopped off onto the smooth white sand. "Good-bye, old friend," he said. "You have been very good to me. Thank you for taking me to the most beautiful place I have ever seen."

"Farewell, Urashima-san," said the old tortoise. "I hope we may meet again some day." Then he turned and crawled slowly back into the sea.

Now that he was in his own village once more, Taro was most anxious to see his parents. He ran along the path which led to their house with his jewel box tucked securely under his arm. He looked up eagerly at each person whom he passed. He wanted to shout a greeting to them, but each face seemed strange and new. "How odd!" thought Taro. "I feel as though I were in some other village than my own. I don't seem to know anyone. Well, I'll soon see Mother and Father," he said, and hurried on. When he reached the spot where the house should have been, there was no house to be seen. There was just an empty lot full of tall green weeds. Taro couldn't believe his eyes. "Why, what has happened to my home? Where are my parents?" he cried. He looked up and down the dusty path and soon saw an old, old woman coming toward him. "I'll ask her what has happened to my home," thought Taro.

"Old woman, please, can you help me?" asked Taro.

The old woman straightened her bent back and cocked her gray head, "Eh, what did you say?" she asked.

"Can you tell me what happened to Urashima Taro's home? It used to be right here," said Taro.

"Never heard of him," said the old woman, shaking her head.

"But you must have," Taro replied. "He lived right here, on this very spot where you are standing."

"Now let me see," she sighed. "Urashima Taro. Yes, it seems I have heard of him. Oh, I remember now. There is a story that he went out to sea in his fishing boat one day and never came back again. I suppose he was drowned at sea. Well, anyway, that was over three hundred years ago. My great-great-grandfather used to tell me about Urashima Taro when I was just a little girl."

"Three hundred years!" exclaimed Taro. His eyes were like saucers now. "But I don't understand."

"Well, I don't understand what you want with a man who lived three hundred years ago," muttered the old woman, and she trudged on down the road.

"So three years in the Palace of the Sea has really been three hundred years here in my village," thought Taro. "No wonder all my friends are gone. No wonder I can't find my mother or father!" Taro had never felt so lonely or so sad as he did then. "What can I do? What can I do?" he murmured to himself.

Suddenly he remembered the little jewel box which the princess had given him. "Perhaps there is something in there that can help me," he thought, and forgetting the promise he had made to the princess, he quickly opened the box. Suddenly, there arose from it a cloud of white smoke which wrapped itself around Taro so that he could see nothing. When it disappeared, Urashima Taro peered into the empty box, but he could scarcely see. He looked at his hands and they were the hands of an old, old man. His face was wrinkled; his hair was as white as snow. In that short moment Urashima Taro had become three hundred years older. He remembered the promise he had made to the princess, but now it was too late and he knew that he could never visit the Palace of the Sea again. But who knows, perhaps one day the old tortoise came back to the beach once more to help his friend.

THE WAVE

The drama of this traditional legend will appeal to children, as will its beautiful evocation of ancient Japan. Margaret Hodges, a gifted storyteller, has adapted it from Lafcadio Hearne's telling. Blair Lent's handsome illustrations make it a distinguished picture book, which was a runner-up for the Caldecott Award in 1965.

Long ago in Japan a village stood beside the sea. When the water was calm, the village children played in the gentle waves, shouting and laughing. But sometimes the sea was angry and waves came tearing up the beach to the very edge of the town. Then everyone, children, fathers and mothers, ran from the shore back to their homes. They shut their doors and waited for the storm to pass and for the sea to grow calm again.

Behind the village there rose a mountain with a zigzag road that climbed up, up through the rice fields. And these rice fields were all the wealth of the people. There they worked hard, drenched by the spring rains that made the mountainside green and beautiful. They toiled up the steep zigzag road in the heat of the summer to care for the rice fields. When the stalks turned gold and dried in the sun, the villagers bent their backs to gather in the heavy harvest, rejoicing that they could eat for another year.

High on the side of the mountain, overlooking the village and the sea, there lived a wise old man, Ojiisan, a name that in Japan means Grandfather. With him lived his little grandson, whose name was Tada.

Tada loved Ojiisan dearly and gave him the obedience due to his great age and great wisdom. Indeed, the old man had the respect of all the villagers. Often they climbed up the long zigzag road to ask him for advice.

One day when the air was very hot and still, Ojiisan stood on the balcony of his house and looked at his rice fields. The precious grain was ripe and ready for the harvest. Below he saw the fields of the villagers leading down the valley like an enormous flight of golden steps.

At the foot of the mountain he saw the village, ninety thatched houses and a temple, stretched along the curve of the bay. There had been a very fine rice crop and the peasants were going to celebrate their harvest by a dance in the court of the temple.

Tada came to stand beside his grandfather. He too looked down the mountain.

They could see strings of paper lanterns festooned between bamboo poles. Above the roofs of the houses festival banners hung motionless in the heavy warm air.

"This is earthquake weather," said Ojiisan.

And presently an earthquake came. It was not strong enough to frighten Tada, for Japan has many earthquakes. But this one was queer—a long, slow shaking, as though it were caused by changes far out at the bottom of the sea. The house rocked gently several times. Then all became still again.

As the quaking ceased, Ojiisan's keen old eyes looked at the seashore. The water had darkened quite suddenly. It was drawing back from the village. The thin curve of shore was growing wider and wider. *The sea was running away from the land!*

Ojiisan and Tada saw the tiny figures of villagers around the temple, in the streets, on the shore. Now all were gathering on the beach. As the water drew back, ribbed sand and weed-hung rock were left bare. None of the village people seemed to know what it meant.

But Ojiisan knew. In his lifetime it had never happened before. But he remembered things told him in his childhood by his father's father. He understood what the sea was going to do and he must warn the villagers.

There was no time to send a message down the long mountain road. There was no time to tell

the temple priests to sound their big bell. There was no time to stand and think. Ojiisan must act. He said to Tada, "Quick! Light me a torch!"

Tada obeyed at once. He ran into the house and kindled a pine torch. Quickly he gave it to Ojiisan.

The old man hurried out to the fields where his rice stood, ready for the harvest. This was his precious rice, all of his work for the past year, all of his food for the year to come.

He thrust the torch in among the dry stacks and the fire blazed up. The rice burned like tinder. Sparks burst into flame and the flames raced through Ojiisan's fields, turning their gold to black, sending columns of smoke skyward in one enormous cloudy whirl.

Tada was astonished and terrified. He ran after his grandfather, crying, "Ojiisan! why? Ojiisan! why?—why?"

But Ojiisan did not answer. He had no time to explain. He was thinking only of the four hundred lives in peril by the edge of the sea.

For a moment Tada stared wildly at the blazing rice. Then he burst into tears, and ran back to the house, feeling sure that his grandfather had lost his mind.

Ojiisan went on firing stack after stack of rice, till he had reached the end of his fields. Then he threw down his torch and waited.

Down below, the priests in the temple saw the blaze on the mountain and set the big bell booming. The people hurried in from the sands and over the beach and up from the village, like a swarming of ants.

Ojiisan watched them from his burning rice fields and the moments seemed terribly long to him.

"Faster! Run faster!" he said. But the people could not hear him.

The sun was going down. The wrinkled bed of the bay and a vast expanse beyond it lay bare, and still the sea was fleeing toward the horizon.

Ojiisan did not have long to wait before the first of the villagers arrived to put out the fire. But the old man held out both arms to stop them.

"Let it burn!" he commanded. "Let it be! I want all the people here. There is a great danger!"

The whole village did come—first the young

men and boys, and the women and girls who could run fastest. Then came the older folk and mothers with babies at their backs. The children came, for they could help to pass buckets of water. Even the elders could be seen well on their way up the steep mountainside. But it was too late to save the flaming fields of Ojiisan. All looked in sorrowful wonder at the face of the old man. And the sun went down.

Tada came running from the house. "Grandfather has lost his mind!" he sobbed. "He has gone mad! He set fire to the rice on purpose. I saw him do it!"

"The child tells the truth. I did set fire to the rice," said Ojiisan. ". . . Are all the people here?"

The men were angry. "All are here," they said. They muttered among themselves, "The old man is mad. He will destroy *our* fields next!" And they threatened him with their fists.

Then Ojiisan raised his hand and pointed to the sea. "Look!" he said.

Through the twilight eastward all looked and saw at the edge of the dusky horizon a long dim line like the shadow of a coast where no coast ever was. The line grew wider and darker. It moved toward them. That long darkness was the returning sea, towering like a cliff and coming toward them more swiftly than the kite flies.

"A tidal wave!" shrieked the people. And then all shrieks and all sounds and all power to hear sounds were ended by a shock heavier than any thunder, as the great wave struck the shore with a weight that sent a shudder through the hills.

There was a burst of foam like a blaze of sheet lightning. Then for an instant nothing could be seen but a storm of spray rushing up the mountainside while the people scattered in fear.

When they looked again they saw a wild white sea raging over the place where their homes had been. It drew back roaring, and tearing out the land as it went. Twice, thrice, five times the sea struck and ebbed, but each time with less strength. Then it returned to its ancient bed and stayed, still raging, as after a typhoon.

Around the house of Ojiisan no word was spoken. The people stared down the mountain at the rocks hurled and split by the sea, at the scooped-up sand and wreckage where houses and temple had been.

The village was no longer there, only broken bamboo poles and thatch scattered along the shore. Then the voice of Ojiisan was heard again, saying gently, "That was why I set fire to the rice."

He, their wise old friend, now stood among them almost as poor as the poorest, for his wealth was gone. But he had saved four hundred lives.

Tada ran to him and held his hand. The father of each family knelt before Ojiisan, and all the people after them.

"My home still stands," the old man said. "There is room for many." And he led the way to the house.

Korea

Korea, once called the **Hermit Kingdom** *during the long period between the late 1500's and late 1800's when she deliberately isolated herself from the world, is in many ways unknown to us. Most of the world knows of her, thanks to a recent long and terrible war, but few people are acquainted with her proud history, her contributions to world culture (such as the invention of movable metal printing type), and her fine artistic and literary traditions. Only one book of Korean folk tales for children exists to unshroud partially the mystery of her folklore. That is Eleanore M. Jewett's* **Which Was Witch?** *and from it we can see that Korean tales are full of ghosts and magic. As interpreted by Miss Jewett, the stories are beautiful in style and content and make a fine contribution to the storyteller's repertory.*

WHICH WAS WITCH?

Despite its witty title, this tale is a good eerie one—especially for Halloween.

There was once a wise and learned man named Kim Su-ik. He lived just inside the south gate of Seoul but he might as well have lived anywhere for all the thought he gave the matter. His mind was entirely taken up with study and books, and one could say of him, as Im Bang said of another scholar, "He used to awake at first cockcrow, wash, dress, take up his book and never lay it aside. On his right were pictures, on his left were books, and he happy between. He rose to be a Prime Minister."

One night Kim Su-ik was absorbed in studying a Chinese classic when he suddenly felt hungry. He clapped his hands to summon a servant, and immediately the door of his room opened.

His wife stepped in.

"What does the master of the house desire?" said she.

"Food," he answered briefly, his attention already returned to the book in his lap.

"I have little in the house but a few roasted chestnuts. If that will suffice I will bring them to you myself. The servants have long since gone to their sleeping quarters."

Kim Su-ik grunted his approval and went on with his studies. In a very short time the door opened again and his wife came in bearing a brass bowl full of hot roasted chestnuts. He helped himself to one and was in the act of putting it into his mouth when once more the door opened and in stepped his wife with a brass bowl full of hot roasted chestnuts.

But his wife was already there, standing beside him with the bowl in her hands!

Kim Su-ik, his mouth still open and a chestnut half in it, looked in astonishment from one to the other of the identical women. They were as like as two pins—faces, features, figures, clothes, the way they stood, the way they used their fingers and moved their shoulders. Never were twins more completely alike. Kim Su-ik passed his hands before his eyes. He must have over-

done his studying, he thought to himself, read too late and too steadily. His eyes were playing tricks on him, that was all. He was seeing double.

But when he looked again the two women were still there, and what was stranger still, they seemed not to be aware of each other, but stood quietly, gracefully, their eyes fastened on him as if waiting to know his pleasure.

The scholar leaped to his feet, choking back the cry of terror that rose in his throat. He knew, suddenly, without a doubt, what this meant. It was midnight, the moon was at the full, ghosts, evil spirits, witches and goblins would be abroad, filled with power. One of these two creatures standing before him was his wife, known and loved by him all his wedded life—and perhaps not quite fully appreciated, he hastily decided. The other must be a witch, able to change into any form she chose in the twinkling of an eye. But *which was which?* How could he protect his wife and drive this evil double from beside her?

Being a quick thinker as well as a learned one, Kim Su-ik plunged into action. He seized the arm of one of the women with his right hand and before the other could realize what he was about, he had her arm fast in his left hand. They turned mildly reproachful eyes upon him but made no effort to free themselves.

"My dear," said one, "too much study has fevered your brain."

"My dear," said the other, "too much reading of books has affected your mind."

Kim Su-ik looked from one to the other. Not a particle of difference was there to give him a hint as to which was wife and which was witch. He shook them gently. They smiled indulgently as at a child. He shook harder. No resentment, no struggle to get free. He was tempted to relax his grip on the two arms, but he knew he must not for a moment do that, and hung on more firmly than ever.

Minutes went by, then hours, the dull slow moving hours between midnight and cockcrow. The three stood silent, motionless, in the same spot. Kim Su-ik grew weary beyond words. So, too, must his wife be weary, but neither of the two women he held so tightly by the arm said anything or showed by any movement or expression of the face that she was tired, puzzled or angry. His wife would have been tired and puzzled—angry, too, perhaps, but she would not have blustered or scolded. Any other woman would, were she witch or human. But surely his wife would say *something*. What in the world had got into her? Was she bewitched? Or walking in her sleep? Perhaps she was not either one of these two women. He wanted to rush into the other part of the house to see if she was there, thus proving that both of these were witches. But he did nothing, just hung on, grimly, silently.

At long last a cock crowed. Immediately the woman at his left tried to wrench her arm free. The other remained quiet. Kim Su-ik dropped the unresisting one and threw all his strength into a struggle with the other. Like a wild thing the creature fought, biting, snarling, spitting, leaping back and forth. Still the scholar held on to her and would not let go. The arm in his hand shrank and grew hairy. The whole figure dwindled, the eyes grew round and green and blazed with fury.

Another cock crowed and another, and the first gray light of dawn melted the dark shadows out of doors. But Kim Su-ik had no thought or time to notice the coming of day. With a hideous shriek the creature changed before his very eyes into a powerful wildcat. In horror he loosed his hold, and she leaped through the window and was gone.

"I still think you are studying too much," said a quiet, familiar voice behind him, and there stood his wife, pale, trembling a little, but smiling confidently.

"Why didn't you let me know which was which?" demanded Kim Su-ik.

His wife laughed. "I don't know what you are talking about! You behaved very strangely, but then, one never knows what to expect of a scholar. Which was which what?"

"Witch!" said Kim Su-ik.

Vietnam

The land of Vietnam, like Korea, is much older than most of us realize. While its first settlers may have been of Chinese origin, the Vietnamese people are not Chinese; for many centuries they have clung to their land and their customs in defiance of the older, more powerful civilization to the north. The history of Vietnam has yet to be written for us, but in the folk tales of this land we find echoes of that history and can discern the spirit of the people. The two tales presented here, retold from oral and printed sources, are but an indication of the unique quality of Vietnam's folklore.

THE LOVE CRYSTAL

This is one of the most exquisite tales to come from the Orient. In Vietnam there is also a song, equally exquisite, that accompanies the story. Although it is an adult kind of tale, it speaks movingly even to youngsters because of its imagery and lyricism.

Long ago in the Serene Land, a beautiful maiden lived in a palace beside a tranquil river.

"The Love Crystal," retold by Mark Taylor. Adapted from *The Fisherman and the Goblet*, by Mark Taylor, Golden Gate Junior Books, 1969

Her father was a great Mandarin. So great was her beauty that it was forbidden anyone but the members of the Mandarin's household to look upon her. In order to keep the girl from the gaze of all others, the Mandarin had her put in the top of a tower which rose above the river. There she passed the lonely hours embroidering and reading, waiting for the man who was destined to come and make her his bride.

Often she would gaze out upon the river below and dream of all the places the river had been in its winding course. As she watched the river one day, she saw a poor fisherman sailing his small boat. She could not see him well from such a height, but he looked from afar to be young and strong. He played a flute, and its melody rose sweet and clear to the tower where the Mandarin's daughter looked down on him. She was struck with joy and wonder at the plaintive sound. It was somehow sad and tender, and as she listened she was deeply moved. The music spoke to her of faraway places she would never see. It spoke to her of feelings for which there are no words. It spoke to her of all the things which make the earth beautiful.

Day after day the fisherman played his flute as his small boat passed beneath the tower where the lonely girl listened in rapture. The pure tones of the flute wound upward like a silver thread of sound. Perhaps, she thought, he was some prince in disguise whom fate meant to be her husband. For the songs he played were like songs of love, especially one which he played over and over until the girl heard it repeated nightly in her dreams. Although she was too shy to send for him, she threw down flower petals to show him her delight.

The fisherman knew that a maiden dwelt high in the tower, and when the flower petals drifted down to the water beside his boat, he knew that she liked his songs. He thought she must be beautiful, even though he had never clearly seen her face.

And so a bond grew between them, a bond made of his songs and her pleasure in them. It was enough. As she listened to his flute and as he caught the softly falling petals, each fancied only the best about the other.

One day the fisherman did not appear. He had learned that it was the Mandarin's daughter who lived in the tower; he dared not return. The girl waited until the sun departed from the sky and would not leave the window until the cool evening breeze swept across the empty river.

When the fisherman did not appear the next day, the girl felt despair. She refused to turn away from the window either to eat or to sleep. All that night she kept vigil with the moon, praying that the fisherman and his flute songs would return. But when the day dawned and waned and the fisherman never came, the girl at last wept. As one day followed after the other, she sat by the window growing pale and thin. At first she wept often; then she became silent. Her loveliness began to pale as does a flower which slowly wilts and fades.

The doctors were summoned in vain to find the cause of her illness. The Mandarin and his wife were frantic. They were not bad people, they merely wanted to protect their beautiful daughter. Now all had somehow gone wrong and she was wasting away. Then the girl's maid could no longer be silent, and whether the Mandarin should be angry or not, she told him about the fisherman whose flute songs had charmed his daughter.

The Mandarin sent for the fisherman. He was brought to the palace. The poor fisherman was indeed young and strong as the girl had imagined, but his face was ugly.

"Although you are only a humble fisherman," said the Mandarin, "your songs hold the key to my daughter's well-being. Perhaps you are the man fate has destined to become her husband. Let us see if she will love you as she has loved your music."

The fisherman was distressed. "I do not want

to have the power of life and death over your daughter," he said. "I only played my songs beneath the tower because she seemed to like them. I have never even gazed upon her face."

The fisherman was taken to the foot of the tower and bade to play his flute. When the girl heard the music, she was filled with joy. She rushed from the tower down the winding stairs to where the fisherman stood. Surely he would be as handsome as his songs were beautiful. Surely he was a prince in disguise. Alas, no! He was ugly. And as she tried to thank him for his music, the maiden turned away in dismay.

When the fisherman saw the Mandarin's daughter, he was struck with love for her. But when she turned from him, he knew such love was hopeless. Sadly he went away, and sadly the girl returned to the top of the tower. Although she was cured, something beautiful had gone from her life.

No more did the fisherman return in his boat. Never again did the girl hear his flute. In time she almost forgot him, except for the echo of his one most beautiful flute song in her dreams. A year passed, and still the girl lived in the tower, waiting for the prince who never came.

But long before the year had passed, the fisherman had died. For soon after he fell in love with the Mandarin's daughter, he died from the utter hopelessness of it. All his beauty was in his music and not in his face, and the girl wanted only his songs.

When the fisherman was to be buried, his family found beside him an exquisite crystal. Everyone realized that the crystal was made from his unanswered love. They put it in the prow of his boat as a remembrance of him whose flute would never be heard and enjoyed again. The flute they gave to the river.

One day, when the Mandarin was boating upon the river, he saw the fisherman's boat with the shining crystal fixed to its bow. When he learned how it came to be there, he was deeply moved and asked to buy it. A good price was paid for the crystal and the Mandarin had it taken to the turner and made into a teacup.

No cup more exquisite had ever been seen! But strange and wonderful to tell, when tea was poured into the cup an image would appear in it. It was the image of the dead fisherman in his boat. And as it sailed around the cup, one could faintly hear his flute.

Thinking to please his daughter, the Mandarin took her the crystal cup. When she saw the fisherman's image and heard the same flute song that haunted her dreams, she was overwhelmed with grief. Hiding her distress, however, she asked to be alone with the cup.

When all had left her, the girl poured tea in the cup and held it in her hands. As she gazed into it she saw the fisherman and heard—as clearly as though he were again on the river—his flute playing his song of love. Then she realized that a heart which can make music is more important than an ugly face. Our faces are given to us, but our hearts are fashioned by our own hands. She knew that the fisherman had loved her enough to die, and her indifference had brought him death.

Quietly the maiden wept, and as she did her tears fell into the cup. Slowly the crystal dissolved, for her tears were made of love and they at last brought peace to the fisherman's soul.

Later they found the girl sitting beside the window. Her soul had left her body, leaving her as still as stone. From the river they faintly heard the sound of someone unseen playing upon a flute. Then all knew that at last the Mandarin's beautiful daughter and the fisherman were together in happiness.

WHY THERE ARE MONSOONS

Not every why *story is as satisfying or as dramatic as this one. There are indeed seasons and times in Vietnam when it seems as though the waters fully intend to overwhelm the land, but Vietnamese children can tell you why they do not.*

Once, very long ago, in the reign of King Hung Vuong XIV, the land of Vietnam almost came to an end. Terrible rains fell from the sky, and the waters of the sea swept over the land as if they would tear to pieces the forests and overwhelm even the mountains. Great destruction was everywhere as the raging waters hurled giant boulders into the air with awful anger. Villages were swept away. The rivers became torrents of

"Why There Are Monsoons." Retold by Mark Taylor and used with his permission

mud. The shrieking storm shook the land in a frenzy of water and wind.

And how did this come to happen? Ah—all because of a beautiful princess and the love which two mighty kings had for her. The princess was the daughter of King Hung Vuong. She was renowned for her virtue and beauty. My Chau was her name.

Many young men came to seek her hand in marriage and thus to find their fortunes, but My Chau could not fall in love with any of them, not even with those princes who were most handsome. As for King Hung Vuong, he made it known that his daughter was worthy of only the most powerful king on earth.

Two such kings lived at that time. One, Son Tien, was King of the Mountains. The other, Thuy Tien, was King of the Waters. They were the most powerful of kings. Son Tien was often called the Genie of the Mountains because of his great powers of magic and healing. Thuy Tien was called the Dragon Prince of the South Sea because he commanded the oceans and made his home far beneath the waves.

How these two kings differed from each other! King Son Tien was not only strong but also just and calm. He brought peace and happiness to those who dwelled on the land, especially among the mountains. King Thuy Tien was equally strong, but he was of a terrible temper. At times he would bring sudden storms at sea, and with them came floods and tidal waves which killed many people. Afterwards he would be sorry and offer to take his unintended victims to his kingdom beneath the sea. But only dead men can dwell in such a kingdom, and King Thuy Tien was not powerful enough to restore life to those from whom he had taken it.

When King Son Tien and King Thuy Tien heard of King Hung Vuong's boast that only the mightiest king on earth could rightfully marry My Chau, each decided that he alone was that king. By chance it happened that they arrived at King Hung Vuong's palace on the same day. When they saw the lovely Princess My Chau they immediately fell in love with her. And when My Chau saw them, she loved them both in return. She found it impossible to choose between them!

King Hung Vuong was in a dilemma. If he were not careful, he would offend one of these two powerful kings, and who could tell what might happen? So King Hung Vuong made an arrangement whereby the two kings would themselves have to prove which was the more powerful and the one entitled to marry My Chau.

"You are both such fine monarchs," he said to them, "that my daughter is equally drawn to you. Neither she nor I would presume to decide which of you she will marry. If you don't mind, you may decide for yourselves."

"How may that be?" asked King Son Tien.

"What makes you doubt that I am not the more powerful?" asked King Thuy Tien in irritation.

"Only you can judge the power of each other," King Hung Vuong explained. "With such power as yours must also come great wisdom. The one who can bring to My Chau the greatest treasures of the earth ought to be the one to marry her."

So it was agreed that in a week each king should bring to the palace three of the greatest treasures which, in his power and wisdom, he could provide.

When a week had passed, King Son Tien, the Genie of the Mountains, returned to the palace with his three treasures. First, he brought a small lacquered box in which there were two perfect gems—one diamond and one jade stone.

"These gems," he said, "are but a token of the beauty which is My Chau's. May they add to her pleasure as her beauty will add to their radiance."

Next, he brought forth the betel, the areca, and the chalk, which are three substances used in all marriage ceremonies in Vietnam. "These simple things are great treasures," he said, "because they stand for my promise of everlasting faithfulness to My Chau, if she becomes my wife."

Last, he took My Chau's hand and placed it over his heart. "My greatest treasure of all," he said, "is the heart within my breast. Without it I could not live. I give it to My Chau forever."

Everyone rejoiced at the wisdom and love which King Son Tien revealed. It was certain that only the greatest of kings could be so humble and true.

Now everyone waited to see what gifts King Thuy Tien, the Dragon Prince of the South Sea, would bring to My Chau. The hours passed and he did not appear. A day passed and still he did not appear. The truth was that King Thuy Tien's kingdom was so vast that he could not make up his mind what three treasures were the finest. He roamed over all the oceans of the world trying to decide. And feeling sure that he was the greatest king of all, he assumed that My Chau would wait until he finally arrived.

But when two days had passed and there was no sign of King Thuy Tien, King Hung Vuong thought that he had been unable to find three perfect treasures and was too ashamed to admit it. Thus it came about that permission was granted for King Son Tien to marry My Chau. The ceremony was brief and simple, and afterward, with King Hung Vuong's joyful blessing, the couple left to make their home in Tan Vien Mountain.

No sooner had they set out for the Kingdom of the Mountains than King Thuy Tien at last arrived at the palace. With him he brought dazzling treasures. First, he brought all the precious gems to be found in the depths of the sea, among them coral and pearls. There were more than could be counted!

Next, he brought the most perfect and beautiful conch shell ever seen, declaring that within it were contained the mighty winds and tempests which could destroy all enemies. One had only to put his ear to the shell to hear the whisper of such winds.

Last, he brought forth a jar made of crystal and coral. It was exquisitely turned and filled with sea water through which the light shimmered in softly changing colors. This, he said, contained the essence of the oceans themselves which would be My Chau's home and kingdom.

"Alas, you come too late," said King Hung Vuong. "We waited, but when you did not return we thought you had changed your mind. My Chau and King Son Tien are now man and wife and have returned to his kingdom. Besides, My Chau has no need of gems to enhance her beauty. Nor has she need of the sea's tempests, for she has no enemies. Nor could she live in the sea, for it would mean death to her."

King Thuy Tien was frenzied with disappointment. "Now you shall see how powerful I truly am!" he cried. "You tell me My Chau has no enemies? I shall be her everlasting enemy! You tell me that to live in the sea she would die? Die she shall!"

Summoning all his powers of wind and water, King Thuy Tien set out in pursuit of King Son Tien and My Chau. Thunderbolts and lightning ran before him. In his wrath he caused the typhoons to blow and the tidal waves to reach up, tearing down the forests, plucking villages into the sea. The rivers rose higher and higher with flood waters, trying to drown the land.

When King Son Tien realized what was happening, he caused the land to rise higher and higher above the reach of the water. He made the mountains a refuge for the people to escape King Thuy Tien's terror. But King Thuy Tien was consumed with the rage of a dragon. He swept in across the land and pursued King Son Tien into the mountains. Protecting himself and My Chau with magic spells which caused clouds and fog, King Son Tien climbed higher and higher. Try as he could, King Thuy Tien could not overwhelm the land. Always King Son Tien climbed higher, and he made the mountains and land so strong that they withstood the fury of the waters.

At last King Thuy Tien could do no more. He was unable to harm King Son Tien and My Chau. In despair the Dragon Prince of the South Sea withdrew from the land. But he could not forget his anger entirely. At times he would suddenly burst out anew with typhoons. However, the sea consoled King Thuy Tien, and when he grew calm he realized that King Son Tien's resistance was more powerful than his rage. He knew, too, that My Chau could not truly live in his kingdom.

It is hard for a great king, however, to lose his beloved to another. King Thuy Tien to this day tries now and then to surprise King Son Tien and perhaps overwhelm the land with water. Thus, when the season of the monsoon rains comes every year, the people of Vietnam know that the Dragon Prince has not given up and is not consoled for his lost love. They know also that he will never succeed.

Of all the rulers on earth, King Son Tien, the Genie of the Mountains, remains the kindest and the greatest. And his love and marriage to My Chau is a promise of his eternal friendship to the people who dwell upon the land.

India

*Until recent years, most of the Indian tales offered to children have
come from two literary classics,* The Panchatantra *(the oldest known collection
of Indian fables) and the* Jatakas *(fables about the many reincar-
nations of Gautama Buddha in animal forms). Both collections are readily
traced to the second and third centuries* B.C., *and both have informed
many of the later tales found in Europe as well as in India.
Of possibly more than 3000* Jataka *tales a fraction have been successfully retold for children. When references to the Buddha are omitted in these,
good talking-beast tales remain. Therefore selections from the* Jatakas
*have been included with the folk tales in this anthology. Recent compilations of
stories from India have moved away from the* Jatakas, The Panchatantra,
and ancient epics like The Ramayana, *and a feeling for the common folk of
India is to be found in the picture-book tale* The Valiant
Chattee-Maker, *a humorous retelling by Christine Price, and* The Beautiful
Blue Jay and Other Tales of India, *by John Spellman. By no means
will such books displace our interest in the old classics, but they will be of aid
in helping children sense something of life and thought in India today.*

THE HARE THAT RAN AWAY

These next three tales are from the Jatakas. *In
each instance they are rather more gentle and
ethical than dramatic. "The Hare That Ran
Away" is obviously the ancestor of "Henny-
Penny." The story may begin without the reference to Buddha, "Once there was a wise Lion
who did much to help his fellow creatures and
he found there was much to be done. For instance, there was a little nervous Hare . . . ."*

And it came to pass that the Buddha (to be)
was born again as a Lion. Just as he had helped
his fellow-men, he now began to help his fellow-
animals, and there was a great deal to be done.
For instance, there was a little nervous Hare who
was always afraid that something dreadful was
going to happen to her. She was always saying:
"Suppose the Earth were to fall in, what would
happen to me?" And she said this so often that at
last she thought it really was about to happen.
One day, when she had been saying over and
over again, "Suppose the Earth were to fall in,
what would happen to me?" she heard a slight
noise: it really was only a heavy fruit which had

"The Hare That Ran Away." From the book *Eastern
Stories and Legends* by Marie Shedlock. Copyright, 1920,
by E. P. Dutton & Co., Inc. Renewal, 1948, by Arthur C.
Jennings. Reprinted by permission of the publisher and
Routledge & Kegan Paul Ltd.

fallen upon a rustling leaf, but the little Hare
was so nervous she was ready to believe anything,
and she said in a frightened tone: "The Earth *is*
falling in." She ran away as fast as she could go,
and presently she met an old brother Hare, who
said: "Where are you running to, Mistress
Hare?"

And the little Hare said: "I have no time to
stop and tell you anything. The Earth is falling
in, and I am running away."

"The Earth is falling in, is it?" said the old
brother Hare, in a tone of much astonishment;
and he repeated this to *his* brother hare, and *he*
to *his* brother hare, and *he* to *his* brother hare,
until at last there were a hundred thousand
brother hares, all shouting: "The Earth is falling
in." Now presently the bigger animals began to
take the cry up. First the deer, and then the
sheep, and then the wild boar, and then the buffalo, and then the camel, and then the tiger, and
then the elephant.

Now the wise Lion heard all this noise and
wondered at it. "There are no signs," he said, "of
the Earth falling in. They must have heard
something." And then he stopped them all short
and said: "What is this you are saying?"

And the Elephant said: "I remarked that the
Earth was falling in."

"How do you know this?" asked the Lion.

"Why, now I come to think of it, it was the Tiger that remarked it to me."

And the Tiger said: "I had it from the Camel," and the Camel said: "I had it from the Buffalo." And the buffalo from the wild boar, and the wild boar from the sheep, and the sheep from the deer, and the deer from the hares, and the Hares said: "Oh! *we* heard it from *that* little Hare."

And the Lion said: "Little Hare, *what* made you say that the Earth was falling in?"

And the little Hare said: "I *saw* it."

"You saw it?" said the Lion. "Where?"

"Yonder by the tree."

"Well," said the Lion, "come with me and I will show you how——"

"No, no," said the Hare, "I would not go near that tree for anything, I'm *so* nervous."

"But," said the Lion, "I am going to take you on my back." And he took her on his back, and begged the animals to stay where they were until they returned. Then he showed the little Hare how the fruit had fallen upon the leaf, making the noise that had frightened her, and she said: "Yes, I see—the Earth is *not* falling in." And the Lion said: "Shall we go back and tell the other animals?"

And they went back. The little Hare stood before the animals and said: "The Earth is *not* falling in." And all the animals began to repeat this to one another, and they dispersed gradually, and you heard the words more and more softly:

"The Earth is *not* falling in," etc., etc., etc., until the sound died away altogether.

GRANNY'S BLACKIE

Once upon a time a rich man gave a baby Elephant to a woman.

She took the best of care of this great baby and soon became very fond of him.

The children in the village called her Granny, and they called the Elephant "Granny's Blackie."

The Elephant carried the children on his back

"Granny's Blackie." From: *The Jataka Tales* by Ellen C. Babbitt, Copyright, 1912, The Century Company. Reprinted by permission of Appleton-Century-Crofts, Division of Meredith Corporation

all over the village. They shared their goodies with him and he played with them.

"Please, Blackie, give us a swing," they said to him almost every day.

"Come on! Who is first?" Blackie answered and picked them up with his trunk, swung them high in the air, and then put them down again, carefully.

But Blackie never did any work.

He ate and slept, played with the children, and visited with Granny.

One day Blackie wanted Granny to go off to the woods with him.

"I can't go, Blackie, dear. I have too much work to do."

Then Blackie looked at her and saw that she was growing old and feeble.

"I am young and strong," he thought. "I'll see if I cannot find some work to do. If I could bring some money home to her, she would not have to work so hard."

So next morning, bright and early, he started down to the river bank.

There he found a man who was in great trouble. There was a long line of wagons so heavily loaded that the oxen could not draw them through the shallow water.

When the man saw Blackie standing on the bank he asked, "Who owns this Elephant? I want to hire him to help my Oxen pull these wagons across the river."

A child standing near by said, "That is Granny's Blackie."

"Very well," said the man, "I'll pay two pieces of silver for each wagon this Elephant draws across the river."

Blackie was glad to hear this promise. He went into the river, and drew one wagon after another across to the other side.

Then he went up to the man for the money.

The man counted out one piece of silver for each wagon.

When Blackie saw that the man had counted out but one piece of silver for each wagon, instead of two, he would not touch the money at all. He stood in the road and would not let the wagons pass him.

The man tried to get Blackie out of the way, but not one step would he move.

Then the man went back and counted out another piece of silver for each of the wagons and put the silver in a bag tied around Blackie's neck.

Then Blackie started for home, proud to think that he had a present for Granny.

The children had missed Blackie and had asked Granny where he was, but she said she did not know where he had gone.

They all looked for him but it was nearly night before they heard him coming.

"Where have you been, Blackie? And what is that around your neck?" the children cried, running to meet their playmate.

But Blackie would not stop to talk with his playmates. He ran straight home to Granny.

"Oh, Blackie!" she said. "Where have you been? What is in that bag?" And she took the bag off his neck.

Blackie told her that he had earned some money for her.

"Oh, Blackie, Blackie," said Granny, "how hard you must have worked to earn these pieces of silver! What a good Blackie you are!"

And after that Blackie did all the hard work and Granny rested, and they were both very happy.

THE BANYAN DEER

There was once a Deer the color of gold. His eyes were like round jewels, his horns were white as silver, his mouth was red like a flower, his hoofs were bright and hard. He had a large body and a fine tail.

He lived in a forest and was king of a herd of five hundred Banyan Deer. Near by lived another herd of Deer, called the Monkey Deer. They, too, had a king.

The king of that country was fond of hunting the Deer and eating deer meat. He did not like to go alone so he called the people of his town to go with him, day after day.

The townspeople did not like this for while they were gone no one did their work. So they decided to make a park and drive the Deer into it. Then the king could go into the park and

"The Banyan Deer." From: *The Jataka Tales* by Ellen C. Babbitt, Copyright, 1912, The Century Company. Reprinted by permission of Appleton-Century-Crofts, Division of Meredith Corporation

hunt and they could go on with their daily work.

They made a park, planted grass in it and provided water for the Deer, built a fence all around it and drove the Deer into it.

Then they shut the gate and went to the king to tell him that in the park near by he could find all the Deer he wanted.

The king went at once to look at the Deer. First he saw there the two Deer kings, and granted them their lives. Then he looked at their great herds.

Some days the king would go to hunt the Deer, sometimes his cook would go. As soon as any of the Deer saw them they would shake with fear and run. But when they had been hit once or twice they would drop down dead.

The King of the Banyan Deer sent for the King of the Monkey Deer and said, "Friend, many of the Deer are being killed. Many are wounded besides those who are killed. After this suppose one from my herd goes up to be killed one day, and the next day let one from your herd go up. Fewer Deer will be lost this way."

The Monkey Deer agreed. Each day the Deer whose turn it was would go and lie down, placing its head on the block. The cook would come and carry off the one he found lying there.

One day the lot fell to a mother Deer who had a young baby. She went to her king and said, "O King of the Monkey Deer, let the turn pass me by until my baby is old enough to get along without me. Then I will go and put my head on the block."

But the king did not help her. He told her that if the lot had fallen to her she must die.

Then she went to the King of the Banyan Deer and asked him to save her.

"Go back to your herd. I will go in your place," said he.

The next day the cook found the King of the Banyan Deer lying with his head on the block. The cook went to the king, who came himself to find out about this.

"King of the Banyan Deer! did I not grant you your life? Why are you lying here?"

"O great King!" said the King of the Banyan Deer, "a mother came with her young baby and told me that the lot had fallen to her. I could not ask any one else to take her place, so I came myself."

"King of the Banyan Deer! I never saw such kindness and mercy. Rise up. I grant your life and hers. Nor will I hunt any more the Deer in either park or forest."

THE TIGER, THE BRAHMAN, AND THE JACKAL

There is a series of jackal stories in which the jackal is generally the trickster who is finally caught and punished, but in this story the tables are turned. Children will be satisfied with the explanation that a brahman is a wise, good man. Further details are unnecessary.

Once upon a time a tiger was caught in a trap. He tried in vain to get out through the bars, and rolled and bit with rage and grief when he failed.

By chance a poor Brahman came by. "Let me out of this cage, O pious one!" cried the tiger.

"Nay, my friend," replied the Brahman mildly, "you would probably eat me if I did."

"Not at all!" swore the tiger with many oaths; "on the contrary, I should be for ever grateful, and serve you as a slave!"

Now when the tiger sobbed and sighed and wept and swore, the pious Brahman's heart softened, and at last he consented to open the door

"The Tiger, the Brahman, and the Jackal." From *Tales of the Punjab* compiled by Flora Annie Steel, copyright 1933 by The Macmillan Company. Reprinted by permission of Macmillan & Co. Ltd.

of the cage. Out popped the tiger, and, seizing the poor man, cried, "What a fool you are! What is to prevent my eating you now, for after being cooped up so long I am just terribly hungry!"

In vain the Brahman pleaded for his life; the most he could gain was a promise to abide by the decision of the first three things he chose to question as to the justice of the tiger's action.

So the Brahman first asked a *pipal* tree what it thought of the matter, but the *pipal* tree replied coldly, "What have you to complain about? Don't I give shade and shelter to every one who passes by, and don't they in return tear down my branches to feed their cattle? Don't whimper—be a man!"

Then the Brahman, sad at heart, went farther afield till he saw a buffalo turning a well-wheel; but he fared no better from it, for it answered, "You are a fool to expect gratitude! Look at me! While I gave milk they fed me on cotton-seed and oil-cake, but now I am dry they yoke me here, and give me refuse as fodder!"

The Brahman, still more sad, asked the road to give him its opinion.

"My dear sir," said the road, "how foolish you are to expect anything else! Here am I, useful to

everybody, yet all, rich and poor, great and small, trample on me as they go past, giving me nothing but the ashes of their pipes and the husks of their grain!"

On this the Brahman turned back sorrowfully, and on the way he met a jackal, who called out, "Why, what's the matter, Mr. Brahman? You look as miserable as a fish out of water!"

Then the Brahman told him all that had occurred. "How very confusing!" said the jackal, when the recital was ended; "would you mind telling me over again? for everything seems so mixed up!"

The Brahman told it all over again, but the jackal shook his head in a distracted sort of way, and still could not understand.

"It's very odd," said he sadly, "but it all seems to go in at one ear and out at the other! I will go to the place where it all happened, and then perhaps I shall be able to give a judgment."

So they returned to the cage, by which the tiger was waiting for the Brahman, and sharpening his teeth and claws.

"You've been away a long time!" growled the savage beast, "but now let us begin our dinner."

"*Our* dinner!" thought the wretched Brahman, as his knees knocked together with fright; "what a remarkably delicate way of putting it!"

"Give me five minutes, my lord!" he pleaded, "in order that I may explain matters to the jackal here, who is somewhat slow in his wits."

The tiger consented, and the Brahman began the whole story over again, not missing a single detail, and spinning as long a yarn as possible.

"Oh, my poor brain! oh, my poor brain!" cried the jackal, wringing his paws. "Let me see! how did it all begin? You were in the cage, and the tiger came walking by——"

"Pooh!" interrupted the tiger, "what a fool you are! *I* was in the cage."

"Of course!" cried the jackal, pretending to tremble with fright; "yes! I was in the cage—no, I wasn't—dear! dear! where are my wits? Let me see—the tiger was in the Brahman, and the cage came walking by—no, that's not it either! Well, don't mind me, but begin your dinner, for I shall never understand!"

"Yes, you shall!" returned the tiger, in a rage at the jackal's stupidity; "I'll *make* you understand! Look here—I am the tiger——"

"Yes, my lord!"

"And that is the Brahman——"

"Yes, my lord!"

"And that is the cage——"

"Yes, my lord!"

"And I was in the cage—do you understand?"

"Yes—no—Please, my lord——"

"Well?" cried the tiger, impatiently.

"Please, my lord!—how did you get in?"

"How!—why, in the usual way, of course!"

"Oh dear me!—my head is beginning to whirl again! Please don't be angry, my lord, but what is the usual way?"

At this the tiger lost patience, and jumping into the cage, cried, "This way! Now do you understand how it was?"

"Perfectly!" grinned the jackal, as he dexterously shut the door; "and if you will permit me to say so, I think matters will remain as they were!"

THE CARTMAN'S STORIES

One can see how this tale reflects the age-old experience and current wisdom of people. It is a great satisfaction to observe how the cartman turns his misfortune into good fortune by simply following three adages. John Spellman took these tales just as he heard them told by Indian mothers to their children.

There once was a very poor farmer who had such a small farm that it was only with great difficulty that he was able to care for his family with its earnings. Still, like most Indian farmers, he lived a happy and contented life. Men are usually self-satisfied and contented with their lot whatever it may be. But that is never true of women. The farmer's wife was always grumbling about her fate and cursed him for his poverty. She urged him to do some side business to add to the small earnings of the farm.

One day he finally got tired of his wife's pestering and decided to do something about it. He took out his cart and put it up for hire. Fortunately he got a customer very soon. The village

"The Cartman's Stories." From *The Beautiful Blue Jay and Other Tales of India* by John W. Spellman, by permission of Little, Brown and Co. Copyright © 1967 by John W. Spellman

merchant wanted to take some merchandise to a nearby village, so he engaged the poor farmer.

After loading the merchandise they both started for the next village. On the way the cartman began to be bored by the complete silence of the merchant. He said to the merchant, "Sir, why don't you talk? Do you know any stories or yarns?"

The merchant was not a talkative fellow. He disliked talk. So, to avoid talking, he told the cartman, "Look, I will give you a story, but I will charge you one *rupee* for each story I tell."

The cartman took it as a joke and said, "Come! Come! Let us hear some nice stories from you. Nobody charges for friendly and free talk." The merchant would not agree and the cartman would not keep quiet. He kept nagging the merchant to tell a story.

The merchant thought he would teach him a good lesson.

"All right," he said. "Listen to my story.

"Never refuse or disobey a request made by the village council.

"My story is over," he said. "Pay me my rupee."

The cartman still thought it was all a joke, so he insisted on having another story. The merchant said, "All right. Listen to my second story.

"Never tell a secret or a truth to a woman.

"My story is over, give me another rupee."

The cartman still took it as a joke and insisted on a nice long yarn that would really entertain him.

The merchant said, "Very well, listen to my third story.

"Never tell a falsehood in a law court.

"My story is over. Give me my third rupee."

Still the cartman took it as a joke and insisted on a really good story. But the merchant would not tell one. He knew the poor cartman had no money to pay, and he did not want to waste his breath for nothing. The fare agreed for the trip was only three rupees. The merchant thought to recover it from the cartman as his payment for the three stories. For a long time he kept on arguing with the cartman, but he would not tell him any more stories.

At last they came to their destination. The cartman unloaded the goods and demanded his fare. The merchant said, "Pay me my three ru-pees for my three stories and I will pay you your fare."

The cartman never expected the joke would be carried so far and so seriously. He was so disappointed and dejected that he did not know what to do. He had no money for food or fodder for his bullocks. And worst of all, what would he tell his wife when he went home? He felt like drowning himself in the river. Dejected, disappointed and weary, the poor cartman started homeward. His fellow cartmen jeered at him for his foolishness, but he listened quietly to all the jeering.

On the way they all came to a village. A destitute beggar had died suddenly, and the village council had met to make arrangements for the disposal of the body. They wanted a cart to carry the body to the cremation ground, but nobody would agree to do it. They disliked the idea of carrying a dead body.

When our cartman was approached, he thought for a moment and then readily agreed, for he was very badly in need of money. Besides, he remembered the merchant's advice in his first story: "Never refuse or disobey a request made by a village council." He decided to see how true it was, since he had paid such a high price for it.

The village council members loaded the dead body into the cart and paid him a rupee for the freight. They told him to take the body to the cremation ground, burn it, throw the ashes into the holy river and then go to his home. The cartman transported the body, put it on the funeral bier, set fire to it and sat down to watch the burning body. When it had completely burned, he went to collect the ashes. To his great surprise he found many tiny, hot bits of glittering gold among the ashes. The gold had been around the waist of the body, hidden under the clothes, left there unknown to anybody. He quickly collected them, put them in his pocket, threw the ashes in the river, and went back to his home in the dead of night.

Before he returned, his companions had already reported the whole story to his wife, so the wife was waiting to scold him. She greeted him with very harsh words, but somehow the poor man succeeded in consoling her. He gave her the rupee he had earned and she was satisfied for the moment. When everybody was asleep he quietly got up and buried the gold in a secret place.

For several days he did not do any work at all but spent his time idling. His wife became very angry, but he did not pay any attention. One day he quietly took out a part of the hidden gold, sold it in the market and bought clothes and provisions for himself and his family.

People were astonished and very curious about his sudden wealth. When they asked him about it, he would say, "God comes in my dreams and gives me money." They would not believe him and planned to force the secret from his wife. But the wife did not know anything either. She was just as curious as the others, and she finally asked her husband. He thought for a time and then remembered the merchant's second story: "Never tell a secret or truth to womenfolk." So he said, "Look, dear, I go into the jungle and drink *dhattura* juice. Then my hairs become gold and I pluck them and sell them."

Now everyone knows that dhattura juice is poisonous, but all the people started to drink it just the same. They all became seriously ill from the poison and some died. Complaints went to the police about this mishap. An enquiry was held and the source was traced to the cartman, who was arrested and put before the court.

When the judge asked the man to explain himself, he thought for a moment and told the whole truth from beginning to end, for he remembered the merchant's third story: "Never tell a falsehood in the law court."

The magistrate was greatly amused by his story and acquitted him, for he was quite innocent. He said, "It served the people right, for they did a foolish thing without considering the effects of their thoughtless actions."

Then the farmer lived very happily ever after.

Oceania and Australia

Although folklorists and anthropologists have been active for several centuries in recording the folklore of the peoples of the Pacific, we have few tales from Oceania and Australia. A great body of material has been gathered, but no really outstanding collection of tales from the islands is yet available for children. From Australia we have only a recent edition of Mrs. K. Langloh Parker's stories taken from the Aborigines of New South Wales, Australian Legendary Tales. *These tales, first published in 1896, were recorded from the now-extinct Euahlayi people with whom Mrs. Parker played as a child. Although folklorists do not consider her work a primary contribution to scholarship, the stories are told simply and honestly as she heard them. It was no easy task to put Aborigine thoughts into English, and many tales in the Parker collection seem strange, falling short of what we think of as "good stories." But they are all we have from the Aborigines that will appeal to boys and girls in the upper grades. As for the folklore of the European settlers in Australia, nothing in the way of tales for children has appeared.*

BEEREEUN THE MIRAGEMAKER

(*Australian*)

Most why *stories explain a single fact or phenomenon, but this one explains several. Moreover, the Aborigine words in it will amuse children with their strange, lyrical sounds and may serve as a small vocabulary study. Note how* much geography and natural history are conveyed by this rather rambling tale.

Beereeun the lizard wanted to marry Bullai Bullai the green parrot sisters. But they did not

"Beereeun the Miragemaker." From *Australian Legendary Tales* collected and edited by H. Drake-Brockman. All Rights Reserved. Reprinted by permission of The Viking Press, Inc., and Angus & Robertson Ltd., Sidney

want to marry him. They liked Weedah the mockingbird better. Their mother said they must marry Beereeun, for she had pledged them to him at their births, and Beereeun was a great wirinun and would harm them if they did not keep her pledge.

When Weedah came back from hunting they told him what their mother had said, how they had been pledged to Beereeun, who now claimed them.

"Tomorrow," said Weedah, "old Beereeun goes to meet a tribe coming from the Springs country. While he is away we will go toward the Big River, and burn the track behind us. I will go out as if to hunt as usual in the morning. I will hide myself in the thick gidya scrub. You two must follow later and meet me there. We will then cross the big plain where the grass is now thick and dry. Bring with you a fire stick. We will throw it back into the plain, then no one can follow our tracks. On we will go to the Big River. There I have a friend who has a goombeelga, a bark canoe. Then shall we be safe from pursuit, for he will put us over the river. And we can travel on and on even to the country of the short-armed people if so we choose."

The next morning ere Goo-goor-gaga had ceased his laughter Weedah had started.

Some hours later, in the gidya scrub, the Bullai Bullai sisters joined him.

Having crossed the big plain they threw back a fire stick where the grass was thick and dry. The fire spread quickly through it, crackling and throwing up tongues of flame.

Through another scrub went the three, then across another plain, through another scrub and onto a plain again.

The day was hot, Yhi the sun was high in the sky. They became thirsty, but saw no water, and had brought none in their haste.

"We want water," the Bullai Bullai cried.

"Why did you not bring some?" said Weedah.

"We thought you had plenty, or would travel as the creeks run, or at least know of a goola-gool, a water-holding tree."

"We shall soon reach water. Look even now ahead, there is water."

The Bullai Bullai looked eagerly toward where he pointed, and there in truth, on the far-side of the plain, they saw a sheet of water. They quickened their steps, but the farther they went, the farther off seemed the water, but on they went ever hoping to reach it. Across the plain they went, only to find that on the other side of a belt of timber the water had gone.

The weary girls would have lain down, but Weedah said that they would surely reach water on the other side of the wood. Again they struggled on through the scrub to another plain.

"There it is! I told you so! There is the water."

And looking ahead they again saw a sheet of water.

Again their hopes were raised, and though the sun beat fiercely, on they marched, only to be again disappointed.

"Let us go back," they said. "This is the country of evil spirits. We see water, and when we come where we have seen it there is but dry earth. Let us go back."

"Back to Beereeun, who would kill you?"

"Better to die from the blow of a boondi in your own country than of thirst in a land of devils. We will go back."

"Not so. Not with a boondi would he kill you, but with a gooweera, a poison stick. Slow would be your death, and you would be always in pain until your shadow was wasted away. But why talk of returning? Did we not set fire to the big plain? Could you cross that? Waste not your breath, but follow me. See, there again is water!"

But the Bullai Bullai had lost hope. No longer would they even look up, though time after time Weedah called out, "Water ahead of us! Water ahead of us!" only to disappoint them again and again.

At last the Bullai Bullai became so angry with him that they seized him and beat him. But even as they beat him he cried all the time, "Water is there! Water is there!"

Then he implored them to let him go, and he would drag up the roots from some water trees and drain the water from them.

"Yonder I see a coolabah. From its roots I can drain enough to quench your thirst. Or here beside us is a bingawingul; full of water are its roots. Let me go. I will drain them for you."

But the Bullai Bullai had no faith in his promises, and they but beat him the harder until they were exhausted.

When they ceased to beat him and let him go, Weedah went on a little way, then lay down, feeling bruised all over, and thankful that the night had come and the fierce sun no longer scorched them.

One Bullai Bullai said to her sister, "Could we not sing the song our Bargi used to sing, and make the rain fall?"

"Let us try, if we can make a sound with our dry throats," said the other.

"We will sing to our cousin Dooloomai the thunder. He will hear us, and break a rain cloud for us."

So they sat down, rocking their bodies to and fro, and beating their knees, sang:

"Moogaray, Moogaray, May, May,
    Eehu, Eehu, Doon-gara."

"Hailstones, hailstones, wind, wind,
    Rain, rain, lightning."

Over and over again they sang these words as they had heard their Bargi, or mother's mother, do. Then for themselves they added:

"Eehu oonah wambaneah Dooloomai
    Bullul goonung inderh gingnee
    Eehu oonah wambaneah Dooloomai."

"Give us rain, Thunder, our cousin,
    Thirsting for water are we,
    Give us rain, Thunder, our cousin."

As long as their poor parched throats could make a sound they sang this. Then they lay down to die, weary and hopeless. One said faintly, "The rain will be too late, but surely it is coming, for strong is the smell of the gidya."

"Strong indeed," said the other.

But even this sure sign to their tribe that rain is near roused them not. It would come, they thought, too late for them. But even then away in the north a thundercloud was gathering. It rolled across the sky quickly, pealing out thunder calls as it came to tell of its coming. It stopped right over the plain in front of the Bullai Bullai. One more peal of thunder, which opened the cloud, then splashing down came the first big drops of rain. Slowly and few they came

until just at the last, when a quick, heavy shower fell, emptying the thundercloud, and filling the gilguy holes on the plain.

The cool splashing of the rain on their hot, tired limbs gave new life to the Bullai Bullai and to Weedah. They all ran to the gilguy holes. Stooping their heads, they drank and quenched their thirst.

"I told you the water was here," said Weedah. "You see I was right."

"No water was here when you said so. If our cousin Dooloomai had not heard our song for his help, we should have died, and you too."

And they were angry. But Weedah dug them some roots, and when they ate they forgot their anger. When their meal was over they lay down to sleep.

The next morning on they went again. That day they again saw across the plains the same strange semblance of water that had lured them on before. They knew not what it could be, they knew only that it was not water.

Just at dusk they came to the Big River. There they saw Goolay-yali the pelican, with his canoe. Weedah asked him to put them over onto the other side. He said that he would do so one at a time, as the canoe was small. First he said he would take Weedah, that he might get ready a camp of the long grass in the bend of the river. He took Weedah over. Then back he came and, fastening his canoe, he went up to the Bullai Bullai, who were sitting beside the remains of his old fire.

"Now," said Goolay-yali, "you two will go with me to my camp, which is down in that bend. Weedah cannot get over again. You shall live with me. I shall catch fish to feed you. I have some even now in my camp cooking. There, too, have I wirrees of honey, and durri ready for the baking. Weedah has nothing to give you but the grass nunnoos he is but now making."

"Take us to Weedah," they said.

"Not so," said Goolay-yali, and he stepped forward as if to seize them.

The Bullai Bullai stooped and filled their hands with the white ashes of the burned-out fire, which they flung at him.

Handful after handful they threw at him until he stood before them white, all but his hands, which he spread out and shook, thus freeing

them from the cloud of ashes enveloping him and obscuring his sight.

Having thus checked him, the Bullai Bullai ran to the bank of the river, meaning to get the canoe and cross over to Weedah.

But in the canoe, to their horror, was Beereeun! Beereeun, whom to escape they had sped across plain and through scrub.

Yet here he was, while between them and Weedah lay the wide river.

They had not known it, but Beereeun had been near them all the while. He it was who had made the mirage on each plain, thinking he would lure them on by this semblance of water until they perished of thirst. From that fate Dooloomai, their cousin the thunder, had saved them. But now the chance of Beereeun had come.

The Bullai Bullai looked across the wide river and saw the nunnoos, or grass shelters, Weedah had made. They saw him running in and out of them as if he were playing a game, not thinking of them at all. Strange nunnoos they were too, having both ends open.

Seeing where they were looking, Beereeun said, "Weedah is womba, deaf. I stole his Doowi while he slept and put in its place a mad spirit. He knows naught of you now. He cares naught for you. It is so with those who look too long at the mirage. He will trouble me no more, nor you. Why look at him?"

But the Bullai Bullai could not take their eyes from Weedah, so strangely he went on, unceasingly running in at one end of the grass nunnoo, through it and out of the other.

"He is womba," they said, but yet they could not understand it. They looked toward him and called him, though he heeded them not.

"I will send him far from you," said Beereeun, getting angry. He seized a spear, stood up in the canoe and sent it swiftly through the air into Weedah, who gave a great cry, screamed "Water is there! Water is there!" and fell back dead.

"Take us over! Take us over!" cried the Bullai Bullai. "We must go to him, we might yet save him."

"He is all right. He is in the sky. He is not there," said Beereeun. "If you want him you must follow him to the sky. Look, you can see him there now." And he pointed to a star that the Bullai Bullai had never seen before.

"There he is, Womba."

Across the grass nunnoo the Bullai Bullai looked, but no Weedah was there. Then they sat down and wailed a death song, for they knew well they should see Weedah no more. They plastered their heads with white ashes and water; they tied on their bodies green twigs; then, cutting themselves till the blood ran, they lit some smoke branches and smoked themselves, as widows.

Beereeun spoke to Goolay-yali the pelican, saying, "There is no brother of the dead man to marry these women. In this country they have no relation. You shall take one, and I the other. Tonight when they sleep we will each seize one."

"That which you say shall be," said Goolay-yali the pelican.

But the sisters heard what they said, though

they gave no sign and mourned the dead Wee-dah without ceasing. And with their death song they mingled a cry to all of their tribe who were dead to help them, and save them from these men who would seize them while they were still mourning, before they had swallowed the smoke water, or their tribe had heard the voice of their dead.

As the night wore on, the wailing of the women ceased. The men thought that they were at length asleep, and crept up to their camp. But it was empty! Gone were the Bullai Bullai!

The men heaped fuel on their fire to light up the darkness, but yet saw no sign of the Bullai Bullai.

They heard a sound, a sound of mocking laughter. They looked around, but saw nothing.

Again they heard a sound of laughter. Whence came it? Again it echoed through the air.

It was from the sky. They looked up. It was the new star Womba, mocking them. Womba who once was Weedah, who laughed aloud to see that the Bullai Bullai had escaped their enemies, for even now they were stealing along the sky toward him, which the men on earth saw.

"We have lost them," said Beereeun. "I shall make a roadway to the skies and follow them. Thence shall I bring them back, or wreak my vengeance on them."

He went to the canoe where were his spears. Having grasped them, he took, too, the spears of Goolay-yali, which lay by the smoldering fire.

He chose a barbed one. With all his force he threw it up to the sky. The barb caught there, the spear hung down. Beereeun threw another, which caught on to the first, and yet another, and so on, each catching the one before it, until he could touch the lowest from the earth. This he clutched hold of, and climbed up, up, up, until he reached the sky. Then he started in pursuit of the Bullai Bullai. And he is still pursuing them.

Since then the tribe of Beereeun have always been able to swarm up sheer heights. Since then, too, his tribe, the little lizards of the plains, make eer-dher, or mirages, to lure on thirsty travelers, only to send them mad before they die of thirst. Since then Goolay-yali the pelican has been white, for ever did the ashes thrown by the

Bullai Bullai cling to him; only where he had shaken them off from his hands are there a few black feathers. The tribe of Bullai Bullai are colored like the green of the leaves the sisters strung on themselves in which to mourn Weedah, with here and there a dash of whitish yellow and red, caused by the ashes and the blood of their mourning. And Womba the star, the mad star, still shines (our Canopus). And Weedah the mockingbird still builds grass nunnoos, open at both ends, in and out of which he runs, as if they were but playgrounds.

And the fire which Weedah and the Bullai Bullai made spread from one end of the country to the other, over ridges and across plains, burning the trees so that their trunks have been black ever since. Deenyi, the iron barks, smoldered the longest of all, and their trunks were so seared that the seams are deeply marked in their thick black bark still, making them show out grimly distinct on the ridges, to remind the Daens forever of Beereeun the miragemaker.

THE PRISONER

(South Seas)

Rarotonga, the island where this tale takes place, is part of the region of Polynesia. The story is a simple etiological tale and a humorous anecdote. Tapa cloth is made by pounding thin the soft inner bark of the mulberry tree.

Once long ago, on the beautiful island of Rarotonga, there lived a girl named Rangi, who was very skillful in the making of tapa cloth from the wet bark of trees. She was especially good at cutting graceful designs with sharp shells on the tapa cloth she fashioned.

Her special place for working was on the open beach of the island, just by the shadow of some wild ginger plants that grew along the shore. Here, almost any day from early in the morning until sunset brought out the first stars, Rangi could be found working away at her tapa designs.

One day, while Rangi worked on the beach, a huge black grouper, a fish almost as big as a small whale, swam up to the edge of the reef from the deep sea. He peered over the reef at the shore, attracted by the splash of brightness made by the ginger blossoms. And when he looked over the reef at the ginger blossoms, he naturally couldn't help seeing Rangi near by, kneeling gracefully and wielding her tapa shells.

The great fish had never seen such a beautiful maiden as Rangi. He fell deeply in love with her in an instant, the way a beast or a fish can sometimes love a human being. And the grouper said to himself, "More than anything in the world, I would like to win that girl for my wife!"

So he set about wooing Rangi in the only way he knew: he swam over the reef into the lagoon on the next high tide, darted as fast as his sluggish body would go toward the beach where Rangi worked, and splashed at the water with his tail and his fins to draw the girl's attention to him.

Rangi looked up and saw him splashing there, near by. And since she was a very friendly girl, she said kindly, "Why, hello there. What a very large fish you are! And pretty, too. Do you mind if I copy some of your markings in my tapa cloth designs?"

"Not at all," returned the grouper, "if you will only consent to marry me."

"Marry you!" Rangi was quite surprised, needless to say. "I couldn't do that."

"Why not?"

"Because you're a fish and I'm a girl, that's why," said Rangi, laughing.

"Please," begged the fish. "I am madly in love with you!"

Rangi shook her head gently. "I'm sorry, fish," she said, "but I must refuse."

At these words, the grouper was very sad, and he slowly swam out toward the reef. Rangi thought he was swimming away forever and wouldn't bother her again, but she was wrong.

The fish swam only as far as the deep water under the reef. Then he went right down to the bottom and lay there, mourning in his heart for the beautiful girl who would not marry him. He decided that he could not give up Rangi as easily as that—he couldn't just swim away forever. So he determined to wait until the next high tide and try his luck again.

The second proposal of marriage, however, was no more successful than his first. Rangi smiled kindly at the grouper but steadfastly refused to consider marrying him. The fish pleaded and begged to no avail. Rangi could not be moved.

Still the fish would not give up. He *had* to have Rangi for his wife. Nothing else would satisfy him. So he decided on a bold plan.

When Rangi turned back to her work and was not looking at him, the fish stretched out a fin as big as a sail and gathered Rangi up in it. He flipped her from the beach into the sea in an instant. Before Rangi had time to do more than gasp and choke a little on the salt water she'd swallowed, the big grouper opened his enormous mouth wide and swallowed Rangi in one big swallow—tapa shells and all.

Rangi wasn't hurt. Not a bit. The fish loved her too much to hurt her. But he was determined to have Rangi for his own. He hoped to be able to talk her around to marrying him in the end. Once Rangi was safe and sound in his warm stomach, the fish swam rapidly through the pass into the open ocean and took her far, far from land.

"Let me out!" shouted Rangi angrily. "Let me out! You are a wicked fish to swallow me and steal me from my home."

"I love you," replied the fish, swimming faster than ever. "That's the only excuse I have. But I can't let you go."

"You must let me go," shouted Rangi up the fish's throat. "You must!"

"Oh, no," said the fish. "Not likely. Not until you agree to marry me."

Rangi, in despair, began to think about how she might escape from the fish's insides. She thought and thought for six days and nights without sleeping. And the only way she could think of to get out of the fish was to cut her way out. She still had with her the sharp cutting shells with which she patterned her tapa cloth. They were stuck into the girdle around her waist.

The first thing Rangi did was to examine very carefully the inside of her prison to find where the flesh was thinnest. She tapped around the walls of the fish's stomach, listening to the sound. She tapped the walls of the fish's throat. And at the upper end of his throat, not far below his enormous mouth, she found the thinnest part of the fish's body. So she began to cut there.

Hour after hour she toiled, drawing the sharp edges of her shells against the flesh of the fish's throat. She decided to make a cut on both sides of his throat, so that she would double her chances of escaping if she ever broke through. She worked very hard. *Cut, cut, cut, cut.*

At length the black grouper, feeling the pain in his throat, called out, "What are you doing in there, Rangi?"

"I'm cutting my way out of you, fish," reported Rangi honestly. "I'll stop if you'll let me out."

But the fish was stubborn. "Go ahead and cut me," he said. "I love you too much to let you out."

So Rangi cut some more.

On the fourth day of her work, she had cut so deeply into both sides of the fish's throat that she could see daylight through the gashes. Only a thin layer of skin now separated her from freedom.

She said to the fish, "You win, fish. I am weary to death of cutting. I shall never get out, I suppose, unless I agree to marry you. So take me to some near-by island where I can get ashore in safety, and I will reconsider marrying you."

"Do you mean it?" asked the grouper, overjoyed. "But how can I trust you?"

"I'm still your prisoner," Rangi reminded him. "How could I escape, even if I wanted to deceive you?"

"That's true," admitted the fish. He swam at once toward the nearest island. "I'm taking you to Mauke," said the fish. "Is that all right?"

"Perfect," said Rangi. "They have beautiful jasmine flowers on Mauke for my bridal bouquet. Let me know when we get there, will you, please?"

"Certainly," said the fish. "You have made me very happy." After an hour, he called out, "We are there, Rangi. Inside the reef at Mauke."

"Close to shore?" asked Rangi. She got her tapa shells ready to make the last cuts in the fish's throat.

"As close as I can get," said the fish.

"Then here I go!" cried Rangi, and slashed the final slash with her shells at each side of the fish's throat. The thin outer skin parted, and through the slits in the fish's gullet, Rangi could see blue sky and green water again. She looked out to see which of her windows in the fish's throat was nearest the shore and jumped quickly through it into the waters of the lagoon. Soon she rose to her feet in the shallow water and ran up on the shore, safely out of reach of her strange suitor.

As for the black grouper, once he became used to the water rushing in and out of his throat through Rangi's cuts, he found it rather a pleasant feeling. He sighed and swam slowly out to sea, vowing never to fall in love with a human girl again.

This story explains why *all* fish have gills in their throats today.

Canada

Aside from the Eskimo and Indian lore, which has been included in this anthology with the tales of all North American Indians, Canada's most distinguishable body of stories and songs comes from the folk literature of French-speaking Canadians. Not many collections are available for young people, however, and much remains to be discovered from the work of Canadian folklore scholars. Though the present offerings are few (see the Bibliography), in them live such unique figures as the loup-garou, *a dangerous supernatural wolf created in the folk imagination, and those colorful, adventurous men out of Canada's early French history—the* voyageurs *and the* coureurs de bois. *They hold a firm place in the folk literature of Canada, and to those of imaginative mind it may seem that they wander still among her rivers, lakes, and forests.*

LITTLE NICHET'S
BABY SISTER

The Nichet stories are traditional tales that Natalie Carlson heard from her French-Canadian uncle. They are also realistic and suggest the friendly spirit in the encounters between Canada's Indians and the French settlers.

That little Nichet, Jean LeBlanc's youngest child, was one to keep his parents as busy as all the other thirteen tied together.

One day the little fellow had a new question for his wise father.

"Papa," said Nichet, "where did the Boulangers get their new baby?"

"That is an easy question," answered Jean LeBlanc. "The good Indians brought her, my little nest egg."

"Did the good Indians bring me to you?" asked Nichet.

"Of course," answered his father. "The good Indians bring all the babies."

Little Nichet thought about this for a while.

"Papa," he asked again, "will the good Indians bring us another baby? I would like to have a little sister like Marie Boulanger."

"*Tatata!*" exclaimed Jean LeBlanc. "Already the good Indians have brought us a houseful. Thirteen brothers and sisters are quite enough for such a little fellow as you. And if we had a new baby, you would no longer be our little nest egg."

But Nichet did not think that thirteen brothers and sisters were enough, especially when they were all older and bigger than he.

One afternoon little Nichet wanted to ask his father more about this. But his father and his mother had driven to town in the two-wheeled cart with his eight sisters squeezed together in back.

It was a lonely day for Nichet because his five brothers were out in the field working. And Grandmère kept falling asleep over the rug she was hooking.

So Nichet bravely decided to go to the Indian

"Little Nichet's Baby Sister." From *Sashes Red and Blue* by Natalie Savage Carlson. Copyright © 1956 by Natalie Savage Carlson. Reprinted by permission of Harper & Row, Publishers

village himself and ask the Indians if they didn't have an extra baby for the LeBlancs.

Nichet started out on his own two short legs. He walked down the river road. He walked up the Indian trail.

At last he came to the Indian village with its houses scattered over the ground like half-melons.

The Indian village was deserted. The Indians must have gone to town too. Then Nichet saw a few squaws working among the corn sprouts on the hillside. He started toward them.

But he never got as far as the cornfields. For there, propped against a tree trunk, was exactly what Nichet wanted. It was a little papoose laced to its cradle board.

Nichet was so excited that he could scarcely unlace the baby from the board. He lifted it carefully in his arms. The baby did not cry like the Boulanger's new Marie. Nichet looked at its brown skin and its black eyes and its straight black hair. He tried to decide whether it looked more like his papa or his mamma.

The little baby waved its tiny brown arms at him.

"You are my little sister," said Nichet. "I think you look most like me. I will take you home to your papa and mamma."

Nichet LeBlanc carried the papoose down the trail to the river road. It was a long walk and Nichet was so tired he did not think he would ever get the baby to its home. But his sturdy legs carried them both there at last.

Papa and Mamma and the girls had not returned from town yet. The boys were still in the field. Nichet took the baby to show her to Grandmère, but the old lady was asleep with her mouth open and her glasses on the end of her nose.

So little Nichet carried the baby into his parents' bedroom. He carefully laid it in the middle of the bright quilt. Then he ran down the lane to wait for his mamma and papa. He wanted to be the first one to tell them the news that they had a new baby.

At first his papa and mamma thought that little Nichet had a fever. Then they thought that he had fallen asleep like Grandmère and had had a bad dream. But when they saw the brown baby with the black hair and black eyes lying on the bed, they knew that Nichet had told the truth.

"Where did this baby come from?" cried Mamma LeBlanc.

"The Indians brought her," said little Nichet. "That is, I went and got her myself so they wouldn't give her to someone else."

Then there was a great *tohu-bohu* of chattering among the LeBlancs.

"We will have to take it right back," said Jean LeBlanc. "If the Indians think we have stolen their baby, they might burn down our house."

Little Nichet was brokenhearted. He begged and begged his parents to keep his little brown sister with the black hair and black eyes who looked so much like him.

But back to the Indians went the little sister. Little Nichet held her in his arms all the way there in the two-wheeled cart.

There was another *tohu-bohu* of chattering going on at the Indian village.

"A bear has carried off one of the babies," a young brave explained to Jean LeBlanc.

"We have your baby here," said Jean. "It was carried off by a very little bear."

Nichet cried and cried at the loss of his Indian sister. He began feeling sorry for himself. He began thinking that if his papa and mamma had returned the baby to the Indians, they might do the same with him someday.

Little Nichet began feeling sorrier than ever for himself. He decided to return to the Indians of his own free will. How his parents would cry when they found he was gone! They would come galloping to the Indian village. They would take him home again—and his baby sister too.

He packed his nightshirt and his willow whistle and his lynx tail into a sack and set out for the Indian village once more. He walked all the way down the river road. He follwed the trail to the houses that were like half-melons.

"I have come back to stay with my little sister," Nichet told one of the Indians.

Then the Indians were as worried as the LeBlancs had been.

"If we keep you here," said one of them, "your papa will think that we have stolen you. He will burn down our lodges."

Little Nichet refused to leave. "I want to stay here and be an Indian like my little sister," he said.

The Indians gathered together and talked their *micmac* talk, which Nichet could not understand. Then one of them turned to him.

"Can you shoot a bow and arrow?" he asked in Nichet's talk.

"No," said little Nichet.

"Can you skin a moose?"

"No," said little Nichet.

"Can you build a birch canoe?"

"No," said little Nichet.

"Then you cannot stay with us," said the brave. "An Indian must be able to do all those things."

So little Nichet sadly turned and started away. But another Indian came running to him with something furry in his hands.

"A gift for you," said the Indian. "A trade for the baby you returned to us."

He dropped a tiny baby animal into Nichet's arms. It had the head of a beaver, the body of a bear, and the tail of a rabbit.

"What is it?" asked Nichet.

"Your wise father will have a name for it," said the Indian, then he began talking his *micmac* talk that Nichet could not understand.

Nichet carried the baby animal home happily.

All the way his busy mind wondered if it was a fox or a beaver or a mink or what.

All the LeBlancs were happy to see that Nichet was home again. For truth, they didn't even know he had gone away until they saw the furry little animal in his arms.

"It is a little whistler," said his wise father, Jean LeBlanc. "Some people call them woodchucks and some people call them groundhogs. But the people back in France call them marmots."

"What is it good for?" asked Grandmère. "Will it give milk or pull a cart or lay eggs?"

"It is good for a lonesome little boy who needs a companion smaller than himself," said Jean LeBlanc. He leaned over Nichet and smiled at the new baby. "Across the ocean in France," he said, "chimney sweeps from the mountains keep whistlers for pets. They teach them to do a little

dance like a bear's."

"Can I be a chimney sweep when I am bigger?" asked little Nichet.

"You may be a chimney sweep tomorrow," said Jean LeBlanc generously. "I am going to take down the stovepipe for your mamma and you may help me clean the soot out of it."

So little Nichet thought that he had made a very good trade with the Indians. The boy picked out the name of Pierrette for his tiny pet, and his father helped him to teach that whistler to dance.

Whenever Nichet whistled a special tune, Pierrette would sit up on her hindquarters and wave her forepaws from right to left as she did her dance of the bear. And from time to time she would make polite curtsies. You may be sure that Pierrette was as popular at the stay-awake parties as old Michel Meloche, the storyteller.

United States: Variants of European Folk Tales

There is no such thing as a typical American folk tale. While we find scattered over the United States pockets of folklore that have grown out of definite ethnic, occupational, and regional situations, the stories in those groups are mostly American adaptations of traditional European tales. Although these have come out of untypical areas, such as the Southern Appalachians and the Ozarks, they are widely known because they have been assiduously recorded and retold in popular books that have delighted adults and children. But our best examples of the European variants are still found in Richard Chase's The Jack Tales *and* Grandfather Tales, *two collections of stories which may easily be traced back to Jacobs, the Grimms, Asbjörnsen and Moe, even to* The Odyssey *and* Beowulf. *Anyone interested in the folklore of the United States must read* American Folklore, *by Richard Dorson, and* Folklore in America, *by Tristram P. Coffin and Hennig Cohen, to see how fascinating and complicated the entire subject is. Meanwhile, we can sit back with the children and enjoy such Americanized versions of European tales as* Journey Cake, Ho! *and "Jack and the Robbers." Since arriving in America the older tales have changed their dress and picked up new and comic vitality.*

JOURNEY CAKE, HO!

Although not strictly a folk tale, created as it was to be a picture book, this rollicking version of the well-known "The Pancake" and "The Gingerbread Boy" makes a fine addition to one's storytelling repertory. If you have the book, by all means share with children Robert McCloskey's genial, lively illustrations for the story.

There were three of them: the old woman, Merry; the old man, Grumble; and Johnny, the bound-out boy. They lived in a log cabin, t'other side of Tip Top Mountain.

The old woman took care of the wool; she

carded and spun and knit it. She laid the fire, tended the griddle, churned the butter, and sang at her work. The song she liked best ran this-wise:

"Ho, for a Journey Cake—
Quick on a griddle bake!
Sugar and salt it,
Turn it and brown it,
Johnny, come eat it with milk for your tea."

The old man tended the garden patch, sheared the sheep, milked the cow, felled the trees, sawed the logs, and grumbled at his work. The grumble he liked best was:

"A bother, a pest!
All work and no rest!
Come winter, come spring,
Life's a nettlesome thing."

And what about Johnny? He split the kindling, filled the woodbox, lugged the water, fed the creatures, fished the brook, and whistled at his work. One tune was as fine as another to Johnny.

Their whole world lay close about them. There were the garden patch, the brook, the logging road that ran down to the valley where the villagers lived, and the spruce woods.

On the tallest tree sat Raucus, the sentinel crow, watching and waiting to caw when surprise or trouble was near.

Nothing happened for a long, long time. They lived snug, like rabbits in their burrow. Then—

One night a fox carried off the hens. "Caw, caw!" called the crow. But it was too late. The next night a wolf carried off the sheep. "Caw, caw, caw!" called the crow. But it was too late.

There came a day when the pig wandered off and got himself lost. Last of all the cow fell into the brook and broke her leg.

All that day the crow cawed and cawed and cawed.

That night the old woman said, shaking her head, "Trouble has come. The meal chest is low, the bin is near empty. What will feed two will not feed three."

The old man grumbled and said, "Johnny, 'tis likely you'll be leaving us on the morrow and

finding yourself a new master and a new ma'm."

The next morning by sunup the old woman had run together a piece of sacking and put straps to it, to hold Johnny's belongings—a knife, some gum from the spruce trees, his shoes and a washing-cloth. On top went the Journey Cake that had been baked for him. It was large, round, and crusty-hard. "Now be off with you!" said the old man, grumbling. "What must be, must be."

"Off with you—and luck follow after," said the old woman sadly.

Johnny said nothing at all. He left his whistle behind him and took the logging road down to the valley.

Right foot, left foot, right foot, left foot. He was halfway down and more when the straps on his sacking bag broke loose. Out bounced the Journey Cake.

It bumped and it bumped; it rolled over and over. Down the road it went, and how it hollered!

"Journey Cake, ho!
Journey Cake, hi!
Catch me and eat me
As I roll by!"

Away and away rolled the Journey Cake. Away and away ran Johnny.

Faster and faster. They passed a field full of cows. A brindle cow tossed her head and took after them. She mooed:

"At running I'll beat you.
I'll catch you and eat you!"

Faster and faster, faster and faster! They passed a pond full of ducks.

"Journey Cake, ho!
Journey Cake, hi!
Catch me and eat me
As I roll by!"

A white duck spread her wings, and away and away she went after them, quacking:

"At flying I'll beat you.
I'll catch and I'll eat you!"

Faster and faster, faster and faster! They came to a meadow where sheep were grazing. A white sheep and a black sheep took after them.

Now they were through the valley and the road began to climb. Slower and slower rolled the Journey Cake. Slower and slower ran Johnny, the brindle cow, the white duck, and the two sheep.

"Journey Cake, hi!
The journey is long.
Catch me and eat me
As I roll along."

They passed a wallows. A spotted pig heard and came a-grunting.

They passed a barnyard, and a flock of red hens flew over the stump fence, squawking. Slower and s-l-o-w-e-r, higher and higher.

At last they came to a mountain pasture where a gray donkey was feeding. Now the Journey Cake was huffing and puffing:

"Journey Cake, hi!
The journey is long.
C-c-catch me and eat me—
As I roll along."

The donkey was fresh. He kicked up his heels and brayed:

"I'll show I can beat you.
I'll catch you and eat you."

Higher went the road. Slower and slower, slower and slower rolled the Journey Cake— t'other side of Tip Top Mountain. Slower and slower and slower, slower and slower came the procession with Johnny at the head. Huffing and puffing, they circled the spruce woods. From his perch on the tallest tree, Raucus, the crow, let out his surprise warning: "Caw, caw, caw!"

Johnny heard. He stopped, all of a quickness. There was the brook; there was the garden patch; there was the log cabin.

He was home again. The Journey Cake had brought him to the end of his journey!

The Journey Cake spun around twice and fell flat. "I'm all of a tucker!" it hollered.

"We're all of a tucker," cried the others. The red hens found a house waiting for them. The cow found her tether rope; the pig found a sty; the duck found a brook; the sheep found a place for grazing, and the donkey walked himself into the shed.

The old woman came a-running.

The old man came a-running.

Johnny hugged them hard. He found his whistle again and took up the merriest tune. "Wheee —ew, wheee—ew!" he whistled. He hopped first on right foot, then on left foot. When he had his breath he said, "Journey Cake did it. Journey Cake fetched me-and-the-cow-and-the-white-duck-and-the-black-and-white-sheep-and-the-flock-of-red-hens-and-the-pig-and-the-gray-donkey. Now they are all yours!"

The old man forgot his best grumble. The old woman picked up the Journey Cake and went inside to freshen it up on the griddle. She went, singing the song she liked best:

"Warm up the Journey Cake;
From now on it's Johnny Cake.
Johnny, come eat it
With milk for your tea!"

JACK AND THE ROBBERS

The tens and elevens will readily recognize "The Four Musicians" in this homespun variant with the realistic conclusion. They should hear Richard Chase tell it in the laconic drawl of a mountain man.

This here's another tale about Jack when he was still a small-like boy. He was about twelve, I reckon, and his daddy started tryin' to make him help with the work around the place. But Jack he didn't like workin' much. He would piddle around a little and then he'd go on back to the house, till one day his daddy whipped him. He just tanned Jack good. Jack didn't cry none, but he didn't like it a bit. So early the next mornin' he slipped off without tellin' his mother and struck out down the public road. Thought he'd go and try his fortune somewhere off from home.

"Jack and the Robbers." From *The Jack Tales* edited by Richard Chase. Copyright, 1943, by Richard Chase. Reprinted by permission of the publisher, Houghton Mifflin Company

He got down the road a few miles and there was an old ox standin' in a field by a rail fence, a-bellowin' like it was troubled over somethin'—

"Um-m-muh!
Um-m-m—muh-h-h!"

"Hello!" says Jack. "What's the matter?"

"I'll just tell you," says the old ox. "I'm gettin' too old to plow and I heard the men talkin' about how they'd have to kill me tomorrow and get shet of me."

"Come on down here to the gap," says Jack, "and you can slip off with me."

So the old ox followed the fence to where the gap was at and Jack let the bars down and the old ox got out in front of Jack, and they went on down the public road.

Jack and the ox traveled on, and pretty soon they came where there was an old donkey standin' with his head hangin' down over the gate, a-goin'—

"Wahn-n-n-eh!
Wahn-n-n-eh!
Wahn-n-n-eh!"

"Hello," says Jack. "What's troublin' you?"

"Law me!" says the old donkey. "The boys took me out to haul in wood this mornin' and I'm gettin' so old and weak I couldn't do no good. I heard 'em say they were goin' to kill me tomorrow, get shet of me."

"Come on and go with us," says Jack.

So he let the old donkey out and they pulled on down the public road. The old donkey told Jack to get up on his back and ride.

They went on a piece, came to an old hound dog settin' in a man's yard. He would bark awhile and then howl awhile—

"A-woo! woo! woo!
A-oo-oo-oo!"

—sounded awful lonesome.

"Hello," says Jack. "What you a-howlin' so for?"

"Oh, law me!" says the old dog. "The boys took me coon-huntin' last night, cut a tree where the coon had got up in it. I got hold on the coon all right, but my teeth are all gone and hit got loose from me. They said they were goin' to kill me today, get shet of me."

"Come on, go with us," says Jack.

So the old dog scrouged under the gate.

The old donkey says to him, "Get up on my back and ride, if you want to."

Jack holp the old dog up behind him, and they went on down the public road.

Came to an old tomcat climbin' along the fence. Hit was a-squallin' and meowin', stop ever' now and then, sit down on the top rail—

"Meow-ow!
Meow-ow-ow!"

—sounded right pitiful.

"Hello!" says Jack. "What's the matter you squallin' so?"

"Oh, law!" says the old cat. "I caught a rat out in the barn this mornin', but my teeth are gettin' so old and bad I let him go. I heard 'em talkin' about killin' me to get shet of me, 'cause I ain't no good to catch rats no more."

"Come on and go with us," says Jack.

So the old cat jumped down off the fence.

The old donkey says, "Hop up there on my back and you can ride."

The old cat jumped up, got behind the dog, and they went on down the public road.

Came to where they saw an old rooster settin' on a fence post, crowin' like it was midnight, makin' the awfulest lonesome racket—

"Ur rook-a-roo!
Ur-r-r rook-a-roo-oo-oo!"

"Hello!" says Jack. "What's troublin' you?"

"Law me!" says the old rooster. "Company's comin' today and I heard 'em say they were goin' to kill me, put me in a pie!"

"Come on with us," says Jack.

Old rooster flew on down, got behind the cat, says, "All right, boys. Let's go!"

So they went right on down the highway. That was about all could get on the old donkey's back. The old rooster was right on top its tail and a-havin' a sort of hard time stayin' on. They traveled on, traveled on, till hit got plumb dark.

"Well," says Jack, "we got to get off the road and find us a place to stay tonight."

Directly they came to a little path leadin' off in the woods, decided to take that, see could they find a stayin' place in there. Went on a right smart piece further, and 'way along up late in the night they came to a little house, didn't have no clearin' around it. Jack hollered hello at the fence but there didn't nobody answer.

"Come on," says the old donkey. "Let's go investigate that place."

Well, there wasn't nobody ever came to the door and there wasn't nobody around back of the house, so directly they went on in. Found a right smart lot of good somethin' to eat in there.

Jack says, "Now, who in the world do you reckon could be a-livin' out here in such a wilderness of a place as this?"

"Well," says the old donkey, "hit's my o-pinion that a gang of highway robbers lives out here."

So Jack says, "Then hit looks like to me we might as well take up and stay here. If they've done stole all these vittles, we got as much right to 'em as they have."

"Yes," says the old dog, "that's exactly what I think, too. But if we stay, I believe we better get fixed for a fight. I expect they'll be comin' back in here about midnight."

"That's just what I was goin' to say," says the old cat. "I bet it's pretty close to midnight right now."

"Hit lacks about a hour," says the old rooster.

"Come on, then," says Jack. "Let's all of us get set to fight 'em."

The ox said he'd stay out in the yard. The old donkey said he'd take up his stand on the porch just outside the door. The dog said he'd get in behind the door and fight from there. The old tomcat got down in the fireplace, and the old rooster flew up on the comb of the roof, says, "If you boys need any help now, just call on me, call on me-e-e!"

They all waited awhile. Heard somebody comin' directly; hit was seven highway robbers. They came on till they got pretty close to the house, then they told one of 'em to go on in and start up a fire so's they could have a light to see to get in and so they could divide out the money they'd stole that day.

One man went on in the house, the other six waited outside the gate.

That man went to the fireplace, got down on his knees to blow up the fire. The cat had his head right down on the hearth-rock and that man thought its eyes was coals of fire. Time he blowed in that old cat's eyes, it reached out its claws right quick and scratched him down both cheeks. The robber hollered and headed for the door. The dog ran out and bit him in the leg. He shook it off and ran on the porch and the old donkey raised up and kicked him on out in the yard. The ox caught him up on its horns and ran to the fence and threw him out in the bresh. About that time the old rooster settin' up there on top of the house started in to crowin' right big.

The other robbers, time they heard all that racket, they put out from there just as fast as

they could run. The one they'd sent in the house finally got up and started runnin' like a streak, caught up with 'em in no time. They said to him, says, "What in the world was that in there?"

"Oh, I'm killed! I'm killed!" says the man. "I won't live over fifteen minutes!"

The other said, "Well, 'fore ye die, tell us what it was caused all that racket back yonder."

"Law me! That house is plumb full of men, and they've even got one on the roof. I went to blow up the fire and a man in the fireplace raked me all over the face with an awl. Started to run and a man behind the door took me in the leg with a butcher knife. Time I got out the door, a man out there hit me with a knot-maul, knocked me clean off the porch. A man standin' in the yard caught me on a pitchfork and threw me over the fence. And then that man up on the roof hollered out,

'Chunk him on up here!
Chunk him on up here.'

Ain't no use in us goin' back there with all of them men in the house. Let's leave here quick 'fore they come after us."

So them highway robbers ran for their life, and kept on runnin' till they were plumb out the country.

Jack and the ox and the old donkey and the dog and the cat and the rooster, they took possession of that house, and just had 'em a big time.

But the last time I was down that way, Jack had gone on back home to his folks. He was out in the yard a-cuttin' his mother a big pile of stovewood.

YOUNG MELVIN

This story seems solely a product of rural America, with its protagonist's naïveté and ultimate sly turning of the tables; but it has its counterparts in other lands and is an old theme in world literature. (See "The Mice That Ate Iron.") This is a perfect example of how a common motif or situation in folklore is adapted to fit the particular circumstances and character of a locality.

After his pappy passed on Young Melvin decided he wanted to travel. He'd always lived back at the forks of the creek and he hadn't ever at no time been farther from there than the crossroads.

So Young Melvin put out the fire and hid the ax and skillet and called up his hound named Bulger and he was on his way. He went over the hill and a good piece further and he come to the crossroads. He went straight to Old Man Bill Blowdy's house there. He knocked on the door.

Old Man Bill Blowdy come to the door and stuck his nose out the crack. "Who's there?" says he, not daring to come out for fear it was somebody he'd beat in some deal.

"It's me," says Young Melvin. "Just me and my hound dog Bulger."

Old Man Bill Blowdy opened the door then and gave Young Melvin a sly look. "Come in and rest and eat a bite," he says, faint-like.

He was a great big fat red man that was always grinning and easy talking, like butter wouldn't melt in his mouth. And he was just about the slickest, double-dealingest old cooter in the country or anywhere else at all. Nobody could beat him in a deal—never had, anyway—or when it come to a law-suit. Always lawing somebody, Old Man Bill Blowdy was.

"Why don't you come in, Young Melvin?" he says.

"Because I'm on my way, Mister Old Man Bill Blowdy. I'm a-going to town for sure. It's forty miles and across two counties but I aim to see that town. That's why I come to see you."

Old Man Bill Blowdy started shutting the door. "Now, now, Young Melvin," he says. "I'm hard up for money right now. I couldn't loan my sweet mother, now in heaven praise be, so much as a penny."

"I don't want no money," says Young Melvin. "I ain't the borrowing kind."

So Old Man Bill Blowdy poked his head out again. "What can I do for you then?"

"Well, it's like this. You're my twenty-third cousin, my only kin in this world. I got a favor for you to do for me."

"Young Melvin." From *God Bless the Devil! Liars' Bench Tales* by James R. Aswell, *et al.* Copyright 1940 by The University of North Carolina Press. Reprinted by permission of the publisher

Old Man Bill Blowdy started sliding that door shut. "No, no favors. I make it a rule to do no favors and don't expect none from nobody."

"It's a favor I'm aiming to pay for," says Young Melvin.

"Oh," says Old Man Bill Blowdy, opening the door once more, "that's different now. Come right in, Young Melvin."

"No sir, no need to come in, for I'd just be coming out again. What I want you to do is keep my fox hound Bulger while I'm off on my travels. I'll pay his keep, I'll pay what's right when I come back to get him."

Old Man Bill Blowdy grinned all over his face. He thought he saw a way to make himself something extry or get him a fox hound one. Everybody knew Young Melvin was simple. Honest as the day's long but simple.

"Why yes," says Old Man Bill Blowdy. "Why yes, I'll keep Bulger for you, Young Melvin, and glad to."

So Young Melvin gave his hound dog over and bid Old Man Bill Blowdy farewell. "I'll be back next week or month or sometime. I don't know how long it'll be, for it's forty miles and across two counties to town."

Well, one day the week or month or anyhow sometime after that, here come Young Melvin down the pikeroad to the crossroads, limping and dusty and easy in mind. He went straight to Old Man Bill Blowdy's house and knocked his knuckles on the door.

Old Man Bill Blowdy stuck his nose out the crack and says, "Who's there?"

"It's me, it's Young Melvin."

"How are you, Young Melvin?"

"Fair to piddling. I walked to town and saw all the sights and then walked back here again. Forty miles and across two counties. Don't never want to roam no more. I'm satisfied now."

Old Man Bill Blowdy started shutting the door. "Glad to hear it, Young Melvin. Next time you come down to the crossroads, drop in and say hello. Any time, just any time, Young Melvin."

"Hold there! Wait a minute!" says Young Melvin.

"I'm busy," says the old man.

But Young Melvin got his foot in the door. "How about Bulger, Old Man Bill Blowdy? How about him?"

Old Man Bill Blowdy kept trying to shut the door and Young Melvin kept shoving his foot in.

"See here!" says Young Melvin. "I mean my fox hound."

"Oh him? Why, I declare to my soul I'd almost forgot that hound dog, Young Melvin. I sure almost had."

"Where is he at?" says Young Melvin, still trying to keep the old man from closing the door.

"I'll tell you," says Old Man Bill Blowdy, still trying to shut it, "I feel mighty bad about it, Young Melvin, but your Bulger is no more."

"How come? What do you mean?"

"Why, he's perished and gone, Young Melvin. The first night after you left I sort of locked him up in that little busted-down house over in the Old Ground. Well sir, Young Melvin, those last renters of mine that lived there was powerful dirty folks. They left the place just lousy with chinch bugs. Them bugs was mortal hungry by this time. So they just eat that Bulger of yours alive. Eat all but the poor thing's bones by morning—and the bones was pretty well gnawed.

"It was my fault in one way. I ought to known better than put your dog in there, Young Melvin. But I done it. So I won't charge you a penny for his keep the night I had him. I aim to do the fair thing."

Well, Old Man Bill Blowdy stuck his sly eye to the crack of the door to see how Young Melvin was taking it. He knew the boy was simple. He figured he had him. Because Old Man Bill Blowdy had Bulger hid out and he aimed to swap him for something to a man he knew in the next county.

So Young Melvin stood there looking like the good Lord had shaken him off His Christian limb. Tears come in his eyes and he sleeved his nose. "That dog was folks to me," he says. "Them chinch bugs don't know what they done to me."

He pulled his foot out of the door and he backed down the steps. He started towards home.

Old Man Bill Blowdy eased out on the porch to watch him go.

About that time Young Melvin turned around. "Mister Old Man Bill Blowdy," he says, "my place is way over the hill and a good piece further. I'm beat out and tired. Wonder if you'd loan me your mule to ride on? I'll bring it back tomorrow."

The old man knew Young Melvin was honest as the livelong day. Besides, he was so tickled with how he'd got him a good hound to swap and it not costing anything that he just called across the way to the crossroads store and got a witness to the loan and let Young Melvin take the mule. It was a fine mule, too, with the three hind ribs showing, the best sort of sign in a mule —shows he's a hard worker.

Next morning Young Melvin never showed up and Old Man Bill Blowdy got worried. He got worrieder still in the middle of the day when no sign of Young Melvin did he see.

But along about afternoon he saw Young Melvin come walking over the hill and down towards the crossroads. He run out on his porch and yelled, "Hey, Young Melvin, where's my mule?"

Young Melvin kept walking. He just shook his head. "I feel mighty bad about that mule, Mister Old Man Bill Blowdy," he called. "I sure do."

"Hey! Wait there!"

But Young Melvin went on, heading for the store at the crossroads.

So Old Man Bill Blowdy was so mad he didn't wait to get his shoes. He just jumped off the porch and run across to Square Rogers, that good old man's house up the road a ways.

"Square," he says, "I want you to handle Young Melvin. He stole my mule."

The Square waked up his deputy and the deputy went down and brought in Young Melvin. Everybody at the crossroads come tagging along behind.

Square said, "Son, they tell me you stole a mule."

"No sir, Square Rogers, I never done it," says Young Melvin.

Old Man Bill Blowdy stomped his bare feet and shook his fists. "He's a bald-faced liar!"

"Curb yourself down, Old Man Bill Blowdy," says the Square, "and let the boy tell his side. Go ahead, Young Melvin."

So Young Melvin told his side, told how he borrowed the mule and started for home. "Well," he says, "you know I live over the hill and a good piece further. I rode that mule to the top of the hill. I was minding my own business and not giving nobody any trouble. Then all on a sudden I see a turkey buzzard dropping down out of the sky. Here it come, dropping fast and crowing like a game rooster.

"First thing I knew that old buzzard just grabbed Old Man Bill Blowdy's mule by the tail and started heaving and the mule's hind legs lifted off the ground and I went flying over his head and hit a rock head-on. I failed in my senses a minute. When I could see straight I saw that buzzard sailing away with the mule, most a mile high and getting littler all the time.

"And that's how it happened. I sure am sorry, but there ain't much you can do with a thing like that, Square."

"Hold on there!" says Square Rogers, that good old man. "I've seen many a turkey buzzard in my time, Young Melvin, but never a one that could crow."

"Well," says Young Melvin, "it surprised me some too. But in a county where chinch bugs can eat up a full-grown fox hound in one night, why I just reckon a turkey buzzard has a right to crow and fly off with a mule if he wants to."

So it all come out and Square Rogers, that good old man, made Old Man Bill Blowdy fork up Bulger and then Young Melvin gave back the mule.

Old Man Bill Blowdy was mocked down to nothing. He just grieved and pined away and it wasn't no more than ten years before he taken sick and wasted away and died.

United States: Tall Tales

England has its giant stories, but the United States of America, with
its national symbols a spread eagle and a super-tall figure of a man called "Uncle
Sam," has expressed its exuberant sense of bigness in a series of tall tales.
Nearly all the morally upright tall tale heroes are products not of the folk
imagination but of the imagination of publicists and writers. Pecos
Bill, a western cowboy; Paul Bunyan of the lumber camps; Stormalong, a New
England sailor, have little or no basis of origin among the folk, either
ethnically, regionally, or occupationally, as do Jesse James and Billy the Kid.
Such heroes as John Henry, Barney Beal of Maine, Casey Jones, Davy
Crockett, and Mike Fink were real people whose legends have outgrown their
biographies—again, thanks in part to the efforts of storytellers and
various writers who helped the legends along.
Two things are certain: first, the American tall tale is largely a manufactured
item; second, the imaginary figures of America's past have intrigued
the American mind and become mass culture heroes who embody what we like
to think of as American traits and philosophy. The general formula
for these stories is that the details shall be meticulously realistic and convincing,
and the whopping exaggeration shall be told with a straight face and
complete gravity. Perhaps the place of these tales in American life (no matter what
their origin and validity) has been best stated by Tristram P. Coffin:
"As a nation becoming almost universally literate before its national folk culture
could form, America had to provide itself with symbols and legends that other
nations would have found ready-made." [1] *We had to, and we did!*

THE CAMP

ON THE BIG ONION

With this introduction to Paul Bunyan, the
mighty logger, children may want Glen Rounds'
delightful book, Ol' Paul, the Mighty Logger. *A*
casual manner in the reading or telling is best
for bringing out the humor of these tales.

That first fall I was workin' for Paul was when
he got the big hotcake griddle. Always in the
woods in them days the boys was mighty fond of
hotcakes—just like men are pretty generally any-
wheres, I guess—and if there was anything could
be said for Paul it was that he tried to treat his
men right. And so, naturally, he wanted 'em to
have hotcakes if there was any way he could fix
it, and then besides, the way he ate 'em after-

wards, he was more'n a little fond of 'em himself.

Well, in camp before that they hadn't never
had hotcakes, because they didn't have no griddle big enough to cook 'em on, and no stove they
could of put the griddle on if they'd of had it
anyway, and so what they had for breakfast before that and what they was havin' when I went
to work for Paul was just sourdough biscuits.
And even so the cook used to have to get up
twenty-six hours before daylight to get the biscuits cooked in time because all he had to cook
'em on was one of them there drumhead stoves
they used to have and he couldn't only cook but
sixty-four drippin' pans full at a time.

But that year Paul made up his mind he was
goin' to have hotcakes for the men and he was
goin' to have a griddle big enough to cook 'em
on. And so he went down to the plow-works at
Moline, Illinois, and contracted for 'em to make
him one to suit him.

The steel that went into this griddle of Paul's
was what would have gone into two hundred
and sixty breakin' plows, and when it was done

[1] Tristram P. Coffin and Hennig Cohen, *Folklore in America*, Doubleday, 1966, p. xx

"The Camp on the Big Onion." From *Paul Bunyan*, copyright 1924, 1952 by Esther Shephard. Reprinted by permission of Harcourt, Brace & World, Inc.

finally, it measured two hundred and thirty-five foot across.

And then the men at the plow-works, of course, didn't have no way to ship it up to Paul and they was out there in the yard at the works figgurin' on how they could build some side-tracks and put several flatcars alongside each other and try to ship it up on them, when Paul happened to come along to see if his griddle wasn't finished yet.

"Never mind that," he says to the men when he seen 'em out there. "Never mind tryin' to build any extra tracks. We couldn't never get enough cars anyway, I don't believe. I'll just raise 'er up on edge and hitch my Blue Ox to 'er, and she'll roll right along."

And so after they'd got out of the way he raised 'er up, and hitched on, and started right out for home.

And when he come to within four or five miles of the camp, like he'd calculated it out before-hand, I guess, he just unhitched the Blue Ox and let the griddle spin on by itself. And here she come, rollin' right along. And when she got to just the right place, where he'd figgured to place her, she begun to spin round and round like spin-the-plate at a play-party and dug a nice big hole for the fire to go in under it, and settled right down and was all ready to go.

Paul had the bull-cooks pile in an acre or two of brush for a good fire, and him and Ole the Blacksmith rigged up a tank for the cook to make his batter in and a flume with a stop-cock in it, so's he could run it out onto the griddle and then shut it off whenever he had enough. Paul got flunkies with slabs of bacon strapped to their feet to skate around on the griddle to keep it greased, and a chicken wire fence all around for 'em to climb up on when the batter come in too thick. We rigged up a kind of block and tackle arrangement to haul the hotcake off with when it was done—that's on that first griddle. Afterwards, like in the camp in North Dakota, Paul, of course, always had donkey engines.

There was four hundred bull-cooks bringin' in the spruce-boughs for the bunks in the big bunkhouse at that first camp I was in; it had eighty tiers of bunks, most of 'em muzzle loaders but the two bottom layers, they was sidewinders. And the men used to go to bed in balloons at night and come down in parachutes in the mornin'.

A pretty sight it used to be to watch 'em comin' down.

"R-o-oo-ool out! Daylight in the swamp!" one of the cookees would yell, and then in a minute or two they'd all be rollin' out of their blankets, and the parachutes would open and they'd all come sailin' down. It sure was a pretty sight— about as fine a show as I ever laid eyes on.

Sometimes in the mornin' I used to stop at the door of the bunkhouse, on my way from the barn, to watch 'em. For Bill and I generally used to be on our way in to breakfast about that time, and Bill'd sometimes take the time to stop for a minute or so.

"I like to see 'em," he'd say to me. "Angus, that's a mighty fine show. They come faster now than they used to when it was just for sourdough biscuits. But we'll have to hustle along and get our hotcakes. We got to get back to the Ox."

That spring on the Big Onion we had an awful lot of trouble with the garlic that growed there where Garlic Crick joins the Big Onion River—a kind of V-shaped tract in there along the loggin' road, that was just full of it. The cook tried to use it all up seasonin' the soup but the Frenchies wouldn't stand for it in their pea-soup after the first week, and even with that he only got the top layer off and then there was four more layers growin' under that one. It beats all how thick that wild garlic can grow when it gets a good start. Everybody that even went by that place was seasoned so strong there wasn't nobody else could live with him and, worst of it, he couldn't stand to live with himself even. And we pretty near just had to break up camp, but then Paul heard that the Italian garlic crop was goin' to fail that year and so we grubbed up the whole piece, every last layer of it, and shipped it all to Italy and that way we got rid of it at last; just in time when a good many of us was goin' on the drive anyway, though.

PECOS BILL
AND HIS BOUNCING BRIDE

Here is one of the children's favorites of all the made-up heroes. The "Western" has become one expression of the American culture, thanks to film and television stories which have little to do with the real cowboy or the real West. But Pecos Bill, in spite of all exaggerations, fits the clichés so dear to our hearts, and Slue-Foot Sue is a comic parody of the determined young lady who loses out to the cowboy's horse.

There were two loves in the life of Pecos Bill. The first was his horse Widow-Maker, a beautiful creamy white mustang. The second, was a girl, a pretty, gay creature named Slue-Foot Sue.

Widow-Maker was the wildest pony in the West. He was the son of the White Mustang. Like his father he had a proud spirit which refused to be broken. For many years cowboys and *vaqueros* had tried to capture him. At last Pecos Bill succeeded. He had a terrible time of it. For a whole week he lay beside a water hole before he could lasso the white pony. For another week he had to ride across the prairies, in and out of canyons and briar patches, before he could bring the pony to a walk. It was a wild ride indeed. But after Bill's ride on the cyclone it was nothing.

At last the white stallion gave up the struggle. Pecos patted his neck gently and spoke to him in horse language. "I hope you will not be offended," he began as politely as possible, "but beauty such as yours is rare, even in this glorious state of Texas. I have no wish to break your proud spirit. I feel that together you and I would make a perfect team. Will you not be my partner at the I.X.L. Ranch?"

The horse neighed sadly. "It must be," he sighed. "I must give up my freedom. But since I must, I am glad that you are the man who has conquered me. Only Pecos Bill is worthy to fix a saddle upon the son of the great White Stallion, the Ghost King of the Prairie."

"I am deeply honored," said Pecos Bill, touched in his heart by the compliment.

"It is rather myself who am honored," replied the mustang, taking a brighter view of the situation.

The two of them went on for several hours saying nice things to each other. Before they were through, the pony was begging Pecos to be

his master. Pecos was weeping and saying he was not fit to ride so magnificent a beast. In the end, however, Pecos Bill made two solemn promises. He would never place a bit in the pony's mouth. No other human would ever sit in his saddle.

When Bill rode back to I.X.L. with his new mount, the second promise was broken. Old Satan, the former bad man, had not completely recovered from his badness. He was jealous of Bill. When he saw the beautiful white stallion he turned green and almost burst with jealousy. One night he stole out to the corral. Quietly he slipped up beside the horse and jumped into the saddle.

Pegasus, as the horse was called, knew right away that his rider was not Pecos Bill. He lifted his four feet off the ground and bent his back into a perfect semicircle. Old Satan flew off like an arrow from a bow. He flew up into the air, above the moon, and came down with a thud on top of Pike's Peak. There he sat howling with pain and fright until the boys at I.X.L. spotted him.

Bill was angry. He knew, however, that Old Satan had had enough punishment. In his kind heart he could not allow the villain to suffer any more than he had to. So he twirled his lasso around his head, let it fly, and roped Old Satan back to the Texas ranch. The former desperado never tried to be bad again.

The cowhands were so impressed by the pony's bucking they decided to change his name. From that time on they dropped the name of Pegasus and called him Widow-Maker. It suited him better.

The story of Bill's other love, Slue-Foot Sue, is a long one. It began with the tale of the Perpetual Motion Ranch. Bill had bought a mountain from Paul Bunyan. It looked to him like a perfect mountain for a ranch. It was shaped like a cone, with smooth sides covered with grassy meadows. At the top it was always winter. At the bottom it was always summer. In between it was always spring and fall. The sun always shone on one side; the other was always in shade. The cattle could have any climate they wished.

Bill had to breed a special kind of steer for his ranch. These had two short legs on one side and two long legs on the other. By traveling in one direction around the mountain, they were able to stand up straight on the steep sides.

The novelty wore off, however, and at last Bill sold the Perpetual Motion Ranch to an English duke. The day that the I.X.L. boys moved out, the lord moved in. He brought with him train-load after trainload of fancy English things. He had featherbeds and fine china and oil paintings and real silver and linen tablecloths and silk rugs. The cowboys laughed themselves almost sick when they saw these dude things being brought to a cattle ranch.

Pecos Bill didn't laugh. He didn't even notice the fancy things. All he could see was the English duke's beautiful daughter. She was as pretty as the sun and moon combined. Her hair was silky and red. Her eyes were blue. She wore a sweeping taffeta dress and a little poke bonnet with feathers on it. She was the loveliest creature Pecos Bill had ever seen.

She was as lively and gay as she was pretty. Bill soon discovered that Slue-Foot Sue was a girl of talent. Before anyone could say "Jack Robinson," she changed into a cowboy suit and danced a jig to the tune of "Get Along, Little Dogies."

Bill soon lost all his interest in cowpunching. He spent his afternoons at the Perpetual Motion Ranch, teaching Sue to ride a broncho. Sue could ride as well as anyone, but she pretended to let him teach her. After several months of Bill's lessons, she put on a show. She jumped onto the back of a huge catfish in the Rio Grande River and rode all the way to the Gulf of Mexico, bareback. Bill was proud of her. He thought she had learned her tricks all from him.

Sue's mother was terribly upset by her daughter's behavior. She didn't care much for Bill. She was very proper. It was her fondest hope that Sue would stop being a tomboy and marry an earl or a member of Parliament.

As soon as she realized that her daughter was falling in love with a cowboy, she was nearly heart-broken. There was nothing she could do about it, however. Slue-Foot Sue was a headstrong girl who always had her own way.

At last the duchess relented. She invited Bill to tea and began to lecture him on English manners. She taught him how to balance a teacup, how to bow from the waist, and how to eat scones and marmalade instead of beans and

bacon. He learned quickly, and soon the duchess was pleased with him. She called him "Colonel."

When the boys from the I.X.L. Ranch saw what was going on they were disgusted. Here was their boss, their brave, big, cyclone-riding Pecos Bill, mooning around in love like a sick puppy. They laughed at his dude manners. They made fun of his dainty appetite. When he dressed up in his finery to call on his girl, they stood in the bunkhouse door. They simpered and raised their eyebrows and said to one another, "La-dee-da, dearie, ain't we fine today!"

But for all their kidding they were broken-hearted. None of them had anything against Sue. They admired the way she rode a horse and played a guitar and danced a jig. But the thought of losing Bill to a woman was too much. Even worse was the thought that Bill might get married and bring a woman home to live with them. That was awful.

In spite of their teasing and the duchess's lessons, Bill asked Slue-Foot Sue to marry him. She

accepted before he could back out. Her father, the lord, had always liked Bill and was terribly pleased at the match.

On his wedding day Pecos Bill shone like the sun in his new clothes. His boys were dressed in their finest chaps and boots for the occasion. Half of them were going to be groomsmen. The other half were going to be bridesmen. At first Bill asked them to be bridesmaids, but they refused. They said that was going too far.

They rode to the Perpetual Motion Ranch in a fine procession, Bill at the head on Widow-Maker. The white horse pranced and danced with excitement.

At the ranch house waited the rest of the wedding party. The lord had sent back to England for a bishop to perform the ceremony. There stood His Eminence in his lace robes. On his one hand stood the duke in a cutaway coat. On his other hand stood the duchess in a stiff purple gown right from Paris.

Down the stairs came the bride. She was a vision of beauty. She wore a white satin dress cut in the latest fashion. It had a long lace train, but its chief glory was a bustle. A bustle was a wire contraption that fitted under the back of the dress. It made the skirt stand out and was considered very handsome in those days.

As Slue-Foot Sue danced down the steps even the cowhands forgot their sorrow. They jumped down from their horses and swept their sombreros from their heads. Pecos Bill lost his head. He leapt down from Widow-Maker and ran to meet her. "You are lovely," he murmured. "I promise to grant you every wish you make."

That was a mistake. A devilish gleam twinkled in Sue's eye. For months she had been begging Bill to let her ride Widow-Maker. Bill, of course, had always refused.

Now Sue saw her chance. Before she allowed the wedding to proceed, she demanded that Bill give her one ride on his white mustang.

"No, no!" cried Pecos Bill. Before he could stop her Sue dashed down the drive and placed her dainty foot into the stirrup. The duchess screamed. The bishop turned pale.

Widow-Maker gave an angry snort. This was the second time the promise to him had been broken. He lifted his four feet off the ground and arched his back. Up, up, up shot Slue-Foot

Sue. She disappeared into the clouds.

"Catch her, catch her!" roared Bill at the boys. They spread themselves out into a wide circle. Then from the sky came a scream like a siren. Down, down, down fell Sue. She hit the earth with terrible force. She landed on her bustle. The wire acted as a spring. It bounced. Up again she flew.

Up and down, up and down between the earth and sky Sue bounced like a rubber ball. Every time she fell her bustle hit first. Back she bounced. This went on for a week. When at last she came back to earth to stay, she was completely changed. She no longer loved Pecos Bill.

The wedding was called off and the boys returned to the I.X.L. with their unhappy boss. For months he refused to eat. He lost interest in cowpunching. He was the unhappiest man Texas had ever seen.

At last he called his hands together and made a long speech. He told them that the days of real cowpunching were over. The prairie was being fenced off by farmers. These "nesters," as he called them, were ruining the land for the ranchers. He was going to sell his herd.

The I.X.L. had its last roundup. Bill gathered all the prime steers together and put them on the train for Kansas City. Then he divided the cows and calves among his boys. He himself mounted Widow-Maker and rode away.

The boys hated to see him go, but they knew how he felt. "Nesters" or no "nesters," the real reason for his going was his broken heart.

None of them ever saw him again. Some of them thought he had gone back to the coyotes. Others had an idea that Slue-Foot Sue had changed her mind and that she and Bill were setting up housekeeping in some private canyon. But they never knew.

Some years later an old cowhand claimed that Bill had died. The great cowpuncher had met a dude rancher at a rodeo. The dude was dressed up in an outfit he had bought from a movie cowboy. The dude's chaps were made of doeskin. His boots were painted with landscapes and had heels three inches high. The brim of his hat was broad enough to cover a small circus. Bill took a good look at him and died laughing.

THE BOOMER FIREMAN'S
FAST SOONER HOUND

Children will enjoy Virginia Burton's pictures in Jack Conroy and Arna Bontemps' book The Fast Sooner Hound. *They will also be entertained by that super horse, recorded in verse by Dick Jones and called* Platonia the Pride of the Plain.

In the days of the old railroad trains before diesel engines were ever thought of the fireman was an important man. A Boomer fireman could get him a job most anytime on most any railroad and was never long for any one road. Last year he might have worked for the Frisco, and this year he's heaving black diamonds for the Katy or the Wabash. He travelled light and travelled far and didn't let any grass grow under his feet when they got to itching for the greener pastures on the next road or the next division or maybe on the other side of the mountains. He didn't need furniture and he didn't need many clothes, and goodness knows he didn't need a family or a dog.

One day when one of these Boomer firemen pulled into the roadmaster's office looking for a job, there was that Sooner hound of his loping after him. That hound would sooner run than eat and he'd sooner eat than fight or do something useful like catching a rabbit. Not that a rabbit would have any chance if the Sooner really wanted to nail him, but that crazy hound dog didn't like to do anything but run and he was the fastest thing on four legs.

"I might use you," said the roadmaster. "Can you get a boarding place for the dog?"

"Oh, he goes along with me," said the Boomer. "I raised him from a pup just like a mother or father and he ain't never spent a night or a day or even an hour far away from me. He'd cry like his poor heart would break and raise such a ruckus nobody couldn't sleep, eat or hear themselves think for miles about."

"The Boomer Fireman's Fast Sooner Hound," by Jack Conroy. From *A Treasury of American Folklore*, edited by B. A. Botkin (New York: Crown Publishers, 1944). Another version of this story is found in *The Fast Sooner Hound* by Arna Bontemps and Jack Conroy (Boston: Houghton Mifflin, 1942). Reprinted by permission of Jack Conroy

"Well, I don't see how that would work out," said the roadmaster. "It's against the rules of the road to allow a passenger in the cab, man or beast, or in the caboose and I aim to put you on a freight run so you can't ship him by express. Besides, he'd get the idea you wasn't nowhere about and pester folks out of their wits with his yipping and yowling. You look like a man that could keep a boiler popping off on an uphill grade, but I just don't see how we could work it if the hound won't listen to reason while you're on your runs."

"Why he ain't no trouble," said the Boomer. "He just runs alongside, and when I'm on a freight run he chases around a little in the fields to pass the time away. It's a little bit tiresome on him having to travel at such a slow gait, but that Sooner would do anything to stay close by me, he loves me that much."

"Oh, is that so? Well, don't try to tell that yarn around here," said the roadmaster.

"I'll lay my first paycheck against a fin [1] that he'll be fresh as a daisy and his tongue behind his teeth when we pull into the junction. He'll run around the station a hundred times or so to limber up."

"It's a bet," said the roadmaster.

On the first run the Sooner moved in what was a slow walk for him. He kept looking up into the cab where the Boomer was shoveling in the coal.

"He looks worried," said the Boomer. "He thinks the hog law [2] is going to catch us, we're making such bad time."

The roadmaster was so sore at losing the bet that he transferred the Boomer to a local passenger run and doubled the stakes. The Sooner speeded up to a slow trot, but he had to kill a lot of time, at that, not to get too far ahead of the engine.

Then the roadmaster got mad enough to bite off a drawbar. People got to watching the Sooner trotting alongside the train and began thinking it must be a mighty slow road. Passengers might just as well walk; they'd get there just as fast. And if you shipped a yearling calf to market, it'd be a bologna bull before it reached the stockyards. Of course, the trains were keeping up

[1] Five dollar bill.—J. C.
[2] Rule forbidding excessive over time.—J. C.

their schedules the same as usual, but that's the way it looked to people who saw a no-good mangy Sooner hound beating all the trains without his tongue hanging out an inch or letting out the least little pant.

It was giving the road a black eye, all right. The roadmaster would have fired the Boomer and told him to hit the grit with his Sooner and never come back again, but he was stubborn from the word go and hated worse than anything to own up he was licked.

"I'll fix that Sooner," said the roadmaster. "I'll slap the Boomer into the cab of the Cannon Ball, and if anything on four legs can keep up with the fastest thing on wheels I'd admire to see it. That Sooner'll be left so far behind it'll take nine dollars to send him a post card."

The word got around that the Sooner was going to try to keep up with the Cannon Ball. Farmers left off plowing, hitched up, and drove to the right of way to see the sight. It was like a circus day or the county fair. The schools all dismissed the pupils, and not a factory could keep enough men to make a wheel turn.

The roadmaster got right in the cab so that the Boomer couldn't soldier on the job to let the Sooner keep up. A clear track for a hundred miles was ordered for the Cannon Ball, and all the switches were spiked down till after that streak of lightning had passed. It took three men to see the Cannon Ball on that run: one to say, "There she comes," one to say, "There she is," and another to say, "There she goes." You couldn't see a thing for steam, cinders and smoke, and the rails sang like a violin for a half hour after she'd passed into the next county.

Every valve was popping off and the wheels three feet in the air above the roadbed. The Boomer was so sure the Sooner would keep up that he didn't stint the elbow grease; he wore the hinges off the fire door and fifteen pounds of him melted and ran right down into his shoes. He had his shovel whetted to a nub.

The roadmaster stuck his head out of the cab window, and —whosh!—off went his hat and almost his head. The suction like to have jerked his arms from their sockets as he nailed a-hold of the window seat.

It was all he could do to see, and gravel pinged against his goggles like hailstones, but he let out a whoop of joy.

"THE SOONER! THE SOONER!" he yelled. "He's gone! He's gone for true! Ain't *nowhere* in sight!"

"I can't understand that," hollered the Boomer. "He ain't *never* laid down on me yet. It just ain't like him to lay down on me. Leave me take a peek."

He dropped his shovel and poked out his head. Sure enough, the Sooner was nowhere to be seen. The Boomer's wild and troubled gaze swept far and wide.

"Don't see him, do you?" the roadmaster demanded. "He's at least seventy-six miles behind."

The Boomer didn't answer. He just threw his head back into the cab and began to shovel coal. He shoveled without much spirit, shaking his head sadly. There was no need for hard work, anyhow, for the Cannon Ball was puffing into the station at the end of the run.

Before the wheels had stopped rolling, the roadmaster jumped nimbly to the ground. A mighty cheer was heard from a group of people nearby. The roadmaster beamed as he drew near them.

"Here I am!" he shouted. "Where are the cameras? Do you want to take my picture in the cab?"

"Go way back and sit down!" a man shouted as he turned briefly toward the railroad official. "You might as well scrap that Cannon Ball. The Sooner has been here a good half hour and time has been hanging heavy on his hands. Look at him!"

The Sooner was loping easily around a tree, barking at a cat which had taken refuge in the branches and was spitting angrily. The Sooner didn't look even a mite tired, and his tongue was behind his teeth.

"I'm through! Enough is enough, boys!" the roadmaster sputtered. "The rule about passengers in the cab is a dead duck from now on. Let the Sooner ride in the cab as often and as far as he wants to."

The Cannon Ball chugged out of the station with the Boomer waving his shovel in salute and the Sooner yelping proudly beside him. The people cheered until the train disappeared around a bend.

United States: Uncle Remus

*The talking-beast tales of Uncle Remus are a priceless treasury of Negro
folk tales. Although it is commonly believed that Joel Chandler Harris wrote
them down just as he heard them told, the truth is that he took elements
of the folk tales that he found among the Southern Negroes and molded them
into polished, literary gems which preserve a form of then current
Southern Negro dialect, a rich vein of humor, and a superb gift for storytelling.
The origins of these stories have been discussed ever since they first
appeared. Although Harris retold them to a great extent, the tales were in
common circulation among plantation Negroes. Folklorists now seem
generally agreed that the tales drew upon earlier African sources (there
are many stories about the hare in Africa), but that for the most part the
stories are from European predecessors. (The best and most authentic
examples of African folk tales in the New World are still the hundreds
of Anansi stories found in the West Indies.)
The hero of these stories is Brer Rabbit, the weakest of all the animals.
He is a trickster, but a lovable one, with no meanness in him, just a love of
playing pranks on his bigger neighbors. Occasionally they turn the
tables on him, but his wit and resourcefulness always save him. Those fortunate
people who can read and understand the rich dialect in which these
stories are recorded should always read or tell them in that form. When put into
everyday English, the tales lose their unique charm. The collection is too
rich for children to miss, and every effort should be made to keep these stories
in circulation. The recordings of some of them, made by Frances Clarke
Sayers for the American Library Association, are an especially fine way to hear
them as they* might *have been told.*

THE WONDERFUL TAR-BABY STORY

*This is the best known of all the stories and a
perennial favorite with children. Be sure to tell
the sequel, "How Mr. Rabbit Was too Sharp
for Mr. Fox," in which Brer Rabbit, as usual,
gets out of his predicament.*

"Didn't the fox *never* catch the rabbit, Uncle
Remus?" asked the little boy the next evening.

"He come mighty nigh it, honey, sho's you
born—Brer Fox did. One day atter Brer Rabbit
fool 'im wid dat calamus root, Brer Fox went ter
wuk en got 'im some tar, en mix it wid some tur-

kentime, en fix up a contrapshun wat he call a
Tar-Baby, en he tuck dish yer Tar-Baby en he
sot 'er in de big road, en den he lay off in de
bushes fer to see what de news wuz gwineter be.
En he didn't hatter wait long, nudder, kaze bimeby here come Brer Rabbit pacin' down de
road—lippity-clippity, clippity-lippity—dez ez
sassy ez a jay-bird. Brer Fox, he lay low. Brer
Rabbit come prancin' 'long twel he spy de Tar-
Baby, en den he fotch up on his behime legs like
he wus 'stonished. De Tar-Baby, she sot dar, she
did, en Brer Fox, he lay low.

"'Mawnin'!' sez Brer Rabbit, sezee—'nice
wedder dis mawnin',' sezee.

"Tar-Baby ain't sayin' nothin', en Brer Fox,
he lay low.

"'How duz yo' sym'tums seem ter segashuate?'
sez Brer Rabbit, sezee.

"Brer Fox, he wink his eye slow, en lay low, en
de Tar-Baby, she ain't sayin' nothin'.

"'How you come on, den? Is you deaf?' sez

Brer Rabbit, sezee. 'Kaze if you is, I kin holler louder,' sezee.

"Tar-Baby stay still, en Brer Fox, he lay low.

"'Youer stuck up, dat's w'at you is,' says Brer Rabbit, sezee, 'en I'm gwineter kyore you, dat's w'at I'm a gwineter do,' sezee.

"Brer Fox, he sorter chuckle in his stummick, he did, but Tar-Baby ain't sayin' nothin'.

"'I'm gwineter larn you howter talk ter 'spect-tubble fokes ef hit's de las' ack,' sez Brer Rabbit, sezee. 'Ef you don't take off dat hat en tell me howdy, I'm gwineter bus' you wide open,' sezee.

"Tar-Baby stay still, en Brer Fox, he lay low.

"Brer Rabbit keep on axin' 'im, en de Tar-Baby, she keep on sayin' nothin', twel present'y Brer Rabbit draw back wid his fis', he did, en blip he tuck 'er side er de head. Right dar's what he broke his merlasses jug. His fis' stuck, en he can't pull loose. De tar hilt 'im. But Tar-Baby, she stay still, en Brer Fox, he lay low.

"'Ef you don't lemme loose, I'll knock you agin,' sez Brer Rabbit, sezee, en wid dat he fotch 'er a wipe wid de udder han', en dat stuck. Tar-Baby, she ain't sayin' nothin', en Brer Fox, he lay low.

"'Tu'n me loose, fo' I kick de natal stuffin' outen you,' sez Brer Rabbit, sezee, but de Tar-Baby, she ain't sayin' nothin'. She des hilt on, en den Brer Rabbit lose de use er his feet in de same way. Brer Fox, he lay low. Den Brer Rabbit

squall out dat ef de Tar-Baby don't tu'n 'im loose he butt 'er cranksided. En den he butted, en his head got stuck. Den Brer Fox, he sa'ntered fort', lookin' des ez innercent ez one er yo' mammy's mockin'-birds.

"'Howdy, Brer Rabbit,' sez Brer Fox, sezee. 'You look sorter stuck up dis mawnin',' sezee, en den he rolled on de groun', en laughed en laughed twel he couldn't laugh no mo'. 'I speck you'll take dinner wid me dis time, Brer Rabbit. I done laid in some calamus root, en I ain't gwineter take no skuse,' sez Brer Fox, sezee.''

Here Uncle Remus paused, and drew a two-pound yam out of the ashes.

"Did the fox eat the rabbit?" asked the little boy to whom the story had been told.

"Dat's all de fur de tale goes,'' replied the old man. "He mout, en den again he moutent. Some say Jedge B'ar come long en loosed 'im—some say he didn't. I hear Miss Sally callin'. You better run 'long.''

OLD MR. RABBIT,
HE'S A GOOD FISHERMAN

The humor here is superb, though it is more gentle than in some of the tales, as both Brer Rabbit and Brer Fox enjoy the joke each has played on the other. Take your time in reading or in telling this one.

"Brer Rabbit en Brer Fox wuz like some chilluns w'at I knows un," said Uncle Remus, regarding the little boy, who had come to hear another story, with an affectation of great solemnity. "Bofe un um wuz allers atter wunner nudder, a prankin' en a pester'n 'roun', but Brer Rabbit did had some peace, kaze Brer Fox done got skittish 'bout puttin' de clamps on Brer Rabbit.

"One day, w'en Brer Rabbit, en Brer Fox, en Brer Coon, en Brer B'ar, en a whole lot un um wuz clearin' up a new groun' fer ter plant a roas'n'year patch, de sun 'gun ter git sorter hot, en Brer Rabbit he got tired; but he didn't let on, kaze he 'fear'd de balance un um'd call 'im lazy, en he keep on totin' off trash en pilin' up bresh, twel bimeby he holler out dat he gotter brier in his han', en den he take'n slip off, en hunt fer cool place fer ter res'. Atter w'ile he come 'crosst a well wid a bucket hangin' in it.

" 'Dat look cool,' sez Brer Rabbit, sezee, 'en cool I speck she is. I'll des 'bout git in dar en take a nap,' en wid dat in he jump, he did, en he ain't no sooner fix hisse'f dan de bucket 'gun ter go down."

"Wasn't the Rabbit scared, Uncle Remus?" asked the little boy.

"Honey, dey ain't been no wusser skeer'd beas' sence de worril begin dan dish yer same Brer Rabbit. He fa'rly had a ager. He know whar he cum fum, but he dunner whar he gwine. Dreckly he feel de bucket hit de water, en dar she sot, but Brer Rabbit he keep mighty still, kaze he dunner w'at minnit gwineter be de nex'. He des lay dar en shuck en shiver.

"Old Mr. Rabbit, He's a Good Fisherman." Reprinted from *Uncle Remus* (Trade-Mark Reg. U.S. Pat. Office) *His Songs and Sayings.* Copyright 1908, 1921 by Esther LaRose Harris. By permission of Appleton-Century, affiliate of Meredith Press

"Brer Fox allers got one eye on Brer Rabbit, en w'en he slip off fum de new groun', Brer Fox he sneak atter 'im. He know Brer Rabbit wuz atter some projick er nudder, en he tuck'n crope off, he did, en watch 'im. Brer Fox see Brer Rabbit come to de well en stop, en den he see 'im jump in de bucket, en den, lo en beholes, he see 'im go down outer sight. Brer Fox wuz de mos' 'stonish Fox dat you ever laid eyes on. He sot off dar in de bushes en study en study, but he don't make no head ner tails ter dis kinder bizness. Den he say ter hisse'f, sezee:

" 'Well, ef dis don't bang my times,' sezee, 'den Joe's dead en Sal's a widder. Right down dar in dat well Brer Rabbit keep his money hid, en ef 'tain't dat den he done gone en 'skiver'd a golemine, en ef 'tain't dat, den I'm a gwineter see w'at's in dar,' sezee.

"Brer Fox crope up little nigher, he did, en lissen, but he don't year no fuss, en he keep on gittin' nigher, en yit he don't year nuthin'. Bimeby he git up close en peep down, but he don't see nuthin' en he don't year nuthin'. All dis time Brer Rabbit mighty nigh skeer'd outen his skin, en he fear'd fer ter move kaze de bucket might keel over en spill him out in de water. W'ile he sayin' his pra'rs over like a train er kyars runnin', ole Brer Fox holler out:

" 'Heyo, Brer Rabbit! Who you wizzitin' down dar?' sezee.

" 'Who? Me? Oh, I'm des a fishin', Brer Fox,' sez Brer Rabbit, sezee. 'I des say ter myse'f dat I'd sorter sprize you all wid a mess er fishes fer dinner, en so here I is, en dar's de fishes. I'm a fishin' fer suckers, Brer Fox,' sez Brer Rabbit, sezee.

" 'Is dey many un um down dar, Brer Rabbit?' sez Brer Fox, sezee.

" 'Lots un um, Brer Fox; scoze en scoze un um. De water is natally live wid um. Come down en he'p me haul um in, Brer Fox,' sez Brer Rabbit, sezee.

" 'How I gwineter git down, Brer Rabbit?'

" 'Jump inter de bucket, Brer Fox. Hit'll fetch you down all safe en soun'.'

"Brer Rabbit talk so happy en talk so sweet dat Brer Fox he jump in de bucket, he did, en, ez he went down, co'se his weight pull Brer Rabbit up. W'en dey pass one nudder on de half-way groun', Brer Rabbit he sing out:

" 'Good-by, Brer Fox, take keer yo' cloze,
 Fer dis-is de way de worril goes;
Some goes up en some goes down,
 You'll git ter de bottom all safe en soun'." *

"W'en Brer Rabbit got out, he gallop off en tole de fokes w'at de well b'long ter dat Brer Fox wuz down in dar muddyin' up de drinkin' water, en den he gallop back ter de well, en holler down ter Brer Fox:

" 'Yer come a man wid a great big gun—
 W'en he haul you up, you jump en run.' "

"What then, Uncle Remus?" asked the little boy, as the old man paused.

"In des 'bout half n'our, honey, bofe un um wuz back in de new groun' wukkin des like dey never heer'd er no well, ceppin' dat eve'y now'n den Brer Rabbit'd bust out in er laff, en ole Brer Fox, he'd git a spell er de dry grins."

North American Indian and Eskimo Tales

On the whole, the stories from the Indian peoples of the North American continent have not proved particularly appealing unless edited (and distorted) to a considerable degree. They often seem to us overly long and formless. One folklorist said that they "give one an impression that their narrators were incapable of even preserving an old tale, to say nothing of inventing a new one." The reason may be that too many collectors and interpreters of the tales were unaware (perhaps deliberately uninformed) of the deep significance of the stories and their style. Taken out of context, the Indian tales have not translated successfully into our culture's terms. This gives us a biting example, however, of how necessary it is to understand a people's mind and ways in order to understand its tales, and not the other way round as has often been averred. To appreciate the Indian's myths and legends, we must first know the Indian.

LITTLE BURNT-FACE

(Micmac)

Little Burnt-Face is the scorched face of the desert in the burning summer. The Great Chief, whose symbol is the rainbow, is the rain. Invisible for a long time, he comes at last and restores beauty to the face of the waiting earth child. This is an interesting variant of the "Cinderella" theme.

Once upon a time, in a large Indian village on the border of a lake, there lived an old man who was a widower. He had three daughters. The eldest was jealous, cruel, and ugly; the second was vain; but the youngest of all was very gentle and lovely.

Now, when the father was out hunting in the forest, the eldest daughter used to beat the youngest girl, and burn her face with hot coals; yes, and even scar her pretty body. So the people called her "Little Burnt-Face."

When the father came home from hunting he would ask why she was so scarred, and the eldest would answer quickly: "She is a good-for-nothing! She was forbidden to go near the fire, and she disobeyed and fell in." Then the father would scold Little Burnt-Face and she would creep away crying to bed.

By the lake, at the end of the village, there was a beautiful wigwam. And in that wigwam lived a Great Chief and his sister. The Great Chief was

* As a Northern friend suggests that this story may be somewhat obscure, it may be as well to state that the well is supposed to be supplied with a rope over a wheel, or pulley, with a bucket at each end.

"Little Burnt-Face." From *Red Indian Fairy Book*, by Francis Jenkins Olcott. Copyright, 1917, by Francis Jenkins Olcott and Houghton Mifflin Company. Reprinted by permission of the publisher

invisible; no one had ever seen him but his sister. He brought her many deer and supplied her with good things to eat from the forest and lake, and with the finest blankets and garments. And when visitors came all they ever saw of the Chief were his moccasins; for when he took them off they became visible, and his sister hung them up.

Now, one Spring, his sister made known that her brother, the Great Chief, would marry any girl who could see him.

Then all the girls from the village—except Little Burnt-Face and her sisters—and all the girls for miles around hastened to the wigwam, and walked along the shore of the lake with his sister.

And his sister asked the girls, "Do you see my brother?"

And some of them said, "No"; but most of them answered, "Yes."

Then his sister asked, "Of what is his shoulder-strap made?"

And the girls said, "Of a strip of rawhide."

"And with what does he draw his sled?" asked his sister.

And they replied, "With a green withe."

Then she knew that they had not seen him at all, and said quietly, "Let us go to the wigwam."

So to the wigwam they went, and when they entered, his sister told them not to take the seat next the door, for that was where her brother sat.

Then they helped his sister to cook the supper, for they were very curious to see the Great Chief eat. When all was ready, the food disappeared, and the brother took off his moccasins, and his sister hung them up. But they never saw the Chief, though many of them stayed all night.

One day Little Burnt-Face's two sisters put on their finest blankets and brightest strings of beads, and plaited their hair beautifully, and slipped embroidered moccasins on their feet. Then they started out to see the Great Chief.

As soon as they were gone, Little Burnt-Face made herself a dress of white birch-bark, and a cap and leggings of the same. She threw off her ragged garments, and dressed herself in her birch-bark clothes. She put her father's moccasins on her bare feet; and the moccasins were so big that they came up to her knees. Then she,

too, started out to visit the beautiful wigwam at the end of the village.

Poor Little Burnt-Face! She was a sorry sight! For her hair was singed off, and her little face was as full of burns and scars as a sieve is full of holes; and she shuffled along in her birch-bark clothes and big moccasins. And as she passed through the village the boys and girls hissed, yelled, and hooted.

And when she reached the lake, her sisters saw her coming, and they tried to shame her, and told her to go home. But the Great Chief's sister received her kindly, and bade her stay, for she saw how sweet and gentle Little Burnt-Face really was.

Then as evening was coming on, the Great Chief's sister took all three girls walking beside the lake, and the sky grew dark, and they knew the Great Chief had come.

And his sister asked the two elder girls, "Do you see my brother?"

And they said, "Yes."

"Of what is his shoulder-strap made?" asked his sister.

"Of a strip of rawhide," they replied.

"And with what does he draw his sled?" asked she.

And they said, "With a green withe."

Then his sister turned to Little Burnt-Face and asked, "Do you see him?"

"I do! I do!" said Little Burnt-Face with awe. "And he is wonderful!"

"And of what is his sled-string made?" asked his sister gently.

"It is a beautiful Rainbow!" cried Little Burnt-Face.

"But, my sister," said the other, "of what is his bow-string made?"

"His bow-string," replied Little Burnt-Face, "is the Milky Way!"

Then the Great Chief's sister smiled with delight, and taking Little Burnt-Face by the hand, she said, "You have surely seen him."

She led the little girl to the wigwam, and bathed her with dew until the burns and scars all disappeared from her body and face. Her skin became soft and lovely again. Her hair grew long and dark like the Blackbird's wing. Her eyes were like stars. Then his sister brought from her treasures a wedding-garment, and she dressed

Little Burnt-Face in it. And she was most beautiful to behold.

After all this was done, his sister led the little girl to the seat next the door, saying, "This is the Bride's seat," and made her sit down.

And then the Great Chief, no longer invisible, entered, terrible and beautiful. And when he saw Little Burnt-Face, he smiled and said gently, "So we have found each other!"

And she answered, "Yes."

Then Little Burnt-Face was married to the Great Chief, and the wedding-feast lasted for days, and to it came all the people of the village. As for the two bad sisters, they went back to their wigwam in disgrace, weeping with shame.

AGAYK AND THE
STRANGEST SPEAR

(Eskimo)

Here is a simple tale with a lesson almost as powerful as the spear of words given the young boy Niklik by the old medicine man. It is a good example of the Eskimo respect for intellect.

One terrible day when the earth was frozen the ground shook. The ice pack cracked on the sea. The floes piled up, grinding and crushing as the huge slabs of frozen ice heaved up on the shore.

The ice smashed the igloo houses of a little fishing village on the frozen shore. The frightened people fled. In their hurry they forgot Agayk, their medicine man, who was too old to run. That is, all forgot him except the boy, Niklik.

Niklik stayed with the old man. Somehow they missed death in the crushing ice, but when the earthquake was over, their troubles did not end.

There was nothing to eat. The polar bear, the seal, and even the fish in the sea had run away from the shaking earth even as the people did.

"Make the fish come back," Niklik said to his companion. "I am very hungry."

"That I cannot do," Agayk said sadly.

"But you are a great *shaman*—magician," the boy said. "Don't the people say that a shaman can walk under the water and talk to the fish and whales?"

"The people say that—yes," Agayk replied, his tired old eyes looking sadly at the boy. "But that is a very difficult thing for me to do. I think we must cross the trail over the great ice mountain and fish in the other bay."

"It is so far. Magic is easier."

The magician's dark face, wreathed in the wolverine fur of his parka, looked sad.

"Yes," he said. "Once I was a great medicine man. I was a friend of Raven who flew to the sun and brought back the spark that made the first fire on earth. And I helped the great black bird with his medicine the day a great wave was going to sweep over the land and he turned this wave into *Denali*, the Great One."

He turned and pointed south where the frozen spire of the great mountain the gold seekers

"Agayk and the Strangest Spear." From *Trickster Tales* by I. G. Edmonds. Copyright © 1966 by I. G. Edmonds. Published by J. B. Lippincott Company. Reprinted by permission of J. B. Lippincott Company, the author, and his agents, Scott Meredith Literary Agency, Inc., 580 Fifth Avenue, New York, New York 10036

would one day call Mount McKinley stuck up high above the land.

"The great bird taught me much magic and medicine, but now I am old and weak. Only the young and strong can make great medicine. This is the way of the world. Raven grew old and left us. The same thing is happening to me."

"Then we will starve," the boy said sadly.

"No, there is fish across the mountains. It is a long way, but we can get there before we starve. Then we have but to cut a hole in the ice and drop in our ivory hooks."

"But the people of the bay are our great enemies," Niklik protested. "They will kill us if we try to fish in their water!"

"Not if we fight them with magic," Agayk replied.

"But you said you were too old to make medicine!"

"I am, but you are young," Agayk said. "You must make the magic."

"I don't know how," Niklik protested.

"I hope I have enough strength left to teach you. Are you willing to learn?"

"Oh, yes!" Niklik said. "Will I be able to walk under the sea and talk to fishes?"

"Well—no," Agayk said. "I am not strong enough to teach you that trick."

"Then maybe you can teach me how to make a fog roll in from the Smokey Sea and hide us. Or will I be able to turn into Nanook the bear and frighten our enemies away?"

"I think the best I can do today is teach you to throw a magic spear."

"Oh, that will be wonderful!" Niklik cried.

"The spear will be made of words."

"Words?" Niklik said uneasily. "That is the strangest spear I ever heard of. Will it work?"

"Because things are as they are—yes, I think so," Agayk said. "Often there is more magic in words than in anything in the world. Had I known this when I was a young man, I would have been an even greater magician than I was."

And so the two climbed the icy trail over the mountain range. It took them five days without food and they were very weak from hunger when they came to the other bay.

There were no fishermen on the ice when they arrived, Niklik chopped a hole in the frozen sea, and dropped an ivory hook into the dark water.

It was night for this was winter and the sun would not shine here above the Arctic Circle for two more months. But the stars were bright and the Northern Lights wove great curtains of soft green, pink, and blue colors through the sky.

This made it as bright as twilight on the ice pack. So it was that they were seen from the shore. All the hunters grabbed their spears and ran to hitch their dog-teams. Two got their dogs in the harness first. They rushed across the ice as if in a mad race to see which could reach the two fishermen first.

"Aiee!" the old medicine man said. "That must be Agarook and Attu. They are the mightiest killers of this village. I have heard it said that they are very jealous of each other. Everytime one does a mighty deed, the other will not sleep until he matches it. They are running a race now to see which will have the honor of killing us."

"Maybe *you* had better use the magic spear," Niklik said uneasily. "They look like very fierce men."

"They are," Agayk admitted. "But the spear would not be powerful enough in my old hands. These men know me. They know I am old and my power gone. Only you can save us now, Niklik-my-son."

"Then give me the spear quickly!" the boy cried.

"They are in these words. When the killers come speak as I tell you."

And the old medicine man then told Niklik what to say. The boy listened, first in surprise and then in alarm.

"We are as good as dead," he said, almost weeping.

"Oh, no," Agayk insisted. "This is good medicine and good magic. Speak as I tell you."

The hunters were almost upon them. Niklik could hear the squeak of the ivory runners as the yelping huskies pulled the racing sleds across the ice pack.

As they came up Agayk pushed back the fur-trimmed hood of his parka so the two hunters could see his face.

"You are the old shaman from across the icy mountains," Agarook cried. "Why do you steal our fish?"

"Our fish ran when the earth shook," Agayk said.

"I will kill you for stealing our fish," Agarook said.

"No *I* will kill them," Attu said jealously.

"Neither of you will kill us," Agayk said firmly. "We are protected by magic."

"You are old. Your magic is weak," Agarook said.

"That is true," Agayk agreed. "But the boy is young. He will save us with his magic."

The two jealous hunters looked at him in amazement. "The *boy?* Who ever heard of a *boy* medicine man!"

"You have heard of one for I have just told you," Agayk said firmly. "Why the boy is such a great shaman he has secret medicine which will bring the seal from the sea and the bear in from the floes so they can be easily killed."

"Tell me this secret or I will kill you!" Attu cried, pointing the ivory tip of his spear at Niklik's heart.

The boy trembled. His throat was so dry with fear that he had trouble speaking the words which Agayk had assured him had magic hidden in them.

Finally he managed to say: "I can give the secret to only one of you. The secret can only be given to the mightiest hunter."

"I am the mightiest!" Attu cried.

"No!" Agarook shouted. "I am greatest of all!"

"I'll show you who is the mightiest!" Attu cried, raising his spear so it pointed at his enemy instead of the boy Niklik. "Too long you have insulted me with your wild bragging!"

"You are the braggart!" his jealous rival cried, raising his own spear.

All the hatred and jealousy of their years of rivalry boiled over. They started to fight, lunging at each other with their spears.

"Who will win?" Niklik asked Agayk.

"Neither," the old medicine man said. "Each is just as strong as the other. So both must win and both must lose."

"That can't be," Niklik said.

"We'll see," the old shaman said.

As he spoke, each man drove his spear into the other. Both men fell into the fish hole and disappeared under the sea.

Soon the rest of the hunters came up. Surprised at finding the two great hunters gone, they asked where the two were. Agayk told them

Niklik had killed them with his magic.

"If a boy can kill such mighty men that even we grown men fear to fight, it must be great magic indeed," their leader said.

"That is right," Agayk said. "He has a magic spear of words. He spoke them and they entered Agarook and Attu and in minutes both men were dead. Would you like him to speak the words to you?"

"Oh, no!" the others said.

"Then let us fish in your waters until the fish return to our own bay and I will beg the boy to spare you."

The fearful villagers agreed.

That is how Niklik learned that there is magic in words. With Agayk as his teacher, he grew even wiser in the use of magic talk. So it was that he became a great and famous man among his people, the Eskimo.

HOW THE LITTLE OWL'S NAME WAS CHANGED

(Eskimo)

This is one of the better and more felicitously styled stories from Charles Gillham's collection of Eskimo tales. It is a why *story which echoes one of mankind's oldest reasons for rejoicing— the return of spring. Even in the bleak far north, as in the warm climes of ancient Greece, the owl is a symbol of life and renewal.*

Every spring in Alaska a little owl would come north with the other birds. It was a tiny owl and flew noiselessly over the tundra on its soft, downy wings. At first the Eskimos called him Anipausigak, which meant "the little owl." Later, after the Eskimos knew more about the bird, they called him Kerayule, which means in their language "the owl that makes no noise when he flies."

In the very early days, before the white men came to Alaska, the Eskimos had no matches and it was very difficult for them to have a fire. Also there was very little wood in the Eskimo country.

"How the Little Owl's Name Was Changed." Reprinted with permission of The Macmillan Company from *Beyond the Clapping Mountains* by Charles E. Gillham. Copyright 1943 by The Macmillan Company

One spring there was one family living all by themselves that had a bit of fire, but there was no place where they could get any if this went out. In the middle of the igloo was a pit, or hole, in the floor. Here a tiny little fire was kept burning at all times. Always someone watched it and tended it. The smoke went curling out of the window in the top of the igloo.

In this igloo were a little boy and a little girl with their mother and father. All times of the day and night someone had to stay in the house and watch the tiny fire. One day when the little girl was all alone—her folks were out hunting seals—some bad people came to the igloo.

"Oh, so you are all alone, little girl," one of them said. "I suppose you are watching the fire so that it does not go out?"

"Yes," said the little girl. "It would be very bad if we lost our fire. We would be very cold and would have nothing to cook by. I must watch it carefully so that when my parents come home there will be a warm house here to greet them."

The bad man laughed. "You will not have to watch your fire any more, little girl, for we have no fire in our igloo and we are going to take yours with us."

How frightened the little girl was and how badly she felt to think she was going to lose the fire! She thought quickly. "Can't I make you some fire on another stick, Mr. Man?" she asked. "Then you can take it with you and I will still have some left for my mother and father and my little brother when they come home from hunting seals."

"I haven't time to wait for you to make new fire," the bad man said, "and, besides, I do not care if you are cold and hungry." With that he grabbed the fire and went away with it, leaving the poor little girl crying and all her fire gone.

When the mother and father and little brother came home they found the igloo cold, and the little girl told them what had happened. Hastily the father took his bow and arrow and set out to the igloo of the bad men to get his fire. When he got there, however, he found that they had two men who guarded the fire day and night. They were big men and had big spears, and bows and arrows too. So the poor man could not get his fire away from them. He begged them to let him

have just a little of it to carry back to his wife and children, but they only laughed at him.

So for several days the good Eskimos had a terrible time. It was very cold and they could not make a fire with anything. At last, one night, the father Eskimo thought of a plan. He called for the little owl, Kerayule, who makes no noise when he flies.

"Please, little owl, will you help us?" the Eskimo man asked him. "You see we have no fire, and we are cold. Please will you get our fire back for us from the bad men who took it away?"

"How can I do that?" asked the little owl. "I would like to help you, but they have spears and bows and arrows. Besides, they are much stronger than I am. Just how do you think I could get the fire?"

"You make no noise when you fly," the Eskimo man replied. "They will not hear you coming in the night. Also you can see in the darkness, and you can go straight to their igloo. The window in the top of it will be open, and you can look in and see how you can get the fire for us."

"I never thought of that," said the little owl. "I think, maybe, I can get the fire for you. I *can* see in the darkness and I make no noise at all when I fly."

So the little owl set off through the dark night to the igloo where the bad men lived.

Carefully the owl flew over the igloo and he did not make a sound. He looked into the window in the top where the smoke came out. He saw the fire—just one small stick burning in the fire pit. Also he saw one of the bad men sitting by it. He seemed to be asleep. The little owl hovered lower and alighted without a sound on the edge of the window. Silently, like a great soft feather, the little owl fluttered down into the igloo.

Right by the fire pit, the little owl landed on the floor and the man did not see him. Maybe he was asleep, but the owl was not sure. Hopping softly across to the stick of fire, the little owl took the unburned end in his mouth and, with a great flutter, flew straight up through the open window in the top of the igloo. As he did, the man awakened. He grabbed his bow and arrow to shoot the little owl, but was too late. Out into the night sailed the little owl, through the black darkness. He flew straight to the igloo of the good Eskimos.

The children were watching for the little owl, and soon they saw the fire come flying through the black sky.

"Look!" shouted the little girl. "See the *sparkling fire* coming!"

And to this day the Eskimos at Hooper Bay call the little owl "sparkling fire owl," or Kennreirk in their language. Sometimes in the springtime, when the sparkling fire owl comes to Hooper Bay and hovers around the people, they will listen closely to see if they can hear him make any noise. Sometimes—very rarely—he makes a little snapping with his beak, or a flutter with his wings. If the people can hear him make any noise they are very glad, for that is the best of good omens. They say the little sparkling fire owl is sending them good luck. If they go hunting they are sure to get a seal, or an eider duck, or a fat fish.

The Eskimo people love the little sparkling fire owl because he brings them good luck and, too, when they see him they know the springtime has come to stay.

The West Indies

In the folklore of the West Indies we find a remarkable fusion of the Old and New Worlds. Anansi stories, direct from Africa, have over the centuries become intermingled with themes from European folk tales. The stories of Uncle Bouqui and Ti Malice, saucy with French overtones, show the European influence, even while containing elements of the rabbit tales from Africa. And some of the tales of Puerto Rico and Cuba reflect the early Spanish dominance in the Caribbean.

The study of West Indian folklore seems rather neglected, but the nuggets of West Indian tales found in collections for children indicate a rich mine to be worked. From the tales of Anansi, of Uncle Bouqui, of the frog in Puerto Rico, and of Juan Bobo as he appears here and there, it would seem that some of the characteristics of the people who inhabit these islands are an irrepressible wit, a delight in harmless trickery, and a love of laughter.

BANDALEE

(Jamaican)

From Aesop to Anansi—or, from Asia to Europe to Africa to the West Indies! Here is the familiar tale of the race between the hare and the

tortoise now firmly a part of Anansi folklore. This story illustrates again that basic themes are *found throughout world folklore, giving us historical evidence that tales have traveled from one continent to the other, even though we cannot always say when or why or how. Older children will enjoy De la Mare's "The Hare and the Hedgehog."*

Whispers went through the forest.

Whenever two of the forest creatures met they put their heads together and whispered. Even those that usually kept far apart could be seen whispering in each other's ears—even Tiger and Goat, Mongoose and Chicken, Dog and Cat were busy whispering to each other.

It was all about Land Turtle. They whispered to each other that Land Turtle had become a very rich man.

Anansi heard the whispers. He believed that they were true, and he made up his mind that he would get some of Land Turtle's money. His eyes shone when he heard of all the money that Land Turtle had. Surely it would not be hard to trick Land Turtle, who looked so slow and stupid.

"I never knew that Land Turtle was so rich," said Anansi to himself. "I thought he was a poor man. He hasn't any sense either, so he has no right to be rich. I've never seen anyone move as slowly as Land Turtle, except Brother Worm. It won't be hard to take some of his money from him."

Anansi crawled under his bed and pulled out from the darkest corner an old calabash that he used to hide his savings. Slowly he counted it, and the counting did not take long because there was so little money. "I must get to work," said Anansi, and he set off for the bank. He lodged his money in the bank and then went to Land Turtle's house.

Now it happened that Land Turtle was a much wiser creature than he seemed. He moved slowly, but he could think fast. When he saw Anansi coming he guessed that there was some reason for the visit, and so he told his wife and children to hide themselves while he talked with Anansi.

"Good morning, Brother Land Turtle," said Mr. Anansi, who was a little breathless because he had walked so fast. "It's a long time since we two met."

Land Turtle bowed but said nothing.

"It's a long time since I paid you a friendly visit," said Anansi.

Land Turtle bowed again, but said nothing.

"Yes, a long time," said Anansi. "To tell you the truth, you would not have seen me today at all; but I went for a long walk, and, as I was tired, I turned in here on my way home to rest a while. Yes, I went to the bank to put in some money because if we do not save we will never have anything."

"That is true," said Land Turtle, who was still wondering why Anansi had come.

"You know, Land Turtle," said Anansi, "perhaps we could make a bargain. You have money in the bank. I have money in the bank. I want more, and you want more. Now suppose we agree to run a race to the bank. The one that wins will get all the money belonging to the two of us."

Land Turtle was silent for a few minutes. He saw through Anansi's scheme.

"That's not fair, Anansi," he said. "Look how fast you walk and how slow I am. You'd get to the bank long before me. But I'll agree to race you if you promise you will run as a spider, and not change yourself into a man." It was well known that Anansi could change himself whenever he wished.

"I'll agree to run the race as a spider," Anansi said.

He knew that even in his spider form, running along his rope, he could run faster than Land Turtle. What a fool Land Turtle was, thought Anansi, to dream of racing me.

"Well, Brother Anansi," said Land Turtle, "since we have made the bargain, the next thing is to decide where we shall start from. As you know, there are two roads that lead to the bank."

"Pshaw," said Anansi, "a road is a road. One is just as long as the other. We can talk about that tomorrow. Let's go to the bank and tell the banker that the one of us that gets there first tomorrow is to have the money, yours and mine put together."

So they went to the bank and explained it all to the banker, and then they went home to get a good night's sleep. Land Turtle called his wife and his sons and his daughters, and told them about the race. "Anansi is very cunning," he said, "but this time Land Turtle is going to be cunning, too. But I will need your help." And then he told them what they must do.

Now Land Turtle knew that Anansi would suggest that each should go by a different road. One road followed the river, and another ran up on the bank a little way. Every little while, there was a crossing that joined the two. Early in the morning of the day of the race, Mr. Land Turtle and his children walked along the river road; and wherever there was a crossing, one of the children sat down to wait. For old Brother Land Turtle and his children looked so much alike that nobody could tell one from another. Mr. Land Turtle's oldest son went to meet Anansi at the starting place, and Mr. Land Turtle himself took up his station at the last crossroads. As soon as he was sure that the race had begun, he planned to run to the bank, get all the money, and go back home through the woods.

All the animals had come out to see the race. Some stood at the starting place, some waited outside the bank. Soon Anansi came along, all smiles and confidence. He could almost feel the weight of Land Turtle's money in his pocket.

Stupid old Land Turtle. Look at him, thought Anansi, as he looked at what he thought was Mr. Land Turtle, but what was in fact Mr. Land Turtle's oldest son.

Just as Land Turtle had thought, Anansi suggested that they run by different roads and call out to each other from time to time. Land Turtle's son nodded his head, to show that he agreed; and Anansi called out—one, two, three—and away they went. Soon Anansi was well ahead of Land Turtle, yet when he came to the first crossing and called out, "You Turtle, you Turtle," he heard a voice reply: "Anansi oh, Anansi oh, bandalee, bandalee."

"Well," thought Anansi, "Land Turtle isn't far behind." And he ran faster. At the next crossing he called out again, "You Turtle, you Turtle," and one of Land Turtle's children answered: "Anansi oh, Anansi oh, bandalee, bandalee."

"I never thought Land Turtle could run so fast," said Anansi to himself. "I must run faster if I'm to get the gold." And away he went.

Once again at the third crossing Anansi called out, "You Turtle, you Turtle!" And once again one of Land Turtle's children called out, "Anansi oh, Anansi oh, bandalee, bandalee."

"Faster still, faster still," thought Anansi to himself. He began to feel anxious. By the time he got to the last crossing he hardly had enough breath to call out, "You Turtle, you Turtle."

This time no answer came.

"At last," said Anansi to himself, "at last I am well ahead. Now for the money at the bank." But at that very moment Land Turtle was leaving the bank with his own money and with the few pence that belonged to Anansi.

Anansi was sure that he had left Land Turtle far behind, so he slowed down and walked into the bank as if he owned it. He asked for his money and Land Turtle's, but the banker told him that he had already given the money to Land Turtle.

"What," panted Anansi, "do you mean that Land Turtle got here first?"

"Yes," said the banker. "Land Turtle came in fifteen minutes ago."

"Are you sure that it was Land Turtle?" asked Anansi.

"Quite sure," said the banker. "I know Land Turtle well, and I gave him the money."

Out rushed Anansi as fast as his legs could carry him. In the distance he could see Land Turtle toiling along.

"To think that slow coach beat me in a race," cried Anansi. "Stop, Turtle, stop."

Turtle did not stop, but Anansi soon caught up with him.

"So you won the race," said Anansi. "Well, well, who could have thought it. Let us walk home together."

Poor Land Turtle was very frightened. However, Anansi was so friendly that soon Land Turtle was calm again. Quietly they walked along until they came to a pond. Anansi saw his chance.

"Let's both dive in," he said, "and see who can stay under the water longest."

Land Turtle was pleased to see how well Anansi had taken his defeat, and he readily agreed. Besides that, he was proud of his diving. This was the one thing in which he felt certain that he could beat Anansi every time. He put down his bag of gold at the edge of the pond, and both Anansi and Turtle dived at the same time.

Land Turtle stayed under for as long as he possibly could. Surely Anansi would lose for the second time in one day. Then he came up but, alas, both Anansi and the money had gone.

UNCLE BOUQUI
AND GODFATHER MALICE

(Haitian)

Again we find that delightful blending of European and African tales. This is nothing more nor less than a variant of the Grimms' "Cat and Mouse Keep House." Compare the two and see how well each pictures the people and place from which it came. Uncle Bouqui's fate is considerably better than that of the mouse in the Grimms' tale.

One time Bouqui and Malice were farming together in the Red Mountains. Every day they went out to their fields with their hoes and machetes, and they worked until the middle of the afternoon when the sun was broiling hot.

Uncle Guinéda, who lived in the village, had chopped down a tree full of honey, and he gave Bouqui a big gourd full of it because Bouqui was godfather to Guinéda's youngest child. Bouqui was very proud and jealous of that gourd of honey, and he hung it up in the rafters of his house, intending to save it for a big holiday, such as Christmas or Dessaline's Day.

Now Ti Malice liked honey just about better than anything. His mouth watered at the sight of that gourd hanging there in the rafters. Four or five times he politely suggested that they sit down and have a glass of honey, but Bouqui shook his head and made an ugly face.

"I'm saving that honey for an occasion," Bouqui said.

"When two good friends get together that *is* an occasion," Malice said.

"Do you think I'm a rich man?" Bouqui said. "I can't eat honey every day."

One hot morning they were out in the field cultivating corn. The earth was dry, and the sun

"Uncle Bouqui and Godfather Malice." From *Uncle Bouqui of Haiti* by Harold Courlander. Copyright 1942 by Harold Courlander and reprinted with his permission

was hot, and Malice became thirstier and thirstier. He began to think of that cool gourd of honey hanging in the rafters of Bouqui's house. Two or three times he stood very still and closed his eyes, just so he could imagine the honey.

Finally he dropped his hoe on the ground.

"Wah!" he said. "Someone is calling me."

"I didn't hear anything but a lamb baaing," Bouqui said, "and it didn't sound like 'Malice.'"

"Wah! There it is again," Malice said. "I'll have to go to see who it is."

He picked up his hat and marched over the hill, and when he was out of Bouqui's sight he turned and headed for Bouqui's house. He went inside and climbed up into the rafters and took down the honey gourd. He poured some honey in a glass, mixed it with water, and drank it. Then he mixed some more and drank it. He kept mixing and drinking until he was so full he couldn't swallow another drop. Then he hung the gourd back in the rafters and went back to the field.

Bouqui was working away with his hoe, and he was mighty hot. He pushed out his lips and made an ugly face.

"You certainly were gone long enough! What happened to you?"

"Wah, Bouqui! Everyone wants me to be godfather to their children. Nobody leaves me alone. I had to go to a baptism."

"Woy, that's different!" Bouqui said, breaking into a smile. "Is it a boy or girl?"

"A girl, and a very nice one indeed," Malice said, licking the honey off his chin.

"Wonderful!" Bouqui said, beaming and resting his arms on the hoe handle. "I like babies. What's her name?"

"Her name?" Malice said. "Oh, yes. Well, I named her *Début*." (Début means "beginning" in Creole.)

"*Début!*" Bouqui gasped. "Woy, what an elegant name! How did you ever think of it?"

"It just came to me," Ti Malice said modestly. And he picked up his hoe and went back to work.

The next day they were weeding the garden with their machetes, and the sun got hotter and hotter, and Malice got thirstier and thirstier. He tried to keep his mind on his work, but all he could think of was that honey gourd hanging in

Uncle Bouqui's rafters. Suddenly he stood up straight and cocked his ear and said:

"Wah, Bouqui, did someone call me?"

"I don't think so," Bouqui answered. "I heard a calf bawling on the next hill, but I don't think he mentioned your name."

"There!" Malice said. "There it is again! I'll have to go see who wants me." He stuck his machete into his belt and marched over the hill.

Bouqui shook his head and mumbled to himself. He rapped his right ear with his knuckles, and then he took hold of his left ear and tweaked it.

"My ears are asleep," he said. "I didn't hear a thing!"

As soon as he was out of sight, Malice turned and ran for Bouqui's house. He climbed up into the rafters and brought down the honey gourd and fixed himself a big drink. He fixed another, and another. He drank and drank and drank until he felt ready to burst. Then he hung the gourd in the rafters again and went down to the field where Bouqui was chopping away in the hot sun.

"Well, what happened?" Bouqui asked impatiently. "You were gone a tremendously long time!"

"Uncle Bouqui, my friends just won't leave me alone. They're always bothering me. It's always Malice-this and Malice-that. They needed me to come and baptise another baby."

"That's a different matter," Bouqui said with a grin. "Boy or girl?"

"A boy this time," Malice said, licking honey off his fingers.

"What's his name?" Bouqui said. "I certainly like babies."

"His name? Oh, well, I called this one *Dèmi*," Malice said. (Dèmi means "halfway" in Creole.)

"*Dèmi!* What a fine name! You certainly have a wonderful imagination. *Dèmi!* It's mighty sweet."

"It certainly is," Malice answered. "There's probably just one more as sweet as that one." And they picked up their machetes and went back to work.

The next day they were out cultivating again. The sun got hotter and hotter. Malice started to sing to keep his mind off the honey, but it was no use. He threw his hoe down on the ground.

"Wah!" he said. "What an imposition!"

"What's the matter?"

"Didn't you hear?" Malice said.

"No, only some dogs barking."

"Someone's calling me again. What do you think they want?"

"People certainly are having babies!" Bouqui said. "Don't be gone long!" He twisted and jerked his ears. "They're half dead," he muttered. "I didn't hear anything but the dogs."

Malice headed over the hill, and then he scrambled for Uncle Bouqui's house. He took down the honey gourd and drank and drank. He drank until the gourd was empty. He stuck his tongue inside and licked it clean as far as he could reach. When he was through, the gourd was dry as an old cornstalk. He hung it up in the rafters and went back to where Uncle Bouqui was sweating and making dark faces in the hot sun.

"Well," Bouqui said, "what was it?"

"Another baby," Ti Malice said. "A girl. I think it's the last one."

"Wonderful!" Bouqui said. "What did you name it?"

"Name it? Oh. Well, I named this one *Sêche*," Malice said. (Sêche means "dry" in Creole.)

"*Sêche!* What an unusual name!" Bouqui said. "Woy, you are just about the best baby-namer in Haiti."

When they went home after work that night Bouqui said, "You know, I think we should celebrate all those babies tonight. Why should I save the honey until Christmas? If we don't drink it the flies will."

He reached up in the rafters and took down the gourd. He stood there a long time looking into it. Then he carried it outside and looked again. He closed his eyes for a minute, then opened them. He turned the gourd upside-down, but nothing happened. He licked the edges, but they didn't even taste like honey. He smelled the gourd, but there wasn't even an odor left.

"Oh-oh!" he said at last. "It's gone!"

He turned around, but somehow Malice seemed to have disappeared too. Uncle Bouqui sat down to think. He thought, thought, thought. He mumbled and argued with himself. He scratched his head first, and then he scratched his chin. He just couldn't make any

and—*pimme!* He clamped his teeth down hard on Malice's big toe. Malice let out a wild yowl and sprang into the air, but Bouqui hung on.

"Ouch!" Malice yelled. "Stop it, you're killing me!"

Bouqui let go with his teeth, and Malice's yelling died down to a moan.

"Uncle Bouqui!" he whimpered. "Uncle Bouqui! What do you call that, anyway?"

"I call that one *Début!*" Bouqui shouted. And he lunged forward, *pamme!* He caught Malice's other big toe right between his teeth.

Malice leaped and jerked and howled, but Bouqui held on. Malice hopped and crawled and jumped, but Uncle Bouqui wouldn't let go.

"Wah!" Malice screamed. "I'm hurt for life!"

Bouqui opened his mouth and made a ferocious face at Malice.

"Uncle Bouqui, Uncle Bouqui!" Malice groaned. "What do you call this business, anyway?"

"I call this one *Dèmi!*" Bouqui shouted. And he lunged forward to get another one of Malice's toes with his teeth.

But Ti Malice came to life. He sprang across the room as though he were running on hot coals. In no time at all he was outside, racing off into the hills.

"Wah!" he howled as he went through the gate. "Wah! There's one thing you'll never do, Bouqui! You'll never be godfather to *Sêche!* Not unless you catch me first!" And he disappeared into the darkness without another word.

Bouqui stood listening until the sound of Malice's feet slapping against the trail had died away. He got to thinking.

"*Sêche,*" he said. "It's a mighty unusual name, at that."

sense out of it. Suddenly he began to tingle. For a moment he sat very still, tingling from head to toe. Then he leaped into the air and howled.

"Wah! The first one was named *Début!* And the second was named *Dèmi!* And the third was named *Sêche!* Beginning, Halfway, and Dry! Wah!" he wailed. "And all the time I was out there working! Beginning, Halfway, and Dry— *of my honey!*"

That night Uncle Bouqui waited until Ti Malice was asleep on his mat, and then he crawled into the house quietly on his hands and knees. "Beginning, Halfway, Dry," he kept saying over and over to himself. When he got to Malice's mat, Bouqui opened his mouth wide

Central and South America

On the whole, the Central and South American folk tales for children
published in this country are not very satisfying (Charles Finger's Tales from
Silver Lands *still remains one of the best collections) and it is difficult to*
find first-rate tales that have drama, local color, and appeal for children. One tale
from Bolivia and another from Costa Rica hardly do justice to the wealth
of material in the folklore archives of some Central and South American
countries. However, much of the best song and story material has not
been translated into English.
As is typical of the folk literature of all the Americas, from northern Canada
to southern Chile, that of Central and South America is a mixture
of native Indian, African, European, and some Asiatic traditions. Out of the
material available to us we can give children a feeling for certain
aspects of these cultures and traditions, but none of it reflects the people as
they are now. Our neighbors to the south have much to tell us in their
tales and their music, much that is wise and pleasing. We are just beginning
to lend them an ear.

THE KING OF THE MOUNTAINS

(*Bolivian*)

This traditional Indian story was told to Mr.
Jagendorf by a Bolivian who was visiting in New
York.

The sun, all gold in the sky, and the condor,[1]
the great and strong bird of the high mountains,
are worshiped and loved in many parts of An-
dean South America. Beautiful temples were
built to the sun, and large monuments were
erected with the condor as the symbol of the
land.

There are many stories about both the bird
and the sun everywhere in that vast land, and
here is one from Bolivia.

This happened long, long ago, soon after the
earth first came into being. The birds in Bolivia
wanted to have a king. But who would be king?

"The King of the Mountains." Reprinted by permission
of the publisher, The Vanguard Press, from *King of the
Mountains: A Treasury of Latin American Folk Stories*
by M. A. Jagendorf and R. S. Boggs. Copyright ©, 1960,
by M. A. Jagendorf and R. S Boggs

[1] The condor is one of the largest birds in existence.
With its wings open in flight, it measures from nine to
ten feet. It is also one of the most graceful birds when
flying and can go for nearly half an hour without moving
its wings—just sailing beautifully through the air. The
bird with jet-black feathers, save for a white frill around
the base of the neck, inhabits the high mountains of the
Andes.

There was so much chattering and arguing
among them about this that the leaves got tired
of listening. There was screaming and whistling
and singing without end. Every bird wanted to
be king.

Finally one wise old bird said, "Let Pachacámac, the great king of the earth, decide; or, better yet, let the one who comes nearest the sun,
where Pachacámac has his golden palace, be king
of the birds."

This made sense to all the birds, and they
agreed, for no one was wiser than Pachacámac.
The birds screamed their desire to Pachacámac,
and the king of the earth spoke: "Yes, let the
bird who flies highest and who comes nearest the
sun and my palace be king. The bird who does
this will have to be very brave."

Then, at a given signal, all the birds rose into
the sky. They were like a great cloud of many
colors, and there were so many of them that the
sun could not be seen.

Up and up they went, streaking and circling
about. Soon some dropped down. Others rose
higher and higher. Then more dropped down.

The higher they went, the fewer there were.
These few circled still higher. And still more
dropped down until there were only three left in
the great blue heaven with the gleaming sun.
They were the eagle, the hawk, and the condor.
Just these three, circling slowly, rising and

rising, getting nearer and nearer to the sun.

Up they went, while all the birds below watched in silence. All the animals were watching, too, for it was a sight worth seeing, those three—the fearless eagle, the keen hawk, and the majestic condor—winging their way silently upward.

Soon those watching below saw one of the three becoming larger and larger, and the other two becoming smaller and smaller. It was the hawk who was coming down, while the eagle and condor kept going up.

"I am beaten by those who are stronger and more fearless than I. The heat was too strong for me," said the hawk.

The birds did not hear. They were watching the two left circling and soaring, soaring and circling, rising higher and higher. The birds and the animals on earth watched silently. Which one would win?

Sometimes the eagle looked at the condor; sometimes the condor looked at the eagle. The eagle looked more often. He was feeling hotter and hotter. His skin was burning dry, his eyes were burning hot. He had to shut them; he could no longer stand the golden fire of the sun, and he began to drop. The condor saw him falling. All the birds and the animals saw him coming down. A great stream of pride surged through the condor's body, and he did not feel the heat at all. He had won!

"I must get nearer the sun!" he cried. So he kept circling, circling, closer and closer to the great, shining sun. The feathers on his head were burned. He kept rising, rising, slowly. The feathers on his neck were burned. It was hard for him to breathe the fiery air, but he kept on rising! His eyes became red as fire! Still, he kept them open and kept on rising.

"I must rise to the sun! It matters not what pain I may feel."

Then, suddenly, there was a cool, sweet wind coming from the yellow, gleaming brightness. There was the Golden City of the Sun. And there, in the center, was Pachacámac, the father of all, sitting on his golden throne.

"Hail, great Malleu, Condor, bird of the sun! Only you had the courage to come so high."

The condor was speechless before all that glory.

"No bird has ever come so close to my City of the Sun. For this you deserve to be king of the birds. You are the king, strong and fearless. Only the strong and fearless can stand the light of the sun that wounds the sight and burns the eyes. You are like me, so I shall take your form when I visit the earth or fly through the air. I am the great king of all that is on the earth, and you will be the great king of all the flying birds. My home is the City of the Sun. Yours will be the highest mountains that are nearest to the sun. Your palace of snow and ice will gleam like my palace of gold. And when you leave the earth, you will come here to me."

Since that time the people of Bolivia know, just as the birds know, that the condor is not only king of all the birds, but that he is sometimes even Pachacámac, king of the earth, flying in the form of the condor; and when they see Malleu, the condor, they look upon him with love, respect, and worship.

To this day wonderful monuments are still built in Bolivia with the condor on top, wings spread wide, as if it were flying to the sun.

THE WITCHES' RIDE

(Costa Rican)

Here is as lively a Halloween story as anyone could ask for. It has a familiar theme—the simpleton who comes out on top—and it is an example of a European tale in Latin America, so untouched by the native culture that it is hardly even Costa Rican in feeling. The Irish "The Voyage of the Wee Red Cap" offers an interesting parallel to this story.

Once, in the days of long ago, there lived in Costa Rica a widow who had an only son. Now this son was considered a *bobo,* or simpleton, because he was lazy and, more than that, because in one way or another he muddled everything he set out to do.

One day the bobo's mother was preparing to cook the *chayote* hash and rice which were to be their supper. She went to the shed for wood to burn in the stove, but the shed was empty. So she told the bobo to go to the forest yonder and bring her some sticks for the fire.

Since it was already late afternoon and a chill wind was blowing, the bobo wrapped himself up in a coarse old blanket, wearing it like a cape. Then he set off. He soon entered the forest, but there were no broken branches at hand and since he had no machete, or long, sharp knife, with him to cut branches from the trees, he went on farther and farther, from one thicket to another. Before long he was deep in the forest.

Soon it grew dark and he lost the path. As he groped his way through the dense underbrush and hanging vines, not knowing which way to turn, he suddenly came upon a hut. He was glad to find a shelter and knocked a good round knock. No one answered. So he opened the door and went in. Finding the hut deserted, he proceeded to make himself at home. In a corner behind a pile of straw he found an old mat woven of reeds, and there he snuggled down. Soon, in good comfort, he was fast asleep.

He slept and slept till at the hour of midnight

"The Witches' Ride." From *The Witches' Ride and Other Tales from Costa Rica,* by Lupe de Osma. Reprinted by permission of William Morrow and Company, Inc. Copyright © 1957 by Lupe de Osma

he was awakened with a start by the sound of merry voices. He raised his head a wee bit and looked around with one eye.

Through the open window of the hut the moonlight shone on the clay floor, turning it white. There the bobo saw twelve black shadows—the shadows of twelve old witches. They were jesting and laughing and having altogether a merry time as each witch took a sip from a big drinking gourd, then smacked her lips and passed it on.

Meantime, the bobo lay quiet and still behind the pile of straw, scarcely daring to draw his breath lest the witches find him and change him into some bird or beast.

And the riot and revelry went on until the gourd ran dry. Then without any warning at all, a witch cried out in a croaking voice, "Time to be off!" At the same moment she picked up a broom from a pile on the floor, placed herself nimbly upon it, and said these magic words:

> "Fly me faster than a fairy,
> Without God—without Saint Mary!"

Away out of the window she flew and soared gracefully up into the air. The others followed quickly—each pouncing upon a broomstick from the pile, then repeating the magic words.

High in the night sky they flew, one behind the other, like a long black waving ribbon. They circled once and again around the big yellow moon and then vanished swiftly from sight beyond the tall mountain peaks.

"A week of Sundays!" cried the bobo in surprise. "Wasn't that neatly done! I wouldn't mind doing it myself! And why not?"

Well, as soon as the last witch had disappeared, up sprang the bobo from the reed mat and straightway went to the corner where the pile of brooms had been. He hoped that the witches might have left one behind. And they had! He snatched it up, and fastening the blanket around his shoulders good and tight, he placed himself upon the stick. Then he shouted with all his might:

> "Fly me faster than a fairy,
> Without God—without Saint Mary!"

These words were scarcely out of his mouth when up he shot into the air like a whizzing arrow, and out of the window he flew. Faster and faster he soared, low over the treetops and high toward the moon, like a bird. And he flew and flew and flew, and the higher he went, the more he liked it—so much that every once in a while he would say the magic words again to the broom.

But, alas, he was not called a bobo for nothing. In his great glee he muddled the words, and said to the broomstick:

"Fly me faster than a fairy,
  Fly with God and good Saint Mary!"

No sooner were these words out of his mouth than the broom began to fall. Fast—and faster than fast—it dropped. The poor bobo had no time to think of the right magic words as he tumbled and somersaulted through the air.

Now then, it so happened that some robbers were hiding at the edge of the forest that night. Their booty was spread out on a large cloth, and they were seated around it, counting out each one's share of the treasure by the weak light of their lantern.

"Ho! The Devil himself must have been with us today," cried one of the robbers in delight.

"Hope he doesn't take a fancy to drop in for his share!"

And at this very moment the bobo, who was coming down full tilt, saw the group and shouted, "Out of the way! Look out there, all of you! Make way for this poor devil!"

The robbers looked up, each and all of them afraid of the strange sight the bobo made. For his blanket flapped and danced behind him like two big black wings as he plunged down upon them. They sprang up in great fear, thinking they had the Devil on their backs.

"The Devil! The Devil is loose! Here he comes!" they cried in terror. "Run! Let us fly! Away . . . away!" They took to their heels as if they were running a race. And they left their booty behind.

The bobo came down in one enormous swoop upon the pile of riches—*plump!* There he sat, gazing rapturously at the heap of gold and silver coins. "Bless my soul! Bless my little soul!" he cried.

Straightway he jumped up and piled the coins together again in the center of the large cloth. Then he made a bundle out of it, slung it over his shoulder, and hobbled home very happy, humming a merry tune.

And as for the robbers, they were never seen again.

Of all forms of fiction, the fable is the most pedantic and the least appealing to children. It is a lesson in behavior, a kind of sugar-coated moral pill, large doses of which are hard to take. Yet presented occasionally, among other and livelier kinds of stories, fables are not unpalatable. They offer a shrewd appraisal of motives and behavior. Their canny and satiric comments on folly are amusing, and wise behavior is picturesquely presented. Such fables as "The Dog in the Manger," "The Wolf in Sheep's Clothing," "The Fox and the Crow," and "The Hare and the Tortoise" are never forgotten. These and many others have come to occupy a permanent place in our thinking and our speech. Children should know the

THE FABLES

fables because they contain the distilled wisdom of the ages in memorable form.

Fables might be defined as brief narratives which attempt to make abstract ideas of good or bad, wise or foolish behavior, concrete and sufficiently striking to be understood and remembered. But because they are concerned with abstract ideas they are not readily understood by most children until the episodes and their significance have been talked over. Sometimes the characters are men, sometimes the elements, but chiefly, they are animals. Whatever they are, the characters of a fable are as impersonal as an algebraic equation. It is never Peter Rabbit with his little brothers and sisters, Flopsy, Mopsy, and Cottontail. It is merely RABBIT, and you never care whether RABBIT has a family or is an orphan. He is simply RABBIT. This abstract, impersonal quality of the fable does not appeal to small children, and the obvious intention of teaching a moral lesson grows tiresome if the fables are used too often or with too heavy a hand.

Since Caxton first published Aesop's fables in English, there have been many editions for children and young people. As one looks through them, it becomes apparent that each editor or compiler of fables had his own notion of what the *moral* for each fable was. Sometimes it was religious, sometimes merely ethical, sometimes highly political. It would seem that fables allow for a wide latitude of interpretation and application. For this reason, then, if for no other, it would be wise not to insist that the children glean one interpretation only from any given fable.

Today there are many editions of Aesop's fables, several of them illustrated by distinguished artists. We also have numerous editions of the fables of La Fontaine, and at least one edition from the Russian fables of Krylov. (See the Bibliography.) Joseph Jacobs' *The Fables of Aesop* has long been a favorite edition and was once practically a household item. His versions are still fun to read. They are spare in treatment and faithful to the Aesopic text of earlier translators from the Latin and Greek manuscripts. James Reeves' *Fables from Aesop* with illustrations in color, sets a much livelier note by having the animals speaking directly. Possibly one of the best renderings of Aesop, however, especially for contemporary children, is to be found in Louis Untermeyer's *Aesop's Fables,* handsomely illustrated by the Provensens. Although only forty fables are included, they are full of verve and humor and present Aesop in a most refreshing manner.

Aesop's Fables

"The Lion and the Mouse" and "The Town Mouse and the Country Mouse" are well liked by the five- and six-year-olds because they are simple little stories and the morals are not too obtrusive. The other fables might well appear in almost any order you like, three or four a year. Perhaps the morals of "The Fox and the Grapes," "The Wolf in Sheep's Clothing," "The Milkmaid and Her Pail," and "The Dog in the Manger" are a little too subtle for young children and are better reserved for the oldest children. Be sure to bring from the library some of the illustrated editions of the fables. In some instances, the fables will lead directly into certain folk tales which are either similar in their point or are expansions of them (such as "Henny-Penny" and "Bandalee"). Many of the fables will also serve to give the children a point of departure for writing and staging brief plays.

THE HARE
WITH MANY FRIENDS

A hare was very popular with the other beasts who all claimed to be her friends. But one day she heard the hounds approaching and hoped to escape them by the aid of her many friends. So she went to the horse, and asked him to carry her away from the hounds on his back. But he declined, stating that he had important work to do for his master. He felt sure, he said, that all her other friends would come to her assistance. She

"The Hare with Many Friends." From *The Fables of Aesop,* selected, told anew, and their history traced by Joseph Jacobs. Macmillan & Co., London, 1894

then applied to the bull, and hoped that he would repel the hounds with his horns.

The bull replied: "I am very sorry, but I have an appointment with a lady; but I feel sure that our friend the goat will do what you want."

The goat, however, feared that his back might do her some harm if he took her upon it. The ram, he felt sure, was the proper friend to apply to. So she went to the ram and told him the case.

The ram replied: "Another time, my dear friend. I do not like to interfere on the present occasion, as hounds have been known to eat sheep as well as hares."

The hare then applied, as a last hope, to the calf, who regretted that he was unable to help her, as he did not like to take the responsibility upon himself, as so many older persons than himself had declined the task. By this time the hounds were quite near, and the hare took to her heels and luckily escaped.

He that has many friends, has no friends.

THE ANT
AND THE GRASSHOPPER

In a field one summer's day a grasshopper was hopping about, chirping and singing to its heart's content. An ant passed by, bearing along with great toil an ear of corn he was taking to the nest.

"Why not come and chat with me," said the grasshopper, "instead of toiling and moiling in that way?"

"I am helping to lay up food for the winter," said the ant, "and recommend you to do the same."

"Why bother about winter?" said the grasshopper. "We have got plenty of food at present." But the ant went on its way and continued its toil. When the winter came the grasshopper had no food, and found itself dying of hunger, while it saw the ants distributing every day corn and grain from the stores they had collected in the summer. Then the grasshopper knew—

It is best to prepare for the days of necessity.

"The Ant and the Grasshopper," "The Shepherd's Boy," and "The Lion and the Mouse." From *The Fables of Aesop,* selected, told anew, and their history traced by Joseph Jacobs. Macmillan & Co., London, 1894

THE SHEPHERD'S BOY

There was once a young shepherd boy who tended his sheep at the foot of a mountain near a dark forest. It was rather lonely for him all day, so he thought upon a plan by which he could get a little company and some excitement. He rushed down towards the village calling out "Wolf, wolf," and the villagers came out to meet him, and some of them stopped with him for a considerable time. This pleased the boy so much that a few days afterwards he tried the same trick, and again the villagers came to his help. But shortly after this a wolf actually did come out from the forest, and began to worry the sheep, and the boy of course cried out "Wolf, wolf," still louder than before. But this time the villagers, who had been fooled twice before, thought the boy was again deceiving them, and nobody stirred to come to his help. So the wolf made a good meal off the boy's flock, and when the boy complained, the wise man of the village said:

"A liar will not be believed, even when he speaks the truth."

THE LION AND THE MOUSE

Once when a lion was asleep a little mouse began running up and down upon him; this soon wakened the lion, who placed his huge paw upon him, and opened his big jaws to swallow him. "Pardon, O King," cried the little mouse; "forgive me this time, I shall never forget it. Who knows but what I may be able to do you a turn some of these days?" The lion was so tickled at the idea of the mouse being able to help him, that he lifted up his paw and let him go. Some time after, the lion was caught in a trap, and the hunters, who desired to carry him alive to the king, tied him to a tree while they went in search of a waggon to carry him on. Just then the little mouse happened to pass by, and seeing the sad plight in which the lion was, went up to him and soon gnawed away the ropes that bound the king of the beasts. "Was I not right?" said the little mouse.

Little friends may prove great friends.

THE FOX AND THE CROW

A fox once saw a crow fly off with a piece of cheese in its beak and settle on a branch of a tree. "That's for me, as I am a fox," said Master Renard, and he walked up to the foot of the tree. "Good-day, Mistress Crow," he cried. "How well you are looking to-day: how glossy your feathers; how bright your eye. I feel sure your voice must surpass that of other birds, just as your figure does; let me hear but one song from you that I may greet you as the Queen of Birds." The crow lifted up her head and began to caw her best, but the moment she opened her mouth the piece of cheese fell to the ground, only to be snapped up by Master Fox. "That will do," said he. "That was all I wanted. In exchange for your cheese I will give you a piece of advice for the future—do not trust flatterers."

The flatterer doth rob by stealth,
His victim, both of wit and wealth.

THE TOWN MOUSE

AND THE COUNTRY MOUSE

Now you must know that a town mouse once upon a time went on a visit to his cousin in the country. He was rough and ready, this cousin, but he loved his town friend and made him

"The Fox and the Crow," "The Town Mouse and the Country Mouse." From *The Fables of Aesop*, selected, told anew, and their history traced by Joseph Jacobs. Macmillan & Co., London, 1894

heartily welcome. Beans and bacon, cheese and bread, were all he had to offer, but he offered them freely. The town mouse rather turned up his long nose at this country fare, and said: "I cannot understand, Cousin, how you can put up with such poor food as this, but of course you cannot expect anything better in the country; come you with me and I will show you how to live. When you have been in town a week you will wonder how you could ever have stood a country life." No sooner said than done: the two mice set off for the town and arrived at the town mouse's residence late at night. "You will want some refreshment after our long journey," said the polite town mouse, and took his friend into the grand dining-room. There they found the re-

from its afternoon work, came up to the manger and wanted to eat some of the straw. The dog in a rage, being awakened from its slumber, stood up and barked at the ox, and whenever it came near attempted to bite it. At last the ox had to give up the hope of getting at the straw, and went away muttering:

"Ah, people often grudge others what they cannot enjoy themselves."

mains of a fine feast, and soon the two mice were eating up jellies and cakes and all that was nice. Suddenly they heard growling and barking. "What is that?" said the country mouse. "It is only the dogs of the house," answered the other. "Only!" said the country mouse. "I do not like that music at my dinner." Just at that moment the door flew open, in came two huge mastiffs, and the two mice had to scamper down and run off. "Good-bye Cousin," said the country mouse. "What! going so soon?" said the other. "Yes," he replied;

"Better beans and bacon in peace than cakes and ale in fear."

THE DOG IN THE MANGER

A dog looking out for its afternoon nap jumped into the manger of an ox and lay there cosily upon the straw. But soon the ox, returning

HERCULES AND THE WAGGONER

A waggoner was once driving a heavy load along a very muddy way. At last he came to a part of the road where the wheels sank halfway into the mire, and the more the horses pulled, the deeper sank the wheels. So the waggoner threw down his whip, and knelt down and prayed to Hercules the Strong. "O Hercules, help me in this my hour of distress," quoth he. But Hercules appeared to him, and said:

"Tut, man, don't sprawl there. Get up and put your shoulder to the wheel."

The gods help them that help themselves.

"The Dog in the Manger," and "Hercules and the Waggoner." From *The Fables of Aesop*, selected, told anew, and their history traced by Joseph Jacobs. Macmillan & Co., London, 1894

BELLING THE CAT

Long ago, the mice held a general council to consider what measures they could take to outwit their common enemy, the cat. Some said this, and some said that; but at last a young mouse got up and said he had a proposal to make, which he thought would meet the case. "You will all agree," said he, that our chief danger consists in the sly and treacherous manner in which the enemy approaches us. Now, if we could receive some signal of her approach, we could easily escape from her. I venture, therefore, to propose that a small bell be procured, and attached by a ribbon round the neck of the cat. By this means we should always know when she was about, and could easily retire while she was in the neighbourhood."

This proposal met with general applause, until an old mouse got up and said: "That is all very well, but who is to bell the cat?" The mice looked at one another and nobody spoke. Then the old mouse said:

"It is easy to propose impossible remedies."

"Belling the Cat," "The Frog and the Ox," and "The Dog and the Shadow." From *The Fables of Aesop*, selected, told anew, and their history traced by Joseph Jacobs. Macmillan & Co., London, 1894

THE FROG AND THE OX

"Oh Father," said a little frog to the big one sitting by the side of a pool, "I have seen such a terrible monster! It was as big as a mountain, with horns on its head, and a long tail, and it had hoofs divided in two."

"Tush, child, tush," said the old frog, "that was only Farmer White's ox. It isn't so big either; he may be a little bit taller than I, but I could easily make myself quite as broad; just you see." So he blew himself out, and blew himself out, and blew himself out. "Was he as big as that?" asked he.

"Oh, much bigger than that," said the young frog.

Again the old one blew himself out, and asked the young one if the ox was as big as that.

"Bigger, Father, bigger," was the reply.

So the frog took a deep breath, and blew and blew and blew, and swelled and swelled and swelled. And then he said: "I'm sure the ox is not as big as——" But at this moment he burst.

Self-conceit may lead to self-destruction.

THE DOG AND THE SHADOW

It happened that a dog had got a piece of meat and was carrying it home in his mouth to eat it

in peace. Now on his way home he had to cross a plank lying across a running brook. As he crossed, he looked down and saw his own shadow reflected in the water beneath. Thinking it was another dog with another piece of meat, he made up his mind to have that also. So he made a snap at the shadow in the water, but as he opened his mouth the piece of meat fell out, dropped into the water and was never seen more.

Beware lest you lose the substance by grasping at the shadow.

THE WIND AND THE SUN

The wind and the sun were disputing which was the stronger. Suddenly they saw a traveller coming down the road, and the sun said: "I see a way to decide our dispute. Whichever of us can cause that traveller to take off his cloak shall be regarded as the stronger. You begin." So the sun retired behind a cloud, and the wind began to blow as hard as it could upon the traveller. But the harder he blew the more closely did the traveller wrap his cloak round him, till at last the wind had to give up in despair. Then the sun came out and shone in all his glory upon the traveller, who soon found it too hot to walk with his cloak on.

Kindness effects more than Severity.

THE FOX AND THE GRAPES

One hot summer's day a fox was strolling through an orchard till he came to a bunch of grapes just ripening on a vine which had been trained over a lofty branch. "Just the thing to quench my thirst," quoth he. Drawing back a few paces, he took a run and a jump, and just missed the bunch. Turning round again with a one, two, three, he jumped up, but with no greater success. Again and again he tried after the tempting morsel, but at last had to give it up, and walked away with his nose in the air,

"The Wind and the Sun," "The Fox and the Grapes," "The Crow and the Pitcher." From *The Fables of Aesop,* selected, told anew, and their history traced by Joseph Jacobs. Macmillan & Co., London, 1894

saying: "I am sure they are sour."

It is easy to despise what you cannot get.

THE CROW AND THE PITCHER

A crow, half-dead with thirst, came upon a pitcher which had once been full of water; but when the crow put its beak into the mouth of the pitcher he found that only very little water was left in it and that he could not reach far enough down to get at it. He tried, and he tried, but at last had to give up in despair. Then a thought came to him, and he took a pebble and dropped it into the pitcher. Then he took another pebble and dropped it into the pitcher. Then he took another pebble and dropped that into the pitcher. Then he took another pebble and dropped that into the pitcher. Then he took another pebble and dropped that into the pitcher. Then he took another pebble and dropped that into the pitcher. At last, at last, he saw the water mount up near him; and after casting in a few more pebbles he was able to quench his thirst and save his life.

Little by little does the trick.

THE HARE AND THE TORTOISE

The hare was once boasting of his speed before the other animals. "I have never yet been
beaten," said he, "when I put forth my full
speed. I challenge any one here to race with me."

The tortoise said quietly: "I accept your challenge."

"That is a good joke," said the hare; "I could
dance round you all the way."

"Keep your boasting till you've beaten," answered the tortoise. "Shall we race?"

So a course was fixed and a start was made.
The hare darted almost out of sight at once, but
soon stopped and, to show his contempt for the
tortoise, lay down to have a nap. The tortoise

plodded on and plodded on, and when the hare
awoke from his nap, he saw the tortoise just near
the winning-post and could not run up in time
to save the race. Then said the Tortoise:

"Plodding wins the race."

THE MILKMAID AND HER PAIL

Patty, the milkmaid, was going to market
carrying her milk in a pail on her head. As she

"The Hare and the Tortoise," and "The Milkmaid and
Her Pail." From *The Fables of Aesop*, selected, told anew,
and their history traced by Joseph Jacobs. Macmillan &
Co., London, 1894

went along she began calculating what she
would do with the money she would get for the
milk. "I'll buy some fowls from Farmer Brown,"
said she, "and they will lay eggs each morning,
which I will sell to the parson's wife. With the
money that I get from the sale of these eggs I'll
buy myself a new dimity frock and a chip hat;
and when I go to market, won't all the young
men come up and speak to me! Polly Shaw will
be that jealous; but I don't care. I shall just look
at her and toss my head like this." As she spoke,
she tossed her head back, the pail fell off it and
all the milk was spilt. So she had to go home and
tell her mother what had occurred.

"Ah, my child," said her mother,

"*Do not count your chickens before they are hatched.*"

THE WOLF
IN SHEEP'S CLOTHING

A wolf found great difficulty in getting at the sheep owing to the vigilance of the shepherd and his dogs. But one day the wolf found the skin of a sheep that had been flayed and thrown aside, so he put it on over his own pelt and strolled down among the sheep. The lamb that belonged to the sheep, whose skin the wolf was wearing, began to follow the wolf in the sheep's clothing; so, leading the lamb a little apart, he soon made a meal off her, and for some time he succeeded in deceiving the sheep, and enjoying hearty meals.

Appearances are deceptive.

The Panchatantra

The fables in the East Indian collections are much longer and more like stories with morals than they are like the spare little abstractions we know as Aesop's fables. The Panchatantra *was really a textbook on "the wise conduct of life" and contained stories within stories. Maude Barrows Dutton retold thirty-four of the best-known tales from* The Panchatantra *and, with the inimitable illustrations of E. Boyd Smith, made an attractive little book called* The Tortoise and the Geese and Other Fables of Bidpai. *The Bidpai fables are the Arabic versions of* The Panchatantra. *The other source of Indian fables is the group called the* Jatakas, *already described in connection with the folk tales of India. As explained, the selections from the* Jatakas *are included with the folk tales because they become good talking-beast tales when references to the Buddha are omitted.*

THE PARTRIDGE AND THE CROW

A Crow flying across a road saw a Partridge strutting along the ground.

"What a beautiful gait that Partridge has!" said the Crow. "I must try to see if I can walk like him."

She alighted behind the Partridge and tried for a long time to learn to strut. At last the Partridge turned around and asked the Crow what she was about.

"Do not be angry with me," replied the Crow. "I have never before seen a bird who walks as beautifully as you can, and I am trying to learn to walk like you."

"Foolish bird!" responded the Partridge. "You are a Crow, and should walk like a Crow. You would look silly indeed if you were to strut like a partridge."

But the Crow went on trying to learn to strut, until finally she had forgotten her own gait, and she never learned that of the Partridge.

THE TYRANT WHO BECAME
A JUST RULER

In olden times there lived a King who was so cruel and unjust towards his subjects that he was always called The Tyrant. So heartless was he that his people used to pray night and day that they might have a new king. One day, much to their surprise, he called his people together and said to them,——

"My dear subjects, the days of my tyranny are over. Henceforth you shall live in peace and happiness, for I have decided to try to rule henceforth justly and well."

The King kept his word so well that soon he was known throughout the land as The Just King. By and by one of his favorites came to him and said,——

"Your Majesty, I beg of you to tell me how it was that you had this change of heart towards your people?"

And the King replied,——

"As I was galloping through my forests one afternoon, I caught sight of a hound chasing a fox. The fox escaped into his hole, but not until he had been bitten by the dog so badly that he would be lame for life. The hound, returning home, met a man who threw a stone at him, which broke his leg. The man had not gone far when a horse kicked him and broke his leg. And the horse, starting to run, fell into a hole and broke his leg. Here I came to my senses, and resolved to change my rule. 'For surely,' I said to myself, 'he who doeth evil will sooner or later be overtaken by evil.'"

THE MICE THAT ATE IRON

The theme of this fable is found among the folk tales of many countries. An American variant, "Young Melvin," appears on pages 246–248.

In a certain town lived a merchant named Naduk, who lost his money and determined to travel abroad. For

> The meanest of mankind is he
> Who, having lost his money, can
> Inhabit lands or towns where once
> He spent it like a gentleman.

And again:

> The neighbor gossips blame
> His poverty as shame
> Who long was wont to play
> Among them, proud and gay.

In his house was an iron balance-beam inher-

"The Mice That Ate Iron." From *The Panchatantra* by Arthur W. Ryder (Chicago: The University of Chicago Press, 1925), p. 474. Copyright 1925 by the University of Chicago Press. Reprinted by permission of the publisher

ited from his ancestors, and it weighed a thousand *pals*. This he put in pawn with Merchant Lakshman before he departed for foreign countries.

Now after he had long traveled wherever business led him through foreign lands, he returned to his native city and said to Merchant Lakshman: "Friend Lakshman, return my deposit, the balance-beam." And Lakshman said: "Friend Naduk, your balance-beam has been eaten by mice."

To this Naduk replied: "Lakshman, you are in no way to blame, if it has been eaten by mice. Such is life. Nothing in the universe has any permanence. However, I am going to the river for a bath. Please send your boy Money-God with me, to carry my bathing things."

Since Lakshman was conscience-stricken at his own theft, he said to his son Money-God: "My dear boy, let me introduce Uncle Naduk, who is going to the river to bathe. You must go with him and carry his bathing things." Ah, there is too much truth in the saying:

> There is no purely loving deed
> Without a pinch of fear or greed
> Or service of a selfish need.

And again:

> Wherever there is fond attention
> That does not seek a service pension,
> Was there no timid apprehension?

So Lakshman's son took the bathing things and delightedly accompanied Naduk to the river. After Naduk had taken his bath, he thrust Lakshman's son Money-God into a mountain cave, blocked the entrance with a great rock, and returned to Lakshman's house. And when Lakshman said: "Friend Naduk, tell me what has become of my son Money-God who went with you," Naduk answered: "My good Lakshman, a hawk carried him off from the river-bank."

"Oh, Naduk!" cried Lakshman. "You liar! How could a hawk possibly carry off a big boy like Money-God?" "But, Lakshman," retorted Naduk, "the mice could eat a balance-beam made of iron. Give me my balance-beam, if you want your son."

Finally, they carried their dispute to the palace gate, where Lakshman cried in a piercing tone: "Help! Help! A ghastly deed! This Naduk person has carried off my son—his name is Money-God."

Thereupon the magistrates said to Naduk: "Sir, restore the boy to Lakshman." But Naduk pleaded: "What am I to do? Before my eyes a hawk carried him from the river-bank." "Come, Naduk!" said they, "you are not telling the truth. How can a hawk carry off a fifteen-year-old boy?" Then Naduk laughed outright and said: "Gentlemen, listen to my words.

Where mice eat balance-beams of iron
    A thousand *pals* in weight,
A hawk might steal an elephant;
    A boy is trifling freight."

"How was that?" they asked, and Naduk told them the story of the balance-beam. At this they laughed and caused the restoration of balance-beam and boy to the respective owners.

Fables of La Fontaine

In France the fables were turned into verse by a skilled poet, Jean de La Fontaine, a contemporary of Charles Perrault. The sources used by La Fontaine were Latin versions of Aesop and The Fables of Bidpai, *and the versions of Marie de France, who introduced the fable into France in the twelfth century. La Fontaine's rhymed moralities were so popular in the France of his day that people called him* le fablier, *"the fable-teller." To translate his witty French verses into English verse is to lose some of their gaiety and charm, so they are usually translated into prose. "The Grasshopper and the Ant" is an example of a metrical translation, and "The Fox and the Crow" and "The Cricket and the Ant" are in the vigorous prose of Margaret Wise Brown. In "The Fox and the Crow" she has used a sing-and-say style that suggests the original verse form but tells the story clearly.*

THE FOX AND THE CROW

Mister Crow sat on the limb of a tree with a big piece of cheese in his mouth.

Old Mister Fox smelled the cheese from a long way off. And he came to the foot of the tree and spoke to the crow.

"Good morning, Mr. Coal Black Crow,
How beautiful and shining your feathers grow,
Black as the night and bright as the sun,
If you sing as well, your fortune is won."

At these words Mr. Crow joyously opened his beak to sing his creaky old crow song.

"The Fox and the Crow" and "The Cricket and the Ant" from *Fables of La Fontaine* translated by Margaret Wise Brown. Copyright 1940 by Harper & Brothers. Reprinted by permission of Western Publishing Company, Inc.

And the cheese fell down to the ground. The fox snapped it up in his mouth.

As he ran away he called back over his bushy tail, "My dear Mr. Crow, learn from this how every flatterer lives at the expense of anybody who will listen to him. This lesson is well worth the loss of a cheese to you."

THE CRICKET AND THE ANT

All through the summer the cricket sang. He sang in the grass when they planted the seed. And he sang in the grass when the flowers bloomed. Why should a cricket work on a sunny day, when he could sing and dance and play? In the early fall when the seeds were blowing in the air the cricket chirped his song. But when winter came and the cold winds blew, the merry little cricket had nothing to eat and nowhere to go.

So he hopped to the house of his neighbor, the ant, who had worked all summer storing up her food for the winter. He knocked at the door and cried, "Oh, dear! Oh, dear! I am starving, hungry, starving! Kind ant, will you lend me some seeds to live on until spring? And I will give you five seeds in the spring for every seed that you give me today."

But the ant was practical—as ants are.

"What did you do in the summer when the days were warm and the flowers were going to seed?" asked the ant. "What did you do in the early fall when the seeds were blowing through the air?"

"Night and day I sang," said the cricket.

"You sang!" said the ant. "Then now you can dance to your own music. I will eat the seed I gathered and the house I have built will keep me warm. Maybe your dancing will keep you warm in the snow."

THE GRASSHOPPER AND
THE ANT

A grasshopper gay
Sang the Summer away,
And found herself poor
By the winter's first roar.
Of meat and of bread,
Not a morsel she had!
So a-begging she went,
To her neighbour the ant,
   For the loan of some wheat,

Which would serve her to eat,
Till the season came round.
  "I will pay, you," she saith
  "On an animal's faith,
Double weight in the pound
Ere the harvest be bound."
The ant is a friend
  (And here she might mend)
  Little given to lend.
"How spent you the summer?"
  Quoth she, looking shame
  At the borrowing dame.
"Night and day to each comer
I sang if you please."
  "You sang! I'm at ease;
For 'tis plain at a glance,
Now, Ma'am, you must dance."

"The Grasshopper and the Ant." From *A Hundred Fables* by Jean de la Fontaine. Reprinted by permission of The Bodley Head, London

Myth and epic are a part of that anonymous stream of folklore which includes the folk tales and the fables. All these once helped to weld people together with a body of common beliefs, customs, morals, and hero cults. They were indeed the "cement of society," holding it together with a moral code and giving it a certain identity.

However, in the light of modern historical and anthropological research, much of what was once thought about myths, their origin and significance, has been called into question. The more that has been discovered about the ancient

THE MYTHS

Greeks, the more we have had to give up our rather simplistic and romantic notions about what their myths meant and what purpose they served. But old notions take a long time to die, and in almost all popularly written books or articles on myths, these older views predominate. It is difficult to understand the full evolution and significance of myths and mythology, and we should be prepared to delve deep and long if we try to do so.

In the meantime, when we speak of myths as literature for children, we refer principally to the myths of the Greeks, Romans, and Norsemen. All peoples have some form of mythology, but the Greeks and Scandinavians created myths that have shaped the mentality, language, and literature of Western man. Not a day passes, hardly an hour of conversation takes place, that we do not use a word or think a thought that draws upon the concepts and tales of these two great mythologies. This is why Shelley could say of us: *"We are all Greeks."* He might have added that we are partly Norse as well.

The origins and possible significance of myths are adult concerns that arise only if one begins to wonder why a myth exists in the first place. Otherwise, the myth may be viewed, as is usually the case, as a kind of ancient adult fairy tale which now appeals more to young people and students of literature than to anyone else. Even so, there are problems about when to introduce the myth to young people and which versions or retellings to use.

Myths generally contain themes which are too adult for young children in the primary grades. Some myths are fables and *pourquoi* tales that may be put into simple form for boys and girls— "Echo and Narcissus," for example. A few myths read like fairy tales, even in their original version, such as "King Midas" or "Baucis and Philemon," and are therefore suitable for the eight- and nine-year-olds. But most myths have complexities that make them more suitable for young people in the upper grades and high school. No blanket decision can be made about them. On the other hand, one must be cautious about those well-intended attempts to adapt and simplify the myths. Such attempts are usually disastrous, sacrificing the spirit of the original and destroying style for the sake of bare plot. The reteller's attitude must also be considered. Hawthorne, in *A Wonder-Book for Girls and Boys* and *Tanglewood Tales for Girls and Boys,* made the myths read like sentimental Gothic fairy tales. Robert Graves, a noted scholar of mythology and a great poet, gave his versions of the myths for young people a decidedly irreverent and cynical flavor. Padraic Colum, in contrast, achieved a bardic feeling in his approach.

The selections here are from older editions in which the writers achieved a good style that will appeal to young people while adhering closely to the more standard translations of the myths as they have come down to us through the writings of Greek and Roman poets, dramatists, and literary commentators. Various editions of the myths are listed in the Bibliography, and by consulting the annotations the reader can determine which editions are most suitable for his specific purposes. Ultimately, however, the adult who steeps himself in the myths by reading many versions and commentaries will come to have his own versions, unique to his understanding of these great tales, and to his attitude toward them.

It is hoped that this small selection of myths will send teachers, parents, and children to whole books of mythology to be used in connection with their study of a people or just for delight in the stories themselves. For to know the beauty of Olympus or Valhalla and to encounter the gods at their best is to dream again some of man's ancient dreams of how splendid life may be for those who dare greatly. There are admirable dreams in the myths. How they came about and whether they are dreams of the past or auguries of the future matters little, for they are couched in symbols whose meaning will grow with children's maturity.

Greek and Roman Myths

When we turn to the Greek myths, Edith Hamilton's observation is undeniable: "The myths as we have them are the creation of great poets." *And it was one of the great accomplishments of the Greeks that their myths for the most part did away with the irrational and fearful elements which characterize many primitive mythologies. Indeed, they acknowledged that the gods were cruel and capricious and that human life was beset by tragedy, but in their myths they made these facts seem understandable and even beautiful. It may be that in making the gods in their own image, they made them not more comprehensible but less fearful, until in time they came to associate with various gods the better aspects and reaches of human reason and virtue.*

CLYTIE

The maiden in the process of transformation is an interesting subject for illustration.

Clytie was a water-nymph and in love with Apollo, who made her no return. So she pined away, sitting all day long upon the cold ground, with her unbound tresses streaming over her shoulders. Nine days she sat and tasted neither food nor drink, her own tears and the chilly dew her only food. She gazed on the sun when he rose, and as he passed through his daily course to his setting; she saw no other object, her face turned constantly on him. At last, they say, her limbs rooted in the ground, her face became a flower (sunflower), which turns on its stem so as always to face the sun throughout its daily course; for it retains to that extent the feeling of the nymph from whom it sprang.

ARACHNE

The gods seem to be especially hard on conceit and boastfulness.

Not among mortals alone were there contests of skill, nor yet among the gods, like Pan and Apollo. Many sorrows befell men because they grew arrogant in their own devices and coveted divine honors. There was once a great hunter, Orion, who outvied the gods themselves, till they took him away from his hunting-grounds and set him in the heavens, with his sword and belt, and his hound at his heels. But at length jealousy invaded even the peaceful arts, and disaster came of spinning!

There was a certain maiden of Lydia, Arachne by name, renowned throughout the country for her skill as a weaver. She was as nimble with her fingers as Calypso, that nymph who kept Odysseus for seven years in her enchanted island. She was as untiring as Penelope, the hero's wife, who wove day after day while she watched for his return. Day in and day out, Arachne wove too. The very nymphs would gather about her loom,

"Clytie." From *The Age of Fable; or Beauties of Mythology*, by Thomas Bulfinch. J. E. Tilton and Company, Boston, 1863

naiads from the water and dryads from the trees.

"Maiden," they would say, shaking the leaves or the foam from their hair, in wonder, "Pallas Athena must have taught you!"

But this did not please Arachne. She would not acknowledge herself a debtor, even to that goddess who protected all household arts, and by whose grace alone one had any skill in them.

"I learned not of Athena," said she. "If she can weave better, let her come and try."

The nymphs shivered at this, and an aged woman, who was looking on, turned to Arachne.

"Be more heedful of your words, my daughter," said she. "The goddess may pardon you if you ask forgiveness, but do not strive for honors with the immortals."

Arachne broke her thread, and the shuttle stopped humming.

"Keep your counsel," she said. "I fear not Athena; no, nor anyone else."

As she frowned at the old woman, she was amazed to see her change suddenly into one tall, majestic, beautiful—a maiden of gray eyes and golden hair, crowned with a golden helmet. It was Athena herself.

The bystanders shrank in fear and reverence; only Arachne was unawed and held to her foolish boast.

In silence the two began to weave, and the nymphs stole nearer, coaxed by the sound of the shuttles, that seemed to be humming with delight over the two webs,—back and forth like bees.

They gazed upon the loom where the goddess stood plying her task, and they saw shapes and images come to bloom out of the wondrous colors, as sunset clouds grow to be living creatures when we watch them. And they saw that the goddess, still merciful, was spinning, as a warning for Arachne, the pictures of her own triumph over reckless gods and mortals.

In one corner of the web she made a story of her conquest over the sea-god Poseidon. For the first king of Athens had promised to dedicate the city to that god who should bestow upon it the most useful gift. Poseidon gave the horse. But Athena gave the olive,—means of livelihood,—

"Arachne." From *Old Greek Folk Stories Told Anew* by Josephine Preston Peabody. Copyright 1897 by Houghton Mifflin Company

symbol of peace and prosperity, and the city was called after her name. Again she pictured a vain woman of Troy, who had been turned into a crane for disputing the palm of beauty with a goddess. Other corners of the web held similar images, and the whole shone like a rainbow.

Meanwhile Arachne, whose head was quite turned with vanity, embroidered her web with stories against the gods, making light of Zeus himself and of Apollo, and portraying them as birds and beasts. But she wove with marvelous skill; the creatures seemed to breathe and speak, yet it was all as fine as the gossamer that you find on the grass before rain.

Athena herself was amazed. Not even her wrath at the girl's insolence could wholly overcome her wonder. For an instant she stood entranced; then she tore the web across, and three times she touched Arachne's forehead with her spindle.

"Live on, Arachne," she said. "And since it is your glory to weave, you and yours must weave forever." So saying, she sprinkled upon the maiden a certain magical potion.

Away went Arachne's beauty; then her very human form shrank to that of a spider, and so remained. As a spider she spent all her days weaving and weaving; and you may see something like her handiwork any day among the rafters.

ORPHEUS AND EURYDICE

This has been one of the more popular of the myths with writers and dramatists, and many European folk tales echo its sorrowful theme.

When gods and shepherds piped and the stars sang, that was the day of musicians! But the triumph of Phoebus Apollo himself was not so wonderful as the triumph of a mortal man who lived on earth, though some say that he came of divine lineage. This was Orpheus, that best of harpers, who went with the Grecian heroes of the great ship *Argo* in search of the Golden Fleece.

"Orpheus and Eurydice." From *Old Greek Folk Stories Told Anew* by Josephine Preston Peabody. Copyright 1897 by Houghton Mifflin Company

After his return from the quest, he won Eurydice for his wife, and they were as happy as people can be who love each other and every one else. The very wild beasts loved them, and the trees clustered about their home as if they were watered with music. But even the gods themselves were not always free from sorrow, and one day misfortune came upon that harper Orpheus whom all men loved to honor.

Eurydice, his lovely wife, as she was wandering with the nymphs, unwittingly trod upon a serpent in the grass. Surely, if Orpheus had been with her, playing upon his lyre, no creature could have harmed her. But Orpheus came too late. She died of the sting, and was lost to him in the Underworld.

For days he wandered from his home, singing the story of his loss and his despair to the helpless passers-by. His grief moved the very stones in the wilderness, and roused a dumb distress in the hearts of savage beasts. Even the gods on Mount Olympus gave ear, but they held no power over the darkness of Hades.

Wherever Orpheus wandered with his lyre, no one had the will to forbid him entrance; and at length he found unguarded that very cave that leads to the Underworld where Pluto rules the spirits of the dead. He went down without fear. The fire in his living heart found him a way through the gloom of that place. He crossed the Styx, the black river that the gods name as their most sacred oath. Charon, the harsh old ferryman who takes the Shades across, forgot to ask of him the coin that every soul must pay. For Orpheus sang. There in the Underworld the song of Apollo would not have moved the poor ghosts so much. It would have amazed them, like a star far off that no one understands. But here was a human singer, and he sang of things that grow in every human heart, youth and love and death, the sweetness of the Earth, and the bitterness of losing aught that is dear to us.

Now the dead, when they go to the Underworld, drink of the pool of Lethe; and forgetfulness of all that has passed comes upon them like a sleep, and they lose their longing for the world, they lose their memory of pain, and live content with that cool twilight. But not the pool of Lethe itself could withstand the song of Orpheus; and in the hearts of the Shades all the old dreams awoke wondering. They remembered once more the life of men on Earth, the glory of the sun and moon, the sweetness of new grass, the warmth of their homes, all the old joy and grief that they had known. And they wept.

Even the Furies were moved to pity. Those, too, who were suffering punishment for evil deeds ceased to be tormented for themselves, and grieved only for the innocent Orpheus who had lost Eurydice. Sisyphus, that fraudulent king (who is doomed to roll a monstrous boulder uphill forever), stopped to listen. The daughters of Danaus left off their task of drawing water in a sieve. Tantalus forgot hunger and thirst, though before his eyes hung magical fruits that were wont to vanish out of his grasp, and just beyond reach bubbled the water that was a torment to his ears; he did not hear it while Orpheus sang.

So, among a crowd of eager ghosts, Orpheus came, singing with all his heart, before the king and queen of Hades. And the queen Proserpina wept as she listened and grew homesick, remembering the fields of Enna and the growing of the wheat, and her own beautiful mother, Demeter. Then Pluto gave way.

They called Eurydice and she came, like a young guest unused to the darkness of the Underworld. She was to return with Orpheus, but on one condition. If he turned to look at her once before they reached the upper air, he must lose her again and go back to the world alone.

Rapt with joy, the happy Orpheus hastened on the way, thinking only of Eurydice, who was following him. Past Lethe, across the Styx they went, he and his lovely wife, still silent as a Shade. But the place was full of gloom, the silence weighed upon him, he had not seen her for so long; her footsteps made no sound; and he could hardly believe the miracle, for Pluto seldom relents. When the first gleam of upper daylight broke through the cleft to the dismal world, he forgot all, save that he must know if she still followed. He turned to see her face, and the promise was broken!

She smiled at him forgivingly, but it was too late. He stretched out his arms to take her, but she faded from them, as the bright snow, that none may keep, melts in our very hands. A murmur of farewell came to his ears—no more. She was gone.

He would have followed, but Charon, now on guard, drove him back. Seven days he lingered there between the worlds of life and death, but after the broken promise, Hades would not listen to his song. Back to the Earth he wandered, though it was sweet to him no longer. He died young, singing to the last, and round about the place where his body rested, nightingales nested in the trees. His lyre was set among the stars; and he himself went down to join Eurydice, unforbidden.

Those two had no need of Lethe, for their life on earth had been wholly fair, and now that they are together they no longer own a sorrow.

PROSERPINE

This myth, sometimes called "Demeter and Persephone," the Greek names for the mother and child, is the story of winter and summer, of the grains maturing below ground in darkness. Robert Graves gives a rather saucy version of it. (See the Bibliography, p. 379.)

When Jupiter and his brothers had defeated the Titans and banished them to Tartarus, a new enemy rose up against the gods. They were the giants Typhon, Briareus, Enceladus, and others. Some of them had a hundred arms, others breathed out fire. They were finally subdued and buried alive under Mount Ætna, where they still sometimes struggle to get loose, and shake the whole island with earthquakes. Their breath comes up through the mountain, and is what men call the eruption of the volcano.

The fall of these monsters shook the earth, so that Pluto was alarmed, and feared that his kingdom would be laid open to the light of day. Under this apprehension, he mounted his chariot, drawn by black horses, and took a circuit of inspection to satisfy himself of the extent of the damage.

While he was thus engaged, Venus, who was sitting on Mount Eryx playing with her boy Cupid, espied him, and said, "My son, take your darts with which you conquer all, even Jove himself, and send one into the breast of yonder dark monarch, who rules the realm of Tartarus. Why should he alone escape? Seize the opportunity to extend your empire and mine. Do you not see that even in heaven some despise our power? Minerva the wise, and Diana the huntress, defy us; and there is that daughter of Ceres, who threatens to follow their example. Now do you, if you have any regard for your own interest or mine, join these two in one."

The boy unbound his quiver, and selected his sharpest and truest arrow; then, straining the bow against his knee, he attached the string, and, having made ready, shot the arrow with its

"Proserpine." From *The Age of Fable; or Beauties of Mythology*, by Thomas Bulfinch. J. E. Tilton and Company, Boston, 1863

barbed point right into the heart of Pluto.

In the vale of Enna there is a lake embowered in woods, which screen it from the fervid rays of the sun, while the moist ground is covered with flowers, and Spring reigns perpetual. Here Proserpine was playing with her companions, gathering lilies and violets, and filling her basket and her apron with them, when Pluto saw her, loved her, and carried her off. She screamed for help to her mother and her companions; and when in her fright she dropped the corners of her apron and let the flowers fall, childlike she felt the loss of them as an addition to her grief. The ravisher urged on his steeds, calling them each by name, and throwing loose over their heads and necks his iron-colored reins. When he reached the River Cyane, and it opposed his passage, he struck the riverbank with his trident, and the earth opened and gave him a passage to Tartarus.

Ceres sought her daughter all the world over. Bright-haired Aurora, when she came forth in the morning, and Hesperus, when he led out the stars in the evening, found her still busy in the search. But it was all unavailing. At length weary and sad, she sat down upon a stone, and continued sitting nine days and nights, in the open air, under the sunlight and moonlight and falling showers. It was where now stands the city of Eleusis, then the home of an old man named Celeus. He was out in the field, gathering acorns and blackberries, and sticks for his fire. His little girl was driving home their two goats, and as she passed the goddess, who appeared in the guise of an old woman, she said to her, "Mother,"—and the name was sweet to the ears of Ceres,—"why do you sit here alone upon the rocks?"

The old man also stopped, though his load was heavy, and begged her to come into his cottage, such as it was. She declined, and he urged her.

"Go in peace," she replied, "and be happy in your daughter; I have lost mine." As she spoke, tears—or something like tears, for the gods never weep,—fell down her cheeks upon her bosom.

The compassionate old man and his child wept with her. Then said he, "Come with us, and despise not our humble roof; so may your daughter be restored to you in safety."

"Lead on," said she, "I cannot resist that appeal!" So she rose from the stone and went with them.

As they walked he told her that his only son, a little boy, lay very sick, feverish and sleepless. She stooped and gathered some poppies. As they entered the cottage, they found all in great distress, for the boy seemed past hope of recovery. Metanira, his mother, received her kindly, and the goddess stooped and kissed the lips of the sick child. Instantly the paleness left his face, and healthy vigor returned to his body.

The whole family were delighted—that is, the father, mother, and little girl, for they were all; they had no servants. They spread the table, and put upon it curds and cream, apples, and honey in the comb. While they ate, Ceres mingled poppy juice in the milk of the boy. When night came and all was still, she arose, and taking the sleeping boy, moulded his limbs with her hands, and uttered over him three times a solemn charm, then went and laid him in the ashes. His mother, who had been watching what her guest was doing, sprang forward with a cry and snatched the child from the fire. Then Ceres assumed her own form, and a divine splendor shone all around.

While they were overcome with astonishment, she said, "Mother, you have been cruel in your fondness to your son. I would have made him immortal, but you have frustrated my attempt. Nevertheless, he shall be great and useful. He shall teach men the use of the plough, and the rewards which labor can win from the cultivated soil." So saying, she wrapped a cloud about her, and mounting her chariot rode away.

Ceres continued her search for her daughter, passing from land to land, and across seas and rivers, till at length she returned to Sicily, whence she at first set out, and stood by the banks of the River Cyane, where Pluto made himself a passage with his prize to his own dominions. The river nymph would have told the goddess all she had witnessed, but dared not, for fear of Pluto; so she only ventured to take up the girdle which Proserpine had dropped in her flight, and waft it to the feet of the mother. Ceres, seeing this, was no longer in doubt of her loss, but she did not yet know the cause, and laid the blame on the innocent land.

"Ungrateful soil," said she, "which I have en-dowed with fertility and clothed with herbage and nourishing grain, no more shall you enjoy my favors."

Then the cattle died, the plough broke in the furrow, the seed failed to come up; there was too much sun, there was too much rain; the birds stole the seeds—thistles and brambles were the only growth.

Seeing this, the fountain Arethusa interceded for the land. "Goddess," said she, "blame not the land; it opened unwillingly to yield a passage to your daughter. I can tell you of her fate, for I have seen her. . . . While I passed through the lower parts of the earth, I saw your Proserpine. She was sad, but no longer showing alarm in her countenance. Her look was such as became a queen—the queen of Erebus; the powerful bride of the monarch of the realms of the dead."

When Ceres heard this, she stood for a while like one stupefied; then turned her chariot towards heaven, and hastened to present herself before the throne of Jove. She told the story of her bereavement, and implored Jupiter to interfere to procure the restitution of her daughter. Jupiter consented on one condition, namely, that Proserpine should not during her stay in the lower world have taken any food; otherwise, the Fates forbade her release. Accordingly, Mercury was sent, accompanied by Spring, to demand Proserpine of Pluto. The wily monarch consented; but alas! the maiden had taken a pomegranate which Pluto offered her, and had sucked the sweet pulp from a few of the seeds. This was enough to prevent her complete release; but a compromise was made, by which she was to pass half the time with her mother, and the rest with her husband Pluto.

Ceres allowed herself to be pacified with this arrangement, and restored the earth to her favor. Now she remembered Celeus and his family, and her promise to his infant son Triptolemus. When the boy grew up, she taught him the use of the plough, and how to sow the seed. She took him in her chariot, drawn by winged dragons, through all the countries of the earth, imparting to mankind valuable grains, and the knowledge of agriculture. After his return, Triptolemus built a magnificent temple to Ceres in Eleusis, and established the worship of the goddess, under the name of the Eleusinian mysteries, which, in the splendor and solemnity of their observance, surpassed all other religious celebrations among the Greeks.

ICARUS AND DAEDALUS

Here would seem to be, according to some people, a lesson for man on the dangers of putting too much stock in his own powers.

Among all those mortals who grew so wise that they learned the secrets of the gods, none was more cunning than Daedalus.

He once built, for King Minos of Crete, a wonderful Labyrinth of winding ways so cunningly tangled up and twisted around that, once inside, you could never find your way out again without a magic clue. But the king's favor veered with the wind, and one day he had his master architect imprisoned in a tower. Daedalus managed to escape from his cell; but it seemed impossible to leave the island, since every ship that came or went was well guarded by order of the king.

At length, watching the sea-gulls in the air—the only creatures that were sure of liberty—he thought of a plan for himself and his young son Icarus, who was captive with him.

Little by little, he gathered a store of feathers great and small. He fastened these together with thread, moulded them in with wax, and so fashioned two great wings like those of a bird. When they were done, Daedalus fitted them to his own shoulders, and after one or two efforts, he found that by waving his arms he could winnow the air and cleave it, as a swimmer does the sea. He held himself aloft, wavered this way and that with the wind, and at last, like a great fledgling, he learned to fly.

Without delay, he fell to work on a pair of wings for the boy Icarus, and taught him carefully how to use them, bidding him beware of rash adventures among the stars. "Remember," said the father, "never to fly very low or very high, for the fogs about the earth would weigh you down, but the blaze of the sun will surely melt your feathers apart if you go too near."

"Icarus and Daedalus." From *Old Greek Folk Stories Told Anew* by Josephine Preston Peabody. Copyright 1897 by Houghton Mifflin Company

For Icarus, these cautions went in at one ear and out by the other. Who could remember to be careful when he was to fly for the first time? Are birds careful? Not they! And not an idea remained in the boy's head but the one joy of escape.

The day came, and the fair wind that was to set them free. The father bird put on his wings, and, while the light urged them to be gone, he waited to see that all was well with Icarus, for the two could not fly hand in hand. Up they rose, the boy after his father. The hateful ground of Crete sank beneath them; and the country folk, who caught a glimpse of them when they were high above the tree-tops, took it for a vision of the gods—Apollo, perhaps, with Cupid after him.

At first there was a terror in the joy. The wide vacancy of the air dazed them—a glance downward made their brains reel. But when a great wind filled their wings, and Icarus felt himself sustained, like a halcyon-bird in the hollow of a wave, like a child uplifted by his mother, he forgot everything in the world but joy. He forgot Crete and the other islands that he had passed over: he saw but vaguely that winged thing in the distance before him that was his father Daedalus. He longed for one draught of flight to quench the thirst of his captivity: he stretched out his arms to the sky and made towards the highest heavens.

Alas for him! Warmer and warmer grew the air. Those arms, that had seemed to uphold him, relaxed. His wings wavered, drooped. He fluttered his young hands vainly—he was falling—and in that terror he remembered. The heat of the sun had melted the wax from his wings; the feathers were falling, one by one, like snowflakes; and there was none to help.

He fell like a leaf tossed down the wind, down, down, with one cry that overtook Daedalus far away. When he returned, and sought high and low for the poor boy, he saw nothing but the bird-like feathers afloat on the water, and he knew that Icarus was drowned.

The nearest island he named Icaria, in memory of the child; but he, in heavy grief, went to the temple of Apollo in Sicily, and there hung up his wings as an offering. Never again did he attempt to fly.

CUPID AND PSYCHE

The theme of this beautiful story is similar to that of "East o' the Sun" and other stories of maidens who doubt and lose their loves but search for them faithfully and successfully.

Once upon a time, through that Destiny that overrules the gods, Love himself gave up his immortal heart to a mortal maiden. And thus it came to pass.

There was a certain king who had three beautiful daughters. The two elder married princes of great renown; but Psyche, the youngest, was so radiantly fair that no suitor seemed worthy of her. People thronged to see her pass through the city, and sang hymns in her praise, while strangers took her for the very goddess of beauty herself.

This angered Venus, and she resolved to cast down her earthly rival. One day, therefore, she called hither her son Love (Cupid, some name him), and bade him sharpen his weapons. He is an archer more to be dreaded than Apollo, for Apollo's arrows take life, but Love's bring joy or sorrow for a whole life long.

"Come, Love," said Venus. "There is a mortal maid who robs me of my honors in yonder city. Avenge your mother. Wound this precious Psyche, and let her fall in love with some churlish creature mean in the eyes of all men."

Cupid made ready his weapons, and flew down to earth invisibly. At that moment Psyche was asleep in her chamber; but he touched her heart with his golden arrow of love, and she opened her eyes so suddenly that he started (forgetting that he was invisible), and wounded himself with his own shaft. Heedless of the hurt, moved only by the loveliness of the maiden, he hastened to pour over her locks the healing joy that he ever kept by him, undoing all his work. Back to her dream the princess went, unshadowed by any thought of love. But Cupid, not so light of heart, returned to the heavens, saying not a word of what had passed.

Venus waited long; then, seeing that Psyche's heart had somehow escaped love, she sent a spell

upon the maiden. From that time, lovely as she was, not a suitor came to woo; and her parents, who desired to see her a queen at least, made a journey to the Oracle, and asked counsel.

Said the voice: "The princess Psyche shall never wed a mortal. She shall be given to one who waits for her on yonder mountain; he overcomes gods and men."

At this terrible sentence the poor parents were half distraught, and the people gave themselves up to grief at the fate in store for their beloved princess. Psyche alone bowed to her destiny. "We have angered Venus unwittingly," she said, "and all for sake of me, heedless maiden that I am! Give me up, therefore, dear father and mother. If I atone, it may be that the city will prosper once more."

So she besought them, until, after many unavailing denials, the parents consented; and with a great company of people they led Psyche up the mountain,—as an offering to the monster of whom the Oracle had spoken,—and left her there alone.

Full of courage, yet in a secret agony of grief, she watched her kindred and her people wind down the mountain-path, too sad to look back, until they were lost to sight. Then, indeed, she wept, but a sudden breeze drew near, dried her tears, and caressed her hair, seeming to murmur comfort. In truth, it was Zephyr, the kindly West Wind, come to befriend her; and as she took heart, feeling some benignant presence, he lifted her in his arms, and carried her on wings as even as a sea-gull's, over the crest of the fateful mountain and into a valley below. There he left her, resting on a bank of hospitable grass, and there the princess fell asleep.

When she awoke, it was near sunset. She looked about her for some sign of the monster's approach; she wondered, then, if her grievous trial had been but a dream. Nearby she saw a sheltering forest, whose young trees seemed to beckon as one maid beckons to another; and eager for the protection of the dryads, she went thither.

The call of running waters drew her farther and farther, till she came out upon an open place, where there was a wide pool. A fountain fluttered gladly in the midst of it, and beyond there stretched a white palace wonderful to see.

Coaxed by the bright promise of the place, she drew near, and, seeing no one, entered softly. It was all kinglier than her father's home, and as she stood in wonder and awe, soft airs stirred about her. Little by little the silence grew murmurous like the woods, and one voice, sweeter than the rest, took words. "All that you see is yours, gentle high princess," it said. "Fear nothing; only command us, for we are here to serve you."

Full of amazement and delight, Psyche followed the voice from hall to hall, and through the lordly rooms, beautiful with everything that could delight a young princess. No pleasant thing was lacking. There was even a pool, brightly tiled and fed with running waters, where she bathed her weary limbs; and after she had put on the new and beautiful raiment that lay ready for her, she sat down to break her fast, waited upon and sung to by the unseen spirits.

Surely he whom the Oracle had called her husband was no monster, but some beneficent power, invisible like all the rest. When daylight waned, he came, and his voice, the beautiful voice of a god, inspired her to trust her strange destiny and to look and long for his return. Often she begged him to stay with her through the day, that she might see his face; but this he would not grant.

"Never doubt me, dearest Psyche," said he. "Perhaps you would fear if you saw me, and love is all I ask. There is a necessity that keeps me hidden now. Only believe."

So for many days Psyche was content; but when she grew used to happiness, she thought once more of her parents mourning her as lost, and of her sisters who shared the lot of mortals while she lived as a goddess. One night she told her husband of these regrets, and begged that her sisters at least might come to see her. He sighed, but did not refuse.

"Zephyr shall bring them hither," said he. And on the following morning, swift as a bird, the West Wind came over the crest of the high mountain and down into the enchanted valley, bearing her two sisters.

They greeted Psyche with joy and amazement, hardly knowing how they had come hither. But when this fairest of the sisters led them through her palace and showed them all the treasures that were hers, envy grew in their hearts and choked their old love. Even while they sat at feast with her, they grew more and more bitter; and hoping to find some little flaw in her good fortune, they asked a thousand questions.

"Where is your husband?" said they. "And why is he not here with you?"

"Ah," stammered Psyche. "All the day long— he is gone, hunting upon the mountains."

"But what does he look like?" they asked; and Psyche could find no answer.

When they learned that she had never seen him, they laughed her faith to scorn.

"Poor Psyche," they said. "You are walking in a dream. Wake, before it is too late. Have you forgotten what the Oracle decreed,—that you were destined for a dreadful creature, the fear of gods and men? And are you deceived by this show of kindliness? We have come to warn you. The people told us, as we came over the mountain, that your husband is a dragon, who feeds you well for the present, that he may feast the better, some day soon. What is it that you trust? Good words! But only take a dagger some night, and when the monster is asleep go, light a lamp, and look at him. You can put him to death easily, and all his riches will be yours—and ours."

Psyche heard this wicked plan with horror. Nevertheless, after her sisters were gone, she brooded over what they had said, not seeing their evil intent; and she came to find some wisdom in their words. Little by little, suspicion ate, like a moth, into her lovely mind; and at nightfall, in shame and fear, she hid a lamp and a dagger in her chamber. Toward midnight, when her husband was fast asleep, up she rose, hardly daring to breathe; and coming softly to his side, she uncovered the lamp to see some horror.

But there the youngest of the gods lay sleeping,—most beautiful, most irresistible of all immortals. His hair shone golden as the sun, his face was radiant as dear Springtime, and from his shoulders sprang two rainbow wings.

Poor Psyche was overcome with self-reproach. As she leaned toward him, filled with worship, her trembling hands held the lamp ill, and some burning oil fell upon Love's shoulder and awakened him.

He opened his eyes, to see at once his bride and the dark suspicion in her heart.

"O doubting Psyche!" he exclaimed with sudden grief,—and then he flew away, out of the window.

Wild with sorrow, Psyche tried to follow, but she fell to the ground instead. When she recovered her senses, she stared about her. She was alone, and the place was beautiful no longer. Garden and palace had vanished with Love. Over mountains and valleys Psyche journeyed alone until she came to the city where her two envious sisters lived with the princes whom they had married. She stayed with them only long enough to tell the story of her unbelief and its penalty. Then she set out again to search for Love.

As she wandered one day, travel-worn but not hopeless, she saw a lofty palace on a hill near by, and she turned her steps thither. The place seemed deserted. Within the hall she saw no human being,—only heaps of grain, loose ears of corn half torn from the husk, wheat and barley, alike scattered in confusion on the floor. Without delay, she set to work binding the sheaves together and gathering the scattered ears of corn in seemly wise, as a princess would wish to see them. While she was in the midst of her task, a voice startled her, and she looked up to behold Demeter herself, the goddess of the harvest, smiling upon her with good will.

"Dear Psyche," said Demeter, "you are worthy of happiness, and you may find it yet. But since you have displeased Venus, go to her and ask her favor. Perhaps your patience will win her pardon."

These motherly words gave Psyche heart, and she reverently took leave of the goddess and set out for the temple of Venus. Most humbly she offered up her prayer, but Venus could not look at her earthly beauty without anger.

"Vain girl," said she, "perhaps you have come to make amends for the wound you dealt your husband; you shall do so. Such clever people can always find work!"

Then she led Psyche into a great chamber heaped high with mingled grain, beans, and lentils (the food of her doves), and bade her separate them all and have them ready in seemly fashion by night. Heracles would have been helpless before such a vexatious task; and poor Psyche, left alone in this desert of grain, had not courage to begin. But even as she sat there, a moving thread of black crawled across the floor from a crevice in the wall; and bending nearer, she saw that a great army of ants in columns had come to her aid. The zealous little creatures worked in swarms, with such industry over the work they like best, that, when Venus came at night, she found the task completed.

"Deceitful girl!" she cried, shaking the roses out of her hair with impatience, "this is my son's work, not yours. But he will soon forget you. Eat this black bread if you are hungry, and refresh your dull mind with sleep. To-morrow you will need more wit."

Psyche wondered what new misfortune could be in store for her. But when morning came, Venus led her to the brink of a river, and, pointing to the wood across the water, said, "Go now to yonder grove where the sheep with the golden fleece are wont to browse. Bring me a golden lock from every one of them, or you must go your ways and never come back again."

This seemed not difficult, and Psyche obediently bade the goddess farewell, and stepped into the water, ready to wade across. But as Venus disappeared, the reeds sang louder and the nymphs of the river, looking up sweetly, blew bubbles to the surface and murmured: "Nay, nay, have a care, Psyche. This flock has not the gentle ways of sheep. While the sun burns aloft, they are themselves as fierce as flame; but when the shadows are long, they go to rest and sleep, under the trees; and you may cross the river without fear and pick the golden fleece off the briers in the pasture."

Thanking the water-creatures, Psyche sat down to rest near them, and when the time came, she crossed in safety and followed their counsel. By twilight she returned to Venus with her arms full of shining fleece.

"No mortal wit did this," said Venus angrily. "But if you care to prove your readiness, go now, with this little box, down to Proserpina and ask her to enclose in it some of her beauty, for I have grown pale in caring for my wounded son."

It needed not the last taunt to sadden Psyche. She knew that it was not for mortals to go into Hades and return alive; and feeling that Love had forsaken her, she was minded to accept her doom as soon as might be.

But even as she hastened toward the descent, another friendly voice detained her. "Stay, Psyche, I know your grief. Only give ear and you shall learn a safe way through all these trials." And the voice went on to tell her how one might

avoid all the dangers of Hades and come out unscathed. (But such a secret could not pass from mouth to mouth, with the rest of the story.)

"And be sure," added the voice, "when Proserpina has returned the box, not to open it, however much you may long to do so."

Psyche gave heed, and by this device, whatever it was, she found her way into Hades safely, and made her errand known to Proserpina, and was soon in the upper world again, wearied but hopeful.

"Surely Love has not forgotten me," she said. "But humbled as I am and worn with toil, how shall I ever please him? Venus can never need all the beauty in this casket; and since I use it for Love's sake, it must be right to take some." So saying, she opened the box, heedless as Pandora! The spells and potions of Hades are not for mortal maids, and no sooner had she inhaled the strange aroma than she fell down like one dead, quite overcome.

But it happened that Love himself was recovered from his wound, and he had secretly fled from his chamber to seek out and rescue Psyche. He found her lying by the wayside; he gathered into the casket what remained of the philter, and awoke his beloved.

"Take comfort," he said, smiling. "Return to our mother and do her bidding till I come again."

Away he flew; and while Psyche went cheerily homeward, he hastened up to Olympus, where all the gods sat feasting, and begged them to intercede for him with his angry mother.

They heard his story and their hearts were touched. Zeus himself coaxed Venus with kind words till at last she relented, and remembered that anger hurt her beauty, and smiled once more. All the younger gods were for welcoming Psyche at once, and Hermes was sent to bring her hither. The maiden came, a shy newcomer among those bright creatures. She took the cup that Hebe held out to her, drank the divine ambrosia, and became immortal.

Light came to her face like moonrise, two radiant wings sprang from her shoulders; and even as a butterfly bursts from its dull cocoon, so the human Psyche blossomed into immortality.

Love took her by the hand, and they were never parted any more.

ATALANTA'S RACE

Even if Prince Meleager had lived, it is doubtful if he could ever have won Atalanta to be his wife. The maiden was resolved to live unwed, and at last she devised a plan to be rid of all her suitors. She was known far and wide as the swiftest runner of her time; and so she said that she would only marry that man who could outstrip her in the race, but that all who dared to try and failed must be put to death.

This threat did not dishearten all of the suitors, however, and to her grief, for she was not cruel, they held her to her promise. On a certain day the few bold men who were to try their fortune made ready, and chose young Hippomenes as judge. He sat watching them before the word was given, and sadly wondered that any brave man should risk his life merely to win a bride. But when Atalanta stood ready for the contest, he was amazed by her beauty. She looked like Hebe, goddess of young health, who is a glad serving-maiden to the gods when they sit at feast.

The signal was given, and, as she and the suitors darted away, flight made her more enchanting than ever. Just as a wind brings sparkles to the water and laughter to the trees, haste fanned her loveliness to a glow.

Alas for the suitors! She ran as if Hermes had lent her his wingèd sandals. The young men, skilled as they were, grew heavy with weariness and despair. For all their efforts, they seemed to lag like ships in a calm, while Atalanta flew before them in some favoring breeze—and reached the goal!

To the sorrow of all on-lookers, the suitors were led away; but the judge himself, Hippomenes, rose and begged leave to try his fortune. As Atalanta listened, and looked at him, her heart was filled with pity, and she would willingly have let him win the race to save him from defeat and death; for he was comely and younger than the others. But her friends urged her to rest and make ready, and she consented, with an unwilling heart.

Meanwhile Hippomenes prayed within himself to Venus: "Goddess of Love, give ear, and

send me good speed. Let me be swift to win as I have been swift to love her."

Now Venus, who was not far off,—for she had already moved the heart of Hippomenes to love, —came to his side invisibly, slipped into his hand three wondrous golden apples, and whispered a word of counsel in his ear.

The signal was given; youth and maiden started over the course. They went so like the wind that they left not a footprint. The people cheered on Hippomenes, eager that such valor should win. But the course was long, and soon fatigue seemed to clutch at his throat, the light shook before his eyes, and, even as he pressed on, the maiden passed him by.

At that instant Hippomenes tossed ahead one of the golden apples. The rolling bright thing caught Atalanta's eye, and full of wonder she stooped to pick it up. Hippomenes ran on. As he heard the flutter of her tunic close behind him, he flung aside another golden apple, and another moment was lost to the girl. Who could pass by such a marvel? The goal was near and Hippomenes was ahead, but once again Atalanta caught up with him, and they sped side by side like two dragon-flies. For an instant his heart failed him; then, with a last prayer to Venus, he flung down the last apple. The maiden glanced at it, wavered, and would have left it where it had fallen, had not Venus turned her head for a second and given her a sudden wish to possess it. Against her will she turned to pick up the golden apple, and Hippomenes touched the goal.

So he won that perilous maiden; and as for Atalanta, she was glad to marry such a valorous man. By this time she understood so well what it was like to be pursued, that she had lost a little of her pleasure in hunting.

BAUCIS AND PHILEMON

Stories of gods walking the earth in disguise have, in the Christian era, become tales of saints walking the earth in disguise. Two good examples are found in Richard Chase's "Wicked John and the Devil" and in "King O'Toole and His Goose."

"Atalanta's Race." From *Old Greek Folk Stories Told Anew* by Josephine Preston Peabody. Copyright 1897 by Houghton Mifflin Company

"Baucis and Philemon." From *The Age of Fable; or Beauties of Mythology,* by Thomas Bulfinch. J. E. Tilton and Company, Boston, 1863

On a certain hill in Phrygia stand a linden tree and an oak, enclosed by a low wall. Not far from the spot is a marsh, formerly good habitable land, but now indented with pools, the resort of fen-birds and cormorants. Once on a time, Jupiter, in human shape, visited this country, and with him his son Mercury (he of the caduceus) without his wings. They presented themselves as weary travellers, at many a door, seeking rest and shelter, but found all closed, for it was late, and the inhospitable inhabitants would not rouse themselves to open for their reception. At last a humble mansion received them, a small thatched cottage, where Baucis, a pious old dame, and her husband Philemon, united when young, had grown old together. Not ashamed of their poverty, they made it endurable by moderate desires and kind dispositions. One need not look there for master or for servant; they two were the whole household, master and servant alike.

When the two heavenly guests crossed the humble threshold, and bowed their heads to pass under the low door, the old man placed a seat, on which Baucis, bustling and attentive, spread a cloth, and begged them to sit down. Then she raked out the coals from the ashes, and kindled up a fire, fed it with leaves and dry bark, and with her scanty breath blew it into a flame. She brought out of a corner split sticks and dry branches, broke them up, and placed them under the small kettle. Her husband collected some pot-herbs in the garden, and she shred them from the stalks, and prepared them for the pot. He reached down with a forked stick a flitch of bacon hanging in the chimney, cut a small piece, and put it in the pot to boil with the herbs, setting away the rest for another time. A beechen bowl was filled with warm water, that their guests might wash. While all was doing, they beguiled the time with conversation.

On the bench designed for the guests was laid a cushion stuffed with sea weed; and a cloth, only produced on great occasions, but ancient and coarse enough, was spread over that. The old lady, with her apron on, with trembling hand set the table. One leg was shorter than the rest, but a piece of slate put under restored the level. When fixed, she rubbed the table down with some sweet-smelling herbs. Upon it she set some of chaste Minerva's olives, some cornel berries preserved in vinegar, and added radishes and cheese, with eggs lightly cooked in the ashes. All were served in earthen dishes, and an earthenware pitcher, with wooden cups, stood beside them. When all was ready, the stew, smoking hot, was set on the table. Some wine, not of the oldest, was added; and for dessert, apples and wild honey; and over and above all, friendly faces, and simple but hearty welcome.

Now while the repast proceeded, the old folks were astonished to see that the wine, as fast as it was poured out, renewed itself in the pitcher, of its own accord. Struck with terror, Baucis and Philemon recognized their heavenly guests, fell on their knees, and with clasped hands implored forgiveness for their poor entertainment. There was an old goose, which they kept as the guardian of their humble cottage; and they bethought them to make this a sacrifice in honor of their guests. But the goose, too nimble, with the aid of feet and wings, for the old folks, eluded their pursuit, and at last took shelter between the gods themselves. They forbade it to be slain; and spoke in these words: "We are gods. This inhospitable village shall pay the penalty of its impiety; you alone shall go free from the chastisement. Quit your house, and come with us to the top of yonder hill."

The old couple hastened to obey, and, staff in hand, labored up the steep ascent. They had reached to within an arrow's flight of the top, when turning their eyes below, they beheld all the country sunk in a lake, only their own house left standing. While they gazed with wonder at the sight, and lamented the fate of their neighbors, that old house of theirs was changed into a *temple.* Columns took the place of the corner posts, the thatch grew yellow and appeared a gilded roof, the floors became marble, the doors were enriched with carving and ornaments of gold.

Then spoke Jupiter in benignant accents: "Excellent old man, and woman worthy of such a husband, speak, tell us your wishes; what favor have you to ask of us?"

Philemon took counsel with Baucis a few moments; then declared to the gods their united wish. "We ask to be priests and guardians of this your temple; and since here we have passed our lives in love and concord, we wish that one and the same hour may take us both from life, that I may not live to see her grave, nor be laid in my own by her." Their prayer was granted. They were the keepers of the temple as long as they lived.

When grown very old, as they stood one day before the steps of the sacred edifice, and were telling the story of the place, Baucis saw Philemon begin to put forth leaves, and old Philemon saw Baucis changing in like manner. And now a leafy crown had grown over their heads, while exchanging parting words, as long as they could speak. "Farewell, dear spouse," they said together, and at the same moment the bark closed over their mouths. The Tyanean shepherd still shows the two trees, standing side by side, made out of the two good old people.

PEGASUS AND THE CHIMAERA

When Perseus cut off Medusa's head, the blood sinking into the earth produced the winged horse Pegasus. Minerva caught and tamed him, and presented him to the Muses. The fountain Hippocrene, on the Muses' mountain Helicon, was opened by a kick from his hoof.

The Chimæra was a fearful monster, breathing fire. The fore part of its body was a compound of the lion and the goat, and the hind part a dragon's. It made great havoc in Lycia, so that the king Iobates sought for some hero to destroy it. At that time there arrived at his court a gallant young warrior, whose name was Bellerophon. He brought letters from Prœtus, the son-in-law of Iobates, recommending Bellerophon in the warmest terms as an unconquerable hero, but added at the close a request to his father-in-law to put him to death. The reason was that Prœtus was jealous of him, suspecting that his wife Antea looked with too much admiration on the young warrior. (From this instance of Bellerophon being unconsciously the bearer of his own death-warrant, the expression "Bellerophontic letters" arose, to describe any species of communication which a person is made the bearer of, containing matter prejudicial to himself.)

Iobates, on perusing the letters, was puzzled what to do, not willing to violate the claims of hospitality, yet wishing to oblige his son-in-law. A lucky thought occurred to him, to send Bellerophon to combat with the Chimæra. Bellerophon accepted the proposal, but before proceeding to the combat consulted the soothsayer Polyidus, who advised him to procure if possible the horse Pegasus for the conflict. For this purpose he directed him to pass the night in the temple of Minerva. He did so, and as he slept Minerva came to him and gave him a golden bridle. When he awoke the bridle remained in his

"Pegasus and the Chimaera." From *The Age of Fable; or Beauties of Mythology*, by Thomas Bulfinch. J. E. Tilton and Company, Boston, 1863

hand. Minerva also showed him Pegasus drinking at the well of Pirene, and at sight of the bridle, the winged steed came willingly and suffered himself to be taken. Bellerophon mounted him, rose with him into the air, soon found the Chimæra, and gained an easy victory over the monster.

After the conquest of the Chimæra, Bellerophon was exposed to further trials and labors by his unfriendly host, but by the aid of Pegasus he triumphed in them all; till at length Iobates, seeing that the hero was a special favorite of the gods, gave him his daughter in marriage and made him his successor on the throne. At last Bellerophon by his pride and presumption drew upon himself the anger of the gods; it is said he even attempted to fly up into heaven on his winged steed; but Jupiter sent a gadfly which stung Pegasus and made him throw his rider, who became lame and blind in consequence. After this Bellerophon wandered lonely through the Aleian field, avoiding the paths of men, and died miserably.

MIDAS

This is the meager source (in translation) from which Hawthorne spun the better-known version that follows it.

Bacchus, on a certain occasion, found his old schoolmaster and foster-father, Silenus, missing. The old man had been drinking, and in that state wandered away, and was found by some peasants, who carried him to their king, Midas. Midas recognized him, and treated him hospitably, entertaining him for ten days and nights with an unceasing round of jollity. On the eleventh day he brought Silenus back, and restored him in safety to his pupil. Whereupon Bacchus offered Midas his choice of a reward, whatever he might wish. He asked that whatever he might touch should be changed into gold. Bacchus consented, though sorry that he had not made a better choice. Midas went his way, rejoicing in his new-acquired power, which he hastened to put to the test. He could scarce believe his eyes when

"Midas." From *The Age of Fable; or Beauties of Mythology,* by Thomas Bulfinch. J. E. Tilton and Company, Boston, 1863

he found a twig of an oak, which he plucked from the branch, become gold in his hand. He took up a stone; it changed to gold. He touched a sod; it did the same. He took an apple from the tree; you would have thought he had robbed the garden of the Hesperides. His joy knew no bounds, and as soon as he got home, he ordered the servants to set a splendid repast on the table. Then he found to his dismay that whether he touched bread, it hardened in his hand; or put a morsel to his lips, it defied his teeth. He took a glass of wine, but it flowed down his throat like melted gold.

In consternation at the unprecedented affliction, he strove to divest himself of his power; he hated the gift he had lately coveted. But all in vain; starvation seemed to await him. He raised his arms, all shining with gold, in prayer to Bacchus, begging to be delivered from his glittering destruction.

Bacchus, merciful deity, heard and consented. "Go," said he, "to the River Pactolus, trace the stream to its fountain-head, there plunge your head and body in, and wash away your fault and its punishment." He did so, and scarce had he touched the waters before the gold-creating power passed into them, and the river sands became changed into gold, as they remain to this day.

Thenceforth Midas, hating wealth and splendor, dwelt in the country, and became a worshipper of Pan, the god of the fields. On a certain occasion Pan had the temerity to compare his music with that of Apollo, and to challenge the god of the lyre to a trial of skill. The challenge was accepted, and Tmolus, the mountain god, was chosen umpire. The senior took his seat, and cleared away the trees from his ears to listen.

At a given signal Pan blew on his pipes, and with his rustic melody gave great satisfaction to himself and his faithful follower Midas, who happened to be present. Then Tmolus turned his head toward the Sun-god, and all his trees turned with him. Apollo rose; his brow wreathed with Parnassian laurel, while his robe of Tyrian purple swept the ground. In his left hand he held the lyre, and with his right hand struck the strings. Ravished with the harmony, Tmolus at once awarded the victory to the god of the lyre, and all but Midas acquiesced in the judgment.

He dissented, and questioned the justice of the award. Apollo would not suffer such a depraved pair of ears any longer to wear the human form, but caused them to increase in length, grow hairy, within and without, and movable on their roots; in short, to be on the perfect pattern of those of an ass.

Mortified enough was King Midas at this mishap; but he consoled himself with the thought that it was possible to hide his misfortune, which he attempted to do by means of an ample turban or head-dress. But his hair-dresser of course knew the secret. He was charged not to mention it, and threatened with dire punishment if he presumed to disobey. But he found it too much for his discretion to keep such a secret; so he went out into the meadow, dug a hole in the ground, and stooping down, whispered the story, and covered it up. Before long a thick bed of reeds sprang up in the meadow, and as soon as it had gained its growth, began whispering the story, and has continued to do so, from that day to this, every time a breeze passes over the place.

THE GOLDEN TOUCH

Once upon a time, there lived a very rich king whose name was Midas; and he had a little daughter, whom nobody but myself ever heard of, and whose name was Marygold.

This King Midas was fonder of gold than of anything else in the world. He valued his royal crown chiefly because it was composed of that precious metal. If he loved anything better, or half so well, it was the one little maiden who played so merrily around her father's footstool. But the more Midas loved his daughter, the more did he desire and seek for wealth. He thought, foolish man! that the best thing he could possibly do for this dear child would be to bequeath her the immensest pile of yellow, glistening coin, that had ever been heaped together since the world was made. Thus, he gave all his thoughts and all his time to this one purpose. If ever he happened to gaze for an instant at the gold-tinted clouds of sunset, he wished that they were real gold, and that they could be squeezed

"The Golden Touch." From *A Wonder Book for Girls and Boys* by Nathaniel Hawthorne

safely into his strong box. When little Marygold ran to meet him, with a bunch of buttercups and dandelions, he used to say, "Poh, poh, child! If these flowers were as golden as they look, they would be worth the plucking!"

And yet, in his earlier days, before he was so entirely possessed of this insane desire for riches, King Midas had shown a great taste for flowers. He had planted a garden, in which grew the biggest and beautifullest and sweetest roses that any mortal ever saw or smelt. These roses were still growing in the garden, as large, as lovely, and as fragrant, as when Midas used to pass whole hours in gazing at them, and inhaling their perfume. But now, if he looked at them at all, it was only to calculate how much the garden would be worth if each of the innumerable rose-petals were a thin plate of gold. And though he once was fond of music the only music for poor Midas, now, was the chink of one coin against another.

At length Midas had got to be so exceedingly unreasonable, that he could scarcely bear to see or touch any object that was not gold. He made it his custom, therefore, to pass a large portion of every day in a dark and dreary apartment, under ground, at the basement of his palace. It was here that he kept his wealth. To this dismal hole —for it was little better than a dungeon—Midas betook himself, whenever he wanted to be particularly happy. Here, after carefully locking the door, he would take a bag of gold coin, or a gold cup as big as a washbowl, or a heavy golden bar, or a peck-measure of gold-dust, and bring them from the obscure corners of the room into the one bright and narrow sunbeam that fell from the dungeon-like window. He valued the sunbeam for no other reason but that his treasure would not shine without its help. And then would he reckon over the coins in the bag, toss up the bar, and catch it as it came down; sift the gold-dust through his fingers; look at the funny image of his own face, as reflected in the burnished circumference of the cup; and whisper to himself, "O Midas, rich King Midas, what a happy man art thou!"

Midas was enjoying himself in his treasure-room, one day, as usual, when he perceived a shadow fall over the heaps of gold; and, looking suddenly up, what should he behold but the figure of a stranger, standing in the bright and narrow sunbeam! It was a young man, with a cheerful and ruddy face. Whether it was that the imagination of King Midas threw a yellow tinge over everything, or whatever the cause might be, he could not help fancying that the smile with which the stranger regarded him had a kind of golden radiance in it. Certainly, although his figure intercepted the sunshine, there was now a brighter gleam upon all the piled-up treasure than before. Even the remotest corners had their share of it, and were lighted up, when the stranger smiled, as with tips of flame and sparkles of fire.

As Midas knew that he had carefully turned the key in the lock, and that no mortal strength could possibly break into his treasure-room, he, of course, concluded that his visitor must be something more than mortal. Midas had met such beings before now, and was not sorry to meet one of them again.

The stranger gazed about the room; and when his lustrous smile had glistened upon all the golden objects that were there, he turned again to Midas.

"You are a wealthy man, friend Midas!" he observed. "I doubt whether any other four walls, on earth, contain so much gold as you have contrived to pile up in this room."

"I have done pretty well,—pretty well," answered Midas, in a discontented tone. "But, after all, it is but a trifle, when you consider that it has taken me my whole life to get it together. If one could live a thousand years, he might have time to grow rich!"

"What!" exclaimed the stranger. "Then you are not satisfied?"

Midas shook his head.

"And pray what would satisfy you?" asked the stranger. "Merely for the curiosity of the thing, I should be glad to know."

Midas paused and meditated. He felt a presentiment that this stranger, with such a golden lustre in his good-humored smile, had come hither with both the power and the purpose of gratifying his utmost wishes. Now, therefore, was the fortunate moment, when he had but to speak, and obtain whatever possible, or seemingly impossible thing, it might come into his head to ask. So he thought, and thought, and

thought, and heaped up one golden mountain upon another, in his imagination, without being able to imagine them big enough. At last, a bright idea occurred to King Midas. It seemed really as bright as the glistening metal which he loved so much.

Raising his head, he looked the lustrous stranger in the face.

"Well, Midas," observed his visitor, "I see that you have at length hit upon something that will satisfy you. Tell me your wish."

"It is only this," replied Midas. "I am weary of collecting my treasures with so much trouble, and beholding the heap so diminutive, after I have done my best. I wish everything that I touch be changed to gold!"

The stranger's smile grew so very broad, that it seemed to fill the room like an outburst of the sun, gleaming into a shadowy dell, where the yellow autumnal leaves—for so looked the lumps and particles of gold—lie strewn in the glow of light.

"The Golden Touch!" exclaimed he. "You certainly deserve credit, friend Midas, for striking out so brilliant a conception. But are you quite sure that this will satisfy you?"

"How could it fail?" said Midas.

"And will you never regret the possession of it?"

"What could induce me?" asked Midas. "I ask nothing else, to render me perfectly happy."

"Be it as you wish, then," replied the stranger, waving his hand in token of farewell. "Tomorrow, at sunrise, you will find yourself gifted with the Golden Touch."

The figure of the stranger then became exceedingly bright, and Midas involuntarily closed his eyes. On opening them again, he beheld only one yellow sunbeam in the room, and all around him, the glistening of the precious metal which he had spent his life in hoarding up.

Whether Midas slept as usual that night, the story does not say. At any rate, day had hardly peeped over the hills, when King Midas was broad awake, and stretching his arms out of bed, began to touch the objects that were within reach. He was anxious to prove whether the Golden Touch had really come, according to the stranger's promise. So he laid his finger on a chair by the bedside, and on various other things, but was grievously disappointed to perceive that they remained of exactly the same substance as before. Indeed, he felt very much afraid that he had only dreamed about the lustrous stranger, or else that the latter had been making game of him. And what a miserable affair would it be, if after all his hopes, Midas must content himself with what little gold he could scrape together by ordinary means, instead of creating it by a touch!

All this while, it was only the gray of the morning, with but a streak of brightness along the edge of the sky, where Midas could not see it. He lay in a very disconsolate mood, regretting the downfall of his hopes, and kept growing sadder and sadder, until the earliest sunbeam shone through the window, and gilded the ceiling over his head. It seemed to Midas that this bright yellow sunbeam was reflected in rather a singular way on the white covering of the bed. Looking more closely, what was his astonishment and delight, when he found that this linen fabric had been transmuted to what seemed a woven texture of the purest and brightest gold! The Golden Touch had come to him with the first sunbeam!

Midas started up, in a kind of joyful frenzy, and ran about the room, grasping at everything that happened to be in his way. He seized one of the bed-posts, and it became immediately a fluted golden pillar. He pulled aside a window-curtain, in order to admit a clear spectacle of the wonders which he was performing; and the tassel grew heavy in his hand,—a mass of gold. He took up a book from the table. At his first touch, it assumed the appearance of such a splendidly bound and gilt-edged volume as one often meets with, nowadays; but, on running his fingers through the leaves, behold! It was a bundle of thin golden plates, in which all the wisdom of the book had grown illegible. He hurriedly put on his clothes, and was enraptured to see himself in a magnificent suit of gold cloth, which retained its flexibility and softness, although it burdened him a little with its weight. He drew out his handkerchief, which little Marygold had hemmed for him. That was likewise gold, with the dear child's neat and pretty stitches running all along the border, in gold thread!

Somehow or other, this last transformation did not quite please King Midas. He would rather that his little daughter's handiwork should have remained just the same as when she climbed his knee and put it into his hand.

But it was not worth while to vex himself about a trifle. Midas now took his spectacles from his pocket, and put them on his nose, in order that he might see more distinctly what he was about. In those days, spectacles for common people had not been invented, but were already worn by kings; else, how could Midas have had any? To his great perplexity, however, excellent as the glasses were, he discovered that he could not possibly see through them. But this was the most natural thing in the world; for, on taking them off, the transparent crystals turned out to be plates of yellow metal, and, of course, were worthless as spectacles, though valuable as gold. It struck Midas as rather inconvenient that, with all his wealth, he could never again be rich enough to own a pair of serviceable spectacles.

"It is no great matter, nevertheless," said he to himself, very philosophically. "We cannot expect any great good, without its being accompanied with some small inconvenience. The Golden Touch is worth the sacrifice of a pair of spectacles, at least, if not of one's very eyesight. My own eyes will serve for ordinary purposes, and little Marygold will soon be old enough to read to me."

King Midas went down stairs, and smiled, on observing that the balustrade of the staircase became a bar of burnished gold, as his hand passed over it, in his descent. He lifted the door-latch (it was brass only a moment ago, but golden when his fingers quitted it), and emerged into the garden. Here, as it happened, he found a great number of beautiful roses in full bloom, and others in all the stages of lovely bud and blossom. Very delicious was their fragrance in the morning breeze. Their delicate blush was one of the fairest sights in the world; so gentle, so modest, and so full of sweet tranquillity, did these roses seem to be.

But Midas knew a way to make them far more precious, according to his way of thinking, than roses had ever been before. So he took great pains in going from bush to bush, and exercised his magic touch most indefatigably; until every individual flower and bud, and even the worms at the heart of some of them, were changed to gold. By the time this good work was completed, King Midas was summoned to breakfast; and as the morning air had given him an excellent appetite, he made haste back to the palace.

On this particular morning, the breakfast consisted of hot cakes, some nice little brook-trout, roasted potatoes, fresh boiled eggs, and coffee, for King Midas himself, and a bowl of bread and milk for his daughter Marygold.

Little Marygold had not yet made her appearance. Her father ordered her to be called, and, seating himself at table, awaited the child's coming, in order to begin his own breakfast. To do Midas justice, he really loved his daughter, and loved her so much the more this morning, on account of the good fortune which had befallen him. It was not a great while before he heard her coming along the passageway crying bitterly. This circumstance surprised him, because Marygold was one of the cheerfullest little people whom you would see in a summer's day, and hardly shed a thimbleful of tears in a twelvemonth. When Midas heard her sobs, he determined to put little Marygold in better spirits, by an agreeable surprise; so, leaning across the table, he touched his daughter's bowl (which was a China one, with pretty figures all around it), and transmuted it to gleaming gold.

Meanwhile, Marygold slowly and disconsolately opened the door, and showed herself with her apron at her eyes, still sobbing as if her heart would break.

"How now, my little lady!" cried Midas. "Pray what is the matter with you, this bright morning?"

Marygold, without taking the apron from her eyes, held out her hand, in which was one of the roses which Midas had so recently transmuted.

"Beautiful!" exclaimed her father. "And what is there in this magnificent golden rose to make you cry?"

"Ah, dear father!" answered the child, as well as her sobs would let her; "it is not beautiful, but the ugliest flower that ever grew! As soon as I was dressed I ran into the garden to gather some roses for you; because I know you like them. But, oh dear, dear me! What do you think has happened? Such a misfortune! All the beautiful roses, that smelled so sweetly and had so many lovely blushes, are blighted and spoilt! They are grown quite yellow, as you see this one, and have no longer any fragrance! What can have been the matter with them?"

"Poh, my dear little girl,—pray don't cry about it!" said Midas, who was ashamed to confess that he himself had wrought the change which so greatly afflicted her. "Sit down and eat your bread and milk! You will find it easy enough to exchange a golden rose like that (which will last hundreds of years) for an ordinary one which would wither in a day."

"I don't care for such roses as this!" cried Marygold, tossing it contemptuously away. "It has no smell, and the hard petals prick my nose!"

The child now sat down to table, but was so occupied with her grief for the blighted roses that she did not even notice the wonderful transmutation of her China bowl. Perhaps this was all the better; for Marygold was accustomed to take pleasure in looking at the queer figures, and strange trees and houses, that were painted on the circumference of the bowl; and these ornaments were now entirely lost in the yellow hue of the metal.

Midas, meanwhile, had poured out a cup of coffee, and, as a matter of course, the coffee-pot, whatever metal it may have been when he took it up, was gold when he set it down. He thought to himself, that it was rather an extravagant style of splendor, in a king of his simple habits, to breakfast off a service of gold, and began to be puzzled with the difficulty of keeping his treasures safe. The cupboard and the kitchen would no longer be a secure place of deposit for articles so valuable as golden bowls and coffee-pots.

Amid these thoughts, he lifted a spoonful of coffee to his lips, and, sipping it, was astonished to perceive that, the instant his lips touched the liquid, it became molten gold, and, the next moment, hardened into a lump!

"Ha!" exclaimed Midas, rather aghast.

"What is the matter, father?" asked little Marygold, gazing at him, with the tears still standing in her eyes.

"Nothing, child, nothing!" said Midas. "Eat your milk, before it gets quite cold."

He took one of the nice little trouts on his plate, and, by way of experiment, touched its tail with his finger. To his horror, it was immediately transmuted from an admirably fried brook-trout into a gold-fish. A very pretty piece of work, as you may suppose; only King Midas, just at that moment, would much rather have had a real trout in his dish than this elaborate and valuable imitation of one.

"I don't quite see," thought he to himself, "how I am to get any breakfast!"

He took one of the smoking-hot cakes, and had scarcely broken it, when, to his cruel mortification, though, a moment before, it had been of the whitest wheat, it assumed the yellow hue of Indian meal. Almost in despair, he helped himself to a boiled egg, which immediately underwent a change similar to those of the trout and the cake. The egg, indeed, might have been mistaken for one of those which the famous goose, in the story-book, was in the habit of laying; but King Midas was the only goose that had had anything to do with the matter.

"Well, this is a quandary!" thought he, leaning back in his chair, and looking quite enviously at little Marygold, who was now eating her bread and milk with great satisfaction. "Such a costly breakfast before me, and nothing that can be eaten."

Hoping that, by dint of great dispatch, he might avoid what he now felt to be a considerable inconvenience, King Midas next snatched a hot potato, and attempted to cram it into his mouth, and swallow it in a hurry. But the Golden Touch was too nimble for him. He found his mouth full, not of mealy potato, but of solid metal, which so burnt his tongue that he roared aloud, and, jumping up from the table, began to dance and stamp about the room, both with pain and affright.

"Father, dear father!" cried little Marygold, who was a very affectionate child, "pray what is the matter? Have you burnt your mouth?"

"Ah, dear child," groaned Midas, dolefully, "I don't know what is to become of your poor father!"

Already, at breakfast, Midas was excessively hungry. Would he be less so by dinner-time? And how ravenous would be his appetite for supper, which must undoubtedly consist of the same sort of indigestible dishes as those now before him.

These reflections so troubled wise King Midas,

that he began to doubt whether, after all, riches are the one desirable thing in the world. But this was only a passing thought. So fascinated was Midas with the glitter of the yellow metal, that he would still have refused to give up the Golden Touch for so paltry a consideration as a breakfast.

Nevertheless, so great was his hunger, and the perplexity of his situation, that he again groaned aloud, and very grievously too. Our pretty Marygold could endure it no longer. She sat, a moment, gazing at her father, and trying, with all the might of her little wits, to find out what was the matter with him. Then, with a sweet and sorrowful impulse to comfort him, she started from her chair, and, running to Midas, threw her arms affectionately about his knees. He bent down and kissed her. He felt that his little daughter's love was worth a thousand times more than he had gained by the Golden Touch.

"My precious, precious Marygold!" cried he.

But Marygold made no answer.

Alas, what had he done? The moment the lips of Midas touched Marygold's forehead, a change had taken place. Her sweet, rosy face, so full of affection as it had been, assumed a glittering yellow color, with yellow tear-drops, congealing on her cheeks. Her beautiful brown ringlets took the same tint. Her soft and tender little form grew hard and inflexible within her father's encircling arms. Oh, terrible misfortune! The victim of his insatiable desire for wealth, little Marygold was a human child no longer, but a golden statue!

Yes, there she was, with the questioning look of love, grief, and pity, hardened into her face. It was the prettiest and most woeful sight that ever mortal saw. All the features and tokens of Marygold were there; even the beloved little dimple remained in her golden chin. But, the more perfect was the resemblance, the greater was the father's agony at beholding this golden image, which was all that was left him of a daughter. It had been a favorite phrase of Midas, whenever he felt particularly fond of the child, to say that she was worth her weight in gold. And now the phrase had become literally true. And now, at last, when it was too late, he felt how infinitely a warm and tender heart, that loved him, exceeded in value all the wealth that could be piled up betwixt the earth and sky!

Midas, in the fulness of all his gratified desires, began to wring his hands and bemoan himself; and now he could neither bear to look at Marygold, nor yet to look away from her. Except when his eyes were fixed on the image, he could not possibly believe that she was changed to gold. But, stealing another glance, there was the precious little figure, with a yellow tear-drop on its yellow cheek, and a look so piteous and tender, that it seemed as if that very expression must needs soften the gold, and make it flesh again. This, however, could not be.

While Midas was in this tumult of despair, he suddenly beheld a stranger standing near the door. Midas bent down his head, without speaking; for he recognized the same figure which had appeared to him, the day before, in the treasure-room, and had bestowed on him this disastrous faculty of the Golden Touch. The stranger's countenance still wore a smile, which seemed to shed a yellow lustre all about the room, and gleamed on little Marygold's image, and on the other objects that had been transmuted by the touch of Midas.

"Well, friend Midas," said the stranger, "pray how do you succeed with the Golden Touch?"

Midas shook his head.

"I am very miserable," said he.

"Very miserable, indeed!" exclaimed the stranger. "And how happens that? Have I not faithfully kept my promise with you? Have you not everything that your heart desired?"

"Gold is not everything," answered Midas. "And I have lost all that my heart really cared for."

"Ah! So you have made a discovery, since yesterday?" observed the stranger. "Let us see, then. Which of these two things do you think is really worth the most,—the gift of the Golden Touch, or one cup of clear cold water?"

"O blessed water!" exclaimed Midas. "It will never moisten my parched throat again!"

"The Golden Touch," continued the stranger, "or a crust of bread?"

"A piece of bread," answered Midas, "is worth all the gold on earth!"

"The Golden Touch," asked the stranger, "or your own little Marygold, warm, soft, and loving as she was an hour ago?"

"Oh, my child, my dear child!" cried poor Midas, wringing his hands. "I would not have given that one small dimple in her chin for the power of changing this whole big earth into a solid lump of gold!"

"You are wiser than you were, King Midas!" said the stranger, looking seriously at him. "Your own heart, I perceive, has not been entirely changed from flesh to gold. Were it so, your case would indeed be desperate. But you appear to be still capable of understanding that the commonest things, such as lie within everybody's grasp, are more valuable than the riches which so many mortals sigh and struggle after. Tell me, now, do you sincerely desire to rid yourself of this Golden Touch?"

"It is hateful to me!" replied Midas.

A fly settled on his nose, but immediately fell to the floor; for it, too, had become gold. Midas shuddered.

"Go, then," said the stranger, "and plunge into the river that glides past the bottom of your garden. Take likewise a vase of the same water, and sprinkle it over any object that you may desire to change back again from gold into its former substance. If you do this in earnestness and sincerity, it may possibly repair the mischief which your avarice has occasioned."

King Midas bowed low; and when he lifted his head, the lustrous stranger had vanished.

You will easily believe that Midas lost no time in snatching up a great earthen pitcher (but, alas me! it was no longer earthen after he touched it), and hastening to the river-side. As he scampered along, and forced his way through the shrubbery, it was positively marvellous to see how the foliage turned yellow behind him, as if the autumn had been there, and nowhere else. On reaching the river's brink, he plunged headlong in, without waiting so much as to pull off his shoes.

"Poof! poof! poof!" snorted King Midas, as his head emerged out of the water. "Well, this is really a refreshing bath, and I think it must have quite washed away the Golden Touch. And now for filling my pitcher!"

As he dipped the pitcher into the water, it gladdened his very heart to see it change from gold into the same good, honest earthen vessel which it had been before he touched it. He was conscious, also, of a change within himself. A cold, hard, and heavy weight seemed to have gone out of his bosom. Perceiving a violet, that grew on the bank of the river, Midas touched it with his finger, and was overjoyed to find that the delicate flower retained its purple hue, instead of undergoing a yellow blight. The curse of the Golden Touch had, therefore, really been removed from him.

King Midas hastened back to the palace; and, I suppose, the servants knew not what to make of it when they saw their royal master so carefully

bringing home an earthen pitcher of water. But that water, which was to undo all the mischief that his folly had wrought, was more precious to Midas than an ocean of molten gold could have been. The first thing he did, as you need hardly be told, was to sprinkle it by handfuls over the golden figure of little Marygold.

No sooner did it fall on her than you would have laughed to see how the rosy color came back to the dear child's cheek! And how she began to sneeze and sputter!—and how astonished she was to find herself dripping wet, and her father still throwing more water over her!

"Pray do not, dear father!" cried she. "See how you have wet my nice frock, which I put on only this morning!"

For Marygold did not know that she had been a little golden statue; nor could she remember anything that had happened since the moment when she ran with outstretched arms to comfort poor King Midas.

Her father did not think it necessary to tell his beloved child how very foolish he had been, but contented himself with showing how much wiser he had now grown. For this purpose, he led little Marygold into the garden, where he sprinkled all the remainder of the water over the rose-bushes, and with such good effect that above five thousand roses recovered their beautiful bloom. There were two circumstances, however, which as long as he lived, used to put King Midas in mind of the Golden Touch. One was, that the sands of the river sparkled like gold; the other, that little Marygold's hair had now a golden tinge, which he had never observed in it before she had been transmuted by the effect of his kiss.

When King Midas had grown quite an old man, and used to trot Marygold's children on his knee, he was fond of telling them this marvellous story, pretty much as I have now told it to you. And then would he stroke their glossy ringlets, and tell them that their hair, likewise, had a rich shade of gold, which they had inherited from their mother.

"And to tell you the truth, my precious little folks," quoth King Midas, diligently trotting the children all the while, "ever since that morning, I have hated the very sight of all other gold, save this!"

Norse Myths

One notices very quickly a difference in mood between the Greek and Norse myths. Greek myth has the bright beauty of a southern country, but Norse myth is somber on a grand and heroic scale. One senses in the tales of Odin and Balder a world before this world, a world somehow doomed. The Greek myths can be humorous and lighthearted on occasion. The Norse myths, while they have joyfulness here and there, are never lighthearted. Can this be due to their having originated in a northern clime? Quite possibly, for the striking change of seasons did not occur in Greece, and it would seem to follow that Norsemen were much more grimly aware of the mystery of ever recurring cycles of life and seeming death in most living things, faced as they were with the stark contrast between flower-filled, light-filled summers, and winters of deepest cold and great darkness. The myth of Balder and his death is an exquisite evocation of that sense of the tragedy of death and the mystery of rebirth, and it is a more despairing symbol of the change of seasons than the Greek story of Demeter and Persephone.

HOW THOR FOUND HIS HAMMER

Rarely does one find outright humor in a Norse myth, and this one is one of the exceptions. There are undertones even to this tale, however, which belong to the province of archaeologists and anthropologists, and it may be that humor was not intended here.

The frost-giants were always trying to get into Asgard. For more than half the year they held the world in their grasp, locking up the streams in their rocky beds, hushing their music and the music of the birds as well, and leaving nothing but a wild waste of desolation under the cold sky. They hated the warm sunshine which stirred the wild flowers out of their sleep, and clothed the steep mountains with verdure, and set all the birds a-singing in the swaying tree-tops. They hated the beautiful god Balder, with whose presence summer came back to the ice-bound earth, and, above all, they hated Thor, whose flashing hammer drove them back into Jotunheim, and guarded the summer sky with its sudden gleamings of power. So long as Thor had his hammer Asgard was safe against the giants.

"How Thor Found His Hammer." Reprinted from *Norse Stories* by Hamilton Wright Mabie by permission of Dodd, Mead & Company

One morning Thor started up out of a long, deep sleep, and put out his hand for the hammer; but no hammer was there. Not a sign of it could be found anywhere, although Thor anxiously searched for it. Then a thought of the giants came suddenly in his mind; and his anger rose till his eyes flashed like great fires, and his red beard trembled with wrath.

"Look, now, Loke," he shouted, "they have stolen Mjolner by enchantment, and no one on earth or in heaven knows where they have hidden it."

"We will get Freyja's falcon-guise and search for it," answered Loke, who was always quick to get into trouble or to get out of it again. So they went quickly to Folkvang and found Freyja surrounded by her maidens and weeping tears of pure gold, as she had always done since her husband went on his long journey.

"The hammer has been stolen by enchantment," said Thor. "Will you lend me the falcon-guise that I may search for it?"

"If it were silver, or even gold, you should have it and welcome," answered Freyja, glad to help Thor find the wonderful hammer that kept them all safe from the hands of the frost-giants.

So the falcon-guise was brought, and Loke put it on and flew swiftly out of Asgard to the home of the giants. His great wings made broad shadows over the ripe fields as he swept along, and the reapers, looking up from their work, wondered what mighty bird was flying seaward. At last he reached Jotunheim, and no sooner had he touched ground and taken off the falcon-guise than he came upon the giant Thrym, sitting on a hill twisting golden collars for his dogs and stroking the long manes of his horses.

"Welcome, Loke," said the giant. "How fares it with the gods and the elves, and what has brought you to Jotunheim?"

"It fares ill with both gods and elves since you stole Thor's hammer," replied Loke, guessing quickly that Thrym was the thief; "and I have come to find where you have hidden it."

Thrym laughed as only a giant can when he knows he has made trouble for somebody.

"You won't find it," he said at last. "I have buried it eight miles under ground, and no one shall take it away unless he gets Freyja for me as my wife."

The giant looked as if he meant what he said, and Loke, seeing no other way of finding the hammer, put on his falcon-guise and flew back to Asgard. Thor was waiting to hear what news he brought, and both were soon at the great doors of Folkvang.

"Put on your bridal dress, Freyja," said Thor bluntly, after his fashion, "and we will ride swiftly to Jotunheim."

But Freyja had no idea of marrying a giant just to please Thor; and, in fact, that Thor should ask her to do such a thing threw her into such a rage that the floor shook under her angry tread, and her necklace snapped in pieces.

"Do you think I am a weak lovesick girl, to follow you to Jotunheim and marry Thrym?" she cried indignantly.

Finding they could do nothing with Freyja, Thor and Loke called all the gods together to talk over the matter and decide what should be done to get back the hammer. The gods were very much alarmed, because they knew the frost-giants would come upon Asgard as soon as they knew the hammer was gone. They said little, for they did not waste time with idle words, but they thought long and earnestly, and still they could find no way of getting hold of Mjolner once more. At last Heimdal, who had once been a Van, and could therefore look into the future, said: "We must have the hammer at once or As-

gard will be in danger. If Freyja will not go, let Thor be dressed up and go in her place. Let keys jingle from his waist and a woman's dress fall about his feet. Put precious stones upon his breast, braid his hair like a woman's, hang the necklace around his neck, and bind the bridal veil around his head."

Thor frowned angrily. "If I dress like a woman," he said, "you will jeer at me."

"Don't talk of jeers," retorted Loke; "unless that hammer is brought back quickly, the giants will rule in our places."

Thor said no more, but allowed himself to be dressed like a bride, and soon drove off to Jotunheim with Loke beside him disguised as a servant-maid. There was never such a wedding journey before. They rode in Thor's chariot and the goats drew them, plunging swiftly along the way, thunder pealing through the mountains and the frightened earth blazing and smoking as they passed. When Thrym saw the bridal party coming he was filled with delight.

"Stand up, you giants," he shouted to his companions; "spread cushions upon the benches and bring in Freyja, my bride. My yards are full of golden-horned cows, black oxen please my gaze whichever way I look, great wealth and many treasures are mine, and Freyja is all I lack."

It was evening when the bride came driving into the giant's court in her blazing chariot. The feast was already spread against her coming, and with her veil modestly covering her face she was seated at the great table, Thrym fairly beside himself with delight. It wasn't every giant who could marry a goddess!

If the bridal journey had been so strange that any one but a foolish giant would have hesitated to marry a wife who came in such a turmoil of fire and storm, her conduct at the table ought certainly to have put Thrym on his guard; for never had a bride such an appetite before. The great tables groaned under the load of good things, but they were quickly relieved of their burden by the voracious bride. She ate a whole ox before the astonished giant had fairly begun to enjoy his meal. Then she devoured eight large salmon, one after the other, without stopping to take breath; and having eaten up the part of the feast specially prepared for the hungry men, she turned upon the delicacies which had been made for the women, and especially for her own fastidious appetite.

Thrym looked on with wondering eyes, and at last, when she had added to these solid foods three whole barrels of mead, his amazement was so great that, his astonishment getting the better of his politeness, he called out, "Did any one ever see such an appetite in a bride before, or know a maid who could drink so much mead?"

Then Loke, who was playing the part of a serving-maid, thinking that the giant might have some suspicions, whispered to him, "Freyja was so happy in the thought of coming here that she has eaten nothing for eight whole days."

Thrym was so pleased at this evidence of affection that he leaned forward and raised the veil as gently as a giant could, but he instantly dropped it and sprang back the whole length of the hall before the bride's terrible eyes.

"Why are Freyja's eyes so sharp?" he called to Loke. "They burn me like fire."

"Oh," said the cunning serving-maid, "she has not slept for a week, so anxious has she been to come here, and that is why her eyes are so fiery."

Everybody looked at the bride and nobody envied Thrym. They thought it was too much like marrying a thunder-storm.

The giant's sister came into the hall just then, and seeing the veiled form of the bride sitting there went up to her and asked for a bridal gift. "If you would have my love and friendship give me those rings of gold upon your fingers."

But the bride sat perfectly silent. No one had yet seen her face or heard her voice.

Thrym became very impatient. "Bring in the hammer," he shouted, "that the bride may be consecrated, and wed us in the name of Var."

If the giant could have seen the bride's eyes when she heard these words he would have sent her home as quickly as possible, and looked somewhere else for a wife.

The hammer was brought and placed in the bride's lap, and everybody looked to see the marriage ceremony; but the wedding was more strange and terrible than the bridal journey had been. No sooner did the bride's fingers close round the handle of Mjolner than the veil which covered her face was torn off and there stood Thor, the giant-queller, his terrible eyes blazing with wrath.

The giants shuddered and shrank away from those flaming eyes, the sight of which they dreaded more than anything else in all the worlds; but there was no chance of escape. Thor swung the hammer round his head and the great house rocked on its foundations. There was a vivid flash of lightning, an awful crash of thunder, and the burning roof and walls buried the whole company in one common ruin.

Thrym was punished for stealing the hammer, his wedding guests got crushing blows instead of bridal gifts, and Thor and Loke went back to Asgard, where the presence of Mjolner made the gods safe once more.

THE DEATH OF BALDER

Here is the Norse equivalent of the Greek myth of Demeter and Persephone, but in much more stark and moving terms. Balder the beautiful, the sun, drifts away in the fiery flames of autumn, leaving the world in darkness.

There was one shadow which always fell over Asgard. Sometimes in the long years the gods almost forgot it, it lay so far off, like a dim cloud

"The Death of Balder." Reprinted from *Norse Stories* by Hamilton Wright Mabie by permission of Dodd, Mead & Company

in a clear sky; but Odin saw it deepen and widen as he looked out into the universe, and he knew that the last great battle would surely come, when the gods themselves would be destroyed and a long twilight would rest on all the worlds; and now the day was close at hand. Misfortunes never come singly to men, and they did not to the gods. Idun, the beautiful goddess of youth, whose apples were the joy of all Asgard, made a resting place for herself among the massive branches of Ygdrasil, and there every evening came Brage, and sang so sweetly that the birds stopped to listen, and even the Norns, those implacable sisters at the foot of the tree, were softened by the melody. But poetry cannot change the purposes of fate, and one evening no song was heard of Brage or birds, the leaves of the world-tree hung withered and lifeless on the branches, and the fountain from which they had daily been sprinkled was dry at last. Idun had fallen into the dark valley of death, and when Brage, Heimdal, and Loke went to question her about the future she could answer them only with tears. Brage would not leave his beautiful wife alone amid the dim shades that crowded the dreary valley, and so youth and genius vanished out of Asgard forever.

Balder was the most god-like of all the gods, because he was the purest and the best. Wherever he went his coming was like the coming of sunshine, and all the beauty of summer was but the shining of his face. When men's hearts were white like the light, and their lives clear as the day, it was because Balder was looking down upon them with those soft, clear eyes that were open windows to the soul of God. He had always lived in such a glow of brightness that no darkness had ever touched him; but one morning, after Idun and Brage had gone, Balder's face was sad and troubled. He walked slowly from room to room in his palace Breidablik, stainless as the sky when April showers have swept across it because no impure thing had ever crossed the threshold, and his eyes were heavy with sorrow. In the night terrible dreams had broken his sleep, and made it a long torture. The air seemed to be full of awful changes for him, and for all the gods. He knew in his soul that the shadow of the last great day was sweeping on; as he looked out and saw the worlds lying in light

and beauty, the fields yellow with waving grain, the deep fiords flashing back the sunbeams from their clear depths, the verdure clothing the loftiest mountains, and knew that over all this darkness and desolation would come, with silence of reapers and birds, with fading of leaf and flower, a great sorrow fell on his heart.

Balder could bear the burden no longer. He went out, called all the gods together, and told them the terrible dreams of the night. Every face was heavy with care. The death of Balder would be like the going out of the sun, and after a long, sad council the gods resolved to protect him from harm by pledging all things to stand between him and any hurt. So Frigg, his mother, went forth and made everything promise, on a solemn oath, not to injure her son. Fire, iron, all kinds of metal, every sort of stone, trees, earth, diseases, birds, beasts, snakes, as the anxious mother went to them, solemnly pledged themselves that no harm should come near Balder. Everything had promised, and Frigg thought she had driven away the cloud; but fate was stronger than her love, and one little shrub had not sworn.

Odin was not satisfied even with these precautions, for whichever way he looked the shadow of a great sorrow spread over the worlds. He began to feel as if he were no longer the greatest of the gods, and he could almost hear the rough shouts of the frost-giants crowding the rainbow bridge on their way into Asgard. When trouble comes to men it is hard to bear, but to a god who had so many worlds to guide and rule it was a new and terrible thing. Odin thought and thought until he was weary, but no gleam of light could he find anywhere; it was thick darkness everywhere.

At last he could bear the suspense no longer, and saddling his horse he rode sadly out of Asgard to Niflheim, the home of Hel, whose face was as the face of death itself. As he drew near the gates, a monstrous dog came out and barked furiously, but Odin rode a little eastward of the shadowy gates to the grave of a wonderful prophetess. It was a cold, gloomy place, and the soul of the great god was pierced with a feeling of hopeless sorrow as he dismounted from Sleipner, and bending over the grave began to chant weird songs, and weave magical charms over it. When he had spoken those wonderful words which could waken the dead from their sleep, there was an awful silence for a moment, and then a faint ghost-like voice came from the grave.

"Who are thou?" it said. "Who breaketh the silence of death, and calleth the sleeper out of her long slumbers? Ages ago I was laid at rest here, snow and rain have fallen upon me through myriad years; why dost thou disturb me?"

"I am Vegtam," answered Odin, "and I come to ask why the couches of Hel are hung with gold and the benches strewn with shining rings?"

"It is done for Balder," answered the awful voice; "ask me no more."

Odin's heart sank when he heard these words; but he was determined to know the worst.

"I will ask thee until I know all. Who shall strike the fatal blow?"

"If I must, I must," moaned the prophetess. "Hoder shall smite his brother Balder and send him down to the dark home of Hel. The mead is already brewed for Balder, and the despair draweth near."

Then Odin, looking into the future across the open grave, saw all the days to come.

"Who is this," he said, seeing that which no mortal could have seen,—"who is this that will not weep for Balder?"

Then the prophetess knew that it was none other than the greatest of the gods who had called her up.

"Thou art not Vegtam," she exclaimed, "thou art Odin himself, the king of men."

"And thou," answered Odin angrily, "art no prophetess, but the mother of three giants."

"Ride home, then, and exult in what thou has discovered," said the dead woman. "Never shall my slumbers be broken again until Loke shall burst his chains and the great battle come."

And Odin rode sadly homeward knowing that already Niflheim was making itself beautiful against the coming of Balder.

The other gods meanwhile had become merry again; for had not everything promised to protect their beloved Balder? They even made sport of that which troubled them, for when they found that nothing could hurt Balder, and that all things glanced aside from his shining form, they persuaded him to stand as a target for their weapons; hurling darts, spears, swords, and battle-axes at him, all of which went singing through the air and fell harmless at his feet. But Loke, when he saw these sports, was jealous of Balder, and went about thinking how he could destroy him.

It happened that as Frigg sat spinning in her house Fensal, the soft wind blowing in at the windows and bringing the merry shouts of the gods at play, an old woman entered and approached her.

"Do you know," asked the newcomer, "what they are doing in Asgard? They are throwing all manner of dangerous weapons at Balder. He stands there like the sun for brightness, and against his glory, spears and battle-axes fall powerless to the ground. Nothing can harm him."

"No," answered Frigg joyfully; "nothing can bring him any hurt, for I have made everything in heaven and earth swear to protect him."

"What!" said the old woman, "has everything sworn to guard Balder?"

"Yes," said Frigg, "everything has sworn except one little shrub which is called Mistletoe, and grows on the eastern side of Valhal. I did not take an oath from that because I thought it was too young and weak."

When the old woman heard this a strange light came into her eyes; she walked off much faster than she had come in, and no sooner had she passed beyond Frigg's sight than this same old feeble woman grew suddenly erect, shook off her woman's garments, and there stood Loke himself. In a moment he had reached the slope east of Valhal, and plucked a twig of the unsworn Mistletoe, and was back in the circle of the gods, who were still at their favorite pastime with Balder. Hoder was standing silent and alone outside the noisy throng, for he was blind. Loke touched him.

"Why do you not throw something at Balder?"

"Because I cannot see where Balder stands, and have nothing to throw if I could," replied Hoder.

"If that is all," said Loke, "come with me. I will give you something to throw, and direct your aim."

Hoder, thinking no evil, went with Loke and did as he was told.

The little sprig of Mistletoe shot through the air, pierced the heart of Balder, and in a moment the beautiful god lay dead upon the field. A shadow rose out of the deep beyond the worlds and spread itself over heaven and earth, for the light of the universe had gone out.

The gods could not speak for horror. They stood like statues for a moment, and then a hopeless wail burst from their lips. Tears fell like rain from eyes that had never wept before, for Balder, the joy of Asgard, had gone to Niflheim and left them desolate. But Odin was saddest of all, because he knew the future, and he knew that peace and light had fled from Asgard forever, and that the last day and the long night were hurrying on.

Frigg could not give up her beautiful son, and when her grief had spent itself a little, she asked who would go to Hel and offer her a rich ransom if she would permit Balder to return to Asgard. "I will go," said Hermod; swift at the word of Odin, Sleipner was led forth, and in an instant Hermod was galloping furiously away.

Then the gods began with sorrowful hearts to make ready for Balder's funeral. When the once beautiful form had been arrayed in grave-clothes they carried it reverently down to the deep sea, which lay, calm as a summer afternoon, waiting for its precious burden. Close to the water's edge lay Balder's Ringhorn, the greatest of all the ships that sailed the seas, but when the gods tried to launch it they could not move it an inch. The great vessel creaked and groaned, but no one could push it down to the water. Odin walked about it with a sad face, and the gentle ripple of the little waves chasing each other over the rocks seemed a mocking laugh to him.

"Send to Jotunheim for Hyrroken," he said at last; and a messenger was soon flying for that mighty giantess.

In a little time, Hyrroken came riding swiftly on a wolf so large and fierce that he made the gods think of Fenrer. When the giantess had alighted, Odin ordered four Berserkers of mighty strength to hold the wolf, but he struggled so angrily that they had to throw him on the ground before they could control him. Then Hyrroken went to the prow of the ship and with one mighty effort sent it far into the sea, the rollers underneath bursting into flame, and the whole earth trembling with the shock. Thor was so angry at the uproar that he would have killed the giantess on the spot if he had not been held back by the other gods. The great ship floated on the sea as she had often done before, when Balder, full of life and beauty, set all her sails and was borne joyfully across the tossing seas. Slowly and solemnly the dead god was carried on board, and as Nanna, his faithful wife, saw her husband borne for the last time from the earth which he had made dear to her and beautiful to all men, her heart broke with sorrow, and they laid her beside Balder on the funeral pyre.

Since the world began no one had seen such a funeral. No bells tolled, no long procession of mourners moved across the hills, but all the worlds lay under a deep shadow, and from every quarter came those who had loved or feared Balder. There at the very water's edge stood Odin himself, the ravens flying about his head, and on his majestic face a gloom that no sun would ever lighten again; and there was Frigg, the desolate mother, whose son had already gone so far that he would never come back to her; there was Frey standing sad and stern in his chariot; there was Freyja, the goddess of love, from whose eyes fell a shining rain of tears; there, too, was Heimdal on his horse Goldtop; and around all these glorious ones from Asgard crowded the children of Jotunheim, grim mountain-giants seamed with scars from Thor's hammer, and frost-giants who saw in the death of Balder the coming of that long winter in which they should reign through all the worlds.

A deep hush fell on all created things, and every eye was fixed on the great ship riding near the shore, and on the funeral pyre rising from the deck crowned with the forms of Balder and Nanna. Suddenly a gleam of light flashed over the water; the pile had been kindled, and the flames, creeping slowly at first, climbed faster and faster until they met over the dead and rose skyward. A lurid light filled the heavens and shone on the sea, and in the brightness of it the gods looked pale and sad, and the circle of giants grew darker and more portentous. Thor struck the fast burning pyre with his consecrating hammer, and Odin cast into it the wonder ring Draupner. Higher and higher leaped the flames, more and more desolate grew the scene; at last they began to sink, the funeral pyre was consumed. Balder had vanished forever, the summer was ended, and winter waited at the doors.

Meanwhile Hermod was riding hard and fast on his gloomy errand. Nine days and nights he rode through valleys so deep and dark that he could not see his horse. Stillness and blackness and solitude were his only companions until he came to the golden bridge which crosses the river Gjol. The good horse Sleipner, who had carried Odin on so many strange journeys, had never travelled such a road before, and his hoofs rang drearily as he stopped short at the bridge, for in front of him stood its porter, the gigantic Modgud.

"Who are you?" she asked, fixing her piercing eyes on Hermod. "What is your name and parentage? Yesterday five bands of dead men rode across the bridge, and beneath them all it did not shake as under your single tread. There is no colour of death in your face. Why ride you hither, the living among the dead?"

"I come," said Hermod, "to seek for Balder. Have you seen him pass this way?"

"He has already crossed the bridge and taken his journey northward to Hel."

Then Hermod rode slowly across the bridge that spans the abyss between life and death, and found his way at last to the barred gates of Hel's dreadful home. There he sprang to the ground, tightened the girths, remounted, drove the spurs deep into the horse, and Sleipner, with a mighty leap, cleared the wall. Hermod rode straight to the gloomy palace, dismounted, entered, and in a moment was face to face with the terrible queen of the kingdom of the dead. Beside her, on a beautiful throne, sat Balder, pale and wan, crowned with a withered wreath of flowers, and close at hand was Nanna, pallid as her husband, for whom she had died. And all night long, while ghostly forms wandered restless and sleepless through Helheim, Hermod talked with Balder and Nanna. There is no record of what they said, but the talk was sad enough, doubtless, and ran like a still stream among the happy days in Asgard when Balder's smile was morning over the earth and the sight of his face the summer of the world.

When the morning came, faint and dim, through the dusky palace, Hermod sought Hel, who received him as cold and stern as fate.

"Your kingdom is full, O Hel!" he said, "and without Balder, Asgard is empty. Send him back to us once more, for there is sadness in every heart and tears are in every eye. Through heaven and earth all things weep for him."

"If that is true," was the slow, icy answer, "if every created thing weeps for Balder, he shall return to Asgard; but if one eye is dry he remains henceforth in Helheim."

Then Hermod rode swiftly away, and the decree of Hel was soon told in Asgard. Through all the worlds the gods sent messengers to say that all who loved Balder should weep for his return, and everywhere tears fell like rain. There was weeping in Asgard, and in all the earth there was nothing that did not weep. Men and women and little children, missing the light that had once fallen into their hearts and homes, sobbed with bitter grief; the birds of the air, who had sung carols of joy at the gates of the morning since time began, were full of sorrow; the beasts of the fields crouched and moaned in their desolation; the great trees, that had put on their robes of green at Balder's command, sighed as the wind wailed through them; and the sweet flowers, that waited for Balder's footstep and sprang up in all the fields to greet him, hung their frail blossoms and wept bitterly for the love and the warmth and the light that had gone out. Throughout the whole earth there was nothing but weeping, and the sound of it was like the wailing of those storms in autumn that weep for the dead summer as its withered leaves drop one by one from the trees.

The messengers of the gods went gladly back to Asgard, for everything had wept for Balder; but as they journeyed they came upon a giantess, called Thok, and her eyes were dry.

"Weep for Balder," they said.

"With dry eyes only will I weep for Balder," she answered. "Dead or alive, he never gave me gladness. Let him stay in Helheim."

When she had spoken these words a terrible laugh broke from her lips, and the messengers looked at each other with pallid faces, for they knew it was the voice of Loke.

Balder never came back to Asgard, and the shadows deepened over all things, for the night of death was fast coming on.

Epics, sagas, and hero tales grow out of and along with myth. They consist of cycles of stories, each cycle centering on some human hero, buffeted by gods and men, who suffers greatly and endures staunchly to the end. Myth is still with us in the early epics, for the gods apparently leave their own affairs in Olympus and Asgard for the express purpose of interfering with man's adventures on earth. But in the epics the center of interest shifts from the gods to the human heroes, from Olympus to earth. After both the

THE EPICS

gods and Olympus had faded from man's dreams, culture heroes still excited man's imagination and gained his belief. Tales of greatness would cluster about a single name until a Roland or a Robin Hood assumed the impressive stature of the epic hero even without the background of warring gods.

The *epic* is strongly national in its presentation of human character. Odysseus is the embodiment of the Greek ideals of manly courage, sagacity, beauty, and endurance. Sigurd is the personification of the Norse code of heroism. King Arthur has come to represent Norman-English chivalry, and Robin Hood, the English love of freedom and justice as well as the ideal of lusty, jovial manhood. Study the epic hero of a nation and you will learn a great deal about the moral code of that nation and era.

Not all epics are suitable for children, but some of them provide a literary and emotional experience as unforgettable as it is precious. *Robin Hood* is certainly the prime favorite with elementary-school children, with the *Odyssey* next in appeal. It is probable that *King Arthur, Roland,* the *Iliad,* and perhaps the *Sigurd Saga* are better postponed for the days of adolescence, although if *told* to children, the Sigurd stories are well liked and so are many of the Arthur cycle. The personification of a great ideal in one hero, the sweep and excitement of epic action, the continuity of the adventures, and the nobility of the stories—these are epic qualities for which there are no substitutes.

Often the epic can be associated with some great poet, who may also have been a bard or minstrel, and this is to be expected when one recalls that the epic is basically defined as a poem which tells the story of heroic men and their deeds. Thus, we think of the Homeric tradition (which was a tradition encompassing many poets and periods of time) in the person of Homer, the blind poet who composed, in elevated poetic style, his account of the Greek and Trojan wars and the wanderings of Odysseus. Taillefer was the great minstrel to William the Conqueror and is said to have accompanied him onto the battlefield at Hastings, reciting to him the *Chanson de Roland.* During certain ages the minstrels did accompany heroes and sovereigns onto the fields of battle that they might later set it all to verse and music.

The *saga,* if we wish to be exact in our terms, is very much like the epic, except that it is in prose and is a term originally applied to the heroic tales of medieval Iceland. As for the *hero tale,* so-called, while it may be either an epic or a saga, it is more likely a story about a rather recent hero (Robin Hood, King Arthur) whose biographical data can more or less be verified, even though the tale may have gone far beyond the realities of his life and acquired much material straight out of myth and folk tale.

Reading epics will give young people some idea of the great antiquity of the epic form and of its enduring appeal. In the epics we can also find much that parallels our own times. After reading of Roland and Robin Hood, older boys and girls may well ask themselves and us: "Who will be *our* epic heroes?" What shall we answer?

from GILGAMESH

Bernarda Bryson

Gilgamesh, *from which this selection is taken, is the oldest written epic known, first recorded in cuneiform nearly 3000 years before Christ. It prefigures much of what was to come later in the Old Testament and in the Greek myths.*

The Monster Humbaba

Perfect was the friendship of Gilgamesh and Enkidu. The wild man asked only to be the servant of the King, but Gilgamesh called him "my younger brother," and Ninsun, the queen, looked upon him almost as a son. Everywhere, they went together and everywhere they were admired. They took part in feats of strength and daring, winning all prizes and all praise. And in all this Enkidu was content.

Not so, Gilgamesh. On one occasion he said to his friend, "Day and night I dream of a great enterprise. Whenever I close my eyes, voices come to me and say: 'Arouse yourself, Gilgamesh, there are great things to be done!' "

Enkidu's mind was full of foreboding.

"You and I, Enkidu, we will climb the mountain and destroy the monster Humbaba!"

Enkidu's eyes filled with tears and he turned away.

"Why should you cry, O Enkidu? Are you not the bravest of men? Are you no longer my friend and brother whom I admire more than anyone at all?"

Enkidu spoke: "I knew the presence of Humbaba even when I was a wild man on the steppes and in the forest. I could hear the sighing of his voice rise over the sound of thunder and high winds. I could hear the beating of his heart and feel the heat of his breath at a distance of five-hundred shar. I do not fear beast or mortal man, O Gilgamesh, but Humbaba is not mortal; he is the appointed servant of the gods, the guardian of the wild cows and the cedar forest. Whoever comes near him will grow weak. He will become paralyzed and will fail."

"The monster is an everlasting evil," said Gilgamesh. "It oppresses the people. Day and night it spreads fires and spews its ashes over the town. It is hated by great Shamash, constantly obscuring his face. O Enkidu, shall my life be as an empty wind? What am I, if I turn aside from the things I want to do? I am nothing, only someone waiting for death! But if I do this thing, O Enkidu, even though I should fail, then they will say, 'Gilgamesh died a hero's death! He died defending his people.' I will have made an everlasting name for myself and my life will not be as an empty wind!"

Still Enkidu turned away.

Gilgamesh then called in the armorers, the makers of spears and shields and axes. They cast for him swords of bronze inlaid with silver and gold. They made powerful long-bows and arrows tipped with stone, and most beautiful of all, a spear with a handle of lapis lazuli and gold inset with many glittering jewels.

Gilgamesh called Enkidu and laid the weapons before him, hoping to tempt him with their beauty. And still Enkidu said no.

Gilgamesh was downcast. "My brother has grown soft and timid. He no longer loves daring; he has forgotten adventure; I will go alone!"

The elders of Uruk, who had long ago forgotten their hatred of the King, now came to him: "O Gilgamesh, do not undertake this thing. You are young; your heart has carried you away. Settle down, O King; take a bride to yourself; let your life be tranquil!"

Gilgamesh laughed. "Save your wise counsel for my friend, Enkidu. He'll listen. You waste your words on me, good fathers!"

The elders came in secret to Enkidu. "If the King stubbornly insists on doing this thing, risking danger and defying the gods, then Enkidu you must accompany him!"

"Indeed, you must go ahead of him," a second elder said, "for it is known that whoever first enters the cedar gate will be the first killed."

"Besides, it is you who know the way, Enkidu.

It is you who have trodden the road!"

"May Shamash stand beside you!"

"May he open the path for you!"

Enkidu went to Gilgamesh. "My head is bowed, O King. I am your brother and your servant; wherever you will go, I will go."

Tears came into the eyes of Gilgamesh; his faith in Enkidu was restored. "Now, my brother, we will go to Ninsun; we will tell our plan and ask her to petition the gods for our success!"

Pale as she was, Ninsun turned more pale. But since she could not dissuade her son, she merely kissed him, giving him her blessing. To Enkidu she said, "Even though you are not my son, O Enkidu, you are like a son to me, and I shall petition the gods for you as for Gilgamesh. But remember, please, that as a man protects his own person, so must he guard the life of his companion!"

The people of Uruk walked with the two friends through the streets admiring their weapons and praising their bold plan: "Praise be to Gilgamesh who dares everything! Praise be to Enkidu who will safeguard his companion!" But Harim the priestess mourned, "May your feet carry you back safely to the city, Enkidu!" And thus they set out.

Ninsun dressed herself in her finest garments. She attached the golden pendants to her ears and set the divine tiara upon her head. She anointed herself with perfumes and carried in her hand an incense that would carry its pleasant odors into the sky. Mounting with stately grace to the roof of her palace, she raised her voice to its highest pitch and called out, "O Shamash, listen to me!" Then waiting a little for her voice to reach the ears of the god, she went on: "O Shamash, why have you given my son Gilgamesh such a restless heart? Why have you made him so eager for adventure? Now he has gone up to fight with the indestructible monster Humbaba. Why have you sent him, O Shamash, to wipe out the evil that you abhor? It is all your plan! It is you who have planted the idea in his head! May you not sleep, O Shamash, until Gilgamesh and his friend Enkidu return to Uruk. If they fail, may you never sleep again!"

Ninsun extinguished the small blaze from under the incense and descended from the roof of the palace.

Gilgamesh and Enkidu walked toward the mountain of the cedar forest. At a distance of twenty double-hours they sat down beside the path and ate a small amount of food. At a distance of thirty double-hours, they lay down to sleep, covering themselves with their garments. On the following day they walked a distance of fifty double-hours. Within three days' time, they covered a distance that it would have taken ordinary men some fifteen days to cover. They reached the mountain and saw before them a towering and magnificent gate of cedar wood.

"Here," said Gilgamesh, "we must pour meal upon the earth, for that will gain us the goodwill of the gods; it will persuade them to reveal their purpose in our dreams!"

They poured meal on the ground and lay down to sleep. After some time Gilgamesh wakened his friend. "Enkidu, I have had a dream; it went like this: We were standing in a deep gorge beside a mountain. Compared to it, we were the size of flies! Before our very eyes the mountain collapsed; it fell in a heap!"

"The meaning of that seems very clear," said Enkidu. "It means that Humbaba is the mountain and that he will fall before us!"

They closed their eyes again and slept. After some time, Gilgamesh again awakened his friend. "I've had another dream, Enkidu. I saw the same mountain this time, and again it fell, but it fell on me. However, as I lay struggling, a beautiful personage appeared. He took me by my feet and dragged me out from under the mountain. Now I wonder what this means? Is it that you will rescue me from the monster, or will someone else come along?"

They pondered a little and went back to sleep. Next Enkidu wakened his brother, Gilgamesh. "Has a cold shower passed over us? Did the lightning strike fires, and was there a rain of ashes?"

"The earth is dry and clean," said Gilgamesh, "you must have dreamed!" But since neither of them could understand the meaning of this dream, they fell asleep again, and soon the day came.

They approached the magnificent gate. "Let's open it, Enkidu! Let's be on our way!"

For a last time, Enkidu tried to persuade his friend to turn back. But since the King would not listen, it was he who went first and placed his hand against the gate to push it open. Enkidu was thrown backward with such violence that he fell to the earth. He rose to his feet. "Gilgamesh, wait! My hand is paralyzed!"

"Put it on my arm, Enkidu! It will take strength from my arm because I am not afraid."

When the two friends threw their weight against the gate, however, it swung inward.

They walked up the mountainside through the sacred trees. And these became closer and thicker until the sky was blotted out. They could hear the giant heartbeat of Humbaba and smell the smoke from his lungs.

To show his daring, Gilgamesh cut one of the cedar trees. The blows of his axe rang out, and from afar the terrible Humbaba heard the sound.

With a crashing of timbers and a rolling of loose stones, Humbaba came down upon them. His face loomed among the treetops, creased and grooved like some ancient rock. The breath he breathed withered the boughs of cedar and set small fires everywhere.

Enkidu's fears now vanished and the two heroes stood side by side as the monster advanced.

He loomed over them, his arms swinging out like the masts of a ship. He was almost upon them when suddenly the friends stepped apart. The giant demon lurched through the trees, stumbled, and fell flat. He rose to his feet bellowing like a bull and charged upon Enkidu. But the King brought down his axe on the toe of Humbaba so that he whirled about roaring with pain. He grasped Gilgamesh by his flowing hair, swung him round and round as if to hurl him through the treetops, but now Enkidu saw his giant ribs exposed and he thrust his sword into the monster's side. Liquid fire gushed from the wound and ran in small streams down the mountainside. Gilgamesh fell to the earth and lay still, trying to breathe. But meanwhile Humbaba grasped the horns of Enkidu and began to flail his body against a tree. Surely the wild man would have died, but now Gilgamesh roused himself. He lanced into the air his long spear with its handle of lapis lazuli and gold. The spear caught Humbaba in the throat and remained there poised and glittering among the fires that had ignited everywhere.

The giant loosened his hold on Enkidu; he cried out. The earth reverberated with the sound, and distant mountains shook.

Gilgamesh felt pity in his heart. He withdrew his sword and put down his axe, while the monster Humbaba crept toward him grovelling and wailing for help. Now Enkidu perceived that the monster drew in a long breath in order to spew forth his last weapon—the searing fire that would consume the King. He leaped on the demon and with many sword thrusts released the fire, so that it bubbled harmlessly among the stones.

Humbaba was dead; the two heroes, black with soot and dirt, were still alive. They hugged each other; they leaped about; and singing and shouting, they descended the mountainside. Gentle rains fell around them and the land was forever free from the curse of the giant Humbaba.

from   THE ODYSSEY

This excerpt from the great Greek epic, The Odyssey, *is one of the most interesting episodes in the life of the hero Odysseus, whose wanderings lasted for ten years.*

The Curse of Polyphemus

Of all the heroes that wandered far and wide before they came to their homes again after the fall of Troy, none suffered so many hardships as Odysseus. Ten years did he fight against Troy, but it was ten years more before he came to his home and his wife Penelope and his son Telemachus.

Odysseus set out from Troy with twelve good ships. He touched first at Ismarus, where his first misfortune took place, and in a skirmish with the natives he lost a number of men from each ship's crew.

A storm then drove them to the land of the Lotus-Eaters, a wondrous people, kindly and content, who spend their lives in a day-dream and care for nothing else under the sun. No sooner had the sailors eaten of this magical lotus than they lost all their wish to go home, or to see their wives and children again. By main force, Odysseus drove them back to the ships and saved them from the spell.

Thence they came one day to a beautiful strange island, a verdant place to see, deep with soft grass and well watered with springs. Here they ran the ships ashore, and took their rest and feasted for a day. But Odysseus looked across to the mainland, where he saw flocks and herds, and smoke going up softly from the homes of men; and he resolved to go across and find out what manner of people lived there. Accordingly, next morning, he took his own ship's company and they rowed across to the mainland.

Now, fair as the place was, there dwelt in it a race of giants, the Cyclopes, great rude creatures, having each but one eye, and that in the middle of his forehead. One of them was Polyphemus, the son of Poseidon. He lived by himself as a shepherd, and it was to his cave that Odysseus came, by some evil chance. It was an enormous grotto, big enough to house the giant and all his flocks, and it had a great courtyard without. But Odysseus, knowing nought of all this, chose out twelve men, and with a wallet of corn and a goatskin full of wine they left the ship and made

"The Curse of Polyphemus." From *Old Greek Folk Stories Told Anew* by Josephine Preston Peabody. Copyright 1897 by Houghton Mifflin Company

a way to the cave, which they had seen from the water.

Much they wondered who might be the master of this strange house. Polyphemus was away with his sheep, but many lambs and kids were penned there, and the cavern was well stored with goodly cheeses and cream and whey.

Without delay, the wearied men kindled a fire and sat down to eat such things as they found, till a great shadow came dark against the doorway, and they saw the Cyclops near at hand, returning with his flocks. In an instant they fled into the darkest corner of the cavern.

Polyphemus drove his flocks into the place and cast off from his shoulders a load of young trees for firewood. Then he lifted and set in the entrance of the cave a gigantic boulder of a doorstone. Not until he had milked the goats and ewes and stirred up the fire did his terrible one eye light upon the strangers.

"What are ye?" he roared then, "robbers or rovers?" And Odysseus alone had heart to answer.

"We are Achaens of the army of Agamemnon," said he. "And by the will of Zeus we have lost our course, and are come to you as strangers. Forget not that Zeus has a care for such as we, strangers and suppliants."

Loud laughed the Cyclops at this. "You are a witless churl to bid me heed the gods!" said he. "I spare or kill to please myself and none other. But where is your cockle-shell that brought you hither?"

Then Odysseus answered craftily: "Alas, my ship is gone! Only I and my men escaped alive from the sea."

But Polyphemus, who had been looking them over with his one eye, seized two of the mariners and dashed them against the wall and made his evening meal of them, while their comrades stood by helpless. This done, he stretched himself through the cavern and slept all night long, taking no more heed of them than if they had been flies. No sleep came to the wretched seamen, for, even had they been able to slay him, they were powerless to move away the boulder from the door. So all night long Odysseus took thought how they might possibly escape.

At dawn the Cyclops woke, and his awakening was like a thunderstorm. Again he kindled the fire, again he milked the goats and ewes, and again he seized two of the king's comrades and served them up for his terrible repast. Then the savage shepherd drove his flocks out of the cave, only turning back to set the boulder in the doorway and pen up Odysseus and his men in their dismal lodging.

But the wise king had pondered well. In the sheepfold he had seen a mighty club of olivewood, in size like the mast of a ship. As soon as the Cyclops was gone, Odysseus bade his men cut off a length of this club and sharpen it down to a point. This done, they hid it away under the earth that heaped the floor; and they waited in fear and torment for their chance of escape.

At sundown, home came the Cyclops. Just as he had done before, he drove in his flocks, barred the entrance, milked the goats and ewes, and made his meal of two more hapless men, while their fellows looked on with burning eyes. Then Odysseus stood forth, holding a bowl of the wine that he had brought with him; and, curbing his horror of Polyphemus, he spoke in friendly fashion: "Drink, Cyclops, and prove our wine, such as it was, for all was lost with our ship save this. And no other man will ever bring you more, since you are such an ungentle host."

The Cyclops tasted the wine and laughed with delight so that the cave shook. "Ho, this is a rare drink!" said he. "I never tasted milk so good, nor whey, nor grape-juice either. Give me the rest, and tell me your name, that I may thank you for it."

Twice and thrice Odysseus poured the wine and the Cyclops drank it off; then he answered: "Since you ask it, Cyclops, my name is Noman."

"And I will give you this for your wine, Noman," said the Cyclops; "you shall be eaten last of all!"

As he spoke his head drooped, for his wits were clouded with drink, and he sank heavily out of his seat and lay prone, stretched along the floor of the cavern. His great eye shut and he fell asleep.

Odysseus thrust the stake under the ashes till it was glowing hot; and his fellows stood by him, ready to venture all. Then together they lifted the club and drove it straight into the eye of Polyphemus and turned it around and about.

The Cyclops gave a horrible cry, and, thrusting

away the brand, he called on all his fellow-giants near and far. Odysseus and his men hid in the uttermost corners of the cave, but they heard the resounding steps of the Cyclopes who were roused, and their shouts as they called, "What ails thee, Polyphemus? Art thou slain? Who has done thee any hurt?"

"Noman!" roared the blinded Cyclops; "Noman is here to slay me by treachery."

"Then if no man hath hurt thee," they called again, "let us sleep." And away they went to their homes once more.

But Polyphemus lifted away the boulder from the door and sat there in the entrance, groaning with pain and stretching forth his hands to feel if any one were near. Then, while he sat in double darkness, with the light of his eye gone out, Odysseus bound together the rams of the flock, three by three, in such wise that every three should save one of his comrades. For underneath the mid ram of each group a man clung, grasping his shaggy fleece; and the rams on each side guarded him from discovery. Odysseus himself chose out the greatest ram and laid hold of his fleece and clung beneath his shaggy body, face upward.

Now, when dawn came, the rams hastened out to pasture, and Polyphemus felt of their backs as they huddled along together; but he knew not that every three held a man bound securely. Last of all came the kingly ram that was dearest to his rude heart, and he bore the king of Ithaca. Once free of the cave, Odysseus and his fellows loosed their hold and took flight, driving the rams in haste to the ship, where, without delay, they greeted their comrades and went aboard.

But as they pushed from shore, Odysseus could not refrain from hailing the Cyclops with taunts, and at the sound of that voice Polyphemus came forth from his cave and hurled a great rock after the ship. It missed and upheaved the water like an earthquake. Again Odysseus called, saying: "Cyclops, if any shall ask who blinded thine eye, say that it was Odysseus, son of Laertes of Ithaca."

Then Polyphemus groaned and cried: "An Oracle foretold it, but I waited for some man of might who should overcome me by his valor—not a weakling! And now"—he lifted his hands and prayed—"Father, Poseidon, my father, look upon Odysseus, the son of Laertes of Ithaca, and grant me this revenge—let him never see Ithaca again! Yet, if he must, may he come late, without a friend, after long wandering, to find evil abiding by his hearth!"

So he spoke and hurled another rock after them, but the ship outstripped it, and sped by to the island where the other good ships waited for Odysseus. Together they put out from land and hastened on their homeward voyage.

But Poseidon, who is lord of the sea, had heard the prayer of his son, and that homeward voyage was to wear through ten years more, with storm and irksome calms and misadventure.

from **THE MERRY ADVENTURES OF ROBIN HOOD**

Howard Pyle

The Robin Hood cycle is a little less "heroic" than the Greek and Germanic epics, but children love Robin Hood and should not miss the stories. Howard Pyle consulted the actual early ballads in order to make his masterful prose version. Anne Malcolmson's Song of Robin Hood *gives us those ballads with their music. The teacher or parent who can sing and play a guitar can give children a unique experience by singing one of the ballads in its entirety.*

Little John and the Tanner of Blyth

It often comes about in this world that unlucky happenings fall upon one in such measure that it seems, as the saying is, that every cat that one strokes flies into one's face. Thus it was with Little John one bright day in the merry Maytime; so listen and you shall hear how Dame Luck so buffeted him that his bones were sore for many a day thereafter.

One fine day, not long after Little John had left abiding with the Sheriff and had come back, with his worship's cook, to the merry greenwood, as has just been told, Robin Hood and a few chosen fellows of his band lay upon the soft sward beneath the greenwood tree where they dwelt.

"Little John and the Tanner of Blyth." From *The Merry Adventures of Robin Hood* by Howard Pyle

The day was warm and sultry, so that whilst most of the band were scattered through the forest upon this mission and upon that, these few stout fellows lay lazily beneath the shade of the tree, in the soft afternoon, passing jests among themselves and telling merry stories, with laughter and mirth.

All the air was laden with the bitter fragrance of the May, and all the bosky shades of the woodlands beyond rang with the sweet song of birds, —the throstle-cock, the cuckoo, and the wood-pigeon,—and with the song of birds mingled the cool sound of the gurgling brook that leaped out of the forest shades, and ran fretting amid its rough, gray stones across the sunlit open glade before the trysting tree. And a fair sight was that halfscore of tall, stout yeomen, all clad in Lincoln green, lying beneath the broad-spreading branches of the great oak tree, amid the quivering leaves of which the sunlight shivered and fell in dancing patches upon the grass.

The good old times have gone by when such men grow as grew then; when sturdy quarterstaff and longbow toughened a man's thews till they were like leather. Around Robin Hood that day there lay the very flower of English yeomanrie. Here the great Little John, with limbs as tough as the gnarled oak, yet grown somewhat soft from good living at the Sheriff's house in Nottingham Town; there Will Stutely, his face as brown as a berry from sun and wind, but, for all that, the comeliest yeoman in the mid-country, only excepting Allan a Dale the minstrel, of whom you shall hear anon. Beside these was Will Scathelock, as lank as a greyhound, yet as fleet of foot as a buck of three years' growth; young David of Doncaster, with great stout limbs only less than those of Little John in size, the tender beard of early youth now just feathering his chin, and others of great renown both far and near.

Suddenly Robin Hood smote his knee.

"By Saint Dunstan," quoth he, "I had nigh forgot that quarter-day cometh on apace, and yet no cloth of Lincoln green in all our store. It must be looked to, and that in quick season. Come, busk thee, Little John! stir those lazy bones of thine, for thou must get thee straightway to our good gossip, the draper, Hugh Longshanks of Ancaster. Bid him send us straightway twentyscore yards of fair cloth of Lincoln green; and mayhap the journey may take some of the fat from off thy bones, that thou hast gotten from lazy living at our dear Sheriff's."

"Nay," muttered Little John (for he had heard so much upon this score that he was sore upon the point), "nay, truly, mayhap I have more flesh upon my joints than I once had, yet, flesh or no flesh, I doubt not that I could still hold my place and footing upon a narrow bridge against e'er a yeoman in Sherwood, or Nottinghamshire, for the matter of that, even though he had no more fat about his bones than thou hast, good master."

At this reply a great shout of laughter went up, and all looked at Robin Hood, for each man knew that Little John spake of a certain fight that happened between their master and himself, through which they first became acquainted.

"Nay," quoth Robin Hood, laughing louder than all, "Heaven forbid that I should doubt thee, for I care for no taste of thy staff myself, Little John. I must needs own that there are those of my band can handle a seven-foot staff more deftly than I; yet no man in all Nottinghamshire can draw gray-goose shaft with my fingers. Nevertheless, a journey to Ancaster may not be ill for thee; so go thou, as I bid, and thou hadst best go this very evening, for since thou hast abided at the Sheriff's[1] many know thy face, and if thou goest in broad daylight, thou mayest get thyself into a coil with some of his worship's men-at-arms. Bide thou here till I bring thee money to pay our good Hugh. I warrant he hath no better customers in all Nottinghamshire than we." So saying, Robin left them and entered the forest.

Not far from the trysting tree was a great rock in which a chamber had been hewn, the entrance being barred by a massive oaken door two palms' breadth in thickness, studded about with spikes, and fastened with a great padlock. This was the treasure-house of the band, and thither Robin Hood went, and, unlocking the door, entered the chamber, from which he brought forth a bag of gold, which he gave to Little John, to pay Hugh

---

[1] The expression *to abide at the Sheriff's* means "to be in jail."

Longshanks withal, for the cloth of Lincoln green.

Then up got Little John, and, taking the bag of gold, which he thrust into his bosom, he strapped a girdle about his loins, took a stout pikestaff full seven feet long in his hand, and set forth upon his journey.

So he strode whistling along the leafy forest path that led to Fosse Way, turning neither to the right hand nor the left, until at last he came to where the path branched, leading on the one hand onward to Fosse Way, and on the other, as well Little John knew, to the merry Blue Boar Inn. Here Little John suddenly ceased whistling, and stopped in the middle of the path. First he looked up and then he looked down, and then, tilting his cap over one eye, he slowly scratched the back part of his head. For thus it was: at the sight of these two roads, two voices began to alarum within him, the one crying, "There lies the road to the Blue Boar Inn, a can of brown October, and a merry night with sweet companions such as thou mayst find there"; the other, "There lies the way to Ancaster and the duty thou art sent upon." Now the first of these two voices was far the louder, for Little John had grown passing fond of good living through abiding at the Sheriff's house; so, presently, looking up into the blue sky, across which bright clouds were sailing like silver boats, and swallows skimming in circling flight, quoth he, "I fear me it will rain this evening, so I'll e'en stop at the Blue Boar till it passes by, for I know my good master would not have me wet to the skin." So, without more ado, off he strode down the path that lay the way of his likings. Now there was no sign of any foul weather, but when one wishes to do a thing, as Little John did, one finds no lack of reasons for the doing.

Four merry wags were at the Blue Boar Inn; a butcher, a beggar, and two barefoot friars. Little John heard them singing from afar, as he walked through the hush of the mellow twilight that was now falling over hill and dale. Right glad were they to welcome such a merry blade as Little John. Fresh cans of ale were brought, and with jest and song and merry tales the hours slipped away on fleeting wings. None thought of time or tide till the night was so far gone that Little John put by the thought of setting forth upon his journey again that night, and so bided at the Blue Boar Inn until the morrow.

Now it was an ill piece of luck for Little John that he left his duty for his pleasure, and he paid a great score for it, as we are all apt to do in the same case, as you shall see.

Up he rose at the dawn of the next day, and, taking his stout pikestaff in his hand, he set forth upon his journey once more, as though he would make up for lost time.

In the good town of Blyth there lived a stout tanner, celebrated far and near for feats of strength and many tough bouts at wrestling and the quarterstaff. For five years he had held the mid-country champion belt for wrestling, till the great Adam o' Lincoln cast him in the ring and broke one of his ribs; but at quarterstaff he had never yet met his match in all the country about. Beside all this, he dearly loved the longbow, and a sly jaunt in the forest when the moon was full and the dun deer in season; so that the King's rangers kept a shrewd eye upon him and his doings, for Arthur a Bland's house was apt to have a plenty of meat in it that was more like venison than the law allowed.

Now Arthur had been to Nottingham Town the day before Little John set forth on his errand, there to sell a halfscore of tanned cowhides. At the dawn of the same day that Little John left the Inn, he started from Nottingham, homeward for Blyth. His way led, all in the dewy morn, past the verge of Sherwood Forest, where the birds were welcoming the lovely day with a great and merry jubilee. Across the Tanner's shoulders was slung his stout quarterstaff, ever near enough to him to be gripped quickly, and on his head was a cap of double cowhide, so tough that it could hardly be cloven even by a broadsword.

"Now," quoth Arthur a Bland to himself, when he had come to that part of the road that cut through a corner of the forest, "no doubt at this time of year the dun deer are coming from the forest depths nigher to the open meadow lands. Mayhap I may chance to catch a sight of the dainty brown darlings thus early in the morn." For there was nothing he loved better than to look upon a tripping herd of deer, even when he could not tickle their ribs with a cloth-yard shaft. Accordingly, quitting the path, he went peeping this way and that through the underbrush, spying now here and now there, with all the wiles of a master woodcraft, and of one who had more than once donned a doublet of Lincoln green.

Now as Little John stepped blithely along, thinking of nothing but of such things as the sweetness of the hawthorn buds that bedecked the hedgerows, or the crab trees that stood here and there all covered with fair pink blossoms, or gazing upward at the lark, that, springing from the dewy grass, hung aloft on quivering wings in the yellow sunlight, pouring forth its song that fell like a falling star from the sky, his luck led him away from the highway, not far from the spot where Arthur a Bland was peeping this way and that through the leaves of the thickets. Hearing a rustling of the branches, Little John stopped, and presently caught sight of the brown cowhide cap of the Tanner moving amongst the bushes.

"I do much wonder," quoth Little John to himself, "what yon knave is after, that he should go thus peeping and peering about. I verily believe that yon scurvy varlet is no better than a thief, and cometh here after our own and the good King's dun deer." For by much roving in the forest, Little John had come to look upon all the deer in Sherwood as belonging to Robin Hood and his band as much as to good King Harry. "Nay," quoth he again, after a time, "this matter must e'en be looked into." So, quitting the highroad, he also entered the thickets, and began spying around after stout Arthur a Bland.

So for a long time they both of them went hunting about, Little John after the Tanner, and the Tanner after the deer. At last Little John trod upon a stick, which snapped under his foot, whereupon, hearing the noise, the Tanner turned quickly and caught sight of the yeoman. Seeing that the Tanner had spied him out, Little John put a bold face upon the matter.

"Hilloa," quoth he, "what art thou doing here, thou naughty fellow? Who art thou that comest ranging Sherwood's paths? In very sooth thou hast an evil cast of countenance, and I do think, truly, that thou art no better than a thief, and comest after our good King's deer."

"Nay," quoth the Tanner boldly,—for, though taken by surprise, he was not a man to be frightened by big words,—"thou liest in thy teeth. I am no thief, but an honest craftsman. As for my countenance, it is what it is; and for the matter of that, thine own is none too pretty, thou saucy fellow."

"Ha!" quoth Little John, in a great loud voice, "wouldst thou give me backtalk? Now I have a great part of mind to crack thy pate for thee. I would have thee know, fellow, that I am, as it were, one of the King's foresters. Leastwise," muttered he to himself, "I and my friends do take good care of our good sovereign's deer."

"I care not who thou art," answered the bold Tanner, "and unless thou hast many more of thy kind by thee, thou canst never make Arthur a Bland cry 'A mercy.' "

"Is that so?" cried Little John in a rage. "Now, by my faith, thou saucy rogue, thy tongue hath led thee into a pit thou wilt have a sorry time getting out of; for I will give thee such a drubbing as ne'er hast thou had in all thy life before. Take thy staff in thy hand, fellow, for I will not smite an unarmed man."

"Marry come up with a murrain!" cried the Tanner, for he, too, had talked himself into a fume. "Big words ne'er killed so much as a

mouse. Who art thou that talkest so freely of cracking the head of Arthur a Bland? If I do not tan thy hide this day as ne'er I tanned a calf's hide in all my life before, split my staff into skewers for lamb's flesh and call me no more brave man! Now look to thyself, fellow!"

"Stay!" said Little John; "let us first measure our cudgels. I do reckon my staff longer than thine, and I would not take vantage of thee by even so much as an inch."

"Nay, I pass not for length," answered the Tanner. "My staff is long enough to knock down a calf; so look to thyself, fellow, I say again."

So, without more ado, each gripped his staff in the middle, and, with fell and angry looks, they came slowly together.

Now news had been brought to Robin Hood how that Little John, instead of doing his bidding, had passed by duty for pleasure, and so had stopped over night with merry company at the Blue Boar Inn, instead of going straight to Ancaster. So, being vexed to his heart by this, he set forth at dawn of day to seek Little John at the Blue Boar, or at least to meet the yeoman on the way, and ease his heart of what he thought of the matter. As thus he strode along in anger, putting together the words he would use to chide Little John, he heard, of a sudden, loud and angry voices, as of men in a rage, passing fell words back and forth from one to the other. At this, Robin Hood stopped and listened. "Surely," quoth he to himself, "that is Little John's voice, and he is talking in anger also. Methinks the other is strange to my ears. Now Heaven forfend that my good trusty Little John should have fallen into the hands of the King's rangers. I must see to this matter, and that quickly."

Thus spoke Robin Hood to himself, all his anger passing away like a breath from the window-pane, at the thought that perhaps his trusty right-hand man was in some danger of his life. So cautiously he made his way through the thickets whence the voices came, and, pushing aside the leaves, peeped into the little open space where the two men, staff in hand, were coming slowly together.

"Ha!" quoth Robin to himself, "here is merry sport afoot. Now I would give three golden angels from my own pocket if yon stout fellow would give Little John a right sound drubbing! It would please me to see him well thumped for having failed in my bidding. I fear me, though, there is but poor chance of my seeing such a pleasant sight." So saying, he stretched himself at length upon the ground, that he might not only see the sport the better, but that he might enjoy the merry sight at his ease.

As you may have seen two dogs that think to fight, walking slowly round and round each other, neither cur wishing to begin the combat, so those two stout yeomen moved slowly around, each watching for a chance to take the other unaware, and so get in the first blow. At last Little John struck like a flash, and, "rap," the Tanner met the blow and turned it aside, and then smote back at Little John, who also turned the blow; and so this mighty battle began. Then up and down and back and forth they trod, the blows falling so thick and fast that, at a distance, one would have thought that half a score of men were fighting. Thus they fought for nigh a half an hour, until the ground was all ploughed up with the digging of their heels, and their breathing grew labored like the ox in the furrow. But Little John suffered the most, for he had become unused to such stiff labor, and his joints were not as supple as they had been before he went to dwell with the Sheriff.

All this time Robin Hood lay beneath the bush, rejoicing at such a comely bout of quarterstaff. "By my faith!" quoth he to himself, "never had I thought to see Little John so evenly matched in all my life. Belike, though, he would have overcome yon stout fellow before this had he been in his former trim."

At last Little John saw his chance, and, throwing all the strength he felt going from him into one blow that might have felled an ox, he struck at the Tanner with might and main. And now did the Tanner's cowhide cap stand him in good stead, and but for it he might never have held staff in hand again. As it was, the blow he caught beside the head was so shrewd that it sent him staggering across the little glade, so that, if Little John had had the strength to follow up his vantage, it would have been ill for stout Arthur. But he regained himself quickly, and at arm's length, struck back a blow at Little John, and this time the stroke reached its mark, and down went Little John at full length, his cudgel flying from his hand as he fell. Then, raising his staff, stout Arthur dealt him another blow upon the ribs.

"Hold!" roared Little John. "Wouldst thou strike a man when he is down?"

"Ay, marry would I," quoth the Tanner, giving him another thwack with his staff.

"Stop!" roared Little John. "Help! hold, I say! I yield me! I yield me, I say, good fellow!"

"Hast thou had enough?" asked the Tanner, grimly, holding his staff aloft.

"Ay, marry, and more than enough."

"And thou dost own that I am the better man of the two?"

"Yea, truly, and a murrain seize thee!" said Little John, the first aloud and the last to his beard.

"Then thou mayst go thy ways; and thank thy patron saint that I am a merciful man," said the Tanner.

"A plague o' such mercy as thine!" said Little John, sitting up and feeling his ribs where the Tanner had cudgelled him. "I make my vow, my ribs feel as though every one of them were broken in twain. I tell thee, good fellow, I did think there was never a man in all Nottinghamshire could do to me what thou hast done this day."

"And so thought I, also," cried Robin Hood, bursting out of the thicket and shouting with laughter till the tears ran down his cheeks. "O man, man!" said he, as well as he could for his mirth, " 'a didst go over like a bottle knocked from a wall. I did see the whole merry bout, and never did I think to see thee yield thyself so, hand and foot, to any man in all merry England. I was seeking thee, to chide thee for leaving my bidding undone; but thou hast been paid all I owed thee, full measure, pressed down and overflowing, by this good fellow. Marry, 'a did reach out his arm full length whilst thou stood gaping at him, and, with a pretty rap, tumbled thee over as never have I seen one tumbled before." So spoke bold Robin, and all the time Little John sat upon the ground, looking as though he had sour curds in his mouth. "What may be thy name, good fellow?" said Robin, next, turning to the Tanner.

"Men do call me Arthur a Bland," spoke up the Tanner, boldly; "and now what may be thy name?"

"Ha, Arthur a Bland!" quoth Robin, "I have heard thy name before, good fellow. Thou didst break the crown of a friend of mine at the fair at Ely last October. The folk there call him Jock o'Nottingham; we call him Will Scathelock. This poor fellow whom thou hast so belabored is counted the best hand at the quarterstaff in all merry England. His name is Little John, and mine Robin Hood."

"How!" cried the Tanner, "art thou indeed the great Robin Hood, and is this the famous Little John? Marry, had I known who thou art, I would never have been so bold as to lift my hand against thee. Let me help thee to thy feet, good Master Little John, and let me brush the dust from off thy coat."

"Nay," quoth Little John, testily, at the same time rising carefully, as though his bones had been made of glass, "I can help myself, good fellow, without thy aid; and, let me tell thee, had it not been for that vile cowskin cap of thine, it would have been ill for thee this day."

At this Robin laughed again, and, turning to the Tanner, he said, "Wilt thou join my band, good Arthur? for I make my vow thou art one of the stoutest men that ever mine eyes beheld."

"Will I join thy band?" cried the Tanner, joyfully; "ay, marry, will I! Hey for a merry life!" cried he, leaping aloft and snapping his fingers, "and hey for the life I love! Away with tanbark and filthy vats and foul cowhides! I will follow thee to the ends of the earth, good master, and not a herd of dun deer in all the forest but shall know the sound of the twang of my bowstring."

"As for thee, Little John," said Robin, turning to him and laughing, "thou wilt start once more for Ancaster, and we will go part way with thee, for I will not have thee turn again to either the right hand or the left till thou hast fairly gotten away from Sherwood. There are other inns that thou knowest yet, hereabouts." Thereupon, leaving the thickets, they took once more to the highway, and departed upon their business.

from THE HOUND OF ULSTER

Rosemary Sutcliff

This selection from The Hound of Ulster *describes the settlement of a long quarrel among the three heroes and comrades (Laery, Conall, and Cuchulain) as to which of them should be called the "Champion of all the Heroes of Ireland." The quarrel was brought about by the lies and maneuverings of the chieftain, Bricrieu, a wily troublemaker. In this episode the three heroes are finally sent by their king, Conor, to Curoi of Kerry, to have him decide the matter, all previous attempts at arbitration having failed.*

The Championship of Ireland

And when Conor the King could make himself heard, he said, coldly angry, 'Then here is my word. You shall go to Curoi of Kerry with this accursed claim; his sight is deeper and his powers older even than those of the Druids, and it may be that he can settle the thing once and for all. Meanwhile, let me hear no more of it.'

So next day the three heroes and their charioteers set out to lay the matter before Curoi the Lord of Kerry.

He was gone from home when they came clattering up the chariot way into the great Dūn on its coastwise headland where he had his palace. But Blanid his wife greeted them softly and warmly, lifting long eyelids at each in turn. And when she had heard what brought them to Dūn Curoi, she said 'Surely that is a thing that can be settled easily enough. But my lord will be three nights from home, and though he has left warriors set about me, I am a foolish woman and grow nervous when he is not by my side. Therefore, let me beg of you as a favour that each of you in turn will watch one night outside the stockade of the Dūn. In that way I shall feel safe.'

That night, when the time came for the warriors to seek their sleeping places, Laery, who was so much the eldest of the three, claimed the first watch, and took up his position outside the big thorn bush that closed the stockade. And Curoi's Queen went to her own chamber and lit a small fire in a brazier and fed it with strange and unholy things until it burned blue; and began to comb her crow-black hair and sing, weaving the

"The Championship of Ireland." From the book *The Hound of Ulster*, retold by Rosemary Sutcliff. Copyright, © 1963 by Rosemary Sutcliff. Reprinted by permission of E. P. Dutton & Co., Inc. and The Bodley Head Ltd.

charm that guarded the gate from all comers after nightfall—and other spells besides.

The night wore on quietly, and Laery was almost asleep leaning on his spear, when he saw a great shadow rising from the sea. Denser and darker and more menacing it grew, until it took the shape of a monstrous human figure, and the moonlight was blotted out behind its shoulders. And Laery saw with a thrill of horror that it carried two war spears whose shafts were branch-stripped oak trees.

'This is a bad night for Ulster,' said the Shadow Giant, and the voice of him boomed hollow as the sea in a cave. And on the word he flung both his spears at Laery the Triumphant; but they passed him by, one on either side, and stood quivering in the massive timber ramparts of the Dūn. Then Laery flung his own spears, and though they were better aimed, he might as well have thrown at a thundercloud as at the great mass towering over him; and with a boom of laughter the monster stooped and caught him up, gripping him so hard in one hand as almost to crush his ribs like egg-shells, and tossed him over the ramparts of the Dūn.

The tumult roused the warriors within, and they came running with Cuchulain and Conall at their head, and found Laery lying just inside the stockade, half dead with his bruises and bubbling for breath; and beyond the stockade the moonlight shining bright and unhindered as before.

The next night Conall took the watch, and all happened in the same way. And when the warriors came running to his aid, he told them of the fight with the giant, just as Laery had done, but like Laery, he could not bring himself to tell how the giant had tossed him contemptuously like a bundle of old rags over the wall. And so, knowing of the spell that Blanid the Queen set every night on the gateway, all men believed that both had jumped the high stockade.

The third night Cuchulain, the youngest, took up his watch outside the Dūn, and the Queen went to her chamber and made her blue fire and let down her black hair to weave the same spells as before, but this time she braided her hair into strange patterns and with each pattern she made another spell that she had not woven last night nor the night before, and little winds ran about the place and small shapeless things squeaked in the corners.

And Cuchulain, leaning on his spear before the gateway, had a quiet watch until midnight. And then he thought he saw nine grey shadows creeping towards him. 'Who comes?' he shouted. 'If you be friends, stand where you are; if you be foes, come on!'

And the nine shadow-warriors raised a great shout and sprang upon him all together, like hounds pulling down a stag; and he fought them all together, shouting his war-cry that made the very timbers of the Dūn shudder behind him, and slew them or drove them back into mist or hacked them into the ground. Then nine more of the shadows leapt upon him, and for the third time, nine more, and all of them Cuchulain dealt with; and then spent and breathless, sat down on a boulder beside the gate to rest.

And as he sat with his head sunk on his breast, he heard a great boom and crash of waves as though of a winter storm beating on the shore, though all about him the night was still. And looking up, he saw a monstrous dragon threshing up from the water. Higher and higher into the air it rose in an arching blaze of fearful glory like a shooting star, and its wings spread half across the sky as it sank with terrible open jaws towards Cuchulain.

Cuchulain's weariness dropped from him like a threadbare cloak, and he sprang to his feet, then made the Hero's Salmon Leap straight up to meet the winged terror, and thrust the full length of his arm down its throat. It was as though his arm was engulfed to the shoulder in living fire, and the hot stinking breath of the creature beat in his face. His hand found the huge pulsing heart and tore it out by the roots.

The monster fell out of the air, black blood bursting from its mouth, and the blaze of its eyes dying out like the red gleeds of a sinking fire. Cuchulain sprang upon the body of the dead monster, and smiting off its head, set it on the pile of three times nine grey snarling warriors' heads he had raised already. And again he sank down on the boulder.

It was almost dawn when he became aware of the shadow coming up from the sea that both Laery and Conall had encountered. Cuchulain

rose to his feet and stood waiting while the shadow darkened and took on giant shape.

'This is a bad night for Ulster,' said the shape, raising the first of the two great spears.

'Yet it may be a worse night for you!' Cuchulain cried.

And the two spears came whistling one after the other, missing him as narrowly as they had missed Laery and Conall, to crash deep into the timber walls of Dūn Curoi; and the monster stooped to grapple with him. But in the same instant Cuchulain sprang up, sword in hand, and leaping as high as the giant's head, flashed in a mighty blow that brought him tumbling to his knees. The giant roared out in a great anguished voice, and with the cry still hanging in the air, was gone like a curl of wood-smoke that the wind whips away.

The first faint light of dawn was broadening over the sea, and Cuchulain knew that there would be no more comers that night, and weary as he was, he thought to go back into the Dūn and rest. But the spells that held the gateway would not yield until the first rays of the sun touched the threshold, and if, as he believed, the other two had leapt the stockade, then so could he. Twice he tried the leap, and twice, with his weariness on him, he failed; and then a great rage rose in him that he could not do what his comrades had done, and with the rage, his utmost strength came upon him, and the Hero light began to flicker like summer lightning about his head, and he took a little run, and vaulting on his spear, went up and over, so high and far that the leap carried him not merely across the wall but into the heart of the Dūn, and he landed on his feet again in the inner court, on the very threshold of Curoi's hall.

He sank down on the door sill, and leaning against the painted doorpost, heaved a great slow sigh.

And Curoi's wife came out from the hall behind him and stooped to touch his shoulder, letting the darkness of her hair trail all across his face. 'That is the sigh of a weary conqueror, not of a beaten man,' she said. 'Come in now, and eat and rest.'

Later, she showed to all three the pile of heads that lay at her gate and said, 'Those are beside the Shadow Giant, who leaves no trace. Now are you content to yield to Cuchulain the Champion's Portion?' she said.

But still the other two would not yield the victory, Laery out of hot jealousy and Conall because by that time he was growing ashamed, and shame always made him the more stubborn. 'No!' said Laery. 'And how should we be content? All men know that Cuchulain was fathered within the Hollow Hills. His own kin among the Lordly People have aided him in this; therefore the contest is an unfair one.'

'Then there is no more that I can do to help you settle the thing,' said Blanid; and she looked just as any other woman whose patience is worn into holes, save that the dark hair on the head of her lifted and crackled like the fur of a black cat that is stroked the wrong way when there is thunder in the air. 'Go home now to Emain Macha, and wait there until my Lord Curoi himself brings you his judgement. But see that you keep the peace with each other while you wait, and whatever the judgement of Curoi may be, see that you accept it, lest Ulster become a laughing stock to Munster and Leinster and Tara and Connacht, for this child's quarrel among her greatest heroes!'

So the three returned to King Conor with the quarrel still unhealed between them, but they kept the peace as Curoi's wife had commanded.

And the days went by and the days went by with no word from Curoi of Kerry. And then one evening when all the Red Branch Warriors were at meat in the King's Hall, save for Conall who was off hunting and his foster brother Cuchulain who had driven down to his own lands of Murthemney to see how the work went on the new house that his men were raising within the old ring-banks of Dūn Dealgan, the door flew open as though at a great blast from the first of the winter gales that was howling like a wolf pack outside. And as all eyes leapt towards it, a terrible figure strode through into the wind-scurried firelight. A creature like a man but taller than any mortal man, horrible to see, and with the yellow eyes of a wolf that glared about the hall as he came. He was clad only in wolfskins roughly sewn together, and a grey mantle over them, and shaded himself from the light of fire and torches with a young oak tree torn up by the roots; and in his free hand he swung a mighty

axe with a keen and cruelly shining edge.

Up the hall strode the horrifying visitor, where every warrior had sprung to his feet, and leaned himself against the massive carved and painted roof-tree beside the central hearth.

'Who are you?' asked Cethern Son of Findtan, striving to make a jest of it. 'Are you come to be our candlestick, or would you burn the house down? Go farther down the hall, my large and hairy friend.'

'Men call me Uath the Stranger, and I am come for neither of those purposes,' returned the giant, in a voice as terrible as his looks. 'I come to see whether, here among the Red Branch Warriors of Ulster, I may find the thing that I have failed to find elsewhere in all Ireland.'

'And what would that be?' demanded Conor the King.

'A man to keep the bargain that he makes with me.'

'And this bargain? Is it then so hard to keep?'

The stranger hunched his great skin-clad shoulders. 'It would seem so.' Then he swung up

the great axe he carried, and held it high, so that all might see the glitter of the firelit blade. 'Behold this axe of mine, is she not fair? But always she is hungry—hungry for the blood of men. Any man bold enough to grasp her tonight may use her to cut my head from my shoulders—provided that he comes here to meet me again tomorrow night that I may return the blow.'

A low murmur of voices, half awed, half angry, sounded all down the crowded benches of the hall; and the stranger looked round him with eyes that blazed like a wolf's when they catch the edge of the firelight. 'The Heroes of the Red Branch are accounted foremost in all Ireland for courage, honour, strength and truth; therefore, let you prove it by finding me, from among you, a man to keep this bargain with me —any man save the King.' His voice rose to a roar like that of a gale among trees. 'If you fail to find me such a champion, then must I say before all men that Ulster has lost her courage and is dishonoured!'

Hardly had he made an end than Laery sprang from his seat. 'Not yet is Ulster without a champion! Give me the axe, and kneel down, fellow!'

'Not so fast! Not so fast, manikin!' Uath the Stranger laughed and began to caress the gleaming axe blade, murmuring over it in a tongue that was strange to all men there. Then handing the weapon to Laery, he knelt and laid his neck over a mighty oak log beside the fire. Laery stood over him, swinging the great axe to test its weight and balance, then brought it crashing down with such force that the stranger's head leapt apart from his body, and the blade bit deep into the log.

Then a horrified gasp broke from all beholders, for as Laery the Triumphant stood back, the body of the stranger twitched, then rose and pulled the axe from the block and picked up its own head from where it had rolled against the hearthstone, and strode down the hall and out into the wild night; and it seemed that the very flames of the torches burned blue behind his passing.

And Laery stood beside the fire, looking as though he had been struck blind.

Next evening the Red Branch Warriors sat at supper in the King's Hall. But they ate little and talked little; and all eyes were turned towards the door. It burst open as before, and in strode Uath the Stranger, with his hideous head set as firmly as ever on his shoulders, and the huge axe swinging in his hand.

As before, he came and leaned against the rooftree and looked about him with yellow eyes under his brows. 'Where is the warrior with whom I last night made a bargain?'

And King Conor Mac Nessa demanded also of his warriors, 'Where is Laery the Triumphant?'

And up and down the benches the warriors looked at each other, but no man had seen Laery the Triumphant that evening.

'So not even among the flower of the Ulster Warriors is there one to keep his word! Never think again to hold your heads high among the Chariot Chiefs of the world, oh small whipped curs of Ulster who cannot count among you one champion whose honour counts as much with him as a whole skin.'

Conall had returned from his hunting and was in the hall that night, and he sprang up, crying, 'Make the bargain afresh, oh Uath the Stranger; make it with me, and you shall not have cause a second time to cry shame on the men of Ulster!'

So the stranger laughed again, and made his magic in a strange tongue, and knelt for Conall as he had knelt for Laery. And again when the blow had been struck, he rose and took up the axe and his own severed head and strode out into the night.

The next evening Conall took his accustomed place among the warriors at supper, white and silent, but determined on his fate. Only when the door burst open as before, and the dreadful figure came striding up the hall, his own courage broke, for it was one thing to die in the red blaze of battle, with company on the journey, and quite another to lay one's head on the block in cold blood, for such an executioner; and he slipped down behind the benches and made for the small postern doorway of the hall.

So when Uath the Stranger called for Conall of the Victories, there was no answer save the click of the falling door pin.

Then Uath looked about him at the shamed and angry faces of King and warriors. 'A pitiful thing it is to see how men such as the Red

Branch Warriors hanker after a great name and yet lack the courage to deserve it! Great warriors indeed you are, who cannot furnish forth *one* man to keep his faith with me! Truly even Cuchulain, though he is nothing but a boy that must stain his chin with bramble juices when he wishes to seem a man, one would think too proud to behave as these two mighty heroes have behaved!'

Cuchulain rose from his place among the Royal kinsmen, and flung his defiance down the hall in a trumpet shout, 'Young I may be, Uath the Stranger, but I keep my word!'

'Come you and prove it, then,' said Uath the Stranger, 'for it is one thing to say and another to do!'

And with a great cry Cuchulain came leaping down the hall and seized the axe from the giant's hand, and springing up from the floor, smote the Stranger's head from his shoulders without even waiting for him to kneel down.

Uath the Stranger lurched like an oak tree in a gale, then steadied, and took back the axe from Cuchulain as though there were nothing odd in the way of it at all, and strode after his head which had bounced like a great hurley ball far off under one of the benches; and so walked down the hall and out into the night, the flames of the torches burning blue behind him.

Next night Cuchulain took his usual place among the warriors. And though the rest, watching him, saw that he was very white and that he scarcely touched the food but drank more than usual of the mead, he had not the look of a man who would take one step backward from the thing that he had come to meet.

Late into the evening, once again the wind rose and the door burst open, and in strode Uath the Stranger, wearing his terrible majesty like a cloud of darkness upon him, and cried out, striking the butt of his axe against the roof-tree, 'Where is Cuchulain? Let him come out to me now, if he would keep his bargain!'

Cuchulain rose in his place and stepped forward. 'I am here.'

'The sadness is in your voice,' Uath said, 'and who shall wonder. Let it be a comfort to you when the axe falls, that you have redeemed the honour of Ulster.' He fingered the axe edge with head cocked, as a harper tuning his instrument.

'Kneel down, now.'

Cuchulain cast one last look round the great hall, seeing Emer's white stone-still face among the women's benches, and the faces of the King, and his friends, and the hounds that he had loved. Then he knelt and laid his head on the great log beside the fire.

'Stretch out your neck farther,' said the voice of Uath, tree-tall above him.

'You are playing with me as a cat plays with a bird!' Cuchulain said angrily. 'Kill me swiftly, for I did not torment you with waiting last night!'

The stranger swung up his axe until the butt of it broke through the rafters with a crash like that of a great tree falling in a storm, then brought it sweeping down in a glittering arc; and the crash of the blow seemed to make the whole hall jump on its foundations. And of the men watching, some covered their eyes, and some could not look away from the horror.

But the young warrior knelt perfectly unharmed, and beside him, no longer the hideous stranger, stood Curoi of Kerry, leaning on his great axe which had bitten deep into the paved floor, smashing the flagstones within a hand's breadth of Cuchulain's head.

'Did I not send you the word through my Queen that I would bring you my decision by and by?' said Curoi. 'Rise up now, Cuchulain.' And as Cuchulain got slowly to his feet and looked about him, as though he were not sure even now that his head was secure upon his shoulders, he said, 'Is the thing still in doubt? Here stands the Champion of all the Heroes of Ireland. The only one among you all, who dared to keep his bargain with death because he gave his word. There is none among the Heroes of Ulster to equal the Hound for courage and truth and honour, and therefore to him I adjudge the Championship and the Champion's Portion at any feast where he may be present, and to Emer his wife, the first place among the princesses of Emain Macha.' For an instant he seemed almost as terrible as Uath the Stranger had been. 'This is the word of Curoi of Kerry, and woe to any warrior who shall dispute it!'

And as he spoke, suddenly it was only his voice that was there, and the firelight shining through the place where he had been. And with the last words spoken, nothing was left of Curoi at all, only the foredoor of the hall crashed shut as though a great wind had blown it to.

For the time that a man might take to draw seven breaths, no one spoke or moved in the hall of Conor the King. And then men began to leave their places and crowd round Cuchulain where he still stood beside the hearth.

Laery came with the rest, and Conall of the Victories to set his arm about Cuchulain's shoulders.

'Why did you speak evil words of me to such as Bricrieu Poison Tongue?' Cuchulain said.

And in the same instant Conall said, 'Why did you speak poison of me to Bricrieu the Gadfly? I would not have spoken so of *you*.'

And Laery grumbled in his russet beard, 'Young cubs, you are, to say scornful things of me to that bird of ill omen, Bricrieu! But I am older, and should have had some wisdom.'

And they looked from one to another in sudden understanding. 'Bricrieu! Of course!' and then began to laugh, and the laughter spread all up and down the hall and broke in waves of mirth against the rafters.

And from that time forward, Cuchulain was acknowledged by all men to be Champion of all the Heroes of Ireland.

Old Magic and Children

One day, early in the 1960's, a seven-year-old boy made a poem:

> I love you, Big World.
> I wish I could call you
> And tell you a secret:
> That I love you, World.[1]

How well this affirmation expresses the natural mood and attitude of young children. They cry out with a great *Yea!* to life, for life impels them to learn and grow. And the duty of adults to children is to foster this impulse. One sure way in which grownups can do this is to take children on what should be a never ending excursion through the realms of literature (especially along the highroads of folk tale and myth), by means of the simple arts of storytelling and reading aloud.

No one can say what the effects of literature may be on a child. Among those who have written of their childhood encounters with books and stories, C. S. Lewis shares the memory of one kind of strong response. In *Surprised by Joy* he describes his experiences in his earliest years with Longfellow's *Saga of King Olaf* and Beatrix Potter's *The Tale of Squirrel Nutkin*. Of the *Saga of King Olaf*, he writes:

> . . . there came a moment when I idly turned the pages of the book and found the unrhymed translation of *Tegner's Drapa* and read
>
> > I heard a voice that cried,
> > Balder the beautiful
> > Is dead, is dead——
>
> I knew nothing about Balder; but instantly I was uplifted into huge regions of northern sky, I desired with almost sickening intensity something never to be described (except that it is cold, spacious, severe, pale, and remote) and then, . . . found myself at the very same moment already falling out of that desire and wishing I were back in it.[2]

Of his first encounter with *The Tale of Squirrel Nutkin*, he writes:

[1] "I Love the World," by Paul Wollner. From *Miracles*, copyright, © 1966, by Richard Lewis, reprinted by permission of Simon and Schuster, Inc. and Penguin Books Ltd.
[2] Clive Staples Lewis, *Surprised by Joy: The Shape of My Early Life*, Harcourt, Brace & World, 1955, p. 17

. . . it administered the shock, it was a trouble. It troubled me with what I can only describe as the Idea of Autumn. . . . And in this experience there was the same surprise and the same sense of incalculable importance. It was something quite different from ordinary life and even from ordinary pleasure; something, as they would now say, "in another dimension."[3]

Of course, not every child will have such acute sensibilities, but every child should have opportunities for encounters with literature so that he may possibly experience this kind of opening up of the mind and spirit. Ideally, these encounters begin in the earliest years and continue throughout life. But such confrontations may never begin, or they may begin needlessly late, unless parents and teachers provide them.

1. WHY TELL STORIES AND READ ALOUD TO CHILDREN

There are four important reasons for telling stories and reading aloud to children: (1) to develop and deepen their enjoyment of literature; (2) to help them achieve competence in the language arts; (3) to promote their psychological well-being; and (4) to expand their social awareness.

Enjoyment of literature

Whenever and however children come into contact with literature, the experience should be pleasurable and arresting. If it is not, they will turn to nonliterary and nonbook forms of entertainment in order to find that other dimension mentioned by C. S. Lewis. Television and motion pictures offer alternatives which may serve to take the place of books altogether. Space does not permit a discussion of the various media in the lives of young people, and a lively discussion it would be! But it would be a sorry day if

[3] *Ibid.*, pp. 16–17

books, for whatever reasons, ceased to be prime vehicles of literary enjoyment.

Why is it necessary to take pains to see that children come in contact with the wealth of folk tales, fables, myths, and epics, especially through storytelling and reading aloud? First, these early forms of literature come out of an oral tradition which is of immeasurable age and only began to diminish less than five centuries ago, following the invention of printing in Europe. Now confined largely to the medium of print, the tales wait to be told and read aloud in order to take on most fully the life they knew for many centuries. Eileen Colwell, an English librarian and a gifted storyteller, clarifies this thought succinctly and well:

> Even in these days of the making and reading of many books, the story that is told by word of mouth holds its own. The spoken word is the memorable word and the voice and personality of the storyteller add richness to the story and lift it from the printed page into life.[4]

Second, if these tales are kept from children, no matter how inadvertently, it is unlikely that the children will ever know them. To miss the folk tales and the myths at the age when they make their greatest impression and offer the greatest delight is to be unknowingly deprived of part of one's rightful cultural inheritance.

Also, the oral presentation of literature must never be thought of as a mere substitute for the child's learning to read for himself. After all, storytelling is an ancient and sturdy art. But if a child never learned to read, a thorough exposure to literature through hearing stories told and read aloud could give him a literary background of lifelong value.

Third, no discussion of literature can avoid questions of taste, judgment, and values; but intellectual and emotional enjoyment should be first goals in our sharing of literature with young people. Call it what you will—fun, excitement, involvement, escape, recreation, experience—intense joy and the sense of surprise are what we all seek in literature. Giving

[4] Eileen Colwell, *A Storyteller's Choice*, Henry Z. Walck, 1964, p. 203

children such delight is the high aim of telling stories and reading aloud to them.

Fourth, perhaps many of the problems children have in learning to read would be more easily surmounted if they got the idea at a very early age that reading and literature are closely connected and highly satisfying. Most children who learn to read with little or no difficulty know this. But all the others who find reading and books a "drag" might change their minds if they found literature in books to be a source of enjoyment. This might provide sufficient motivation for them to *want* to learn to read no matter what.

Long before children can read independently, we can give them every opportunity to be ecstatic and grow through literature. Even after they have mastered the mysteries of print, we should continue to do so. The constant encounter with literature is, after all, one of the finest contributions the process of education can make to young people. And if this encounter can be made a total immersion, a high point in the education of the young will have been reached.

Growth in language arts skills

While it is difficult to assess what happens when children are plunged deeply and continually into valid literature experiences, it is somewhat easier to ascertain how storytelling and reading aloud contribute to their growth in language arts skills. We can observe how attention spans increase, how words and phrases are incorporated into daily speech, how syntax patterns are acquired and used, and how the stories elicit all kinds of responses and engender creativity in play, conversation, and writing.

Through hearing stories told and read, children are aided in developing an ear for style, from the mind-tingling styles of Hans Christian Andersen or Ella Young to Kipling's and Sandburg's rib-tickling displays of language. From the new and old collections of great folk tales come the nuances of many cultures' thought and spirit, nuances which linger unforgettably in our minds because they issue from the deep feeling and strong poetic utterances of men and women close to the wellsprings of life. As a child hears these tales, he perceives the infinite variety of language as it is used in literature, and he begins to know style for what it is, the distinguished use of language to say best what has to be said.

Patterns of literature, of thought, of language are more easily and vividly grasped by children as they listen to stories. It is these patterns which they readily imitate and which help them develop certain standards of literary taste and acquire competence in speaking and writing. Through enjoying the literature they hear, children not only pick up hundreds of new words but become aware of how words in combination connote an infinite array of ideas and feelings. Take Kipling's description of the Elephant's Child's near fatal encounter with the Crocodile (this is at the point where the Crocodile has caught the Elephant's Child by the nose and is pulling him into the water):

> Then the Bi-Coloured-Python-Rock-Snake came down from the bank, and knotted himself in a double-clove-hitch round the Elephant's Child's hind legs, and said, "Rash and inexperienced traveller, we will now seriously devote ourselves to a little high tension, because if we do not, it is my impression that yonder self-propelling man-of-war with the armour-plated upper deck" (and by this, O Best Beloved, he meant the Crocodile), "will permanently vitiate your future career."[5]

It is doubtful that very many children could define most of the words used by the Bi-Coloured-Python-Rock-Snake, but they know what he means—especially when they *hear* the story. They also get a feeling for what those words mean individually and are likely to understand them even in different contexts. Also, when children hear adults use long and strange words in the pleasurable situation of storytelling and reading aloud, they discover that words come in all shapes and sizes and convey an infinite variety of ideas, attitudes, implications, feelings, and remarkable ambiguities.

The Kipling example is admittedly an exceptional demonstration of language delightfully

[5] Rudyard Kipling, *Just So Stories,* Doubleday, 1902, p. 72

employed to achieve drama and rather satirical humor on the child's level. But the old folk tales, when told carefully, simply, and well, also give children the awareness that words are interesting, beautiful, powerful, and that language well spoken is refreshing and rewarding.

Books that children might reject if they tried to read them independently can have startling impact when children hear them read aloud. Think of the myriad folk tales which children needlessly miss because they never hear them told. Ask any twelve acquaintances to identify Espen Cinderlad or Anansi, and you will be lucky if any of the twelve is able to do so.

How Espen and Anansi and all their kin thrive when they are freed from the confines of a book! Can the good-natured, humorous inefficiency and incredible luck of Gudbrand on the Hill-side really come across with full dimension unless the storyteller tells him into life (see p. 127)? Does the deep foreboding of disaster for the fisherman's greedy wife assume its full and awful proportions without actual utterance of the fisherman's ritualistic summoning of the enchanted fish (see p. 68)? Yes, for the minority of adults and children who are good readers and can inwardly give these tales life through their own silent reading of them. But what of all the others? When the words of the tale are spoken, when gestures and intonation are added, when the cadences and rhythms are voiced, when the storyteller and his listeners share in the adventure, then, for good readers and nonreaders alike, a high point of literary experience is reached, a measure of magic is given. In addition, children are making the connections between reading, speaking, listening, and writing.

If more children found in literature a doorway to delight, they might very well begin to write, independently of assignments, and to tell stories themselves. Both activities developed impressively in the North Ranchito School of the El Rancho School District in Pico Rivera, California. In a program of remedial reading for fourth-, fifth-, and sixth-grade youngsters, a reading specialist initiated a unique project. He felt that the children needed to strengthen their self-images and that success in reading would surely help them do so. Taking a volunteer group of some twenty boys and girls, he helped them learn to read aloud and to tell fairly easy-to-read stories. The children met regularly as a group to learn and practice. They also talked with a writer and an adult storyteller. Then they went into the classrooms of all the grades to read and tell stories to other children. What happened? Plenty! The original group of youngsters, finding considerable success in their venture, began to overcome their own reading difficulties, to build self-confidence, and to generate enthusiasm about books. Other children who were already good readers were attracted to the project. Before the year was out, a group of able readers, as well as those with problems, had voluntarily formed themselves into the "Weavers of Tales." Teachers' and children's responses to their efforts were so enthusiastic that a teachers' sign-up sheet had to be provided to schedule the services of these youngsters.

The results of this experimental adventure were far reaching. Not only did the children find that their own immersion in literature was enriching, but they found they could share their discoveries of delight. And the teachers of the district, impressed by what happened, worked with all their pupils to develop an "Authors' Workshop," the children being the authors. At the end of the school year a book fair was held, displaying several hundred books written, illustrated, and bound by the children. What kind of books? They ranged from poetry, fiction, and true adventure to anthologies and picture books. In addition, an anthology of poetry by numerous children was printed and a copy given to each parent who attended the open house held in connection with the "Authors' Workshop."

Later, the entire workshop became a part of the summer and regular school sessions. Thus, the children in one district became more involved with literature and books than they might have become. They learned how writers work. They learned how to interpret literature more carefully, knowing from their own experience that self-expression is demanding but satisfying. And they underscored the fact that adults, to a great extent, are able to create an environment in which children can, from their earliest years, participate in the uniquely human need for literary expression and nourishment.

Psychological benefits

Less obvious but equally important are the psychological events that take place within children when they hear stories told and share them with adults who read aloud. These inner happenings cannot be measured. If we know what we are about, however, they can be mostly beneficial.

It is true that reading aloud and storytelling greatly increase the power of a tale or book to arouse strong emotions in children. The storyteller sets up between himself and his young audience an intense artistic and psychological dialogue, so charged with deep-drawn energies that teller and listener are united in a mutual re-creation of a literary event. Powerful impressions and powerful reactions are bound to result from the stretching of spirit, the inflaming of feeling, and the engendering of ideas which the oral communication of literature promotes.

It is not appropriate in these pages to undertake a long discussion of psychological theories about the significance and effects of literature upon children. But let it suffice here to note that the folk tales and myths give form to deep unconscious needs and problems which are fairly common to a cultural group.

The idea of a Universal Man assumes that each of us is a particular reflection of him. It is this Universal Man, the hero, who appears in one guise or another in world literature. It has been suggested by such psychologists as Carl G. Jung that the myths are in a way the dreams of man and that our own personal dreams share their content. As Joseph Campbell writes in *The Hero with a Thousand Faces:*

> Dream is the personalized myth, myth the depersonalized dream; both myth and dream are symbolic in the same general way of the dynamics of the psyche. But in the dream the forms are quirked by the peculiar troubles of the dreamer, whereas in myth the problems and solutions shown are directly valid for all mankind.[6]

This is pretty heavy stuff which one is hardly

[6] Joseph Campbell, *The Hero with a Thousand Faces,* Bollingen Foundation, Pantheon Books, 1949, p. 19. Meridian paperback, 1956, p. 19

likely to apply in any direct way in the class-room. But look at it this way: although man's connection to the myths and folk tales is no longer as close and vital as it once was, the witches, monsters, helpful spirits, fearful giants, captive princesses, and rescuing heroes abound-ing in world folklore exist in various forms in our own fantasy life and in children's play. In a sense they help keep us sane.

Civilized life in modern societies requires that much of the child's natural feelings and wishes be suppressed or transformed into behavior which is acceptable. The suppressed energies and desires have a way of reappearing in the form of dreams, fantasies, play, fears, and anx-ieties. The folk tales assist children by allowing them to project many of the unfulfilled wishes and guilt-ridden desires into the characters and events of the tale. The child contains in himself the "good" and "bad" which the tales present. The story helps him act out in imagination what he could not act out in real life or accept as being really part of himself.

For these reasons, then, a very strong argu-ment can be made for letting children experi-ence the horror as well as the beauty which exists in folk literature. Any number of commentators have pointed out that when children are given only a one-sided view of life (positive) through literature and education, they often create their own dark worlds quite spontaneously in their dream and fantasy life. What is then likely to happen is that the child who has to invent his own monsters may do so, but without any re-deeming heroes to save the world and restore it to peace and harmony. The folk tales and the myths, with their balance of good and evil, help children maintain psychological balance.

An English psychologist, whose *I Could a Tale Unfold* deserves a wider audience, writes:

Though the stories cannot supplant play, they can, and must, supplement play. Through the art form, tales perform a treble function: they bring to chil-dren experience as yet unknown to them, they demonstrate manipulation of that internalized ac-tion which we call thought, and above all they break down the isolation of phantasy life in all its lonely guilt-ridden anxiety.[7]

At the time of this writing there is tremen-dous concern over the occurrence of violence on television and the prevalence of it in our na-tional life. The issue is not really one of whether children should be exposed to violence or not, but one of how they are exposed. Life con-tains violence, a fact children cannot long es-cape. When violence is seen on the streets and viewed in a television newscast, it is senseless and deeply upsetting. But when violence is met through the filter of art and literature, it is given aesthetic distance and perspective so that the child may view it with some sense of understand-ing. Storytellers can often go one step further to see that children are not overwhelmed by the horrific elements which literature, as well as life, offers. By the very manner in which their telling reassures children that the horror is not engulf-ing and by the fact that they accept and react to events in certain ways, they set children at ease while allowing them to "enjoy" the deliciously scary episodes.

By all means take time to read the books of Kornei Chukovsky, Carl G. Jung, and P. M. Pickard which are listed in the Bibliography. They provide ideas and examples of the psycho-logical uses of literature which every adult work-ing with children and books would do well to consider. After all, in manipulating the external environment of children, the adult has an obli-gation to be aware of what happens to children inwardly. Our understanding of what happens is far from complete, but intelligent reading and reflection, together with experience and intui-tion, will help you discern those reasons why storytelling and reading aloud are important to the psychological well-being of children.

Social awareness

If listening to the telling and reading of folk literature creates in children a feeling for lan-guage and literature and gives them a way of dealing with their internal realities, it already has gone far to make them aware of man and so-ciety. Because adults take time to read aloud and participate in the enjoyment of stories, children

[7] P. M. Pickard, *I Could a Tale Unfold: Violence, Hor-ror, and Sensationalism in Stories for Children,* Barnes and Noble, 1961, p. 154

are more inclined to view grown-ups not so much as taskmasters from whom they are alienated but as friends with whom they share a common humanity.

It is an honor which every youngster deserves, the sharing of feelings and ideas with adults which storytelling and reading aloud permit. It can result in a better classroom atmosphere which probably helps you and your pupils be generous to one another in going through the requirements of an established curriculum. And it brings children directly into the timeless fellowship of sensitive and well-read men and women.

The telling of folk tales (as well as the independent reading of them) helps prepare a young person for his own adulthood and world citizenship. He sees how adults view the world. Hearing the tale "Rapunzel," for instance, he will begin to grasp such concepts as fate, tragedy, justice. In the tales of such tricksters as Brer Rabbit and Anansi he may begin to understand the rebel nature of man which he later encounters in the myth of Prometheus.

Through familiarity with myth, folk tale, fable, and epic, and through the intense experiencing of them which storytelling and reading aloud favor, children can at an early age begin to perceive the connections between folk literature, language, history, philosophy, and their own lives. Exposure such as this will bring young persons to the realization that mankind is one species.

The idea of wickedness and human malice is common to all cultures. For example, people everywhere recognize that mothers are not always perfect. But generally such a recognition is repressed, split off from consciousness as it were, and it goes underground in the psyche, to emerge later in the form of wicked stepmothers, evil queens, and witches.

As stated above, our folk literature acknowledges the rebellious side of human nature. How else do we account for the eternal popularity of the devil and of characters such as Peer Gynt, saucy Espen Cinderlad, jaunty Jack of the Southern Appalachians, and all their cousins? And love is such a universal theme, such a basic need, that the Cinderella story is found around the world, expressing in countless versions the di-

lemma of being unloved and the fear of being unlovable. To this and most tales we give happy endings because man, no matter how cruelly reality disappoints him, feels that existence not only needs but deserves this promise that ultimately, as it is affirmed in the Mormon hymn, *all is well!*

The special contribution of telling stories and reading aloud is that vivid life is given to some of the world's oldest and greatest literature. When this happens, children take part in the story of man's soul and are touched by the fire, ice, storm, and lyric of his inner and outer life.

Bernarda Bryson, writing about why stories are important, has forcefully and passionately set forth not only the justification of stories but the very driving need we have of the storyteller's art:

A story is probably the most human thing about a human being. A story is the inalienable and hereditary wealth of the poor man, however deprived he may be of other goods; and a story is something without which the rich man would still be threadbare. It is the story that truly educates the child, orients him into his world and opens up the imaginative paths of his future life, that makes him moral, compassionate and visionary.

It is the story and the stories of any society that give it cohesion, mutual understanding, a common language of reference, of imagery, humor, and tragedy. The stories of Homer alone, the majestic and awful House of Atreus, provided the Greeks with some thousand years of literature, art, music and drama, and after that time continued to illuminate the hearts and minds of an entire world, and still continue to do so. The stories of the ancient Jews knit that people with bonds that no span of time or of space could sever.

Whatever use may be made of the story, whether it may become a vehicle for verse, the thread upon which a philosophy is hung, a theme for music or the dance, the substance of art or drama, such embellishments are only added treasure; but the story persists and is self-sufficient and stands alone, and is enough by itself without all this.[8]

[8] Bernarda Bryson, in *Owlet Among the Colophons,* Vol. 3, Issue 1, April 1968. Prepared by Corporate Library Services Department at Holt, Rinehart and Winston, Inc.

2. TELLING STORIES AND READING ALOUD

When and where should you tell stories and read aloud to children? Actually the best kinds of storytelling occasions and the most receptive moods may occur under almost any conditions and circumstances. In a shelter at a rained-out picnic; in the midst of a city's cacophony on a busy playground; in the quiet, secure moments before bedtime; in a crowded classroom, as well as in a quiet library corner—all can be best times and places for storytelling and reading aloud.

At school

Parents, librarians, playground personnel, and camp counselors may find it easy to be flexible about when and where they share stories and books with children, but the teacher may have difficulty in finding time for "fun" of this sort. The school day is a busy one and the requirements of the set curriculum usually contend with the individual and group needs of the children. When and where you tell stories and read aloud hinge upon certain necessities. You must:

1. Create a good climate in the classroom for the oral communication of literature;
2. Take time for preparation;
3. Have a wide selection of materials from which to choose;
4. Develop your talent and technique for telling stories and reading aloud.

Your audience may be a captive one, but that hardly helps. You must play the Pied Piper successfully or even your captive audience can escape by tuning you out. But even if you do pipe the tune well, you must create and capture the best moments for piping.

Today, creating the right climate for telling stories is not always easy. If teaching is the process of helping children discover the world and themselves, then the enjoyment of listening to stories told and books read aloud must also be discovered. Children's innate desire to be told a story can be distorted by the great exposure they have to television and films. By the time they reach school, they may need aid in learning how to sit and listen to the spoken word. The quiet voice of books and storytelling takes time to be heard against the frenetic clamor of the electronic media.

Children are not automatically good listeners. They are naturally bouncy, and the attention span required by television programs interrupted by many commercials is not long. Films and television are further intensified by much physical action, dramatic dialogue, and a constant use of music and sound effects to punctuate what is happening. You have none of these aids when you tell stories and read aloud. But never forget that you, as a storyteller and communicator, can be one of the most effective all-around audio-visual media ever devised!

If the children are not accustomed to listening to stories, you may at first have to use few and fairly short materials, letting the children get used to listening to narration. It is helpful to talk informally about the story or the book, letting the children respond as they will. Try to avoid directing their thinking about a story. And don't pry into their reactions. Let them question and comment as they will. This kind of easy and free association may provide your clue to their true interests and needs. How we react to literature tells pretty well who and how we are.

Whether the children are just learning to listen to literature, or whether they have already become skilled at it, your finest effort is required. This does not mean that you need to compete with the devices and effects of television and film, but it does mean you must perfect your techniques, one of which is "setting the stage." This is done partly by your enthusiasm and skill in presenting books orally, partly by the kinds of books you choose, and partly by the mood of relaxation and anticipation you establish.

It is a sound practice to have a planned *daily* period for telling stories, reading aloud, sharing poetry, or talking informally and freely about books and reading. This should be a first step. *Consider literature as an indispensable part of the curriculum.* The sharing of literature must not be something tacked onto the day's activities for good behavior or after lessons are finished, or set aside for Friday afternoon. Do not make the reading-aloud period an occasion for "teaching."

Let it be enjoyable for its own sake. Insights gained, lessons learned, questions asked should come of their own accord as the children feel and reveal them.

Your classroom program may make the last period in the morning or the afternoon the best time of day for storytelling and reading aloud, although some may object to these times, especially since the dismissal bell often means a rather abrupt and chaotic halt to the schoolday and to any storytelling. It is wise to have a long enough block of time in which to be flexible. An hour seems excellent for junior-high grades, while a half hour can be adequate for elementary grades. But do not cut the time so close that only short materials can be used. With longer periods, you can make sure that there is time to read complete chapters without hurrying or breaking them off in awkward places. If the chapters are short, read several. If the allotted time is sufficient, you may read, tell, and discuss stories and books in a leisurely enough fashion that the period may seem to be the best and the shortest of the day.

With a large block of time, you can get through long or hard-to-put-down books more quickly. Also, if you take a subject approach to literature, you will have enough time to present an idea or subject adequately in one session, reading from different types of literature which enable the children to see how a poet approaches an idea as contrasted with the way a writer of fiction or the teller of a folk tale or myth approaches an idea. One hour for reading aloud can be a splendid antidote for the frustrating and frequent fragmentation of our lives. And a special time for reading aloud and storytelling lends the activity unassailable status.

Planning and scheduling have other advantages. The children know what to expect and tend to devote themselves to their classwork more readily, if they know that a reading-aloud time is coming, and probably they return to classwork more refreshed after such a period. Also, you are able to organize and prepare for the session. This is essential: you cannot read aloud on the spur of the moment from *unfamiliar* material with any degree of skill of interpretation, nor can you tell stories well, without careful preparation. Planning also helps

you arrange the schedule so that the children are not cheated out of hearing literature. These pointers do not mean that you should not spontaneously seize upon a mood or event and fit a book or story to it. But in being spontaneous, it is still imperative to have behind you skills and awareness based on preparation.

Indeed, spontaneity is as important as a plan and a schedule. The best moments of life—and of literature—seem to be unexpected. If you know a wide variety of books, folk tales, and poetry, you are prepared to act on the moment and to give it focus or emphasis through reading and telling. In the middle of disaster, in the face of personal or national tragedy, at a time of happiness, there is, if one but knows it, the story which fits the occasion and lends it significance, or there is the poem or song which gives it emotional sense. Many of us who work with children in school found this so when President Kennedy was assassinated; we turned to poetry and to other literature then and afterwards to find solace and understanding, as indeed our nation did.

There are many moments in history when the oral expression of literature has lent depth and dignity to events. During the inauguration of President Kennedy the entire nation touched greatness as Robert Frost spoke from his own poetry. During the televised funeral of Martin Luther King the nation was moved to tears as thousands of voices expressed their anguish and hope in the singing of "We Shall Overcome"—a folk hymn.

As nations turn to literature in this way, so should we in the search to bring literature and life together in the classroom. Of course, this demands that you have a good knowledge of books. When a story or poem or song can be connected with an item of study, a lesson in social problems, or the study of a country, then real connections take place for the child as life and literature do reveal to him their relationship.

At home

Parents, too, should make a habit of sitting down with children for times of reading and talking about books. In her classic *"Bequest of*

Wings," Annis Duff describes how one family turned to and lived with books. This is not putting television down. Both television and books bring life to us and us to life, but a balance should and can be maintained, a kind of cooperative system, as it were, of taking from each of the media what it can best offer. Writing a brief for books and for sharing them in the family, Mrs. Duff says:

> People have often said to us, "How does it happen that your children know so many books? Mine have never asked for them." It does not just "happen"; children seldom do *ask* for books, as an initial stage in learning to love them. Reading, for young children, is rarely a pleasure in isolation, but comes through shared pleasure and constant discerning exposure to books so that they fall naturally into the category of pleasant necessities, along with food, sleep, music and all out-of-doors. If the parents really want a child to have the fun of being a great reader, or if the child feels any need of it at all, I am fairly confident that it can be managed with a little intelligent effort. The important thing to remember, is that "you can lead a horse to water but you cannot make him drink." We have the greatest respect for a child's independence in his choice and judgment of books . . . .[9]

Who is to say when is the best time at home for reading aloud? Before dinner could be ideal, giving the family a chance to unwind from a busy day, changing the gears from the push of daytime to the slower pace of evening. But more practical moments probably come at other times. At bedtime, of course, a short story told or retold, a chapter read from a favorite book, a poem or two said before putting out the lights —these are good guarantees of pleasant dreams and lifelong pleasant memories. Anyone who has experienced as a child the security and comfort of a bedtime story knows how satisfying it is and how this ritual draws child and parent close in friendship and pleasure. But there are all the other times that each family knows best: a walk to the grocery store or to the park is a good time to share a story, or during long household chores like ironing and washing dishes or

windows. And when tempers are short and nervous excitement runs high, reading aloud and storytelling can again bring life to a quieter tempo—not duller, but quieter, as youngsters fall under the spell of a good book.

You who are parents of preschool children should take special care to share literature with them. Literature for this age level has to be hunted out, but it exists and public librarians are glad to help you discover it. Every year the number of good picture books for children increases. And from the many editions of nursery rhymes comes a wealth of literary enjoyment. There are also simple folk tales and songs which the younger child loves to hear over and over. The parent and teacher who reads and learns these tales and sings the songs, in a short time can develop a rather extensive repertory which will be good for many reruns!

Astute observers of young children have said for many years that the most important and critical period in the language development of children is in the years before kindergarten. During these years, though, not only language development but an interlocking process of psychological and social development is taking place. Sharing literature with the child contributes inestimably to these processes. Extensive research on literature experiences and language development in young children has yet to be undertaken, but it is known that children who have been read to regularly at home have a readier interest in and enjoyment of books than children who have not been read to, and that the children who have learned early to enjoy books tend to maintain this lead throughout the grades.

At the library

There is consternation over the fact that children are great users of the library but grow up to be nonusers. Possibly more than half the circulation of a public library's books consists of children's books (the figures run from forty to sixty per cent). One factor which may account for this disturbing paradox seems to be that many parents do not use libraries with their children. All statistics about libraries consistently reveal that only ten per cent or less of the

[9] Annis Duff, *"Bequest of Wings": A Family's Pleasures with Books,* Viking, 1944, p. 17

adult populace regularly uses the library.

There might be startlingly positive results in the next generation, if a majority of parents now took time to go to the library once or twice a month just to see how things are done and to get to know the children's librarian. Parents, as a rule, are not permitted to attend story hours, but they can see to it that their children are given every opportunity to attend them.

Story hours have been a traditional part of public library services to children in the United States. To three generations of children's librarians go thanks for keeping alive for millions of youngsters the art of storytelling. But the story hours are now less frequent and well attended than a generation or two ago, largely because there are serious shortages of facilities and trained librarians and also because children are more involved in extracurricular pursuits. While story hours for older boys and girls have had to fight for time and attendance with the distractions of mid-twentieth-century America, the story hours for preschoolers have gained favor. If one must choose between the two, story hours for the youngest should have priority. Such hours give the library an opportunity to work with mothers of young children while their offspring are being entertained and enriched and are learning to get along with other children in a somewhat formal group situation.

Whether or not the library is able to play a significant role in the oral approach to literature, it certainly is equipped and geared to help parents and teachers do so. Too many adults, however, are unaware of the books and services the public library can give them in sharing literature with children. Somehow this situation needs to be changed.

3. HOW TO TELL STORIES AND READ ALOUD

This section will offer brief suggestions on how to select, prepare, and tell or read stories aloud. There are several fine books on telling stories (see the Bibliography), and anyone would do well to study one or more of them with careful attention.

Selection

The first thing to decide is whether the story you want to use is best told or read aloud—a decision that depends upon the material to be shared, the time you have for preparation, and the age of the children. However, do not assume that storytelling is just for very young children. There is no age, no level of sophistication, at which storytelling cannot be a captivating experience. Even teen-agers enjoy hearing stories told, and it is regrettable that they rarely come in contact with a storyteller. Of course, storytelling is one of the best ways to begin sharing literature with boys and girls, but it is not merely a technique to be limited to the nursery school.

The stories which are better read than told are, generally speaking, picture books, short stories that require the author's exact words and style to be effective, and full-length books which have a complicated narrative structure and are too long to tell in one or two sessions. Certain books, like *The Wind in the Willows,* would require immense effort to learn to tell (even a chapter would make terrific demands on you), and yet how they take on life when read aloud! Some books, like James Thurber's *The Great Quillow,* for example, both tell and read aloud well. With *The Great Quillow* the storyteller's judicious cutting in no way detracts from the children's enjoyment of the tale. And Dorothy Hosford's version of Beowulf, *By His Own Might,* lends itself very well to telling in two or three sessions—but, of course, this story is close to the folk-tale tradition.

A major factor in selection, of course, is the worth of the material. Will it help you create an experience of literature for the children? Probably you should favor those stories which have high literary quality and which the children might conceivably not encounter on their own. In this way, you open new vistas, new ways, new challenges that they might otherwise miss. This is why reading aloud and telling stories to young people are so exciting. In seemingly only entertaining them, you are giving them one of the finest possible gifts—an encounter with greatness. And lest this sound too serious, remember that literature contains all the adventure and lightness of heart which some children think can be found only in books of lesser artistic merit. Furthermore, those moments of shared pleasure in the classroom reach into the future. A university professor writes: ". . . I believe it was in elementary school that I first heard stories and first fell in love with literature."[10]

There is also value in sharing with children the books that really need no selling. When you read from books which children already love, you create a camaraderie between them and yourself. Books like those about Pippi Longstocking permit you to share with children the natural feelings thay have of rebellion against adult authority, as together you enjoy the hilarious ways in which Pippi represents all children in her rebellion against the world of grown-ups and demonstrates the delicious improbability of a child's competent outmatching of blundering adults. *Charlotte's Web* gives the children and you the opportunity to draw together not only in the spirit of deep-shared humor but in the knowledge that life is ironic and often sad.

Probably, your reading aloud and telling should include in large measure the folk tales, the fables, the hero tales, the epics, and the myths. And you should take these stories from the best-known and most highly recommended editions, not from the myriad indifferent and inferior retellings which flood the market. You can easily select stories from the collections of tales made by collectors and editors who have reputations for careful, scholarly, literate work. Among all the persons who compile folk tales for children, only a few belong to this group of dependable and gifted retellers and selectors. Sorche Nic Leodhas (LeClaire Alger) in the past decade has produced fine retellings of Scottish folklore. Harold Courlander has compiled many excellent collections representing all parts of the world. Virginia Haviland, a distinguished children's librarian, has retold some of the better and best-known folk tales for children in grades two through five. Ruth Sawyer, a great American storyteller and a writer for young people, has

brought us some priceless tales from Irish and Spanish folk literature. And Richard Chase has given us delightful folk tales of the Southern Appalachians in *The Jack Tales* and *Grandfather Tales,* two volumes which have become near classics and in which not a false note or dull story is to be found. These collectors, compilers, and editors and others of their caliber (see the Bibliography) not only respect scholarship and authenticity but also have the ability to preserve in their retellings the qualities of dialect or idiomatic distinctiveness or folk poetry which make their tales a delight to tell and to listen to.

In addition to the tales from the traditional literature, you should choose from the works of such master storytellers as Eleanor Farjeon, Hans Christian Andersen, Frank R. Stockton, Carl Sandburg, Lawrence Housman, Rudyard Kipling, and Walter de la Mare. Their stories almost demand to be heard; indeed, they sound as if the writers had spoken aloud as they wrote. Unless these stories are told expertly, they are best read aloud. Stories from these writers and others are found in various collections, including the companion book *Time for New Magic,*[11] and should certainly be part of every teacher's telling and reading-aloud program.

Materials sometimes overlooked as part of the story hour are poetry, ballads, and songs. *Time for Poetry*[12] has many suggestions on how to use poetry in ways which will enhance any program of reading aloud. Also, many folk songs are exquisite poetry. Singing them is preferable, but innumerable songs come across very well if they are spoken. These materials bring a lyrical note to reading aloud and storytelling and richly enhance your literature program.

One admonition: Choose only those books and stories which you are enthusiastic about and which you really want to share with children. Your reading aloud and your telling can never be better than the delight you feel about the literature you share. Perhaps this delight is the most important thing you do share. Perhaps it is better to tell a poor story really well than to

[10] Edmund J. Farrell, "Listen, My Children, and You Shall Read. . . ." *English Journal,* January 1966, p. 39

[11] May Hill Arbuthnot and Mark Taylor, *Time for New Magic,* Scott, Foresman and Company, 1970
[12] May Hill Arbuthnot and Shelton L. Root, Jr., *Time for Poetry,* Scott, Foresman and Company, 1968

tell or read a good one badly. It is to be hoped, though, that personal taste and good literature will coincide in what you bring to boys and girls.

This anthology has been compiled with one purpose uppermost—to bring under one cover a wide and representative world collection of good folk tales, fables, myths, and epics—and in the extensive Bibliography to provide an even more comprehensive selection of books to choose from.

But your own wide reading is necessary. The world is so full of stories that not even a group of professional anthologists could locate them all or meet all tastes and needs. One tremendous source for any adult who wishes to expand his repertory of stories is the public library. Librarians who specialize in work with children are some of society's unsung heroes. They are the resource persons who keep us supplied with the newest and best materials. It is imperative that you keep up-to-date on books and stories for children. Too many people get stuck with their old favorites and forget that a new book could be better than an old and treasured one, or at least deserve a place alongside it. For example, retellings of *Aesop* in recent years have been more lively and contemporary in appeal than earlier "classic" editions, and many new versions of the myths are truer to the originals and better stated for the contemporary child than older versions. Librarians can generally guide you through the maze of new and old editions, and since many of them are storytellers, they can provide parents and teachers with good suggestions from their repertories. Also, they can help you avoid a bias toward tales only from the Western world. Many people seem to think of folk tales solely in terms of Jacobs, the Grimm brothers, Andersen, and Perrault, which of course leaves out three fourths of the earth and a majority of its inhabitants.

Several large public libraries in the United States have published lists of stories to tell, with accompanying bibliographies of collections of folk tales and books to read aloud. The lists of the New York Public Library, the Carnegie Library of Pittsburgh, and the Enoch Pratt Library of Baltimore are included in the Bibliography.

One last caution: When checking over recommended books and folk-tale collections and when looking over new ones, read some of the stories aloud. Many times a story will seem unappealing in print and yet will be superb in the telling. On the other hand, sometimes a story which can be enjoyed when read silently does not tell well.

Preparation

Probably no two persons prepare a story for telling, or a book for reading aloud, in the same manner. We may have rules for such preparation, but each of us must find his own way. Two things must somehow get together—you, the storyteller, and the story. Since you communicate not just the story and its words but your own feelings and attitudes about it, it is vital that you, the presenter of a piece of literature, get it into yourself so that it becomes your own true possession. Who can say how long this takes? Love and appreciation of the material, individual abilities of absorption and retention, a schedule or deadline for telling the tale—these are some of the factors at work. Experience, also, helps you prepare stories with greater ease and speed and at the same time reveals to you ever higher standards of preparation and performance.

Whether to memorize or not is something only you can best decide. Some people memorize easily and with good results. Others who make no effort to memorize nevertheless come up with versions of tales which vary only slightly from one telling to the other. Do whatever is easiest for *you* in order to get a story inside yourself. If you memorize easily, you are soon free of the printed page and have the story in your head so that you can "read" it and work on it whenever and wherever you will. Gradually, it will become part of the very fabric of your mind. Often, we simply absorb the general outline and content of a story and when we come to tell it, it is pretty much in our own words.

But whether or not you memorize a story, you must avoid a mechanical manner in the telling. You must *know* the story. Memorization by rote is not knowing the story but merely having its words. You need to know your story so well that even if you forget a phrase or paragraph, you are not brought to a halt. Look at it this way: A good storyteller, no matter how he acquires his material, can tell it naturally and without forgetting, because the story is a part of him.

Should you not memorize the entire story, you will want to memorize certain colorful and fresh phrases which lend authentic flavor to even a simple folk tale. And of course, you should always give special attention to the beginnings and endings of stories, deciding how best to get your listeners into the tales and how best to end the tales effectively. Storytellers as a rule, regardless of the method they use to prepare their stories, believe that the beginnings and endings should be memorized.

Certain procedures are helpful, no matter how you learn your story or prepare to read aloud. First, work out in your mind the sequence of events. Most stories for telling proceed linearly, without flashbacks or digressions. Getting the simple sequence in mind is not difficult. Begin with the major events, the points at which the story takes its principal turns and shifts, the large bones of the skeleton. Then work at adding the smaller sequences necessary to remembering the tale. This procedure helps in reading aloud, too, giving you a good idea of how to pace the reading and when and where to pause or even break off if time grows short or the children become restless.

Next, get a firm idea of the characters, even if they are only the two-dimensional ones found in the folk tales. Know what they essentially stand for, how they contrast with other characters in the story, like one instrument in an orchestra against the other instruments—all working into a final blending and texture. This familiarity with the characters will help in the way you interpret by unconscious gesture and intonation—of great importance in storytelling or reading aloud. If the characters do not live as individuals for you, your reading will be wooden and confusing.

Strange or difficult words and unusual or archaic phrases can bewilder and distract children. Learn how to pronounce the words and all proper names and always pronounce them in the same way. If you do not know the pronunciation of a word, try to find it in a footnote, a glossary, or a dictionary. Often the Reference Department of a public library can help you, over the telephone, if you cannot go to the library. Should these measures fail, and they often do with folk tales, decide for yourself how the words might be pronounced. Remember that many languages have pure vowel sounds, so try that approach. However, let your own ear be your guide, but don't come up with unpleasant pronunciations. Spelling, unfortunately, is often no guide at all. *Oisin* and *Fionn*, two Gaelic names which baffle most non-Gaelic speakers, are pronounced *u-SHEEN* and *fin,* but you could probably make a fairly mellifluous pronunciation by guessing.

You must also decide which words should be explained beforehand. If a word is essential to understanding the story, make sure the children know its meaning in context. Sometimes it is best to explain words only when they are basic to the story's meaning or when they will distract the children's attention from the story. Sometimes a strange word can be made clear merely by the way you say it in the context of the tale. In Joseph Jacobs' "Tom Tit Tot" (see p. 19), the young woman is referred to as a "gatless girl." If you say "gatless" in the right way, the children will know she was lazy and didn't use her wits. Sometimes it is easy to paraphrase a strange or difficult word or expression immediately after using it. For instance, the word "pipkin" appears in some translations of Hans Christian Andersen's "The Swineherd." The storyteller can simply say, "Then the swineherd made a pipkin—that's a small earthen pot." The children not only know what the swineherd made but have learned a new word.

In addition to words and phrases, you often need to clarify unfamiliar backgrounds and traditions. The setting of a tale and the milieu of ideas and customs in which it originated often need to be described. In telling about the Gubbaun Saor in Ella Young's *The Wonder Smith and His Son* (see Bibliography, page 380), you should explain briefly his place in early Irish folklore. For an Anansi story it may be necessary to tell the children who Anansi is, what he is like, and where he comes from as a character in folklore. This kind of prefatory material, which can be made part of the story, will keep an audience from becoming confused or from missing the real punch and humor of a tale.

Voice, diction, gesture, and pacing

Before the actual presentation, you should think through voice projection, diction, gesture, pacing—all the "tricks of the trade." These should be worked out in your rehearsal periods. No storyteller can afford to lose power by thinking about technique during actual performance.

One of the first considerations is your voice. Do you talk to the back row? If so, no one will have difficulty in hearing you. Do you have a resonant, firm, controlled voice, neither too high and harsh nor too low and indistinct? So many books have been written about voice and diction that it is unnecessary to go into detail here. The thing to aim for is the best possible use of your own voice. Some people pitch their voices lower than is natural for them and lose valuable overtones. Some people, under stress, pitch their voices too high and become shrill and breathy. A simple technique for improving one's voice is to hum so softly that the sound can hardly be heard, even by you. Say "mm" and let it be a hum that causes the lips to vibrate very slightly. Do not force the humming or all its good effect will be undone. Hum this way, whenever you can, sometimes running up and down simple scales, neither too high nor too low. Often say "mm-hmm" to yourself. This kind of hum tends to place the voice automatically where it will best use the head, throat, and chest resonators. The results are a more rounded voice, a voice which has the "m" hum within it.

Diction is another matter for serious attention. Most people speak too fast under ordinary circumstances and even faster when in a public-speaking situation. A good way to improve your diction is to take time to enjoy the sounds of words. Some people do not speak as carefully as they could. We overlook much about language because we use it mostly for utilitarian purposes, mostly unconsciously, rarely with deliberate aesthetic intent. Take random words and say them over and over, until they become words you physically *feel*. If you enjoy and savor words, your listeners will too.

Speak nursery rhymes to yourself. Say poetry aloud. Recognize the fact that words communicate just by their sounds. Give a word time, when you say it, to have its full value. There is hardly any danger of dragging out words unduly, but words that are clipped short, swallowed, or slurred plague the general speech. Good storytellers must have a feeling for words and use them lovingly.

Matters of gesture often trouble people. The best advice is not to think about gestures at all. Planned gestures are definitely undesirable. Storytelling is not elocution, and reading aloud is not a formal dramatic presentation. Some persons will use many gestures, others few or none. It does not matter. We gesture unconsciously with our entire bodies—a tilt of the head, a half smile, a shrug of the shoulder, a slight movement of the hands. The best gestures come on their own, aiding the interpretation but not distracting the audience—or the storyteller. Probably the face is the best means of physical expression and the eyes the most effective single asset—eyes that look first at this person and then at that one, eyes that express the mood of the teller and the tale. Neither age nor dress can diminish the power of a face that is alive, interesting, and interested.

Another concern is pacing. Don't think *slow* as to speaking; rather, think *easy—easy—easy*. You must give children and yourself time to experience the story. If you live the story as you tell it, you will achieve great power in your telling, and pacing will tend to take care of itself. In the early stages of learning to tell stories and read aloud, you may have to be conscious of pacing, to experiment with it, and with the pause—one of the most effective of all speaking techniques. But let it be a technique, not a device. It should come naturally. If you really feel what you are telling and reading, pauses will come as they should.

Presentation

When you feel that the story or the book has become a part of you, you are ready to share it. You know this by being aware that you are almost bored by it, almost but not quite. It is the feeling you have that you could tell the story backward, step by step, or that you could wake from a sound sleep and begin the telling at any point of the narrative. If you have the story this thoroughly in hand, it will have conviction, even if it is the tallest of tall tales. Children will sense this. Complete familiarity with your story makes the difference in style and effectiveness which sets off one storyteller from another.

People sometimes try to imitate others who read aloud well and tell stories well. Why? Does any storyteller have time to imitate another person and still attend to his story? The question of style is simple: it is a matter of being oneself. The more you are yourself, the more you discover and use your own approach, the better and more distinctive will be your style. If you have prepared well, you won't need to worry about style.

What children look for are the twinkle in your eye and the relaxed air that promise a good time ahead. Keep your hands free of handkerchiefs, pencils, or any other impedimenta which might cramp some of the small, natural gestures most storytellers use. Having possibly practiced your storytelling in front of a mirror, you should have a good idea of how you look, sitting or standing, so that you make an alert but easy and agreeable picture. If you are telling to a large group, your clothes should be the kind the audience forgets the moment the tale begins. Women need to beware of chains or dangles which they may be tempted to finger, and men need to avoid putting their hands in their pockets (from which hands can seldom be recalled once they have disappeared therein). These are all details of general admonition, not to be lingered over but to serve as a reminder to you to avoid clothing and physical mannerisms which break the spell of storytelling.

In a small group, especially of very young children, it is good to sit on a low chair or stool, if they too are sitting on chairs or on the floor. There are times when it is best to sit on the floor with them. In the classroom, you may sit on the corner of a desk—sit, not slouch. When the group is larger and older, you may certainly stand before it, striving always to keep a sense of relaxation and ease. Avoid seeming to tower over the children. An intimate feeling is usually best for storytelling and reading aloud.

When reading aloud, it is wise in the beginning, as you introduce the author and the book, to show the book so that all the children may see it comfortably. Jackets and bindings of books are usually colorful and attractive, and pick up the spirit or general mood of the story. If there are pictures which will really help the children visualize the story, show them before you begin. However, if the pictures are too small for a group to see easily or do not contribute anything to the story, make no point about showing them. And while reading, maintain as much eye contact with the children as possible. If you have prepared well for the reading, it is easy to look up from the page often and for a considerable length of time. Try to take as much of the *reading* out of reading aloud as you can.

When telling a story, don't worry about occasional mistakes. If you forget a choice phrase, who is to know but you? If you leave out a portion of the necessary action and remember it later on, where knowledge of it is necessary to understanding what is about to happen, you can always back up and put all in order, simply by saying, "Now, as you may not have known . . . ." Remember this always: You, the storyteller, are the keeper and the revealer of a mystery and a delight—a story.

When telling and reading aloud, welcome children's participation, their comments, their questions, their expressions of feeling. Don't fear to be interrupted and asked to explain a word or passage or to repeat it. This need not break the narrative. Those who conduct story hours for preschoolers soon discover that all kinds of interruptions are usual, but they rarely disturb the children. More than once in his career, a storyteller to young children will have to answer an enthusiastic child's outburst: "Yes, Bobby, I think it *is* exciting that your daddy goes scuba diving. Oh, your daddy, too, Rhoda? That's wonderful. Now—what do you suppose the little old woman did next?"

It is a thrilling lesson to watch Richard Chase tell stories. He not only handles children's comments and questions superbly, he invites their participation in the story. Before he is very far into a story, the children are joining him in refrains and are guessing about what is coming. The effect is one of intense dialogue between teller and listener, and each storytelling session with him is unique. One of the highest compliments you can be paid as a storyteller is to have children so caught up in the story that they give you every kind of reaction—from total, hushed silence, to giggles or fearful gasps.

4. NEW DIMENSIONS FOR THE ORAL APPROACH TO LITERATURE

Audio-visual extensions of books, stories, and storytelling (through films, filmstrips, and recordings) can add color and interest to the story hour. Graphics and realia can make attractive displays in the classroom and the library, and they can tie in well with your storytelling and reading aloud. Indeed, it is not only possible but very exciting to add to storytelling such other media as music, puppetry, dance, and mime. When these art forms are combined with storytelling and literature, children can play as active a role as the adult. The involvement of children in dramatizing their favorite stories and books—through writing scripts and acting them out—is immensely enjoyable and valuable. As A. S. Neill declares in his book *Summerhill:* "Acting is a *necessary* part of education [italics the editors']."[13] Neill goes on to indicate how important and beneficial it is to children of all ages to write and act in their own plays, often based on their favorite literature. It is certain that if children are allowed this kind of involvement, the passivity too often engendered in the usual approaches to books and stories is avoided.

In the mid-1950's, as one of the authors recalls, Pearl Primus, the American modern dancer and student of anthropology, provided a fine ex-

[13] A. S. Neill, *Summerhill, a Radical Approach to Child Rearing*, Hart Publishing Company, 1960 (paperback), p. 68

ample of how storytelling, song, dance, and pantomime can be merged into a total literature experience. At one point in her dance concert, Miss Primus said she would do something not usual in a dance recital—she would tell stories. They would be, she said, African folk tales, presented with some artistic heightening and embellishment as she had seen them done in West African villages.

Once upon a time, in many small African communities, everyone would gather in the center of the village to enjoy the closing of the day. Families had finished their evening meal. The day's work was done, and the men were in from the fields and from hunting. The children were tired and ready to be quiet. As the shadows deepened, it was quite possible that people would begin to exchange jokes about various things, including the "they say" type of anecdotes about the wily rabbit, or about the prankster-thief Anansi the spider man. Always there were those who, by talent or by training, were the acknowledged tale tellers of the community. They would know *all* the tales and songs about Anansi, and they would know how to tell them in the best way. It would not be long, then, before attention would be focused on such a storyteller, as he told about the never ending exploits of the spider man. Perhaps, as he narrated, there would be moments in the story where a bit of chant or a fragment of song would fit in, or perhaps the narration would have strongly rhythmical passages. At these times, the listeners would join with the storyteller in telling, singing, and chanting the story back and forth. The strong rhythms of the tale and the chants would lead to strong pantomimic gestures and dance movements. Before long, what had begun as casual swapping of jokes about Anansi would have become a great community sharing of story, song, and dance! We envy those who grow up with such encounters with literature. Would that we could bring this kind of thing to pass in our classrooms, on our playgrounds, in our libraries.

Using puppets in combining the media

Puppetry offers one easy way of bringing together storytelling, dramatization, song, and music, to extend children's enjoyment of their favorite books and stories. With the children making and manipulating their own puppets and supplying their voices, the satisfactions in everyone's participating are immense. Such an undertaking can be a creative way of helping children develop language arts skills.

Since there are many books on making and using puppets, it will suffice here to point out that puppets can be made from anything—from paper bags to pipestem cleaners. Those the children make are often more delightful and interesting than any that can be purchased. However, a store-bought puppet can be modified and turned into a unique creation.

There is one technique for producing a spontaneous script and sound track with which some teachers have had success. It does require two tape recorders, however; knowledge about how to cut and edit tape; and facilities for duplicating tape sound tracks. When well used, it enables you to bring stories, music, puppets, and the children's own efforts to a pleasing culmination. First, tell a number of stories and let the children decide which one they would most like to "produce." As soon as a story has been selected, get out the tape recorder, set up the microphone (better read a book, first, on how to place microphones and set voice levels!), and proceed as follows: Let the children talk about the story, why they like it, what they think of the characters, how they would expect them to talk. Have them begin to assume various roles and to speak for the characters. You can "play around" with this, letting the children respond to the story as they feel it. Sooner, or later, you can get the entire tale into dialogue form and recorded on tape. It is then a fairly simple matter (once you know how) to edit the tape so that the dialogue runs smoothly. Thus, the children have produced their own rough sound track! You may even want to use it as the basis for doing a more finished product.

After the puppets are made and the sound track prepared (with music worked in where you need it), you and the children are ready to rehearse. In putting these elements together, children and adults learn to work with one another, and the barriers between teacher and students are easily hurdled in a creative enterprise.

The children may want to work out a written script to read from in live performance. This can be managed so that all of them are involved in some aspect of the writing and production and all can take turns in presenting the play and watching it. If your school has closed-circuit television or portable videotape recording and playback facilities, the puppet play can be presented to other classes, and the children can see and hear how they perform. Many teachers have reported that shy and withdrawn children, once they are behind puppets, speak and express themselves forthrightly and well. But think what such activities can mean to *all* children in terms of literary appreciation, oral expression, and cooperative group creation.

You can also make good use of hand puppets in your storytelling. A puppet may represent a character from a book or folk tale or song, or it may be an original human or animal personality. It is not difficult at all to work with a hand puppet. It can make very few movements, of course: It can bow, nod yes and no, clap its hands, raise a hand, point, turn its head, cover its face with its hands, wave, bob, and twist. However, surprisingly, this minimal range of movements can create an entire vocabulary of expression.

Hand puppets need not talk. Indeed, non-talking puppets often seem more real than those that do talk. An audience tends to read into a puppet all kinds of personal projections. Thus, the storyteller may serve as a kind of foil for the puppet, taking directions from it about which stories to tell or songs to sing. Also, while the storyteller is presenting the stories, the puppet can listen along with the children, turning from time to time to look at the storyteller. And the hand puppet will ably help you hold a picture book, turn its pages, and point to the text or pictures. Many didactic elements, such as asking the children to be quiet, or explaining certain words and ideas, can be handled by talking them over with the puppet.

Children quickly identify with such a puppet and look forward to its joining them in the story hour. They tend to follow the puppet's leadership, and they most willingly suspend their disbelief. In time, the puppet becomes *real* to them.

Music may be used most effectively in the presentation of literature. We usually leave it to those who we think know more about music than we do. What a mistake! Literature has always been as present in song as it has been in poetry and prose. The ballad and the folk song are prime examples of the fusing of music and poetry. Some of the books in the Bibliography suggest how literature, music, and creative dramatics and games can be used together. But you, the classroom teacher, can bring these elements together in a way children will remember with deep pleasure all their lives.

Sing folk songs! You can. You don't need a great voice, and you don't need to be an accomplished instrumentalist. Many teachers are finding out that they can learn to play the guitar and, after a few weeks of lessons and diligent practice, play enough simple chords, using simple strums, to accompany themselves and the children in singing dozens of folk songs. By the simple device known as a *capo* (a movable strip fastened across the fingerboard to permit changing the pitch of all the strings at once) you can play the same easily fingered chords in any key comfortable for singing. Some teachers use autoharps, because the autoharp is easy to play. But it is far more difficult to tune and keep tuned than a guitar. Even if you do not play an instrument such as the guitar or a recorder, it is still possible to sing folk songs *without* accompaniment. Group singing is very satisfying and beautiful.

You may ask about the piano, since so many collections of songs give piano arrangements as well as indicate guitar chords (see the Bibliography). Generally speaking, the piano overwhelms the folk song and it overwhelms young children. Also, it is impossible to play the piano and sing with the children in the intimate and enjoyable fashion which the guitar not only permits but invites. You need not worry about having an untrained voice. All you need to do is carry a tune, and the children's singing with you will improve everything.

A last resort for introducing music in the storytelling milieu is the use of records—if they are used sparingly. Perhaps you should play one song to set the mood or help establish a theme, or to help the children learn the song so that they can sing it by themselves. Singing along with a record, or with a filmstrip version of a song (with accompanying record), can be fun and give variety to the occasion.

The basic rule to follow in using any of the media is this: *Do not use them unless they add something of value.* Why show a filmstrip of a picture book, if reading and showing the book to the children is more effective? Why listen to a recorded folk song if you and the children can sing it yourselves? Why listen to a recording of someone telling a story, when you can do it just as well and have the advantage of being live and spontaneous? The filmstrips and the records can play an important role, but they should never become substitutes for what you can best do yourself.

The "mediated" story hour

As more schools develop professionally staffed Instructional Media Centers, replete with books, films, records, realia (objects related to a people or a subject under study), and carrels (individual cubicles), which connect with computers and have audio-video facilities, we shall be reading more and more about the "multi-media approach to the story hour." However, the multi-media approach is as yet a limited one because we lack a wide range of materials and equipment which can be easily and effectively used. Any kind of multi-media program requires sound planning, careful preparation, skilled execution—and plenty of opportunities for the children's participation. Participation does not always mean *doing* something physically; however, it does mean something more than passive acceptance of what is being presented. For example, when children listen to stories and sing along with an adult or with one another, there is participation. Remember that the storytelling situation itself demands an intellectual and emotional give-and-take between storyteller and listeners.

Your use of the story hour format in the classroom will be less formal and structured than that of librarians, let us say. When you are preparing your multi-media approach for the presentation of literature, however, you will do well to seek the assistance of public and school librarians. They and the media specialists can keep you informed about new books, records, films, filmstrips; they can help you find materials from which to make attractive and effective transparencies; and they can assist you in making up a worksheet for each of your "mediated" story hours. The worksheet should indicate what you tried to do and whether you succeeded or not. Such worksheets can be an excellent feedback for building a sound program of "mediated" story hours and revealing what materials are most desirable.

The following three story hours are designed to give you an idea of how you can extend the literature program by using a simple multi-media approach. A subject arrangement is loosely employed in these samples, but you should experiment with your own ways of building a program. A very good article on presenting these kinds of story hours is "Summer Happening," by Sandra Stroner and Florence E. Burmeister, in *Top of the News,* April 1969, pages 291–300. The programs therein described follow a subject and theme approach, but they avoid being too rigid in this respect. Remember, after all, that a potpourri will allow for variety and good pacing. Just because your children are working on a unit about volcanoes, it does not follow that the story hour should be all about volcanoes! Life is not a simplified unit of study, and literature should not be either.

For younger children (kindergarten through grade two)

PROGRAM 1

Subject: Foxes (or Traveling)
Selections and materials:
1. Picture book: *The Fox Went Out on a Chilly Night,* illustrated by Peter Spier (Doubleday, 1961).
2. Sound filmstrip: *The Fox Went Out on a Chilly Night.* Song, with pictures from the book of the same name (see above). Produced by Weston Woods Studios.
3. Poems: "The Little Fox," by Marion Edey and Dorothy Grider (in *Time for Poetry,* comp. by May Hill Arbuthnot and Shelton

L. Root, Jr., Scott, Foresman, 1968, p. 64). "Four Little Foxes," by Lew Sarrett (*ibid.,* p. 64). "The Three Foxes," by A. A. Milne (in *When We Were Very Young,* by A. A. Milne, Dutton, 1924, pp. 38–40).
4. Story: "The Travels of a Fox" (p. 12).
5. Sound filmstrip: *The Camel Who Took a Walk.* Narration and music, with pictures from book of the same name (*The Camel Who Took a Walk,* by Jack Tworkov, illustrated by Roger Duvoisin, Dutton, 1951). Produced by Weston Woods Studios.

Suggestions for using the materials:

Open with a quiet sharing and reading aloud of the picture book, *The Fox Went Out on a Chilly Night.* Afterwards, play the sound filmstrip. Children will enjoy seeing this book in a new dimension and hearing the jolly music, which is very well sung. They will easily be able to sing along part of the time, even on a first hearing. Those children who can read will be able to follow the text as it appears on the screen with the pictures. Then change the pace with two or three appropriate poems, combined with spontaneous and relaxed talk about what the story and song have brought to mind. It doesn't *have* to be talk about foxes! By this time, the children should have quieted down after the stimulation of a filmstrip and music. Read, preferably *tell,* "The Travels of a Fox." This story generally provokes laughter, and it can make a ready lead-in to the next filmstrip, *The Camel Who Took a Walk.* Have the picture book with you, and tell the children they may read it for themselves and that you will share it with the entire group on a future occasion. Since the fox went traveling in both the song and the story, it is easy to tie in the story of the camel who took a morning walk. You might even have a foxlike hand puppet assist you in presenting the story hour, to hold the book with you, and to help with the explanations and discussions.

PROGRAM 2

Subject: Eating!
Selections and materials:
1. Story: "The Three Billy-Goats Gruff" (p. 115).

2. Picture book: *The Three Billy Goats Gruff,* illustrated by Marcia Brown (Harcourt, 1957).
3. Sound filmstrip: *The Three Billy Goats Gruff.* Narration, music, and pictures from the book of the same name (see above). Produced by Weston Woods Studios.
4. Story: "Sody Sallyraytus" (in *Grandfather Tales,* by Richard Chase, Houghton Mifflin, 1948).
5. Sound filmstrip: *I Know an Old Lady Who Swallowed a Fly.* Song. Produced by Weston Woods Studios.

Suggestions for using the materials:

The first three selections will give children the chance to enjoy the same story in three different ways. Begin by telling "The Three Billy-Goats Gruff." Then show the picture-book treatment of it by Marcia Brown, but do not read it aloud. The children will probably make comments on the pictures and the story. Next, show the filmstrip, which together with the music casts it into a somewhat new mold. "Sody Sallyraytus" is a wonderful story to tell and has the same theme as "The Three Billy-Goats Gruff," but there are four people and a pet squirrel who cross over a bridge under which lives a "mean old Bear." Here you and the children can have great fun in dramatizing this absurd tale, using simple puppets, or having the children act out the story. You could use shadow puppets or have the children give a shadow play. A happy way to end the story hour would be to show the filmstrip of the hilarious and ridiculous song, *I Know an Old Lady Who Swallowed a Fly.* This is so repetitious, so simple, and so infectious that children can easily sing along the very first time they hear it, and the pictures add immensely to the fun.

For older children (grades three and up)

This story hour is about North American Indians and is a combination book talk, lesson, and storytelling session with films. It would run almost an hour, unless you omit the film *Paddle-to-the-Sea.* This film and *The Loon's Necklace* should be readily available from libraries and the film circuit to which many metropolitan, county, and state library systems belong. It would be desirable if every school system had these and other films in their own collections or in a central audio-visual department.

Subject: North American Indians—life and lore
Selections and materials:
1. A brief talk about the Indians, their ways of life, their philosophy, their encounter with the white man.
2. Stories: "Little Burnt-Face" (p. 259) and other Indian tales (see the Bibliography).
3. Book: *Paddle-to-the-Sea,* by Holling C. Holling (Houghton Mifflin, 1941).
4. Film: *Paddle-to-the-Sea* (Canadian Film Board, 1967).
5. Film: *The Loon's Necklace* (Canadian Film Board, 1955).

Suggestions for using the materials:

In introducing the subject, have available books about Indians, as well as collections of Indian stories. Indian artifacts would aid in arousing interest. An overhead projector (using transparencies) will enable all the children to see any illustrative materials you wish to show. The film *The Loon's Necklace* is an exquisite presentation of a Pacific Northwest Indian *pourquoi* story, telling why the loon has a white ring around its neck. Traditional masks made by the Indians were used in the film. You may wish to show the film after the introduction rather than at the end of the program. If so, follow it by reading, preferably telling, several short Indian nature myths or a longish story. Next, show the children Holling's *Paddle-to-the-Sea* and discuss its story and illustrations. You may even wish to read or paraphrase a short portion. This will be a good introduction to the film of *Paddle-to-the-Sea,* a good film in that it retains the color and excitement and true spirit of the book.

5. FOLK TALES, FABLES, MYTHS, AND EPICS

"Dead are all the gods," wrote the German philosopher Friedrich Wilhelm Nietzsche more than three quarters of a century ago, at a time when interest in the old gods of Indo-European mythology ran strong. Here is a paradox, as real now as it was then. The people and world which produced our most familiar classical myths are, like their gods, dead; yet the present-day study of folklore is a serious scientific discipline.

The power of the old gods and the vitality of the folk tales are proved in the way we still allude to them in language, literature, and habits of thought. Everyday words and expressions utilize them: "Don't be a dog in the manger"; "She is a siren"; "That's a herculean job." The Oedipus complex is a familiar term and concept. Our rockets and missiles and spacecraft are named Titan, Gemini, and Apollo. Our days of the week and names of the months are taken from the names of various Norse and Greek divinities. Common words like *cereal, tantalize, gas,* and *chaos* hearken back to the early Greeks.

Even though most Americans are cut off from any viable oral literary tradition, everyone knows "Beauty and the Beast," "Cinderella," and "Snow-White." And it is less than half a century since the world was torn asunder when a modern European nation attempted to use its myths to justify collective madness.

The theories of folk-tale origin, of the genesis of myths, of the historical significance of fable and epic are complicated and contradictory at times. *Children and Books,* by May Hill Arbuthnot, offers a brief review of the major theories and developments in the study of folklore (pp. 252 ff.). Stith Thompson's *The Folktale* is a scholarly and lengthy treatment of the subject which serves as an excellent introduction and reference work. And Edith Hamilton's *Mythology* is indispensable to any adult seriously desiring to study Greek, Roman, and Norse mythology. These and other books listed in the Bibliography will amply repay the time spent in studying them.

Likewise, a bibliographical-biographical review of the outstanding collectors (and collections) of folk tales is beyond the province of this anthology. But the life and scholarly contributions of such great folklorists as the brothers Grimm, Asbjörnsen and Moe, Lang, and Afanasiev (see *Children and Books,* Part Three), make a fascinating history of scholarship com-

bined with a delightful occupation—the gathering and recording of the "old tales." This kind of work goes on today, more avidly and with more thoroughness than ever before.

The folk tales

Of the four kinds of traditional literature represented in this book, the folk tales offer the most numerous examples and are the most popular with children. Folk tales are the stories which are circulated and kept alive, usually among unlettered people, by word of mouth, handed down from generation to generation by professional storytellers, traveling merchants, soldiers and seamen, old wives, and grandmothers.

Various theories on the origin and diffusion of the tales have been advanced over the past one hundred fifty years. Some have been bizarre, and none has been totally accepted by scholars. Douglas G. Haring, Professor of Anthropology, Syracuse University, says:

> Historical evidence probably never will be obtained to settle many . . . questions of origin, and it is unlikely that a single archetype of any widespread tale can be reconstructed and attributed positively to a specific people or area. Nevertheless, evidence of the continuous and widespread diffusion of folklore is conclusive.[14]

Obviously, much that has been written about the folk tale is highly speculative. The following remarks (many of which are based on information supplied in Stith Thompson's *The Folktale*) will serve as the briefest kind of recapitulation of major theories advanced since the time of the brothers Grimm.

First, it might be well to note that scholars nowadays minimize the difference in content between the myth and the folk tale, especially since the myths were once believed to be the sources of folk tales. Suffice it to say that the "classic" myths (Greek, Roman, and Norse) were written and shaped by skilled literary men and were not the anonymous products of illiterate persons. It would seem, according to Franz Boas (1858–1942), that there is "a continual flow of material

[14] Douglas G. Haring, "Folklore," *Encyclopedia Americana,* 1969, Volume 11, p. 422f

from mythology to folk-tale and *vice-versa,* and that neither group can claim priority." [15]

The Grimms advocated the idea that the folk tales of Europe were inherited from a common Indo-European language and culture and were broken-down myths which could be understood only by reconstructing the original myths. This theory, referred to as *monogenesis,* admitted of a single origin for the tales.

A variation of this theory (see Thompson, pp. 376–379) was held by T. Benfey, who believed that the folk tales originated in India and spread westward into Europe by three routes: (1) the oral tradition before the tenth century; (2) the literary tradition, from the tenth century onward, through the literary writings of Islamic civilization; and (3) the Mongol invasions which brought Buddhistically inspired tales to Europe.

Andrew Lang, known to thousands of children over the past eighty years for his still-in-print "color" fairy books, was a serious folklorist who worked out his own theories. He has wrongly been credited by some writers as advancing an extreme theory of *polygenesis* (many origins), which theory holds that specific types of tales appear at certain stages of evolution in human cultures (see Thompson, p. 380). This theory is rather appealing and would seem to account for the numerous variants of "Cinderella" (of which there are several hundred). But it is now recognized that although widely separated people may tell similar stories, the stories do not necessarily mean the same thing.

Lang did advance the survival theory of the folk tale. He believed that the folk tale was a key to primitive mythology, being a survival of earlier and more savage states of man. To some extent this is true, but the arguments for and against it entail a good deal of detailed scholarship.

Sir James Frazer and others thought they saw in the folk tales and myths identical worldwide patterns of thought, but they drew undiscriminatingly from very diverse sources and tried to lump them all together on the basis of supposed similarities (see Thompson, p. 382). As Stith

Thompson observes:

. . . identical simple ideas arise over and over. . . . If men tell tales at all they must sometimes hit upon the same motifs. And no copyright office even today prevents this.[16]

Other nineteenth-century theorists saw the folk tales and myths as great fantasies about forgotten historical events. In recent years archaeological discoveries have made this theory even more plausible. It is probable that certain hero tales (Jason, Theseus) are built around the lives and exploits of individual or composite leaders of antiquity.

Yet another approach to the folk tale and the myth has been that of psychologists. This approach yields fascinating material, and two of the most interesting writers on the subject are Carl G. Jung and Joseph Campbell (see the Bibliography). But as in reading about any theories, one must study their hypotheses with a certain degree of skepticism. Whereas Jung's ideas on the significance of folklore may be very helpful to the psychotherapist and his patient, they may on the other hand be of little value to the folklorist who seeks verifiable data.

At any rate, theories about folk tales have been drawn from the researches, findings, and speculations of anthropologists, psychologists, philologists, archaeologists, and comparative mythologists. The most certain thing we know about the folk tales is that they have existed from remote times and have great similarities regardless of where or when they supposedly originated, and they are remembered and disseminated in large part by the common man.

It is agreed that the folk tales represent the "cement of society." They teach kindness, industry, courage. They are carriers of the moral code. Consequently, the folklore of a people can only be understood by understanding their particular religious beliefs, history, and social behavior. It is for this reason that the tales have great value for contemporary children. They carry in them ideas and attitudes which are now somewhat outmoded, but they also contain implicit clues on how to view life and how to behave. Modern children learn from these old tales something

[15] Franz Boas, *Race, Language and Culture,* New York, 1940, p. 405, quoted in Stith Thompson, *The Folktale,* Dryden, 1946, p. 389

[16] Stith Thompson, *The Folktale,* p. 385

about their own behavior in relation to other people. They learn that it is well to use your head. Henny Penny was nearly gobbled up because of her gullibility, but the third little pig prospered because he had courage and used his wits. Children learn that you must look beyond appearances. The prince discovered this to his sorrow when he accepted the false maid as his princess in "The Goose-Girl." Beauty found her true love because she looked beyond the ugliness of the poor beast to his kindness. And Boots accomplished the impossible because he had the courage to wonder, to investigate, and to tackle things for himself. To the sophisticated, such philosophy may not seem to be borne out by the hard facts of modern life. But actually, gangsters and dictators are still coming to bad ends. Children are going to inherit plenty of dragons, ogres, and giants to be exterminated. They also need some of the cement of society to be found in the folk tales, a belief in the moral code of decency, courage, and goodness.

Predominant types of folk tales

In *The Folktale,* Stith Thompson gives the folklorist's formal classification of folk tales (pp. 7–10). In *Children and Books,* a classification more useful to the teacher is offered (pp. 269–272). The folk tale, as we are most familiar with it, and which appears most frequently in this anthology, is generally referred to by scholars as a *Märchen.* We call it a folk tale; children call it a fairy tale. It is the story which has some touch of exaggeration or of the supernatural, best represented by such tales as "The Fisherman and His Wife" (p. 68) and "East o' the Sun and West o' the Moon" (p. 135). But one may put the tales under all kinds of headings, and always there is some overlapping, for few tales belong to just one category.

Accumulative or *repetitional* stories appeal to children four to six years old or even seven. In these stories, plot is at a minimum and action takes its place. The episodes follow each other in logical order and are related in a repetitional cadence that is almost like a patter-song. These stories grow imperceptibly from mere chants like "The Old Woman and Her Pig" to such plot stories as "The Four Musicians."

Talking beast stories are usually prime favorites. Sometimes the animals talk with human beings, as in "Puss in Boots" or "The Travels of a Fox," and sometimes they just converse with other animals. Occasionally there is a talking beast who is no beast at all but an unhappy prince or princess under a wicked spell. That is, of course, quite a different matter. But the talk of the three billy-goats Gruff, Brer Rabbit, and all the pigs, bears, and foxes of the folk tales is quite as understandable and perhaps a shade more reasonable to the child than much of the talking-to he receives from grown-ups.

The *drolls* or *humorous stories* were obviously told for sheer entertainment. Stories of the sillies and the numskulls are ancestors of Lucretia Hale's *The Peterkin Papers* and of the moron tales. Fortunately, the humor of the folk tales is not confined to such foolish ones as "Clever Elsie" (p. 63) but progresses to the gaieties of "King O'Toole and His Goose" (p. 38) and "Tom Tit Tot" (p. 19).

Realistic stories, wherein everything that happens might conceivably be so, are few and far between in the folk tales commonly told to children. The old storytellers were fond of the fabulous. Generally, the more realistic tales have subtleties of humor and ethics which do not readily get across to children. However, Dick Whittington is a very possible hero of flesh-and-blood proportions. On the whole, folk tales pay scant attention to everyday actualities and are far happier and more numerous in the field of the impossible.

Some *religious tales* of long ago have been appropriated by the children. In the Middle Ages, the stories which grew out of the morality plays often included the devil, the saints, or occasionally the Virgin or the Christ Child. The devil stories were invariably humorous, with the devil getting the worst of it at the hands of resourceful human beings, oftentimes scolding wives. The stories of the saints were generally grave, although this collection includes one that is broadly comic, "King O'Toole and His Goose."

Tales of magic, as already stated, are the heart of the folk tales. Fairies and fairy godmothers, giants, water nixies, lads who ride up glass hills, impossible tasks which are nonchalantly performed, three wishes, three trials, enchanted men or maidens—these are just a suggestion of fairy-tale motifs and atmosphere. These give the tales an unearthly quality, often so beautiful that they come close to poetry.

The fables

At first glance, the fables would seem to be a very particular kind of folk tale, and they are. Yet, most fables as we know them (Aesop, the Bidpai, La Fontaine) are the products not of the folk but of men who used these short beast tales for skillful literary, social, and political commentary. There is no question that they probably borrowed from earlier existing folk tales.

The fable is a brief, didactic anecdote, generally with animal characters, who thinly disguise human traits—greed, sloth, patience, wisdom. They point up human faults and virtues and offer practical precepts for successful living. What has been said about fables in *Children and Books* is worth quoting at length:

> Fables have a teasing likeness to proverbs and parables. All three embody universal truths in brief, striking form; and all three are highly intellectual exercises, as exact as an equation. Of the three, the *proverb* is the most highly condensed commentary on human folly or wisdom. . . .
>
> . . . Perhaps the fable grew out of the proverb, to dramatize its pithy wisdom in story form.
>
> The *parable* is like the fable in that it tells a brief story from which a moral or spiritual truth may be inferred. But its characters, unlike the personified animals or objects of most fables, are generally human beings . . . .[17]

The great fable sources are *Aesop, The Panchatantra,* the *Jatakas,* and the works of La Fontaine (see *Children and Books,* pp. 300–303); but to most English-speaking people, fables and Aesop are synonymous. Various encyclopedias will give what actual information is known about the source and history of *Aesop,* and Stith Thompson's *The Folktale* offers additional clues. Actually, no one knows who Aesop was and whether, like Homer, the name stands for one man or for a literary tradition.

[17] May Hill Arbuthnot, *Children and Books,* Third Edition, Scott, Foresman, 1964, p. 299

One of the first books printed in English by William Caxton was *Aesop's Fables* (1484). Caxton's text still remains a good one, being a translation from a French edition and preserving a straightforward style. It is interesting to think that at the very outset of English printing, a book now associated primarily with children should have led the grand parade of books and literature that has followed.

Whatever we may or may not discover about the sources and transmission of the fables, it is clear that for over two thousand years, century after century, fables have delighted and instructed men from India to Iceland. From the mountains of ancient Kashmir and the long-crumbled temples of India, from the vanished manuscripts of forgotten Arab writers, from the great succession of translators and copyists, these compact, trenchant tales speak clearly, unhampered by any bounds of time and space and tongue. In them, children see men as they have been and as they continue to be beneath layers of sophistication, discovering thereby that men of all times and places make up the one family of man.

The myths and epics

Writings on mythology abound. Edith Hamilton's *Mythology* has already been suggested as a good basic introduction to the classic myths. Her impeccable scholarship, fine literary discernment, and clear account of how Greek, Roman, and Norse myths arose and developed serve as excellent guidelines for a study of this literary genre.

What do we know about myths? We know that they are accumulations of folk tales, epics, fables, historical legends, religious legends, *pourquoi* stories, and pure make-believe all melded into a fairly coherent system or tradition of tales in which gods and goddesses play major roles. We know that the classic myths are not products of uncivilized minds or savage states of society but are, rather, the work of poets who take the stuff of folk tale and religious belief and ritual and make of it a body of literature we call myths.

What is a myth? According to William Reginald Halliday, the myth in general attempts to explain, for the most part symbolically, the vital outlines of existence:

(1) cosmic phenomena (e.g., how the earth and sky came to be separated); (2) peculiarities of natural history (e.g., why rain follows the cries or activities of certain birds); (3) the origins of human civilization (e.g., through the beneficent action of a culture-hero like Prometheus); or (4) the origin of social or religious custom or the nature and history of objects of worship.[18]

This is, of course, a rather loose definition of myth, since folk tales, fables, and epics serve many of the same purposes. Robert Graves holds a view which he admits is his own hypothesis but which he insists is supported by archaeological and anthropological findings:

True myth may be defined as the reduction to narrative shorthand of ritual mime performed on public festivals, and in many cases recorded pictorially on temple walls, vases, seals, bowls, mirrors, chests, shields, tapestries, and the like.[19]

And Dr. Jung, the great psychological interpreter of myths, makes this claim:

Myths go back to the primitive storyteller and his dreams, to men moved by the stirring of their fantasies. These people were not very different from those whom later generations have called poets or philosophers. Primitive storytellers did not concern themselves with the origin of their fantasies; it was very much later that people began to wonder where a story originated. Yet, centuries ago, in what we now call "ancient" Greece, men's minds were advanced enough to surmise that the tales of the gods were nothing but archaic and exaggerated traditions of long-buried kings or chieftains. Men already took the view that the myth was too improbable to mean what it said. They therefore tried to reduce it to a generally understandable form.[20]

[18] William Reginald Halliday, "Folklore," *Encyclopaedia Britannica,* 1963. Reprinted by permission, copyright *Encyclopaedia Britannica,* 1963
[19] Robert Graves, *The Greek Myths,* Braziller, 1955, Vol. 1, p. 10
[20] Carl G. Jung, "Approaching the Unconscious," in *Man and His Symbols,* edited with an introductory chapter by Carl G. Jung, Doubleday, 1964, p. 90

These three writers all express perfectly valid views, and it probably doesn't matter in the least whether we call "Narcissus and Echo" a myth or an early Greek folk tale, or a narrative account of a religious ritual. What we do know about the Greek, Roman, and Norse myths is that they give us a fairly unified view of how the people who developed them explained *metaphorically* the world about them, their own history, and their ideas of man and society.

Edith Hamilton offers a nice summation:

The [classical] myths as we have them are the creation of great poets. The first written record of Greece is the *Iliad.* Greek mythology begins with Homer, generally believed to be not earlier than a thousand years before Christ. The *Iliad* is, or contains, the oldest Greek literature; and it is written in a rich and subtle and beautiful language which must have had behind it centuries when men were striving to express themselves with clarity and beauty, an indisputable proof of civilization. The tales of Greek mythology do not throw any clear light upon what early mankind was like. They do throw an abundance of light upon what early Greeks were like—a matter, it would seem, of more importance to us, who are their descendants intellectually, artistically, and politically, too. Nothing we learn about them is alien to ourselves.[21]

It is safe to say, then, that the myths are first, transmogrified historical records in narrative form. Second, they have in them what appear to be early poetic attempts at giving some logical explanation for cosmic and natural phenomena. Third, they are literature because they tell stories which are interesting and enjoyable in themselves. Fourth, the myths reflect the religious, philosophical, and political ideas of their creators.

One may note in the Greek myths various levels of sophistication, indicating perhaps that they come from different ages and stages of Greek civilization. Traces of primitive belief in unknown powers controlling nature appear in those myths and rituals which acknowledged and propitiated various powers residing in trees, rocks, springs, and animals. We see traces of such

[21] Edith Hamilton, *Mythology,* Little, Brown and Company, 1942, p. 7

primitive beliefs in a youngster's small superstitions about stepping on cracks, uttering certain words, and performing certain expiatory actions to avoid dangers.

Another degree of abstraction is to be found in those myths in which the forces of nature are ascribed to various deities. Apollo was the symbol of the sun, with all its warmth, power, beauty. Thunderbolts were said to be hurled by an angry Zeus, though it can be questioned that anyone literally believed this. There were picturesque ways of describing the powers of the universe, just as the Old Testament pictured God as a shepherd and men as His sheep.

As poets and playwrights and others took the myths and used them for their own purposes, it seems to have come about that gods and goddesses were more reflections of man than philosophical abstractions. And yet, there seems to be a later stage in the evolution of Greek myths when the divinities stood for certain abstract virtues. Apollo, for example, became not only the sun god but a god of health and healing and finally a symbol of the abstraction of purity and purification.

For this collection, the simpler stories have been selected, and the Greek and Roman stories predominate not only because they are, on the whole, more interesting, but also because they are the source of innumerable allusions which the child will encounter now and later on.

A word needs to be said about the epics in particular. They are a special kind of literary genre which nevertheless is closely tied to the myths. The epics with which we are most familiar are the literary epics whose authorship is known. In *Robin Hood* and *Beowulf* we have examples of the folk epic, cyclic hero tales very close to the folk tale and the myth.

The epic embodies the national character and its moral code. It may have as its nucleus real events and real heroes no longer traceable through authentic historical records, or it may be a personification of certain ideals and notions which a people cherishes. Closely related to the epics are those cycles of folk tales and myths about such heroes as Theseus, Sigurd, and even Davy Crockett. Strictly speaking, however, the epic is not a cycle of hero tales but is rather a long narrative poem, in dignified style, which presents the adventures and deeds of a hero or a band of heroes. In many such epics, just as in the myths, the gods of Olympus and Asgard participate in the affairs of men. Although the epics of Robin Hood and King Arthur do not show any real connection with supernatural beings, the heroes themselves seem to live on an exalted level of existence and are either touched by something beyond the scope of the here-and-now or possess superhuman abilities. The epics are larger than life, and we speak of larger-than-life events as having epic proportions. In the epic the bounds of humanity are stretched, broken, and extended beyond the ordinary limits.

Not to know something of myths and epics is to be deprived of a rich source of cultural nourishment. It is to be denied an appreciation of linguistic, literary, artistic, commercial, and even scientific references which draw directly from the myths. Not to know the myths is to lose touch with certain ready-made symbols which have possible psychological import for the adult as he gains self-insight and his mind hearkens back to the myths which once ignited his imagination. Not to know the myths is to know less than we should of the spiritual and physical history of the people who developed them and whose heirs we are. Not to know the myths is to miss adding important dimensions to our own lives.

6. ENVOY

Take time for *Time for Old Magic*. There is treasure here that time itself cannot steal. You need not be an academician to appreciate these tales for what they most truly are. To know them is to understand them. To share them with children is to pass them on to the next generation and beyond. As long as men and children live to enjoy them, these tales tell of man's odyssey and impart knowledge and wisdom to us all for carrying on the great journey. Surely they will go with us even as we press outward to new worlds among the beckoning stars.

Bibliography

The Bibliography has been prepared with the help of Miss Lois Miller, District Librarian, Unified School District, Montebello, California. The authors are grateful for her able assistance.

Among the books listed are collections of folk songs with music, and single folk songs in picture-book form. Those entries are preceded by the symbol ♪. (See pp. 355–357 for discussion and examples of the use of music in story hours.)

Few picture-book versions of single folk tales are annotated, since the ones included are already well known and loved or have received recognition for excellence in translation, illustration, or graphic design. Such books represent the work of some of our best illustrators and deserve attention for their artistic merit as well as for their literary value.

Every effort has been made to include important and first-choice books, and for several areas of the world such are available in abundance. However, for many countries there is a scarcity of folklore in printed form for children. For the sake of wide coverage, therefore, we have included some items which are not of superior literary quality, but which, through judicious use, will broaden background and awareness of world folklore. In other words, many serviceable books do have undesirable features. To a great extent their value depends upon the use made of them by the teacher or parent.

Several awards and honors are mentioned in the Bibliography. They are explained briefly in the paragraphs below.

The Caldecott Medal is awarded for distinguished illustration, by an American, of a book for children; the Newbery Medal, for distinguished writing for children by an American author. Both medals are awarded annually by the American Library Association. Comparable awards—the Kate Greenaway Medal for illustration and the Carnegie medal for writing—are made by the British Library Association for outstanding works by British subjects.

The Hans Christian Andersen International Children's Book Medal, or Hans Christian Andersen Award, was created by the International Board on Books for Young People and is given to a living author of children's books in recognition of the entire body of his work. For the Hans Christian Andersen Honor List, the representatives of each national group nominate books from their country. The awards jury of the board considers the nominees and selects the books for the honor list.

ALA Notable Children's Books are selected annually by a committee of the Children's Services Division of the American Library Association. The list consists of fifty or more titles chosen as representing the best children's books of the previous year.

"Fanfare" is *The Horn Book Magazine* honor list, published in each October issue of that periodical. The books are selected from the publications of the preceding year. In this Bibliography the term *HB Fanfare* designates books that have been selected for this list.

For the Lewis Carroll Shelf Award, created by the School of Library Science at the University of Wisconsin, publishers may nominate any book from their list which they think worthy to sit on the shelf with *Alice in Wonderland*. A distinguished panel of judges awards a limited number of places each year.

FOLK TALES

Worldwide Collections: General

ASSOCIATION FOR CHILDHOOD EDUCATION, *Told Under the Green Umbrella*, ill. by Grace Gilkison, Macmillan, 1962. Twenty-six excellent tales for reading aloud or storytelling. 5–7

BAKER, AUGUSTA, comp., *The Golden Lynx and Other Tales*, ill. by Johannes Troyer, Lippincott, 1960.
The Talking Tree and Other Stories, ill. by Johannes Troyer, Lippincott, 1955.
The compiler, a storyteller of distinction, selected from her own repertoire and from out-of-print sources forty-four stories of proven interest to children. The first volume contains sixteen stories; the second, twenty-eight. 8–11

BLEECKER, MARY N., ed., *Big Music: or Twenty Merry Tales to Tell*, ill. by Louis S. Glanzman, Viking, 1946. Traditional, imaginative stories from many lands. 9–12

CHILD STUDY ASSOCIATION OF AMERICA, *Castles and Dragons: Read-to-Yourself Fairy Tales for Boys and Girls*, ill. by William Pène du Bois, Crowell, 1958. Eighteen amusingly illustrated stories selected for their interest to the young independent reader. 9–12

DE LA MARE, WALTER, *Tales Told Again*, ill. by Alan Howard, Knopf, 1959. Felicitously worded versions of nineteen widely known stories. A valuable book for the storyteller. 9–12

FENNER, PHYLLIS R., comp., *Adventure, Rare and Magical*, ill. by Henry C. Pitz, Knopf, 1945.
Giants and Witches and a Dragon or Two, ill. by Henry C. Pitz, Knopf, 1943.

Princesses and Peasant Boys: Tales of Enchantment, ill. by Henry C. Pitz, Knopf, 1944.
Excellent collections enjoyed by the reader and story-teller. 9–12

FILLMORE, PARKER, *The Shepherd's Nosegay, Stories from Finland and Czechoslovakia,* ed. by Katherine Love, ill. by Enrico Arno, Harcourt, 1958. Favorites selected from three of the author's out-of-print books. 9–13

HUTCHINSON, VERONICA S., ed., *Candlelight Stories,* ill. by Lois Lenski, Putnam, 1928.
Chimney Corner Fairy Tales, ill. by Lois Lenski, Putnam, 1926.
Chimney Corner Stories, ill. by Lois Lenski, Putnam, 1925.
Well-selected tales set in large print suitable for beginning readers. 7–9

JACOBS, JOSEPH, *The Pied Piper and Other Tales,* ill. by James Hill, Macmillan, 1963. An attractive edition with good illustrations and large print. 10–12

LANG, ANDREW, ed., *Fifty Favorite Fairy Tales,* ill. by Margery Gill, Watts, 1964. Selected from the many volumes collected by this great folklorist. (Andrew Lang's "color fairy books" have been favorites over the years and have been published in various editions by different publishers. Longmans published excellent editions during the 1940's. They are still in print and include such titles as *Blue Fairy Book, Crimson Fairy Book, Green Fairy Book,* and *Yellow Fairy Book.* McGraw-Hill Book Company and Dover Publications have undertaken publication of facsimile editions of the twelve original titles. Users should be aware that a few stories in these editions are unacceptable to minority groups.) 9–12

MANNING-SANDERS, RUTH, comp., *The Red King and the Witch: Gypsy Folk and Fairy Tales,* ill. by Victor G. Ambrus, Roy, 1965. Entertaining versions of familiar tales. 9–11

RACKHAM, ARTHUR, comp., *Arthur Rackham Fairy Book,* ill. by compiler, Lippincott, 1950. A famous artist chose his favorite stories to illumine with his matchless illustrations. 8–10

ROSS, EULALIE S., comp., *The Buried Treasure and Other Picture Tales,* ill. by Joseph Cellini, Lippincott, 1958. Twenty-two favorite tales from the out-of-print Picture Tales series. 7–10
The Lost Half-Hour, ill. by Enrico Arno, Harcourt, 1963. A collection of traditional and modern fanciful stories chosen for their appeal when told aloud. 9–11

UNITED NATIONS WOMEN'S GUILD, *Ride with the Sun: An Anthology of Folk Tales and Stories from the United Nations,* ed. by Harold Courlander, ill. by Roger Duvoisin, McGraw-Hill, 1955. Each of the sixty tales included was approved by the U.N. delegate of the country from which it comes. 10–12

WIGGIN, KATE DOUGLAS, and NORA A. SMITH, eds., *The Fairy Ring,* rev. by Ethna Sheehan, ill. by Warren Chappell, Doubleday, 1967. Forty-six tales from fifteen countries are contained in this new edition of a time-honored favorite. 9–12

WITHERS, CARL, comp., *A World of Nonsense; Strange and Humorous Tales from Many Lands,* ill. by John E. Johnson, Holt, 1968. An outstanding collection of nonsense stories. ALA Notable Children's Book. 9–11

Worldwide Collections: Special Topics

ADAMS, KATHLEEN, and FRANCES E. ATCHINSON, comps., *The Book of Giant Stories,* ill. by Robert W. Lahr, Dodd, 1926. Fourteen tales gathered from various countries. 10–11

BELTING, NATALIA M., *Cat Tales,* ill. by Leo Summers, Holt, 1959.
Elves and Ellefolk: Tales of the Little People, ill. by Gordon Laite, Holt, 1961.
The Earth Is on a Fish's Back: Tales of Beginnings, ill. by Esta Nesbitt, Holt, 1965.
Three excellent collections. 8–12

CARPENTER, FRANCES, *Wonder Tales of Dogs and Cats,* ill. by Ezra Jack Keats, Doubleday, 1955. The wit and wisdom of cats and dogs are well portrayed in this unusual collection of tales from seventeen nations. 9–12

DE LA MARE, WALTER, *Animal Stories,* Scribner's, 1940. This valuable collection for storytellers contains forty-two stories and forty-six rhymes and ballads about animals. 10–up

HARDENDORFF, JEANNE B., comp., *Tricky Peik, and Other Picture Tales,* ill. by Tomie de Paola, Lippincott, 1967. Tricksters from eight countries are introduced in this assemblage of tales from the out-of-print Picture Tales series. Teachers and others who tell many stories will find this a valuable source. 8–10

JAGENDORF, M. A., and C. H. TILLHAGEN, *The Gypsies' Fiddle and Other Gypsy Tales,* ill. by Hans Helweg, Vanguard, 1956. A unique and useful collection of stories gathered from Gypsy sources. 9–12

LEACH, MARIA, *How the People Sang the Mountains Up: How and Why Stories,* ill. by Glen Rounds, Viking, 1967. Imaginative tales from primitive cultures, retold by one of America's well-known folklorists. Sources and backgrounds are explained in the notes. 9–12

MANNING-SANDERS, RUTH, *A Book of Dragons,* ill. by Robin Jacques, Dutton, 1965.
A Book of Dwarfs, ill. by Robin Jacques, Dutton, 1964.
A Book of Giants, ill. by Robin Jacques, Dutton, 1963.
A Book of Mermaids, ill. by Robin Jacques, Dutton, 1968.
A Book of Witches, ill. by Robin Jacques, Dutton, 1966.
Excellently illustrated collections. 8–12

SAWYER, RUTH, *Joy to the World: Christmas Legends,* ill. by Trina Schart Hyman, Little, 1966.
The Long Christmas, ill. by Valenti Angelo, Viking, 1941.
Two fine collections of stories well told by a master storyteller. 8–12

SPICER, DOROTHY GLADYS, *13 Ghosts,* ill. by Sophia, Coward, 1965. This diverting collection presents tales of ghouls, ghosts, and other supernatural creatures. 9–11

Europe

Jewish Folk Tales

ISH-KISHOR, SULAMITH, *The Carpet of Solomon; a Hebrew Legend,* ill. by Uri Shulevitz, Pantheon, 1966. An excellent retelling of the ancient legend in which King Solomon, exultant over his magic flying carpet, compares himself to God. 9–11

SIMON, SOLOMON, *The Wise Men of Helm,* ill. by Lillian Fischel, Behrman, 1945.
More Wise Men of Helm; and Their Merry Tales, ill. by Stephen Kraft, Behrman, 1965.
Funny tales about a mythical Jewish community in Poland. 10–12

SINGER, ISAAC BASHEVIS, *When Shlemiel Went to Warsaw*

and Other Stories, tr. by Elizabeth Shub and the author, ill. by Margot Zemach, Farrar, 1968. Eight lively, appealing stories. ALA Notable Children's Book. 9–up
Zlateh the Goat and Other Stories, tr. by Elizabeth Shub and the author, ill. by Maurice Sendak, Harper, 1966. Seven skillfully told stories. HB Fanfare, runner-up for Newbery Medal. 10–up

British Isles: General Collections

MANNING-SANDERS, RUTH, ed., *A Bundle of Ballads*, ill. by William Stobbs, Oxford (in U.S. by Lippincott), 1959. This fine compilation of ballads from the British Isles received the Kate Greenaway Medal. 11–15
PICARD, BARBARA LEONIE, *Tales of the British People*, ill. by Eric Fraser, Criterion, 1961. Nine stories which represent the lore of the various peoples who invaded the British Isles. 10–12
♪RITCHIE, JEAN, *From Fair to Fair: Folk Songs of the British Isles*, photographs by George Pickow, piano arrangements by Edward Tripp, Walck, 1966. Sixteen songs woven together by a story about Jock, a wandering minstrel. The piano and guitar arrangements add to the value of this volume. 9–13
YOUNG, BLANCHE C., ed., *How the Manx Cat Lost Its Tail, and Other Manx Folk Stories*, ill. by Nora S. Unwin, McKay, 1959. A unique collection of stories gathered from the inhabitants of the Isle of Man. 7–12

British Isles: Cornwall and Wales

JONES, GWYN, *Welsh Legends and Folk-Tales*, ill. by Joan Kiddell-Monroe, Walck, 1955. Retellings of ancient sagas as well as folk and fairy tales are included. 11–14
MANNING-SANDERS, RUTH, *Peter and the Piskies: Cornish Folk and Fairy Tales*, ill. by Raymond Briggs, Roy, 1966. A sprightly and diversified group of Celtic tales filled with the deeds of the spriggans, demons, knockers, piskies, and other supernatural beings. 8–11
SHEPPARD-JONES, ELISABETH, *Welsh Legendary Tales*, ill. by Paul Hogarth, Nelson, 1960. Well-told tales of mortals' encounters with mermaids, monsters, wizards, dragons, and other mythical creatures of Wales. 9–12
TREGARTHEN, ENYS, *Piskey Folk; A Book of Cornish Legends*, collected by Elizabeth Yates, Day, 1940. A rare compilation of Cornish tales. Although out of print, the book is available in many public libraries. 9–11

British Isles: England

BROOKE, L. LESLIE, ed., *The Golden Goose Book*, ill. by editor, Warne, n.d. Contains "The Golden Goose," "The Three Bears," "The Three Little Pigs," and "Tom Thumb." 5–7
CHAUCER, GEOFFREY, *Chanticleer and the Fox*, adapted and ill. by Barbara Cooney, Crowell, 1958. Caldecott Medal, ALA Notable Children's Book. 6–9
Dick Whittington and His Cat, adapted and ill. by Marcia Brown, Scribner's, 1950. ALA Notable Children's Book, runner-up for the Caldecott Medal. 4–8
ELKIN, BENJAMIN, *Six Foolish Fishermen*, based on a folk tale in Ashton's *Chapbooks of the Eighteenth Century*, ill. by Katherine Evans, Childrens Press, 1957. 5–7
HAVILAND, VIRGINIA, ed., *Favorite Fairy Tales Told in England*, ill. by Bettina, Little, 1959. An attractive edition of six familiar tales based on versions by Joseph Jacobs. Minor changes make the stories easier for children to read. ALA Notable Children's Book. 6–11

JACOBS, JOSEPH, ed., *English Folk and Fairy Tales*, ill. by John Batten, Putnam, n.d.
More English Folk and Fairy Tales, ill. by John Batten, Putnam, n.d.
Good sources for the favorite tales, appealing in format and illustration. 9–12
Mr. Miacca, an English Folktale, ill. by Evaline Ness, Holt, 1967. 5–7
Tom Tit Tot, ill. by Evaline Ness, Scribner's, 1965. Runner-up for Caldecott Medal, ALA Notable Children's Book. 5–8
LEFÈVRE, FÉLICITÉ, *The Cock, the Mouse, and the Little Red Hen*, ill. by Tony Sarg, Macrae, 1947. Lewis Carroll Shelf Award. 5–8
♪*London Bridge Is Falling Down*, ill. by Ed Emberley, Little, 1967. The verses, the tune, the rules, and the historical background of this favorite game accented with glowing illustrations. 5–8
♪*London Bridge Is Falling Down!* ill. by Peter Spier, Doubleday, 1967. Eighteenth-century London lives again in this splendid picture book. 6–8
The Old Woman and Her Pig, ill. by Paul Galdone, McGraw-Hill, 1960. 3–6
STEEL, FLORA ANNIE, *English Fairy Tales*, ill. by Arthur Rackham, Macmillan, 1962. First published in 1918. Although the style is somewhat more formal and literary than that of Joseph Jacobs, the book is an excellent one for both readers and storytellers. 9–12
The Story of the Three Bears, ill. by L. Leslie Brooke, Warne, 1934. 3–6
The Story of the Three Little Pigs, ill. by L. Leslie Brooke, Warne, 1934. 3–6
The Three Little Pigs, in verse, author unknown, ill. by William Pène du Bois, Viking, 1962. 4–7
The Three Wishes, ill. by Paul Galdone, McGraw-Hill, 1961. 4–7
ZEMACH, MARGOT, *The Three Sillies*, ill. by author, Holt, 1963. 5–8

British Isles: Ireland

COLUM, PADRAIC, *The King of Ireland's Son*, ill. by Willy Pogány, Macmillan, 1962, 1944, 1916. Each exciting story in this volume is concerned with the daring deeds of the King's son. 10–12
The Stone of Victory and Other Tales of Padraic Colum, ill. by Judith Gwyn Brown, McGraw-Hill, 1966. The author selected these stories from seven of his earlier works, six of which are no longer in print. Thus, a new generation of children is privileged to know the work of this master storyteller. 9–12
HAVILAND, VIRGINIA, ed., *Favorite Fairy Tales Told in Ireland*, retold from Irish storytellers, ill. by Artur Marokvia, Little, 1961. A discriminating selection of five tales for the younger reader. 7–10
JACOBS, JOSEPH, ed., *Celtic Fairy Tales*, ill. by John D. Batten, Putnam, n.d.
More Celtic Fairy Tales, ill. by John D. Batten, Putnam, n.d.
Both volumes include Welsh, Scotch, Cornish, and Irish tales. 9–12
MACMANUS, SEUMAS, *The Bold Heroes of Hungry Hill*, ill. by Jay Chollick, Farrar, 1951.
Hibernian Nights, ill. by Paul Kennedy, Macmillan, 1963.
The Well o' the World's End, ill. by Richard Bennett, Devin-Adair, 1954.

Fascinating tales which the author collected by the hearths of Donegal and other Irish counties. Three out-of-print collections worth seeking in libraries are: *Donegal Fairy Stories, Donegal Wonder Book,* and *In Chimney Corners.*   10–up

O'FAOLAIN, EILEEN, *Children of the Salmon and Other Irish Folktales,* selected and tr. by the author, ill. by Trina Schart Hyman, Little, 1965.
Irish Sagas and Folk-Tales, ill. by Joan Kiddell-Monroe, Walck, 1954.
Two useful books. The cadence of the Gaelic has been preserved in the latter.   10–up

PICARD, BARBARA LEONIE, *Celtic Tales: Legends of Tall Warriors and Old Enchantments,* ill. by John G. Galsworthy, Criterion, 1965. Nine robust tales with special appeal for boys. Source and background are given for each story.   10–12

PILKINGTON, FRANCIS MEREDITH, *The Three Sorrowful Tales of Erin,* ill. by Victor Ambrus, Walck, 1966. The handsome illustrations match in mood and style these highly competent retellings of third-century legends. ALA Notable Children's Book.   11–13

YOUNG, ELLA, *The Unicorn with Silver Shoes,* ill. by Robert Lawson, McKay, 1957. The tale of Ballor, the King's son, and his adventures in the Land of the Ever Young is told in beautifully cadenced prose.   9–12

British Isles: Scotland

ARMSTRONG, GERRY and GEORGE, *The Magic Bagpipe,* A. Whitman, 1964. Includes the MacCrimmon piping tune.   6–8

HAVILAND, VIRGINIA, ed., *Favorite Fairy Tales Told in Scotland,* ill. by Adrienne Adams, Little, 1963. Six action-packed stories retold with a simplicity that retains the Scottish atmosphere.   7–10

NIC LEODHAS, SORCHE (pseud. of LeClaire Alger), *By Loch and by Lin: Tales of the Scottish Ballads,* ill. by Vera Bock, Holt, 1969.
Claymore and Kilt: Tales of Scottish Kings and Castles, ill. by Leo and Diane Dillon, Holt, 1967.
Gaelic Ghosts, ill. by Nonny Hogrogian, Holt, 1964.
Ghosts Go Haunting, ill. by Nonny Hogrogian, Holt, 1965.
Heather and Broom: Tales of the Scottish Highlands, ill. by Consuelo Joerns, Holt, 1960.
Sea-Spell and Moor-Magic: Tales of the Western Isles, ill. by Vera Bock, Holt, 1968.
Thistle and Thyme: Tales and Legends from Scotland, ill. by Evaline Ness, Holt, 1962.
These delightful volumes have made a great body of Scottish lore accessible to children.   9–12
Sorche Nic Leodhas has also written for younger children four picture books based on folklore of Scotland: *All in the Morning Early,* ill. by Evaline Ness, 1963; *Always Room for One More,* ill. by Nonny Hogrogian, 1965; *Kellyburn Braes,* ill. by Evaline Ness, 1968; *The Laird of Cockpen,* ill. by Adrienne Adams, 1969. All published by Holt.   5–8

SHEPPARD-JONES, ELISABETH, *Scottish Legendary Tales,* ill. by Paul Hogarth, Nelson, 1962. An extensive compilation of stories about the fairypeople and other small folk of Scotland.   10–13

WILSON, BARBARA KER, *Scottish Folk-Tales and Legends,* ill. by Joan Kiddell-Monroe, Walck, 1954. Contains examples of many types of Scottish folk tales.   11–13

Finland

BOWMAN, JAMES CLOYD, and MARGERY BIANCO, *Seven Silly Wise Men,* from a tr. by Aili Kolehmainen, ill. by John Faulkner, A. Whitman, 1964. A picture-book version of a story often called "The Wise Men of Holmola."   5–8
Tales from a Finnish Tupa, from a tr. by Aili Kolehmainen, ill. by Laura Bannon, A. Whitman, 1936, 1964. An interesting group of Finnish tales.   10–14

France

BROWN, MARCIA, *Stone Soup,* ill. by author, Scribner's, 1947. ALA Notable Children's Book, runner-up for Caldecott Medal.   5–8

COONEY, BARBARA, *The Little Juggler,* adapted and ill. by author, Hastings, 1961. A beautiful adaptation of the legend about the boy who was inspired to amuse the Virgin and Child with his best juggling act. HB Fanfare.   8–11

D'AULNOY, COMTESSE, *The White Cat and Other Old French Fairy Tales,* ed. and tr. by Rachel Field, Macmillan, 1967, 1928. A fine collection that has long deserved republication.   8–11

HAVILAND, VIRGINIA, ed., *Favorite Fairy Tales Told in France,* retold from Charles Perrault and other French storytellers, ill. by Roger Duvoisin, Little, 1959. Five well-told stories that many children will enjoy reading for themselves.   7–11

LANG, ANDREW, *The Twelve Dancing Princesses,* ill. by Adrienne Adams, Holt, 1966. This version of the tale, drawn from French sources, is more elaborate and fanciful in tone than that recorded by the Grimms.   5–9

PERRAULT, CHARLES, *Cinderella; or The Little Glass Slipper,* ill. by Marcia Brown, Scribner's, 1954. Caldecott Medal, ALA Notable Children's Book.   5–9
Perrault's Complete Fairy Tales, tr. by A. E. Johnson and others, ill. by W. Heath Robinson, Dodd, 1961. This edition is not very attractive to children, but adults should be aware of it because the "moralities" of Perrault are included and the illustrations are excellent.   10–up
Puss in Boots, ill. by Marcia Brown, Scribner's, 1952. ALA Notable Children's Book.   6–9
Puss in Boots, adapted and ill. by Hans Fischer, Harcourt, 1959.   5–8

PICARD, BARBARA LEONIE, *French Legends, Tales, and Fairy Stories,* ill. by Joan Kiddell-Monroe, Walck, 1955. A rich source of French folklore.   10–14

Germany

A Boy Went Out to Gather Pears, ill. by Felix Hoffmann, Harcourt, 1966. An outstanding pictorial interpretation of this cumulative verse-tale. ALA Notable Children's Book.   5–8

GRIMM, JACOB and WILHELM, *The Brave Little Tailor,* adapted by Audrey Claus, ill. by E. Probst, McGraw-Hill, 1965.   6–9
Fairy Tales, tr. by Lucy Crane, Marian Edwardes, Mrs. Edgar Lucas, and others, ill. by Jean O'Neill, World, 1947. Sixty stories selected from the vast collection of the Grimms.   9–12
Favorite Fairy Tales Told in Germany, retold by Virginia Haviland, ill. by Susanne Suba, Little, 1959. Seven well-known stories retold in a style appealing to the younger reader.   7–11
The Fisherman and His Wife, ill. by Margot Zemach, Norton, 1966.   6–8

The Four Clever Brothers, ill. by Felix Hoffmann, Harcourt, 1967. 5–8

Gone Is Gone, retold and ill. by Wanda Gág, Coward, 1935. The familiar tale of the man and wife who exchanged chores. 5–8

The Good-for-Nothings, ill. by Hans Fischer, Harcourt, 1957. 5–8

The Goose Girl, a new tr., ill. by Marguerite de Angeli, Doubleday, 1964. 5–8

Grimm's Fairy Tales, based on the Frances Jenkins Olcott edition of the English translation by Margaret Hunt, Follett, 1968. This beautiful edition is notable for its illustrations, which were chosen from artwork submitted by children of many nations. Frances Clarke Sayers, author and storyteller of distinction, has contributed an eloquent foreword. 7–up

Grimm's Fairy Tales, tr. by Lucy Crane and others, ill. by Fritz Kredel, Grosset, 1945. Based on some of the best English translations of the tales, this edition is thoroughly satisfying to children. 9–12

The House in the Wood, ill. by L. Leslie Brooke, Warne, 1944. The illustrations and large type make this edition popular with young readers. 8–10

Household Stories, tr. by Lucy Crane, ill. by Walter Crane, McGraw-Hill, 1966 (paperback ed., Dover, 1964). Unabridged republication of the work first published by Macmillan in 1886. 10–up

Nibble, Nibble Mousekin, ill. by Joan Walsh Anglund, Harcourt, 1962. 5–7

Rapunzel, ill. by Felix Hoffmann, Harcourt, 1961. 6–8

The Seven Ravens, ill. by Felix Hoffmann, Harcourt, 1963. ALA Notable Children's Book. 6–9

The Shoemaker and the Elves, ill. by Adrienne Adams, Scribner's, 1960. 5–9

The Sleeping Beauty, ill. by Felix Hoffmann, Harcourt, 1960. 6–11

Snow-White and Rose-Red, retold and ill. by Barbara Cooney, Delacorte Press, 1966. 6–10

Snow-White and the Seven Dwarfs, ill. by Wanda Gág, Coward, 1938. Runner-up for the Caldecott Medal. 5–9

Tales from Grimm, freely tr. and ill. by Wanda Gág, Coward, 1936.

More Tales from Grimm, freely tr. and ill. by Wanda Gág, Coward, 1947.

Three Gay Tales from Grimm, freely tr. and ill. by Wanda Gág, Coward, 1943.

The stories in the preceding three collections retain the essential qualities of folk tales and are enhanced by Wanda Gág's deft illustrations. 8–12

JAGENDORF, M. A., *Tyll Ulenspiegel's Merry Pranks,* ill. by Fritz Eichenberg, Vanguard, 1938. A large collection of tales about the exploits of that legendary figure who championed the cause of the underdog and embarrassed his enemies with jokes and pranks. 9–11

PICARD, BARBARA LEONIE, *German Hero-Sagas and Folk-Tales,* ill. by Joan Kiddell-Monroe, Walck, 1958. Despite the title of this volume from the Oxford Myths and Legends series, the content is predominantly folklore. 10–12

Italy

BASILE, GIOVANNI BATTISTA, *Old Neapolitan Fairy Tales,* selected and retold by Rose Laura Mincieli, ill. by Beni Montresor, Knopf, 1963. These stories are retold from a seventeenth-century collection, *Il Pentamerone.* Chil-

dren will enjoy the variants of "Cinderella" and "Rapunzel." 8–10

CHAFETZ, HENRY, *The Legend of Befana,* ill. by Ronni Solbert, Houghton, 1958. An ancient Christmas legend well told and illustrated. 5–9

HAVILAND, VIRGINIA, *Favorite Fairy Tales Told in Italy,* ill. by Evaline Ness, Little, 1965. Two of the six tales in this collection are variations on the themes of "Cinderella" and "The Three Little Pigs." 7–11

JAGENDORF, MORITZ ADOLF, *The Priceless Cats and Other Italian Folk Stories,* ill. by Gioia Fiamenghi, Vanguard, 1956. An attractive, gaily illustrated collection which children will enjoy reading for themselves. 10–13

TOOR, FRANCES, *The Golden Carnation,* ill. by Anne Marie Jauss, Lothrop, 1961. Includes Italian versions of Greek myths, historic legends, and variations of well-known stories from other countries. 10–12

VITTORINI, DOMENICO, *Old Italian Tales,* ill. by Kathryn L. Fligg, McKay, 1958. Twenty short tales alive with humor and wisdom. 7–12

ZEMACH, HARVE, *Too Much Nose; an Italian Tale,* ill. by Margot Zemach, Holt, 1967. The theme of the three sons who set out to make their way in the world is again encountered in this highly entertaining book. 6–9

Poland

BORSKI, LUCIA M., and KATE B. MILLER, *The Jolly Tailor, and Other Fairy Tales Translated from the Polish,* ill. by Kazimir Klepacki, McKay, 1928, 1956. An excellent source for the storyteller, but tales should be selected from this collection with discretion, for some may offend minority groups. 9–12

HAVILAND, VIRGINIA, ed., *Favorite Fairy Tales Told in Poland,* ill. by Felix Hoffmann, Little, 1963. Six stories which merit more attention in this country. ALA Notable Children's Book. 8–11

Scandinavian Countries

ASBJÖRNSEN, PETER C., and JÖRGEN E. MOE, *East of the Sun and West of the Moon, and Other Tales,* ill. by Tom Vroman, Macmillan, 1963. The unsurpassed tales of Scandinavia that were collected in mid-nineteenth century by the scholarly authors and translated by Sir George Dasent. 10–14

Norwegian Folk Tales, tr. by Pat Shaw Iversen and Carl Norman, ill. by Erik Werenskiold and Theodor Kittelsen, Viking, 1960. Excellent stories and some of the incomparable illustrations of earlier Scandinavian artists. Invaluable to the storyteller. 10–up

The Three Billy Goats Gruff, ill. by Marcia Brown, Harcourt, 1957. ALA Notable Children's Book. 7–9

AULAIRE, INGRI and EDGAR PARIN D', eds., *East of the Sun and West of the Moon,* ill. by eds., Viking, 1969. Reissue of an earlier edition, also based upon work of P. C. Asbjörnsen and J. E. Moe. 8–12

FEAGLES, ANITA, *Autun and the Bear: An Old Icelandic Legend,* ill. by Gertrude Barrer-Russell, W. R. Scott, 1967. 7–9

HATCH, MARY C., *13 Danish Tales,* ill. by Edgun (pseud.), Harcourt, 1947.

More Danish Tales, ill. by Edgun (pseud.), Harcourt, 1949.

Two fine compilations of amusing and wittily illustrated stories. 9–12

HAVILAND, VIRGINIA, ed., *Favorite Fairy Tales Told in Nor-*

way, ill. by Leonard Weisgard, Little, 1961.

Favorite Fairy Tales Told in Sweden, ill. by Ronni Solbert, Little, 1966.

The stories in both books are told in simple, direct style, well illustrated, and set in readable type for the younger reader. 7–11

JONES, GWYN, *Scandinavian Legends and Folk-Tales*, ill. by Joan Kiddell-Monroe, Walck, 1956. Contains a few well-known stories along with hero tales and some unusual examples of folklore. 8–12

OLSEN, IB SPANG, *The Marsh Crone's Brew*, tr. by Virginia A. Jensen, ill. by author, Abingdon, 1960. A fantastically humorous tale concerning the "little people" of Denmark. 6–8

THORNE-THOMSEN, GUDRUN, *East o' the Sun and West o' the Moon*, rev. ed., ill. by Gregory Orloff, Row-Peterson, 1946. Though out of print, this book is included because it is an outstanding rendition of Norwegian folk tales by a storyteller who represented the highest and most artistic achievement in her field. It is available in many libraries. 9–13

UNDSET, SIGRID, ed., *True and Untrue, and Other Norse Tales*, ill. by Frederick T. Chapman, Knopf, 1945. Twenty-seven striking Norwegian tales based on the collections of Asbjörnsen and Moe. The foreword is especially valuable to adult students of folklore. 10–14

ZEMACH, HARVE, *Nail Soup*, retold; ill. by Margot Zemach, Follett, 1964. See also the French variant on this theme, *Stone Soup* (Bibliography, p. 370). 5–8

Spain

BOGGS, RALPH STEELE, and MARY GOULD DAVIS, *Three Golden Oranges and Other Spanish Folk Tales*, ill. by Emma Brock, McKay, 1936, 1964. Romantic and exciting stories for older children. Includes one remarkable ghost story. 10–12

DAVIS, ROBERT, *Padre Porko, the Gentlemanly Pig*, ill. by Fritz Eichenberg, Holiday, 1948. The activities of the kindly pig who delights in helping his friends, both human and animal, are retold in these eleven tales. 8–12

HAVILAND, VIRGINIA, ed., *Favorite Fairy Tales Told in Spain*, ill. by Barbara Cooney, Little, 1963. Six of the best-loved stories of the Spanish people, enhanced with charming illustrations by a noted artist. 7–10

Turkey [1]

DOWNING, CHARLES, *Tales of the Hodja*, ill. by William Papas, Walck, 1965. Nasreddin Hodja, the invincible, half-wise, half-foolish personality from Turkey, is the hero of each of these short tales. 8–11

EKREM, SELMA, comp., *Turkish Fairy Tales*, ill. by Liba Bayrak, Van Nostrand, 1964. These twelve Turkish tales, never before published in the U.S., were heard by the Turkish-born author from her nurse in Istanbul. 9–12

ENSOR, DOROTHY, *The Adventures of Hatim Tai*, ill. by Pauline Baynes, Walck, 1962. Colorful, romantic tales about the legendary feats of Hatim Tai. 9–11

KELSEY, ALICE GEER, *Once the Hodja*, ill. by Frank Dobias, Longmans, 1943. Humorous tales about Nasr-ed-Din Hodja, who combines wisdom and foolishness but always manages to come out on top. ALA Notable Children's Book. 8–11

WALKER, BARBARA K., *Hilili and Dilili*, adapted from a tr. by Mrs. Neriman Hizir, ill. by Bill Barss, Follett, 1964. 5–7

Just Say Hic! adapted from a tr. by Mrs. Neriman Hizir, ill. by Don Bolognese, Follett, 1965. 5–7

Union of Soviet Socialist Republics [2]

ALMEDINGEN, EDITH MARTHA, *The Knights of the Golden Table*, ill. by Charles Keeping, Lippincott, 1964. These twelve stories about Prince Vladimir of Kiev and his knights are filled with the color and flavor of early Russia. 12–14

ARTZYBASHEFF, BORIS, *Seven Simeons; a Russian Tale*, retold and ill. by author, Viking, 1961. The 1937 edition of this humorous tale was runner-up for the Caldecott Medal. 7–10

BLOCH, MARIE HALUN, ed., *Ukrainian Folk Tales*, tr. by editor from the original collections of Ivan Rudchenko and Maria Lukiyanenko, ill. by J. Hnizdovsky, Coward, 1964. These twelve short animal stories, rich with unforced peasant humor, will be new to most American children. 8–12

CARRICK, VALERY, *Picture Tales from the Russian*, tr. by Nevill Forbes, Dufour, 1963 (Stokes, 1915). Eleven little animal stories for the five- and six-year-olds. 5–6

DEUTSCH, BABETTE, and AVRAHM YARMOLINSKY, eds., *Tales of Faraway Folk*, ill. by Irene Lorentowicz, Harper, 1952. *More Tales of Faraway Folk*, ill. by Janina Domanska, Harper, 1963.

These unique collections come mainly from Russia and other Asiatic lands.

DOWNING, CHARLES, *Russian Tales and Legends*, ill. by Joan Kiddell-Monroe, Walck, 1957. Authoritative versions of Russian tales. 9–11

DURHAM, MAE, *Tit for Tat and Other Latvian Folk Tales*, retold from the tr. of Skaidrite Rubene-Koo, ill. by Harriet Pincus, Harcourt, 1967. Twenty-two distinctive stories which portray the Latvian peasant's philosophy of life. 9–11

HAVILAND, VIRGINIA, ed., *Favorite Fairy Tales Told in Russia*, ill. by Herbert Danska, Little, 1961. Five old stories, expertly retold and fittingly illustrated, which show the cunning and humor characteristic of Russian folklore. 7–11

RANSOME, ARTHUR, *Old Peter's Russian Tales*, ill. by Dimitri Mitrokhin, Nelson, 1917. This is the teacher's most practical source for the Russian tales. 8–12

The Fool of the World and the Flying Ship; A Russian Tale, retold; ill. by Uri Shulevitz, Farrar, 1968. Caldecott Medal, ALA Notable Children's Book. 8–11

REYHER, BECKY, *My Mother Is the Most Beautiful Woman in the World; a Russian Folktale*, retold; ill. by Ruth Gannett, Lothrop, 1945. Runner-up for the Caldecott Medal. 6–9

ROBBINS, RUTH, *Baboushka and the Three Kings*, ill. by Nicolas Sidjakov, Parnassus, 1960. Caldecott Medal, Hans Christian Andersen Honor List, ALA Notable Children's Book. 5–9

SMALL, ERNEST, *Baba Yaga*, ill. by Blair Lent, Houghton, 1966. 5–8

The Story of Prince Ivan, the Firebird, and the Gray Wolf, tr. by Thomas P. Whitney, ill. by Nonny Hogrogian, Scribner's, 1968. ALA Notable Children's Book. 8–10

---

[1] Included in this section are stories from Asian Turkey.

[2] Included in this section are stories from Asian sections of the Union of Soviet Socialist Republics.

TASHJIAN, VIRGINIA A., *Once There Was and Was Not,* based on stories by H. Toumanian, ill. by Nonny Hogrogian, Little, 1966. A captivating array of Armenian tales, all of which deserve to be better known. ALA Notable Children's Book, HB Fanfare.　　9–12

TOLSTOY, LEO, *Russian Stories and Legends,* tr. by Louise and Aylmer Maude, ill. by Alexander Alexeieff, Pantheon, 1967. Eight folk tales grouped around the theme of brotherhood.　　10–up

TRESSELT, ALVIN, *The Mitten,* adapted from the version by E. Rachev, ill. by Yaroslava Mills, Lothrop, 1964.　5–8

ZEMACH, HARVE, *Salt: A Russian Tale,* adapted from Benjamin Zemach's literal translation of the Russian of Alexei Afanasev, ill. by Margot Zemach, Follett, 1965. ALA Notable Children's Book, HB Fanfare.　　6–8

Other Countries of Europe

AMBRUS, VICTOR G., *Brave Soldier Janosh,* ill. by author, Harcourt, 1967.
The Three Poor Tailors, ill. by author, Harcourt, 1965. Two Hungarian tales. Both books are notable for glowing illustrations. *The Three Poor Tailors* received the Kate Greenaway Medal.　　5–9

DUVOISIN, ROGER, *The Three Sneezes, and Other Swiss Tales,* ill. by author, Knopf, 1941. Lively and humorous tales, many of them variants of stories from other countries.　　9–11

FILLMORE, PARKER, *The Laughing Prince,* ill. by Jan Van Everen, Harcourt, 1921. This interesting group of Yugoslavian stories is full of fun, humorous inventions, and imaginative detail.　　9–12

HAVILAND, VIRGINIA, ed., *Favorite Fairy Tales Told in Czechoslovakia,* ill. by Trina Schart Hyman, Little, 1966. Five Slavic tales in a volume attractive to the young reader and useful to the storyteller.　　7–11

MANNING-SANDERS, RUTH, *Damian and the Dragon; Modern Greek Folk-Tales,* ill. by William Papas, Roy, 1966. Superior and extremely interesting retellings of several gay tales in which the brave, steadfast, and wise are aided by a variety of magical creatures.　　9–11

MÜLLER-GUGGENBÜHL, FRITZ, *Swiss-Alpine Folk-Tales,* tr. by Katharine Potts, ill. by Joan Kiddell-Monroe, Walck, 1958. One of the collections in the useful Oxford Myths and Legends series.　　10–14

NESS, EVALINE, *Long, Broad, and Quickeye,* ill. by author, Scribner's, 1969.　　6–10

PRIDHAM, RADOST, *A Gift from the Heart: Folk Tales from Bulgaria,* ill. by Pauline Baynes, World, 1967. A good collection of tales that reflect the Oriental and Western heritage of the Bulgarian people. The introduction provides background for the stories.　　9–11

PRODANOVIC, NADA CURCIJA, *Heroes of Serbia,* ill. by Dušan Ristic, Walck, 1964. An excellent contribution to the study of folklore. Scholarly comments on background and sources.　　11–up
Yugoslav Folk-Tales, ill. by Joan Kiddell-Monroe, Walck, 1957. One of the books in the Oxford Myths and Legends series.　　10–14

Africa

AARDEMA, VERNA, *Tales from the Story Hat: African Folk Tales,* ill. by Elton Fax, Coward, 1960.
More Tales from the Story Hat, ill. by Elton Fax, Coward, 1966.
In West Africa the storyteller wears a broad-brimmed

hat from which dangle tiny objects representing his tales of magic, wonder, and fun.　　7–11

APPIAH, PEGGY, *Ananse the Spider: Tales from an Ashanti Village,* ill. by Peggy Wilson, Pantheon, 1966. These interesting stories are a trifle more formal than those presented by Courlander and will be attractive to older readers.　　11–14

ARKHURST, JOYCE COOPER, *The Adventures of Spider: West African Folk Tales,* ill. by Jerry Pinkney, Little, 1964. A book of amusing folk tales, dashingly illustrated, which many youngsters will be able to read for themselves.　　7–10

ARNOTT, KATHLEEN, *African Myths and Legends,* ill. by Joan Kiddell-Monroe, Walck, 1963. Contains stories representative of nineteen African nations and of several tribes south of the Sahara.　　9–12

BURTON, W. F. P., *The Magic Drum; Tales from Central Africa,* ill. by Ralph Thompson, Criterion, 1962. Thirty-eight tales heard from storytellers in Congo villages during the author's term of service as a missionary.　　9–12

CARPENTER, FRANCES, *African Wonder Tales,* ill. by Joseph Escourido, Doubleday, 1963. Twenty-four tales from various parts of Africa. Includes a pronunciation guide for African names.　　8–11

COURLANDER, HAROLD, *The King's Drum and Other African Stories,* ill. by Enrico Arno, Harcourt, 1962.　9–11

COURLANDER, HAROLD, and EZEKIEL A. ESHUGBAYI, *Olode the Hunter, and Other Tales from Nigeria,* ill. by Enrico Arno, Harcourt, 1968.　　8–12

COURLANDER, HAROLD, and GEORGE HERZOG, *The Cow-Tail Switch, and Other West African Stories,* ill. by Madye Lee Chastain, Holt, 1947. Runner-up for the Newbery Medal.　　10–12

COURLANDER, HAROLD, and WOLF LESLAU, *The Fire on the Mountain and Other Ethiopian Stories,* ill. by Robert W. Kane, Holt, 1950.　　10–14

COURLANDER, HAROLD, and ALBERT PREMPEH, *The Hat-Shaking Dance, and Other Tales from the Gold Coast,* ill. by Enrico Arno, Harcourt, 1957.　　9–11
Harold Courlander and his collaborators on the volumes listed above have contributed greatly to our knowledge of African folklore and to our understanding of the great continent of Africa.

DAVIS, RUSSELL, and BRENT ASHABRANNER, *The Lion's Whiskers: Tales of High Africa,* ill. by James Teason, Little, 1959. Thirty-one tales from Ethiopia and its borderlands.　　11–15

DAYRELL, ELPHINSTONE, *Why the Sun and the Moon Live in the Sky: An African Folktale,* ill. by Blair Lent, Houghton, 1968. ALA Notable Children's Book.　5–8

GILSTRAP, ROBERT, and IRENE ESTABROOK, *The Sultan's Fool and Other North African Tales,* ill. by Robert Greco, Holt, 1958. Eleven stories concerned with the deeds of sultans, caliphs, camel drovers, merchants, and scheming wives.　　10–12

GUILLOT, RENÉ, *Guillot's African Folk Tales,* ill. by William Papas, Watts, 1965. Tales of the days when men and animals, trees and plants, and the sun and the moon walked and talked with one another.　　11–up

HARMAN, HUMPHREY, comp., *Tales Told Near a Crocodile: Stories from Nyanza,* ill. by George Ford, Viking, 1967. Tales gathered from the storytellers of six tribes who live in the vicinity of Lake Victoria.　　9–11

HEADY, ELEANOR B., *Jambo Sungura! Tales from East Africa,* ill. by Robert Frankenberg, Norton, 1965.　7–11

When the Stones Were Soft; East African Fireside Tales, ill. by Tom Feelings, Funk and Wagnalls, 1968. 9–12 These collections feature stories about the animals of East Africa and contain some *why* stories of the region.

Asia

General Collections

CARPENTER, FRANCES, *The Elephant's Bathtub; Wonder Tales from the Far East,* ill. by Hans Guggenheim, Doubleday, 1962. An entertaining group of twenty-four tales gathered from many Oriental sources. Each carries the atmosphere of the country in which it originated. 9–11

COURLANDER, HAROLD, *The Tiger's Whisker and Other Tales and Legends from Asia and the Pacific,* ill. by Enrico Arno, Harcourt, 1959. Brevity and simple concepts make these tales suitable for telling to groups in which the children vary widely in age. 9–12

Arabian Countries

BROWN, MARCIA, *The Flying Carpet,* ill. by author, Scribner's, 1956. 7–10

COLUM, PADRAIC, *The Arabian Nights: Tales of Wonder and Magnificence,* ill. by Lynd Ward, Macmillan, 1953. This attractive group of stories, selected by a noted storyteller, will appeal to older readers. 10–14

KELSEY, ALICE GEER, *Once the Mullah,* ill. by Kurt Werth, McKay, 1954. Stories told by the Mullah give insight into Persian life and folklore and are often exceedingly funny. 9–12

LANG, ANDREW, ed., *Arabian Nights,* ill. by Vera Bock, McKay, 1946. Attractive format, fine design and illustrations. 10–12

LARSON, JEAN RUSSELL, *Palace in Bagdad,* ill. by Marianne Yamaguchi, Scribner's, 1966. Human ingenuity and invention, not magic spells and enchantment, solve the problems in these stories. 9–12

MEHDEVI, ANNE SINCLAIR, *Persian Folk and Fairy Tales,* ill. by Paul E. Kennedy, Knopf, 1965. Stories authentically Persian in their portrayal of character but universal in topic. ALA Notable Children's Book. 9–12

The Seven Voyages of Sindbad the Sailor, ill. by Philip Reed, Atheneum, 1962. A beautiful book, illustrated with handsome, colored woodcuts, brings new interest to the tale of this extremely durable merchant. 7–10

China

CARPENTER, FRANCES, *Tales of a Chinese Grandmother,* ill. by Malthé Hasselriis, Doubleday, 1937. Thirty folk tales, told with quiet charm, reveal customs, beliefs, and home life in the China of long ago. 8–11

HUME, LOTTA CARSWELL, *Favorite Children's Stories from China and Tibet,* ill. by Koon-chiu, Tuttle, 1962. Nineteen stories collected in China over a period of twenty years. Many familiar themes. 8–11

KNIGHT, MARY, *The Fox That Wanted Nine Golden Tails,* ill. by Brigitte Bryan, Macmillan, 1969. 7–10

LIN, ADET, *The Milky Way, and Other Chinese Folk Tales,* ill. by Enrico Arno, Harcourt, 1961. A collection of twelve stories translated from original sources. 9–12

MOSEL, ARLENE, *Tikki Tikki Tembo,* ill. by Blair Lent, Holt, 1968. ALA Notable Children's Book. 4–7

India

BABBITT, ELLEN C., *The Jataka Tales,* ill. by Ellsworth Young, Appleton, 1912.
More Jataka Tales, ill. by Ellsworth Young, Appleton, 1912.
These fables from India have more elaborate plots and characterization than Aesop's fables, and they are often rather humorous. 6–10

GRAY, JOHN E. B., *India's Tales and Legends,* ill. by Joan Kiddell-Monroe, Walck, 1961. Skillfully told and well-illustrated tales and fables from the ancient epics and folklore of India. 11–13

JACOBS, JOSEPH, ed., *Indian Folk and Fairy Tales,* ill. by John D. Batten, Putnam, n.d. First published in 1892 with the title *Indian Fairy Tales.* 9–11

MACFARLANE, IRIS, *Tales and Legends from India,* ill. by Eric Thomas, Watts, 1966. Tales retold with respect for their basic humor and the ancient oral tradition of the village storytellers. 8–11

PRICE, CHRISTINE, *The Valiant Chatteemaker,* ill. by author, Warne, 1965. 5–8

QUIGLEY, LILLIAN, *The Blind Men and the Elephant,* ill. by Janice Holland, Scribner's, 1959. 6–9

REED, GWENDOLYN, *The Talkative Beasts: Myths, Fables and Poems of India,* ill. with photographs by Stella Snead, Lothrop, 1969. The culture of India is reflected in this volume. All ages

SPELLMAN, JOHN W., *The Beautiful Blue Jay, and Other Tales of India,* ill. by Jerry Pinkney, Little, 1967. Stories that mothers tell to their children, collected firsthand by the author. The first appearance in print for many of the tales. 5–8

WYATT, ISABEL, *The Golden Stag, and Other Folk Tales from India,* ill. by Anne Marie Jauss, McKay, 1962. Sixteen amusing tales full of India's ancient wisdom. 9–11

Indonesia

BRO, MARGUERITTE HARMON, *How the Mouse Deer Became King,* ill. by Joseph Low, Doubleday, 1966. An excellent collection of eleven stories about Kantjil, the mouse deer, Indonesian counterpart of Brer Rabbit. 9–11

COURLANDER, HAROLD, *Kantchil's Lime Pit, and Other Stories from Indonesia,* ill. by Robert W. Kane, Harcourt, 1950. Twenty-three tales with notes on their origins and a glossary and pronunciation guide. 9–11

DELEEUW, ADÈLE L., *Indonesian Legends and Folk Tales,* ill. by Ronni Solbert, Nelson, 1961. An enjoyable collection gathered from the storytellers of Indonesia. 10–11

Japan

BARUCH, DOROTHY W., *Kappa's Tug-of-War with Big Brown Horse,* ill. by Sanryo Sakai, Tuttle, 1961. 6–8

HAVILAND, VIRGINIA, ed., *Favorite Fairy Tales Told in Japan,* ill. by George Suyeoka, Little, 1967. Five interesting stories appropriately illustrated. 7–10

HODGES, MARGARET, *The Wave,* adapted from Lafcadio Hearn's *Gleanings in Buddha-fields,* ill. by Blair Lent, Houghton, 1964. Runner-up for Caldecott Medal. 6–9

ISHII, MOMOKO, *Issun Boshi, the Inchling, an Old Tale of Japan,* tr. by Yone Mizuta, ill. by Fuku Akino, Walker, 1967. 7–9

MC ALPINE, HELEN and WILLIAM, *Japanese Tales and Legends,* ill. by Joan Kiddell-Monroe, Walck, 1959. Traditional tales of Japan's legendary past, folk tales, and the epic of the Heike. 10–15

MATSUI, TADASHI, *Oniroku and the Carpenter*, ill. by Suekichi Akaba, tr. from the Japanese by Masako Matsuno, Prentice-Hall, 1963. 6–9

PRATT, DAVIS, and ELSA KULA, *Magic Animals of Japan*, Parnassus, 1967. Twelve stories that describe the legendary animals of Japan. Decorated with handsome woodcuts. 8–10

STAMM, CLAUS, ed., *Three Strong Women: A Tall Tale from Japan*, ill. by Kazue Mizumura, Viking, 1962. Hilarious story of the wrestler who trained with three women of superhuman strength. 6–10
The Very Special Badgers: A Tale of Magic from Japan, ill. by Kazue Mizumura, Viking, 1960. 6–10

UCHIDA, YOSHIKO, *The Dancing Kettle and Other Japanese Folk Tales*, ill. by Richard C. Jones, Harcourt, 1949.
The Magic Listening Cap, ill. by author, Harcourt, 1955.
Tales in the two books are well told, moralistic, and full of magic. 9–12
The Sea of Gold and Other Tales from Japan, ill. by Marianne Yamaguchi, Scribner's, 1965. A handsome book in which the tales reflect age-old concepts of morality. 9–11

YAMAGUCHI, TOHR, *The Golden Crane*, ill. by Marianne Yamaguchi, Holt, 1963. Allegorical story about a young deaf mute and his guardian who nurse one of the sacred cranes back to health. 9–10

YASHIMA, TARO, *Seashore Story*, ill. by author, Viking, 1967. 5–9

Other Countries of Asia

HITCHCOCK, PATRICIA, *The King Who Rides a Tiger, and Other Folk Tales from Nepal*, ill. by Lillian Sader, Parnassus Press, 1966. A dozen Nepalese folk tales were selected and handsomely illustrated for this volume. 10–12

JEWETT, ELEANORE MYERS, *Which was Witch? Tales of Ghosts and Magic from Korea*, ill. by Taro Yashima, Viking, 1953. Fourteen stories with sparkle and suspense, excellent for storytelling. ALA Notable Children's Book. 9–12

MERRILL, JEAN, *High, Wide, and Handsome*, adapted from a Burmese folk tale, ill. by Ronni Solbert, W. R. Scott, 1964. 7–9
Shan's Lucky Knife, ill. by Ronni Solbert, W. R. Scott, 1960. A Burmese folk tale. 7–11

SIDDIQUI, ASHRAF, and MARILYN LERCH, *Toontoony Pie and Other Tales from Pakistan*, ill. by Jan Fairservis, World, 1961. Twenty-two authentic tales from the regions of the Punjab and Bengal. 8–11

Oceania and Australia

BROWN, MARCIA, *Backbone of the King*, ill. by author, Scribner's, 1966. Linoleum-block prints were employed to enhance this presentation of an old Hawaiian legend. HB Fanfare. 10–12

COLUM, PADRAIC, *Legends of Hawaii*, ill. by Don Forrer, Yale University Press, 1937. Nineteen tales, some selected from the author's *At the Gateways of the Day* and *The Bright Islands*. 11–up

HOLDING, JAMES, *The Sky-Eater and Other South Sea Tales*, ill. by Charles Keeping, Abelard, 1965. Tales of the origin of the moon, the mango, and the coconut, and other stories with the flavor of the South Seas. 6–9

PARKER, CATHERINE SOMERVILLE (FIELD), *Australian Legendary Tales*, collected by K. Langloh Parker, sel. and ed. by H. Drake-Brockman, ill. by Elizabeth Durack, Viking, 1966. Not suitable for children, but valuable for folklorists, teachers, and storytellers. Adult

SECHRIST, ELIZABETH HOUGH, *Once in the First Times*, ill. by John Sheppard, Macrae, 1969. Fifty folk tales from the Philippine Islands. 8–12

THOMPSON, VIVIAN L., *Hawaiian Myths of Earth, Sea, and Sky*, ill. by Leonard Weisgard, Holiday, 1966. Twelve nature myths retold with artful simplicity. 8–10

North and South America

General Collections

COTHRAN, JEAN, *The Magic Calabash: Folk Tales from America's Islands and Alaska*, ill. by Clifford N. Geary, McKay, 1956. A useful collection of tales from Hawaii, Puerto Rico, the Virgin Islands, and Alaska. 8–10

LEACH, MARIA, *The Rainbow Book of American Folk Tales and Legends*, ill. by Marc Simont, World, 1958. Tall tales, Indian legends, and scary stories from all regions of North and South America are found in this useful volume. 9-12

North America: Indian and Eskimo Tales

BELTING, NATALIA, *The Long-Tailed Bear, and Other Indian Legends*, ill. by Louis F. Cary, Bobbs, 1961. Twenty-three animal legends retold from the lore of various Indian tribes. Bibliography and notes on tribal sources are included. 7–9

CHAFETZ, HENRY, *Thunderbird, and Other Stories*, ill. by Ronni Solbert, Pantheon, 1964. Three tales from American Indian mythology. The illustrations are reminiscent of Navaho sand paintings. 9–11

CURRY, JANE LOUISE, *Down from the Lonely Mountain: California Indian Tales*, ill. by Enrico Arno, Harcourt, 1965. Twelve tales concerning the creation, the way men obtained fire, and the outwitting of enemies. 8–10

FISHER, ANNE B., *Stories California Indians Told*, ill. by Ruth Robbins, Parnassus, 1957. Legends collected by an eminent anthropologist, Dr. C. Hart Merriam, who in turn related them to the author. 8–12

GILLHAM, CHARLES EDWARD, *Beyond the Clapping Mountains: Eskimo Stories from Alaska*, ill. by Chanimun, Macmillan, 1943. 9–10
Medicine Men of Hooper Bay: More Tales from the Clapping Mountains of Alaska, ill. by Chanimun, Macmillan, 1946. 9–11
Unusual and highly imaginative tales of the animals and folk heroes of the Eskimos. Unfortunately, the author's language tends to detract from the dignity of the stories.

HARRIS, CHRISTIE, *Once Upon a Totem*, ill. by John Frazer Mills, Atheneum, 1963. Five tales of the Northwest Indians which will help boys and girls understand an interesting people. 10–14

HILL, KAY, *Glooscap and His Magic: Legends of the Wabanaki Indians*, ill. by Robert Frankenberg, Dodd,

1963. Amusing stories of the mythical Indian hero, his people, and his animals. 8–11

♩HOFMANN, CHARLES, *American Indians Sing*, ill. by Nicholas Amorosi, John Day, 1967. An excellent introduction to the ceremonials of American Indians by a collector of folk materials for the Library of Congress. Includes transcribed music and a recording. 10–14

♩HOFSINDE, ROBERT, *Indian Music Makers*, ill. by author (Gray Wolf), Morrow, 1967. Describes the use of music in the ceremonies and in the everyday life of the Indian. 9–11

HOUSTON, JAMES, *Tikta'liktak: An Eskimo Legend*, ill. by author, Harcourt, 1965.

The White Archer: An Eskimo Legend, ill. by author, Harcourt, 1967.

Stories that reflect the Eskimo's courage and his will to survive adversity. 9–11

HUNT, WOLF ROBE, and HELEN RUSHMORE, *The Dancing Horses of Acoma, and Other Acoma Indian Stories*, ill. by Wolf Robe Hunt, World, 1963. Twelve legends and stories of the Pueblo Indians reveal the customs and character of a proud and complex people. 10–12

LEEKLEY, THOMAS B., *The World of Manabozho: Tales of the Chippewa Indians*, ill. by Yeffe Kimball, Vanguard, 1965. These stories retain the flavor of the original tales as told by Indian storytellers. 9–11

MARTIN, FRAN, *Nine Tales of Coyote*, ill. by Dorothy McEntee, Harper, 1950.

Nine Tales of Raven, ill. by Dorothy McEntee, Harper, 1951.

The first volume draws upon the legends of the Nez Percé Indians; the second upon the tales which came via the Eskimos and Canadian Indians. 9–11

PENNEY, GRACE, *Tales of the Cheyennes*, ill. by Walter Richard West, Houghton, 1953. Long-ago legends explaining nature and customs, and a group of humorous tales. 10–14

REID, DOROTHY N., *Tales of Nanabozho*, ill. by Donald Grant, Walck, 1963. Twenty-one short Indian tales about the great creator-magician, Nanabozho (Hiawatha) of the Ojibwas. Pronunciation guide and extensive bibliography. 9–12

Canada

BARBEAU, MARIUS, *The Golden Phoenix, and Other French-Canadian Fairy Tales*, retold by Michael Hornyansky, ill. by Arthur Price, Walck, 1958. These stories are quite easily recognized as variants of well-known European tales, and little about them is distinctively French-Canadian. 9–11

CARLSON, NATALIE, *The Talking Cat and Other Stories of French Canada*, ill. by Roger Duvoisin, Harper, 1952. This array of genuinely funny stories has been adapted from tales told within the author's family circle. ALA Notable Children's Book. 9–11

HOOKE, HILDA MARY, *Thunder in the Mountains; Legends of Canada*, ill. by Clare Bice, Walck, 1947. Seventeen tales which draw upon three major sources: Indian legends, stories of the coming of white men, and variants of European tales. 9–12

Mexico, Central and South America

BARLOW, GENEVIEVE, *Latin American Tales: From the Pampas to the Pyramids of Mexico*, ill. by William M. Hutchinson, Rand, 1966. Most of these stories, translated from Spanish sources which are cited, come from the Indian tribes of South America. Four have not previously been published. 8–11

BRENNER, ANITA, *The Boy Who Could Do Anything, and Other Mexican Folk Tales*, ill. by Jean Charlot, W. R. Scott, 1942. These curious tales are distinguished for their authentic idiom. They evoke the setting and style of Mexico and its people. ALA Notable Children's Book. 9–11

EELLS, ELSIE SPICER, *Tales of Enchantment from Spain*, ill. by Maud and Miska Petersham, Dodd, 1950. Fifteen tales which originated in Spain but were collected for this volume in South America. 9–11

Tales from the Amazon, ill. by Florence Choate and Elizabeth Curtis, Dodd, 1966, 1927. Twenty-six Indian legends and fairy tales from South America. 9–11

FINGER, CHARLES J., *Tales from Silver Lands*, ill. by Paul Honore, Doubleday, 1924. Nineteen Indian legends and folk tales from South America transcribed as the author heard them on his travels. Newbery Medal. 10–12

JAGENDORF, M. A., and RALPH S. BOGGS, *The King of the Mountains: A Treasury of Latin American Folk Stories*, ill. by Carybé, Vanguard, 1960. An impressive gathering of sixty-five tales from various parts of Latin America. 9–12

ROSS, PATRICIA FENT, *In Mexico They Say*, ill. by Henry C. Pitz, Knopf, 1942. Fourteen tales that reflect the social life and customs of Mexico. 9–12

♩YURCHENCO, HENRIETTA, *A Fiesta of Folk Songs from Spain and Latin America*, ill. by Jules Maidoff, Putnam, 1967. Over thirty folk songs and singing games from Spain and the Spanish-speaking American nations. Melody line and chords are indicated for accompaniment. 5–11

United States: General Collections [3]

COTHRAN, JEAN, ed., *With a Wig, With a Wag, and Other American Folk Tales*, ill. by Clifford N. Geary, McKay, 1954. Fifteen stories gleaned from many parts of the United States, felicitously worded for telling or reading aloud. 8–10

FIELD, RACHEL, ed., *American Folk and Fairy Tales*, ill. by Margaret Freeman, Scribner's, 1929. A highly satisfactory collection of Indian legends, Negro stories, Louisiana folk tales, mountain stories, and tall tales. 12–13

JAGENDORF, MORITZ ADOLF, ed., *The Ghost of Peg-Leg Peter and Other Stories of Old New York*, ill. by Lino S. Lipinsky, songs of old New York selected by June Lazare, Vanguard, 1966. An amusing potpourri of tales about one of our greatest cities. 10–13

The Marvelous Adventures of Johnny Caesar Cicero Darling, ill. by Howard Simon, Vanguard, 1949. The tales of Johnny Darling are a good addition to American frontier humor. 10–adult

United States: Folk Songs in Picture-Book Form

♩CHASE, RICHARD, *Billy Boy*, verses selected by Richard Chase, ill. by Glen Rounds, Golden Gate, 1966. 5–9

♩EMBERLEY, BARBARA, *One Wide River to Cross*, adapted by author, ill. by Ed Emberley, Prentice-Hall, 1966. Runner-up for the Caldecott Medal. 5–8

♩*The Fox Went Out on a Chilly Night; an old song*, ill. by Peter Spier, Doubleday, 1961. 4–8

[3] Three books of Hawaiian tales are listed among the collections from Oceania and Australia (p. 375).

♪LANGSTAFF, JOHN, *Frog Went a Courtin'*, ill. by Feodor Rojankovsky, Harcourt, 1955. Americanized version of an old Scottish ballad. Caldecott Medal. 3–9

♪*Over in the Meadow*, ill. by Feodor Rojankovsky, Harcourt, 1957. ALA Notable Children's Book. 5–7

♪*The Swapping Boy*, ill. by Beth and Joe Krush, music set down by Cecil Sharp, Harcourt, 1960. 5–9

♪ROUNDS, GLEN, *The Boll Weevil*, ill. by author, Golden Gate, 1967. 7–up

ZEMACH, HARVE, *Mommy, Buy Me a China Doll*, adapted from an Ozark children's song, ill. by Margot Zemach, Follett, 1966. HB Fanfare. 3–7

United States: Afro–American Tales

COURLANDER, HAROLD, *Terrapin's Pot of Sense*, ill. by Elton Fax, Holt, 1957. American Negro stories collected in several widely spaced rural areas of the U. S. Notes give sources of different versions of the stories. 8–11

FELTON, HAROLD W., *John Henry and His Hammer*, ill. by Aldren Watson, Knopf, 1950. 10–13

HARRIS, JOEL CHANDLER, *Brer Rabbit: Stories from Uncle Remus*, adapted by Margaret Wise Brown with the A. B. Frost pictures redrawn for reproduction by Victor Dowling, Harper, 1941. Twenty-four stories suitable for younger children. The dialect has been modified slightly to make it more comprehensible to the young reader. 8–11

The Complete Tales of Uncle Remus, comp. by Richard Chase, ill. by A. B. Frost and others, Houghton, 1955. A monumental collection of interest to folklorists and storytellers. Adult

Uncle Remus: His Songs and His Sayings, rev. ed., ill. by A. B. Frost, Appleton, 1921. This version of the Uncle Remus stories is more acceptable to children than the preceding volume, but probably only the best readers will tackle it. 10–up

United States: Tall Tales

BLAIR, WALTER, *Tall Tale America: A Legendary History of Our Humorous Heroes*, ill. by Glen Rounds, Coward, 1944. The authenticity is questionable but this should not detract from enjoyment of the book. 10–14

BOWMAN, JAMES CLOYD, *Mike Fink*, ill. by Leonard Fisher, Little, 1957. 11–15

Pecos Bill, ill. by Laura Bannon, Whitman, 1937. Collections of tales about two American superheroes whose folk origins are doubtful. 11–15

CARMER, CARL, *The Hurricane's Children*, ill. by Elizabeth Black Carmer, McKay, 1967. A reissue of an excellent collection of American tall tales first published in 1937. 9–11

CREDLE, ELLIS, *Tall Tales from the High Hills, and Other Stories*, ill. by Richard Bennett, Nelson, 1957. Twenty amusing tales from the Blue Ridge Mountains. 9–12

FELTON, HAROLD W., *Bowleg Bill, Seagoing Cowpuncher*, ill. by William Moyers, Prentice-Hall, 1957. 8–10

John Henry and His Hammer, ill. by Aldren Watson, Knopf, 1950. 10–13

Mike Fink, Best of the Keelboatmen, ill. by Aldren Watson, Dodd, 1960. 10–12

New Tall Tales of Pecos Bill, ill. by William Moyers, Prentice-Hall, 1958. 10–13

Pecos Bill, Texas Cowpuncher, ill. by Aldren Watson, Knopf, 1949. 10–13

Sergeant O'Keefe and His Mule, Balaam, ill. by Leonard Everett Fisher, Dodd, 1962. 10–12

Lively accounts of five tall-tale heroes appear in the six collections listed above.

KEATS, EZRA JACK, *John Henry, an American Legend*, ill. by author, Pantheon, 1965. 6–8

MC CORMICK, DELL J., *Paul Bunyan Swings His Axe*, ill. by author, Caxton, 1936. 9–11

Tall Timber Tales; More Paul Bunyan Stories, ill. by Lorna Livesley, Caxton, 1939. Stories about the exploits of the legendary logger. 9–12

MALCOLMSON, ANNE, *Yankee Doodle's Cousins*, ill. by Robert McCloskey, Houghton, 1941. This is one of the finest and most satisfying collections of real and made-up heroes from all sections of the United States. 10–14

MALCOLMSON, ANNE, and DELL J. MC CORMICK, *Mister Stormalong*, ill. by Joshua Tolford, Houghton, 1952. Bulltop Stormalong's adventures at sea are told with verve and imagination. 9–12

PECK, LEIGH, *Pecos Bill and Lightning*, ill. by Kurt Wiese, Houghton, 1940. A brief edition with copious illustrations to aid and comfort the slow reader. 8–12

ROUNDS, GLEN, *Ol' Paul the Mighty Logger*, ill. by author, Holiday, 1949. Paul Bunyan stories retold with an earthy, exuberant zest. 10–adult

SHAPIRO, IRWIN, *Heroes in American Folklore*, ill. by James Daugherty and Donald McKay, Messner, 1962. These tales of five heroes were originally published in separate volumes. 9–12

SHEPHARD, ESTHER, *Paul Bunyan*, ill. by Rockwell Kent, Harcourt, 1941. This is an early version of the Paul Bunyan epic. 10–14

STOUTENBERG, ADRIEN, *American Tall Tales*, ill. by Richard M. Powers, Viking, 1966. Covers many of the characters found in Malcolmson's *Yankee Doodle's Cousins* but is more modestly written. 9–11

WADSWORTH, WALLACE, *Paul Bunyan and His Great Blue Ox*, retold; ill. by Enrico Arno, Doubleday, 1964, 1926. A gravely told story about the great logger who, some say, followed the logging industry from Maine to the Northwest. 10–12

United States: Variants of European Folk Tales

CHASE, RICHARD, ed., *Grandfather Tales*, ill. by Berkeley Williams, Jr., Houghton, 1948.

The Jack Tales, ill. by Berkeley Williams, Jr., Houghton, 1943.

Two fine collections of tales from the mountains of the South. Priceless contributions to American folklore. 10–up

Jack and the Three Sillies, ill. by Joshua Tolford, Houghton, 1950. 5–9

JAGENDORF, MORITZ ADOLF, *New England Bean-Pot; American Folk Stories to Read and to Tell*, ill. by Donald McKay, Vanguard, 1948. The dry humor characteristic of the New England people is found in these folk tales from six states. 10–13

SAWYER, RUTH, *Journey Cake, Ho!* ill. by Robert McCloskey, Viking, 1953. Runner-up for Caldecott Medal. 6–10

West Indies

BELPRÉ, PURA, *Perez and Martina*, new ed., ill. by Carlos Sanchez, Warne, 1961. A Puerto Rican folk tale. 7–9

The Tiger and the Rabbit, and Other Tales, ill. by Tomie de Paola, Lippincott, 1965. This book, originally published by Houghton in 1946, contains eighteen Puerto Rican stories which echo themes and characters from other national folklore. 9–11

COURLANDER, HAROLD, *The Piece of Fire: And Other Haitian Tales*, ill. by Beth and Joe Krush, Harcourt, 1964. Twenty-six tales which capture the humor and mischief of this island people. 9–11

Uncle Bouqui of Haiti, ill. by Lucy Herndon Crockett, Morrow, 1942. This delightful array of folk tales from Haiti is now out of print. It should, however, be available in some libraries and is well worth searching out, for the tales reflect the happy collision of African and European folklore. 9–11

SHERLOCK, PHILIP M., *Anansi, the Spider Man*, ill. by Marcia Brown, Crowell, 1954. These stories, told by Jamaicans, have their roots in Africa. ALA Notable Children's Book. 9–12

The Iguana's Tail; Crick Crack Stories from the Caribbean, ill. by Gioia Fiammenghi, Crowell, 1969. A group of humorous animal tales. 8–12

West Indian Folk-Tales, Retold, ill. by Joan Kiddell-Monroe, Walck, 1966. Twenty-one West Indian *how* and *why* stories, eight of them new tales about the wily spider man, Anansi. 9–11

FABLES

AESOP, *The Miller, His Son, and Their Donkey*, ill. by Roger Duvoisin, McGraw-Hill, 1962. 5–9

ARTZYBASHEFF, BORIS, ed., *Aesop's Fables*, ill. by editor, Viking, 1933. Ninety fables selected by the editor-illustrator and embellished with beautiful wood engravings. 12–14

The Book of Fables, ill. by Will Nickless, Warne, 1963. An attractive selection, mainly from Aesop, but also from later fabulists of England, France, Germany, Russia, and India. 9–11

BROWN, MARCIA, *Once a Mouse*, Scribner's, 1961. A fable from *The Hitopadesa*, illustrated with vivid woodcuts. Caldecott Medal, Lewis Carroll Shelf Award, U.S. nominee for Hans Christian Andersen Honor List. 5–9

FRASCONI, ANTONIO, *The Snow and the Sun: La Nieve y el Sol*, ill. by author, Harcourt, 1961. 6–9

GAER, JOSEPH, *The Fables of India*, ill. by Randy Monk, Little, 1955. Selected from three collections of Indian fables—*The Panchatantra*, *The Hitopadesa*, and the *Jatakas*. ALA Notable Children's Book. 10–14

JACOBS, JOSEPH, ed., *The Fables of Aesop*, ill. by David Levine, Macmillan, 1964. Contains over eighty fables and Jacobs' history of them. 9–11

KRYLOV, IVAN ANDREEVICH, *Fifteen Fables of Krylov*, tr. by Guy Daniels, ill. by David Pascal, Macmillan, 1965. The translator has rendered these fables into sophisticated English verse. 12–up

LA FONTAINE, *The Hare and the Tortoise*, ill. by Brian Wildsmith, Watts, 1967.

The Lion and the Rat, ill. by Brian Wildsmith, Watts, 1963.

The North Wind and the Sun, ill. by Brian Wildsmith, Watts, 1964.

The Rich Man and the Shoemaker, ill. by Brian Wildsmith, Watts, 1966.

Each of the above fables is beautifully illustrated in glowing colors. *The Rich Man and the Shoemaker* was selected as an ALA Notable Children's Book. 5–8

REEVES, JAMES, *Fables from Aesop, Retold*, ill. by Maurice

Wilson, Walck, 1962. In this collection the narrator has chosen to have the animals speak. 8–12

SHOWALTER, JEAN B., *The Donkey Ride*, a fable adapted by author, ill. by Tomi Ungerer, Doubleday, 1967. 5–9

WERTH, KURT, *The Monkey, the Lion, and the Snake*, retold and ill. by author, Viking, 1967. 6–9

UNTERMEYER, LOUIS, ed., *Aesop's Fables*, selected and adapted by editor, ill. by Alice and Martin Provensen, Golden Press, 1965. Forty fables in a large picture book with refreshing illustrations. 6–9

WHITE, ANNE TERRY, *Aesop's Fables*, retold; ill. by Helen Siegl, Random, 1964. These fables are retold in an easy, contemporary style. 8–10

MYTHS, EPICS, AND HERO TALES

General Collections

ASIMOV, ISAAC, *Words from the Myths*, ill. by William Barss, Houghton, 1961. Explains the mythological origins of many words in common usage and thus deepens the reader's understanding of the myths and their pervasive influence in literature and art. 9–14

GREEN, ROGER LANCELYN, ed., *A Book of Myths*, selected and retold by editor, ill. by Joan Kiddell-Monroe, Dutton, 1965. A useful reference for children because it gives parallels and variants of myths from many ancient lands. 9–12

HAMILTON, EDITH, *Mythology*, ill. by Steele Savage, Little, 1942. Probably the most valuable single source of information for the reader who needs background in the myths. 12–up

HAZELTINE, ALICE I., ed., *Hero Tales from Many Lands*, ill. by Gordon Laite, Abingdon, 1961. A judicious selection from well-known retellings of the stories about great epic heroes. Includes sources, background notes, a glossary, a pronunciation guide, an index, and a bibliography. 10–14

Babylonian Epic

BRYSON, BERNARDA, *Gilgamesh*, ill. by author, Holt, 1967. An exceptionally fine retelling of the ancient story of the proud King Gilgamesh. (See "The Monster Humbaba," p. 319.) 11–up

FEAGLES, ANITA, ed., *He Who Saw Everything: The Epic of Gilgamesh*, ill. by Xavier Gonzáles, W. R. Scott, 1967. This epic antedates the earliest Hebrew and Greek writers by at least fifteen centuries. It was evidently known by the Greeks, for the stories of Gilgamesh and Odysseus have many parallels. The flood story in Gilgamesh also echoes in the story of Noah in the Old Testament. 9–13

Greek and Roman Myths and Epics

AULAIRE, INGRI and EDGAR PARIN D', *Ingri and Edgar Parin d'Aulaire's Book of Greek Myths*, ill. by authors, Doubleday, 1962. A book with appeal for the younger readers. The Greek myths are told in a simple narrative beginning with the Titans and finishing with the heroes. A large volume illustrated with beautiful lithographs. 8–11

BENSON, SALLY, *Stories of the Gods and Heroes*, ill. by Steele Savage, Dial, 1940. A selection of stories from

Thomas Bulfinch's *Age of Fable.* ALA Notable Children's Book. 10–12

BULFINCH, THOMAS, *A Book of Myths,* selections from Bulfinch's *Age of Fable,* ill. by Helen Sewell, Macmillan, 1942. Striking illustrations suggestive of ballet postures and movement distinguish this collection. 10–14

COLUM, PADRAIC, *The Children's Homer,* ill. by Willy Pogány, Macmillan, 1918, 1962. A distinguished version in cadenced prose. 10–14

The Golden Fleece and the Heroes Who Lived Before Achilles, ill. by Willy Pogány, Macmillan, 1962. A good-looking modern edition of this famous retelling. 11–15

COOLIDGE, OLIVIA E., *Greek Myths,* ill. by Edouard Sandoz, Houghton, 1949. A retelling of the most widely known Greek myths. Here the gods are not idealized—indeed the book opens with an unappealing tale of trickery—but the stories have authenticity. 10–14

The King of Men, ill. by Ellen Raskin, Houghton, 1966. A robust and absorbing narrative based on stories about Agamemnon. ALA Notable Children's Book. 12–15

DE SÉLINCOURT, AUBREY, *Odysseus the Wanderer,* ill. by Norman Meredith, Criterion, 1956. A lusty, modern retelling of *The Odyssey.* 12–up

GRAVES, ROBERT, *Greek Gods and Heroes,* ill. by Dimitris Davis, Doubleday, 1960. This sardonic interpretation is excellent for young people who are familiar with the standard treatments of the myths. 12–up

HAWTHORNE, NATHANIEL, *The Complete Greek Stories of Nathaniel Hawthorne,* ill. by Harold Jones, Watts, 1963. 10–12

The Golden Touch, ill. by Paul Galdone, McGraw-Hill, 1959. 7–10

Tanglewood Tales, ill. by S. Van Abbé, Dutton, 1952. 9–12

A Wonder Book and Tanglewood Tales, ill. by Maxfield Parrish, Dodd, 1934. 9–12
Hawthorne's treatment of the myths, though often criticized, has helped to interest many children in mythology. His work is well presented in the editions listed above.

KINGSLEY, CHARLES, *The Heroes,* ill. by Joan Kiddell-Monroe, Dutton, 1963. Narrative versions of Hercules' twelve labors and of the legends about Perseus, the Argonauts, and Theseus. 10–14

The Heroes, ill. by Vera Bock, Macmillan, 1954. Thirty tales are beautifully retold and make a fine cycle for the storyteller. 10–14

MC LEAN, MOLLIE, and ANNE WISEMAN, *Adventures of the Greek Heroes,* ill. by Witold T. Mars, Houghton, 1961. Parents or teachers in need of simply written versions of the myths will find this book valuable. 8–11

SELLEW, CATHARINE F., *Adventures with the Gods,* ill. by George and Doris Hauman, Little, 1945. Sixteen popular myths are included in this volume. 9–11

SERRAILLIER, IAN, *The Clashing Rocks; the Story of Jason,* ill. by William Stobbs, Walck, 1964.

A Fall from the Sky; the Story of Daedalus, ill. by William Stobbs, Walck, 1966.

The Gorgon's Head; the Story of Perseus, ill. by William Stobbs, Walck, 1962.

The Way of Danger; the Story of Theseus, ill. by William Stobbs, Walck, 1963.
The handling of these legends is direct and vigorous, and the illustrations are dramatically strong. 10–up

Norse Myths and Epics

ALMEDINGEN, E. M., *The Treasure of Siegfried,* ill. by Charles Keeping, Lippincott, 1965. This is an adequate version of the Niebelungenlied. It is faithful to the original plot, although the author has omitted some of the cruel and barbaric incidents. 11–14

AULAIRE, INGRI and EDGAR PARIN D', *Norse Gods and Giants,* ill. by authors, Doubleday, 1967. Retells for younger children the dramatic, exciting, and often humorous tales of Norse mythology. 8–11

COLUM, PADRAIC, *The Children of Odin: The Book of Northern Myths,* ill. by Willy Pogány, Macmillan, 1920, 1962. This incomparable retelling of Norse mythology has been given a new format and new type, but the distinctive Pogány illustrations remain. 11–15

HOSFORD, DOROTHY G., *Thunder of the Gods,* ill. by Claire and George Louden, Holt, 1952. The author successfully combines the dramatic form of the folk tale and the formal language appropriate to the telling of the myths. ALA Notable Children's Book. 9–11

SELLEW, CATHARINE F., *Adventures with the Giants,* ill. by Steele Savage, Little, 1950. A discriminating selection of stories for younger readers. 8–11

Adventures with the Heroes, ill. by Steele Savage, Little, 1954. The Volsung saga retold in simple language. 9–12

English Epics and Hero Tales

HOSFORD, DOROTHY, *By His Own Might; the Battles of Beowulf,* ill. by Laszlo Matulay, Holt, 1947. A retelling especially suitable for children in upper grades of elementary school. 10–12

LANIER, SIDNEY, *The Boy's King Arthur,* ill. by N. C. Wyeth, Scribner's, 1942. An authoritative and popular version, the best one to use for reading or telling. 10–14

King Arthur and His Knights of the Round Table, ill. by Florian, Grosset, 1950. An attractive and inexpensive edition. 10–14

MAC LEOD, MARY, *The Book of King Arthur and His Noble Knights,* ill. by Henry C. Pitz, Lippincott, 1949. A version, faithful to the original, which presents the legend in an easily understood manner. (Other editions by this author were published by Dodd, 1953; Macmillan, 1963; World, 1950.) 9–13

MC SPADDEN, J. WALKER, *Robin Hood and His Merry Outlaws,* ill. by Louis Slobodkin, World, 1946. Lively accounts of the outlaw and his band. 9–12

♪MALCOLMSON, ANNE, ed., *Song of Robin Hood,* music arr. by Grace Castagnetta, ill. by Virginia Lee Burton, Houghton, 1947. A handsome book containing eighteen songs. Runner-up for Caldecott Medal, ALA Notable Children's Book. 11–14

PICARD, BARBARA LEONIE, *Hero Tales of the British Isles,* ill. by John G. Galsworthy, Criterion, 1963. Eleven stories about the ancient heroes of the Isles. Helpful notes give perspective on each hero's place in history and folklore. 10–13

Stories of King Arthur and His Knights, ill. by Roy Morgan, Walck, 1955. An absorbing retelling that evokes the atmosphere and spirit of the Middle Ages without the use of archaic language. 10–12

PYLE, HOWARD, *The Merry Adventures of Robin Hood of Great Renown in Nottinghamshire,* ill. by author,

Scribner's, 1946. This version has gone through many editions and remains a favorite with readers. A fine source for reading aloud. 12–14

Some Merry Adventures of Robin Hood, rev. ed., ill. by author, Scribner's, 1954. Twelve stories, each somewhat abridged, from the longer version above. 10–13

The Story of King Arthur and His Knights, ill. by author, Scribner's, 1903. One of the great versions of the Arthurian legends. Also available in paperback edition from Dover Publications. 10–12

SERRAILLIER, IAN, *Beowulf, the Warrior,* ill. by Severin, Walck, 1961. One of the better versions, told in verse form. 12–14

SUTCLIFF, ROSEMARY, *Beowulf,* ill. by Charles Keeping, Dutton, 1962. The battles with Grendel and Grendel's mother, and the final combat with the fire-drake are covered in this account. 12–14

TREASE, GEOFFREY, *Bows Against the Barons,* ill. by C. Walter Hodges, Meredith, 1967. A newly illustrated reissue of a version published in 1934. Robin Hood is presented as leader of a band of serfs in rebellion against the feudal lords. 10–12

Irish Epics and Hero Tales

HULL, ELEANOR, *The Boy's Cuchulain,* ill. by Stephen Reid, Crowell, 1910. This out-of-print version is often available in libraries and is included because it offers excellent material for the storyteller. 11–14

SUTCLIFF, ROSEMARY, *The High Deeds of Finn Mac Cool,* ill. by Michael Charlton, Dutton, 1967. A vivid recounting of the legends of the Fianna by a superb storyteller. 11–14

The Hound of Ulster, ill. by Victor Ambrus, Dutton, 1964. A finely written account which incorporates the many legends about Cuchulain into one consecutive narrative. (See "The Championship of Ireland," p. 330.) 11–14

YOUNG, ELLA, *The Tangle-Coated Horse and Other Tales,* ill. by Vera Bock, Longmans, 1929. Tales of Finn told by one of Ireland's most gifted storytellers. 11–14

The Wonder Smith and His Son, a Tale from the Golden Childhood of the World, ill. by Boris Artzybasheff, McKay, 1957. Fourteen tales, which have Gaelic as their mother tongue, told with incomparable verve and beauty by one who had the poet's touch. Runner-up for the Newbery Medal. 10–13

Other National Epics

BALDWIN, JAMES, *The Story of Roland,* ill. by Peter Hurd, Scribner's, 1930. The romantic story of Charlemagne's most trusted peer. 12–up

DAVIS, RUSSELL, and BRENT K. ASHABRANNER, *Ten Thousand Desert Swords; the Epic Story of a Great Bedouin Tribe,* ill. by Leonard Everett Fisher, Little, 1960. Eleven tales from the great group of legends surrounding the Bani Hilal, a powerful tribe of Bedouin warriors. 11–13

DEUTSCH, BABETTE, *Heroes of the Kalevala,* ill. by Fritz Eichenberg, Messner, 1940. A version with literary distinction and continuity. ALA Notable Children's Book. 10–14

GAER, JOSEPH, *The Adventures of Rama,* ill. by Randy Monk, Little, 1954. This is a retelling of one of the best-loved epics of India. ALA Notable Children's Book. 12–14

GOLDSTON, ROBERT C., *The Legend of the Cid,* ill. by Stephane, Bobbs, 1963. The adventures and brave deeds of this Spanish hero are presented in a simple prose narrative enhanced by strong illustrations. 10–13

SAWYER, RUTH, and EMMY MOLLÈS, *Dietrich of Berne and the Dwarf King Laurin; Hero Tales of the Austrian Tirol,* collected and retold by authors, ill. by Frederick T. Chapman, Viking, 1963. This intriguing hero tale, a complex blend of historical fact and legend, concerns Dietrich of Berne, who became Theodoric the Great, Emperor of Rome. HB Fanfare. 9–13

The Song of Roland, tr. by Merriam Sherwood, ill. by Edith Emerson, McKay, 1938. A version that begins with Ganelon's treachery and ends with the triumph of Charlemagne over the Saracens. 11–up

ADULT REFERENCES [4]

ARBUTHNOT, MAY HILL, *Children and Books,* Scott, Foresman, 1964. Folk tales, fables, myths, and epics are discussed in Chapters 10 and 11. Chapter 13 contains a comprehensive discussion on storytelling and reading aloud.

AUSUBEL, NATHAN, ed., *A Treasury of Jewish Folklore,* Crown, 1948. A lengthy compilation of over seven hundred stories and seventy-five songs of the Jewish people.

♪BAILEY, CHARITY, *Sing a Song with Charity Bailey,* Plymouth Music Co., 1955. Twenty easy songs with piano arrangements, chords for guitar and autoharp, and some drum rhythms. 5–8

♪BONI, MARGARET BRADFORD, ed., *Favorite American Songs,* arr. by Norman Lloyd, ill. by Aurelius Battaglia, Simon and Schuster, 1956. 10–up

♪*Fireside Book of Folk Songs,* sel. and ed. by Margaret Bradford Boni, arr. by Norman Lloyd, ill. by Alice and Martin Provensen, Simon and Schuster, 1947, 1966. 10–up

BOTKIN, BENJAMIN A., ed., *A Treasury of American Folklore,* Crown, 1944. The stories, ballads, and traditions of the people are grouped under such headings as "Heroes and Boasters," "Boosters and Knockers," "Songs and Rhymes."

A Treasury of New England Folklore, Crown, n.d.

A Treasury of Western Folklore, Crown, 1951.

A Treasury of Southern Folklore, Crown, 1949.

♪BRAND, OSCAR, ed., *Singing Holidays,* music arr. by Douglas Townsend, ill. by Roberta Moynihan, Knopf, 1957. Ninety interesting folk songs for American holidays. 12–up

BULFINCH, THOMAS, *Bulfinch's Mythology: The Age of Fable; The Age of Chivalry; Legends of Charlemagne,* ill. by Elinore Blaisdell, Crowell, n.d., 3 vols. in 1. This adult work, first published in 1855, has much value as a basic reference.

CAMPBELL, JOSEPH, *The Hero with a Thousand Faces,* rev. ed., Princeton Univ. Press, 1968 (Pantheon Books, 1949). The author explores the mythology of many peoples and attempts to show that all the myths are really one great story. In discussing the symbolism of the myths, he draws somewhat upon all schools of

[4] Numbers at the end of an entry marked ♪ in this section suggest the age level of the children with whom the songs in that collection can best be used.

psychoanalysis. See also the author's four-volume work, *The Masks of God*—vol. 1, *Primitive Mythology* (1959) ; vol. 2, *Oriental Mythology* (1962) ; vol. 3, *Occidental Mythology* (1964) ; vol. 4, *Creative Mythology* (1969)—published by Viking.

♪CARMER, CARL, comp., *America Sings,* music arr. by Edwin John Stringham, ill. by Elizabeth Black Carmer, Knopf, 1942.   11–16

CATHON, LAURA E., and others, eds., *Stories to Tell to Children,* 7th ed., Carnegie Library of Pittsburgh, 1960. The subtitle indicates the scope of this helpful booklet: "A selected list for use by libraries, schools, clubs, and by radio and television storytellers, with a special listing of stories for holiday programs."

♪CHASE, RICHARD, *American Folk Tales and Songs,* New American Library, n.d. This excellent contribution to American folklore, by a renowned collector and teller of tales, has been given new life by its recent reissue in a paperback edition.

CHUKOVSKY, KORNEI, *From Two to Five,* tr. and ed. by Miriam Morton, Univ. of Calif. Press, 1963. This work, by a great Russian educator, critic, and writer, was first published in Russia in 1925 and was addressed to teachers and parents. In it the author discusses the importance of literature for the child between the ages of two and five. He stresses the importance of poetry, folk tales, and fantasy in the development of imagination and creativity.

COLUM, PADRAIC, ed., *A Treasury of Irish Folklore,* 2nd rev. ed., Crown, 1967. The legends, ballads, stories, and superstitions of the Irish people, compiled and edited by an eminent authority on the subject.

♪DIETZ, BETTY WARNER, and THOMAS CHOONBAI PARK, eds., *Folk Songs of China, Japan, Korea,* Day, 1964. A valuable volume for teachers and others who are interested in helping children understand the culture of the Orient. Many of the songs can be effectively used with the folk tales of the countries named in the title.   9–11

DORSON, RICHARD, *American Folklore,* Univ. of Chicago Press, 1959. A volume in the Chicago History of American Civilization series, this work surveys the entire field of American folklore from colonization to mass culture. Based upon field collection and research, the text includes folkways, jests, boasts, tall tales, folk and legendary heroes, and ballads.
Buying the Wind: Regional Folklore in the United States, Univ. of Chicago Press, 1964. A supplement to *American Folklore.* Includes the folklore of Maine Down Easters, the Pennsylvania Dutch, Southwest Mexicans, Utah Mormons, southern mountaineers, Louisiana Cajuns, and Illinois Egyptians. For each regional group, the text provides narratives, proverbs, riddles, beliefs, folk dramas, and folk songs.
See also Folktales of the World series, ed. by Richard Dorson, Univ. of Chicago Press. The series contains the following titles: *Folktales of China,* ed. and tr. by Wolfram Eberhard (1965) ; *Folktales of England,* ed. by Katharine M. Briggs and Ruth L. Tongue (1965) ; *Folktales of Germany,* ed. by Kurt Ranke (1966) ; *Folktales of Hungary,* ed. by Linda Degh (1965) ; *Folktales of Ireland,* ed. by Sean O'Sullivan (1966) ; *Folktales of Israel,* ed. by Dov Noy (1963) ; *Folktales of Japan,* ed. by Keigo Seki (1963) ; *Folktales of Norway,* ed. by Reidar Th. Christiansen (1964). This series is of outstanding value to the adult who is interested in authentic versions of folk tales. The storyteller seeking

new material from the countries represented will be well rewarded by study of these volumes.

DUFF, ANNIS, *"Bequest of Wings": A Family's Pleasures with Books,* Viking, 1944. A charming and intimate account of one family's experience with books. It is included here because of the excellent discussion on the problem of violence and evil in fairy tales (Chap. 14). The author also has much to say on the value of reading aloud and discussing books with children.

EASTMAN, MARY HUSE, *Index to Fairy Tales, Myths, and Legends,* Faxon, 1926. First supplement, 1937. Second supplement, 1952. Useful for locating various sources in which individual tales may be found. There are geographical and racial groupings and lists for storytellers.

♪ENGVICK, WILLIAM, ed., *Lullabies and Night Songs,* music by Alec Wilder, ill. by Maurice Sendak, Harper, 1965.   4–8

♪FELTON, HAROLD W., ed., *Cowboy Jamboree: Western Songs and Lore,* arr. by Edward S. Breck, ill. by Aldren A. Watson, Knopf, 1951.   9–15

♪FUKUDA, HANAKO, comp. and tr., *Favorite Songs of Japanese Children,* ill. by Katsuya Kay Nishi, Highland Music Company, 1965. Fifteen delightful songs presented with dancing, dramatization, and games, just as they would be performed in Japan.   6–10

♪GLAZER, TOM, comp., *Treasury of Folk Songs,* ill. by Art Seiden, arr. for piano by Stanley Lock and Herbert Haufrecht, Grosset, 1964.   All ages

GREENE, ELLIN, comp., *Stories; a List of Stories to Tell and to Read Aloud,* New York Public Library, 1965. An excellent aid for the beginning storyteller. Contains an annotated list of stories and their sources, a list of poetry and books for reading aloud, a bibliography for the storyteller, a subject index, and a name index.

HARDENDORFF, JEANNE B., ed., *Stories to Tell: A List of Stories with Annotations,* 5th ed., Enoch Pratt Free Library, 1965. In addition to a well-annotated list of stories for telling, this book contains a list of picture books for TV storytelling, suggested programs for story hours, a list of stories by subject, and a list of poetry collections.

♪HAYWOOD, CHARLES, ed., *Folk Songs of the World,* ill. by Carl Smith, Day, 1966. Songs in this global array are presented in their native languages and in English. Notes add commentary on the musical life of each country and a description of each song. Chords for instrumental accompaniment are also indicated.   10–up

HAZARD, PAUL, *Books, Children and Men,* tr. by Marguerite Mitchell, Horn Book, 1944. An eminent member of the French Academy discusses national traits in relation to children's books and gives special attention to folklore, fairy tales, nursery rhymes, and poetry.

HUCK, CHARLOTTE S., and DORIS YOUNG KUHN, *Children's Literature in the Elementary School,* rev. ed., Holt, 1968. In Chapter 8 the authors discuss folk tales, fables, myths and legends, and modern fantasy. Bibliographies are fairly extensive and up-to-date.

♪HURD, MICHAEL, *Sailors' Songs and Shanties,* ill. by John Miller, Walck, 1965. Includes a brief but informative discussion of the purposes and origins of various sea shanties.   10–up

♪IVES, BURL, *The Burl Ives Song Book,* Ballantine, 1953.
♪*Sea Songs of Sailing, Whaling, and Fishing,* Ballantine, 1956. This collection is out of print but is available in many libraries.

♪*More Burl Ives Songs,* Ballantine, 1966.

JOURNAL OF AMERICAN FOLKLORE, *Folklore in America,* sel. and ed. by Tristram P. Coffin and Hennig Cohen, Doubleday, 1966. This interesting compilation of verified folk pieces, reprinted from the *Journal of American Folklore,* is divided into the following categories: tales, songs, superstitions, proverbs, riddles, games, folk dramas, and folk festivals.

JUNG, CARL, and others, eds., *Man and His Symbols,* Doubleday, 1964. The chapter "Ancient Myths and Modern Man" should be read for the insight which it gives into the importance of myth. This book serves as the best introduction to Jung's psychology to have appeared so far.

♪KNUDSEN, LYNNE, comp., *Lullabies from Around the World,* arr. by Carl Bosley, ill. by Jacqueline Tomes, Follett, 1967. This very specialized collection is excellent for use with young children. Guitar and simple piano accompaniments are included, and a brief, informative introduction precedes each song.   3–6

♪KRONE, BEA and MAX, *Cantemos, Ninos,* Neil Kjos, 1961. A compilation of folk songs, singing games, and dances. Lyrics are printed in Spanish and in English. Simple accompaniments and chords for guitar and autoharp are included. Excellent for use with stories from Spain and Latin American countries.   10–up

LEACH, MARIA, ed., *Funk and Wagnalls Standard Dictionary of General Folklore, Mythology and Legend,* 2 vols. Funk and Wagnalls, 1949–1950. The tremendous extent and variety of the world's folklore is made known in this fine reference work which serves the general reader as well as the expert.

♪LLOYD, NORMAN, *The New Golden Song Book,* Golden Press, 1962.   6–7

♪LOMAX, ALAN, *The Folk Songs of North America,* Doubleday, 1960.   12–up

♪*Hard Hitting Songs for Hard-Hit People,* music transcribed and ed. by Pete Seeger, Oak, 1967.   12–up

♪LOMAX, ALAN, and ELIZABETH POSTON, *Penguin Book of American Folk Songs,* Penguin, 1964.   12–up

♪LOMAX, JOHN A., ed., *Folk Song: U.S.A.,* Duell, 1948.   10–up

MOORE, VARDINE, *The Pre-School Story Hour,* Scarecrow Press, 1966. Gives the basic necessities for planning and conducting story hours in all kinds of libraries. Especially useful for its listings of finger games, recordings, and picture books. A practical and authoritative work, unfortunately marred by an abundance of typographical errors.

MORTON, MIRIAM, ed., *A Harvest of Russian Children's Literature,* Univ. of Calif. Press, 1967. An anthology of one hundred selections from literature published for Russian children from 1825 to the present. The twenty-one folk tales represent various regions of the Soviet Union.

OPIE, IONA and PETER, *The Oxford Dictionary of Nursery Rhymes,* Oxford, 1951. An authoritative and highly interesting work which gives much of the folklore surrounding the nursery rhymes.

♪PAZ, ELENA, *Favorite Spanish Folk Songs,* Oak, 1965. Forty-five traditional songs from Spain and Latin America. Included are literal English translations, notes on the songs, and guitar chords.   10–up

PICKARD, P. M., *I Could a Tale Unfold: Violence, Horror, and Sensationalism in Stories for Children,* Barnes and Noble, 1961. This perceptive and scholarly account by a British psychologist deals with the relationship between the comics and traditional literature and with the child's need for stories of various kinds, including fantasies and tales with aspects of horror.

♪REYNOLDS, MALVINA, *Little Boxes and Other Handmade Songs,* ill. by Jodi Robbins, Oak, 1964.

♪*Tweedles and Foodles for Young Noodles,* Schroder Music Co., Berkeley, Calif.

These two books contain songs by a well-known ballad maker. Although they are not folk songs, they comment upon life and the social scene in much the same manner as folk songs. Not all songs in the first volume are suitable for use with children, but in many cases the author suggests variants. Songs in the second book were written especially for children.   8–up

♪RITCHIE, JEAN, *Folk Songs of the Southern Appalachians,* Oak, 1965.   10–up

♪*Jean Ritchie's Swapping Song Book,* piano arr. by A. K. Fossner and Edward Tripp, ill. by George Pickow, Walck, 1952.   9–12

♪*Singing Family of the Cumberlands,* Oak, 1963.   10–up

RYDER, ARTHUR W., tr., *The Panchatantra,* Univ. of Chicago Press, 1925. Adult students will be interested in discovering in these Indian fables the sources of many Aesop and La Fontaine fables.

♪SACKETT, S. J., *Cowboys and the Songs They Sang,* W. R. Scott, 1967. A group of familiar favorites from the West of the 1870's and '80's. The book is illustrated with photographs of the period and contains descriptive background on the songs. A book that should have special appeal for boys.   8–13

♪SANDBURG, CARL, ed., *American Song Bag,* Harcourt, 1927. *New American Song Bag,* Broadcast Music Inc., 1950.   10–up

SAWYER, RUTH, *The Way of the Storyteller,* Viking, 1962. A great storyteller discusses the art and technique of successful storytelling and shares eleven of her best stories.

♪SEEGER, PEGGY, *Folk Songs of Peggy Seeger,* Oak, 1964. Over eighty traditional American folk ballads and songs from the repertoire of Peggy Seeger. Rare versions and unusual tunes. Guitar chords and introductory notes are included.   12–up

♪SEEGER, PETE, *American Favorite Ballads,* Oak, 1961. Eighty-four traditional songs as sung by this noted wandering minstrel.   12–up

♪SEEGER, RUTH CRAWFORD, *American Folk Songs for Children,* ill. by Barbara Cooney, Doubleday, 1948.   5–12

♪*American Folk Songs for Christmas,* ill. by Barbara Cooney, Doubleday, 1953.   5–12

♪*Animal Folk Songs for Children; Traditional American Songs,* ill. by Barbara Cooney, Doubleday, 1950.

These three books should assuredly form the nucleus of any collection of folk songs for children. The tunes and piano accompaniments are simple and appealing. *American Folk Songs for Children* contains an especially helpful discussion on the values and uses of folk songs. Each book includes a classified index and an index of titles and first lines.   5–12

SHEDLOCK, MARIE, *The Art of the Story-Teller,* 3d ed., bibl. by Eulalie Steinmetz, Dover, 1951. A master British storyteller discusses the techniques of storytelling and presents eighteen stories as she would tell them.

♪SHEKERJIAN, HAIG and REGINA, *A Book of Ballads, Songs and Snatches,* Harper, 1966. A book that is graphically beautiful and musically excellent. Many unusual and little-known songs can be found here. Piano arrangements are tasteful and guitar chords are given. The coverage is international. 10–up

♪SILBER, IRWIN, and E. ROBINSON, *Songs of the Great American West,* Macmillan, 1967. Each of eight chapters is prefaced by a short historical essay. In addition, documentary notes on sources are provided for the ninety-two songs, which cover the decades from 1840 through the 1920's. Adult

SMITH, LILLIAN, *The Unreluctant Years,* American Library Association, 1953. An inspiring book on all types of literature for children. Chapters 4, 5, and 6 deal with fairy tales, myths, and epics.

THOMPSON, STITH, *The Folktale,* Holt, 1960 (Dryden Press, 1946). The author, one of the world's foremost authorities on the subject, discusses the universality of the folk tales, and analyzes types of tales and their place in a primitive culture. The final section concerns ways of studying the folk tale on a worldwide basis.

Motif-Index of Folk Literature, ed. by Stith Thompson, rev. and enl. ed., 5 vols., Indiana Univ. Press, 1955. A reference work valuable for analyzing and categorizing folk literature of the world. Volume 1 includes a bibliography of all works examined for motifs.

TOOR, FRANCES, *A Treasury of Mexican Folkways,* ill. by Carlos Merida, Crown, 1947. Although published over twenty years ago, this comprehensive book has much of value on the customs, myths, fiestas, dances, and songs of the Mexican people.

U.S. LIBRARY OF CONGRESS, *Children's Literature: A Guide to Reference Sources,* Supt. of Documents, U.S. Government Print. Off., 1966. An "annotated bibliography [which] describes books, articles, and pamphlets selected on the basis of their estimated usefulness to adults concerned with the creation, reading, or study of children's books" (preface). The section on storytelling (pp. 183–200) and the one on folk tales, myths, and legends (pp. 201–226) are of most importance to the user of this bibliography.

♪VON SCHMIDT, ERIC, *Come for to Sing,* piano arr. by Robert Freedman, Houghton, 1963. An amusing collection of folk songs with easy piano arrangements and guitar chords. Pathways of Sound, Inc., has produced a recording of all songs in this book.

♪WEAVERS, THE, eds., *The Weavers' Song Book,* arr. by Robert De Cormier, Harper, 1960. 10–up

♪*Travelin' On with The Weavers,* arr. for piano and guitar by Herbert Haufrecht, Harper, 1966. 10–up

♪WHITE, FLORENCE, and KAZUO AKIYAMA, *Children's Songs from Japan,* ill. by Toshihiko Suzuki, Edward B. Marks Music Corp., 1960. Approximately fifty songs make up this interesting collection. 6–10

WILLCOX, ISOBEL, *Reading Aloud with Elementary School Children,* Teachers Practical Press, Atherton, 1963. Designed especially for the classroom teacher, this brief booklet discusses various aspects of reading aloud. In addition, it contains useful suggestions for scheduling and recommends appropriate post-reading activities.

♪WINN, MARIE, and ALLAN MILLER, *The Fireside Book of Children's Songs,* arr. by Allan Miller, ill. by John Alcorn, Simon and Schuster, 1966. 6–10

♪ZEITLIN, PATTY, *Castle in My City,* ill. by Lucille Krasne and the children in Watts, Golden Gate, 1968. A group of original songs composed and tested by the author in her nursery school classes. The title song refers to the famous Watts Towers in Los Angeles. Most of the songs are easy for young children to sing and will be very useful in connection with the story hour. 4–8

GLOSSARY AND PRONUNCIATION GUIDE

The following list contains foreign words and phrases and the names of authors, places, and story characters selected from Parts One and Two. Words that can be found in a standard college dictionary are not included. Definitions are limited to those that apply in this book and are given only if meanings have not been supplied in context.

Symbols used in the pronunciation are as follows: a as in *hat;* ā as in *age;* ã as in *care;* ä as in *father;* e as in *let;* ē as in *see;* ėr as in *term;* i as in *pin;* ī as in *five;* o as in *hot;* ō as in *go;* ô as in *order, all;* oi as in *oil;* ou as in *house;* th as in *thin;* th as in *then;* u as in *cup;* ù as in *full;* ü as in *rule;* ū as in *use;* zh as in *measure;* ə as in the unaccented syllables of *about, taken, pencil, lemon, circus;* H as in the German *ach;* N as in the French *bon* (not pronounced, but shows that the vowel before it is nasal); œ as in the French *peu* and the German *könig* (pronounced by speaking ā with the lips rounded as for ō); Y as in the French *du* (pronounced by speaking ē with the lips rounded as for ü). All other symbols represent the consonant sounds that they commonly stand for in English spelling.

AFANASIEV (ä fä nä′syif)
AGAYK (ä gī′ik)
ALEIAN (ä′lā ən), a plain in Lycia
ANANSI (ə nan′sē)
ANTEA (an tē′ə)
ARHA (är′hä)
ARRA (ar′ə), a mild Irish expletive, equivalent to "Really!"
ARTZYBASHEFF (är tsi ba′shif)
ASBJÖRNSEN (äs′byėrn sen)
ASIMOV (a′si mov)
AULAIRE, D' (dō lãr′)
AULNOY, D' (dō nwä′ or dōl nwä′)

BALLAGHADEREEN (bä lä hä′də rēn)
BARBEAU, MARIUS (bär bō′, ma′rē ys)
BARGI (bär′gē), grandmother
BASILE, GIAMBATTISTA (bä zē′lā, jäm′bät tēs′tä)
BEAUMONT, DE (də bō mōN′)
BEEREEUN (bā rā ün′)
BIALKA (byäl′kä)
BIDPAI (bid′pī)
BINGAWINGUL (bing′ə wing′əl), an Australian shrub; scrub
BLANID (blô)

BOADAG (bō′ag)
BOGATIR (bō gä tēr′), hero; valiant knight
BOONDI (bün′dē), a club-headed weapon
BORSKI, LUCIA MERECKA (bōr′skē, lü′syä mə res′kä)
BOULANGER (bü län zhä′)
BOUQUI (bü kē′)
BRANDIS (bran′dis), a three-legged iron stand used to support a cooking vessel over a fire; a trivet
BREIDABLIK (brī′də blik)
BRICRIEU (brik′rü)
BUDULINEK (bə dü′lə nek)
BULLAI BULLAI (bul′ī bul′ī)

CARABAS (ka′rə bas)
CELEUS (sē′lē əs)
CETHERN (kãr′ən)
CHAYOTE (chä yōd′ē), the fruit of a tropical vine of the cucumber family, used as a vegetable
CHEELD-WHIDDEN (chēld′ hwid′ən), baby
CHINKERINCHEE (ching′kə rin′chē), South African perennial with starry white blossoms; commonly known as *star-of-Bethlehem*
CHUI (chü′ē)
CHUKOVSKY, KORNEI (chu kôf′skē, kôr nä′)
CHURA (chü′rä)
CLOAM (klōm), earthenware
CLYTIE (klī′tē)
CONALL (kon′əl)
CONNLA (kon′lə)
COOLABAH (kü′lə bä), eucalyptus
CORAN (kō′rən)
CORNCRAIK (kôrn′krāk), a hand rattle used to frighten birds from sown seed or growing corn; also, the European land rail, a bird with a harsh grating voice heard among the grain fields
CROOM (krüm), crumb
CROOM OF A CHEELD (krüm əv ə chēld), a very small child
CUCHULAIN (kü hul′in)
CUROI (kü′roi)
CURRAGH (kėr′əH or kėr′ə), an open boat made of skin or canvas
CYANE (sī′ə nē)

DAEN (dä′ən), an aborigine of Australia
DASENT (dā′sənt)
DEALGAN (däl′gən)
DEENYI (dēn′yē)
DÈMI (dem′ē)

DEUTSCH, BABETTE (doich, bab et′)
DINKY (ding′kē), very small; a small creature, i.e., fairy
DOOLOOMAI (dü′lü mī′)
DOON-GARA (dün′gä rä)
DOOWI (dü′wē), dream spirit
DRAUPNER (droup′nér)
DREXEL (drek′səl), threshold
DUIRMUID (dir′mid)
DUMMUTS (dum′its), twilight
DŪN (dün), fort
DURRI (dur′ē), cake of grass-seed flour

EE (ä), yes
EEHU (ē′hü)
EER-DHER (ēr′ᵗher)
EMAIN MACHA (em′ôn ma′hä)
ENCELADUS (en sel′ə dəs), in Greek mythology, a hundred-armed giant
ENKIDU (en′kə dü)
ENNA (en′ə), in Greek mythology, the vale of Enna was Persephone's home on earth
ERYX (er′iks), a city and mountain in Sicily
ESU (ä′sü), an African interjection, equivalent to "Good!" or "Wonderful!"

FALADA (fä lä′dä)
FIONN (fin)
FY (fī), faith

GÁG (gäg)
GALLAND, ANTOINE (gə län′, än twon′)
GATLESS (gat′lis or gôt′lis), shiftless; careless; thoughtless
GIDYA (gid′yä), a shrub of the genus *Acacia*, which gives off a sickening odor in damp weather or when in bloom
GILGUY HOLE (gil′gī hōl), a water hole
GIOCONDO DE' FIFANTI (jō con′dō dā fi fän′tē)
GIUFA (jü′fə)
GLEED (glēd), a glowing coal
GOO-GOOR-GAGA (gü′gür gä′gä), an Australian bird with a raucous cry, commonly known as *laughing jackass*
GOOLA-GOOL (gü′lä gül′)
GOOLAY-YALI (gü′lä yä′lē)
GOOMBEELGA (güm bēl′gä)
GOOWEERA (gü wē′rä)
GOTHEL (gôt′əl)
GRAINNE (grôn′yə)
GRANDMERE (grän mär′)
GUDBRAND (gud′bränd or gud′bränt)
GUINEDA (gē nä′də)
GURAGÉ (gü′rä gä′), a group of people in central Ethiopia and the region in which they live

HAILU (hī′lü)
HAPTOM HASEI (hap′təm hä sē′)
HAZARD, PAUL (a zar′, pôl)
HELHEIM (hel′hām)
HERMOD (her′müd or her′məd), a son of Odin
HIISI (hī′si), in Finnish folklore, the Evil Power
HIITOLA (hī′tō lä), the dominions of Hiisi
HODER (hō′dér)
HOLLE (hôl′lə)
HUNG VUONG (hun vwun)
HYRROKEN (hī′rō kin)

INJERA (in jä′rä), a pancake-style bread
IOBATES (ī ob′ə tēz)
ISMARUS (is′mə rəs)

ISS (is), yes
ISS FY (is fī), by my faith

JATAKA (jä′tə kə)
JEAN LEBLANC (zhän lə blän)

KIBOKO (ki bō′kō), a rhinoceros-hide whip
KNOWE (nou or nō), knoll
KOPPIE (kop′ē), hill
KRYLOV (kril ôf′)
KWAKU ANANSI (kwa′kü ə nan′sē)

LAERY (lē′rē)
LAIVA (lī′vä)
LING BROOM (ling brüm), a broom made of heather
LIU (lyü)
LOKE (lō′kē)
LÖNNROT, ELIAS (lérn′rôt, ə lī′əs)

MAEVE (māv)
MALICE (mä lēs′)
MÄRCHEN (mär′ʜən)
MARMOT (mar mō′)
MAROOSIA (mä rü′sē ə)
MBWEHA (əm bwä′hä)
MEDIO POLLITO (mä′dē ō pō lyē′tō)
METANIRA (met ə nī′rə)
MICHEL MELOCHE (mē shel′ mä lôsh′)
MJOLNER (myôl′nér)
MOE, JÖRGEN (mōə, yér′gən)
MURTHEMNEY (mir them′nē)
MUSTAPHA EFFENDI (mus′tä fä i fen′di)
MY CHAU (mē jou)

NANNA (nä′nä)
NASR-ED-DIN HODJA (näs′red din′ hôd′yə)
NICHET (nē shä′)
NIC LEODHAS, SORCHE (nik lē ō′əs, sôr′ä)
NUNNOOS (nun′üs)
NYODU (nə yō′dü)

O'FAOLAIN (ō fwä′lôn)
OISIN (u shēn′), great legendary Irish hero who went to the Land of the Ever Young
OJIISAN (ō jē sän)
ORMANINI (ôr′mä nē′nē)

PADRE PORKO (pä′thre pôr′kō)
PANCHATANTRA (pän chə tän′trə)
PENTAMERONE (pen tä mä rō′nä)
PERRAULT, CHARLES (pe rō′, sharl)
PIACEVOLI NOTTI, LE (lä pyä chä′vô lē nôt′tē)
PICARD (pē kar′)
PIES (pyesh)
PIRENE (pī rē′nē)
POLYIDUS (pol′ē ī′dəs)
PROETUS (prō ē′təs)

RAPUNZEL (rə pun′zəl), rampion, a European plant having a tuberous root used for salad

SADKO (säd′kô)
SEANACHIE (shän′ə hē)
SÊCHE (sesh)
SHMELKA (shmel′kä)
SHMELKICHA (shmel′ki chä)

SKILLY-WIDDEN (skil'i wid'ən), a Piskey baby
SLEIPNER (slăp'nir), the eight-legged steed of Odin
SLOAN (slōn), sloe, the fruit of the blackthorn
SLOOGEH (slü'gə), Saluki, the long-eared desert hound
SMOLICHEK (smol'i chek)
SON TIEN (shun tin)
SPIEWNA (shpyev'nä)
STRAPAROLA (strä pä rō'lä)
SUNGURA (sün gü'rä)

TAILLEFER (tä'yə fär')
TASHJIAN (täs jun)
THOK (thôk)
THORNE-THOMSEN, GUDRUN (tôrn tom'sen, gü'drun)
THRYM (thrim or trēm)
THUY TIEN (tủ'ē tin)
TIRE-WOMAN (tīr' wům'ən), one who sells and provides
    headdresses
TMOLUS (tə mō'ləs)
TOIVO (toi'vō)

TOLKIEN (tôl'ken)
TUPA (tú'pä)

UATH (ü'ä)
UCHIDA, YOSHIKO (ü chē dä, yō shē kō)
URASHIMA TARO (ü rä shē mä tä rō)
URUK (ü'ruk), an ancient Sumerian city
USNA (us'nə)

VILLENEUVE (vēl nœv')
VLEI (flā), meadow, marsh

WEEDAH (wē'dä)
WIRINUN (wir'ē nun), sorcerer; medicine man
WOMBA (wom'bä)

YGDRASIL (ig'drə sil), in Norse mythology, the world tree
    in Neflheim which binds together heaven, earth, and
    hell
YHI (yē)

INDEX OF AUTHORS AND TITLES